Dostoevsky

Dostoevsky

HIS LIFE AND WORK

BY KONSTANTIN MOCHULSKY

TRANSLATED, WITH AN INTRODUCTION, BY

MICHAEL A. MINIHAN

PRINCETON UNIVERSITY PRESS

To Helene Iswolsky
with gratitude and deep affection

Translator's Introduction

Dostoevsky: His Life and Work by Konstantin Mochulsky, originally published in Russian by the YMCA Press, Paris, in 1947, was recognized soon after its appearance as a classic in its field; it has been called "the best one-volume study of Dostoevsky available in any language." Most Russian scholars abroad have been unreserved in their praise; yet at a time when literally dozens of books about the author are appearing every year, I should like briefly to analyze the importance and uniqueness of this work in several of its major aspects.

Mochulsky's basic approach is to offer a detailed critical investigation of Dostoevsky's writings, individually and in relation to one another. He devotes separate chapters to each of his major works, beginning with the writer's first literary creations, the novels *Poor People* and *The Double*, up through his last articles published posthumously in *The Diary of a Writer*. Works such as *Netochka Nezvanova*, *The Village of Stepanchikovo*, *Notes from the House of Death*, *The Humiliated and Wronged*, and *Winter Notes on Summer Impressions* are here examined for the first time in real depth, and lesser known novels, stories, and essays are introduced to the general reader in illuminating discussion. However, to illustrate my specific point by a few examples, we might turn first to *Notes from Underground*, "the philosophical preface to the cycle of the great novels," and to those five novels themselves which, following Ivanov, Mochulsky calls "novel-tragedies."

The critic brilliantly explores the ideational content of the *Notes*, interprets the author's examination of the consciousness of modern man in its tragic isolation and dichotomy, and affirms Dostoevsky's opposition of "will" to "rationally understood advantage"; he shows how the origins of the underground man's struggle lie in his repudiation of the premises of "utopian socialism," and underlines Dostoevsky's affirmation of the individual, personality, and freedom. But here Mochulsky goes further. Western criticism often accepts the "underground" as Dostoevsky's own final word on "freedom." Mochulsky cites a letter (March 26, 1864) in which the writer complains to his brother Mikhail that the "essential thought" of his work was obscured by the censors: "Where I mocked at everything and sometimes *blasphemed for form's sake*—that's let pass, but where from all this I deduced the *need of faith and Christ*—that is suppressed." Dostoevsky's understanding of "freedom" and the "highest development of individuality" was religious, and the fullest expression of its formula is presented in the chapter on *Winter Notes.*

Pursuing Ivanov's description of Dostoevsky's novels as modern "vehicles of Dionysius," Mochulsky analyzes *Crime and Punishment* in terms of classical tragic form: as a five-act tragedy with a prologue and epilogue; and even further he refers to the three classical "unities" and shows how the artist observes them throughout his work. In the chapter on *The Idiot* he offers an incisive study of Dostoevsky's failure to create a "positively beautiful individual," and defines the roots of this failure on both the empirical and metaphysical (mythological) planes.

Many critics in America regard *The Devils* as a caricature, not based on reality, as the product of a warped reactionary imagination. Mochulsky presents the most thorough and discerning interpretation that has yet appeared. On one side, he authenticates the novel's factual basis in the Nechayev affair, produces evidence as to how Dostoevsky first learned many of the circumstances through his brother-in-law, and as well, conclusively demonstrates the seriousness of Dostoevsky's own involvement in revolutionary activity during the forties. As for the work itself, Mochulsky penetrates the personality of the "fascinating demon" Stavrogin and establishes it as one of the writer's greatest creations. He examines the excluded chapter *Stavrogin's Confession* and argues how it is absolutely integral to the plot and that its elimination distorts the novel's design. Critics who counter that Dostoevsky never reestablished the chapter in subsequent editions are answered by the fact that in general he did not rewrite his published works, but rather turned to new projects, and that he incorporated elements of the suppressed chapter in his later novels.

Often *A Raw Youth* is simply dismissed as an inferior work because of its structural flaws. However, in terms of our times and the young generation which is experiencing many of the problems of the "Raw Youth," such as that of "identity," and witnessing the "disintegration of family structure," the "unsightliness of their fathers," and the absence of traditional forms, it touches us, as readers, very closely. Granting its artistic shortcomings, here for the first time, its importance is recognized and evaluated.

The two chapters which Mochulsky devotes to *The Brothers Kara-mazov* are brilliant, and completely absorb the reader. After a discussion of the novel's architectonics, the separate characters are considered in detail. We move from Fyodor Pavlovich, in whom the "earthly Karamazov force" remains at the level of primeval sexual drives, not even rising to "Eros," and arrive at Alyosha's Christian love, inspired by the Elder Zosima's teaching.

Having glanced at these illustrations, we must now turn to another extremely significant aspect of Mochulsky's book, his study of the development of Dostoevsky's art, the interrelationship of themes throughout his creative work and the evolution that took place within those themes. For example, Dostoevsky considered the idea of the "double," which first appeared in his second novel, one of his most important discoveries in literature. This theme is shown in its subsequent formulations: in the relationship of Svidrigailov to Raskolnikov, Rogozhin to Myshkin, and finally in Stavrogin's "scrofulous imp with a cold" and Ivan Karamazov's devil and Smerdyakov. Many of Dostoevsky's early works are involved with the problem of "romantic dreaming" (*The Landlady, White Nights, A Faint Heart*), but Mochulsky demonstrates how after the "illusions" of the forties, the dreamer "remained seated alone in his corner" and grew into the "spiteful" *man from underground*; how the underground man's theories of personal rights, when unqualified by the concept of brotherhood, suggest the idea that "everything is permitted" to Raskolnikov, to Stavrogin, to Ivan Karamazov. The critic traces Dostoevsky's efforts to create a "positively beautiful individual" from his first draft, Colonel Rostanev (*The Village of Stepanchikovo*), to Prince Myshkin in *The Idiot*, and his later attempts: Bishop Tikhon in *The Devils*, Makar Dolgoruky in *A Raw Youth*, Alyosha and the Elder Zosima in *Brothers Karamazov*.

The devices Dostoevsky employed in his writing are also treated. Mochulsky draws a distinction between Dostoevsky's art, which he terms "expressive," as opposed to the "descriptive art" of Tolstoy, Goncharov, and Turgenev. Dostoevsky's work is dramatic, not epic in form. This distinction, originating with Ivanov, has been treated in American criticism by George Steiner. But Mochulsky goes into a more subtle and involved analysis on the basis of the text, untranslated notebooks, and the author's own statements. He follows the images that pervade Dostoevsky's novels: the "crystal palace," the "anthill," spiders, the "slanting rays of the sun," "little sticky green leaves," "the little tear of a child," and the great symbol and concept of "living life" which is first mentioned in *Notes from Underground*, and recurs in the later novels.

Before this book perhaps only two studies have even alluded to Dostoevsky's style *as such*. (This is, of course, related to the question of translation, which I will deal with later.) Mochulsky shows how Dostoevsky's art grows out of dialogue, how he masterfully portrays a character's intonations, verbal style. Detailed examples of this are given in reference to each work. The general question of narrative form is discussed and quotations are drawn from the author's notebooks illustrating the importance which he attached to this difficult problem which determined the tone as well as the structure of his novels.

Many documents, letters, sketchbooks, and early drafts, vital to the study of Dostoevsky, here appear in English for the first time. We enter into the creative process itself.

All this extensive material is presented against the background of Dostoevsky's biography. Konstantin Mochulsky maintains in his preface that "the life and work of Dostoevsky are inseparable. He 'lived in literature' . . . His works unfold before us as one vast confession, as the integral revelation of his universal spirit." An approach that would eliminate the biographical elements *which shed further light upon an author's work*, is one-sided, incomplete, and can ultimately lead to grievous distortions. The exclusive study of the text itself must often be complemented by other critical factors. This is especially true in the case of Dostoevsky. Not only his personal life, but also the political, social, literary, and philosophical life of his period are frequently unfamiliar to the reader. And this affects our understanding of his novels. Mochulsky succeeds in preserving this "spiritual unity" of the writer's life and work.

But Dostoevsky was not merely a *littérateur*; he was one of the world's greatest religio-philosophical thinkers. His ideas cannot be artificially separated from his creative work, for they are categorically fundamental to his writing and to any real understanding of it. His characters proceed out of ideas, these ideas form the dialectic of his novels. The problems are posed: does an "exceptional man" have the right to "transgress" the moral law, to kill another human being even if the latter is "of no use to anyone at all"? What is our ultimate responsibility toward others? May a man remain "isolated in proud solitude"? Does God exist, and if so how does one explain or justify "the tears of a five-year-old girl, tortured by her sadist-parents"? Is the soul immortal? What is the meaning of suffering? What is the nature of beauty? Does man's ultimate happiness lie in his physical well-being and lack of responsibility? What is the foundation of the state? And with these questions we immediately see emerging the figures of the "underground man," Raskolnikov, Myshkin, Stavrogin, Kirilov, Ivan Karamazov, the Grand Inquisitor, and the Elder Zosima.

Often these questions of theodicy, ethics, historiosophy, and aesthetics in themselves are not new. They have been raised innumerable times by men throughout history. All really great art is concerned with the same "ultimate questions." But Dostoevsky has posed them in a new way, in a way that is immediately relevant to our age, perhaps even more relevant than the nineteenth century could understand or bear.

Here, in my opinion, lies the final greatness and value of Mochulsky's critical study. He has understood Dostoevsky's work in the light of his primary intuition, his idea, and has analyzed it in terms of the natural synthesis of its form and content.

We might not entirely agree with a few conclusions that Mochulsky draws. One problem lies in his discussion of Akaky Akakyevich and Gogol's *Greatcoat* in the chapter *Poor People*. The critic overstates a very valid and necessary point regarding Dostoevsky's transformation of Gogol; the difficulty here is not in our understanding of Dostoevsky and what he was doing, but rather in our interpretation of Gogol. I should point out that Mochulsky has written an excellent book on Gogol which deals with the author on his own terms and perhaps more fairly (*Dukhovny put Gogolya* [Gogol's Spiritual Way], YMCA Press, Paris 1934).

And I cannot concur with Mochulsky on one other interpretation: that Raskolnikov's conversion was a "pious lie" written for the readers of Katkov's "well-meaning" journal. I think the seeds of a *metanoia* are planted in Raskolnikov from the beginning on the basis of the fact that he ultimately never lost his *ability to love*. Svidrigailov and Stavrogin, for example, are incapable of love and must perish in the dialectic of Dostoevsky's thought. However Raskolnikov's conversion seems completely possible on the theoretic plane. The problem, it seems to me, is rather a technical one. In the amount of space that Dostoevsky allotted to indicating this inner change, we do not find the psychological evidence convincing in itself. "But," as the author writes, "this begins a new story. . . ."

Perhaps a few words are needed regarding one point that may pose some problems to the reader. In his chapters on *The Idiot, The Devils, A Raw Youth,* and *Karamazov,* Mochulsky continually refers to the use of myth in Dostoevsky's writing (Psyche and her liberator, the Mother of God–Mother Earth, the Eternal Feminine–Sophia). In this he is largely dependent upon Vyacheslav Ivanov, the Symbolist poet, scholar, and critic.

The "new" Russian Symbolists—Aleksandr Blok, Ivanov, Andrey Bely—began to publish in the early years of this century. Their intuition was quite different from their Western European counterparts. They looked for religious and metaphysical symbolism in life itself; life was to become creativity, and creativity life, not in a metaphorical, but in an ontological sense. They were greatly influenced by the Russian philosopher, Vladimir Solovyov, the friend who accompanied Dostoevsky to Optina Pustyn. Solovyov found the "spirit of the world" in the "feminine principle," in "Sophia," which at times he identified with Divine Wisdom, at times with the Holy Spirit, with the earth, the Church, or the Mother of God. His complex thesis (which, for our purposes, I am just briefly indicating) lies at the root of Ivanov's "Sophiac" criticism. In 1911 the poet wrote a brilliant book in which he discusses three aspects of Dostoevsky's work: "Tragedic" (which we noted in our definition of "novel-tragedy"), "Mythological," and "Theological." In his remarks on μυθολογούμενα Ivanov states:

Dostoevsky has a peculiarly characteristic conception of life as a drama which, both in the fate of the individual and in the history of the world, is enacted invisibly—beneath the empirically recognizable pragmatism of events and the surface of spiritual impulses—by God and the innermost human Ego. And from this conception arises, of itself, that inherent symbolism of his epic-tragedy, that "realism in the higher sense," as he himself calls it, which we shall term realistic symbolism. . . .

Truly realistic symbolism, based on the intuition of a higher reality, acquires a principle of life and movement . . . within the intuition itself as a comprehension of the dynamic principle of intelligible substance: as a discernment of its actual form, or, what is the same thing, a discernment of its universal actuality and its activity in the world.

The more the writer has the feeling for *realiora in realibus*—that pathos which breaks out in Goethe's "All that is transient is but an allegory"—the more naturally, of course, does he meet and conform with the original imaginative patterns of the essential train of thought that lives on in the obscure memory of the ancient myth. Conversely, the more deeply the poetic conception is rooted in the native soil of the myth, the more significant and intrinsically true does it seem to us—that is, if we have not yet lost the sense of its magnetic force, so that Goethe's words "truth was discovered long ago" can still be fully applied to poetic truth.[1]

He distinguishes three primeval myths which Dostoevsky employs: "the enchanted bride," "the revolt against Mother Earth," and "the stranger." These themes are what Mochulsky illustrates in his analysis.

Konstantin Vasilyevich Mochulsky was born in Odessa, in the south of Russia, on January 28, 1892. His father held the chair of Russian Letters at Novorossiisky University. As a child his health was poor and he was educated privately; he early expressed a deep love of poetry and the theatre. At eighteen after completing his studies at the Gymnasium in Odessa, he entered the philological faculty of St. Petersburg University. There he distinguished himself as a perceptive and serious student. Upon finishing his degree, he remained at the University and continued his work in Romance literatures. In 1918, after the Revolution, he was appointed lecturer at Saratov University, but as the result of various complications, could not assume his post. His first lectures were delivered in the same university where his father had taught, in Odessa. In 1919 he left Russia and carried on his promising academic career, lecturing first at the University of Sofia from 1920 to 1922, and then moving to Paris to teach at the Sorbonne.

Unfortunately, the enthusiasm and interest in Paris that first surrounded the Russian faculty, staffed by many eminent scholars of the recent emigration, began to dwindle, and though Mochulsky remained associated with the University until 1941, his lectures on Russian literature were on the whole poorly attended. His books on Vladimir Solovyov and on Dostoevsky grew out of courses which he gave during those years. The writer Helene Iswolsky, who attended both these courses, has described his character to me: he was, apparently, very genial, affable, kind, witty, and sincere. He was well liked in society, both French and Russian. He often frequented the literary circles in Montparnasse. About this time he began to write and was associated

[1] Ivanov, Vyacheslav, *Freedom and the Tragic Life. A Study in Dostoevsky* (trans. by Norman Cameron), The Noonday Press, New York 1957, pp. 49, 52.

with the weekly *Zveno* (The Link). He published articles on literature and the theatre, and also wrote short stories under the pen name *Versilov*. However, by disposition he refused to become a "journalist" or "critic"; he remained more of a classical feuilletonist and wrote about those things "which interested him personally."

At the end of the twenties, the beginning of the thirties, Mochulsky underwent some sort of spiritual crisis, a religious "conversion." Everyone noted a change in him. He no longer went to Montparnasse, but started attending the meetings of Berdyayev's Religio-Philosophical Academy. His thinking was greatly influenced by Father Sergy Bulgakov. He began to contemplate monasticism, and to dispose of his possessions and books. But like Alyosha in the *Brothers*, in the end he decided to remain "a monk serving in the world." Perhaps this is related to his meeting with Mother Mariya, a Russian nun, one of the most remarkable figures of the spiritual life in Paris. In temperament Mother Mariya was the exact opposite of Mochulsky. She felt that all of God's world was the monk's cell, that the religious must go to the world, "the world was burning for salvation." Working with Mother Mariya, Mochulsky devoted himself to the society of Orthodox Action. He was active in the League of Orthodox Culture, the Student Christian Movement, and the Fellowship of St. Alban and St. Sergius; he served on the faculty of St. Sergius Theological Academy until the year before his death.

In 1940 the Germans occupied Paris. Mochulsky remained in the city and heroically suffered all the privation of that period. Mother Mariya, along with many of her co-workers, was arrested by the Gestapo, and died in a Nazi concentration camp. The events of those years and personal hardships undoubtedly affected his health. In 1946 it was found that he was in an advanced stage of tuberculosis. At first his doctors sent him to a sanatorium at Fontainebleau, then to Cambo in the Pyrenees. In 1947 he returned to Paris for a brief time, and then went back to Cambo, where he died on March 21, 1948.[2]

His bibliography includes *Dukhovny put Gogolya* (Gogol's Spiritual Way), 1934; *Vladimir Solovyov*, 1936; *Dostoevsky: His Life and Work*, written 1942, published 1947; *Aleksandr Blok*, 1948; *Andrey Bely*, 1955; *Valery Bryusov*, 1962.

When I began this translation, I set myself a difficult task: to give

[2] For many of the facts about Mochulsky's life, I am indebted to Helene Iswolsky and to M. Kantor's essay which appears in *Aleksandr Blok*, YMCA Press, Paris.

a literal rendition of the Russian, hopefully preserving all the nuances and flavor of the original, and at the same time to present this in the form of flowing English prose. As is obvious, it is a long book, and also a very complicated book as regards translation. Literally hundreds of set "formulae" appear throughout the work, and I have tried to keep them uniform; this is also true of quotations and fragments of quotations which I have only varied where the Russian itself is inconsistent. Mochulsky frequently uses dialogue from the novels to illustrate peculiarities of characters' speech patterns, and here I have attempted to retain the intonation of the originals. All the quotations from Dostoevsky, as well as from other authors, I have translated myself. The problems of formulae being abstracted from such quotations and sometimes the tonality of various renditions have necessitated my doing this.

The English reader who turns to translations of Dostoevsky's novels might find a few words about the existing versions helpful. The best are decidedly those of Jessie Coulson; however, she has done only *Crime and Punishment* and *Memoirs from the House of the Dead*. Boris Brasol's translation of *The Diary of a Writer*, though in a completely different genre, is also extremely good. As standard translations of Dostoevsky's other writings, I would still recommend Constance Garnett's. She is always accurate, does not merely paraphrase, conveys the spirit of the works, although at times she does "tone down" the Russian with "Victorianisms."

I have occasionally departed from Mrs. Garnett's choice of titles, although I do have precedents. I have done this for the sake of literalness and also because of allusions in the text itself. So *The Friend of the Family* (sic) appears as *The Village of Stepanchikovo*, *The Insulted and Injured* as *The Humiliated and Wronged*, *The Possessed* as *The Devils*. Other variants should be obvious to the reader.

Russian names I have always left exactly as they appear in the text, first of all because, while Michael Dostoevsky is *perhaps* permissible, Michael Mikhailovich or Michael Michaelovich has always struck me as impossibly strange; secondly, the usage of names conveys connotations: e.g., the name and patronymic is polite and formal, diminutives or nicknames express endearment or familiarity. I have maintained this principle throughout with two exceptions: Peter the Great and Catherine the Great. Surnames in the feminine add "-a," or, when the masculine is "-sky," "-skaya." All foreign names I have left in their original spellings, except Vrangel and Fonvizina.

Transliteration from the Cyrillic to the Latin alphabet always presents a problem, and it is impossible to be absolutely consistent without reverting to a system that would provide the general reader with unnecessary complications. I have tried to employ a fairly uniform and uninvolved pattern. I have left the spelling "Dostoevsky," and not "Dostoyevsky," because of common usage.

As regards punctuation, at times I have followed the Russian text, especially in quotations from Dostoevsky who often "strewed" his pages with commas and colons. Dates follow the Julian calendar, except in instances when they are specifically marked "new style." In the nineteenth century, these dates were twelve days earlier than if they were calculated by the Gregorian calendar. I have footnoted only what seemed necessary to me, hoping to avoid the Scylla–Charybdis of pedanticism and obscurity. My footnotes are indicated by numerals, those of the author by letters.

I would like to acknowledge my indebtedness to:

Helene Iswolsky, who years ago introduced me to Mochulsky's work and who helped and reassured me through the trials of translating it;

Professor Richard Burgi of Princeton University, who first encouraged me to begin this project;

Professor George Krugovoy, who continually sustained my efforts with his advice, insights, and understanding;

Professor Roger DeGaris of Northwestern University and Professor Clarence Brown of Princeton, who read through sections of the manuscript;

Mr. Norman Weinstein, who accomplished the *podvig* of preparing my index;

the President of Bard College and my colleagues in the Department of Languages and Literature, who displayed great generosity, cooperation and understanding;

to my mother, my sister Denise, and friends for their support and encouragement when I needed it most;

and especially to Mrs. James Holly Hanford, of Princeton University Press, without whose selfless, untiring efforts and generosity I could not have completed this work.

Michael A. Minihan

Annandale-on-Hudson
October 10, 1967

Author's Preface

Dostoevsky's life was profoundly tragic. It was enveloped in vast solitude and loneliness. The universal problems which concerned the author of *Crime and Punishment* were all but inaccessible to his contemporaries. They regarded him merely as a preacher of humanitarianism, as the voice of "poor people," of the "humiliated and wronged." The 19th century found Dostoevsky's world fantastic. While Turgenev, Goncharov, and Lev Tolstoy painted grand epics of the impregnable order of the Russian "cosmos," Dostoevsky cried out that this cosmos was unstable, that beneath it chaos was already beginning to stir. In the midst of general prosperity, he alone spoke of the cultural crisis and of the unimagined catastrophes that awaited the world. Contemporaries dismissed these "ravings" and the despair of the author of *Notes from Underground* as the outgrowth of fanaticism and sickness. Dostoevsky was dubbed "a sick, cruel talent"[1] and quickly forgotten. The writer's spiritual ties with the generation of the 1880's and 1890's were rent in two. At the beginning of the 20th century, before the first Revolution, the Symbolists "discovered" Dostoevsky. The historical bulwarks of Russian life were beginning to waver; new souls, with a new tragic world-sense, were being born. The author of *The Devils* became their spiritual mentor. They were caught up by his prophetic anxiety. It was in the books and articles of N. Berdyayev, D. Merezhkovsky, S. Bulgakov, A. Volynsky, V. Ivanov, and V. Rozanov that Dostoevsky's philosophical dialectic was brought to light for the first time, that the spiritual revolution he had effected was considered and evaluated. The writer's works acquired a third dimension: metaphysical

[1] The term *cruel talent* was first used by the critic Nikolay Mikhailovsky (1842-1904) in an article published under that name in 1882. Mikhailovsky's philosophical views, based largely on Comte, were directed against metaphysical idealism and sought in scientific positivism and personalism a comprehensive world-view. As a "populist" he was affronted by the "libel" in *The Devils* and in 1882, when Vladimir Solovyov was proclaiming Dostoevsky the prophet of the Russian people, Mikhailovsky set about demonstrating that from his earliest works Dostoevsky had been fascinated by "cruelty" and the sensual pleasure involved in torturing. He completely failed to grasp Dostoevsky's concepts of the personality and of suffering and basically misunderstood his major characters. Through his influence upon Gorky, Mikhailovsky's criticism became a dominant line of Soviet critical studies until the late fifties; but what is more incomprehensible and unfortunate is that a number of American and English critics have till today continued naively to pursue this "trend."

depth. The merit of the Symbolists in overcoming a purely psychological approach to the creator of the 20th century's "novel-tragedy,"[2] was to see in Dostoevsky not only a talented psychologist, but a great religious thinker as well.

The second "discovery" of Dostoevsky took place after the Revolution of 1917. In 1905 there had been only a foreboding of catastrophe and it had made itself manifest in dull, underground rumblings; in 1917 it burst forth. Ties with the self-satisfied, "cultured" prosperity of the 19th century were severed once and for all. Russia, and with her the entire world, entered upon a terrible era of hitherto unknown social and spiritual ordeals. The presentiments of the author of *The Devils* were proved correct. The catastrophic world-outlook of this "sick talent" became the spiritual climate of the times.

The year 1921, the centennial of his birth, is an important date in the history of Dostoevskian studies. There appeared, both in Russia and abroad, a whole group of young scholars (A. Dolinin, V. Komarovich, L. Grossman, G. Chulkov, V. Vinogradov, Yu. Tynyanov, A. Bem) who set about laying the foundations for the scientific, historic, and literary study of the great writer's works.[3] Archives were published. Some of Dostoevsky's little known or forgotten works appeared in print. A complete collection of his letters came out.[4] The publication of various memoirs significantly enriched critical research. Numerous

[2] The term *novel-tragedy* originated in a study published in 1911 by Vyacheslav Ivanov (1866-1949). Ivanov was a major Russian poet, the leading theorist of the St. Petersburg Symbolists, a talented philologist, historian, professor, and critic. His remarkable essays on Dostoevsky (which have been collected and published in English by Noonday Press, New York 1952, under the title *Freedom and the Tragic Life*) present the writer as the great modern creator of myths. Ivanov analyzes Dostoevsky's novels in the light of classical and Shakespearean tragedy and demonstrates how his purposes, construction, devices, and the ultimate effects produced by his work follow the patterns of tragic rhythm: suffering, death, and rebirth through purification.

[3] The value to Dostoevskian scholarship of these critics' research and publications cannot be overestimated. Among many other works, attention should be drawn to A. S. Dolinin's publication of Dostoevsky's letters, the notebooks to *A Raw Youth* and *The Brothers Karamazov*, as well as of various archives and materials; to Chulkov's analysis of Dostoevsky's creative processes; to Tynyanov's brilliant essay on Gogol and Dostoevsky; and Vinogradov's study of the evolution of the Russian "natural school." A special place in Dostoevskian scholarship belongs to Leonid Grossman for his many volumes of source and biographical material and for his own critical analyses. His book *Dostoevsky*, published in Moscow 1962, is of major importance. The emigré scholar A. Bem at the end of the thirties edited in Prague three excellent volumes of studies on Dostoevsky which include his own writings on the influences upon Dostoevsky.

[4] Four volumes of Dostoevsky's letters were published in Moscow and Leningrad under A. S. Dolinin's editorship in 1928, 1930, 1934, and 1959. Professor Joseph Frank and David Goldstein are presently preparing an English translation of these letters for Rutgers University Press.

monographs and collections of studies were written. Among these new publications the printing of Dostoevsky's notebooks is of the greatest importance.[5] The rough drafts and notes for the "great novels" are full of reflections of absorbing interest. Here we find Dostoevsky's laboratory. We see before our very eyes the birth, growth, and development of his ideological and artistic plans. The genesis of the "novel-tragedy" and the laws of its structure have now been made accessible to research.

The Symbolists discovered Dostoevsky the philosopher. Contemporary scholars are discovering Dostoevsky the artist. The myth about the lack of aesthetic form and the stylistic carelessness of the author of *The Karamazovs* has at last been cast aside. In studying the writer's poetics, his composition, techniques, and style, we enter the aesthetic world of the great novelist.

The life and work of Dostoevsky are inseparable. He "lived in literature." It was his life's concern and his tragic fate. In all of his works he resolved the enigma of his personality; he spoke only of those things which he himself had personally experienced. Dostoevsky was always drawn to confession as an artistic form. His works unfold before us as one vast confession, as the integral revelation of his universal spirit. In the course of our study we have tried to preserve this spiritual unity of life and work.

K. Mochulsky

[5] The notebooks for *Crime and Punishment* were published by Glivenko (*Iz arkhiva Dostoevskogo. Prestuplenie i nakazanie*), Moscow and Leningrad, 1931; for *The Idiot* by Sakulin and Belchikov (*Iz arkhiva Dostoevskogo. Idiot. Neizdannye materialy*), Moscow, 1931; for *The Devils* by Konshina (*Zapisnye tetradi F. M. Dostoevskogo*), Moscow and Leningrad, 1935; for *A Raw Youth* by Dolinin (*V tvorcheskoy laboratorii Dostoevskogo*), Moscow, 1947; and for *The Brothers Karamazov* by Dolinin (*Dostoevsky, materialy i issledovaniya*), Leningrad, 1935. The University of Chicago Press has announced its intention to publish an English translation of the notebooks, the first volume of which series, *The Notebooks for Crime and Punishment*, has already been issued under the editorship of Edward Wasiolek.

Contents

Translator's Introduction   vii

Author's Preface   xvii

   I. Childhood and Youth   3

  II. *Poor People*   24

 III. *The Double* and *Mister Prokharchin*   40

 IV. Works of 1847-1848   69

  V. The First Attempt at a Novel:
Netochka Nezvanova   99

 VI. Dostoevsky the Revolutionary   114

VII. The Fortress and Penal Servitude   133

VIII. Exile · First Marriage · *Uncle's Dream*
The Village of Stepanchikovo   155

 IX. *Notes from the House of Death*   182

  X. *The Humiliated and Wronged*   198

 XI. The Journal *Time* (1861-1863)
Winter Notes on Summer Impressions
His Intimacy with A. Suslova   219

XII. The Journal *Epoch*
Notes from Underground   242

XIII. *Crime and Punishment*   270

XIV. *The Gambler* · Second Marriage
Life Abroad (1866-1868)   314

XV. *The Idiot*   334

XVI. Florence and Dresden
The Eternal Husband and
The Life of a Great Sinner   382

XVII. Work on the Novel *The Devils*   404

XVIII. *The Devils*   433

XIX. The Epoch of *The Citizen*
The Diary of a Writer for 1873   470

XX. *A Raw Youth*   488

XXI. *The Diary of a Writer* (1876-1877)   535

XXII. The Final Years · The History of
The Brothers Karamazov   565

XXIII. *The Brothers Karamazov*   596

XXIV. The Pushkin Speech · Death   637

Conclusion   649

Appendix   652

Index   681

Dostoevsky

I

Childhood and Youth

In the course of the 17th century, the Dostoevskys, one of the branches of an old Lithuanian family, settled in the Ukraine.[1] The writer's grandfather was a priest; his father, Mikhail Andreyevich, as a boy of fifteen ran away to Moscow, where he completed his studies at the Academy of Medicine. He took part in the War of 1812, and from the year 1821 served as head physician at the Mariinsky Hospital in Moscow. A man of extremely difficult temperament, sullen, contentious, suspicious, the elder Dostoevsky was subject to attacks of depression. His personality was a fusion of cruelty and sensibility, piety and avarice. His wife, Mariya Fyodorovna, came from a family of merchants, the Nechayevs. A gentle and sickly woman, she venerated her husband. Fyodor Mikhailovich used to keep a miniature that had belonged to his mother. On it was pictured an angel flying, and the words:

> J'ai le coeur tout plein d'amour,
> Quand l'aurez-vous à votre tour?

The correspondence between Dostoevsky's parents is full of tenderness and feeling. His father wrote: "Don't forget me, poor as I am, and without a home"; "don't forget me, a poor, wretched soul." His mother replied: "Don't be disturbed, my pet. . . . But tell me, my life, what is this depression, what are these melancholic thoughts, and what torments you, my dearest love? My heart sinks when I imagine you in such a depressed state of mind. I implore you, my angel, my divinity, preserve yourself for my love. . . ."

Dostoevsky's father proceeded quickly from sentimental outpourings to household problems: after Mariya Fyodorovna's departure to the

---

[1] There has been some controversy in the past as to whether the Dostoevsky family originally migrated from Lithuania or whether they were of Tartar stock. Soviet scholars today are inclined to the former theory on the basis of Ukrainian documents and records. Grossman cites the fact that in 1506 the family was granted a charter to the village of Dostoevo in Pinsk district.

country with the children, he took a thorough inventory of the soup-spoons, bottles, decanters, and his wife's dresses. He suspected that the servants might be stealing. "Write me," he asked his wife, "if you didn't leave some of your dresses, some dickies, caps, or anything like that, and as well, what we have in the store-room. Try to remember, and write me in detail, because I'm afraid that Vasilisa might have robbed us." He was constantly complaining about poverty. "Alas, how sad it is," he wrote his wife, "that because of my present state of poverty, I can't send you anything for your name's day. My soul languishes." But his poverty was purely imaginary. Mikhail Andreyevich received a salary of 100 paper rubles, had a private practice, a rent-free apartment from the government, seven servants, and four horses. In 1831 he purchased an estate consisting of two villages, Darovoye and Chermashnya, in the province of Tula.

Fyodor Mikhailovich Dostoevsky was born in Moscow on October 30, 1821. His brother Mikhail was older than he by a year, while his sister Varvara was one year younger. According to the author's wife, Anna Grigoryevna, "Fyodor Mikhailovich liked to recall his happy, serene childhood, and he would speak of his mother with great fervor. He especially loved his older brother Misha and his sister Varenka. His younger brothers and sisters failed to leave any strong impression on him."

Anna Grigoryevna's memoirs contain a hagiographical touch. Dostoevsky's childhood was hardly that serene. His mother used to call Fedya "a regular ball of fire." The conflicts with his father, his fear of him, and a latent ill-will borne toward him developed a reticence and lack of straightforwardness early in the boy's life. "I am astonished, my love, at Fedya's pranks," Mariya Fyodorovna wrote to her husband, "for one has always to expect such things from him." And the elder Dostoevsky used to tell his son: "Eh, Fedya, watch out. You'll get it yet. You'll wear the red hat."[2] Even though this threat of conscription was made in jest, all the same it does not attest to any particular tenderness on the parent's part.

The children used to tremble before their father, fearing his angry outbursts. He taught Latin to Mikhail and Fyodor. Andrey Mikhailovich, Dostoevsky's younger brother, recalls: "When my brothers were with father, which was frequently for an hour or more, they not only

[2] Red hats were worn by privates in the Siberian line battalions. The elder Dostoevsky's remark proved tragically prophetic; Dostoevsky did serve as a private in Siberia from March 1854 to the fall of 1855 as a result of his involvement in the Petrashevsky Affair.

did not dare sit down, but even lean their elbows on the table. They used to stand like little idols, declining in turn, *mensa, mensae,* or conjugating *amo, amas, amat."* During the summer, when the doctor would rest after lunch, one of the children used to shoo the flies away with a lime-tree branch.

The family's patriarchal regime was in singular accord with the sentimental style of the epoch. The saccharine exuberance of Dostoevsky's letters to his father produce a tedious impression. In 1838 he wrote to Mikhail Andreyevich: "Most beloved Papa! My God, how long have I not written to you! How long have I not tasted these minutes of true, heart-felt beatitude, true, pure, sublime . . . Beatitude which is experienced only by those who know with whom to share their hours of delight and of afflictions, to whom they can confide all that is fulfilled in their hearts. . . . Oh, how greedily now I revel in this beatitude! . . ." The letter ends with a request for money.

All of Dostoevsky's letters to his father from the School of Engineering are replete with exclamations, moral reflections, and complaints about his needs. In order to move the harsh old man, the youth artfully played upon his more sensitive chords. "The camp life of every pupil in a military academy," he wrote in 1839,

> costs at very minimum, forty rubles. (I write you all this because I'm talking to my own father.) In this sum I do not include such wants as, for example, to have tea, sugar, and so on. This sum, even without that, is indispensable, and is indispensable not merely for propriety's sake, but out of sheer need. When in foul weather, the rain soaks you in your linen tent, or in such weather coming back from the exercises, tired, frozen through, one can fall sick without tea. This happened to me last year during maneuvers. But all the same I respect your need, and so will not drink tea. I only want that which is indispensable for two pairs of ordinary boots, — sixteen rubles.

In another letter the threat of not being able to drink tea is reinforced by moral aphorisms: "Children, when they understand their parents' concerns, ought themselves to share everything with them — joy and sorrow. In every respect children should support their parents' needs. I will not ask much of you. So what! Because one has not drunk tea, one won't die from hunger. I'll live somehow. . . ."

The son's diplomacy grew less innocent when, in order to catch his father, he turned to more serious motives than that of being deprived of tea. "I have just taken Communion," he wrote. "I borrowed money for the priest. For a long time now I've been without a kopeck." The dualism of Dostoevsky's nature and the complex contradictions of his soul are already in evidence to some degree in these early letters.

After the death of his wife, whose humble love had assuaged his despotic disposition, Mikhail Andreyevich retired, and settled on his country estate. There he turned to drink and debauchery, and began to torture his peasants. One of the peasants from Darovoye, Makarov, in recalling the elder Dostoevsky, stated: "The man was a beast. His soul was dark, — that's it. . . . The master was a stern, unrighteous lord, but the mistress was kind-hearted. He didn't live well with her; beat her. He flogged the peasants for nothing." In 1839 his peasants killed him. Andrey Dostoevsky gives an account of it in his memoirs: "Father flew into a rage and began to shout terribly at the peasants. One of them, being more daring than the rest, answered this shouting with a strong vulgarity and thereupon being frightened of the consequences of such audacity, he yelled out, 'Boys, let's finish him off.' And with these cries, about fifteen peasants fell upon father and in an instant, naturally, put an end to him." The writer's daughter, Lyubov Dostoevskaya, adds: "They found him later half-suffocated with a pillow from the carriage. The coachman had disappeared together with the horse."

In Dostoevsky's correspondence we do not find a single reference to the tragic death of his father. There is something frightening in this unyielding silence throughout the course of his entire life. A close friend of the writer, Baron Vrangel, let it be known that "Dostoevsky categorically did not like to talk about his father and asked not to be questioned about him." A. Suvorin alludes to "a tragic incident in his family life." He adds: "The epilepsy with which Dostoevsky had been afflicted since the days of his childhood, profoundly intensified the thorny way of his life. Something frightening, unforgettable, agonizing, happened to him in childhood as the result of which epilepsy appeared."[3]

The testimony of Doctor S. Yanovsky fully confirms this. "It was in

[3] Sigmund Freud's famous essay *Dostoevsky and Parricide* (reprinted in *Dostoevsky*, ed. René Wellek, in the "Twentieth Century Views" series, Prentice-Hall, Inc., 1962) is particularly interesting in this regard. Freud draws a distinction between organic and "affective" epilepsy, the second being not an alien disturbance, but an expression of the individual's mental life itself. He then goes on to propose that Dostoevsky's attacks were of this latter type and to relate them to the oppressive atmosphere of his childhood and finally to the effect of his father's murder upon the writer.

fact during his childhood that Fyodor Mikhailovich underwent some gloomy and depressing experience such as never passes in maturity without some effect, and which imprints the subject with a temperament which is prone to nervous ailments and, consequently, even epilepsy, as well as to sullenness, reticence, and suspiciousness. This latter usually manifests itself as a struggle against privation, even though such privation does not exist, at least, not to any terrifying degree."

That "frightening" experience about which Suvorin and Yanovsky speak was his father's violent death. But they were mistaken in extending this occurrence back to the writer's childhood. Dostoevsky was then eighteen years old. A jarring change in his character can be traced precisely to that age. The lighthearted and playful boy, the "regular ball of fire," was transformed into an unsociable, contemplative youth. This is how his comrades at the School of Engineering painted him. The characteristics that Yanovsky noted — the sullenness, the reticence, and suspiciousness — were part of Dostoevsky's legacy from his father. The son's imagination was deeply shaken not only by the dramatic circumstances of the older man's death, but also by a feeling of his own guilt before Mikhail Andreyevich. He did not love him; he used to complain about his stinginess; shortly before his death he had written him an irritating letter; and now he felt himself to a degree responsible for his father's death. This moral trauma prepared the way for his initial epileptic seizures. The problem of fathers and children, of crime and punishment, of guilt and responsibility met Dostoevsky at the very threshold of his conscious life. This was a physiological and moral trauma in his being; and it was only at the end of his life in *The Brothers Karamazov* that he freed himself of it by transforming it into a creative work of art.

This, of course, does not mean that Fyodor Pavlovich Karamazov is a portrait of Mikhail Andreyevich. Dostoevsky was freely in command of the materials which life provided. But the "idea" of the Karamazov father was doubtlessly inspired by the image of Dostoevsky's father. The writer's daughter, Lyubov Fyodorovna, observes in her memoirs: "I have always felt that while Dostoevsky was creating the character of the old Karamazov, he was thinking of his own father." In his father's house, under the respected forms of a strictly ordered life, the boy early began to detect falsehood and insecurity. All of Dostoevsky's novels are, in a profound sense, autobiographical, and, of course, in the manuscript of *A Raw Youth* he is writing about his own family: "There are children who, while still in childhood, begin to reflect upon their families, who begin in childhood to be offended by their fathers' unsightliness, their fathers' and their surroundings', and above all, who in childhood already begin to understand the disorder and haphazardness of the very foundation of their whole life, the absence of established forms and ancestral tradition." The family of staff-physician Dostoevsky, the impoverished noble and petty landowner, completely conforms to the designation "a haphazard household."

As Dostoevsky grew older, he liked to recall the memories of his childhood. In order to refresh them, he went to visit his father's estate, which long before had been sold. There he was reminded of the poor idiot Agrafena who for a whole year walked about in a single shirt, who passed the nights in the cemetery, and used to tell everyone about her dead child. The "idea" of the father, which served as the impetus for the novel *The Brothers Karamazov*, gave rise also to the image of the idiot Agrafena from the village of Darovoye (Stinking Lizaveta) and the name of the village Chermashnya. There is an indirect confirmation in this of the bond between Fyodor Pavlovich Karamazov and Dostoevsky's father.

The closed little world of the family, with its unvarying rules of life; and, behind the lattice in the garden, the hospital park in which the patients in their nightcaps and dressing gowns walked about taking the air; his nurse Lukerya's stories about the Fire-Bird and Ivan the Tsarevich; on Sundays, standing through the interminable Liturgy, in the evenings, the family reading — this was Dostoevsky's childhood. He treasured the memory of his stout old nurse Alyona Frolovna who, when he was a child of three, taught him to pray: "I place all my hope in Thee, Mother of God; preserve me under Thy protection." The decorous summer promenades in Mary's Grove, which his father combined with edifying conversation, and the annual pilgrimages to the Trinity–St. Sergius Monastery were the big events in the boy's life. The church architecture, the harmonious singing of the choir, and the crowds of pilgrims left a strong impression on the boy. Later in life, he recalled that he had seen women who were suffering from fits, cured there. "That truly amazed and astonished me as a child." His mother taught him the alphabet through *The Holy History of the Old and New Testament*, illustrated with pictures. Later on the deacon took up the children's education, and used to tell them magnificent stories "from the Scriptures."

The Dostoevskys never visited, nor did they receive guests; the brothers lived without any playmates of their own age, almost without contact with the outside world. Two or three times they were taken to the theatre. Dostoevsky remembered one presentation *Jacot, or the Brazilian Monkey*, and later he saw Mochalov's performance in Schiller's *The Robbers*. From that time on — he was then ten years old — he expressed a passionate enthusiasm for Schiller. Fyodor and Mikhail, being isolated from life, began early to immerse themselves in "fantasy." The verses of Derzhavin, Zhukovsky, Pushkin, Karamzin's narratives, and the novels of Walter Scott opened their eyes to the magic world of fiction. They raved over sentimental heroes and medieval knights. Mikhail wrote some verses on the sly, while Fyodor dreamed that he was Waverly or Quentin Durward. His imagination was flooded with pictures of Venice, Constantinople, and the fabled East. The brothers knew Pushkin by heart. After the poet's death, Fyodor used to say: "If our own family had not been in mourning [their mother died in 1837], I would have asked father's permission to wear mourning for Pushkin."

The young Dostoevsky devoured books: *Yury Miloslavsky, The House of Ice, The Kholmsky Family*, the tales of the Cossack Lugansky the novels of Narezhny and Weltmann, and especially, Karamzin's histories and his narratives — the boy read everything and retained everything. His was not a mere curiosity, but a genuine passion for literature. In the rough draft of his unwritten novel *The Life of a Great Sinner*, the writer notes: "A detailed psychological analysis of how the works of various authors influence the child, and so on. *Hero of Our Time*. He reads a prodigious amount (Walter Scott and so forth). Is greatly developed and knows many things. Gogol he knows, and Pushkin. He used to know the entire Bible. Without fail, how the Gospels influence him. In agreement with Gospels. Reading about Suvorov. Arabian tales. Fancies." There can be no doubt but that this notation is autobiographical.

The impressions which the young Dostoevsky gleaned from literature, were far more important to him than those offered by life. His acquaintance with Scott or Schiller determined his inner formation to a much greater degree than the influence of nature or the atmosphere of his family life. By his very nature he was an introspective, withdrawn individual. The interior always prevailed in his personality over the exterior. The intensity of his inner life posed a threat to equilibrium, and set the stage for the tragedy of the dreamer vainly searching for "living life." The problem of the "underground man" is contained in the writer's "abstract," bookish youth.

In 1833 the Dostoevsky brothers were enrolled in the boarding school of Monsieur Souchard, a poorly enough educated Frenchman, who together with his wife somehow taught French grammar. Life at this curious establishment has been described by the writer in *A Raw Youth*. After a year the boys transferred to the "proper," patriarchal boarding school of Leonty Ivanovich Chermak, which was staffed by the best professors in Moscow. The teacher of Russian letters was the famous scholar Davydov. Fyodor did not have any friends at school; he was unable to get along with his contemporaries. Every Saturday a carriage from the hospital used to come for the brothers to take them home, where their beloved books were waiting for them. Their mother died of consumption. She passed away in 1837; her death affected Dostoevsky much less than did Pushkin's.

Mikhail Andreyevich now decided to take the younger children and move to the country, while placing the older boys, Mikhail and Fyodor, in the School of Engineering in Petersburg. In May of the year 1837 he took them to the capital, and established them in Koronad Filippovich Kostomarov's boarding school so they could prepare for the entrance examinations. In *The Diary of a Writer* Dostoevsky reminisces upon this journey.

At that time, my brother and I were longing for a new life; were desperately dreaming of something, of all that is "beautiful and noble" — at that time, these little words were still fresh and uttered without irony. We passionately believed in something, and although we both knew perfectly well that all they would ask us about on the examination was mathematics, nonetheless we dreamed only of poetry and of poets. My brother was writing verses. Every day he composed three poems, even while we were traveling, and I was continually formulating the mental draft of a novel about Venetian life. Only two months before, Pushkin had passed away, and on the road my brother and I agreed that once we had arrived in Petersburg, we would immediately go down to the spot where the duel had been held, and make our way to Pushkin's former apartment in order to see the room in which he had given up his spirit.

The Venetian novel was abruptly cut short by a confrontation with Russian reality. At a posting-station in the province of Tver, Dostoevsky met an official courier, "a well-built, strong fellow," who, with his clinched fist, was methodically beating a postillion over the back of the head. "That disgusting picture," the writer noted, "has always lingered in my memory. I can never forget that courier, and somehow unwillingly, and for a long time afterward, I was inclined to explain — from what was of course already too one-sided a viewpoint — much that is shameful and cruel in the Russian people." Such was the young idealist's first awakening from the world of dreams. Dostoevsky had the courier in mind when he created the image of cruelty in Raskolnikov's dream (a poor nag being beaten to death by Mikolka).

At Kostomarov's boarding school, the Dostoevsky brothers were plunged into geometry and the study of fortification. Fyodor passed his examination, and in January 1838 entered the School of Engineering. Mikhail, however, was not accepted, on the grounds of poor health, and he set out for Reval to join an engineering detachment there. A lively correspondence now began between the brothers. The years of study in the Palace of Engineering were devoid of any noteworthy occurrences. Without the least enthusiasm, the boy drudged through the lectures, examinations, the camping exercises; he submitted with difficulty to the stringent drilling; he crammed for the detested mathematics courses. In this depressing palace where Emperor Pavel I was killed, the traditions of discipline, military valor, and tours of service were carefully preserved. But there also existed a "secret spirit": two of the students, the musician Chikhachyov and Ignaty Bryanchaninov, once they had finished the officers' courses, entered St. Sergius' Monastery as novices. Among the students of the school, they were known derogatorily as "Bryanchaninovites." It is altogether possible that this mystical stream touched even young Dostoevsky.

This romantic period of the writer's life was marked by his literary enthusiasms and his ardent cult of friendship. In Petersburg he became acquainted with Ivan Nikolayevich Shidlovsky, a young civil servant in the Ministry of Finance and a poet. Shidlovsky wrote verse in a mystical and nebulous vein: he suffered as the result of a sublime and exalted love, talked about the Heavenly Kingdom with true inspiration, and at the same time was enthralled by the dream of self-destruction. He was disillusioned. Even his beloved did not know how to inspire him to great creative acts; even she "did not wrest harmonious chords from his reed-pipe upon which a spell has been cast by the fragrance of an unexpected flower." In his soul the verses of Schiller and Novalis resounded; the unbodied shades of Zhukovsky's poetry wafted gently; the ideas of Schelling's "Naturphilosophie" had their response. He believed that "man is the means through which the sublime will become manifest in humanity; that the body, that clay pitcher, will sooner or later be smashed to pieces." Dostoevsky wrote to his brother about Shidlovsky with ecstatic delight. In his letters, the romantic literary style is carried almost to the point of parody. The youth not only saw everything through the eyes of his friend, but literally felt with his feelings. Here for the first time we encounter the writer's capacity for artistic metamorphosis.

In 1840 he informed Mikhail Mikhailovich:

> If only you had seen him [Shidlovsky] last year. . . . But to glance at him — there is a martyr! He was fearfully emaciated; his cheeks hollowed; his once-moist eyes were dry and burning. The spiritual beauty of his face was exalted by his physical decline. He was suffering, suffering terribly. My God, how he loves a certain girl. . . . Without this love he would not be such a pure, exalted, disinterested priest of poetry. . . . Before me there stood a beautiful, sublime creature, the true sketch of a man, such as both Shakespeare and Schiller have presented to us. But even then he was prepared to succumb to the gloomy mania of Byronic characters. Frequently we sat up together whole evenings in conversation about God knows what. Oh, what a candid, pure soul! Tears now flow when I remember the past. . . . Spring came upon us; it enlivened him. His imagination began to create dramas, and what dramas, my brother! . . . And his lyric poems! . . . At our last meeting, we strolled about Yekaterinhof. Oh, how we passed that evening! We recalled our winter life when we used to talk about Homer, Shakespeare, Schiller, Hoffmann. . . . Last winter I was in a state of rapture. My acquaintance with Shidlovsky gave me so many hours of a better life.

Soon the friends were parted forever. We are informed about the subsequent fate of Shidlovsky, the Russian romantic-mystic, through a letter written by his daughter-in-law to Anna Grigoryevna Dostoevskaya in 1901. Shidlovsky soon gave up writing verse and began to work on a history of the Russian Church.

But scholarly work was not enough to absorb the entirety of his moral activity. Inner discord, a dissatisfaction with all about him, these supposedly were the reasons that prompted him during the 50's to enter the Valuy Monastery. Apparently not finding satisfaction and peace of mind even here, he undertook a pilgrimage to Kiev, where he appealed to a certain spiritual director who advised him to return home to the country, where he lived until his death, though even there not taking off the monastic habit of a novice. His strange life, so full of vacillations, bears witness to his strong passions and stormy nature. Ivan Nikolayevich's profound moral sense stood frequently in contradiction to several strange turns of behavior. His sincere faith and religious tenor alternated with temporary skepticism and negation.

At his estate Shidlovsky sometimes dissipated with the dragoons, sometimes preached homilies. "For a long time, in the distant regions of Kharkov Province, one could see a tall man dressed in pilgrim's garb, standing at the entrance to a tavern, preaching the Gospel to a crowd of muzhiks."

Russian romanticism in all the intricacies of its diverse aspects is one of the fundamental ideas of Dostoevsky's work. From his enthusiastic veneration of it, through his unmasking and struggle with it, he came finally at the end of his life to a recognition of its worth. But the writer created not abstract schemes, but living people — "the bearers of ideas." He had experienced romanticism in his deep personal friendship with the romantic, Shidlovsky; he had perceived it in an actual human image. Ordynov in the tale *The Landlady* heads the line of Dostoevsky's romantic heroes; Dmitry Karamazov, declaiming Schiller, closes it. Throughout his whole life, Fyodor Mikhailovich treasured the tender memory of the friend of his youth. Anna Grigoryevna tells us that he first became attracted to Vladimir Solovyov because the latter reminded him of Shidlovsky.

A second romantic friendship can be dated about 1840. Its hero was Dostoevsky's senior classmate, Ivan Berezhetsky. One of the instructors, A. Savelyev, has described him as an effeminate fop. "It happened more than once," he wrote, "that I saw, even during class hours and at the time when the conductors would take their airing, F. M. Dostoevsky either alone or with somebody, but never anyone other than the conductor of the senior class, Iv. Berezhetsky. Frequently under the pretext of being ill, they would stay behind either by the little table by the bed, occupied with reading, or walking together about the room. Unfortunately, then, even as now, it was difficult to determine the actual significance of this friendship between the two young men. . . . Berezhetsky was considered to be a person of substance; he liked to play the fop by exhibiting his wealth (he wore a watch, diamond rings; had money) and distinguished himself by his social upbringing, playing the fop in his dress, toilette, and especially in the delicacy of his mannerisms in dealing with others." K. D. Khlebnikov in his *Notes* informs us: "I remember how F. M. Dostoevsky and Berezhetsky became strongly attached to one another by reading, if I am not mistaken, Schiller together. They used to read, read, and suddenly begin to argue and then soon, soon they would go through all our rooms and dormitories, one ahead of the other, as though running away in order not to hear the other's retort — this Berezhetsky usually did, and Dostoevsky would follow him in an attempt to finish expounding his opinion."

In the friendship with Shidlovsky, Dostoevsky was only a pupil restrained by the genius of his poetic friend. In his relations with the dandy, Berezhetsky, on the other hand, his was the dominant role. With the voice of authority he impressed upon the worldly youth the greatness of Don Carlos and the Marquis de Posa. In the former instance, he was the reincarnation of Shidlovsky; here he transformed Berezhetsky into the heroes of Schiller. He wrote his brother:

> *I had* a companion near me, the only creature that I have ever loved so. You wrote to me, dear brother, that I have not read Schiller; you're mistaken, brother! I learned Schiller by heart; his was my voice; he was my delirium. And I think that fate has never acted more opportunely in my life than to have introduced me to the great poet at this very period of my life; later I could never have known him as I do now. While reading Schiller *with him,* I find the noble, fiery Don Carlos and the Marquis de Posa and Mortimer verified *in him.* This friendship has brought me so much grief and delight. From now on I will be eternally silent about it. The name of Schiller has become a part of me, as some magic sound summoning forth as many dreams. But they are bitter, my dear brother. That is why I did not speak to you about Schiller, about the impressions that he has produced in my soul. I am pained when I but hear the name of Schiller.

In the letters to his brother, no mention was ever made of his life at school, the activities, or the teachers. The dreamer took no notice of dreary reality; he lived in a world of literature, poetry — and he inhabited it with passionate enthusiasm. The friendship with Berezhetsky was not to last, and the dreams about Schiller that were intimately bound to it soon became "bitter." Probably, Don Carlos–Berezhetsky disappointed his exacting friend. His companions at school described the young Dostoevsky as being pensive and taciturn. K. Trutovsky wrote:

He was well-built, thick-set; his gait was quick and somehow jerky. He had a sort of greyish complexion. His glance was always pensive, and for the most part his expression remained intent. In some way or other he just did not seem to go with the military uniform. He always held himself aloof, and he struck me as being almost constantly apart from the others, pacing in one direction or another, backward and forward, and with an expression that seemed lost in contemplation. . . . He always had a serious look about him, and I simply cannot imagine him laughing or having fun with a group of friends. I don't know why, but at school we dubbed him "Photius."[4]

In 1841 the instructor Savelyev described Dostoevsky in the following manner:

Pensive, readily prone to fits of depression, one might say reserved, he rarely joined any of his comrades. His favorite place to work was the embrasure of the window in the company's corner dormitory, which looked out upon the Fontanka. In this spot isolated from the other desks, F. M. Dostoevsky used to sit and occupy himself. It frequently happened that he would not notice anything that was going on about him. At the regular set time his comrades would fall in line to go off to supper. They would pass through the circular room on their way to the dining hall; then with a great deal of noise, they would go into the recreation hall for their prayers; and finally once again they would pass through the room as they dispersed and went their separate ways. Dostoevsky would put his books and notes away into the desk only when the drummer, who had already gone through the rooms and sounded the evening tattoo, would compel him to leave off his work. In the dark of night you could still find F. M. sitting at his desk working. Having thrown a blanket about himself over his underwear, he hardly seemed conscious of the icy wind that blew in from the window next to which he was sitting.

[4] "Photius" may refer to the fanatical archimandrite (in the world Pyotr Spassky) who regarded himself as "the Savior of the Church and the Fatherland," and exercised an unfortunate influence over Aleksandr I, or perhaps to the great 9th century Byzantine Patriarch and champion of the Eastern Church.

A young writer enrolled by fate in a military academy, the first flares of inspiration born to the accompaniment of marching and the roll of drums — this is an image of his spiritual solitude in the School of Engineering. The young man drank in the air of mystical romanticism, of the religion of the heart, of the dream of a golden age. The borders of Christian art for him were very broad; they embraced Homer and Hugo, Shakespeare and Schiller, and Goethe. He wrote his brother:

> Homer (a man of legends, perhaps, like Christ, made flesh by God and sent to us) can find his parallel only in Christ, and not in Goethe. . . . Why, in the *Iliad* Homer presented all the ancient world with an organization for both its spiritual and earthly life (with absolutely the same force as Christ was to exercise regarding the new). . . . Victor Hugo, as a lyric poet, has a purely angelic character, has a poetic tendency that is both Christian and childlike — and in this no one can touch him, not Schiller (however much of a Christian poet we find Schiller) nor the lyric Shakespeare nor Byron nor Pushkin (Homer alone resembles Hugo).

In this letter with what awe and reverence do we find the apprentice kneeling before the "geniuses"! What an admixture of immature enthusiasm and hazy Christianity! Dostoevsky was acquainted with the romantic cult of the demigod Homer. He repeats the fashionable idea of an "organization" of mankind. He had heard something about Hugo's Christianity. With no less a passion he extolled the classics of Racine and Corneille. "Racine has no poetry?" he exclaims. "Racine, the fiery, passionate Racine, in love with his ideals, he has no poetry? And one can in fact ask this? Now about Corneille. . . . And do you know that through the vastness of his characters, the spirit of romanticism, he is almost a Shakespeare? Have you read *Le Cid*? Read it through, pitiable wretch, read it and fall in the dust before Corneille. You have abused him." After Corneille, Balzac steps forward as the synthesis of the spiritual development of all mankind. "Balzac is great," wrote Dostoevsky, "His characters are the fruit of a universal mind. Not the spirit of the times, but rather whole millenniums have by their struggles prepared for such a denouement in man's soul." Under the phrase "a universal mind" it is not hard to discern "the world spirit" of German Idealism.

Dostoevsky's enthusiasm for Balzac was to last throughout his entire life; the author of *Eugénie Grandet* was one of his most constant companions. Nor was the influence of Hoffmann any less profound. The fantastic world of the German romantic exercised a secret force to captivate the young man; though fully awake, he entered the delirious dreams of Hoffmann's strange and dreadful heroes. "I have a project," he informed his brother, "to go mad. Let people rage, try to cure me, let them try to bring me to reason. If you have read all of Hoffmann, then surely you remember the character Alban. It is hideous to behold a man who has the unintelligible in his power, a man who does not know what he must do, and plays with a toy which is God." Thus Dostoevsky's life was absorbed in literature; that which he read, he relived in his own being. Each encounter with a writer was a reality to him. Inasmuch as he had not received a systematic education, the youth, feverishly, impetuously, tried to assimilate world culture. The great names flashed but for a moment; enthusiasms changed and were replaced. His imagination seethed. But within this chaotic variation of impressions and enthusiasms, little by little a central theme was emerging, and his future vocation was being discerned. In all of German "Naturphilosophie," in Goethe's cosmic poetry, in Schiller's "noble and beautiful," and in the social novels of Balzac, Dostoevsky was searching for a single thing: man and his secret. The duality in human nature struck him early. In 1838 he wrote to his brother: "The atmosphere of man's soul consists in a fusion of heaven with earth; and man is a kind of illegitimate child. The law of man's inner nature is beyond him. It seems to me that our world is a purgatory for heavenly spirits who have been saddened by a sinful thought. It seems to me that our world has been given a negative significance, and from a lofty, fine spirituality, only satire has come forth. . . . How faint-hearted is the creature man! Hamlet! Hamlet!" And so here, for the first time, we find him confronted, though in a misty, romantic form, with the enigma of the Fall of Man and of Evil.

By the following year he already knew his vocation. The purpose of his life had been discovered. "My soul is now inaccessible to the raging squalls that used to shake it. In it, all is at peace as in the heart of a man who harbors a deep secret. To study the meaning of man and of life — I am making sufficient progress here. I have faith in myself. Man is a mystery. One must solve it. If you spend your entire life trying to puzzle it out, then do not say that you have wasted your time. I occupy myself with this mystery because I want to be a man." These prophetic words were uttered by an eighteen-year-old boy.

Dostoevsky's life at school became more agonizing with each passing day. He felt creative forces within himself, and was wretched because it was impossible to actualize them. "How miserable your life becomes," he complained to his brother, "when a man, conscious of vast forces within himself, sees that they are being spent in activity that is false and essentially contrary to your nature . . . in a life fit for a pigmy and not a giant, for a child and not a man."

These complaints were continually repeated: "Oh, my brother! Dear brother! Sooner to dock, sooner to freedom! Freedom and one's vocation are a great thing. I dream of it and imagine it as never before . . . somehow my soul is expanding that I might understand the grandeur of life."

Mikhail Mikhailovich came to Petersburg to take his officers' exam. On their last evening together before parting, Dostoevsky read him some excerpts from his dramas *Mary Stuart* and *Boris Godunov*. Of these first literary attempts, only the titles have come down to us. The influence of Shidlovsky, who had written a play *Mariya Simonova*, his passion for Schiller and Pushkin, and his devotion to the actor Samoylov account adequately for the origins of these sketches. They were quickly forgotten. Yet even in later life the writer came back more than once to this intended project — to write a play. However, this dream was never to be realized.

In 1842 Dostoevsky was promoted to the rank of sublieutenant, and he quit the Palace of Engineering. He rented a good-sized apartment on Vladimir Street. After the death of his father, his sister Varvara's husband Karepin, who was trustee of the estate, had been sending him each month his share of the income. Together with his salary, this constituted no meager sum: about 5,000 paper rubles a year.[5] But Dostoevsky never found any given amount of money sufficient. He lived freely. In the morning he used to attend lectures for the officers; he frequently passed his evenings at the theatre. He was captivated by Samoylov, the concerts of Rubini and Liszt, and Glinka's opera *Ruslan and Lyudmila*. Sometimes his fellow officers would gather at his place. They used to play Preference and other card games, and drink punch. For a while his younger brother Andrey lived with him. In his memoirs he complains that "Fyodor assumed supercilious airs in relations with him for fear he might carry his head too high" and that Dostoevsky did not enter him in Kostomarov's boarding school "because of monetary

[5] Paper rubles were worth slightly less than one-third as much as silver rubles.

considerations." It is difficult to determine just to what extent these reproaches are justified. Living with Andrey was without doubt a burden to Fyodor, and they parted without any regrets. In 1842 Andrey enrolled in a school for civil engineers.

In the spring of 1843 Dostoevsky passed his final examinations, and left to spend the summer in Reval with Mikhail. There he acted as godfather for his brother's first child. His health was shattered. His complexion had a claylike cast; his voice was hoarse and he had a dry cough. Mikhail and his wife Emiliya Fyodorovna had to look after his laundry and clothes. Upon his return to Petersburg, Dostoevsky moved into an apartment which he shared with a Dr. Riesenkampf. He was now working as a draughtsman in the Engineering Corps. Riesenkampf sketched this portrait of him: "A rather nicely rounded, fair, blondish chap with a roundish face and a slightly turned-up nose. He wore his light chestnut hair cut short. Under his high forehead and thin, sparse eyebrows his small, rather deep-set, greyish eyes were hidden. His cheeks were pale and freckled; his complexion was sickly, clay-colored; his lips thickish. He was far more lively, active, spirited than his sedate brother. . . . He loved poetry with a passion, but wrote only prose because his patience wasn't up to cultivating the form. Thoughts were born in his head much like sprays in a whirlpool."

The honorable doctor went to great lengths to inspire his roommate with some principles of household economy, but without success. Dostoevsky lived in hopeless extravagance and disorder. Now he regaled the doctor with a "sumptuous" dinner in fashionable Lerch's Restaurant on Nevsky Prospect; then for several months he remained without a cent. Having received a thousand rubles from his trustee in Moscow, he promptly lost it at billiards. Chance partners and questionable "friends" robbed him. He entered into conversations with Riesenkampf's patients and supplied them with money. He became involved with a vagrant whom he questioned about the life of the dregs of the capital. He borrowed money from pawnbrokers, and immediately lost it gambling. Dostoevsky's personality is accurately summed up by Riesenkampf in his memoirs: "good, generous, trusting, and completely unfit for life's realities — and this is how he will remain forever." But his disorderly existence did not hinder the writer from seriously occupying himself with literature. His military duties weighed upon him. In his letters to his brother this was the eternal complaint: "my duties are tiresome," "my duties have become as tiresome as potatoes."

Finally, in October 1844 he retired from the service. "As regards my life, don't be troubled," he wrote Mikhail. "I will find a piece of bread soon. I'll work hellishly. Now I'm free."

The former sublieutenant engineer Dostoevsky now became a professional writer.

His first steps along this new path were difficult. He was not earning any money; and on the other hand, debts were mounting. Dostoevsky wrote to his trustee, Pyotr Andreyevich Karepin, proposing that, for the sum of 1,000 silver rubles, he renounce all rights to his father's estate. Karepin did not approve of his retirement from the service. He could not cursorily effect an allotment of the property, and he urged him to think things over. Dostoevsky was enraged and denounced his rich relation. His letter resounds with savage irony. He dramatizes his own situation, describing himself as sick, impoverished, and dying of hunger. At this time he was working on his first novel *Poor People*, and almost imperceptibly he transformed himself into his hero, the half-starved civil servant Makar Devushkin. In a sporting fashion Karepin had admonished and tried to reform him; Dostoevsky retorted with malicious sarcasm. The trustee's reproaches, and they were fully deserved, wounded Dostoevsky's self-pride. The novelist's impression converted this honorable philanthropist into the figure of an exploiting bourgeois. Literature and reality were merged into one. The future author of *Poor People* had been aroused and inflamed by social pathos, and Karepin became the victim of his accusations.

We may illustrate the tone in which Dostoevsky wrote to his trustee, with the following excerpt:

> I am informing you, Pyotr Andreyevich, that I have an unqualified need for clothes. The winters in Petersburg are cold, and autumn is extremely damp and injurious to one's health. From this it obviously follows that one cannot go about without clothes, and if there aren't any, one can just give up the ghost. . . . Since I will not have an apartment, for I'm certainly going to have to vacate the old one for nonpayment of rent, then my fate will be to live on the street or to sleep under the colonnade of the Kazan Cathedral. But since this is unwholesome, I will need an apartment. In conclusion, I need to eat because not to eat is unwholesome. I have requested, asked, and implored you for three whole years to turn over to me that portion of my dead father's estate which is coming to me. You did not answer

me. You did not want to answer me. You have tormented me, humiliated me; you have mocked at me. I have borne it all with patience; I
have contracted debts; I have used up all my money. I have endured
shame and grief; I have endured sickness, hunger, and cold. Now my
endurance has ended, and I have no choice but to employ all the
means which the law and nature itself have placed at my disposal,
so that you will listen to me, and listen to me with both ears.

This picture of his own wretched existence ("shame, hunger, and
cold") and of the persecutions he must endure at the hands of his relations was transposed into Dostoevsky's biography out of his novel
Poor People. This, nonetheless, was not a conscious effort on his part
to distort the facts. Entranced by his own ideas, the young author
actually imagined himself dying of hunger on the streets of Petersburg.
On the other hand, however, Karepin was definitely not the savage and
heartless bourgeois that appears in Dostoevsky's representation. This is
what the writer's brother, Andrey Mikhailovich, had to say about him:
"Pyotr Andreyevich Karepin was a little over forty and a widower. He
had served as an administrator in the chancellory of the Governor-
General of Moscow, as an auditing-secretary for the Ladies' Committee for Prisons and on the Charity Committee which superintends all
the estates of the Princes Golitsyn. He was the very best of our best
men — not simply good, but evangelically good. He came from the
people, and achieved everything by his own intelligence and activity."
A rich, elderly widower by the name of Bykov marries a poor young
girl in Dostoevsky's novel *Poor People*. In his short story *A Christmas
Tree Party and a Wedding*, a wealthy man in his fifties, Yulian Mastakovich, is portrayed as the fiancé of a seventeen-year-old girl. We
find Dunya's fiancé, Luzhin, a man who is well-to-do and not especially
young in *Crime and Punishment*. Perhaps in Raskolnikov's hatred for
his sister's fiancé there are traces of the author's own hostility toward
his sister Varya's husband Karepin. Of course, psychologically there is
as little in common between Bykov, the willful and unreasonable landowner, and Karepin as there is between the civil servant Devushkin
and Dostoevsky himself. In his creation of the "Bykov-Luzhin" type,
the writer was attempting to give artistic embodiment to the idea of
the power of money, and of the coercive force of the strong over the
weak. The trusteeship of Karepin, that man who has "wronged" the
poor heirs, served as the focal point around which the author's personal feelings and his literary influences crystallized. Perhaps it was

also as a result of this association of Karepin with Bykov that the heroine of *Poor People* was given the name Varenka (in his letters Dostoevsky used to call his sister Varvara, who had married Karepin, "Varenka").

During this period, just at the beginning of his career, the young writer's literary work was haphazard and disorderly. His grandiose plans for dramas, translations, and publications quickly faded. At one time he wrote to his brother and proposed a translation and publication of Eugène Sue's *Mathilde;* at another he informed him that he had just finished a new play, *The Jew Yankel;* then he wrote that he had discarded the play. "You say," he added, "my salvation is the drama. Yes, but putting one on takes time and money as well." At his insistence Mikhail translated Schiller's *Robbers* and *Don Carlos,* while Fyodor toyed with the idea of publishing a complete edition of the German poet's works translated into Russian.

In 1843 Balzac spent three months in Petersburg. The journals sang his praises; this was the full flowering of his glory in Russia. Dostoevsky decided to profit by the French novelist's success, and he translated *Eugénie Grandet.*

In January 1844 he wrote his brother: "Apropos of Reval *we will think on it,* 'nous verrons cela' (an expression of *papa Grandet*). . . . You should be informed that during the holidays I have translated Balzac's *Eugénie Grandet.* (Miracle! Miracle!) My translation is incomparable." The translator intensified the emotional tone of the novel, and did not hesitate to employ effective similes and picturesque epithets. Under his pen the story of Eugénie's sufferings is transformed into a tale of "the unfathomable and horrifying tortures" of a poor young girl whose image for some reason or other he compares with an ancient Greek statue. This first literary attempt after the editors had abridged it by a third, appeared in *Repertoire and Pantheon.*

Dostoevsky's entrance into the literary world under the aegis of Balzac has its symbolic significance. He had become acquainted with the author of the *Comédie humaine* through installments of *The Library for Reading* in which *Le Père Goriot* had been translated. The journals presented Balzac to the Russian public as the voice of the contemporary city with its contrast of palaces and slums, as a preacher of compassion toward the unfortunate and the destitute. Père Goriot, who was made an object of derision by the inhabitants of a miserable, squalid boarding house in the Latin Quarter, and who was the victim of his own passionate love for his ungrateful daughters — especially captivated the young writer. From this hero of Balzac, there descends the whole line of Dostoevsky's "humiliated" old civil servants, and his grotesque and pitiable "poor people." In his first novel we meet two variants of this type: the old Pokrovsky cowering before his educated son, and Devushkin who perishes out of love for the orphan Varenka. In *Le Père Goriot*, Balzac touched upon problems of the strong personality, and this too was to become a central theme of the Russian novelist's work. Rastignac is Raskolnikov's spiritual brother.

Dostoevsky the romanticist considered the works of the author of *Eugénie Grandet* to be the apex of all Christian art. Did not Balzac himself say that his Goriot was the "Christ of fatherly love," and did he not compare his sufferings to "the Passion endured by the Savior of Mankind for the salvation of the world"? From the French writer, Dostoevsky learned the technique of the novel; he studied his style. His letters of this period are liberally sprinkled with Balzacian expressions: "c'est du sublime," "irrévocablement," "un homme qui pense à rien," "nous verrons cela"(an expression of papa Grandet), "assez cause" (Vautrin).

I I

Poor People

While working on his translation of *Eugénie Grandet,* Dostoevsky discerned the course which he was to pursue as a writer. He now abandoned his former intentions to write in the dramatic genre and, inspired by Balzac's narration about an unfortunate young girl, began to sketch outlines of his own tale *Poor People.*[1] In September 1844 he informed his brother: "I have one hope. I am finishing a novel of the same dimensions as *Eugénie Grandet.* The novel expresses adequate originality. I'm already making a copy, and in all likelihood, I should even receive a decision regarding it somewhere around the 14th. I will send it to *Fatherland Notes.* I'm pleased with my work. Perhaps I will get about 400 rubles for it. So there it is, the source of all my hopes."

During the autumn of that year Dostoevsky began to share an apartment with a friend of his from the School of Engineering, the young writer D. V. Grigorovich. They had funds sufficient for only the first half of the month; for the remaining two weeks they lived on rolls and coffee brewed from barley. They did not have a servant, and were forced to set up the samovar themselves. "When I began to live with Dostoevsky," Grigorovich relates,

---

[1] In Russian, a *povest* as a generic form stands somewhere between a *rasskaz* (short story) and a *roman* (novel). In distinction to a *rasskaz,* a *povest* usually depicts not one, but a series of events, illuminating a whole period in the life of its main character. Consequently, life is reflected in more of its complexity than in the *rasskaz,* but with less diversity of characters and events than in the novel. Somehow the English terms *novelette, short novel* or even Henry James' *nouvelle* are not quite exact or suitable. I have chosen the word *tale* as a translation of this generic term, and use it consistently throughout whenever the word *povest* is found (as opposed to *rasskaz* – story, short story). I feel further justified in this since in ancient Russian literature the term *povest* served to designate any narrative about historical or private events (e.g., the earliest chronicle, *The Tale of Bygone Years*). A short story (*rasskaz*) is sometimes called in Russian a *novella* and this word is also applied to some foreign short stories. This does not appear frequently in the text, and when it does, I use the term *novella.*

he had just finished his translation of Balzac's *Eugénie Grandet*. Balzac was our favorite author. . . . Dostoevsky used to sit at his desk for entire days and part of the night. He did not say a word about what he was writing; he used to answer my inquiries tersely and only with reluctance. Knowing how reserved he was, I finally stopped prodding him with questions. I could see only a mass of sheets covered with that handwriting which was so characteristic of Dostoevsky. The letters poured out from his pen just like little pearls, as if they had been drawn. As soon as he would leave off writing, immediately a book would be in his hands. For a time he took a liking to the novels of F. Soulié. *The Notes of a Demon* especially delighted him. This strenuous work and his persistent sitting at home proved utterly pernicious to his health. It all aggravated that sickness which had already occurred several times while he was still a young man living at school. Several times during our infrequent walks he was subject to fits. Once while we were walking along together on Trinity Lane, we met a funeral procession. Dostoevsky quickly turned back. He wanted to return home, but before we got more than a few paces, he had a fit of such violence that I had to carry him with the help of some passersby into a nearby dairy-shop. We could hardly bring him to his senses. Such fits were usually followed by a state of spiritual depression that would last for about two or three days.

The novel was finished in November 1844. In December he completely reworked it; in February 1845 there was even a second revision. "I actually finished it, it seems to me, somewhere around the end of November," Dostoevsky informed his brother. "In December, however, I decided to revise the whole thing. I revised and rewrote it; but in February I began again to clean and polish it anew, to make additions and to eliminate certain things. About the middle of March I was finally ready and satisfied with it."

He was tortured by a passionate thirst for perfection. "I want each of my works," he declared, "to possess a distinct excellence." With regard to this he cited Pushkin and Gogol, Raphael and Vernet, who used to spend long periods of time perfecting their creations. This propensity to be thorough, this unending dissatisfaction with form, was to haunt Dostoevsky throughout his life. Necessity forced him to work by demand, and this was the greatest tragedy of his life. Once and for all let us put an end to the legends about Dostoevsky's stylistic carelessness. The innumerable revisions and reworkings to which he subjected his novels more than adequately testify to the seriousness and severity with which he approached artistic creation.

The new version of *Poor People* satisfied him. He wrote: "I am sincerely pleased with my novel. It is forceful and well-developed. There are, however, terrible shortcomings."

The pressure of literary activity, his affairs in a complete muddle, the specter of poverty gaping over his shoulder, broken health — these are the conditions that surrounded the beginnings of Dostoevsky's literary career. His entire fate depended on the success of this novel. "The fact is, I hope to redeem all this by the novel. If things don't turn out well, perhaps I will hang myself." These words so terrifying in their calm, introduce us into the young writer's tragic world. The loftiest note is unhesitatingly sounded, the question is posed in terms of life and death, and immediately "incipit tragoedia." Dostoevsky was conscious of his vocation, and had a presentiment of his way of the cross. The following remark to his brother can serve as the epigraph to his birth as a writer: "I have just finished reading an article in *The Invalid* about German poets who have died of hunger and cold, and in mad-houses. There were about twenty of them; and what names! Even now I am still terrified by it. . . ."

A month and a half passed by. The novel was revised for a third time. On the fourth of May he wrote his brother: "Up till this very moment I've been hellishly busy. This novel of mine, which has tied me up hand and foot, has given me so much work that had I but realized it, I would never have started it at all. I decided to go through and correct it once again, and by God, for the better. It has picked up almost double its worth. But it is finished now and this revision was the last. I give my word, I will not touch it again."

And again the somber forebodings and thoughts about suicide: "The most agonizing thoughts often keep me from sleeping entire nights. I will not succeed with my novel; so perhaps into the Neva with me as well. I will not survive the death of my *idée fixe*."

The author was overcome by his own work. After the brief joys of inspiration, there followed that long and agonizing period during which the words must be given flesh and bone. He could not "free himself from the bonds" that tied him to the novel. It became a fixed idea and linked with the thought of death. Literature was Dostoevsky's tragic fate. The revisions of *Poor People* testify to his intense spiritual labor. In the course of the years 1843-1845, a profound change occurred in the writer's soul. He hinted at it in a letter to his brother: "I read a terrible amount, and I'm terribly affected by my reading. I now reread something that I had read a long time ago, and, as though vitalized by new forces, I apprehend everything. My understanding is clear and sharp, and I myself extract the ability to create. . . . Dear brother, in respect to literature, I am not the same person that I was two years ago. That was merely childishness, rubbish. These two years of study have brought much to me and taken much away."

Dostoevsky's romantic youth, that period of his friendship with the poet Shidlovsky and of the ecstatic tears poured over Schiller's poetry, had decisively come to an end; now began his literary maturity under the aegis of the magician Gogol. The writer who not so long before was dreaming of medieval knights and Venetian beauties, now wrote the history of a wretched civil servant from Petersburg, Makar Devushkin. This change of literary orientation reflects certain factors which have their origins in the very depths of his consciousness. Dostoevsky's concept of the world was gradually changing. It is not impossible to conjecture that the earlier variations of *Poor People* proved unsatisfactory because of their failure to correspond adequately to his new attitudes toward life. While he was revising his novel, he was also groping about in search of his own self. Then finally the semiconscious process was ended in one instant of dazzling clarity. The expression for the confused activity of his soul was found. A new word had been born.

Up until this moment Dostoevsky had lived in a world of romantic dreams. Far-off lands and distant times, the exotic and heroic had completely captivated him. He was blind to reality, and everything that was mysterious, fantastic, and out-of-the-ordinary would lure him into its captivating sphere: the knights' castles in the novels of Radcliffe and Walter Scott, the tales of Hoffmann, the diabolism in Soulié. . . . Then suddenly his eyes were opened and he understood: *there is nothing more fantastic than reality.* He calls this moment his birth. It happened in the fantastic city of Petersburg. Gogol, the author of *Nevsky Prospect,* was the newborn's godfather. In an article written in 1861, *Petersburg Dreams in Verse and Prose,* Dostoevsky describes his "vision on the Neva."

I remember once on a wintry January evening I was hurrying home from Vyborg.[2] I was still very young then. Coming up to the

___

[2] A section of Petersburg across the River Neva from the center of the city. At the beginning of the 19th century it still remained somewhat rural in character.

Neva, I stopped for a minute and cast a searching glance down the river, into the murky distance thick with frost, which suddenly had flushed with the last purple of sunset, burning itself out on the misty horizon. Night settled down over the city, and with the sun's last gleam, all the boundless expanse of the Neva's glade, which had swollen out of the frozen snow, crumbled apart in infinite myriads of sparks emitting from the needle-pointed rime. It turned to frost at 20 degrees. . . . The frozen vapor fell in clouds from the tired horses, from the running people. The close air vibrated at the tiniest sound, and columns of smoke from all the roofs on both banks arose like giants, and were carried upward through the cold heaven, intertwining and unwinding on their way so that, it seemed, new buildings were rising over the old ones, and a new city was being assembled in the air. . . . It seemed, in the end, that all this world, with all its inhabitants, both the strong and the weak, with all their habitations, whether beggars' shelters or gilded palaces, at this hour of twilight resembled a fantastic, enchanted vision, a dream which in its turn would instantly vanish and waste away as vapor into the dark blue heaven. Suddenly a certain strange thought began to stir inside me. I started and my heart was as if flooded in that instant by a hot jet of blood which had suddenly boiled up from the influx of a mighty sensation which up until now had been unknown to me. In that moment, as it were, I understood something which up to that time had only stirred in me, but had not as yet been fully comprehended. I saw clearly, as it were, into something new, a completely new world, unfamiliar to me and known only through some obscure hearsay, through a certain mysterious sign. I think that in those precise minutes, my real existence began. . . . Tell me, gentlemen, have I not been a fantast, have I not been a mystic since my very childhood? Nothing, nothing whatever, one sensation. . . .

Up until that instant he had lived in a world of myths, "in a world of inflamed daydreams." After "the vision" he began to dream other dreams.

I began to look about intently and suddenly I noticed some strange people. They all were strange, extraordinary figures, completely prosaic, not Don Carloses or Posas to be sure, rather down-to-earth titular councilors and yet at the same time, as it were, sort of fantastic titular councilors. Someone was grimacing in front of me, having hidden himself behind all this fantastic crowd, and he was fidgeting some thread, some springs through, and these little dolls moved, and he laughed and laughed away. And then another scene began to form in my mind, in some dark corners, the heart of some titular, upright and pure, moral and devoted to his superiors, and along with him a certain young girl, wronged and sad, and their story in all its poignancy tore deep into my heart.

This forgotten page is one of the supreme examples of Dostoevsky's lyricism. It is intimately related to Gogol. In *Nevsky Prospect* the mysteriousness of Petersburg grows with the coming of night.

Then [at twilight] a mysterious interlude will fall when the lamps will cast a certain alluring, wonderous light upon everything. . . . Everything is an illusion; everything is a dream; nothing is that which it seems. . . . At all times it is deceitful and false, this Nevsky Prospect, but especially when night will press upon it in a thickened mass and sort out the white and the straw-colored walls of the houses; when the whole city will be transformed into thunder and streaks of light; the myriads of carriages tumble down over the bridges; postillions cry out and spring on the horses; and when the demon himself lights the lamps only that he might show everything in an unreal guise.

A "completely new world" was opened to Dostoevsky: a fantastic world ready "to waste away as vapor," a world inhabited by strange people, by marionettes dancing to a demon's laughter. Gogol the magician had bewitched all Russian literature with his strange merriment, and it was he who woke Dostoevsky from his romantic dream. *He now saw that reality was unreal.* The rupture of these two planes of existence provided his work with its necessary direction. Dostoevsky was to learn the art of words from Gogol, but he was not to become his slave as all Russian literature in the 1830's and 1840's had been. He reacted both with love and hatred toward Gogol, and even while imitating him, he was struggling with him. As Strakhov has aptly pointed out, Dostoevsky's early works comprise "a bold and resolute correction of Gogol."

The "vision on the Neva" necessarily leads us to the conception of *Poor People.* The story of "the heart of a titular, upright and pure, and of a young girl, wronged and sad" is in fact the story of Makar Devushkin and Varenka. For his tale, Dostoevsky adopted one of the most commonplace themes of Gogol's "natural school." In his tale *The Greatcoat,* Gogol describes a poor civil servant, Akaky Akakyevich, dull-witted, beaten-down, and speechless. At the price of unbelievable privations, he saves his money to buy a new greatcoat. It is, however, stolen from him, and he dies of despair. The hero of *Poor People*, Makar Devushkin, is also a poor, wretched civil servant.[3] His entire life has also been spent transcribing papers. His fellow-workers mock and ridicule him, while his superiors upbraid him. Even in his external appearance, his dress, his boots, he is like the hero of *The Greatcoat*. Dostoevsky assimilated all of Gogol's devices, heightening and developing them, but at the same time, the student rose in open revolt against his master. He resented Gogol's relation to his own unfortunate hero. Is not *The Greatcoat* but a murderous derision of the "poor civil servant"? Is Akaky Akakyevich not a walking automaton, a dull-witted being whose highest ideal is a warm greatcoat? Dostoevsky having mastered the technique of Gogol's school, demolished it from within. *He turned the ludicrous hero into a human being.* During the 1840's Russian society was keenly influenced by French social novels with their appeal to humanism and social justice (Balzac, Georges Sand), and *Poor People*, in its turn, responded to this new disposition in the reader. Dostoevsky effected a simple but ingenious change in Gogol's composition. In place of an object (the greatcoat), he incorporated a living human person (Varenka), and a miraculous transformation resulted. The ludicrous self-abnegation of Akaky Akakyevich for the sake of a greatcoat, his asceticism, which had become so meanly degraded by its unworthy object — these are translated into Makar Alekseyevich's exalted and touching attachment to his Varenka. Out of Bashmachkin's mania, Dostoevsky created Devushkin's disinterested love. (The name Bashmachkin has the connotation of a simple object; the name Devushkin, on the other hand, implies something personal and human.)[4]

The battle with Gogol was waged on two different planes, that of literature and that of life itself. Devushkin, the civil servant, by his life, his love, his heroism, unmasks the "defamation of man" in Gogol's tradition; Devushkin, the man of letters, engages Gogol the writer in a polemic. Dostoevsky transformed the poor civil servant into a writer who attends to his letters and "formulates his own style."

[3] At the beginning of the 18th century Peter the Great formulated a "Table of Ranks" for the civil service which corresponded to the fourteen ranks of the military. They ranged from Chancellor of the Empire (the first rank) to Collegiate Registrar (the Fourteenth). In Dostoevsky's *chinovnik* (civil servant) stories we most frequently encounter Collegiate Assessors (the eighth rank) and Titular Councilors (the ninth). The functions of civil servants of these categories often were the transcribing and registering of official documents, etc.

[4] *Bashmak* in Russian = shoe; *deva*, a virgin or maid; *devushka* a young girl.

Makar Devushkin reads *The Greatcoat* and takes it very much to heart. He is deeply offended by this "pasquil" and complains of it to Varenka: "And why write such things? And why is it necessary? . . . Well, it's a nasty little book, Varenka. It's simply unheard of because it's not even possible that there could be such a civil servant. No, I will complain, Varenka, I will formally complain." Devushkin recognizes his own self in all the particulars of Akaky Akakyevich's existence. All the details have been copied from nature, and they are all "simply unheard of." The "natural school" is tried and condemned. Everything is just as it really is, but it lacks the spark of life; these are not people, they are "dead souls." Dostoevsky contrasts Gogol's spirit with that of Pushkin. Devushkin reads Pushkin's story *The Stationmaster,* and writes to Varenka: "I have never before in all my life read such a splendid book. One reads along in it — it's as though I had written it myself. It's as if, so to speak, I had taken my own heart, such as it is, and turned it inside out for all the world, and even described it in detail — just like that! No, it's really natural! You read it. It's natural! It has life."

Devushkin recognizes his own self both in the hero of *The Greatcoat* and in the hero of *The Stationmaster.* However, he recoils from the first in horror. It is the likeness of a dead mask with a living face. He is readily drawn to the latter: "my own heart."

Dostoevsky joins the Gogolian theme of the poor civil servant to the plot of *The Stationmaster.* Simeon Vyrin, like Makar Devushkin, is a good and simple man with an ardent and loving heart. The one has a passionate attachment to his daughter; the other a selfless love toward an orphaned relation. A seducer appears in both of the stories. Vyrin wants to save his Dunya. He goes to reason with her seducer and "is thrown out onto the stairs." Devushkin goes to the officer who has abused Varenka, and he is also "thrown out." Once he has lost Dunya, Vyrin takes to drink and dies. Devushkin, unable to help Varenka, abandons himself to "debauchery." It is almost impossible for him to survive his parting from her. Thus, in both Pushkin and Dostoevsky, the story is built around the tragic love of "an ardent heart." Its heroes are not the medieval knights of a romantic novella, but rather modest, inconspicuous people — an insignificant civil servant and a stationmaster. The tragic conflict has become an interior one. *Poor People* is the story of its hero's inner life, of his love, his sufferings, and his ruin. Dostoevsky mastered the art of the psychological short story through the mentorship of Pushkin.

The young author effected a bold revolution in literature. He succeeded in combining Gogol's genre with that of Karamzin. Makar Devushkin no longer is the "speechless civil servant"; rather, he is transformed into a "sentimental lover." The result is an effective contrast between the hero's unassuming outward appearance and his tender and sensitive soul. The elderly civil servant in his bedraggled uniform and mended boots treasures a little book of tender verses, and he dreams of becoming "a composer of literature and a poet." He writes to Varenka: "Now there, for example, let's suppose that from neither here nor there, a book suddenly came out with the title *The Poems of Makar Devushkin!* Well, what would you say then, my little angel?" The hero himself underlines the humor of this contrast: "Well, what would it be like when everybody learned that there the author Devushkin has boots with patches? Why, some contessa-duchess would find out, and, my heart, what would she say?"

The sentimental hero loves flowers, little birds, idyllic pictures of nature, a tranquil and peaceful life. Everything touches and delights him, moves him to a state of compassion. "They have opened the window here," he writes Varenka, "The dear sun is shining; the little birds are chirping. The aromas of spring are floating in the air, and all nature has come to life." He dreams "pleasantly enough," and compares Varenka "with a little bird from heaven, sent for the delight of all and for the adornment of created nature." Varenka finds good-natured amusement in the excessive tenderness of her honorable friend. The embarrassed dreamer apologizes for his impulsiveness: "It's most unpleasant that I have written to you so figuratively and stupidly. . . . And why did I have to ride there on Pegasus. . . . In my old age, with only tufts of hair left, to set out for amours — and that equivocally."

The novel is built upon such ascents of tender lyricism and lapses into the wretched state of existence. Dostoevsky succeeded brilliantly in resolving his problem. What could be a more original concept than to provide the hero of *The Greatcoat*, Akaky Akakyevich, with the tender soul of a Grandisson or a Saint-Preux? But we have still not exhausted the artistic significance of the story. The author has broadly expanded its framework by introducing in it the social pathos of the French novel. The modest story of Devushkin's love for Varenka has blossomed forth into a tableau depicting social evil and injustice. The contrast between the two literary styles, sentimentalism and naturalism, only serves to deepen the second contrast between wealth and poverty. Under Dostoevsky's pen, this psychological story acquires the character of a social novel. The critic Belinsky specifically noted this side of *Poor People,* and it was this that brought such resounding success to Dostoevsky's work.

With his description of the tragedies of poverty, the young writer truly came into his own. His apprenticeship was finally over, and for the first time we hear the voice of the author of *Crime and Punishment.* Makar Devushkin lives in the corner of a kitchen behind a partition. "Imagine, for example," he writes,

> a long corridor, absolutely dark and very dirty. Along its right hand there will be a blank wall, while on the left all doors and doors, just like in a hotel, and behind each of these there is a little room. There are two and three people living in each one of them. . . . The black staircase is damp, filthy; the steps are broken; and the walls are so greasy that your hand sticks when you lean against them. On each landing stand trunks, chairs, and broken cupboards; rags are strewn all over, and windows smashed in; washtubs stand filled with all kinds of dirt, filth, and litter, with eggshells and with fish entrails. The smell is ugly.

We find existence depicted in bold, acrid strokes such as these. But Devushkin's physical sufferings, his life of semistarvation in the kitchen with its fumes and odors, his walking to work in tattered boots, the mechanical transcribing of papers are all utterly insignificant in contrast to the mental tortures which poverty has inflicted upon him. His inability to come to Varenka's assistance when malnutrition and death threaten her, when she is sick and abused by persons with evil intent — this is what drives the quiet, meek Makar Devushkin to despair and revolt. He is in debt to his landlady; he has sold his overcoat. It becomes embarrassing for him even to appear at the office. He is driven out of his meager living-quarters. His fellow-workers ridicule him, dubbing him "the rat." Varenka breaks down under her heavy load of work, and yet everything could have been set aright if only there had been a little money. The very best pages of the story are devoted to Devushkin's dreams of a loan, his hopes and plans, his visit to a moneylender, his failure, his despair, and then "debauchery."

Poverty is at the root of Devushkin's own personal tragedy; but all of Petersburg, with its streets, back-alleys, and slums, reflects the exact same image. The houses, the embankments and bridges cry out with poverty. Devushkin wanders about the city. "Scores of people were walking along the canal bank," he relates, "and as fate would have it, the people's faces were all so terrible and dejected; drunken peasants; snub-nosed old Finnish hags in boots, with nothing on their heads; street urchins; some locksmith's apprentice in a striped work-coat, underfed, frail, with his face bathed in grease and a lock in his hand; a retired soldier seven feet tall. . . . On the bridges sit old women with soggy ginger cakes and rotten apples, and they are all such dirty, soggy old women!" Then an organ-grinder appears. He puts all his force and effort into his work and does not grovel before anyone. "He is a beggar, a beggar, it's true, a beggar all the same, but then he's a noble, honorable beggar." There is a boy about ten years of age, sick, frail, having only a little shirt on, barefooted. With his mouth gaping, he listens to the music, and there is a note in his hand: "Everybody knows what was written: 'My benefactors, a mother with children is dying. Three children are starving, so now, you help us.' Over there a man is standing close to a fence, begging, 'Good sir, give me a penny for the sake of Christ!' And in such a harsh, broken voice that I shuddered with a feeling of horror. . . ."

Devushkin not only experiences poverty as a personal and human tragedy in his life, but further he even analyzes it as *a specific mental state*. Poverty means helplessness, intimidation, humiliation. It strips man of his dignity, and turns him into "a rag." The poor man is trapped in his shame and pride. His heart grows bitter, and he becomes suspicious and "demanding." "Poor people are capricious," Devushkin writes.

He, the poor man, he is demanding. He even views God's world in a peculiar fashion and looks askance at each passerby while at the same time he casts about an embarrassed glance and listens attentively to each word that is uttered: whether they are not talking about him, whether they are not remarking what an unsightly sort he is. . . . If you will forgive an ill-mannered expression, Varenka, then I will tell you that on that score, the poor man has the very same girlish embarrassment that you, speaking by way of example, have.

The "meek" and "quiet" little Devushkin begins to rebel. "Liberal" ideas enter into his head. He asks someone, why are some happy and rich, while others are poor and miserable? Why is there such inequity? "Why does it happen that for instance, a good man finds himself left to ruin and perdition? And then, on the other hand, happiness frequently falls to some half-wit Ivanushka. They tell him: 'You, Ivanushka the half-wit, dive into your grandfather's money bags; eat, drink, make merry, and you, one way or other, have only to lick your chops.'" But having posed the question, he is immediately terrified by it: "I know, I know, my dear lady, it's not good to think such things. It's freethinking. . . ." "It's sinful, my good lady, it's sinful to think like that, and whether you will or nill, a sin is thrust upon your soul. . . ." The author holds his humble hero in check; the role of a freethinker is not becoming to the figure of a poor "departmental rat." But nonetheless Devushkin is Dostoevsky's first "rebel." With trepidation he mumbles that which later Raskolnikov will proclaim loudly and boldly.

But *Poor People* is even more than a social novel. Had poverty alone determined Devushkin's fate, the situation would not have been so desperate and hopeless. Let us suppose for a moment that he were to receive a substantial inheritance, settle his affairs, and provide for Varenka; would this have resolved his sufferings? On the contrary, freed from the turmoil of financial cares, they would only have become more obvious. Devushkin is unhappy not only because he is poor; he loves Varenka with undivided affection. His very first letter breathes forth his infatuation. He is "happy, immeasurably happy, impossibly happy" that she had but slightly raised the curtain on her window; it means she was thinking about him. "In my imagination your little smile now began to glow, my angel, your good, warm little smile; and in my heart I had exactly the same feeling as that time when I kissed you, Varenka."

But her answer is light-hearted and jocular, and he immediately changes his tone. No, she had not understood him correctly; he had been lost in his own feelings. "And you were mistaken about those feelings of mine, my dear relation! You took my outpouring of them in utterly the wrong way. Paternal affection prompted me, purely a paternal affection." Varenka values him as a friend and benefactor. She is grateful and devoted to him, and will pray for him always . . . but she does not love him. In all innocence she even tells him about her semichildish romance with the student Pokrovsky, never once imagining how this tears at his heart. When the landowner Bykov who has already wronged her, now proposes marriage, she consents, hoping by this means to restore her good name and "as a security against poverty, privation, and unhappiness in the future." She does not even ask Devushkin's advice. "The decision which you have just read," she writes him, "is unalterable, and I shall immediately inform Bykov of it." Intent upon resolving her own fate, she does not bestow a single moment's reflection upon his misery and grief. Before Makar Alekseyevich had to conceal his love under the guise of paternal affection; now he is forced to devise various pretexts, though they be naive and ineffectual, in order to dissuade Varenka. During the final days before their parting, she is more preoccupied with gowns and dressmakers than with her benefactor's despair. Only on the very eve of her departure, does there awaken in her a grateful tenderness toward him. "But I have seen it all," she writes, "I have known how you love me."

Devushkin's last letter is the groan of a dying man, the incoherent mutterings of a raving love: "My sweet, Varenka, my little dove, my precious one! They are carrying you away; you are going! Now it would be better if they tore the heart out of my breast than to take you away from me! How can you! See, you are crying, and you are going! So you do not want to go; *so you loved me!*" It is no longer a game of familial regards. Devushkin does not survive the loss of his Varenka. He takes to drink, and dies.

The motif of an old man's loving a young girl with its vague interweaving of eroticism and "paternal affection," is one of Dostoevsky's favorite themes. Devushkin is the purest and most honorable of the "old lovers." He sublimates his passion to the heights of self-abnegation and disinterested service; at the diametrically opposite pole is Fyodor Pavlovich Karamazov with his passion for Grushenka.

In *The Diary of a Writer* (1877) Dostoevsky describes his sudden, unexpected fame. Upon the advice of his friend, the writer Grigorovich, he took the manuscript to the poet Nekrasov. Nekrasov and Grigorovich were simply unable to set it down, and read the whole novel through aloud. At four o'clock in the morning, they came running to the author and in sheer ecstasy, almost crying, rushed upon him and embraced him. After they left, Dostoevsky who was very much excited, could not get back to sleep. "What ecstasy, what a success, and above all, the sentiment was dear. I remember distinctly." Nekrasov gave the manuscript to Belinsky who insisted upon meeting the young writer. Dostoevsky quotes Belinsky's long speech with its keen analysis of the personality of the novel's hero. The critic began to speak heatedly with eyes burning:

Why, this unfortunate civil servant of yours — why he has already so exhausted himself in the service and reduced himself to such a state that he no longer even dares to consider himself unhappy —

out of humility. And he feels that the slightest complaint is almost an act of freethinking. He does not even dare to acknowledge his right to be unhappy. And when a kind man, his general, gives him those hundred rubles, he is completely reduced, overcome with amazement, that "their excellency" could take pity on such a one as himself. Not "his excellency," but "their excellency," as it is expressed in your story. And that torn-off button, that minute when he kisses the general's hand — why this is no longer compassion for an unfortunate man; it's horror, horror! Its horror lies in this very gratitude! *This is a tragedy!* Truth has been revealed and proclaimed to you as an artist; it has been apportioned to you as a gift. So, value your gift and be faithful to it, and you will be a great writer.

Dostoevsky left Belinsky "in a state of rapture."

I stopped at the corner of his house, looked up at the sky, at the bright day, at the passersby, and I felt with my whole being that a solemn moment had occurred in my life, a break forever; that something completely new had begun, but such a thing as I had not envisioned even in my most passionate dreams. . . . "Oh, I will be worthy of these praises, and what men! What men! That's where men are! I will strive to merit their respect. I will do my all to become as wonderful as they. I will remain 'faithful.' " . . . All of these thoughts passed through my mind. I recalled that moment with the fullest vividness, and since then I have never been able to forget it. It was the most blissful moment of my entire life. When I was serving my sentence of hard labor, merely recalling it strengthened me spiritually. Even now I still remember it with ecstasy.

The most blissful moment of his entire life! And perhaps the only moment of pure happiness that the writer was ever to experience. It was short-lived. Soon after this "prologue in heaven," he was to begin his descent through the spheres of hell. The beginning of Dostoevsky's journey was bathed in light. Afterward everything was plunged into darkness. And only at the very end of his life, one single day, the solemn day of the Pushkin speech, was to be illuminated by the setting sun.

This episode in *The Diary* is not only an historical document, but a genuine artistic creation as well. The white night in Petersburg, a night spent without sleep, during which Nekrasov and Grigorovich came running to the young writer; the bright spring day when, upon

his leaving Belinsky "in a state of rapture," he looked up at the sky —
such are the poetic images with which he colors the "solemn moment"
of his life. This moment marked the writer's birth.

In 1861 Dostoevsky employed this same autobiographical material
in his novel *The Humiliated and Wronged.* The novice writer Ivan
Petrovich recounted:

> And then at last my novel came out. Long before its appearance
> it had raised noise and a hubbub in the literary world. B. was
> delighted as a child when he read my manuscript. No! If I ever have
> been really happy, it was not during those first ravishing minutes of
> my success, but when I still had not read or even shown my manu-
> script to anyone; on those long winter nights, midst solemn hopes
> and dreams and a passionate love for my work, when I had merged
> with my fancy, with the characters whom I myself had created, just
> as if they were my own family, as though they were real human
> beings. I loved them. I shared their sorrows and their joys, and at
> times, I even shed the most genuine tears over my unpretentious
> hero.

Here we have an important account of the writer's work during this
first period of his life, the "sentimental" period. The episode about the
two literary figures spending the night reading his novel was effectively
employed in the plot of *The Humiliated and Wronged:* Ivan Petrovich
reads his work to the Ikhmenyev family, and everyone weeps. "I read
them my novel at one sitting," he recalls.

> We started immediately after tea, and we sat up until two in the
> morning. At first the old man just scowled. He was expecting some-
> thing incomprehensibly sublime, something, I suppose, which even
> he himself would fail to understand, but which nonetheless, would
> be without doubt sublime. And instead of this he suddenly heard
> such mundane things, and everything so totally familiar, precisely
> the same as were happening about him every day. And it would
> have been nice if the hero had been a great or interesting man, or
> some historical figure, but here it turned out to be some little, down-
> trodden, and even somewhat ridiculous civil servant who had lost the
> buttons on his uniform. And it was all described in such a simple
> style, nothing added, nothing taken away, no better than we our-
> selves talk. . . . It's strange! . . . And what happened? Before I
> had finished reading half of it, tears were streaming from the eyes

of all my listeners. . . . The old man had already abandoned all his dreams of anything sublime. "From the first step it's clear that the woodcock still has a long way till Peter's day;[5] and the same is true of you. It's just a little story. But then it grasps at your heart," he said. "For it becomes clear and fixed in one's mind what's going on all about you, and you realize that even the most down-trodden, the humblest person is also a man, and that he is called my brother!" Natasha listened, cried, and furtively squeezed my hand under the table.

This is how the author himself evaluated his work. In *Poor People,* the canon of romanticism (something "incomprehensibly sublime") is overthrown; an everyday subject and an ordinary simple style are introduced; the sentimental manner ("it grasps at your heart") is renovated; and we encounter a humanistic-philanthropic tendency ("the humblest person is also a man").

Dostoevsky's first literary work was an event in the history of Russian literature.

[5] Russian expression meaning: one still has a long way to go. "Peter's day" is the feast of Sts. Peter and Paul, June 29.

I I I

The Double and *Mister Prokharchin*

After having spent the summer of 1845 at his brother Mikhail's in Reval, Dostoevsky returned to Petersburg in August. His "state of rapture" had passed and he was now preoccupied with grim forebodings. Here for the first time we encounter a manifestation of his mystical gift that seemed to accord him a certain foreknowledge of the future. The young writer, entering upon his career under such brilliant auspices, suddenly, in an instant of illumination, envisioned the terrible trials that awaited him in life, and pleaded for death. "How dejected I felt as I entered Petersburg," he wrote his brother. "Petersburg and my future life here appeared so terrible, so desolate and dismal, and necessity so ruthless, that if my life had ended at that moment, I believe I would have died with genuine delight."

While in Reval he had begun a new tale *The Double*, and now he continued working on it in Petersburg. As with Devushkin in *Poor People*, the hero of this new work, Golyadkin, emerged and developed out of the verbal element. First the writer had to assimilate his character's intonations; he had to learn to speak for him, to penetrate the rhythm of his sentences and the peculiarities of his language. Only then would the author discern his character's personality. Dostoevsky's heroes are born out of speech; this is a general law in his creative processes. In a letter to Mikhail, he practiced the manner in which his Golyadkin was to speak:

> Yakov Petrovich Golyadkin upholds his character to perfection. A terrible rascal, one simply can't get to him. By no means does he want to go forward, pretending that, why, he is just not ready yet, and that for the present he is who he is, that he is nothing, not on your life, and that, I dare say, if it's already come to that, then so can he, and why not, for what reason not. Why, he's just like everybody else. He's simply who he is, but then just the same as everybody

else! What's it to him! A rascal, a terrible rascal! Before the middle of November it's simply out of the question for him to acquiesce and end his career.

This assimilation of his character's style was carried to the point of possession. Dostoevsky himself confessed: "Now I am truly Golyadkin."
A friendship was formed with Belinsky and with the circle of writers who collaborated in the publishing of *Fatherland Notes*. The writer informed his brother: "I go to Belinsky's with great frequency. No one could be better disposed toward me, and in all seriousness, he sees in me a demonstrative argument set before the public and a vindication of his opinions. . . . Belinsky urges me to finish writing my book about Golyadkin. He has already announced it to the whole literary world and practically concluded an arrangement with Krayevsky. Meanwhile half of Petersburg is already talking about *Poor People*."
His letters to his brother during this period (the winter of 1845 and spring of 1846) are filled with endless conceit and a childish braggadocio: Dostoevsky ingenuously admits that now he is "almost enraptured by [his] own personal glory," that he is a "braggart" and can write only about himself. One would almost think that some of these letters had issued from the buoyant pen of the Gogolian hero Khlestakov.[1]
On November 16, 1845, he wrote to Mikhail:

Really, brother, I think that my fame will never again rise to such a peak as now. Everywhere I am greeted with unbelievable esteem; everyone is terribly curious about me. I've been introduced to a galaxy of people, and these of the very best society. Prince Odoyevsky asks me to favor him with a visit, while Count Sologub tears his hair out in despair. Panayev has assured him that this is a talent which will trample them all down into the muck. Everyone receives me as a living wonder. No longer can I open my mouth, lest it be repeated in all corners that Dostoevsky said such and such, Dostoevsky wants to do such and such. Belinsky has the greatest possible affection and regard for me. . . .

---

[1] Khlestakov is the hero of Gogol's great comedy *The Inspector General*. An insignificant minor official, he arrives in a remote provincial town, and is there mistaken for an incognito governmental inspector. He is the embodiment of *poshlost*, an almost untranslatable Russian word meaning crude, vulgar, but eminently self-satisfied and ambitious banality. He sets in motion a tumult of confusion, meaningless and undirected activity through his flighty irresponsibility.

The young writer's *amour-propre* was particularly indulged by his friendship with the handsome and aristocratic Turgenev.

A few days ago the poet Turgenev returned from Paris (you, of course, have heard), and from the very first he became attached to me by such close bonds, by such friendship, that Belinsky explains it by saying that Turgenev has fallen in love with me. But, brother, what a man he is! And I in turn, have almost fallen in love with him. A poet, a talent, an aristocrat, handsome, rich, brilliant, cultured, 25 years old — I can't imagine what nature has refused him. Lastly, he has a character that is absolutely upright, splendid, formed in the grand school. . . .

And so the course of Dostoevsky's protracted enmity with Turgenev had its beginnings in a bond of mutual affection. Out of the squalid atmosphere of Mariinsky Hospital, out of the dismal, closed world of the School of Engineering, from poverty and obscurity, the morbidly egocentric writer now suddenly moved into a "world of society." He was fascinated by Turgenev's rank as a gentleman; later he came to detest it.

Nekrasov contemplated publishing a humorous almanac *The Scoffer* and commissioned Dostoevsky to prepare an announcement to this effect. The young writer assumed the role of the Balzacian hero Lucien de Rubempré, the social lion and brilliant feuilletonist. "The notice has created a sensation," he informed his brother, "for this is the first time that such levity and such humor have been employed in things of this type. It reminded me of Lucien de Rubempré's first feuilleton."

Dostoevsky attempted to acclimate the Parisian *flâneur* to the streets of Petersburg. The scoffer is a young man, "gay, quick-witted, cheerful, noisy, playful, loud, light-hearted, ruddy-cheeked, rotund, satisfied." Petersburg strikes him as a "magnificent illustrated almanac which one can look through only at one's leisure, out of boredom, after dinner — to yawn over or to smile at." The subtle wit of the Parisian boulevardier and the pose of the exquisite dandy were not quite suited to the author of *Poor People*. Fortunately for Dostoevsky, Nekrasov's almanac never materialized.

His next literary experience was even more dismal. "A few days ago," he wrote his brother,

since I didn't have any money, I dropped in on Nekrasov. While I was sitting in his room, I got the idea for a novel in nine letters.

Upon arriving home, I wrote this novel in one night. In the morning I brought it to Nekrasov and received 125 paper rubles for it. That evening my novel was read at Turgenev's to our entire circle, that is, to twenty people, at a minimum, and it created a furor. You yourself will see whether it's at all inferior to, for example, Gogol's *The Lawsuit.* Belinsky remarked that now he has absolute confidence in me, for I can adapt myself to completely different elements. . . . I have a mass of ideas. . . . Dear brother, if I were to begin to enumerate all my triumphs to you, why, I simply wouldn't have enough paper. Golyadkin is turning out capitally; this will be my chef-d'oeuvre.

A Novel in Nine Letters is the story of two friends, Pyotr Ivanovich and Ivan Petrovich, who formed a sort of partnership to cheat at cards. Pyotr Ivanovich has borrowed an advance of 350 rubles from his "associate," and now employs various cunning pretexts to avoid meeting him. Ivan Petrovich combs the entire city in search of his friend and having finally become convinced of his perfidy, writes him an accusing letter. Events at the end take a most unexpected turn when it is discovered that all the while the wives of both swindlers have been unfaithful. Dostoevsky has adopted his basic theme from Gogol's *The Gamblers;* the motif of the "auntie's" sickness and death has been borrowed from the same writer's *The Lawsuit.* The story was written hurriedly while Dostoevsky was in the process of working on *The Double.* The shrewd scoundrel Pyotr Ivanovich bears some resemblance to Golyadkin Sr.; the righteous indignation of the other scoundrel suggests Golyadkin Jr.'s complaints.[2] It is hard, however, to understand how such an impotent work could "create a furor" among Belinsky's friends.

Success continued to intoxicate Dostoevsky. It seems that he was seriously beginning to fancy himself a fashionable dandy and litterateur after the manner of Lucien de Rubempré. Now the only thing that the image lacked was success with women and an elegant rakishness. But then even these came his way:

Yesterday I was at Panayev's for the first time, and I suppose, have fallen in love with his wife. She is a clever, pretty little thing, and moreover affable and absolutely sincere. Those precious Minas, Klaras, Mariannas, and so forth have grown prettier than ever, but they cost a terrible amount. Not long ago Turgenev and Belinsky

[2] Perhaps in this instance Mochulsky may have intended the reverse regarding Golyadkin Sr. and Jr.

really took me over the coals about my irregular life. These gentle-men simply don't know how to prove their affection for me. One and all, they love me. . . .

He had lost all sense of reality; dream had come to triumph over fact. Dostoevsky "became the reincarnation" of Rubempré; counts and princes courted his favor; the entire capital was thrown into ecstasy upon reading his works; fashionable courtesans worshipped him. . . . But under the mask of the self-satisfied dandy, one can distinguish yet another face: that of the lonely dreamer insatiably yearning for love and happiness. The young, inexperienced heart opened itself trustingly to people; it had faith in their goodness and sincerity. And there was much touching, candid nobility in this nai-veté: "These gentlemen simply don't know how to prove their affection for me." Waking from this celestial dream was to prove a horrifying experience. The disillusion which Dostoevsky was to suffer at the hands of his friends would aggravate his nervous ailment. Avdotya Panayeva immediately perceived the nature of her new admirer. "At first glance," she writes in her memoirs,

> you could discern that Dostoevsky was a terribly nervous and sensi-tive young man. He was of slight build, short, fair, with a sickly complexion. His small grey eyes would rather restlessly flit from object to object, while his pale lips twitched nervously. Because of his youth and his nervousness he did not know how to conduct himself, and he would only too clearly express his conceit in the fact that he was an author. He held his own literary talent in very high repute. Inasmuch as he had been overawed by his unexpectedly brilliant entrance into the literary world, and having had the praise and commendation of competent men in literature lavished upon him, he, as a sensitive person, could not conceal his pride before other young writers who were making modest advances in the pro-fession with their works.

The "nervous young man" whom Panayeva describes, bears little resemblance to Balzac's hero; and Count Sologub's portrait of the real Dostoevsky is still further removed from this myth.

In a little apartment on one of the more remote streets of Petersburg, I think it was on Sands, I found the young man, pale and sickly in appearance. He was wearing a rather shabby smoking-jacket with unusually short sleeves as though the thing had been tailored for someone else. . . . He was embarrassed, became quite confused, and offered me the only armchair that was to be found in the room. It was old and rather outmoded. I immediately perceived that he was by nature shy, reserved, and conceited, yet talented and sympathetic to the highest degree. I sat with him for about twenty minutes and then rising, I invited him to come and dine with me informally. Dostoevsky became quite sincerely alarmed. "No, Count, forgive me," he said in utter dismay, wringing his hands, "but really I have never in my life been in society, and it's impossible for me to make up my mind. . . ." It was only about two months later that one day he decided to put in an appearance at my "menagerie."

It would appear that "those exquisite Minas, Klaras, and Mariannas" were also fanciful imaginings. More than likely they wandered in from the pages of Balzac's *Illusions perdues* as the indispensable accessory to a dandy's erotic life. At any rate Dr. Riesenkampf considered them "pure fabrication." He wrote: "Young people in their twenties usually pursue some feminine ideal; they find themselves attracted to good-looking women. It is extraordinary that in the case of Fyodor Mikhailovich nothing like this seems to have occurred. He always appeared to be indifferent to the company of women and, in fact, all but had a kind of aversion toward it." Was not even the infatuation with Panayeva invented as the result of snobbishness? In February 1846 Dostoevsky confided to his brother: "I was quite seriously in love with Panayeva; now it is passing, but I still don't know. . . ." This love passed quickly and painlessly.

In *The Diary of a Writer* Dostoevsky reflects how in December 1845 he read several chapters of *The Double* at Belinsky's. "For this purpose he [Belinsky] even arranged a soirée (which was something he almost never did) and invited his intimates. I remember Iv. Ser. Turgenev's being at the soirée. He listened to only a half of what I read. He praised it and left, being very much in a hurry to go off some place. The three or four chapters which I read delighted Belinsky (although in fact, they were not worth it)."

Grigorovich and Annenkov have also left references to this reading. The former wrote: "Belinsky sat opposite the author. He greedily drank in his every word, and simply could not hide his delight at certain passages, repeating over and over that only Dostoevsky could hit upon such wondrous psychological subtleties."

Annenkov's observations were different; he noted a "reservation" on the part of the critic. "Belinsky was pleased with this story because of its style and its treatment of an original and strange theme, but it struck me, and I was present at the reading, that the critic still had some reservation which he did not deem necessary to express at that given moment. He continually called Dostoevsky's attention to the need of limbering up his fingers, as they say, for literary endeavors."

More than likely, Annenkov was right. Belinsky's attitude toward *The Double* at his first encounter with this strange work, was evasive. Otherwise it is very difficult to explain the critic's brusque transition from praise to a merciless damnation of the novel.

On January 15, 1846, the almanac *Petersburg Collection* published *Poor People;* on January 30 *The Double* appeared in *Fatherland Notes.*

Once again we find ourselves with Gogol's civil servants, chancery offices, departments, papers, and Their Excellencies; once again we are in the fantastic city of Petersburg with its human marionettes. Dostoevsky does not step out beyond the magic circle of Gogol's images and diction. The young writer's contention against the author of *Notes of a Madman* still continued; and even while imitating him, he struggled to overcome this temptation. Contemporary critics noted the imitation, but they failed to appreciate the "revolt." Their appraisal was harsh and unjust. K. S. Aksakov wrote: "Quite plainly we do not even understand how this tale could appear. Gogol is known to all of Russia, known almost by heart — and here, right under everyone's eyes, Dostoevsky paraphrases and literally reproduces Gogol's very expressions." S. Shevyryov remarked ironically: "There at the beginning one is continually nodding one's respects to some acquaintance out of Gogol: first to Chichikov, then to the Nose, then Petrushka, to the Indian Cock in the form of a samovar, then to Selifan."

Dostoevsky makes extensive use of Gogol's device of mechanized movements. His hero is depicted in the form of a doll that operates by an internal spring. His gestures and movements are violent, fatuous, and unreflected. This provides the narrative with a comic effect.

The Double is a story of the civil servant Golyadkin's mental derangement; it is an expansion of the theme of Gogol's *Notes of a Madman.* Poprishchin is in love with a general's daughter; Golyadkin, with Klara Olsufyevna, his director's daughter. The scintillating Teplov, a Gentleman of the Bedchamber, is favored over Poprishchin; the young man-of-the-world Vladimir Semyonovich is preferred to Golyadkin. In both Gogol and in Dostoevsky a section-head conspires against the civil servant. But in Gogol, it is only at the conclusion of the story that, as a denouement, the hero goes mad. Dostoevsky, on the other hand, makes this his basic theme, and in the very first chapter of his tale he depicts his hero in a state of incipient madness. Gogol employs the motif of insanity only as the vehicle of a clever stylistic game (the diary and the dogs' correspondence). Dostoevsky probes into the psychology of a madman, into the genesis of the disease and the process of its development. He transforms his teacher's study of the fantastically grotesque into a psychological novel. The motif of a split in an individual's conscious faculties is suggested by another of Gogol's short stories *The Nose*. The collegiate assessor Kovalyov has also been "split in two." His feature has acquired an independent existence. It wears a uniform, rides in a carriage. The nose, now that it has become detached from its owner, functions as a sort of double. Kovalyov explains to the clerk in the newspaper office: "Well, I am not asking you to publish an advertisement about a poodle, but about my own nose, which happens to be almost the same as about my very self."

Dostoevsky discards the anecdotal element (the nose) and provides the horrifying phenomenon of the double. But the genetic bond relating Golyadkin to Kovalyov remains. Here is how Gogol describes the first appearance of the double in his story: "Suddenly he [Kovalyov] *stopped dead in his tracks* at the doors of one of the houses. Right before his very eyes a *most inexplicable* occurrence had just taken place: a gentleman had jumped out, stooping over, and had run up the stairs. Now what was *the horror and, at the same time, astonishment* of Kovalyov when he recognized that this was his very own nose." And in *The Double* we read: "With *inexplicable* apprehension he began to look about in all directions *He stopped short, dead in his tracks*. Shuddering, he considered carefully and then screamed out *in astonishment and horror*. His legs gave way under him. It was the very same passerby with whom he was acquainted."

Thus by combining Gogol's thematic schemes, that of Poprishchin's madness and of the split in Kovalyov's consciousness, Dostoevsky succeeded in creating his own *Double*. It appears that after having studied and pondered the fantastic stories of the author of *Dead Souls,* he wanted to reason out Gogol's idea for himself. Why did Poprishchin go mad? What made Kovalyov split in two? How can this take place? Dostoevsky posits as his purpose the task of "rethinking" Gogol.

The titular councilor Yakov Petrovich Golyadkin is a creature of the putrid, damp fog of Petersburg, a phantom living in a phantasmal city. He revolves in the bizarre world of departments, chancery offices, of associations, of papers that are being issued, of administrative "upbraidings," complicated intrigues, of civil grades and official reports. He is a little "cog" in the state machinery, an insignificant grain of sand that is lost in the crowd of civil servants. Nikolai I's bureaucratic regime bore down with its ponderous mass upon the human personality. The state knew numbers and grades, but it did not know persons. The schema of human values was replaced by the table of ranks. All civil servants were indistinguishable one from another, and their significance was determined not inwardly by their respective worth, but externally by their position, by their function. Relations between people became purely mechanical, and people themselves were transformed into mere objects. Golyadkin's double makes his appearance in the department and not a single civil servant even remarks at this "wonder of nature." No one even looks at the man's face, for after all do objects really have faces? Objects are mutually interchangeable and no one is surprised that Golyadkin has been replaced by his double.

And what of the man who has been crushed and devoured by this bureaucratic machinery? What must he suffer as he faces the impending dissolution of his personality? Why, it is impossible for him not to be aware of the fact that beyond this kingdom of "paperwork" there no longer remains any real bond uniting him with people, that he exists in a vacuum, in an infinite solitude. Such a man must live in a constant state of fear, fear of being menaced on all sides. How can he defend himself? How can he demonstrate that he is in fact himself, one unique person without any duplication; that it is impossible for him to be replaced or exchanged? How can he affirm his identity? Golyadkin tries to save his personality by screening it from others, by individualizing it from the impersonal masses, by isolating himself. Like the harassed mouse, he hides in his underground nest.[3] He is Dostoevsky's first "man from underground." He wants to be "off to the side" so that no one will disturb him, to be "like everyone else" so as not to attract anyone's attention.

"I want to say," he mumbles confusedly, "that I am going my own way, my individual way. I live apart, and so to that degree it seems to

[3] Reference is to the *Notes from Underground*. *Podpolye* literally means in Russian a cellar under the house used for storage of food, etc. Allusion to the "mouse" is obvious.

me, I am not dependent on anyone. . . . Even though I'm a peace-loving man, nonetheless my road goes off apart." The self-abasement, the anxious fright of a man deprived of his personality is expressed in maniacal utterances: "I am absolutely nothing at all; I am who I am, like everyone else. In any case, my little hut stands off apart by itself. . . . I don't want to know anyone. Don't bother me, and I won't bother you. I'm off to the side."

That "I'm off to the side" savors of cowardly weakness. Golyadkin realizes that he will not be able to defend himself, that he will not succeed in scurrying off underground, that he has no "strength of character," that his personality has long since been crushed and suppressed. He fears life and its responsibilities, and with anxiety he longs to "disappear," to "vanish from sight." "He looked as though he wanted to hide from himself somewhere, as though he wants to run far away from himself." Golyadkin goes riding in a hired carriage, and suddenly he meets his superior, Andrey Filippovich. In a state of "indescribable anguish," he deliberates: "Shall I greet him or not? Or shall I pretend that I am not really me, that I'm someone completely different, though strikingly like me. . . . Simply not me, not me, and that's all." And so fear and a craving for security give birth to the first intimation of a split personality. It swells in the hero's raving consciousness, and finally realizes embodiment in the image of Golyadkin Jr. The "underground man" seeks to isolate himself, but outside the realm of social reality tragedy awaits him. Fleeing from the machinery which threatens to grind him to pieces, he finds a gaping vacuum in his own self. There is nothing to rescue; it is too late. His personality has already wasted away. Golyadkin still bustles about and fidgets, but these are the convulsive throes of a mouse that has been trampled upon. He cries out that he is a man, that he has "his own rightful place," that he is not just "a rag" . . . "I will not submit to being tossed about like a rag. I have not submitted to being tossed about even by such people; much less will I permit a man who is completely depraved to attempt it. I am not a rag; I, my good sir, am not a rag." But the narrator, parodying Golyadkin, adds insidiously: "Perhaps if someone had so desired, if, for example, someone so longed and positively craved to turn Mr. Golyadkin into a rag, why he would have succeeded, he would have succeeded without resistance and with impunity (Mr. Golyadkin himself sometimes felt this), and the result would have been a rag, and not Golyadkin. And so the result would have been a vile, filthy rag."

The underground man, goaded and insulted, lives through repressed feelings. His self-love approaches madness; his insecurity and "ambition" know no bounds. His unfulfilled wishes turn into obsessions; engender paranoia; are resolved in insanity. Golyadkin suspects everyone; trusts no one. He is surrounded by powerful enemies; all around him there are intrigues, "underminings," and "plots." They want to "kill him morally," to "exclude him from all the spheres of life." He loves talking about his "reputation," his noble intentions and honor, yet at the same time he is contriving plots to slander his rival. His double embodies all the baseness and meanness that is secreted in his soul. And Golyadkin Sr., even while railing against Golyadkin Jr., recognizes in him his own self. "He is of such a playful, nasty character. . . . He's such a villain, so fidgety, a bootlicker, a toady; *he is such a Golyadkin.*"

Yes, it would be easy to turn Golyadkin into a rag, but the narrator adds: "That rag would have had impulses and feelings, albeit only timid ambition and timid feelings, and these secluded deep in the filthy folds of the rag, but nonetheless feelings."

"A rag with ambitions," — this is a succinct image of Golyadkin. It was only years later that Dostoevsky realized the social significance of this type. In an 1865 edition, *The Double* was given the subtitle "A Petersburg Poem." Golyadkin is intimately bound to "the Petersburg period of Russian history"; he is clearly a product of the Russian "enlightenment." One can see in him the first caricature of the rationalized "universal man" whom Dostoevsky so despised. Of no less significance as regards the writer's work was the germination of the idea of the double, linked as it is with the problem of personality. From Golyadkin stem not only Dostoevsky's "underground men," but also those divided characters struggling for the integration of their personality: Versilov, Stavrogin, Ivan Karamazov. Reflecting upon this early work Dostoevsky writes in *The Diary of a Writer* (1877): "Most assuredly I utterly failed with this tale; however, its idea was quite lucid, and I have never developed anything in literature that is genuinely more serious than this idea. But the form of the story was an utter failure. I greatly amended it afterward, about fifteen years later, for the then 'general collection' of my works, but even at that time I again came to the conclusion that the thing was a complete failure; and were I to take up this idea now and expand it afresh, I would adopt a totally different form. But in '46 I did not succeed in finding this form, and failed to master the tale." In 1846, at the beginning of his literary career, Dostoevsky was unable to free himself from the poetics of the "natural school." He modified them by introducing new content within the traditional forms, but nevertheless Gogol's comic grotesque was patently unsuited to his new ideological and psychological art. The opposition of form and content had already been noticeable in *Poor People*; in *The Double* it became outrageous. The devices of mechanized movements expressing the transformation of a man into a rag, the endless repetitions, enumerations, the conglomeration of details, the uniformity of circumstances and the insufferable length of the descriptive passages, all serve to make the tale cumbersome and tedious. The writer recognized these deficiencies and was endlessly tormented by the thought that he had spoiled his "lucid" idea.

In 1859 he wrote his brother from Tver: "In mid-December I will send you (or I'll bring personally) a revised copy of *The Double*. Brother, believe me, this revision provided with a preface will amount to a new novel. Now at last the meaning of the double will be made clear! I hope to do more than merely create interest. In a word, I'm throwing down a challenge to all of them, and, lastly, if I don't revise *The Double* now, then when will I revise it? Why should I let a choice idea like this just slip out of my hands? This is a monumental type as regards its social importance, and I was the first to discover it, the first to herald it." But Dostoevsky's plan to rewrite the story never materialized. In Stellovsky's edition of 1865, *The Double* appeared with extensive abridgments which, in fact, seem at times to be haphazard and nonorganic, only tending to obscure the thought. No "new novel" was ever produced. In Dostoevsky's sketchbooks, however, there are several notations written, more than likely, during the years 1861-1864, which are valuable in indicating the subsequent development of the idea of Golyadkin. The tale mentions a certain Karolina Ivanovna, the proprietress of an eating-house, whom Golyadkin had first promised to marry and later deceived. In one of the notebooks we read: "A poor, very poor German woman with a limp, who lets out rooms for rent; she once helped Golyadkin, and Junior has succeeded in tracking her down; Senior is afraid to admit that once he was acquainted with her. The story of his relations with her pathetically recounted to Junior. The latter proves false and betrays him." Another notation reads: "Mr. Golyadkin at Petrashevsky's; Junior is making a speech . . . the system of Fourier. Noble tears. They embrace. *He will inform the police.*" "The following day Golyadkin goes to Petrashevsky's; he finds him lecturing the house-porter and his men about the system of Fourier and declares that Junior will inform the police." And finally the laconic notation: "Golyadkin Jr., he is the personification of baseness." Let us compare these statements: Golyadkin Jr., "the personification of baseness," is Golyadkin Sr.'s double. He is a tittering, restless and constantly fidgeting intriguer, a member of a secret society, and an informer. He assumes the personality of Antonelli, an agent of the Third Section[4] who denounced the Petrashevsky group, and ultimately he is embodied in the immortal figure of Pyotr Stepanovich Verkhovensky, the "petty devil," agent provocateur and double of Stavrogin (*The Devils*). Now one readily understands why the poor German woman Karolina Ivanovna, with whom Golyadkin Sr. had some sort of vague romantic affair, is portrayed as having a limp. In her shadowy image we already see the features of the lame Marya Timofeyevna emerging. Dostoevsky began to envision a novel of enormous scope, *The Devils*, and dropped his plans to revise *The Double*. This new idea demanded a totally different form, a totally different scale. Even further: in the 1865 text of *The Double* Dostoevsky carefully suppressed all traces of its conceptual relationship with *The Devils*. The idea of "imposture" is reserved for the great novel. Corresponding passages in the tale are left out, for example: "But imposture and shamelessness, dear Sir, are not accepted in our times. Imposture and shamelessness, my dear Sir, lead to no good, but rather bring one to the noose. Grishka Otrepyev[5] was the only one, my good Sir, who succeeded as an impostor. He deluded a blind people, but even then it was not for long." The wretched, pitiable Golyadkin falls far short of the idea of spiritual treachery; this is reserved for the powerful and terrible demon — Stavrogin. It is at him that the lame Marya Timofeyevna will cry out: "Grishka Otrepyev — anathema!"

After publication of *The Double,* Dostoevsky wrote his brother: "Golyadkin is ten times greater than *Poor People*. Our friends all say that since *Dead Souls* there hasn't been anything like it in Russ, that it is a work of genius, and they go on and on and on! They all look to me with such great expectations! Believe me, Golyadkin has carried me to the very heights of success."

[4] The Third Section of the Imperial Chancery was the secret police.

[5] Grishka Otrepyev, the "False Dmitry," was a run-away monk whom the Poles accepted as Dmitry, the son of Ivan IV, the lawful heir to the Russian throne. In 1604 he led a Polish army against the forces of the elected tsar Boris Godunov, defeated him with popular support, and was crowned Tsar of Moscow. A few months later he was killed in a riot. At the time he was marching into Russia, he had been anathematized by the Patriarch of Moscow.

In February 1846 Belinsky reviewed *Poor People* and *The Double* for the journal *Fatherland Notes*. The praise which he lavished upon the second tale, was accompanied by rather mild criticism. "And so," Belinsky wrote, "the hero of the novel is a madman. A daring concept and rendered by the author with wondrous skill." But he immediately added: "Albeit so, the Petersburg reading public has voiced the almost unanimous opinion that this novel is intolerably drawn out and consequently terribly boring, from which it follows that they had reason to raise some racket about the author." Belinsky tried rather unsuccessfully to defend the young writer. He explained that "there is an abundant number of excellent passages in *The Double, but one and the same thing*, however excellent it may be in itself, tends to weary the reader and becomes boring." It was his opinion that all of the story's shortcomings resulted from the excessive fecundity of an insufficiently matured talent which lacked an adequate sense of "tact, measure and harmony."

This critique, though completely well-meaning in its designs, cast the sensitive and impressionable Dostoevsky into utter despondency. Like his second Golyadkin, he lapsed quickly from a state of rapture into despair; felt himself affronted and persecuted. "What I find most nasty and tormenting," he wrote his brother,

> is that our own, our friends, Belinsky and everybody are displeased with Golyadkin. Their first impression was spontaneous enthusiasm, talk, noise, rumors. The second, criticism. It's just that *everybody, everybody*, from what's being said — i.e., our friends and all the public — has found Golyadkin so boring and lifeless, so drawn out, that it's simply impossible to read. . . . And on my part, for some time now I've been just plunged into despondency. There is a terrible defect in my personality, *a boundless self-love and vanity*. The very idea that I have failed to justify their expectations and that I have spoiled a thing which could have been a great work simply kills me. Golyadkin has become repugnant to me. A great deal of it was written in haste and when I was overly tired. Side by side some brilliant pages there is smut, garbage. It revolts one's soul; one does not even want to read it. This thing has simply cast me in hell for a time, and I've fallen sick from my distress.

But by the end of the letter the young writer's vanity once again rears its head: "Meanwhile, I'm still in first place, and I hope that's so forever."

This statement is extraordinary. Dostoevsky is, as it were, echoing his Golyadkin: the same lack of "strength of character," the same immoderate ambitions, the sudden transitions from childish self-sufficiency to utter self-contempt, the sensitiveness, mistrustfulness, the paranoia ("everybody, everybody") and the escape from inner "hell" to sickness. It is difficult within the framework of the writer's life to discern the boundaries which separate his biography from his art. In one instance, the author is duplicating his heroes; in another, these heroes are mimicking the author.

Dostoevsky's nervous ailment grew steadily worse. On April 26 he wrote his brother: "I was most violently ill, owing to an aggravation of my whole nervous system, and this malady centered upon my heart, producing an inflow of blood and inflammation of the heart." On May 16 he again wrote about his condition: "I have absolutely never had such a hard time with myself. Boredom, melancholy, apathy, a feverish, convulsive longing for something better, these torment me. And then this sickness still. . . ." V. N. Maikov introduced him to Dr. S. D. Yanovsky who treated him for several months. Throughout his entire life Dostoevsky cherished feelings of friendship and gratitude toward him. In 1872 he wrote the doctor: "You loved me and troubled yourself over me, a man sick with a mental illness (why, I recognize this now) up until the time of my journey to Siberia, where I was cured." In his memoirs Yanovsky describes his patient's external appearance with professional preciseness:

In height he was shorter than average. He had broad bones and was especially broad in his shoulders and chest. His head was well-proportioned, though his forehead was extremely developed, with noticeably prominent protuberances. His eyes were small, bright grey, and extremely lively. His lips were delicate and he invariably held them compressed together, with the result that his whole face expressed a sort of concentrated goodness and kindness. His hair was more than light, almost whitish, and extremely fine and soft. His hands and feet were noticeably large.

During this Balzacian period of his life, Dostoevsky dressed with dandyish elegance. "His clothes were always neat and immaculate," Yanovsky writes, "and you could say fashionable. He used to wear an excellently tailored black frock coat of excellent cloth, a black cassimere waistcoat, irreproachably white Holland linens, and a Zimmerman top hat. If there was anything that marred the harmony of his toilette, then it was his utterly unhandsome footwear and the fact that he tended to carry himself somewhat sluggishly." From behind the shoulder of the Russian Lucien de Rubempré, the civil servant Makar Devushkin was furtively peeping out.

During the summer of 1846 Dostoevsky set out for Reval, and there stayed with Mikhail Mikhailovich's family. Afterward he looked back upon this journey with depression. He wrote to his brother about his reservedness and duality:

> At times I am tormented by such anxiety. I remember at times how crude and difficult I was when I stayed with you in Reval. Dear brother, I was sick. I remember how once you said to me that the manner in which I treat you, precludes any mutual equality. . . . But mine is such a foul, repulsive character. . . . Sometimes when my heart is brimming with love, you will not draw a tender word out of me; at such times my nerves simply do not obey me. I am ludicrous and vile, and accordingly I am forever suffering from the unfair conclusions that are necessarily drawn about me. They say that I am cold and without a heart.

His summer spent resting in Reval did nothing to improve his condition. Upon his return to Petersburg, he felt so badly that he looked now upon his unpleasant stay with his brother as though it were paradise. "Here I have the most terrible melancholia," he wrote his brother on September 17, "and so work suffers. I lived with you and your family as though in paradise, and the devil knows: give me something good, and without fail I'll spoil it by my character."

During this period of his nervous ailment he became completely self-centered and doted on the torturous contradictions in his nature. In October everything became so unbearable that he finally decided to leave for Italy. "I am going not to have a spree, but rather to be treated," he informed his brother. "Petersburg is hell for me. It is so oppressive, so oppressive living here. And my health is noticeably worse. Moreover I have terrible fears. . . ."

In Italy he would write a novel; afterward from Rome he would take a short trip to Paris. . . . It was possible to raise the money — he would have only to publish all his works in a single volume. This plan was obviously fantastic. Once again the writer refers to his fears: "I am now in a state of fear that almost borders on panic, in regard to my health. The palpitations of my heart are simply terrifying, just as in the first phase of my sickness."

Suddenly he announced that the journey was being postponed. "All of this is so frustrating to me, brother, that I'm just going crazy. . . . Dear brother, I absolutely must have a spectacular success; without this there will be nothing."

The nervous strain resulting from two years of intense work on *Poor People* and *The Double*, combined with the emotional impact of the resounding success of the former and the not less resounding failure of the second, undermined his health. One can infer from Yanovsky's memoirs that Dostoevsky stood poised on the verge of mental illness. The doctor once came upon his patient on Senate Square. "Fyodor Mikhailovich was without a hat; his frock coat and waistcoat were unbuttoned. He was being helped along by some clerk from the War Office, and he cried with all his might, 'There is the one who will save me!' " These reflections about his nature, the analysis of the various sensations that accompanied his attacks and his thoughts on "a state of fear that borders on panic" — all of which are scattered throughout the letters of 1846 — later provided the writer with material for the characteristics of Ivan Petrovich, the young author in the novel *The Humiliated and Wronged*. From the point of view of biographical detail, Ivan Petrovich is very close to Dostoevsky. He is also a young writer, the author of a tale about a poor civil servant, which is extolled by the critic B. He also plunges from the height of glory into obscurity; he writes stories in great haste for an "entrepreneur" and falls sick from a nervous ailment. In describing his hero's mental state, the writer remolds autobiographical material within artistic form. All of Dostoevsky's heroes are flesh of his flesh, and their respective fates aid us in unraveling the enigma of their author.

Ivan Petrovich is sick, downcast; he cannot write.

I threw my pen down and sat by the window. The darkness of evening was descending, and I felt more and more melancholy. Various depressing thoughts beset me. I became convinced that in the end I should perish in Petersburg. Spring was drawing near: in like manner I should also come back to life, I guess. The thought ran through my mind — if only I could dig my way out of this shell into the light of heaven, if I could breathe the smell of the fresh fields and the forests — but I have not seen them for so long. I remember, the thought also struck me — how nice it would be, if by some magic or miracle I could completely forget everything that was, that has been lost in these past years; to forget everything, to freshen my mind, and to begin again with new strength. In those days I still dreamed of it and longed for a resurrection from the dead. Perhaps I could go into a madhouse or something, I decided finally so that somehow all my brains might be shaken up in my head and rearranged in a new order, and then be cured again. For I still had a thirst for life and faith in it.

In his letters to his brother we encounter the same feeling of perishing in Petersburg, the same longing "to dig his way out" of it, the journey to Reval, the plan of traveling to Italy. Even the thought of madness which had flashed across the writer's imagination in 1838 upon reading Hoffmann's *The Magnetizer*, finds its artistic adaptation in this novel. Lastly, the fear that Dostoevsky mentions so frequently in his letters here reveals its authentic mystical nature.

. . . As the darkness lowered and spread itself, my room became, as it were, more spacious; it seemed to extend further and further. . . . And then, at that very instant, I experienced something which made a great impression upon me. However, I must make an openhearted confession of everything: whether it was from my nervous affliction, or from new impressions in my new apartment, or from a recent attack of depression — but little by little with the first approach of twilight, I gradually began to succumb to that state of soul which now comes to me so frequently at night, in my sickness, and which I call *mystical terror*. It is a most oppressive, tormenting fear of something that I myself cannot define, of something that is not understood and that does not exist in the natural order of things, but that without fail, perhaps this very minute, will happen, as though in mockery of all the arguments of reason, and will come to me and stand before me as an undeniable fact, horrible, unseemly, and implacable. This fear usually grows more and more intense in spite of the arguments advanced by my intellect, so that finally the mind, in spite of the fact that at these times it assumes perhaps an even greater clarity, nonetheless is stripped of all power to resist these sensations. It goes unheeded. It becomes useless, and this inner split serves only to intensify that frightening anguish of anticipation. I guess that it is somewhat like the anguish of people who are afraid of the dead. But in the anguish that I experience, the uncertainty of the danger intensifies my suffering even more.

This was not fear concerning one's health (as Dostoevsky wrote to his brother), nor fear in the face of impending madness, nor even fear of death. This was still more terrifying. On the basis of his personal experience with this malady in 1846, the writer began for the first time in *The Humiliated and Wronged* to appraise it as a metaphysical problem. Something "unseemly and implacable" stands at the threshold of consciousness and is ready to thrust itself into our "reasoned" world. This something does not exist and at the same time can happen at any given moment, can stand before a man as "an undeniable fact." It does not follow the laws of logic (it both exists and does not exist); reason repudiates it with terror, but in mockery of reason, it nonetheless asserts itself in all its "unseemliness." It is nothing, but it is; nonbeing, but it exists; a dark abyss before which understanding breaks down, but which the heart understands. Nonbeing was Dostoevsky's most torturous nightmare. It pursues his heroes: Svidrigailov, Stavrogin, Versilov, Ivan Karamazov. In an effort to free himself from this phantom, the writer searched for *mystical reality*, for genuine being. His art is a struggle with the phantasms of consciousness, a search for the ontological basis of existence.

In October 1846 Dostoevsky's health began to improve somewhat. His relations with *The Contemporary* and its contributors grew more and more strained. He submitted his new story, *Mister Prokharchin*, not to Nekrasov but to Krayevsky, the editor of *Fatherland Notes*. A quarrel ensued. In November 1846 he wrote his brother: "Let me tell you that I had the unpleasant experience of quarreling decisively with *The Contemporary*, in the person of Nekrasov. . . . Now they are spreading the story that I am eaten up with self-love, that I have grown too big for my boots and am going over to Krayevsky because Maikov panders to my ego. . . . And as for Belinsky, he is such a weakling that even his literary opinions are swayed by every passing breeze."

In his imagination this breach with *The Contemporary* swelled into a struggle to the very death *with everybody*. Once again we hear the voice of Golyadkin. "I really feel," he confesses, "that I have instituted proceedings against all our literature, our journals and critics . . . and even this year I am going to confirm my primacy to spite all those who wish me ill."

The literary world was repelled by the young writer's conceit and his defiant arrogance. They began mercilessly to badger him; lampoons and epigrams came pouring down. The literary circles of those times frequently enough resorted to such "dethronements" of various celebrities. Avdotya Panayeva writes:

> Several young writers joined our circle and it was a genuine misfortune for anyone who chanced to fall prey to their derision, but Dostoevsky, as though by design, used to give them every opportunity, with his irritable disposition and arrogant tone, as if implying that he was incomparably greater than they because of his talent. And so they would proceed to pick away at him, to nettle his conceit with various cutting remarks in the course of their conversations. Turgenev was indisputably a master at this. He would contrive to draw Dostoevsky into a dispute and then drive him to the ultimate limits of exasperation. The latter would finally be ready to climb up the walls and would heatedly defend what were sometimes absurd notions about things, which he would blurt out in passionate rage, while Turgenev would snatch them up and thoroughly entertain himself. Dostoevsky grew terribly suspicious. He began to suspect that everyone was envious of his talent and he used to see in almost every innocent word uttered, some hidden design to belittle his works, to cast aspersions upon him. Even at this time, when he would come to join us, one could obviously sense his feelings of resentment. He used to find fault with what was said so that he might vent upon those who were envious of him all the bile that had gathered up and been choking him. Instead of merely looking upon him with some condescension as a sick, nervous man, they continued to harass him even more with their lampoons.

Grigorovich completes the picture of the badgering which this "sick man" had to endure:

> The abruptness of the transition from the worship paid to the author of *Poor People*, exalting him almost to the level of a genius, to the hopeless denunciation of all his literary talents could have crushed a man who was much less impressionable and conceited than Dostoevsky. He began to avoid those persons who were associated with Belinsky's group. He became completely withdrawn, even more so than before, and grew hopelessly irritable. When face to face with Turgenev, Dostoevsky unfortunately could not restrain himself and gave vent to the indignation that had been boiling up within him. He said that none of them frightened him, that only give him time, and he would trample them all down into the dirt. . . . After this

scene with Turgenev the final rupture between Belinsky's circle and Dostoevsky took place. He no longer came to call on him. Witticisms, caustic epigrams were showered upon him. They accused him of being monstrously conceited, of being envious of Gogol.

Turgenev spread a rumor to the effect that Dostoevsky had insisted upon having *Poor People* printed in an edition with gold edgings. Grigorovich, Panayev, and Annenkov all repeat this ridiculous gossip in their memoirs. In 1888 Leontyev reported that Turgenev used to tell him this story at the time when Dostoevsky was serving his sentence of hard labor. "Young people such as you," he would say, "because of their intrinsic worth do not have to make a display of self-conceit when they achieve their first successes. Take, for example, what happened to this unfortunate Dostoevsky. When he first submitted his novel for publication to Belinsky, he got so carried away that he said to him: 'You know, we're going to have to have my tale edged with some kind of little border.'" *Belinsky's Missive to Dostoevsky* can be ascribed to the collective efforts of Turgenev and Nekrasov. It begins with the strophe:

> Knight of mournful figure,
> Dostoevsky, you dear blow-hard,
> You redden the nose
> Of literature like a new pimple. . . .

In conclusion Belinsky asks:

> To secure my future acclaim,
> (The need, you see, is great),
> Of your unpublished works
> Keep *The Double* for yourself.
>
> I will pamper you like an old nurse,
> I will play the role of your toady,
> I'll edge you with a border,
> I'll set you up in the end.[6]

Turgenev told I. Pavlovsky that on one occasion Dostoevsky came into his apartment at the precise moment when all the assembled guests (Belinsky, Ogaryov, Herzen) were laughing at a certain piece of nonsense. He interpreted this as being on his account. He bolted

[6] This poem, and those following in other chapters, are rhymed in the original. In the translation no attempt has been made to preserve the rhyme scheme. The "knight of mournful figure" refers, of course, to Don Quixote.

out the door and for an hour walked about the streets in the freezing cold. Later when Turgenev chanced to find him, he exclaimed: "My God! It's just impossible! Wherever I go, everywhere they are laughing at me. Unfortunately, from the doorway I happened to see how you began to laugh when you noticed me. And aren't you even ashamed?" The story probably is without any factual foundation, but it succeeds in conveying the "atmosphere" which surrounded the tormented writer. The memoirs of I. Panayev exude an open spite: "We bore him [Dostoevsky] in triumph through the boulevards and squares of the city, and as we presented him to the public, we cried out: 'Behold a little genius who has just come to life. In time he will put an end to all present and past literature through his own works. Bow down to him! Bow down!'" According to I. Panayev's wife, Avdotya Panayeva, Nekrasov had a fierce time explaining the poem *The Knight of Mournful Figure* to Dostoevsky. Dostoevsky ran out of his apartment "pale as a sheet" and after he had left, Nekrasov complained to Panayeva: "Dostoevsky has simply gone out of his mind! . . . He came and threatened me not to dare review his work in the next issue. And he has gotten wind of a rumor that I am going about everywhere reading a pasquil in verse that I have composed against him! He flew into a rage."

The pages of our literary life are shamefully soiled by Dostoevsky's conflict with *The Contemporary* and by the badgering to which he was subjected by such noted personages as Turgenev and Nekrasov. For the rest of his life Dostoevsky continued to regard Belinsky and Turgenev with abhorrence as the very embodiment of all the evil in "the Petersburg period of Russian history." This enmity, in great measure, determined the future development of his world-outlook.

Toward the end of 1846 Dostoevsky began to cultivate an entirely new circle of acquaintances. After his quarrel with Belinsky's group he became friends with the Beketov brothers and joined the sizable and convivial company which used to gather at their hospitable home. Lively conversations were carried on there; literary news was exchanged and discussed. They used to take airings together. Grigorovich relates: "Once the whole lot of us agreed to embark upon a real excursion, to set out on foot for Pargolovo and to pass the night on Mt. Salutation overlooking the lake."

During the course of the same year the writer was introduced into the literary salon of the Maikovs. According to Dr. Yanovsky, Dostoevsky used to criticize the characters of Gogol's and Turgenev's works there and those of his own *Prokharchin* "with a sort of atomistic analysis that was peculiar to him." "And at times," Yanovsky writes, "all this would go on to the accompaniment of good music and singing, but for the most part with discussions and argumentation, until three, and even at times till four o'clock in the morning. . . ." Throughout his entire life Dostoevsky valued the friendship of Apollon Maikov.

We pass to a new year, 1847. The author of *The Double* admitted with bitterness that "his glory had diminished in the journals" and he totaled up the sad reckoning of his literary career. "You will not believe me," he wrote his brother,

> but here I have been writing as a profession for three years already, and I am completely in a fog. I do not see life; I have no time really to collect myself. Knowledge and capability are slipping away because there is no time. I would so like to become established. The reputation which has been set for me, is uncertain, and I don't know how long this hell will go on. All around poverty, pressing work — if only I could get some rest!

And after *Crime and Punishment*, after *The Idiot*, and even after *The Devils*, Dostoevsky would still be talking about his "uncertain reputation"; he would still long "to become established." It seems that he could never believe decidedly in his own fame. Side by side the "boundless vanity" there was an unfathomable humility.

During this tragic year, 1846, though sick and under great strain, Dostoevsky worked on two things: *The Shaved Whiskers* and *The Story of the Suppressed Chancery Offices*. He assured his brother that "both of them excite an astonishing tragic interest and are succinct to an unbelievable degree." Financial difficulties forced him to interrupt this work and to begin a short story for Krayevsky. On April 26 he informed his brother: "There's a story that I have to complete before my departure [for Reval], not a long one, for the money which Kravevsky advanced me, and then I'll ask him for another advance."

Once having written this item (*Mister Prokharchin*), he resumed work on *The Shaved Whiskers*. On October 17 the tale was "still not completely finished." His dream of publishing an edition of all his works in a single volume came to naught. In the course of this same month he wrote his brother: "All my plans have come crashing down and of their own selves have been demolished. The edition is not going to materialize. . . . I'm through writing even *The Shaved Whiskers!* I threw everything out. . . ." Of the two proposed stories, only the titles have come down to us. From these we can conclude that, as in the case of his earlier works, Dostoevsky was still held within the bounds of the "natural school's" themes.

The work of an entire year — and all that survived is one rather short tale, *Mister Prokharchin,*[A] and that in a form mutilated by the censor. The author complained: "Prokharchin has been terribly disfigured in a certain place. These gentlemen from you know where, have even prohibited the use of the word 'civil servant' and God knows for what reason. As it stood it was too innocuous and now they have slashed through it everywhere. All that was lively has disappeared. Only the skeleton of what I read to you remains. I renounce my own story."

Semyon Ivanovich Prokharchin is of the same cast of insignificant civil servants as Makar Devushkin in *Poor People* and Akaky Akakyevich in *The Greatcoat.* The motif of the squalor and misery of his existence is sharply underlined. He lives in a corner of a room, and pays five rubles a month for this closet. He eats only half a dinner, and does not send his linen to the laundry. The peculiarities of his impeded speech are also heightened; the stammerings of Gogol's Akaky Akakyevich are accentuated in original fashion. "When he [Prokharchin] did happen to manage a long sentence, then to the extent that he became absorbed in it, each word seemed to give birth to still another word, that other word, immediately upon its birth, to a third, the third to a fourth, etc., etc., so that his mouth was stuffed full. He would begin to clear his throat slightly and the crowding words would finally begin to fly out in the most picturesque disorder." This speech characteristic leads us immediately to the psychology of a maniac.

Like his confreres Devushkin and Bashmachkin, Prokharchin serves as a target for ridicule. His fellow-boarders fabricate various stories while he is in the room so as to intimidate him. They remove the screens from around his bed and place a doll upon it. Two of his "friends" try to kidnap his cherished little trunk. This morose individual's constant badgering by his derisive fellow-lodgers reflects not only Akaky Akakyevich's and Makar Devushkin's misfortunes in the chan-

---

[A] Published in *Fatherland Notes* (1846).

cery offices, not only the "machinations" of Golyadkin's "enemies," but also the personal drama of Dostoevsky who was "tormented" by the group that formed *The Contemporary*. Just like the author himself, Prokharchin is a "stubborn, uncommunicative" individual; he "does not know how to get along with people." Before this, he used to live in "dense, impenetrable solitude." He silently kept to his bed behind a screen for fifteen years and "did not have anything to do with anyone." The "lucid idea" which Dostoevsky by his own admission "had spoiled" in *The Double*, once again appears in *Prokharchin*. We again are presented with the problem of the loneliness of the human soul, of the solitude of consciousness, the escape underground. In *The Double* a man's estrangement from reality is disclosed within a psychological framework. Golyadkin is a madman; Prokharchin is only a crank who has "a fantastic turn of mind" and is surrounded by a certain "mysteriousness." By modifying the tonality in this manner, the author has overcome the main inadequacy of *The Double*. This new story is not a record of delirious ravings, but the concise delineation of a character. Dostoevsky is, as it were, reconsidering his resolution of the problem of "loneliness." He no longer finds escape in madness as the inevitable fate of the underground man. He sees other possibilities of "self-affirmation." Protecting himself against a hostile and alien world, rescuing himself from the vacuum of his own "loneliness," the solitary can dream of power and might; the pauper can hypnotize himself with the idea of riches. Prokharchin is a miser. Like Akaky Akakyevich, he half-starves himself. He deprives himself of the very necessities. Ascetically he serves his "idea." But his idea cannot be compared with the pitiable dream of a warm greatcoat. His idea is majestic. He is a *covetous knight*.

Years later, in his feuilleton *Petersburg Dreams in Verse and Prose* (1861), Dostoevsky set forth a detailed account of the origins of the wealthy pauper Prokharchin's image and of his connection with Pushkin's *The Covetous Knight*. In the course of the article he relates how once he had read the story of a certain miser in the newspapers. "Suddenly there emerged a new Harpagon who had died midst the most awful poverty, lying upon heaps of gold. This old man was a certain retired titular councilor named Solovyov. For three rubles he used to rent a screened-off corner of a room for himself. Solovyov lived for more than a year in his filthy corner. He remained without any activities or occupation, and used to complain continually about his meager finances. True to the character of his apparent poverty he even failed to pay for his lodgings on time, being a year behind in his rent at the time of his death. . . . He used to deny himself fresh food, even during the last days of his life. Solovyov died on a heap of rags amidst shocking and foul poverty, and after his death they found among his papers 169,022 rubles in banknotes and ready cash. . . .

"And there in the crowd," continues the author,

a certain figure, not real, but fantastic, flashed for an instant before me. . . . The figure wore an old and threadbare greatcoat of cotton wadding, which without doubt its owner used in place of a blanket at night — that was evident even at first glance. Shreds of grey hair thrust themselves out from under his hat and fell onto the collar of the greatcoat. The old fellow supported himself on a cane. He would chew on his lips, and with his eyes fixed on the ground, he hurried along to some place or other. Having come up alongside of me, he cast a glance at me and winked an eye, a dead eye, without light or vitality, just as if the eyelid of a corpse had been opened before me, and immediately it came to me that this was that very Harpagon who had died with half a million on his pile of rags. . . .

And there before me an image suddenly emerged, very much like that of Pushkin's *Covetous Knight*. Suddenly I felt that my Solovyov was a colossal personage. He had left the world and withdrawn from all its allurements into himself behind the screen. What did all this inane splendor, all this magnificence of ours mean to him? What is rest and comfort? . . . No, he does not need anything; he has all this there under the pillow, the covering of which has not been changed since last year. He will sprawl there, and everything that he needs will docilely come crawling to him. He will have a desire for something and a number of people will satisfy him with an attentive smile. He is beyond all desires. . . . But when I imagined such an image, I felt that I was not going to the point of stealing from Pushkin. . . .

The man who has shut himself off from the world hangs suspended in a vacuum; the solitude of "I" is his moral void. He affirms himself in "power and might" when faced with the fear of nonbeing. If he is rich, he "has everything." But Dostoevsky did not want to "steal from" Pushkin and he developed the latter's idea independently. He concerned himself not with the aspect of power in miserliness, but with *the aspect of fear*. He believed that Solovyov in his youth was just like everybody else: he loved some Luiza or other; used to go to the theatre; and then suddenly he underwent one of those experiences which in an instant change a man.

"Perhaps he passed through some moment or other when suddenly, as it were, he began to see clearly into something and lost his courage before something. And here like Akaky Akakyevich, he begins to save up half-kopeck pieces for a martin coat and he sets aside from his wages, and he saves, saves for a dark day—he does not know for what — but only not for the coat. He sometimes even trembles and fears and wraps himself up in the collar of his greatcoat when he walks along the streets, so as not to be frightened of anyone, and in general, he looks as if they had just taken him over the coals." And the more he saves, the more he fears. "It is both a delight and a horror to him; and fear oppresses his heart more and more until he suddenly realizes his fortune and hides himself in some poor corner. . . ."

Fear has turned Prokharchin into a miser. In him, paradoxically, we find the covetous knight's majestic image united to the wretched figure of Akaky Akakyevich. Prokharchin fears life and "secures" himself by being thrifty in regard to his personal needs. But once "having lost his courage" he can no longer return to his former feeling of security. Fear lies buried deep in his soul and waits only for the opportunity to flare up and consume the man who has lost his courage. The lodgers' pranks and teasing appear as just such an opportunity. "Prokharchin's face began to wear a troubled expression; his glances became anxious, sheepish, and a little suspicious." He would go off somewhere with his friend, "a drunken beggar," and return in a state of psychological stupor. He was plagued by the thought that the chancery office in which he served would be suppressed.

At the same time that he was writing *Prokharchin*, Dostoevsky was working on *The Story of the Suppressed Chancery Offices*. It is altogether possible that he made use of the theme of this unfinished work in *Prokharchin*. The unfortunate civil servant dies all alone as the result of his fear. In the story of this "wealthy pauper" the problem of loneliness is related to the idea of guilt and responsibility. He affirms his "ego" without any reference to the world beyond his self, and this is his sin. Prokharchin's fellow-boarder Mark Ivanovich replies to his complaints and apprehensions: "And who do you think you are? You sheep! Without house or home. What, are you the only person on earth? What, was the world made for you? What, are you some kind of Napoleon? What are you? Who are you? Are you a Napoleon, eh? Napoleon or not? Tell me, sir, are you Napoleon or not?" Prokharchin's sin consists in his living as though he were the only person on earth, as though he had no neighbor, no mutual responsibility of human suffering or of human love. And his feelings of guilt are to be found embodied in the delirium which precedes his death. His coworker Andrey Yefimovich, with whom he has not passed a word for twenty years, appears to him. This latter is counting over his rubles and mumbling: "There won't be any more, and there won't be any kasha, and I, good sir, have seven children." And Prokharchin feels that he himself is precisely to blame that Andrey Yefimovich has seven hungry children. . . . Then he chances upon a fire. He stands sandwiched up against a fence, and a certain muzhik in a torn smock arouses "all God's people" against him. He recognizes the muzhik as a cab driver whom five years ago he "had cheated in a most inhuman way." The enraged crowd "winds about him, presses upon him, suffocates him." Prokharchin's dream is the most powerful passage in the entire story. This is the first instance in which Dostoevsky touches upon his basic theme: "All men are guilty for everyone," and in which he advances his moral evaluation of solitude as an offense against the human family. Prokharchin's dream reminds us of Mitya's vision on the road to Mokroye.

In Mark Ivanovich's harsh response one word arrests our attention. It opens unexpected perspectives for us into the writer's future conceptions. Why does Prokharchin's fellow-boarder so obstinately interrogate him: "Are you a Napoleon, eh? Napoleon or not?" What does the wretched denizen of corners have in common with the great commander? We find the answer to this question in that same feuilleton of 1861 *Petersburg Dreams.* Dostoevsky describes another civil servant, humble, silent, "an absolutely blameless individual." At home he had an aunt whose cheek was bandaged up, a querulous wife, and six children. Fault-findings, tears, reproaches finally lead him to the point of despair.

> The poor man suddenly raised his head and spoke like Balaam's ass, but he talked so strangely that they put him away in a mad-house. And how could it ever have entered his head that he was *Garibaldi!* He almost never spoke to anyone, and then suddenly he began to be upset, to be puzzled, to pose questions all about Garibaldi and about conditions in Italy, just as Poprishchin did about Spanish affairs. . . . And here, little by little, he began to be irresistibly convinced that he was in fact Garibaldi, a filibuster and transgressor of the natural

order of things. . . . He saw only one thing no matter where or at what he looked: his crime, his shame and infamy. . . . And then one morning suddenly he threw himself at the feet of His Excellency. "Pardon me," he said. "I'll make a full confession. I am Garibaldi. Do with me what you wish!" . . . Well, and so they did with him . . . what they had to do.

Strange and fearful thoughts are born to the man who exists in solitude and social humiliation. At times even the meek and humble Makar Devushkin feared his own tendency toward freethinking. For many years the civil servant–Garibaldi had repressed his thoughts "about the natural order of things" that was proceeding to transform him into a rag. Then these considerations evolved into a fixed idea. He himself is a "transgressor of order," a criminal. Prokharchin is also such a transgressor. Is not the "natural order" violated when a civil servant whose salary consists in but a mere pittance, becomes a millionaire? Vaguely he feels that his secret wealth is a crime, and pangs of conscience and fear haunt him. The author substitutes the forceful name "Napoleon" for the less suggestive image the "filibuster Garibaldi." When Mark Ivanovich questions Prokharchin as to whether or not he is Napoleon, he is penetrating the innermost recesses of the latter's secret.

However, Devushkin the freethinker, the civil servant–Garibaldi, and Prokharchin-Napoleon are still but pale shadows. It was only after Dostoevsky's sentence of hard labor that the real insurgent and criminal entered the writer's world. It is the fate of Raskolnikov that bestows upon the name Napoleon, the "transgressor of the order of things," its full significance as an idea.

I V

Works of 1847-1848

With the failure of *Mister Prokharchin* Dostoevsky's "fame" underwent a complete "reversal." Belinsky, who had been so forbearing in his criticism of *The Double,* completely failed to understand *Prokharchin* and was unjust in his condemnation of it. In *The Contemporary* (1847) he wrote in reference to the remarkable tale: "There are flashes of talent gleaming in it, but in so dense a gloom that their light yields nothing to the reader. It was not inspiration, not free and ingenuous creativity, that begot this strange tale, but something in the nature of . . . how shall we put it? — ostentation and pretension . . . or else it would not be so affected, mannered, incomprehensible, more like some actual but strange and complicated incident than a poetic creation."

The final two years before his arrest Dostoevsky lived continually in a state of financial need, dependent upon the "day-labor" that was given him by the editor of *Fatherland Notes,* Andrey Aleksandrovich Krayevsky. He owed the latter a large sum of money, and had to eke out his bare existence from advance to advance. "What a misfortune to have to work as a hired laborer," he complained to his brother. "You destroy everything, your talent and youth and hope. Work becomes repulsive, and you end up, finally, a dabbler and not a writer." He envisioned the prospect of writing a long novel in six parts, but instead, owing to the burden of finances, he was forced to compose "light" things. In the life of Dostoevsky the year 1847 was relatively without events. Yet two of them were to play a decisive role in his fate: his final quarrel with Belinsky and his acquaintance with Petrashevsky.

In April 1847 he began to write the feuilletons entitled *Petersburg Chronicle* for the *Saint-Petersburg Gazette.* The critics of *The Contemporary* finally convinced him that the style practiced by the "natural school" was decidedly unsuited to his purposes. And after *Prokharchin* even he himself felt that he had exhausted all the possibilities of Gogolian naturalism. The feuilletonist of the *Saint-Petersburg Gazette*, E. I. Hubert, died at this time and Dostoevsky was offered his position. He readily accepted the proposal, remembering his first "brilliant" appearance in the character of a feuilletonist (the announcement of the almanac *The Scoffer* in 1845). Merely contributing to this aristocratic-conservative newspaper, which was hostile to the Gogolian trend and preserved the Pushkin tradition, extended a challenge to his recent friends of *The Contemporary*. However, he was primarily attracted by the free and ample form of the feuilleton, the tone of natural conversation, intimate and lively. The author presented himself as a "Petersburg *flâneur*," described genre scenes; discussed books he had read; sketched portraits in passing; conveyed his impressions of theatrical performances and concerts; combined ironic observations with reflections and personal admissions. Under Dostoevsky's pen the feuilleton ceased to be "a collection of urban news flavored with amiable banterings," as Polevoy called it, and became a lyric confession. The *Petersburg Chronicle* is the first *Diary of a Writer*, the first attempt made at ordering the author's inner experiences within an artistic form. It is from this reservoir of ideas and emotions that the writer drew the material for his stories of 1847-1848 (*The Landlady, White Nights, A Faint Heart, A Christmas Tree Party and a Wedding, The Jealous Husband*). The random remarks of the *Chronicle* are unified by the image of its main hero: the fantastic and gloomy city Petersburg. The *flâneur* tuned his ear to its mysterious life:

> . . . There I was going through the Hay Market,[1] deliberating upon what to write. Despondency gnawed at my being. It was a damp and foggy morning; Petersburg had gotten up nasty and peeved, like an irritable young socialite. . . . It was depressing to look at its huge damp walls, and at its marbles, bas-reliefs, statues, the columns which, so it would seem, also were vexed at the foul weather . . . at the naked wet granite of the pavement which lay cracked, as though maliciously, under the feet of passersby, and finally, at the passersby themselves, pale green, stern, somehow terribly angry. . . . All Petersburg's horizon looked so sour, so sour. . . . Petersburg was sulking. . . . It was evident that it was nursing a *terrible desire* to run off somewhere far away from here and on no account to remain in this grim Ingermanland marsh.[2]

[1] In Dostoevsky's day a slum area in Petersburg.
[2] The Finnish marshland on which, at the beginning of the 18th century, Peter the Great constructed his new capital, Petersburg.

The *Petersburg Chronicle* helped provide Dostoevsky with a new artistic theme: that of romantic dreaming. It evolved out of the concept of "isolated consciousness," a concept fundamental to all the writer's work. However, within the natural school's poetics this theme had been linked to the image of the "poor civil servant," and was reduced to the dismal or comic-grotesque (Golyadkin, Prokharchin). Now Dostoevsky found it necessary to return to the romantic tradition in order to disclose its more lofty poetic aspect. In the *Petersburg Chronicle* we find pages of brilliant lyricism devoted to this daydreaming. His works of this period are filled with the inspiration of their pathos.

This is how the Petersburg dreamer characterizes himself:

Do you have any idea what a dreamer is, ladies and gentlemen? It is a Petersburg nightmare, it is sin personified, it is a tragedy, speechless, mysterious, sullen, ferocious, with all its raging horrors, with all its catastrophes, peripeteias, intrigues, and denouements, and we say this in utter seriousness. You sometimes meet an individual who is lost in his own thoughts, who has a vaguely expressionless look about him, whose face is frequently pale and worn. He always seems taken up with something terribly onerous, with some affair that is simply racking his brain. Sometimes he is weary, exhausted, as though from heavy labors, but in fact he does not produce a single given thing. This is how the dreamer appears outwardly. The dreamer is always troublesome because he is inconsistent to excess: now he is too gleeful, now he is morose, now crude, now attentive and tender, now he is an egoist, now capable of the most noble sentiments. . . . They settle themselves for the most part in a deep solitude, in inaccessible corners, as though trying to hide themselves from people and from light, and in general when they first glance at them, something melodramatic springs to their eyes. . . . They love to read . . . but usually after the second or third page they lay the reading aside for they are completely satisfied. Their fantasy, animated, soaring, light, is already stimulated, an impression has been fashioned; and an entire dream world with its joys, with sorrows, with hell and paradise, with its captivating women, with heroic exploits, with noble pursuits, always with some sort of gigantic struggle, with crimes and all sorts of horrors, suddenly seizes possession of the dreamer's whole being. The room disappears, and space as well; time comes to a halt or flies so quickly that an hour seems as though it were but a minute. Sometimes they pass entire nights in indescribable pleasures. Frequently within several hours they live through a paradise of love or an entire life, huge, gigantic, unheard-of, wonderful, like a dream, magnificently beautiful. In accord with some unknown arbitrary force the pulse quickens, tears gush forth, the pale, moistened cheeks burn with feverish fire. . . . The moments of sobering are horrible: the poor wretch cannot endure them and immediately starts to take his poison in new increased dosages. . . . He goes out onto the street with head cast down, paying little attention to the surroundings, but if he does notice anything, the most commonplace, mundane trifle takes on a fantastic coloring for him. . . . His imagination has been set in motion: straightway an entire story, a tale, a novel is born. . . . Frequently reality produces an onerous impression, one hostile to the dreamer's heart, and he hastens to withdraw into his own inviolable golden nook. . . . Imperceptibly the *talent* for real life begins to be deadened within him. . . . At last, in his delusion he completely loses that moral instinct by means of which an individual is capable of perceiving all the beauty of the real, and in his state of apathy lazily folds his hands and does not want to know that human life is the continual contemplation of self in nature and in day-by-day reality. . . . And is not such a life a tragedy! Is it not a sin and a horror! Is it not a caricature! And are we not all to one degree or other dreamers!

The last sentence discloses the narrator's pseudonym: it is the *dreamer* narrating about his own self, or to put it more exactly, Dostoevsky is making an intimate confession to the reader about his own character (troublesome, inconsistent — now tender, now crude), about his own romantic youth when he dreamed of heroic exploits and a "paradise of love," about his lack of sociability and loneliness. The *flâneur*-feuilletonist forgets that he is not a novelist and confesses that in his imagination every mundane trifle is transformed "into a tale, a novel. . . ." Fourteen years later, in his collection *Petersburg Dreams*, Dostoevsky again turned to the material of the *Chronicle*. The myth of the *flâneur* was abandoned and the narration was presented in the first person. The dreamer is the author himself. . . . "And what dreams did I not have in my adolescence. . . . I was so lost in dreams that my whole youth passed by without my ever noticing it. . . ." And so *Petersburg Chronicle* is the author's confession. We find in it the creation of a new art form: lyric-pathetic, with a touch of melodrama and moralism.

The theme of dreaming brings us to the tale *The Landlady*. The schematic origins of this work arose toward the end of 1846. After the failure of *Prokharchin* Dostoevsky rejected the techniques of the natural school and destroyed his attempt *The Shaved Whiskers*.

"I threw the whole thing out," he wrote his brother, "for all of it is nothing but a repetition of old items that I've already said long ago. Now I'm forced to put more original, lively, and lucid thoughts upon paper. When I finally came to the end of *The Shaved Whiskers*, I suddenly realized all this. In my position uniformity means ruin. I'm writing another tale and the work is going as it sometimes did in *Poor People*, freshly, with ease and success."

This "other tale" — *The Landlady* — had already taken hold of his imagination, and it soon began to express itself stylistically. The author who when writing to his brother not very long ago had simulated Golyadkin's manner of speech, now talks the language of Ordynov, the hero of his new story. . . . "Independence, a situation, and, finally, work for Holy Art, work holy, pure, in a simplicity of heart which has never so trembled and stirred within me as now, before all the new images which are created in my soul. Dear brother, I am being reborn not only morally, but physically as well. Never have I known such profusion and clarity, so much stability of character, so much physical health." This letter alone seems to indicate that the tale will be sublimely romantic ("Holy Art") with a forced emotional strain ("my heart trembles and stirs").

In February 1847 Dostoevsky wrote his brother: "Wish me success. I'm writing my *Landlady*. Even now it is turning out better than *Poor People*. . . . My pen is guided by a flow of inspiration driving its way straight from out my very soul." This not altogether adept phrase ("my pen is guided by a flow") could well have been written by the romantic Marlinsky.[3] The author of *Poor People* returns to the idols of his youth. *The Landlady* was published in the October and November issues of *Fatherland Notes* for the year 1847.

The hero of the tale, the young scholar Ordynov, is a Petersburg dreamer. "He had not known his parents. Because of his strange, unsociable character he suffered inhuman and harsh treatment from his schoolmates, with the result that he became genuinely unsociable and morose, and little by little surrendered himself to a state of self-

[3] Marlinsky was the pen name of Aleksandr Bestuzhev (1797-1837), a romantic novelist and poet whose work, while nearly forgotten now, enjoyed great popularity at the beginning of the 19th century.

imposed isolation." When once he had received his degree, he settled somewhere in a corner "as though he were closing himself off in a monastery, as though removing himself from the world. After two years he became completely withdrawn." Like Dostoevsky himself, Ordynov lives in poverty "on an insignificant sum" that his guardian has given over to him. His sole passion is science; he is writing a treatise on the history of the Church. At this point the author's story of his own romantic youth is interwoven with memories of that strange companion of past years, the poet Ivan Shidlovsky, who also had been writing a work on the history of the Church. The substitution, however, of science for literature remains purely external. Ordynov is an "artist in science"; the author is analyzing the creative imagination not of a scientist, but of an artist. His admissions strikingly approach the agitated tone of a confession. "He was devoured by the deepest, the most insatiable passion, one exhausting a man's whole life. . . . This passion was science. Meanwhile it was consuming his youth, infecting his night's rest with its slow, intoxicating poison, cutting him off from nourishing food and fresh air." Like the *flâneur* of the *Petersburg Chronicle*, Ordynov loves to stroll about the city streets. "He used to stare at everything like a *flâneur*." But the *flâneur*'s sterile imaginings are severely condemned in the *Chronicle*. (Such a life is a "tragedy and a caricature".) Dostoevsky's attitude toward Ordynov's daydreaming is different: this is a tragedy, but in any event not a caricature. The author suddenly came to see his "insatiable passion" in a different light, and as if for the first time evaluated its creative power. This "fire," this "ecstasy," the artist's "burning fever" is bought at a costly price: estrangement from reality, spiritual solitude; but nonetheless it is a gift, terrible and sublime. Creative imagination is by no means the common trait of all the denizens of Petersburg "corners," but rather the special portion of the artist. The arbitrary generalization made in the feuilleton is set aside and the theme, precisely delineated, is considered on a more profound and acute level. Dostoevsky discusses the nature of his own artistic imagination. It lies on the boundary of prophetic clairvoyance and titanic might. With magic force, thought, idea, sensation are directly embodied in grandiose forms; whole worlds appear, whole peoples and races come to life. An immense universe, summoned into existence by his fiery spirit, threatens to crush its creator. This magic of art breathes in it majesty and horror.

He saw how everything, starting with the vague fantasies of his childhood, all his thoughts and dreams, all that he had experienced in life, all that he had read in books, all the things that long ago he had forgotten, all were coming to life, all were being put together, were taking on bodies and rising before him in colossal forms and images, were moving and swarming round about him; he saw sumptuous magic gardens being spread out before him, whole cities being built and destroyed before his eyes, entire cemeteries yielding up to him their dead, who now began life once more; whole races and peoples came, were born, and passed their lives before his eyes; finally, every one of his thoughts, every immaterial fantasy became embodied, became embodied almost at the instant of its conception; at last he saw that he was thinking not in immaterial ideas, *but in whole worlds*, whole creations; saw that he was being borne along like a particle of dust in all this endless, terrible world from which there was no escape.

Among Dostoevsky's letters there exists plentiful evidence to confirm this inspired self-portrait: *he is a creator of embodied ideas, the maker of new worlds*.

The author having described his own dream-filled youth in the character of Ordynov, attempts to expose in the plot the tragic conflict within the hero's soul. Ordynov is sovereign in a world of fantasy and "a child as regards external life." He soars freely in the heavens and does not know how to tread upon earth. In a letter to his brother (1847) Dostoevsky precisely formulizes the "idea" of his hero: "The *exterior* must keep a steady balance with the *interior*. Otherwise, in the absence of exterior phenomena, the interior will assume too dangerous an upperhand. Nerves and fantasy will occupy a very great place in one's being." It is this reflection made by the author regarding his own self, that serves as a basis for the plot of *The Landlady*. Ordynov is forced to find a new apartment. After having lived so long in solitude, he finds himself out upon the noisy streets. He is blinded by the brilliance of this "alien life"; is intoxicated and frightened. A feeling of loneliness and a longing for human love overcome him. His meeting with Katerina in the church comes in answer to this depression. Exteriorly it is a chance occurrence; inwardly it is necessity. The pure, lonely dreamer experiences "an extreme impressionability, a nakedness and defenselessness regarding his feelings." In his "impulsive" heart he bears his own downfall. Ordynov's love for Katerina is presented as an event of his interior life in which reality is interwoven with delirium and dreams, the external is refracted in the internal, is "embodied in colossal forms." At times the border line between dream and reality completely disappears. The dynamism of sensation that has accumulated in his isolated soul bursts forth in violent and destructive force. There is neither light nor joy in this, the young man's first love; it is an oppressive passion, an affliction, a sickness. The author presents a succession of analogies between love and sickness. Upon first seeing Katerina, Ordynov goes after her "scourged by some sweet, unknown feeling." After he has moved into the apartment of old Murin, Katerina's mysterious protector, he breaks down under the strain of his inner agitation. " 'No, better death,' he thinks; 'better death,' he whispers with feverish, trembling lips." Then later he falls into the "agonizing unconsciousness of illness"; the following morning he wakes up healthy. "However, he was still very weak. A chill ran down his back, all his limbs ached and felt as though they had been broken." Katerina kisses him. . . . "He weakly uttered a cry and fell unconscious." All the subsequent events are plunged in the obscurity of delirium. Ordynov feels that he is "condemned to live in a kind of long, interminable dream, full of strange, fruitless anxieties, of struggles and sufferings." As in a dream he listens to Katerina narrate her half-mad confession; a sick, frantic passion rises up within him after her story.

"A kind of agonizing feeling, an unaccountable, unendurable trepidation discharged itself like poison through all his veins and grew with every word of Katerina's story; a hopeless yearning, a craving and unbearable passion seized possession of his thoughts, disquieted his feelings." After parting with Katerina, Ordynov "fell sick and only after three months could he get up from his bed."

Ordynov's sickliness has its counterpart in the sickliness of Murin and Katerina. The old man suffers from epilepsy: a "feverish brilliance" glows in his eyes and his face has a "deathlike bluish cast." His wife is "unbalanced," "bewitched." This pathology conveys a uniformly somber tonality to the tale. All that remains of the characters' feverish exaltation is the remembrance of an agonizing nightmare. The tale's artistic defect is explained, although at the same time it is not completely justified, by the subject which the author undertook to develop. Having broken with the "natural school," Dostoevsky here was attempting to put new life into romantic forms that had become outdated.

The heroes' emotional intensity is increased to the point of frenzy and it serves to motivate the half-fantastic, half-melodramatic character of their story. In his searchings for a subject the author once again collides with Gogol, the author of romantic tales. Defeated on the plane of "naturalism," the magician Gogol continued to hold his rebellious pupil captive. *The Landlady* was written under the direct influence of *The Terrible Vengeance*. Dostoevskian scholars Yu. Tynyanov, V. Komarovich, and A. Bem have conclusively demonstrated this relationship. The motif of an old man–father's illicit love for his daughter is developed along parallel lines both by Gogol and by Dostoevsky. Gogol's sorcerer summons forth Katerina's soul by evil charms and tortures it with his impure passion. The evil old man, Murin, who is endowed with mysterious power, tyrannizes the timid heart of his wife-daughter Katerina. In Gogol, the fabulous and supernatural character of an "old legend" is underlined; Dostoevsky interprets Murin's demonism psychologically. The heroine's confession in *The Landlady* carries all of the devices of the "terrible" romantic tale to the very border of parody. It is a story of robbers on the Volga. A storm in the forest, the burning of a factory, a wayward daughter who runs away from home with her mother's lover, her father's ruin and the mother's curse; a terrible old man "with a beard black as pitch and eyes burning like coals"; the murdering of a young merchant while crossing the storming river in a boat — crimes, horrors, spells are amassed in this incoherent tale. It seems that Dostoevsky's Katerina is paraphrasing the story of Gogol's Katerina, refracting it in her own sick imagination.

The author of *The Landlady* tried to create a new narrative style corresponding to his subject on the basis of Russian folklore. Katerina's "verbal image" develops from the broad drawl of the Russian folk song. Her speech is prompted by her past. Murin calls her a "peasant girl": she grew up in a forest on the far side of the Volga, " 'mongst bargemen and factory workers"; she lives in a world of legends and songs. Murin's power over her soul is linked to his "whispered tales." "Katerina would look at him with attentive eyes filled with childish wonder and, it seemed, would listen with inexhaustible curiosity, overcome with expectation, to what Murin was telling her."

Here is an example of her rhythmical speech: "Beloved or not beloved you came to me; to know, it is not for me to know that, but truly for another senseless, shameless girl that dishonored her maiden room in the dark night, sold her soul for a mortal sin, and did not restrain her demented heart." . . . In all the scenes in which Katerina appears, the features of her speech prevail over the verbal style of her interlocutors. Murin's speech characterizes him as a member of the artisan class. He says to Ordynov: "You see, regarding that, Your Honor, I made bold to inconvenience Their Honor somewhat on your account. It comes from the fact, sir — you know yourself — the mistress and I, that is, we would be glad with all our heart and soul. . . . What do we need? To have enough to eat, to be healthy; complain, *we do not complain*. . . ." In the presence of Katerina, however, this same Murin succumbs to her singsong cadences and talks in the same manner as she. "And you must not grieve, must not mourn for it, for the tear-drop, the drop of heavenly dew. You will yet shed it with interest, your pearly tear-drop in the long night, in the grief-filled night." Such a transition in the case of Murin, the sorcerer-story-teller, from an artisan's level of speech to these singsong measures, is psychologically intelligible. But when the Petersburg dreamer, the young scientist Ordynov, alters his literary mode of expression and begins to speak like Katerina, the stylistic transition is strikingly unexpected. Here is an example: "Who are you, who are you, my very own? From where do you come, my sweet dove? Out of what heaven have you flown into my skies? . . . What were your dreams, what visions did you have of the future, what proved false and what didn't prove false for you — tell me everything. For whom did your maiden heart first begin to ache, and for what did you give it?"

What is the origin of this folklore material in Dostoevsky? The stylistic influence of Gogol's *The Terrible Vengeance* is beyond dispute, yet this tale does not exhaust the forms of verbal expression contained in *The Landlady*. Childhood memories occupy a large place in Ordynov's dreams. He muses upon "the tender, peacefully spent years of his early childhood" when "his mother would make the sign of the cross, kiss him, and sing him a soothing little lullaby." Perhaps this tale serves to reflect the writer's own childhood memories, his mother's songs, the stories that Lukerya, his foster-mother, and his nurse Alyona Frolovna used to tell.[4]

In the composition of *The Landlady* two worlds collide one with another: the world of the Petersburg dreamer and the world of the terrible folk tale, the world of Ordynov and the world of Katerina. Despite the author's attempt to bring them into some kind of harmony, they stand in jarring opposition to one another. This fusion of heterogeneous elements roused Belinsky's indignation. He informed

---

[4] In Russia a *mamka* was a foster-mother or wet nurse; later the child was watched over by a *nyanya*, a nurse or the English nanny.

Annenkov: "Dostoevsky has written a story *The Landlady* — just terrible rubbish. In it he sought to reconcile Marlinsky with Hoffmann, after he had tossed in a bit of Gogol." In *The Contemporary* the critic commented on Dostoevsky's new work: "Is it surprising that what came out was something monstrous, something reminiscent of the now fantastic stories of Tit Kosmokratov who used to entertain the public with them in the twenties of the present century. In this entire tale there is not a single simple, living word or expression. Everything is affected, strained, set on stilts, artificial, and false."

Dostoevsky's tale was misunderstood and rejected by his contemporaries. It is only now that we are coming to realize its artistic worth. If in *The Landlady* the author had opposed these two worlds simply for the sake of an effective contrast, Belinsky would have been proved right. The tale would have come down in literature as a kind of "monster." However, Belinsky failed to recognize that these worlds are organically united through an artistic idea, one of the most profound in all of Dostoevsky's work. Both Ordynov and Katerina embody on different planes a sole theme, *that of the faint heart*. Ordynov stands defenseless before the passion which has swept down upon him; in his soul, enfeebled through its existence of solitary dreaming, the sensation immediately assumes a destructive force leading not to life, but to death. An inner tension paralyzes action and dissipates itself in the phantoms of erotic imagination. When Ordynov is faced with having to contend for his own happiness, with having to save Katerina from her evil genius, he undergoes a shameful defeat. In the struggle for Katerina it is Murin who remains the victor. Ordynov raises a knife to him, but he does not have the strength to strike the evil magician. "The knife dropped out of his hands and resounded upon the floor." Murin philosophizes upon the "faint heart's" lack of spirit: "Let him have his sweet will, the weak individual; he'll wrap it up himself, he'll carry it back to you. . . . He'll pick up a knife in his anger . . . and let 'em put this knife into your own hands, and your enemy himself, let him throw out his broad chest right before you: and just so you'll draw back." In this tirade Murin is talking both about Ordynov and about Katerina; he joins them together through the derisive expression "weak individual."

Katerina is Murin's captive, a prisoner of this person of demonic passion and terrifying willpower. She is a gentle, pure dove, of "unbounded piety," with a fervent, childlike heart. Murin overcomes her soul by infecting it with mystical terror of a crime which perhaps she committed. Her parents perished at the time of the fire; this terrible old man had carried her off from the house and made her his wife. Since that time she has been "wronged." "I am corrupt, I have been corrupted," she cries, "I've been ruined. It is he who has ruined me. I sold my soul to him. I am his, I am sold to him through my soul. He is powerful. His word is mighty."

Katerina's sensitive conscience and superstitious piety are nurtured by Murin with horrifying tales, the reading of schismatic books,[5] threats of judgment and punishment. "He says," she confesses, "that when he dies, he will come for my sinful soul. . . . He tormented me, he read to me from his books, he says that I have done a terrible sin. . . . He always reads such stern, threatening things." The old husband enchains his young wife by means of a *mystical terror*. His love is tyranny, a licentious pleasure derived from exercising power over an individual's living soul.

It is only after he has parted from Katerina and is slowly beginning to comprehend the experience which he has lived through that Ordynov comes to understand his beloved's tragic fate. "He felt that Katerina's mind was sound, but that in his own way Murin was right when he called her a *faint heart*. . . . His dreams were constantly filled with this abysmal, desperate tyranny over a poor, defenseless creature. He felt that to the frightened eyes of her suddenly aroused soul the idea of her fall had cunningly been presented, her poor faint heart had cunningly been tortured, the truth had been interpreted to her in topsy-turvy fashion, and, where it was necessary, she had been purposely kept blind, the impetuous inclinations of her inexperienced, troubled heart had been deftly flattered. Little by little the free, unconstrained soul was clipped of its wings until, at last, it remained unfit either to revolt or to make a free movement into real life."

In this analysis of a demonic individual's tyranny over a "faint heart," in the exposure of passion as a *love of power*, we see the penetration of Dostoevsky's genius. He here touches upon one of the great themes of his creative work. Katerina realizes that Murin has "ruined" her;

[5] Murin was Old Believer or Schismatic. In the 17th century a schism occurred in the Russian Church when Patriarch Nikon revised certain liturgical books and practices on the basis of present Greek usage. The dissenters refused to accept Nikon's reforms because of the temporary union of Constantinople with Rome after the Council of Florence, and after government persecution, many of them migrated to the far North and the Volga regions. A good number of them were of the conservative merchant classes, and so a tradition developed in 19th century romantic literature about the Old Believer merchants from the Volga which is comparable to the romantic themes of the gypsies or the Georgians, or in English literature to the tales about Scotland.

she hates him and dreams of freeing herself from his diabolic sway. Ordynov, pure, brilliant, and young, appears to her as a savior. Trustingly, she at once confides her heart to him. However, the bird's wings are clipped and freedom proves too much for the faint heart. At her first word, Murin swears, with a sense of cold calculation, that he will release "her love and her cherished golden will." He knows that she will not have the strength to bear freedom. When triumphantly Katerina bids him farewell, he pretends to be magnanimous and affectionately gives her leave. And suddenly "she throws herself upon the old man's bosom, winds her arm around his neck and looks at him with a burning, feverish gaze." She turns upon her savior Ordynov with hatred and cries: "Go away! You are drunk and evil! I don't want you as my guest!" The old man laughs with "shameless laughter" and Ordynov, horrified, shudders. "Deceit, calculation, cold, jealous tyranny and intimidation of a poor, torn heart — that is what he understood in this shameless laughter now no longer even concealed."

The "faint heart's" tragedy lies in the fact that it is incapable of coping with freedom. In slavery it encounters a shameful bliss. Katerina herself is glad to set aside her "cherished golden will." "What I find bitter and rends my heart," she confesses, "is that I am his dishonored slave, that my dishonor and shame are dear to me, completely shameless being that I am, that it is dear to my craven heart to recall my sorrow just as a joy and happiness; my sorrow lies in there being no strength in it and there being no anger against the offense that I've undergone."

And so Ordynov and Katerina, the Petersburg dreamer and the wild creature from the Volga, are bound to one another through the common tragedy of the faint heart, the tragedy of being helpless in the face of life and incapable of coping with freedom. The philosophy of the story is placed in the mouth of the sorcerer Murin.

"Come, admit it, sir: a weak individual just can't manage by himself. Now give him everything; he'll come of himself, will give it all back. Give him half the kingdom of the world to possess — try it, what do you think? He'll hide himself at once there in your shoe; he'll make himself so small. *Let him have his sweet will, the weak individual; he'll wrap it up himself, he'll carry it back to you.* To a foolish heart even his own will is of no use."

Inadvertently one is reminded of another image, one more majestic and powerful, of other words, the most profound of all Dostoevsky's words. It is the Grand Inquisitor speaking to Christ: "Man knows no concern more tormenting than finding that individual to whom he may most quickly surrender that gift of freedom with which the wretched creature is born. . . . There are three forces, three forces alone on earth, capable of overcoming and captivating once and for all the conscience of these *enfeebled rebels* for the sake of their happiness. These forces are miracle, mystery and authority."

This early tale of Dostoevsky's, which Belinsky evaluated as "terrible rubbish," already poses the problems of personality and freedom.

———————

Dostoevsky was overcome by Belinsky's criticisms and ultimately persuaded by them. His letters of 1849 to A. Krayevsky complain bitterly of the conditions of "day-labor" under which he was forced to work in the preceding year: "Because, in order to fulfill my word and deliver on time, I drove myself, and wrote among other things such bad works or such a bad work as *The Landlady* with the result that I fell into misgivings and self-deprecation, and for a long time afterward I was unable to bring myself to write anything serious or worthwhile. Every one of my failures has caused me to fall ill." . . . "In order to repay my debt to you, I hastily wrote another tale and risked my own signature, which is my only capital." . . . "I failed to polish my work sufficiently and wrote for a deadline, i.e., I sinned against art. My health was not spared, and I made excruciating efforts in order to 'settle accounts.'" Such is the severity with which the author evaluates his compositions of 1848. His "self-deprecation" proved excessive and unfair. Dostoevsky was always inclined to a harsh appraisal of himself. He always felt that he had "failed to polish his work sufficiently," that he was "sinning against art." He was no more satisfied with *The Idiot* and *The Devils* than with *The Landlady*. However, the tales of 1848 suffer not merely from a lack of sufficient polish: we see reflected in them the author's confusion, his "misgivings"; they are experimentings, searchings, trials. Dostoevsky was living through a crisis and painfully sought to find his own literary style. And in this creative crisis, external factors, his need, the indebtedness to Krayevsky, his having to work and meet deadlines, played only a secondary role.

The least successful of the eight works written in 1848 are the first two, *Another Man's Wife* and *The Jealous Husband*. The author subsequently combined them for the edition of 1865, entitling the single tale *Another Man's Wife and the Husband under the Bed. An Unusual Happening.*[A]

[A] Published in *Fatherland Notes* (1848).

The piquant adventures of a jealous husband whose wife is deceiving him are described by the author in the light manner of Paul de Kock. Dostoevsky avidly read this then fashionable writer and sought to imitate his Parisian *esprit*. The hero of the tale, Ivan Andreyevich, complains that his wife has "Paul de Kock invariably under her pillow," and in his agitation jumbles Glafira Petrovna together with literature. "I am saying a certain lady of honorable conduct, that is, of frivolous content — excuse me, I am so confused, just as though I were talking of literature. You see, it was felt that Paul de Kock was of frivolous content, and all the trouble comes from Paul de Kock, sir . . . you see!" The comic effect is compounded on such questionable witticisms and verbal puns. In the first chapter (which corresponds to the story *Another Man's Wife*), the elderly husband (a gentleman in racoon furs), standing on the street before a certain "house of an interminable number of stories," encounters his wife's lover (a gentleman in a short wadded overcoat). After a protracted dialogue that pretends to an elevated humor, it is discovered that Glafira Petrovna is presently engaged in being unfaithful, at one and the same time, to both her husband and her lover. In the second chapter (which corresponds to the story *The Jealous Husband*), this same Ivan Andreyevich in an attempt to track down his wife chances upon another man's apartment and is forced to hide under the bed where he finds a certain young man already lying concealed. Once again a piquant dialogue follows. The young man turns out to be his wife's lover; he has also made a mistake regarding the correct floor. After the lover's escape, the respectable Ivan Andreyevich creeps out from under the bed and finds himself face to face with an enraged "His Excellency" into whose apartment he has chanced by mistake. The following scene in which the confused civil servant explains himself to the "general" is the one lively episode in the story. Ivan Andreyevich's incoherent, frightened and subservient blathering, the "upbraiding" pronounced by the general, together with his wife's hysterics, do succeed in producing a comic impression. The author forgets about Paul de Kock and reverts to civil-servant literature's hackneyed theme of the comic civil servant– deceived husband. Dostoevsky's partiality for theatrical form is most characteristic; the entire story is made up of dialogues and developed in the genre of light vaudeville. The epic element is introduced only in the context of the author's stage remarks. *Another Man's Wife* is Dostoevsky's first attempt at a *tale-comedy*; he was to return to this form in *Uncle's Dream* and *The Village of Stepanchikovo*. The rough sketch of the comic figure of the enfeebled, dotardly old man whom the "jealous husband" takes for a prince and calls "Your Highness," was later to provide the author with material for the image of another prince, also enfeebled and senile — the hero of the tale *Uncle's Dream*.

The second tale written in 1848 *A Faint Heart* is of incomparably greater worth than the playsome farce about the jealous husband.[B] In his perplexity after the failure of *The Landlady* the author decided that he had made a false start, that he had failed in his attempt to revive the romantic genre, and that he ought not venture beyond the limitations of the "natural school" to which he was indebted for his first and only triumph, the success of *Poor People*. After his excursion into the realm of folklore and the adultery novel, he returned humbly to the small familiar world of "civil-servant literature."

In the *Petersburg Chronicle* the author speaks of an important civil servant, Yulian Mastakovich, whom he calls "my good acquaintance, who in times past always sought my benefit and even to a certain extent watched over me." He is about fifty years of age and is preparing to get married to a seventeen-year-old girl. "One evening Yulian Mastakovich was walking about his office, his hands crossed behind his back, with such an insipid, dirty, and sour look on his face that if the civil servant who sat in the corner of that same office, laboring over some pressing, weighty affair, had in his character even a touch of the insipid, then immediately it would have turned sour as the inevitable result of one of his protector's glances." This reference serves as a point of departure for the plot of *A Faint Heart*. Yulian Mastakovich, the little civil servant Vasya Shumkov's superior and benefactor, has directed him to copy out a voluminous work. Reference is also made in passing to the "patron's" marriage: "he himself has gotten married not long ago." This subject is joined to a theme already familiar to us, that of the civil servant who is going mad. An exemplary and humble individual suddenly begins to feel that he is a criminal, a "transgressor of order" and urges the authorities to punish him. (The civil servant–Garibaldi in *Petersburg Dreams*.) Vasya Shumkov fails to meet his deadline in transcribing the papers; the awareness of his guilt drives him out of his mind. He imagines that "they intend to induct him into the army as a result of his improper execution of the affair" and consequently surrenders himself over to the hands of the authorities.

[B] Published in *Fatherland Notes* (1848).

In Yulian Mastakovich's study, "Vasya was standing, pale, with head erect, having stretched himself taut as a thread, like a recruit before a new commander, with his feet together and his hands held down along the seams." Dostoevsky was relentlessly haunted by the problem of "the weak individual." Why did Prokharchin "start to cringe," why did the civil servant–Garibaldi and Vasya Shumkov lose their minds? The tale *A Faint Heart* contains within the framework of a most elemental plot a complex psychological subject. It is not merely one aspect of the basis of madness that is introduced, but a whole network. The simple explanation proves to be not at all simple: one cause draws after it another, one more profound, but even this does not exhaust the enigmas of the personality. Vasya Shumkov, "a modest, quiet young man . . . had tried to study, sought to educate himself . . . through his own efforts he had risen out of his lowly status." He serves in a ministerial department; his handwriting is like samples of calligraphy; he receives three hundred rubles a year salary. His superior and benefactor Yulian Mastakovich gives him some transcribing to do overtime, and his magnanimity attains to such bounds that he presents Shumkov with fifty rubles, this for the first time after he has worked for four months without pay. Vasya is overcome with gratitude. "I poured forth tears," he tells his friend Arkady. He reveres his superior, who is unscrupulously exploiting him, as "a great man," almost as his own father, and is touched by his goodness. Moreover, he has fallen in love with a charming young girl who has agreed to marry him though he is unworthy of her: he has a low grade in the service and a physical defect (a curvature on one side resulting in limping). Lizanka's love, the friendship of Arkady, the benevolence of Yulian Mastakovich, all this exorbitant happiness suddenly crushes down upon Vasya. The weak individual fails to survive and loses his mind. The feeling of his own unworthiness overflows into a consciousness of guilt; he did not copy out the papers, he deceived his benefactor's trust, he responded to his love with black ingratitude. Yulian Mastakovich asks: "'And how has this — how has this happened to him? What has driven him out of his mind?' 'Gra-grati-tude!' was all Arkady Ivanovich was able to utter." The individual who is oppressed by society develops an inferiority complex which, upon an aggravation of conscience, can readily pass over into a feeling of guilt. In this sense, Vasya Shumkov is a blood-brother of Makar Devushkin.

But the "faint heart" is likewise an "ardent heart." Vasya is a *dreamer*. Arkady says to him: "You're such a good, tender soul . . .

moreover, a dreamer as well, but now this too is not good. One can simply throw one's self out of joint, brother." His sensitivity, his exuberance, his life which is animated exclusively by the heart, are all rooted in the sphere of "dreams." He lives with his friend Arkady in a kind of "amorous paradise"; they coo like love birds and exhaust themselves in the dulcet outpourings of sentiments. "Tears trickled out of Vasya's eyes onto Arkady's hands." . . . "If you but knew, Vasya, how much I love you." . . . "Yes, yes, Arkady, I don't know because I don't know how you came to love me so. Do you know how many times, especially when I would be lying down to sleep, I used to think about you, I used to pour myself out in tears and my heart would shudder because . . . well, because you love me so, while I could not relieve my heart in any way, I could in no way thank you."

We find still greater sensibility in the description of Lizanka's virtuous family, the fiancé's meeting with his betrothed, of their reciprocal gifts. Vasya presents Lizanka with a "little love of a cap" in tulle "with a cherry-colored ribbon," and she prepares a surprise for him, a papercase embroidered in beads — on one side of which is depicted a stag, and on the other "a famous general." Arkady's dreams are equally touching. "You've seen right through me, Vasya," said Arkady Ivanovich, "Yes! I love her as much as you; she will be my angel as she is yours since your mutual happiness will come pouring out onto me as well, and it will offer me warmth." This is the tone set throughout the entire story. The heroes' emotional exaltation borders upon a parody of the sentimental genre. Vasya's "ardent heart" swims in ecstasy, tenderness, tears of love. The dreamer conceives of all men as being excellent, noble, and good; he observes an amiability toward himself even on the part of Yulian Mastakovich. The author pokes good-natured fun at his tearful and rapturous hero much in the same way a grown man with a smile recalls his youth. The young Dostoevsky, brought up on Karamzin and infatuated with Schiller, also used to shed tears over all the "noble and beautiful," also relished his friendship for Shidlovsky; he too dreamed of love's happiness. And he knew how dangerous it was to surrender to dreams: "one can throw one's self out of joint."

Vasya is without restraint in regard to his happiness since it is not enough for him to have Lizanka, Arkady, and Yulian Mastakovich; instinctively he craves for universal happiness, for *paradise on earth*. He is not to be reconciled with less; this already is the nature of a dreamer. The tragedy of the "ardent heart" is exposed by Arkady:

Come now, listen, why I know what you would like! You would like, for example, for Yulian Mastakovich to be beside himself, and further, I suppose, to give a ball in his joy that you are getting married. . . . You would want that no one on earth would any longer be unhappy now that you're getting married, that I, for example, your best friend, would all of a sudden fall into a fortune of 100,000, that all enemies, whatever there are on earth, would suddenly for neither rhyme nor reason, make peace with one another, that all of them would joyfully embrace in the middle of the street, and then they might, I suppose, come here as guests to the apartment. Because you are happy, you want everyone, absolutely everyone, to become happy at once . . . it is painful, difficult for you to be happy alone.

This singularly penetrating characterization of the dreamer relates first of all to Dostoevsky himself. Since his youth he had cherished and venerated the idea of universal happiness, and he never ceased dreaming about an "earthly paradise," "world harmony," the Kingdom of God on Earth. No matter to what extent he would later deride and ridicule utopianism and utopians, nonetheless this remained his greatest and most radiant ideal. In the year 1848, during which the tale *A Faint Heart* was written, Dostoevsky used to frequent the Petrashevsky circle and became captivated by utopian socialism. The mark of this enthusiasm is imprinted on Vasya Shumkov.

If it is not possible for all enemies directly to make peace with one another, for all people to become happy and all mankind to embrace, the happiness of one sole individual becomes unlawful and is condemned as a sin and blameworthy. Vasya says in "a voice full of muffled sobs": "Arkady, I'm not worthy of this happiness! I hear, I feel it! Just look, how many people, how many tears, how much grief, how much day-to-day routine without a holiday! And I . . ."

And this anguish, thinking about everyone, drives him out of his mind. The "weak individual" Vasya Shumkov finds a safe coverture from "unlawful" happiness in madness. The strong individual Ivan Karamazov proudly renounces it and "returns his ticket." But both the one and the other do not admit happiness if it is not for all.

The tale *Polzunkov* was written for I. Panayev's and N. Nekrasov's *Illustrated Almanach*. The type of Polzunkov, this "comic martyr," had already been delineated in *Petersburg Chronicle*. In one of his feuilletons the author talks "about our home-grown jesters, parasites, and entertainers."

Suddenly and well, not simply out of petty vulgarity, a man ceases to be a man, and turns himself into a midge. . . . He looks you in the eyes, give or take, just like a little pug-dog that is waiting for a tidbit. Furthermore, in spite of the fact that he is wearing an excellent frock coat, he lies down on the floor in a fit of sociability, gaily beats his little tail, squeals, licks himself . . . and what is most amusing of all, what is most pleasing of all, he does not impair his worth a bit. This is by no means a base soul — it is an intelligent soul, an amiable soul, a soul taken from society, a soul that wishes to receive, a soul that is searching, a fashionable soul, one, it is true, that has begun to run ahead a little, but nonetheless a soul — I will not say, such as all have, but as many have.

Dostoevsky employs this sketch in the creation of the figure Polzunkov. The hero of this tale "earned his bread by being a buffoon to all the world." But this strange and ludicrous man was not "a buffoon by profession." "It seems to me," adds the author, "his whole longing to be of service emanated more readily from a good heart than because of material profit." Polzunkov would endure mockery, but he suffered at the thought that his listeners were so ignobly cruel as to be capable of laughing not *at the thing itself*, but at him, at his whole being. He would live on tokens of charity, was endlessly borrowing money, yet he could not "begin to cast himself down into complete and utter debasement." The consciousness of his own worth struggled within him against the feeling of his insignificance. "This was the most honest and noble individual on earth" who could accomplish a vile act with personal disinterest "solely for the sake of pleasing his neighbor." One can surmise that Dostoevsky conceived of Polzunkov as a comic *pendant* to Vasya Shumkov. He too is an "ardent heart," a good and noble individual, full of love for his neighbor; he too would like to please everyone, to make everyone happy; he is a soul taken from society that craves to love and be loved. In a word he is the same type of sensitive utopian as Vasya Shumkov. "If he had been persuaded in his heart," the author notes, "that all his listeners were the kindliest people in the world who were laughing only at something amusing and not at the expense of his personality, then he would have delightedly taken off his coat, somehow put it on inside out and, to please the others and for his own enjoyment, would go up and down the streets in this costume if only to make his patrons laugh and afford them all pleasure." Ultimately, however, this excellent, generous individual fails to emerge as a benefactor of mankind, but results in a "most useless and consequently most comic martyr." Dostoevsky examines the dangers which threaten the "good heart," this daydream love of mankind. The philanthrope-madman (Shumkov) and the philanthrope-buffoon (Polzunkov) — these are the heroes of his stories. In them we find his artistic response to the questions that were troubling him during the period of his relations with Petrashevsky: he sensed that utopian socialism was too theoretic and bookish, that it lacked sufficient relation to life and society. Why was the "good heart's" fate so unhappy? In the *Petersburg Chronicle* Dostoevsky answers: "Only by recognizing those generalized interests that are in sympathy with the masses of society and with their direct, immediate demands — and not by dozing off into slumber, not in that unconcernedness that is resulting in the disintegration of the masses, not in isolated seclusion — is it possible to polish into a precious, into a lustrous diamond their treasure, their capital, their 'good heart'!" This is the author's first statement in regard to "social questions." It is evident that he had been reading a good number of scholarly books on socialism. The "good heart" is brought to destruction through solitude; once again we are faced with the "sin of romantic dreaming." In order to depict Polzunkov's nature in action, the author contrived a plot that was relatively unsuccessful. The "well-intentioned buffoon" recounts the story of his friendship with his superior Fedosey Nikolayevich and his courtship of the latter's daughter, Mariya Fedoseyevna. It is a touching idyll full of the most lofty sentiments which, however, do not deter the subordinate from writing a denunciation against his superior, and the superior through a skillful intrigue of removing the subordinate from his office. Well, we already know that this most noble man is capable of a vile act "solely for the sake of pleasing his neighbor."

In the fifty-seventh issue of *Fatherland Notes* of 1848 there appeared *Stories of a Man of Experience. From the Notes of an Unknown:* the first under the title *The Veteran,* the second being *An Honest Thief.* For the edition of 1865 the author suppressed the essay *The Veteran,* retaining only the two pages of introduction. The subject of this story was an old soldier's description of the campaigns of 1812-1814, of the partisan Figner, of the battle of Leipzig, and the entry of the Russians into Paris. In his memoirs Dr. Yanovsky informs us: "Even at that time Dostoevsky had living with him in the capacity of a servant a retired noncommissioned officer, Yevstafy, who was well known to us all and very much loved by us. Fyodor Mikhailovich singles out his name with a warm word in one of his tales." In the story *An Honest Thief*, the narrator is a retired soldier Astafy Ivanovich. The mode of speech — half folkish, half soldierlike — of the "man of experience" is reproduced with great skill; his unaffected account breathes with simplicity and sincerity. One can suppose that the author made use of some of his servant's actual conversations. Astafy Ivanovich rented a corner from a certain "little old woman" and employed himself as a tailor. He began to receive frequent visits from Yemelya, an "utterly God-forsaken individual," a "no-good drunk and worthless creature." The latter was of a quiet temperament, "such a warmhearted, good soul." He felt ashamed to beg. He latched on to Astafy Ivanovich and, in the end, came there to live with him. "I wonder, wonder, what am I going to do with him?" the old soldier asks. "Just to kick him out is shameful, pitiful; such a pitiful, God-forsaken individual, that even — good Lord! And so silent; he doesn't ask, just sits himself down like a little puppy, and looks into your eyes." The man of experience attempted to teach him comprehension, reasoning, to train him to work; nothing came of it: he would disappear for several days, would return in rags, having partaken of a little too much. Astafy Ivanovich finds that a pair of "riding breeches" are missing. He accuses his companion of taking them, but Yemelya resolutely denies it and for about two weeks abandons himself uninterruptedly to drink. Finally he returns sick and before his death confesses to the theft.

Employing an extraordinary economy of means this brief story portrays the simple and humble goodness of the Russian whose origins lie in the people. The drunkard Yemelya has thrust himself upon the poor soldier, but the latter finds it "shameful" to throw him out and he shares his last piece of bread with him. "I sat down there, sir, and began to consider would he, a vagabond like that, be of much trouble to me? And it turned out on second thought that the trouble wouldn't cost me much." And Astafy came to love his dissolute comrade. It hurt him that Yemelya had stolen the "riding breeches" from him, he rebuked him, but then also forgave him. And when Yemelya disappeared, he began to search for him in the taverns. "I got frightened; I was upset with worrying: I couldn't drink, couldn't eat, couldn't sleep. The man just totally disarmed me."

Even more considerate and sensitive is the character of Yemelya himself. How he exerts himself to please his benefactor, how he would like to reform, to set about working, how his conscience torments him that "he has brought down shame upon him." "And what am I to do, Astafy Ivanovich," he says, "why even I myself know that I'm always a drunk and of no use anywhere." "And then suddenly how his blue lips would start to quiver, how a little tear rolled down his white cheek, how this tear trembled on his unshaven, stubbly chin, and how my Yemelyan would choke up, would suddenly burst forth in a regular handful of tears. . . . 'Ah, you sensitive soul, and I never should have thought it.' "

Both the heroes of the story are sensitive individuals. Their sensitivity, however, is not akin to the dreamer s good heart." The weak individual Yemelya is brought to ruin not by an illusory guilt, as in the case of Vasya Shumkov, but as the result of an actual one (theft). He is the victim of a vice (drunkenness) and not of a disordered imagination. Astafy Ivanovich is not an ardent dreamer like Ordynov; his love is living and active: he has sympathy and forgives. *An Honest Thief* is Dostoevsky's first "populist" work and Astafy Ivanovich his first "just man" from the people. The opposition of the people and of the intelligentsia was perceived by the writer even before his servitude in Siberia.

The subject of the next story, *A Christmas Tree Party and a Wedding. From the Notes of an Unknown,*[c] once again is drawn from the stock of the *Petersburg Chronicle*. The author complains that the "villains of the old melodramas and novels" have disappeared from literature. "And now God knows what story-tellers write about. Now, all of a sudden, it somehow turns out that the most meritorious individual, and moreover the one in a sense most incapable of doing evil, all of a sudden emerges as a thorough out-and-out villain, and moreover without discerning it himself." That important civil servant Yulian Mastakovich with whom we are already acquainted, makes his appearance. In his "judicious years" he is preparing to marry a very young girl. "Each evening he dresses himself in his white waistcoat, his wig, all his decorations, buys a bouquet and candy, and goes to win the favor of Glafira Petrovna, his fiancée, a girl of seventeen, completely innocent and utterly naive. The thought alone of this last circumstance already brings the flakiest little smile to Yulian Mastakovich's sugary lips." And the author adds that his hero has a "very kind heart" and "will live out his life in contentment and happiness." Accordingly, Dostoevsky illustrates his thought with an example of "un-

[c] Published in *Fatherland Notes* (1848).

conscious evil-doing": "As though in our time it were some kind of prodigy to have a good heart!" The image of an old man in love with young girls and doting on their innocence with a "flaky little smile" developed in his imagination long before the great novels. From Yulian Mastakovich is descended the series of "sensualists," Prince Volkovsky, Svidrigailov, Totsky, Fyodor Pavlovich Karamazov. In Dostoevsky the concept of sensuality is intimately related to the violation of a young girl or even a child (Stavrogin's confession). In the story *A Christmas Tree Party and a Wedding* the motif of sensuality is masked by that of greed. Yulian Mastakovich's betrothed is the daughter of a wealthy lease-contractor[6] and has a dowry of 300,000 rubles. While at a children's party[7] the future fiancé meets this eleven-year-old girl, "sweet, like a little Cupid, retiring, dreamy, pale." His decision is taken; he will marry her in five years. In a hushed voice almost totally overcome with emotion and impatience, he asks her: "And will you love me, dear little girl, when I come and visit your parents?"

Five years later the author happens upon a church during a marriage ceremony. He recognizes the bridegroom as Yulian Mastakovich, "well-nourished, ruddy, thick-set, with a little paunch, with fleshy legs." In the unhappy bride's face "something altogether naive, youthful, without entreaties, implores on its own behalf for mercy."

Here for the first time, in his description of the children's party held in this rich house, Dostoevsky approaches one of his favorite themes: the psychology of children. "I very much like to observe children," he writes, "Life's first independent manifestation in them is extraordinarily curious." In the crowd of nicely attired children he notices a "forgotten and frightened little boy, the son of the governess of the master's children." A certain insolent youth had struck him a blow, but the child "dared not start to cry." A poor, harassed boy will appear in *Netochka Nezvanova* (Larya), and will accompany the writer to the very end of his life (Ilyusha in *The Brothers Karamazov*).

The tale *White Nights*[D] bears two subtitles: *A Sentimental Novel.* (*From the Recollections of a Dreamer.*) Its literary form was directly suggested by the genre of the feuilleton; as in the *Petersburg Chronicle* the narration is presented in the first person in the tone of a

[6] A lease-contractor was one who, in return for a sum of money, acquired certain rights on the collection of government revenues and taxes.

[7] The word *yolka* means both a Christmas tree and a children's Christmas party.

[D] Published in *Fatherland Notes* (1848).

free, spontaneous chat with the reader. In the *Chronicle* we find: "They say that it's spring in Petersburg. Now is this altogether true? But then it is even possible that it's so. Actually, there are all the signs of spring. . . . However, let's leave all this. Better let us wish ourselves a fine summer. We might in that case take a stroll, relax a bit. Where will we go, ladies and gentlemen?" In *White Nights:* "It was a wonderful night, such a night as is only really possible when we are young, kind reader. . . . *And so you understand, reader, in what sense I am acquainted with all Petersburg!*" The *paysage* in the tale is the same as that of the feuilleton: Petersburg in springtime, the city is becoming empty, everyone is setting out for his summer home. Lastly it is not difficult to recognize the author of the *Petersburg Chronicle* in the very hero of *White Nights*. He is also a "half-sick city dweller, *flâneur*, and dreamer." He loves his city, wanders about the streets, knows each house, and the houses enter into conversation with him. One says to him: "How are you feeling? I'm to be repaired tomorrow"; another: "I nearly burned down and on the occasion was in a terrible fright."

Sometimes excerpts are taken from the feuilleton and with insignificant stylistic corrections are carried over into the tale. In the *Chronicle* we read:

> There is something indescribably naive, even something touching in our Petersburg nature when, all of a sudden, as though unexpectedly, it will display all its vigor, will dress itself in green, will burst into leaf, will adorn itself, will besprinkle itself with colors and flowers. I don't know why, it reminds me of that young girl, consumptive and ailing, at whom you look sometimes with compassion, sometimes with kind of a tender-hearted love, sometimes you simply do not notice, but who suddenly, in an instant, and somehow unexpectedly, will make herself wonderfully, inexpressibly beautiful, and you are astonished, surprised. Involuntarily you ask yourself: what force impelled these eyes, always so pensively sad, to gleam with such fire, that drew the blood into these pale cheeks. . . .

This whole lyrical tirade is included in *White Nights:* "There is something indescribably touching in our Petersburg nature when, with the approach of spring, all of a sudden it will display all its vigor, all the powers bestowed on it by heaven, will burst into leaf, will adorn itself, will besprinkle itself with colors and flowers. Somehow involuntarily it reminds me of that young girl . . . , etc."

White Nights develops the theme of romantic dreaming that is presented in the *Chronicle*. The form of intimate conversation flows most naturally into that of confession. Upon his chance encounter with Nastenka on a Petersburg street during a white night,[8] the hero opens his soul to her. "Listen, do you want to know what sort of person I am. . . . If you like, I am a type. . . . A type, it's an original, it's such a ludicrous individual! . . . It's such a character. . . . Listen, do you have any idea what a dreamer is?" The material of the *Chronicle* is freely reworked to suit the hero's confession. We find motifs with which we are already acquainted: a dreamer's life is "a mixture of something fantastic, fervently idealistic and along with that dully prosaic." The dreamer is not a man but a creature of some intermediate sort; he settles himself off in an inaccessible corner, is afraid of people and does not know how to respond to them. When once he returns from work into his own four walls, "which are invariably painted green," he sets about living "his own individual life." "Now the 'goddess of fantasy' (if you have read Zhukovsky, my dear Nastenka) has already begun with capricious hand to spin her golden warp and started to unfold before him patterns of an extraordinary, phantasmic life." The book falls from his hands and a "new enchanted life" is spread open before him. The "dream world's" characteristics were denoted in the *Chronicle* in terms of their general features. In the *Tale* they receive concrete substantiality as an *emotional experiencing of literary and historic images*. "You'll ask, perhaps, what does he dream about? What reason is there to ask? Why, about everything. . . . About the role of the poet, at first unrecognized, then afterward exalted, about friendship with Hoffmann; St. Bartholomew's Night, Diana Vernon, a hero's part in the taking of Kazan by Ivan Vasilyevich, Clara Mowbray, Effie Deans, the council of prelates with Huss before them, the rising of the dead in *Robert* (do you remember the music? It smells of the churchyard!), Minna and Brenda, the battle of Berezina, the reading of a poem at Countess V. D.'s, Danton, Cleopatra *e i suoi amanti*, the little house in Kolomna, one's own little corner, and close by a dear creature who listens to you on winter evenings, opening her little mouth and eyes. . . ." These confidences are autobiographical. Under the likeness of romantic dreaming Dostoevsky is describing his own *creative meditations* on literature and history. As a consequence his moral evaluation of this disposition is doubly important. As in the case of the *Chronicle* he continues to assert that such a

[8] Because of the far northern latitude, in late spring and early summer, it remains light in Petersburg (Leningrad) throughout most of the night.

life of illusion is a sin, that it draws the individual away from actual reality — and yet at the same time he underscores its enormous *aesthetic value*. . . . "He is himself the artist of his own life and creates it for himself every hour in accord with some new whim." This mode of duality is understandable: behind the hero of *White Nights*, the little civil servant and fantast, there stands the author himself, the writer, filled with inspiration and vast designs. Gradually the problem of idle dreaming is supplanted by the more profound problem of creative activity. The eccentric civil servant speaks about his nightly reveries, but we hear another voice, that of the artist, talking about inspiration. "Why is it then that entire sleepless nights pass like a brief instant in inexhaustible pleasure and happiness, and when dawn shines its rose-colored beam into the windows, our dreamer worn out, weary, throws himself onto his bed and falls asleep in a swoon from the ecstasy of his morbidly overwrought spirit and with such an oppressively sweet pain in his heart." Echoes of the creative crisis which ensued upon the failure of *The Double* are clearly heard in the dreamer's most penetrating confidences: "One feels that it, this 'inexhaustible fantasy,' is at last getting tired, is exhausted in the endless strain, because, why, you are attaining maturity, you are outgrowing your former ideals; they are shattering into dust, into fragments; and if there is no other life, so then you must build one up out of these very fragments. . . ."

Perhaps, precisely because the hero of *White Nights* can virtually be identified with the author, never again do we find the theme of romantic dreaming presented by Dostoevsky with such a magic, poetic luster, with such an enchantment of youth, infatuation, spring. There is nothing of the "underground," nothing stale or musty, in the image of the young poet. His confession is illumined by the gentle light of Petersburg's white nights. His love for Nastenka is innocent, trusting, and pure. He is a youthful idealist with an ardent heart and a fiery imagination; a lonely individual and unloved — not from pride, but out of a shy timidity. However, when he meets Nastenka, how ample his heart proves to be! Reticence is only a form of moral chastity: it stems not from deficiency, but from wealth. He worships before the shrine of love, his soul overflows with it; each girl he chances upon, he is prepared humbly to beg for love. This is the reason that his acquaintance with Nastenka saves him from the "sin" of dreaming and satiates his longing for real life, "eternally renewing itself, eternally young." The hero encounters his first romance; Nastenka initiates him into the mystery of life. And despite the fact that she does not respond to his affection and loves another, nonetheless this *éducation sentimentale* serves to transform him. Nastenka with simple-hearted candor speaks of this: "See now, all that you told me about your dreamer then is completely untrue, that is — I want to say, it has no relation to you at all. You are returning to health; you are, in fact, a completely different person than you described yourself. If some time you fall in love, then God give you happiness with her! And for her I don't wish anything, because she will be happy with you."

Having probed into all the declivities and distortions latent in the "good heart," Dostoevsky at last found a true course for the sensitive hero. Boldly and without irony he called his tale a "sentimental novel." After his saunters into the realm of the "natural school," of melodramatic romanticism and folklore, he now returned to his unique success — the tale *Poor People*. In it, he had endeavored to remold the traditional Gogolian manner by introducing an influx of sentimentalism. In *White Nights* the sentimental genre is purged of all the admixtures of naturalism: departments, uniforms, Their Excellencies. The general scheme of the plot is the same but without the former's social disposition and tragic illumination. The tale is written in radiant, springlike tones. In place of the old man, Devushkin, there stands the young dreamer, in place of the sick and cheerless Varenka — the seventeen-year-old Nastenka, a "most enchanting little brunette," brimming with youthful vitality. Varenka is compromised by Bykov, whom she marries despite her not loving him. The man to whom she has given her affection leaves Nastenka, but the injury proves to be merely passing: he returns "in love" and the novel ends with a happy marriage. The fate of Makar Devushkin upon his "rejection" is tragic. The dreamer in love with Nastenka suffers a sad, yet enlightening, experience. The former, once he has parted with Varenka, is doomed to drink and ruination; the other, after Nastenka's wedding, blesses his kind genius: "May your sky be clear, may your dear smile be bright and untroubled, may you be blessed for the moment of bliss and happiness which you gave to another, lonely, and grateful heart! My God! An entire moment of happiness! And really is this not enough even if it be for the whole of a man's life!"

In Dostoevsky's creative work, *White Nights* strikes a chord of serene and joyful melody. It penetrates the whole of the tale's composition. The dreamer takes a walk out of the city, goes out "among the tilled fields and meadows" and at once his spirits enliven. "I used to walk along and sing because when I'm happy, invariably I start humming to myself. . . ." He dictates a letter for Nastenka when she tries to write to her fiancé, but it turns out that the letter had already been composed just as in *The Barber of Seville*. " 'R, o-Ro, s, i-si, n, a-na!' I began. 'Rosina!' we both started to sing, I nearly embracing her in my delight, while she blushed as only she could blush." The musical character of the tale's structure is evidenced in the hero's words: "When I woke up it seemed to me as though some musical motif, long familiar, heard somewhere in the past, forgotten and delightfully sweet, had now come back to me. . . ."

The "loving friendship" of the dreamer and Nastenka, the white nights, Rossini's melody, the fleeting moment of happiness — such is the translucent and delicate fabric of this tale. Nastenka is the first female image in Dostoevsky that breathes with life. In *Poor People*, Varenka exists as but a pale shadow. She is too traditionally virtuous and impersonal, too much a "victim of social injustice." Katerina in *The Landlady* is more like the vision of an emotionally excited imagination and the heroine of a terrible tale, than she is akin to a living woman. Nastenka is the embodiment of life and youth. She is full of genial cunning, graceful vigor, naive coquettishness. In her there is in fact something of Rosina from the *Barber of Seville*. The tale is divided into four nights and a morning. The dialogues of the "nights" and the "morning" denouement correspond to the five acts of classical comedy; and in this dramatically structured tale Nastenka determines the action. She is openly unaffected and astute: it is with difficulty that she comprehends the dreamer's literary manner of speech, but unerringly she reads into his heart. After their first meeting she agrees to see him again "upon a condition." " 'But mind you, come upon the condition, first of all (only be kind, do what I ask you — you see, I'm speaking frankly), don't fall in love with me. . . . This is impossible, I assure you. I'm prepared for friendship; here is my hand. . . . But you mustn't fall in love, I beg you.' 'I swear to you,' I cried, gripping her dear, little hand. . . . 'Hush, don't swear; why, I know you're just ready to burst forth and explode like gunpowder.' "

Nastenka lives with her old grandmother who is unable to keep proper watch over the mischievous child and for that reason she pins the girl's dress onto her own. She falls in love with a tenant and when she discovers that he is moving away, ties up her clothing in a little bundle and goes to him in his room. She resolves upon such an action because she is in love and believes in his love. And he does not deceive her. In his absence she becomes acquainted with the dreamer who in spite of all his oaths, falls passionately in love with her. Nastenka is filled with empathy toward him, loves him like a brother, and in her farewell note writes: "Oh, God! If I could but love both of you at once! If only you were he! You will not desert us, you will forever remain a friend, a brother to me. . . . *Do you love me as before?*"

How enchanting do we find this simple-hearted question! It is in point not to the dreamer, but rather to Nastenka, guileless and naive, that the author finally entrusts his own inviolable dream *of universal brotherhood*. "But listen," she says, "why is it that we all aren't like that, like brothers dealing with brothers? Why is it that the very finest individual is always, as it were, concealing something from the other person and keeping silently removed from him? Why not just tell me straight out what is in your heart?"

V

The First Attempt at a Novel:
Netochka Nezvanova

Dostoevsky began very early to envisage the idea of a full-length novel. Within three months after his first appearance in literature he was already informing his brother of his plans to write a "big novel for Nekrasov" (April 1, 1846). During his illness which ensued upon the failure of *The Double,* he dreamed of "just running away from everything," of going off to Italy and there at leisure of "writing a novel" for himself. This fantastic scheme was sketched out with precise detail. "I will spend eight months [in Italy]. I'll send the first part of the novel to *The Contemporary,* receive 1,200 r. and from Rome will take a trip to Paris for two months, and then back again. Upon my return I'll directly bring out the second part; and I will continue writing the novel up till the fall of 1848, and then bring out its 3rd or 4th parts. The first, a prologue, will have already been printed in *The Contemporary* in the form of a prologue. I have now both the plot (also the prologue) and the thought worked out in my mind" [October 7, 1846].

At the end of the same month he notified his brother: "Now that I have written my tale *The Landlady,* I'm going to leave off publishing entirely until next year, but I am writing a novel which even at this early point gives me no peace." The title is mentioned for the first time in a letter of December 17, 1846. "I am presently overburdened with work and I guaranteed to deliver the 1st part of my novel *Netochka Nezvanova* to Krayevsky by the 5th of January." In January 1847 the writer was still confident that the novel would appear shortly. "You'll soon read *Netochka Nezvanova,*" he informed his brother. "It will be a confession, like Golyadkin, though in a different tone and manner." The novel's appearance, however, was delayed. His work on *The Landlady* diverted Dostoevsky from *Netochka.* Then for financial reasons he was forced to undertake writing feuilletons for the *Saint Petersburg*

Gazette. And yet, he hoped that his novel would be published by the end of the year (1847). "It will culminate the year," he writes, "it will come out right at subscription time and most important, it will be, if I'm not mistaken at this point, the choicest piece of the year and will just rub the noses of our friends, the contemporaries, who have resolutely set upon burying me." But even at the end of the year the novel did not appear. The whole of 1848 was taken up with "light" things, with day-labor which the author accounted as a "sin against art." It was only in his scattered moments of leisure that he continued working on *Netochka.* At last, in February 1849, upon settling his affairs with the "entrepreneur" Krayevsky and persuading him to forward an advance of 100 rubles on the novel, Dostoevsky proudly declared: "I am writing . . . because 1) I love my novel, 2) because I know that I am writing a good thing, such as will not incur a risk but rather the reader's favor (I am not given to boasting, allow me now in short to tell the truth, I am called upon to tell it). . . . And I am finishing it up: the proof is that in the second part I have discarded an entire printed sheet and a half of things that were not at all bad, so as to round out the work, i.e., I blot out and abridge, and do not write continuously as a person would do who does not set value upon his work. . . . In the third part there will be no less than five sheets. . . ."[1]

The novel was planned on a grandiose scale: six first parts were projected and in some measure roughly outlined. The published fragment, Netochka's childhood, according to the author's design, constituted only the prologue. It appeared in *Fatherland Notes* in 1849. The writer's arrest and exile cut short his work on this composition, and he never again returned to it.

Netochka Nezvanova is written in the form of a "personal" account which the heroine presents of her own life. The narrative breaks off at a dramatic episode in her early youth. The novel is composed of three independent tales externally interrelated through the continuing presence of the narrator. These include the story of the musician Yefimov, that of Netochka's friendship with young Princess Katya, and that of her benefactress Aleksandra Mikhailovna. The first two tales are within themselves completed entities: the tragedy of the deranged musician concludes with his death, the friendship of the two girls is interrupted

---

[1] A technical printer's term used in Russia as a measure of length of a literary work. A "printed sheet" consists of 40,000 typographical units or sixteen pages of printed text. Dostoevsky was paid by the "printed sheet."

at their separation; the third episode has been left in part unfinished. The tales are distinct one from another not only as regards their individual subject matter, but also in their literary style. The author failed in his desire to achieve either compositional or stylistic unity. This is probably the reason that subsequently he never attempted to complete this rather unsuccessful work. But for all that, *Netochka* maintains a prominent place in Dostoevsky's writings as his first experiment in the realm of the psychological novel.

The first tale, that of the musician Yefimov, the heroine's stepfather, is conceived in the romantic spirit. We must remember that the author wrote it in the year 1847 at a time when he was disenchanted with the "natural school," and that work on it was interrupted by his composition of *The Landlady*. The theme of the eccentric musician — the mad musician stemming from Hoffmann's facile hand — had succeeded in altogether engulfing Russian romantic literature. Music and insanity hold an honored place in Prince V. Odoyevsky's *The House of Madmen* and *Russian Nights;* there is also Polevoy's tale *The Bliss of Insanity;* Gogol proposed to write a short story entitled *Notes of a Mad Musician* which subsequently appeared under the name *Notes of a Madman.* Beyond this, Dostoevsky could refer to the novella of his beloved Balzac, *Gambara,* in which an Italian musician composes a new form of music and devises new musical instruments. The insane enthusiast travels about Europe accompanied by his devoted wife, undergoes hunger, failures, but remains true to his inviolable madness. In the end, he chances upon a theatre where Meyerbeer's opera *Robert the Devil* is being presented, and this revelation of genuine music astounds him: just one more instant and he, it appears, will regain his vision. But his mania proves stronger than truth, and Gambara once again plunges into his musical delirium. Hoffmann's insane musician, proceeding through Balzac's romantic novella, is transformed by Dostoevsky into the dissolute violinist Yefimov. The narrator, Netochka, speaks of him as of a romantic hero: "His lot was very remarkable: this was the strangest, the most wonderful man of all whom I have ever known." And later, reflecting upon the years spent in her stepfather's house, she underlines the romantic features of her own childhood: "Though my story was very *exceptional,* and a great part was played in it by fate, by various, let us even suppose, *mysterious* paths, and in general there was much in it that was interesting, *inexplicable,* even something *fantastic,* nonetheless I myself turned out, as though in despite of all these *melodramatic* surroundings, a most ordinary child."

This is the manner in which the author evaluates his tale, this is how he wanted to see it: mysterious, exceptional, fantastic. However, only its beginning corresponds to these characteristics — Yefimov's past. His present, his drunken and dissolute life, with a sick wife and hungry daughter, departs further and further from romantic mysteriousness and draws ever closer to realistic melodrama.

Yefimov was the son of a poor musician and used to play the clarinet in an orchestra that had been organized by a certain landowner. The "mysterious" enters his life in the form of an Italian bandmaster, a "wicked man," who leaves him his violin. This inheritance is associated with some sort of crime, some diabolic force. Yefimov, up till now a mediocre clarinetist, is suddenly transformed into an exceptionally gifted violinist; he falls into melancholy and becomes obstinate and ill-tempered. He says to the landowner when parting from him: "Your house is not the place for me to live! I tell you that the devil has fastened himself on me. I'll set fire to your house if I stay. It just comes upon me. Now you'd better let me be, sir. It's all from the time when *that devil* began to act the brother with me."

After so Hoffmannesque an introduction with its bandmaster-devil, the story of the musician's downfall is related, yet here there is not even a trace of the supernatural. Yefimov squanders away all his funds, roves about from one provincial orchestra to another, and finally comes to Petersburg, a beggar. His talent, at first real, is undermined by his disorderly, poverty-stricken life. "When he arrived in Petersburg, even then he was proceeding almost unconsciously . . . and even he himself scarcely knew what prospects would await him in the capital. His enthusiasm was of a spasmodic nature, jaundiced, impulsive, as though he sought to deceive himself by this enthusiasm and through it, assure himself that his first strength, his first fire, his first inspiration as yet had not been spent within him!"

In Petersburg Yefimov becomes friends with the musician B., and before long the latter comes to perceive what lies at the core of his problem: after seven years of dissolute living the violinist has in fine lost his talent. "B. saw clearly that all this impetuosity, feverishness, and impatience were nothing other than unconscious despair at the thought of his wasted talent; that moreover, ultimately this very talent had been, perhaps even at the beginning itself, not at all so great, that there had been in it a great deal of blindness, of empty self-confidence, of premature self-satisfaction and incessant fancying, incessant illusion regarding his own genius. . . . But what astounded him most of all was that this man, in view of his utter helplessness, possessed such a profound, such a forceful and, one might even say, instinctive understanding of art. . . . He so very intensely felt it and understood it himself, that consequently it is no wonder that he was mistaken in his own judgment of himself, and took himself not merely for a profound, instinctive critic of art, but rather for a priest of that art itself, for a genius."

This exposure of Yefimov's "secret" serves to introduce the story of his tragic ruin. Romantic devilry is left behind; the author strikes upon a theme that is his own, a language proper to himself. The precision of his observations and the agitation of tone at once impress the reader: this is a confession. In 1847 the theme of an artist whose talent is spent was a theme personally immediate to Dostoevsky. His own sudden triumph had been followed by a series of failures. After that of *The Double*, every new work only tended to worsen his situation. Belinsky wrote in a letter to Annenkov: "We certainly were duped, my friend, with Dostoevsky the genius. I'm not speaking of Turgenev — in this he was his very own self — but really of me, the old hell-fiend. There's nothing even to say on it, but for a good caning. I, the foremost critic, here played the role of an ass squared to the second power." And from "self-satisfaction" Dostoevsky now passed into a state of self-disparagement. He believed the critics, had misgivings about his talent, began to entertain regrets, and fell sick in despair. Perhaps, he thought, even at the very beginning his talent "was not so great"; perhaps it was the talent of a critic and not of an artist. The crisis ultimately found its resolution in his writings. Yefimov was born out of the painful sufferings of the artist's imagination, from the plaguing idea that his talent of itself had been consumed. His own spiritual state became embodied in the image of the insane musician, and thereupon unfolded as the fate of an entire life. The hours of Dostoevsky's doubting and despair were transformed into the very tragedy of Yefimov's life. It is in his creative work that the writer *realized the possibilities of his own spirit.* The *possibility* of the author's having lost his talent and of ruin became a *reality* in the case of his hero.

This is the reason why there is so much "anguished torment" in Dostoevsky's psychological approach. He analyzed his own self not for the sake of dispassionate knowledge, but as a *therapy*. The allure of fame (the "incessant illusion regarding his own genius"), his impatience, his lack of courage, the impossibility of polishing his works, his "inner helplessness" — these are the "sins against art" which he had to expiate. Naturally, Yefimov is not Dostoevsky, but he is a specific state of Dostoevsky's inner life which has been embodied as a person and given its own respective fate.

The musician B., upon parting with Yefimov, forewarns that he will have a difficult life. The bitter personal recollections of the author himself resound in these predictions.

At this point you are still of no use to anyone, no one even cares to know you. This is the way the world is. But wait a bit, before long it will be different once they find out you possess a gift. Envy, petty meanness, and worst of all, stupidity will weigh upon you more heavily than poverty. Talent needs sympathy, it needs it in order to be understood; but you will see what sort of people will crowd about you when once you have attained even a fraction of your goal. They'll regard as worthless and look with contempt upon what you have achieved through hard labor, privations, hunger, sleepless nights. They won't encourage, won't console you — your future comrades; they'll not point out to you what is good and true in you; but with malicious glee will grasp at your every mistake, will point out precisely where you are wrong, where you are mistaken, and under an outward show of coolness and contempt toward you, will revel, as though it were a festive occasion, at your every mistake. So you are conceited, often at inopportune times you are proud and capable of insulting some egoistic nonentity, and then there is trouble. You will be alone, but there are many of them: they will torment you with their pinpricks.

This entire tirade is utterly superfluous to the story. The musician B., having already concluded that Yefimov has lost his talent, now for no reason speaks to him of his "gift" and of the trials that face the artist. Surely he knows that his predictions will not be fulfilled. Here the author's confession intrudes upon the plot of his tale. In complaining of the badgering to which he was subjected by the associates of *The Contemporary* ("they will torment you with their pinpricks"), Dostoevsky for the time forgets about his hero.

Once parted from his friend and benefactor B., Yefimov sinks lower and lower. He marries, for various calculated reasons, a widow with a two-year-old daughter, Netochka. "This was an unhappy woman. In the past she had been a governess, had been very well educated, good-looking, and through poverty had married an old civil servant, my father." In the features of this "dreamer and enthusiast," stricken with consumption and exhausted from overwork, we see glowing the image of another sufferer, Katerina Ivanovna Marmeladova. The author portrays her misery through the symbolism of her movement. "She used to walk continuously, without tiring, back and forth about the room whole hours on end, often even during the night when she could not sleep — an affliction which tormented her; she would walk whispering something to herself as though she were alone in the room, now flinging her arms wide apart, now folding them upon her breast, then wringing her hands in a certain terrible, relentless anguish." It is in this same movement and with these gestures that Katerina Ivanovna likewise is depicted. The author later transferred the description of this impoverished life in a garret, of a sick, hard-working mother, a drunken father, and a frightened daughter (Yefimov, his wife, Netochka) into his novel *Crime and Punishment*. Marmeladov too steals from his wife and squanders away in drink the last of her funds as does Yefimov.

Now having gotten married, the depraved musician declares that it is marriage which has destroyed his talent, and attributes all his failures to his wife. He vows that he will not take a violin into his hands until her very death. It is at this point that actual insanity begins systematically to develop: "the resolute idea that he is the first of all violinists, that he is harassed by fate, affronted — owing to various intrigues, misunderstood and existing in obscurity."

Eight years pass in this fashion. Netochka comes to an awareness of herself; she feels as though she is waking up from a deep sleep. The hostile relations between her parents trouble her childlike imagination. "My heart was wounded from the first moment," she says, "and with inconceivable, exhausting speed my development set in motion." The author reflects upon the tragedy of the child growing up in a "peculiar household," examines the rupture in its soul when faced with the "unsightliness" of its parents. The "wounded heart" develops quickly and morbidly; its sensitivity and imagination are given a false start. "I am not surprised," says Netochka, "that in the midst of such peculiar people as my father and mother, I myself turned out such a strange, fantastic child." Dostoevsky bore a deep trauma from the time of his childhood, and his thoughts always tended to the question of the family. In the original edition of *Netochka Nezvanova* we find some curious observations made by the heroine in regard to the novels of Walter Scott which she had read avidly while living in the house of Prince Kh. "My life in this new family was too intensely reflected in the first impressions of my heart, and as a result, the feeling of family — so poetically rendered in the novels of Walter Scott, the feeling in the name of which they were created, this feeling, carried to its most sublime historical significance, presented as the very postulate for the preservation of all mankind, conveyed through all his novels with such love — was too sweetly, too strongly compressed within my heart in response to my own memories, my own sufferings."

Bitter recollections about his own childhood and the poetic cult of "family" in Walter Scott compelled Dostoevsky to consider the *problem of the Russian family;* it is treated in all his great novels, and with unsurpassed force in *A Raw Youth* and *The Brothers Karamazov.* Arkady Dolgoruky belongs to a "haphazard household," is continually affronted by his "fathers' unsightliness"; *The Brothers Karamazov* is the tragic chronicle of a "haphazard household." Hostility between parents is perversely refracted upon the consciousness of their children. Together with her stepfather Netochka begins to hate her poor tormented mother and dreams of her death. She is drawn to her father with a morbid affection. "From that moment I began to feel a certain boundless love for my father, but a strange love, as it were, not at all childlike. I'd say that it was rather a kind of compassionate, motherly feeling." At times she is aware of the wrong which she is doing to her mother, is tormented by pangs of conscience, as though realizing the sinfulness of her disposition, yet unhesitatingly she steals money from her mother at her stepfather's promptings. "Little by little," she confesses, "my love — no, better, I will say passion, for I know no word strong enough and able fully to convey the irrepressible feeling which I had toward my father and which proved an anguish to myself — developed to the point of a sort of morbid exasperation. There was only one pleasure I had — thinking and dreaming about him; only one desire — to do everything that could provide him with even the slightest satisfaction. . . . By degrees I began to dominate him and, conscious of how dependent he was upon me, sometimes even played coquettishly with him. In fact, this attachment that I had, did bear some resemblance to a *romance."* In his subsequent writings, Dostoevsky never again attempted so bold an analysis of the erotic element in a child's soul. The innocent Netochka experiences a most complicated feeling as regards her stepfather: motherly concern, childlike attachment, adult passion. In this precocious fullness of emotion we as yet have not crossed beyond the boundary of the normal and the abnormal.

The composition of this tale devoted to the violinist Yefimov is Dostoevsky's first attempt to construct a full-scale novel; the slow and detailed psychological preparation is brought to its culmination in the outburst of the catastrophe. It is apparent that destructive forces have gradually been building up in the musician's tiny flat, that the air which his family breathes is becoming more and more impregnated with electricity. The hero's ruin is foretold by his friend B. This latter says to the music enthusiast Prince Kh.: "He is, despite everything, convinced that he is the foremost musician in the entire world. Convince him that he is not an artist, and I tell you, he will die on the spot as though struck down by a clap of thunder, for it is a terrible thing to have to part with a fixed idea for which one has offered one's entire life as sacrifice."

The renowned violinist S. comes to Petersburg; Yefimov induces Netochka to steal the last of her mother's money so that he might buy a ticket for the concert. The final scene, intensely dramatic, is not devoid of its own somber, ominous grandeur. Having returned from the concert, Yefimov plays his violin in the presence of his wife's corpse. "The music began. . . . But it was not music. . . . These were not the sounds of a violin, but as though the horrible voice of some being had begun for the first time to reverberate in our dismal lodgings. . . . I heard groans, a human cry, weeping. The whole of despair was poured forth in these sounds." Netochka's stepfather taking her, runs away; she falls down in the street and loses consciousness. They apprehend him outside the city in a fit of raving insanity. After two days he dies in a hospital. "He died because such a death was a necessity to him, the natural consequence of all his life. . . . The truth blinded him with its unbearable radiance, and what had been a lie was proved a lie even to the man himself. In his last hour he had heard a marvelous genius who had revealed his own self to him and condemned him for ever. . . . The blow was fatal."

———————

The second part of *Netochka Nezvanova* is also an independent tale. After her parents' death the heroine is brought rather fortuitously into the home of Prince Kh., and there her fate sustains a drastic change. Her youth remains completely unrelated to her childhood. The break between these two worlds is underlined by the heroine's protracted illness. In place of a continued organic development within the action we are faced with an entirely new episode. The novel has been left severed in fragments, and this compositional defect is not offset by psychological unity. Netochka is too pale a figure, too much the narrator and not the heroine. With discreet modesty she invariably yields the foreground to other individuals and is incapable of focusing the novel's events on her own personality. She relates the story of her life, but it is her fate to act as an accessory to the lives of people more significant than herself.

The second part of the novel, devoted to Netochka's life in the Prince's home, underwent a substantial abridgment in the final edition. The author eliminated the episode of the boy Larenka, a poor orphan, whom, as in the case of Netochka, the Prince has brought into the shelter of his home. This is also a "wounded heart." Larenka is convinced that he is the cause of his parents' death; he dwells on how he used to torment his mother. This feeling of guilt results in his developing a nervous ailment. Netochka tenderly watches over the sick boy, but his health continually grows worse and the Prince finally sends him away to relatives in Little Russia.[2] The author enters into a detailed analysis of the child's overstrung emotionality with its frequent lapses into "sensualism." Leaving Freud's school far behind, he takes the soul's initial wound (the trauma) and from it deduces the origins of consciousness. "I have observed such children," Netochka remarks, "who, for the sake of gratifying a depraved sensualism, the outgrowth of a falsely developed sensitivity, have emerged as utter tyrants at home, and have brought their refinement of pleasure to such a point as, for example, intentionally to torture domestic animals in order that they might, at the time of the very process of torment, experience a certain inexplicable pleasure that was comprised of the sensation of feeling remorse, feeling pity, and the awareness of their own inhumanity." A morbid sensitivity ultimately degenerating into sadism is peculiar to all the children in Dostoevsky's writing (*The Idiot, A Raw Youth, The Brothers Karamazov*).

In the final version, these observations regarding a child's soul, along with the episode about Larenka, have disappeared. Druzhinin had reproached Dostoevsky for having imitated Dickens; in actual fact, Netochka's attachment to Larenka does bear some resemblance to the friendship of Florence and Paul in the novel *Dombey and Son*. After Larenka was removed from the story, the Prince's daughter, Katya, who is the same age as Netochka, became the principal character of the second part. She has been visiting with her grandmother in Moscow, and returns to Petersburg at the point of Netochka's recovery.

[2] Little Russia = the Ukraine.

Through his juxtaposition of these two young girls, the fair, blue-eyed Netochka and dark, impassionate Katya, the author succeeded in creating a psychological format to which he would forever remain faithful. Netochka, morbid, sensitive, patiently enduring, shy and given to tears, stands at the head of a whole line of meek women in Dostoevsky. With tender irony Katya says about her: "Now there, you pale little thing, with your blonde hair; yourself a dear silly child, such a crybaby, with your blue eyes; you are my li-ttle or-phan girl." This class of meek women is represented by Sonya Marmeladova in *Crime and Punishment*, Dasha in *The Devils*, Sofya Andreyevna in *A Raw Youth*, the heroine of the tale *The Meek One*. From young Princess Katya there extends the series of "proud women": Polina in *The Gambler*, Nastasya Filippovna in *The Idiot*, Liza in *The Devils*, Katerina Ivanovna in *Brothers Karamazov*. In contrast to the former's gentle amiability there stands the "astonishing" beauty of these latter. Netochka says of Katya: "Picture to yourself a little face, one ideally charming, an astonishing, dazzling beauty, one of those before which you suddenly come to a stop as though transfixed in delightful wonderment, shuddering with rapture." The "proud woman" in Dostoevsky is always a dazzling beauty who transfixes the soul with aesthetic rapture. Upon first glance Netochka falls passionately in love with Katya. . . . "Perhaps," she writes, "for the first time an aesthetic sense, a sense of the lovely, was astonished within me; for the first time it manifested itself, aroused by beauty, and it was for this reason that my love came forth into being." Prince Myshkin sees a portrait of Nastasya Filippovna, and her beauty astonishes him; in the same way, Akhmakova's beauty "disturbs" Versilov, the beauty of Grushenka "transfixes" Mitya. In *Netochka* we already see intimations of Dostoevsky's profound theme of the "terrible force of beauty."

The gay, boisterous Katya is indifferent to Netochka with all her constant weeping. Her girl friend's loving affection is disturbing, and annoys her. Their governess holds up the diligent orphan as an example. Pride flares up in Katya and she begins to torment her gentle companion, questions her about her parents, laughs at her poverty, her wretched clothing, her not knowing how to dance and play the piano. Netochka cries; Katya is punished and ordered to beg forgiveness for having offended her. From that point on she develops an "unfathomable" aversion toward Netochka.

At the end of the tale the puzzle is resolved: the young princess suddenly realized that Netochka loved her, and a corresponding feeling was born in her own heart. But for a long time the proud girl had been unwilling to acknowledge this love and because of it, inflicted her resentment on both herself and on Netochka. Her cruelty only served to strengthen Netochka's devotion: "I scarcely understood what was happening to me," she writes. "Everything within me was in a state of agitation as the result of some new, inexplicable sensation, and I will not exaggerate if I say that I suffered, was tortured by this new feeling. More precisely — and may I be forgiven for saying this — I was in love with my Katya. Yes, it was love, real love, love with its tears and joys, passionate love." It was almost in these very same terms that Netochka spoke of her affection for her father. The author here for the second time portrays the child's sensitivity as an erotic element bordering on the verge of pathology.

After such involved peripeteias the love quarrel between Netochka and Katya draws to its denouement. Katya does something seriously wrong, and Netochka takes the blame upon herself. The young princess is overcome; at night, when in bed, an explanation takes place between the two girls: "We hugged and greedily squeezed one another. The young princess began almost to dissolve me in kisses. 'Netochka,' whispered Katya through her tears, 'you are my angel; why, I've loved you for so long, for so long. . . . Listen. I had very much wanted to love you, and then suddenly *I would begin wanting to hate you,* and I hated you so, hated so! . . . And then too I saw that you couldn't live without me and I thought: here now I will torment her to despair, the nasty thing. . . . Why, I've always loved you! Always loved you! Only later did the whole thing become unbearable. I thought, I will kiss her some day or I'll end up just pinching her to death.' " In the confession of this naive young girl there lies an element of bold candor. Love opens out upon a dark abyss of cruelty, hatred, pride, and the urge to dominate. "Dazzling beauty" is a demonic force. "Transfixing" the heart, it feeds upon its blood; its victims — Rogozhin, Versilov, Mitya Karamazov — are doomed to the bliss of destruction.

The story of Katya is interrupted by her having to leave for Moscow. A new break occurs within Netochka's life. The prince's family moves to Moscow, while the heroine is left with the princess' daughter by her first marriage, Aleksandra Mikhailovna. She is a "woman of about twenty-two, quiet, tender, loving." Four years before she had married "a man, rich and holding a significant rank." The novel's third part embraces the eight years Netochka spends in the family of Aleksandra Mikhailovna; it is introduced by the heroine's words: "Now there begins a new story." And in actual fact, this part, just as the first two, stands as a distinct tale. It is built on the same device as in those preceding: a lengthy psychological preparation and an effectively dramatic scene at the point of denouement. The literary tone in which it is written is distinguished by an exaggerated sensibility. Netochka's new life unfolds "serenely and calmly" as in a monastery. She studies with fervent zeal, becomes enthusiastically absorbed in reading, takes singing lessons. No particular events take place in her life; there is nothing to mark her inner development. The monotony of the narrative is further increased by the fact that Netochka's new friend and benefactress is, like herself, a "meek" type. The end result is a duplication of one and the same psychological tonality. Both Netochka and Aleksandra Mikhailovna suffer, feel dejected, dream mournfully, are touched by their mutual friendship, embrace one another, and cry. Netochka tries to solve the mysterious secret of her second mother, and with this eight years pass. It is only as the conclusion draws near that the action becomes animated; the story is broken off at a highly melodramatic scene.

To all appearances, Aleksandra Mikhailovna passionately loves her husband, Pyotr Aleksandrovich, "but in his presence she carefully weighs her every movement, acts diffidently towards him, is embarrassed and afraid before his stern glance." There is something of childlike innocence, of helplessness in this "wounded heart" overflowing with love and tenderness. It is as though "the memory of something painfully tormenting to her conscience, would flare up in her soul." Aleksandra Mikhailovna's husband is "a tall, thin man who seems intentionally to conceal the look in his eyes behind large, green spectacles." He is reticent, dry, and finds little subject for conversation, even in private with his wife. He views his wife with a patronizing condescension and cold feelings of pity. Chance leads Netochka to the explanation of Aleksandra Mikhailovna's secret: in Walter Scott's novel St. Ronan's Well, which she has taken from their library, she finds an old letter addressed to her protectress. Herein some unknown individual bids his final farewell to that one who through her pure friendship had elevated him to her own level, who had transformed him, a coarse and simple man, through her compassionate love. "Yes, you love me very much, you have loved me as a sister loves her brother; you have loved me as your own creation, because you have raised my heart from the dead, awakened my mind from its slumber and have infused sweet hope in my breast. But I could not, dared not, I have never till now called you my sister, since I could not be your brother, since we were not equal, since you were deceived in me." Their love, however, was discovered: "Their gossip, their cries have arisen." He must leave her, but believes that her husband will protect his innocent wife from slander. "I have just now met your husband," he continues. "We are both unworthy of him, although we remain innocent before him. He is aware of everything. . . . He has heroically set himself behind you; he will save you. . . ." And Netochka understands the "innocent sinner's" tragedy. Pyotr Aleksandrovich has saved his wife, but he has not forgiven her for having fallen in love. He has converted his generosity into an instrument of torture and on his compassion has built up a refined system of spiritual tyranny. "I came to envision," says Netochka, "the prolonged, hopeless suffering, the martyrdom, the sacrifice which was tendered submissively, docilely, and unavailingly. It struck me that the man to whom this sacrifice was being offered despised it and laughed at it. It seemed as though here I was watching a criminal pardoning the sins of a just man."

The idea that a meritorious individual can prove himself to be a terrible villain had already been remarked by Dostoevsky in the *Petersburg Chronicle* and illustrated through the example of the honored Yulian Mastakovich (*A Christmas Tree Party and a Wedding*). In *Netochka Nezvanova*, written at the same period, the theme of the "good heart" finds its artistic culmination. The hypocritical just man and virtuous executioner Pyotr Aleksandrovich, "concealing the look in his eyes behind large, green spectacles," merits his place among the ranks of Dostoevsky's most terrifying, demonic heroes. In the story of Aleksandra Mikhailovna the motif of a strong individual's tyranny over a weak soul reverberates with no less tragic force than in the tale *The Landlady*. But here it is freed of romantic legends and the fantastic. Aleksandra Mikhailovna is a lady of Petersburg society, and not a half-mad wild creature from the Volga; Pyotr Aleksandrovich is a "rich man, holding a significant rank," and not a sorcerer and black magician like Murin. The tragedy of the "faint heart" is depicted on a psychological plane, and this succeeds in heightening its artistic import.

The novel's denouement has been left unfinished. Pyotr Aleksandrovich realizes that Netochka has discerned his true character, and he decides to avenge himself. He comes unexpectedly upon her in the library holding the fatal letter in her hands, and thereupon accuses her, in the presence of Aleksandra Mikhailovna, of immoral behavior. "Believe me, madam," he says to his wife, "I know my duty, and how ever generously you may excuse me, I shall say as before, that *crime will always remain crime, that sin will always be sin,* shameful, hideous, dishonorable, no matter to what height of grandeur you may raise the depraved feeling." Inexhaustible malice and vengefulness finally burst forth from this hero of morality; he inflicts a final, mortal blow upon his victim.

Dostoevsky was unsuccessful in his attempt to create the format of a full-scale psychological novel. *Netochka Nezvanova* is not a single novel, but three distinct tales. The narrator proved too colorless a being to pretend to the role of heroine. But what a complex wealth of ideas, images, and devices is gathered in this work! *Netochka Nezvanova* is the laboratory in which the ideology and technique of the great novels were worked out.

Dostoevsky the Revolutionary

Dostoevsky's youth was passed under the dominance of romantic "daydreaming," the idealism of Schiller, and French utopian socialism. Through the influence of George Sand and Balzac he early developed an interest in social questions. Belinsky rapturously hailed the author of *Poor People* as the originator of the first Russian social novel. A protest against social injustice and the defense of the "humiliated and wronged" are constantly introduced in all his early works. In the *Petersburg Chronicle* we already encountered an appeal to public endeavor ("the generalized interests, the sympathy with the masses of society and with their direct, immediate demands"). Dostoevsky not only studied French socialist theories, but also tried to apply them to life. In the winter of 1846 he and his friends, the Beketov brothers, experimented in forming an "association."

"The Beketovs, with their company, have cured me," he wrote his brother. "In the end, I suggested that we live together. A large apartment was found, and the entire expense for all the particulars of housekeeping — the sum total — does not exceed 1,200 paper rubles an individual for the course of a year. So great are the benefits of an association." And later: "Do you see what an association means? Working apart individually, we will falter, be intimidated, our spirit will be reduced to poverty. But two banded together for a single purpose — that's another matter." The transition from romantic idealism to socialism was perfectly natural. The young writer lived in an atmosphere of mystical expectations, of faith in the imminent approach of the golden age and in the complete transfiguration of life. It seemed to him that a new Christian art (Victor Hugo, George Sand, Balzac) was ordained to renew the world and provide for the happiness of mankind; he believed that the systems of Saint-Simon, Fourier, and Proudhon would fulfill the promises of romanticism, would gratify this longing for a better life. Socialistic utopianism appeared to the generation of the forties as a continuation of Christianity, as the attainment of evangelical truth. It was a translation of the Christian Apocalypse into contemporary "social" terms.

Reflecting upon his ardent youth Dostoevsky writes in the *Diary of a Writer* (1873):

At that time the matter was still conceived in a most *rosy and paradisiacally moral light*. It is in fact true that socialism in its nascency was compared even by some of its ringleaders with Christianity and was regarded only as a corrective and improvement of the latter in conformity with our age and civilization. All of these then new ideas were wholeheartedly received by us in Petersburg, seemed to the highest degree holy and moral and, most important of all, *universal to mankind,* the future law of all men without exception. Long before the Paris revolution of '48 we were already consumed by the fascinating influence of these ideas.

In his "explanation" submitted to the commission of inquiry Dostoevsky boldly admitted his enthusiasm for utopian socialism. "Fourierism," he wrote, "is a peaceful system: it *charms the soul* with its refinement, *seduces the heart* by that love for mankind which animated Fourier when he composed his system, and *astonishes the mind* with its proportioned harmony. It draws adherence not through bilious assaults, but by animating with a love for mankind. In this system there is no hate."

Dostoevsky was never to disavow this utopia of the transfiguration of the world, this *Christian socialism.* The concept of a golden age and of world harmony was his most inviolable, most "sacred" idea; it stands at the center of his world-outlook and creative work.

Upon becoming acquainted with Petrashevsky in the spring of 1846, he set about borrowing books of a social-Christian content from his library: Saint-Simon's *Le nouveau Christianisme,* Cabet's *Le vrai Christianisme suivant Jésus-Christ,* Proudhon's *De la célébration du dimanche.*

In 1847 he began to frequent Petrashevsky's circle, and in it met many individuals upholding the same ideas: A. P. Milyukov revered Lamennais and translated his *Paroles d'un croyant* into Church Slavonic; K. I. Timkovsky "promised that on one of the Fridays he would demonstrate in a purely scientific fashion the divinity of Jesus Christ, the necessity of His coming into the world for the purpose of salvation, and His birth of a Virgin"; the poet A. N. Pleshcheyev wrote:

I sit surrounded by a noisy crowd
At a great feast, I hear the sound of chains;
And there appears far in the distance, like a vision before me,
Crucified upon a cross, the Great Nazarene.

Another Petrashevist, Yevropeus, stated at the inquiry that "the character of Fourier's theory is *religious*,' harmonious, scientific, and peaceful, in opposition to all violent overthrowals, revolutions, and disorders." Debout likewise regarded Fourierism in this manner. "The theory of Fourier," he testified, "contains nothing that is injurious to society; on the contrary, it reconciles people of all classes and standings, upholds *religious sentiments* and disposes to the preservation of order."

The Petrashevist D. Akhsharumov was also a fervid Christian socialist; at a dinner in honor of Fourier (April 7, 1849) he declared: "And here were to be found men with an ardent love for all people, for the whole of mankind, and likewise *for God*, who dedicated their entire lives in an attempt to discover an ordering of society wherein all would be rich, happy, and content; where our very life, its every day, hour, and minutes, would be a thanksgiving hymn to the *Creator*; where there would be neither tears nor crimes; and at their head there stands the lofty genius Fourier." The exalted aim of the Petrashevists was to restore man's image in all its grandeur and beauty . . . "to cover the whole of the impoverished earth with palaces, fruits, and to adorn it with flowers." This speech fully conveys the new movement's utopian spirit, its religious-humanistic pathos. Dostoevsky could have signed his own name beneath every word of this manifesto. The Russian Fourierists had no political program, were opposed to violent overthrowals, recognized private ownership in "association" and the hierarchical structuring of labor. In this sense it is impossible for one to term them either revolutionaries or even socialists. The name by far most applicable to them is that of *philanthropic liberals*.

No Petrashevsky conspiracy in fact ever existed. All Petersburg knew of their gatherings at his apartment on Fridays. D. Akhsharumov says in his *Notes* that "it was an interesting kaleidoscope of the most varied opinions about contemporary events. . . . City news was related; everything was brought under loud discussion without the slightest constraint. . . ." Balasoglo calls Petrashevsky's Fridays "simple gatherings of acquaintances who were closely bound together through their mutual feelings and relationships."

Liprandi, a functionary on special commission from the Ministry of Internal Affairs, wrote in his memorandum regarding the Petrashevsky affair: "In the majority of the young people one sees manifest a certain radical embitterment against the existing order of things, due not to any personal motivations, but solely to an infatuation with the *illusory utopias* which hold sway in Western Europe and up until now have without hindrance infiltrated us by way of literature and even the very teaching in our schools. Blindly dedicating themselves to these utopias, they imagine that they have been called upon to renovate all of social life, to remodel all mankind and are prepared to be the *apostles and martyrs* of this unfortunate self-delusion." It would be impossible to give a more precise delineation of the intellectual outlook that prevailed among the "dreamers" and "freethinkers" of the forties. In his explanation before the commission of inquiry Dostoevsky declared: "Yes, if to desire that which is better, is liberalism, freethinking, then in that sense perhaps I am a *freethinker*. I am a freethinker in the same sense in which every individual can be termed a freethinker who in the depths of his heart feels himself to possess the right to be a citizen, feels himself to possess the right to desire that which is good for his fatherland."

Utopian socialism, however, was not for long to remain the dominant current in this decade. A new movement rose up against it out of Germany, where Hegelian idealism at this time was undergoing a profound crisis. The left-wing Hegelians following Feuerbach and Marx broke with abstract metaphysics and laid the foundations of future materialistic socialism. Hegel's philosophy was now interpreted in the context of an appeal to social revolution; Christianity we find rejected as an outmoded superstition hindering the progress of this new society. Herzen, Botkin, and Bakunin saw in atheism the liberation of the spirit. Herzen wrote: "Hegel's philosophy is the algebra of revolution; it uniquely frees man and does not leave a stone upon a stone of the Christian world, of the world of legends which have outlived their time." In the mid-forties Belinsky, under Feuerbach's influence, rejected Hegel, turned enthusiastically to the natural and exact sciences and became a militant atheist. "To hell with metaphysics," he exclaimed, "this word connotes the supernatural, hence, absurdity. . . . Liberating science from phantoms, transcendentalism, and theology; demonstrating the frontiers of the mind within which its activity is fertile; tearing it away once and for all from everything fantastic and metaphysical — here is what the founder of the new philosophy will accomplish." In 1845 he wrote Herzen: "I have acquired the truth, and in the words *God and religion* I see darkness, obscurity, chains, and the knout."

Belinsky, out of his love for mankind, revolted against God and refused to believe in the creator of an imperfect world. He was a fanatic insofar as his love for people was concerned: "Sociality, sociality or death! This is my motto," he declared. If to ensure the happiness of the majority, one were forced to cut off a hundred thousand heads — he would cut them off. He himself related his bloodthirsty philanthropy to the tradition of Marat. Belinsky's influence was ultimately to determine the fate of Russian socialism: atheistic materialism succeeded in trampling down Christian utopianism; the way was being prepared for Marxist Communism. In this turbulent Russian tragedy Dostoevsky was destined to play a role that remained far from insignificant. He was guilty of a renunciation, and atoned for it by ten years of Siberia. In this lies his "crime and punishment."

In *The Diary of a Writer* (1873) he relates in detail how in 1846 Belinsky "rushed head-on to convert [him] to his belief." "I found him a passionate socialist, and he promptly embarked upon *atheism* with me. For me there is much that is significant in this — namely, his amazing insight and his unusual ability to become permeated, in the most profound sense, with an idea. . . . He knew that moral principles are the basis of all things. He believed in the new moral bases of socialism to the point of delirium and without any reflection: here there was nothing save ecstasy. Yet as a socialist, he had before all else to dispose of Christianity; he knew that the revolution must necessarily begin with atheism. He was forced to dispose of this religion which had given rise to the moral foundations of the society which he was rejecting. The family, property, the individual's moral responsibility — these he rejected radically.

"At this juncture, however, there remained the radiant personality of Christ Himself with which it was most difficult of all to contend. He, as a socialist, was bound absolutely to destroy Christ's teaching, to call it fallacious and ignorant philanthropy brought to nought by contemporary science and economic principles; but for all that, there remained the most lustrous image of the God-man, its moral inaccessibility, its wonderful and miraculous beauty. In his incessant, inextinguishable ecstasy Belinsky did not stop even before this insurmountable obstacle. . . .

" 'But do you know,' he screamed one evening (at times if he became very excited, he used somehow to scream), 'do you know that it is wrong to charge a man with sins and encumber him with obligations and the turning of cheeks when society is so vilely constituted that it is impossible for man not to commit misdeeds, when economically he is brought to misdeeds, and that it is absurd and cruel to demand from a man that which, according to the very laws of nature, he is incapable of carrying out, even if he wanted to.'"

And turning to a second guest, Belinsky pointed to Dostoevsky and continued: "I am even touched to look at him. Every given time that I'll mention Christ like this, *his whole countenance changes just as though he were on the verge of breaking into tears.* But believe me your Christ, if He were born in our time, would be the most inconspicuous and ordinary individual; likewise He would even vanish from sight before our present-day science and before the propellers of mankind!" And Dostoevsky concludes: "During the last year of his life I stopped visiting him. He had taken a dislike to me; *but at that time I passionately accepted all his teaching.*"

An extraordinary confession: Dostoevsky *passionately* accepted the atheistic teaching of Belinsky. In another essay included in the same *Diary of a Writer* for 1873, the author delineates still more precisely the character of Belinsky's "teaching." "All these convictions about the immorality of the very foundations (Christian) of contemporary society, *about the immorality* of religion, the family, about the immorality of the right of property; all these ideas about the obliteration of nationalities in the name of a universal brotherhood of men, about contempt for one's fatherland, etc., etc. — all these were influences such as we were not able to overcome and which, to the contrary, seized our hearts and minds in the name of a certain magnanimity." These words leave no possibility of doubt: Belinsky did convert Dostoevsky to his belief; he "passionately" accepted all his *atheistic communism.* The "philanthropic liberal" abandoned his Christian utopianism and renounced the "radiant personality of Christ." And this did not constitute a passing delusion, but was rather a prolonged inner tragedy. Eight years after he had embraced Belinsky's "atheistic belief," Dostoevsky wrote from Omsk to the wife of the Decembrist Fonvizin:[1] "I

---

[1] Following the Napoleonic Wars, the Russian Forces of Occupation came in close contact with many of the democratic and social ideas prevailing in Western Europe, such as those of the Italian *Carbonari* or the German *Tugendbund.* Upon their return to Russia secret societies were formed, lengthy debates were held, but no precise, constructive program was ever agreed upon. This movement, headed by Pavel Pestel, did not involve popular support, but was exclusively of an idealistic, aristocratic character. After the sudden death of Emperor Aleksandr I, an

will tell you regarding myself that I am a child of the age, *a child of nonbelief and doubt, up till now* and even (I know it) until my coffin closes."

This man who was responsible for the most brilliant argumentation ever written in defense of atheism (Ivan Karamazov), this man whom "throughout [his] entire life God tormented," combined within his heart the most ardent faith with the greatest disbelief. All the religious dialectic of his novels stems from this tragic duality.

After having confessed in *The Diary of a Writer* that he had been a partisan of communistic ideas, Dostoevsky drew from this a terrible conclusion: "How do you know that the Petrashevists could not have become the Nechayevists, that is, have set themselves on Nechayev's very path, *in such an instance, were things to have taken a similar turn?* Of course, at that time it was impossible even to imagine how things could develop and take such a turn. But permit me to speak concerning myself only: probably I could never have become a *Nechayev,* but a *Nechayevist,* this I do not vouch; it is possible, I too could have become one . . . *in the days of my youth.*" And in conclusion he asks himself pensively how he could have succumbed to such a fallacy. "I am descended from a Russian and a pious family. . . . We in our family knew the Gospel almost from our earliest childhood. . . . Every time I used to visit the Kremlin and the Moscow cathedrals, it was to me a solemn and festive occasion."

But the faith of his childhood proved fragile. His initial impressions of churches, the Divine service, liturgical chants were more aesthetic than religious. His parents' ritualistic piety related only to the surface of the boy's soul. And later, in his youth, Christian humanism and romantic mysticism for a long time contented the "dreamer's" religious yearning. The young Dostoevsky's understanding of Christianity was clouded and vague. He compared Homer to Christ, considered Victor Hugo a lyricist with a "Christian, childlike poetic tendency." Finally — and this is most noteworthy — religious questions are never posed in any of his works prior to his servitude in Siberia. In *The Landlady,* Ordynov is composing a treatise on the history of the Church, but this bears no reflection upon his life. Pious individuals

---

uprising demanding a constitution was staged on December 14, 1825, in Senate Square. The poorly organized rebellion was quickly suppressed and five of the Decembrist leaders were sentenced to death, while over a hundred were exiled to Siberia. The wives of a number of these men voluntarily and heroically followed their husbands into the trials of prison life. Their memory has been immortalized in Russian literature. Mme Fonvizina was one of these.

are cast as hypocrites and tyrants (M⸱rin in *The Landlady*, the old princess in *Netochka Nezvanova*). In Dostoevsky's writings of this period, God finds no mention. This is the reason why the young writer was left helpless before Belinsky's influence, and why it "seized his heart." His own encounter with Christ took place in penal servitude through his communion in the sufferings of the Russian people. "However," writes the author of *The Diary*, "this did not occur right away, out gradually, by degrees, and after a very, very long time." Even the scaffold and exile did not avail immediately to shatter his convictions. "We, Petrashevists," he continues, "stood on the scaffold and listened to our sentence without the slightest repentance. . . . If not each single one, then, at any rate, the overwhelming majority of us would have considered it a dishonor to renounce his convictions. The affair for which they had condemned us, those thoughts, those ideas which governed our spirit, were regarded by us not only as not requiring repentance, but even as something purifying, a martyrdom, for which much would be forgiven us. And so it continued for a long time. Not the years of exile, not the sufferings succeeded in breaking us. On the contrary, nothing broke us, and our convictions only upheld our spirit by the realization of a duty fulfilled." This essay from *The Diary of a Writer* for 1873 is an act of public penance unprecedented in the history of Russian spirituality. There is a grandeur in this boldness and ardor of spirit. Dostoevsky confessed to everything to which he could confess, and hinted at that which in his time it was impossible to relate. Until the present, this allusion has remained obscure and it is only now, thanks to the publication of new material, that we are able to comprehend its meaning.

"Probably," says Dostoevsky, "I could never have become a *Nechayev*, but a *Nechayevist*, this I do not vouch; it is possible, I too could have become one . . . in the days of my youth." As we know, Nechayev was the founder of a revolutionary society in the sixties and the author of *The Catechism of a Revolutionary*. The Nechayevists sought to enmesh the whole of Russia in a network of secret cells, to stir up the masses, organize a bloody insurrection, overthrow the government, and abolish religion, the family, property. Dostoevsky stigmatized these fanatics of destruction in his novel *The Devils*. How then are we to understand the statement that he could have "become a Nechayevist" in the days of his youth? What is meant by that enigmatic phrase: "in such an instance, were things to have taken a similar turn"?

Dostoevsky's "revolutionary activity" was not confined to the Petrashevsky circle. Through its agent Antonelli, the commission of inquiry was well informed about what took place at Petrashevsky's on Fridays, but it knew little regarding the work of the Durov group. Let us begin, however, by elucidating the "open" side of the "Dostoevsky affair." In the spring of 1846 he was introduced to Petrashevsky by the poet Pleshcheyev, and from Lent 1847 took to attending his Fridays. In his "explanation" presented to the inquiry commission, the writer declared that he was never intimate with him. "I maintained relations with Petrashevsky," he wrote, "precisely to the point that civility demanded, that is, I used to visit him from month to month, and sometimes even less frequently. . . . Last winter, starting from September on, I was at his apartment no more than eight times. . . . Moreover, I always respected him as an honorable and noble individual." Dostoevsky argued that there was nothing blameworthy in his conduct. . . . "In point of fact, even now I still do not know what charges have been brought against me. I have only been informed that I took part in general discussions at Petrashevsky's, spoke as a 'freethinker' and, finally, that I read aloud a literary essay *Belinsky's Correspondence with Gogol.*" The accused brilliantly defended himself from these two vague charges: "Who saw what was in my soul? . . . I spoke three times: twice I spoke about literature and once about a theme totally unrelated to politics: the personality and human egoism."

And as to "freethinking," here we find it reduced to an instance of "desiring that which is good for one's fatherland." Then further, what person in our time does not talk about politics, about the West, about censorship? "In the West a terrible spectacle is taking place, an unprecedented drama is being enacted [the February Revolution]. . . . Really, is it possible to bring accusations against me because I view with a token of seriousness the crisis from which poor France is suffering and being torn in two?" He adheres, however, to the tradition of autocracy in Russia and looks only for those reforms which come "from above, from the throne." One may well question the sincerity of this last avowal; a passionate student of Belinsky could hardly at that time have been so well-intentioned a monarchist. It proved more difficult for Dostoevsky to exonerate himself of the second charge: reading Belinsky's famous letter to Gogol apropos of the latter's *Correspondence With Friends.* The spy Antonelli submitted in his report: "At the meeting held on April 15 [1849] Dostoevsky read Gogol's correspondence with Belinsky, and notably, Belinsky's letter to Gogol. This letter summoned a considerable amount of enthusiastic approval from the society, in particular on the part of Balasoglo and Yastrzhemb-sky, especially at that point where Belinsky says that religion has no basis among the Russian people. It was proposed that this letter be distributed in several copies."

In point of fact, having read this letter, Dostoevsky's position was seriously compromised. Belinsky had written to Gogol: "You have failed to observe that Russia sees her salvation not in mysticism, not in asceticism, but in the achievements of civilization, enlightenment, humanitarianism. What she needs is not sermons (she has heard enough of them!) or prayers (she has repeated them over and over to excess!), but an awakening in the people of a sense of their human dignity. . . . Look about you a little more attentively and you will come to see that it [the Russian people] is by nature a *profoundly atheistic people.*"

Dostoevsky acquitted himself confusedly, in verbose and unconvincing fashion.

Whatever the date and month I don't remember (it seems that it was in March), I called on Durov between two and three in the afternoon, and found Belinsky's correspondence with Gogol, which had been sent to me. There on the spot I read it to Durov and Palm. Toward six o'clock Petrashevsky dropped in and stayed for a quarter of an hour. He questioned: "What is the notebook?" I said that it was Belinsky's correspondence with Gogol, and *injudiciously* promised to read it at his home. I did this under the influence of my first impression. Then, after Petrashevsky had left, some other people came. Quite naturally, the conversation turned to Belinsky's essay and I read it a second time. . . . I read it at Petrashevsky's because I had given my word and at that point was unable to retract it. I read it, taking pains not to show partiality either to the one or to the other correspondent.

And so, Dostoevsky read Belinsky's letter *three times*. Furthermore, Filippov had testified before the commission that he made a second copy of the letter from the one that he had received from Dostoevsky, after which the latter had taken both copies himself. The defendant tried to prove that he read Belinsky's essay "as a literary monument, neither more nor less," that he was not in agreement with the letter, he had quarreled with him, etc., etc. All this is quite unlikely, in fact, farfetched. The reading of the letter had evoked an overwhelming response from among those present, and surely Dostoevsky, who read it three times, shared this enthusiasm. The accused's "explanation" amounts simply to a clever diplomatic device: he assumed the role of a professional litterateur defending the theory of pure art, exposed the Petrashevsky circle in an inoffensive, ludicrous guise, depicted Fourierism as a system that was "laughed at, unpopular, hissed, and contemptuously forgotten," minimized the degree of his own intimacy with the "good-hearted dreamer" Petrashevsky, did not betray any of his comrades belonging to the group; he obscured the incident of his having read Belinsky's letter and above all, mentioned not a single word about the other group — Durov's.

The matter could have ended here had the commission not unexpectedly learned of the existence of Durov's circle. Dostoevsky was required to furnish additional testimony. His position immediately took a turn for the worse: he was charged with taking part in a revolutionary cell that had proposed establishing a secret printing press. He was forced to contrive an entire story in order to pacify his interrogators' suspicions. He wrote:

> I frequently went to Durov's soirées. My acquaintance with Durov and Palm began the previous winter. Our similarity of thoughts and tastes drew us together: both of them, Durov and especially Palm, created a most pleasant impression upon me. Not having a large number of friends, I valued this new acquaintance and did not want to lose it. The circle of Durov's acquaintances was *purely artistic and literary*. Shortly thereafter we — that is I, my brother, Durov, Palm, and Pleshcheyev — decided to publish a literary miscellany and as a result, began to see each other more frequently. . . . Soon our meetings developed into literary soirées in which music also played a part.

And then it happened that Filippov made a suggestion that they lithograph the various writings of the group without initially submitting them to the censors. Durov was very displeased with this proposal; Mikhail Mikhailovich Dostoevsky immediately threatened to withdraw from the group, while Fyodor Mikhailovich convinced everyone to reject Filippov's plan. "After this we met no more than once. It was already past Holy Week. . . . Owing to Palm's illness the soirées were completely discontinued." Such was the version set forth by Dostoevsky: an innocent literary-musical group; Filippov suggested establishing a secret printing press in order to publish literary works, but this ridiculous plan was resolutely spurned by all. Throughout this entire story Dostoevsky enacted the most honorable and well-intentioned role.

This is the "open" side of the Dostoevsky affair. Its "clandestine" side was uncovered only in the most recent times. Durov's circle was by no means quite that innocent. It was organized by the most radical element from among those who attended Petrashevsky's Fridays, individuals who were not content with the moderation exhibited by the majority. Petrashevsky himself was not an "overt fighter." He repudiated revolutionary tactics, advocated the use of peaceful propaganda in order gradually to influence the masses and was prepared to admit a constitutional monarchy. The report submitted by the agent Antonelli regarding the meeting of April 1, 1849, is very curious: "At the meeting held on April 1 the discussion centered about freedom of the press, an emendation of legal and court procedures and liberation of the peasants. Golovinsky maintained that the peasants must be freed first, while Petrashevsky argued that securing reforms in the court system was far less dangerous and closer at hand. In the course of these discussions Golovinsky said that the change of government could not take place suddenly and that it would at first be necessary to provide for a dictatorship. Petrashevsky stood up strongly against this and in conclusion said that he would be the first to raise his hand against a dictator."

Among the Petrashevists a radical minority moved to the side and entered into violent opposition to Petrashevsky and the greater part of his clique. This breach noticeably attracted the attention of the prosecuting magistrate, Liprandi. In his official report he wrote that the majority of the Petrashevists were moderate, but that "several members could in fact actually be conspirators." "One could see that it was their intention to act resolutely, without any fear of consequent crime, provided only that it could secure their desired goal, but not everyone was like that. The vast portion of the members proposed to go more slowly but more surely and, in particular, by way of propaganda acting upon the masses." The radical faction stood in favor of revolutionary tactics and set as its objective the liberation of the serfs "even if it were through means of an uprising." A. Milyukov informs us: "Above all we were occupied with the question of liberating the peasants and at our soirées continually discussed by what course and when it could be resolved. Some individuals expressed the opinion

that, faced with the reaction which had set in as a result of the revolutions in Europe, the government would hardly move to decide this
matter and, in all probability, action could be expected sooner from
below than from above. Others, on the contrary, said that our people
would not follow in the steps of the European revolutionaries and
would patiently look to the highest authority for the decision of its
fate."

In the fall of 1848 the "revolutionaries" formed a group centered
about Durov; it included Durov, Speshnyov, Golovinsky, Palm, Pleshcheyev, Filippov, Mombelli, Lvov, Grigoryev, Dostoevsky, and others.
The aim of the society was to prepare the people for an uprising; with
this in view, it is decided clandestinely to set up a printing operation.
A committee of five members was to exercise control. In order to safe-
guard the secret, they found it "necessary to include in one of the para-
graphs of the preliminary indoctrination the threat of punishment
by death in the case of treason; the threat [would] reinforce the secret
even more rigidly, thereby securing it." This resolution reminds us of
Nechayev's *Catechism of a Revolutionary.* Thus Dostoevsky, together
with the Durovists, followed the first step "along Nechayev's path."
The commission of inquiry named Durov "a revolutionary, that is, an
individual who has sought to accomplish reforms by way of violence."

Regarding the student P. Filippov, author of *An Interpretation of
the Ten Commandments,* Dostoevsky stated: "He is still a very young
man, passionate and utterly inexperienced, ready to abandon himself
to the first unreasoned folly, and will think better of it only then
when once he has already created a misfortune. Nonetheless, he does
have many very fine qualities for which I have come to like him —
namely: honesty, a cultured refinement, integrity, valor, and open-
hearted sincerity."

Grigoryev composed a brochure, *Soldiers' Talk,* which was directed
at fomenting agitation. In it he instructed soldiers to set right their
accounts with the tsar. Dostoevsky was an active member of the Durov
group. Palm testifies to his revolutionary bent of mind: "On one occasion when the controversy was reduced to the question: 'Well, and
if it should prove impossible to liberate the peasants otherwise than
through an insurrection?' Dostoevsky with his wonted impressibility
cried out: 'That's right, even if it has to be through an insurrection!'"
In his novel *Aleksey Svobodin,* Palm reproduces several of Dostoevsky's features: "Svobodin calmly and slowly remarked: 'The emancipation of the serfs assuredly will be the first step toward our great

future.'" Milyukov recalls how Dostoevsky, flowing with his usual energy, read Pushkin's poem *The Village.* "As though it were now, I hear the exultant voice with which he read the closing couplet:

> "'Will I see, o friends, my people unoppressed.'"[A]

P. Semyonov-Tyan-Shansky while resolutely denying Dostoevsky's actual revolutionary involvement, nonetheless admits the possibility of his being "carried away." "Dostoevsky was never a revolutionary," he writes, "and he could not be [?], but as a man of sentiment, he was capable of being carried away by feelings of indignation and even by rage at the sight of violence being inflicted upon the humiliated and wronged, which took place, for example, when he saw or learned how a sergeant-major in the Finnish Regiment had been forced to run the gauntlet. It was only during moments of such outbursts that Dostoevsky *was capable of going out onto the square with a red standard.* . . ."

According to N. P. Grigoryev's assertion Dostoevsky undertook to "explicate socialism" at one of the meetings of Durov's circle. We know nothing about the character of this society's gatherings; not one of its participants revealed the secret. However, it is possible to formulate a notion of its revolutionary tactics on the basis of Liprandi's report: it relates to conversations which were conducted at Petrashevsky's among the radical members.

> At the meetings they engaged in deliberations as to how to arouse people of various classes to discontent and indignation against the government, how to incite the peasants against the landowners, against the authorities, how to profit from the schismatics' fanaticism, and in other classes of society to undermine and destroy all religious feelings which they themselves have already utterly dismissed, preaching that religion impedes the development of the human mind and consequently, even of happiness; and here they deliberated with regard to special measures, how to proceed in the Caucasus, in Siberia, in the Pre-Baltic Provinces, in Finland, Poland, in Little Russia.

If Liprandi was accurately informed about the meetings at Petrashevsky's, then we can with reason surmise that this was the same program propounded by the radicals in Durov's circle. In order to ac-

---

[A] A. Milyukov's memoirs are exceedingly unreliable. He depicts Dostoevsky in the forties as the conservative monarchist which he was in the seventies.

complish these ends, it was resolved that they should organize a secret printing operation.

Two important documents shed light on the active role which Dostoevsky played in this conspiracy. These are Speshnyov's testimony before the inquiry commission and a letter of Apollon Maikov to P. A. Viskovatov written in the year 1885.

During the course of the investigation Speshnyov declared: "In November or the last part of October 1848 several persons who for one reason or other were displeased with Petrashevsky's society, decided to stop visiting there and to open their own salon. So Pleshcheyev and Dostoevsky at one time came to me and said that they would like to meet with their acquaintances some other place and not at Petrashevsky's, where it was both boring and no one talked about anything — that is about scholarly topics — and the people on the whole were unknown, and it was dreadful even to utter a word." This shrewd, cautious statement discloses how several individuals who were "displeased," separated themselves from Petrashevsky's group and proposed to open their own salon. The initiative in this measure was undertaken by Dostoevsky and Pleshcheyev.

In 1885 Apollon Maikov wrote to Viskovatov:

One day, I think in January of 1848,[B] F. M. Dostoevsky came to see me and stayed to pass the night — I used to live alone then in my own apartment. My bed was near the wall, while opposite there was a divan which had been made up for Dostoevsky. And now he began to tell me that he had been delegated to approach me with a proposition: Petrashevsky, he said, was an imbecile, an actor, and an empty chatterer — he can never come out with anything intelligent; and that those of his visitors who were somewhat more capable had on their own conceived of a venture which he knew nothing about and into which he would not be admitted, namely: Speshnyov, P. Filippov (these have died, so I am naming them; the others, it appears, are still living and for that reason will continue to pass over them in silence as I have for thirty-seven whole years remained silent up till now about the entire episode) and then five or six more, I don't remember, included among whom was Dostoevsky. And they had decided to ask yet a seventh or eighth member, that is myself. They intended to set up a secret printing operation and to publish, etc. I argued the imprudence, the danger of such an activity, and

[B] Not 1848, but 1849.

that they were headed for what was obvious destruction. And besides, this was my principal argument, both you and I are poets, consequently, people who are not practical, and we have not even succeeded in setting our own affairs in order, whereas political activity is in the highest degree a practical efficiency, and so forth. And I remember — there Dostoevsky sat, like dying Socrates in front of his friends, wearing a nightshirt with unbuttoned collar, and exerting all his eloquence *as regards the holiness of this affair, our duty to save the fatherland,* etc., so that I finally began to laugh and joke. "And so it's no?" he concluded. "No, no, and no!" Next morning, after tea, he said as he was leaving: "You don't need talk about this — not a word." "That goes without saying." Afterward I found out that a hand printing press had been ordered in various parts of the city in accord with a sketch prepared by Filippov, and a day or two before the arrest had been brought and assembled in the apartment of one of the principals, M-v,[o] whom, it seems, I did not even know. When he was arrested and a search was conducted, they failed to take any note of this apparatus. He had a number of physical and other instruments and equipment standing there in a closet. However, they placed an official seal upon the door. After the commission had departed and he had been led away, his servants were able to take the door off its hinges without impairing the seals, and secretly removed the press. In this way the evidence was destroyed. The commission knew nothing about this entire affair, nor did Petrashevsky, and of all those avoiding arrest, I was the only one who also knew.

In the light of these facts, which have only recently been disclosed, the confession contained in *The Diary of a Writer* for 1873 now stands revealed in all its extraordinary candor and we have come to understand what is meant when the author declared that "he could have become a Nechayevist in the days of his youth." This revolutionary cell with its secret printing press and program of propagandizing insurrection is in actual fact not far removed from Nechayev's organization. In his novel *The Devils* Dostoevsky accused and expelled many devils from possessed Russia, but he remembered that even he himself at one time could have been included among that number.

Toward the end of his life the writer told D. Averkiyev that he "accounted the Petrashevists and *himself in that number* as the origina-

[o] Perhaps Mordvinov.

tors and disseminators of revolutionary teaching." After the "regeneration of his convictions" he considered the revolutionary period in his life as a renunciation of Christ and a sin against the Russian people. When once it was contended: "Nevertheless, how unjust it was to have exiled you!" he protested in annoyance: "No, it was just; the people would have condemned us." Yet for all that, it was only out of his love for the people, for the sake of their liberation, that he did enter upon the destructive "way of Nechayev." The commission of inquiry was right in classifying Dostoevsky as "one of the most important."

The central figure in Durov's circle was Speshnyov, a person exercising a vast and mysterious influence upon Dostoevsky. V. Semevsky[D] compiled some curious information regarding him. Speshnyov came from a rich family, studied at the Lyceum, though he left it without having completed his course of study. He had a love affair with Savelyeva who abandoned her husband and two children in order to go abroad with him. There she poisoned herself out of jealousy. Speshnyov lived abroad for four years (1842-1846) and in Dresden was reputed the lion of foreign, especially Polish, society. According to Bakunin, "Ye. P. Yazykova, her daughter and all their lady-friends, even a certain 70 year-old Polish countess, were in love with him. However, not only the women, but even young Polish men, for the most part those of Czartoryski's aristocratic faction, were delirious about him. His inseparable Seid was Edmond Choietski." Ogaryova-Tuchkova wrote about him: "His sympathetic outward appearance attracted universal attention to him. He was tall, had regular features. Dark-blond curls fell in billows onto his shoulders; his eyes, large and grey, were covered with a kind of quiet sadness." In 1845, in Dresden, Speshnyov wrote a tract on secret societies and studied the history of primitive Christianity. "He was struck at the time by the world influence and utter success of this ancient secret society," and began to contemplate the creation of a corresponding society in our modern world. His work was divided into four chapters: 1) the Essenian school and the growth of primitive Christian society, 2) a history of several modern secret societies, 3) the differences to be found in the activity of this Christian society as opposed to the secret societies, 4) the optimum structuring of a secret society consonant with conditions in Russia.

He also considered editing a free journal in Russian to be published abroad. Upon returning to Petersburg, Speshnyov began to frequent

[D] V. I. Semevsky, M. V. Butashevich-Petrashevsky i petrashevtsi (M. V. Butashevich-Petrashevsky and the Petrashevists), Moscow 1922.

Petrashevsky's, but the milieu there failed to appeal to him. He was one of the first Russians who had become acquainted with Marx and Engel's *Communist Manifesto*. At Petrashevsky's "he gave only one lecture which, it appears, proved both dry and concise, with the result that he was not prepared to broadcast his irreligious ideas any further and chose decidedly not to present any more interpretations, but to write for himself." In his lecture he had preached "socialism, atheism, terrorism, everything, everything that is good on earth." According to Mombelli's statement, "Speshnyov declared that he was a communist, but in general he did not like to express his opinions and held himself *somewhat mysteriously*. This especially was annoying to Petrashevsky. The latter frequently complained of Speshnyov's reticence and said that he always wanted to appear not in fact as he really was." Even at his home Speshnyov used to talk only "as much as proved necessary in order to prompt others to speak, to sustain the conversation, while he himself would merely listen. . . . He was courteous and attentive to his guests, but always cold, immovably calm; his exterior never changed its expression."

It is understandable that the communist Speshnyov could find no interest in the liberal chatter that occupied Petrashevsky's circle. Very likely it was precisely on his initiative (and not at all on Dostoevsky's) that the Durov group withdrew. It is further possible that it was this theoretician of secret societies who composed the statutes of this new body and functioned as its primary leader. When his apartment was searched, a "compulsory pledge" was found: "I, the undersigned, of my own will, after sound reflection and in accord with my own desire, enter this Russian society and take upon myself the following obligations which I will carry out explicitly." Here is the first of these obligations: "When the executive committee of the society upon having considered the society's resources, the circumstances and the opportunity which is presented, shall determine that the time for the uprising has come, then I pledge, without sparing myself, to take full open part in the rebellion and fighting." There can be no doubt that on one of these affirmations Dostoevsky's signature was also to be found.

Cold, handsome, and mysterious, Speshnyov attained an unlimited power over the writer's soul. In 1854 Dostoevsky wrote about him: "The wondrous fate of that man; wherever and however he makes his appearance, the most unconstrained, the most impervious people immediately surround him with devotion and respect." Pleshcheyev in a letter to Dobrolyubov (1860) said, regarding Speshnyov: "One can assert positively that out of all our number this was *the most remarkable personality.*"

Dostoevsky felt not only this strange individual's captivating charm, but also his demonic force. Speshnyov was his evil genius. Doctor S. Yanovsky in his *Memoirs* writes: "Shortly before his arrest Dostoevsky became rather apathetic, more irritable, more easily offended and prone to find fault over the most insignificant trifles, began especially often to complain of dizzy spells. The reason for this, according to Dostoevsky's own admission, was his familiarity with Speshnyov, or to put it more exactly, a loan which he had made from him." To the doctor's assurances that this gloomy state of mind would pass, Dostoevsky once replied: "No, it will not pass, but will continue on and on to torment me because of my having taken money from Speshnyov (in this respect he named a sum of about 500 rubles). *Now I am with him and his.* And I'll never be in a position to recoup this sum, but then he wouldn't even take the money back; that's the kind of individual he is. Do you understand that from now on I have *my own Mephistopheles.*"

Dostoevsky was tormented by the thought that he had sold his soul to the "devil." "Now I am with him and *his.*" From now on he had his own Mephistopheles just as Ivan Karamazov has his devil. Speshnyov prodded him on to sin and crime; he was his somber "double."

Nikolay Speshnyov was rich and handsome, an aristocratic gentleman with a turbulent romantic past; for a long time he lived abroad; upon returning to Russia, he preached atheism and motivated a secret revolutionary society. He was cold, reserved, dissembling; "his exterior never changes its expression." We recognize familiar features here: Dostoevsky conferred immortality upon him in the image of Nikolay Vsevolodovich Stavrogin (*The Devils*).

V I I

The Fortress and Penal Servitude

The secret police maintained a watch on the Petrashevists. Antonelli, an artist's son, who was a former student at Petersburg University, used to submit reports on their activities to Liprandi, an official in the Ministry of Internal Affairs. On April 22, 1849, the chief of gendarmes Count Orlov advised the Sovereign that the "conspirators" were to be arrested. On his memorandum Nikolai I noted: "I have read everything; the matter is important for if it was but only foolish prattle, even then it is in the highest degree criminal and intolerable. Set about the arrest as indicated. Go with God! May His will be done!"

In the year 1860 Dostoevsky wrote an account of his arrest in an album belonging to A. P. Milyukov's daughter:

The 22nd or better to say 23rd of April, I returned home sometime around four o'clock from N. P. Grigoryev's, lay down in bed, and immediately fell asleep. Not more than an hour passed when I felt, as though in a dream, that some strange and suspicious persons had entered my room. There was the clatter of a saber accidently knocking against something. What on earth is going on? With effort I open my eyes and hear a soft, sympathetic voice: "Get up!" I look: there is a quarter or district superintendent of police with a handsome pair of side whiskers. But it was not he who had spoken; the gentleman who spoke was dressed in light blue, wearing a lieutenant-colonel's epaulettes. "What's happened?" I asked, raising myself in bed. "At the command of . . ." I look: it actually was "at the command. . . ." At the door a soldier was standing, also in blue. It was then his saber that had rattled. . . .

After a search the prisoner was taken out. "At the entrance a carriage was waiting; the soldier, myself, the police officer and the lieutenant-colonel got into the carriage. We proceeded to the Fontanka in the direction of the Chain Bridge by the Summer Gardens.[1] There we encountered much bustling about and groups of people. I met many acquaintances."

That night Petrashevsky and thirty-three members of his circle were arrested. By mistake even Dostoevsky's younger brother, Andrey Mikhailovich, was taken into custody and for two weeks was detained in the fortress. Mikhail Mikhailovich, his older brother, who had now and again attended Petrashevsky's Fridays, was also held. Owing to lack of evidence, he was released after two months. The trial began: the writing of "explanations," of supplementary explanations, the interrogations of the inquiry commission, the encounters with General Rostovtsev, who characterized Dostoevsky as "clever, independent, crafty, headstrong." Lyubov Dostoevskaya has suggested that her father had this his prosecuting magistrate in mind when he created the figure of Porfiry Petrovich in *Crime and Punishment*. The defendant's tactics consisted in concealing, refuting, portraying everything in the most innocent light, not mentioning anyone's name.

For eight months Dostoevsky sat confined in the Alekseyevsky ravelin of Petropavlovsky Fortress. In his dungeon cell, in the darkness and quiet, the prisoner was cut off from the world. At first the accused were not even allowed to receive books. Many did not survive: Grigoryev and Katenev went mad; Yastrzhembsky attempted to commit suicide; Akhsharumov put aside a nail with which to hang himself. Later Dostoevsky told Vsevolod Solovyov: "When I arrived in the fortress, I thought that this was the end for me too, thought that I would not last three days, and all at once I grew perfectly calm. Now what did I do there? I wrote *A Little Hero* — read it, really is there any trace in it of bitterness, sufferings? I used to dream peaceful, kind, good dreams, and later, as time went on, the better things became."

Only on July 11 did the prisoner receive a first letter from his brother Mikhail Mikhailovich; answering him, he wrote:

I am not despondent; it is, of course, boring and loathsome, but what can one do! And besides, it's not always even boring. . . . Naturally, I drive all seductive thoughts from my imagination, but other times there'll be no controlling them and so my old life breaks in upon my soul with its former impressions and again I relive the past. . . . I haven't lost time to no avail: *I've thought out three tales and two novels*. I'm writing one of them now, but am afraid of over-

[1] I.e., they were driving to the offices of the Third Section.

working. . . . This work, especially if it is done with pleasure (and I have never toiled so *con amore* as now), has always proved exhausting and had an effect upon my nerves.

In the casemate the writer's inner life was not weakened, but to the contrary attained even greater intensity. This force of imagination and creativity is astounding. Three tales and two novels! And he worked with such enthusiasm as to be forced to restrain himself. . . . He was depressed that throughout the entire summer he would not see the "green leaves." "Do you remember how sometimes for our walks we used to be taken out into the little garden during May? It was just beginning to turn green then. . . ."

Leaves, "little, sticky green leaves," are a favorite symbol of Dostoevsky's. For him all the beauty of God's world is contained in this humble image. A little green leaf is to his heroes the most irrefutable proof of the existence of God and of the coming transfiguration (*The Brothers Karamazov*). In his next letter (August 27) the prisoner complained that "especially at night" his impressionability had increased. "I constantly feel that the floor is swaying beneath me, and to sit in my room is like being in a ship's cabin. From all this I conclude that my nerves are in disorder." And he makes a very important admission regarding the nature of his creative activity: "When in the past such a *'nervous state'* would come upon me, I made use of it in order to write — you will always write better and more in such a condition — but now I hold back so as not once and for all to destroy myself." Dostoevsky's inspiration was related to a nervous impulse which "exhausts" and can "destroy." In a third letter (September 14) he writes still more explicitly about this onslaught of thoughts and images. "It's just like being under an air-pump which is forever drawing off the air. Everything has gone out of me into my head, and from my head into thought — everything, absolutely everything — and in spite of this, the work gets greater every day. Books are but a drop in the sea, yet nonetheless they help. While my own work, it seems, simply squeezes out the last juices. *Otherwise though, I'm happy with it.*" Looking through the writer's notebooks and rough drafts, we understand what literary work meant to him. Tens of plot variations, hundreds of situations and images would rush past in his mind; he lacked the force to set them onto paper; he succumbed beneath these whirlwinds of imagination. However overburdened his novels may be, they are still only an insignificant part of the original designs. He actually did think "in whole worlds." Reading was to his creative fantasy only a "drop in the sea"; the prisoner continually asked his brother to send him books and journals. He read *Fatherland Notes*, Shakespeare, the Bible, two accounts of journeys to the Holy Land, the works of St. Dmitry of Rostov. On October 1 Mikhail Mikhailovich sent him four volumes of Russian authors (apparently in the Smirdin editions),[2] three volumes of Dahl's works (*Tales of the Cossack Lugansky*) and Sakharov's *Legends of the Russian People*. Dostoevsky's interest in the Bible and spiritual themes is significant. The journeys through the Holy Land and the writings of St. Dmitry of Rostov later would be reflected in the style of the elder Zosima's life. During the whole of the eight months' imprisonment few events took place. In August he was permitted to walk about in the yard where there were seventeen trees, and in the evening was given leave to have a candle; in September, with the approach of autumn, his "hypochondria" became more aggravated. "Now the sky has begun to frown, and it was that bright patch of sky, visible from my casemate, which guaranteed my health and complacent frame of mind." And nonetheless, in spite of all the hardships, sicknesses, the nervous disorder, and exhausting work of thought — he was full of life. "I anticipated much worse," he confessed to his brother, "and now I see that *there is within me such a store of vitality, that it cannot even be consumed. . . .*"

He had in him that indestructible vital force which Ivan Karamazov mockingly calls the "indecent Karamazov thirst for life." This mysterious gift helped Dostoevsky to sustain his terrible fate and his superhuman genius.

Of the "three tales and two novels" conceived in Petropavlovsky Fortress, one tale was written, *A Little Hero. From Unknown Memoirs.*[A] It appeared in print only eight years later. In the prison, while awaiting the decision of his fate, Dostoevsky created one of his brightest and most joyous works. At the village of the rich landowner T-v, near Moscow, a gay and numerous society had gathered together. "It seemed like a holiday which had even begun with the thought of never coming to a close." Dances, music, singing, picnics, riding parties, amateur theatre, "the diversions followed one after another." The author compares the relations of one lovely lady and her admirer to Benedick and Beatrice's amorous contention in Shakespeare's comedy *Much Ado about Nothing*. In the fortress he had been reading Shake-

---

[2] The publisher Smirdin issued standard, popular editions of the Russian authors.
[A] Published in *Fatherland Notes* (1857).

speare, and the poetic joy of life that imbued the Renaissance was reflected in his description of the "eternal holiday" in the village near Moscow. Against this background of music, laughter, jousts of wit, among charming women and gallant young men, an eleven-year-old boy comes to an awakening of love. Chivalry is inherent in a child's pure heart: the boy falls in love with the beautiful Mme M. and becomes her "*cavalier servant.*" The teasing which his bashful sentiment encounters reduces him to despair. "The first untried, as yet uncultivated feeling had been harshly wounded in me, in a child; the first fragrant, virginal shame had so early been exposed and insulted." Like a mediaeval page he serves his lady faithfully, and in order to win her regard, performs an heroic feat: he mounts and rides a raging horse. "Really there was in all this, as it were, something truly chivalrous." The author insists upon this image: "All my *chivalry*, however, began and ended in less than an instant, or else it would have gone badly for the *knight.*" When the hero, scarcely breathing, is taken down from the horse, his glance meets the eyes of Mme M., who has turned pale. Now as befits the "lady of one's heart," she presents her page with a "crimson gauze scarf." All around, shouts arise: "De Lorge! Toggenburg!"[3] But Mme M. loves another. By chance the boy sees her tearfully bid farewell to N. and drop a letter which she has received from him. He saves her from disgrace and ruin by a most "chivalrous gesture": in a bouquet of flowers he returns to her the envelope that he has found. Schiller's romanticism triumphs; the "noble and beautiful" are spontaneously disclosed in the child's first love. The tale ends with a "revelation of the heart." "And all at once my bosom heaved," relates the little hero, "began to ache as if from something that had pierced it, and tears, sweet tears, poured from my eyes. I hid my face in my hands and, trembling like a blade of grass, freely surrendered myself to the first consciousness and *revelation of my heart,* to the first yet vague apprehension of my nature. My early childhood ended with that instant." The heart opening itself to love, opens as well to the entire world. In this tale written in prison, we find that which is almost always absent in Dostoevsky's works: the sky, the sun, air. And in what an exalted romantic tone is the *paysage* itself described:

The sun had risen high and luxuriantly was floating above us through the deep, dark-blue sky, as though melting away in its own fire. The

---

[3] Knights, heroes of two of Schiller's poems.

reapers had already moved far off; behind them endless furrows of mown grass crept without interruption, and from time to time a faintly stirring breeze wafted its fragrant exhalation toward us. Round about there was the unbroken concert of those who "neither reap, nor sow," but are unconstrained as the air they cleave with their frolicsome wings. It seemed that at this moment every flower, the last blade of grass, as it consumed itself in sacrificial aroma, was saying to the One Who created it: "Father! I am blessed and happy!"

In its composition *A Little Hero* is related to *Netochka Nezvanova*. The novel was left unfinished, but its idea — the awakening of consciousness within a young being — continued to disturb the author. And after his arrest, instead of proceeding with work on *Netochka*, he turned to a new tale employing this same theme. His tearful and lifeless heroine is replaced by a "little hero." The action, extending in the novel over eight years, is concentrated in the tale to a period of several days; two successive stages of development (the episode with Katya and that of Aleksandra Mikhailovna) are merged together. The structure is the same: at its center stands a young being who for the first time experiences love, is credulous, ardent, untried; surrounding it we find two female images embodying two aspects of love: love-torture and love-sacrifice. In the novel these are Princess Katya and Aleksandra Mikhailovna, in the tale the "blonde" and Mme M.

For a long time Katya torments Netochka with her derision, feigned indifference and coquetterie; the "blonde" abuses the eleven-year-old boy, taking pleasure in his sufferings and shame. At a private theatrical she abruptly suggests that he sit down on her lap. "Completely unexpectedly, to my greatest surprise, she most painfully squeezed my hand in her mischievous warm fingers and began to wring my fingers, but so painfully that I exerted all my strength so as not to cry out. . . . The rascally creature guffawed right in my face, like a mad woman, and meanwhile pinched and wrung my poor fingers ever more and more violently." From that evening she kept after him "without measure or conscience," became his "persecutor and tyrant." Netochka performs a courageous deed, assumes Katya's blame, and thereafter the young princess' hostility is abruptly changed into the most ecstatic tenderness. The little hero mounts the raging horse; the "blonde" rushes to embrace and kiss him, "moved, proud of me, joyful." Then she puts him to bed and touchingly looks after him. "Saying goodnight to her, I fervently and ardently embraced her as my dearest, as my closest friend. . . . I almost cried pressing myself to her bosom. . . ."

Katya "astonishes" with her dazzling beauty, "one of those before which you suddenly come to a stop as though transfixed." The "blonde" likewise "was wonderously pretty, and there was something in her beauty that struck one's eye even at first glance. Something like lightning used to dazzle in this face. . . ." These "proud beauties" accordingly resemble one another in their gay laughter and as well in their cruel tormenting.

Mme M. in the tale is a blood sister of the novel's Aleksandra Mikhailovna. She too is a wounded heart, a "meek sufferer." "Her large, sad eyes, full of fire and strength, used to look timid and anxious, as though every minute afraid of something hostile and threatening, and this strange timidity at times cast so despondent a veil over her peaceful, *meek* features, which recalled the luminous faces of Italian Madonnas, that looking at her, one soon also became sad." Such women, continues the author, "are like sisters of mercy in life." Netochka learns of Aleksandra Mikhailovna's unhappy love from a letter which she accidently finds; the denouement of Mme M.'s romance takes place before the eyes of the "little hero." Parting with N., "she stood white as a handkerchief, and great tears broke forth from her eyes." The letter motif recurs. Mme M. loses her beloved's farewell letter; the boy finds and returns it to her. The heroine of the tale's love is as innocent and sacrificial as that of the heroine in the novel. "This relationship," notes the author, "was not perhaps such as one could imagine at first glance. Perhaps this kiss was in farewell, perhaps it was the last faint reward for the sacrifice that had been made to her peace and honor. N. was going away; he was leaving her perhaps for good."

Mme M.'s husband continues the development of Yulian Mastakovich in *A Christmas Tree Party and a Wedding* and of Aleksandra Mikhailovna's husband in *Netochka Nezvanova*. The author displays this type as "a good heart which can prove itself the greatest of villains." M. M. is "jealous not out of love, but from self-love." He expounds on "a philanthropy, sound and rationally justified," but in point of fact, is a hypocrite and egoist. His characteristics are enriched by several new features: he is a "European, a man of the times with samplings of new ideas and modish phrases." Speaking about this "Tartuffe and Falstaff," the author unexpectedly falls into a bilious and irritable tone; we remark in his words personal affront and vindictiveness. This odious "wit, chatterer, and storyteller," sarcastic and self-centered, carries a sharp suggestion of his recent friend, now his enemy: Ivan Sergeyevich Turgenev. If this conjecture is true, one can consider the figure of M. M. as a first caricature of the celebrated novelist and a rough sketch for the portrait of Karmazinov in *The Devils*.

The sentimental tale *A Little Hero* ends Dostoevsky's creative work prior to his sentence of penal servitude. His last word was an affirmation of the "noble and beautiful" in the Schillerian spirit. On the threshold of a new life, Siberia and exile, the writer bade good-bye to his romantic youth. In parody Turgenev called him a "Knight of Mournful Figure." Dostoevsky took up the challenge: his tale is devoted to a "knight" . . . to a "little hero."

At last the inquiry regarding the Petrashevsky affair was completed. The Auditoriat General's verdict declared:

Retired Lieutenant Dostoevsky for having taken part in criminal designs, having circulated a letter by the writer Belinsky which was filled with impertinent expressions against the Orthodox Church and the sovereign power and for having attempted, together with others, to circulate works against the government through means of a private printing press, is to be stripped of all the rights owing to his station[4] and to be exiled to penal servitude in a fortress for eight years.

The Emperor appended the decision: "For four years, and then into the ranks."[5] Although having pardoned the conspirators who were sentenced to death, Nikolai I ordered that this reprieve be announced on the square after the formalities of an execution had taken place. All the particulars of the ceremony were set forth in "highly secret documents." The Sovereign entered personally into all the details: the scaffold's dimensions, the uniforms to be worn by the condemned, the priest's vestments, the escort of carriages, the tempo of the drum-roll, the route from the fortress to the place of shooting, the breaking of the swords, the putting on of white shirts, the executioner's functions, the shackling of the prisoners. The instructions were revised three times. On December 22, 1849, this terrible mock execution was staged. On the same day Dostoevsky wrote to his brother Mikhail:

Today, December 22, we were driven to Semyonovsky Parade Ground. There the death sentence was read to us all, we were given the cross to kiss, swords were broken over our heads, and our final toilet was arranged (white shirts). Then three of us were set

[4] At the time of his mock-execution Dostoevsky was stripped of all his rights as a noble; he was reinstated only when he was promoted to officer.
[5] As a private soldier.

against the posts so as to carry out the execution. We were summoned in threes; consequently I was in the second group, and there was not more than a minute left to live. I remembered you, my brother, and all yours; at the last minute you, you alone, were in my mind, and it was only then that I realized how much I love you, my dearest brother! I also succeeded in embracing Pleshcheyev and Durov, who were beside me, and bade farewell to them. Finally the retreat was sounded, those who had been tied to the posts were led back, and they read to us that His Imperial Majesty granted us our lives. Thereupon followed the actual sentence. . . .

Brother, I'm not depressed and haven't lost spirit. Life everywhere is life, life is in ourselves and not in the external. There will be people near me, and to be a human among human beings, and remain one forever, no matter what misfortunes befall, not to become depressed, and not to falter — this is what life is, herein lies its task. I have come to recognize this. This idea has entered into my flesh and blood. Yes, it's true! That head which created, lived by the highest life of art, which acknowledged and had come to know the highest demands of the spirit, that head has been cut from my shoulders. Memory remains, and the images I have created and still not molded in flesh. They will leave their harsh mark upon me, it is true! But my heart is left me, and the same flesh and blood which likewise can love and suffer and desire and remember, and this is, after all, life. On voit le soleil! Well, good-bye, brother! Do not grieve for me. . . . Never till now have such rich and healthy stores of spiritual life throbbed in me. But whether the body will endure, I don't know. . . .

My God! How many images which I have experienced, have created anew, will be lost, will be darkened in my mind or like poison overflow in my blood! Yes, if I'm not permitted to write, I shall perish! . . . There is no bitterness or malice in my soul; at this moment I gladly would love and embrace be it anyone from my past. It is a consolation; I experienced it today when in the face of death I said farewell to those dear to me. . . . As I look back upon the past and think how much time has been spent to no avail, how much of it was lost in delusions, in mistakes, in idleness, in not knowing how to live; what little store I set upon it, how many times I sinned against my heart and spirit — for this my heart bleeds. Life is a gift, life is happiness, every moment could have been an age of happiness.

Si jeunesse savait! Now, upon changing my life, I am being born again in a new form. Brother! I swear to you I will not lose hope and will preserve my spirit and my heart in purity. I'll be reborn to the better. This is my entire hope, all my consolation!

This letter was written within several hours after the scaffold. Here are the words of a man who has just seen death before him. In the letter the bewilderment of soul and joyous excitement of a return to life are sounded. Trials and sufferings are nothing in comparison to the *supreme value* of life. "Life is a gift, life is happiness." At this moment Dostoevsky felt intensely the divine mystery of existence, the *grace of life*. This *mystical naturalism* rests at the base of his philosophy. The grace of life, which is greater than understanding, greater than its justification, is also spoken of by Prince Myshkin and Ippolit in *The Idiot*, Makar Dolgoruky in *A Raw Youth*, and by the elder Zosima in *The Brothers Karamazov*. Dostoevsky's sinners are saved through their love of "living life" (Raskolnikov, Ivan Karamazov); hearts that are apathetic and numb perish despite all their wisdom (Kirilov, Stavrogin). As he went forth into exile, the writer swore loyalty to the ideal of his youth: religion of the heart. The "highest demands of the spirit," art, creative work had been taken away, but the "heart was left" and "that is, after all, life"! To the blessing of life is joined the glorification of love; this is the leitmotif of *ecstasies* in Dostoevsky (Alyosha in a transport of love kisses the ground). In the letter we encounter the French phrase: *"On voit le soleil!"* Sentenced to death, he remembered Victor Hugo's work, *Dernier jour d'un condamné.*[B] "Je veux bien les galères. Cinq ans de galères, et que tout soit dit — ou vingt ans — ou à perpétuité avec le fer rouge. Mais grâce de la vie! Un forçat, cela marche encore, cela va et vient, *cela voit le soleil!*" The same expression, "I see the sun," is also repeated by Mitya Karamazov upon being condemned to penal servitude.

Lastly, we learn from the letter that several sheets of manuscript, the rough drafts of a play and a novel plus the completed tale *A Child's Story* were confiscated from the prisoner. *A Child's Story* is the original title of *A Little Hero;* the rough outlines of the play and novel have been lost.

The scaffold proved a crucial event in the writer's inner life. His life was "split in two," the past was ended, there began another existence, a "rebirth in a new form." In order to realize the full significance of this second birth, long years were demanded. From the day of mock execution almost twenty years passed before Dostoevsky was able to transpose his personal experience into the language of artistic forms.

[B] A Bem was the first to draw attention to this quotation from Hugo.

In the novel *The Idiot* Prince Myshkin tells of the last minutes of a man condemned to death. In this description motifs are developed which were already remarked in the letter written to his brother December 22, 1849: the circumstances of the execution are dramatized, the condemned's inner state is analyzed with greater depth, and the mystical feeling of life is intensified.

Here is Prince Myshkin's story:

This man had once been led out together with others to the scaffold, and a sentence of death was read to him: he was to be shot for a political crime. About twenty minutes later a reprieve was read and another degree of punishment was allotted; but nonetheless the time intervening between the two sentences, twenty minutes or at least a quarter of an hour, he passed in the undoubted conviction that in several minutes he suddenly would die. . . . He remembered everything with extraordinary clarity and used to say that he would never forget anything that occurred during those minutes. About twenty paces from the scaffold around which soldiers and people were standing, three posts had been set in the ground inasmuch as there were several criminals. The first three were brought to the posts, tied, the death garment (long white smocks) was given them, and white hoods were pulled over their eyes so that the rifles would not be seen; then a detachment of several soldiers was drawn up opposite each post. My acquaintance was standing eighth in the line so that his turn was in the third group. A priest went about to each of them with a cross. It appeared that he had not more than about five minutes to live. He told me that these five minutes seemed like an endless stretch of time, an enormous wealth; he felt that during those five minutes he would live through so many lives that now there was as yet no need to think of the last instant, so that he made various calculations: he set aside time to take leave of his comrades — for this he reckoned about two minutes — then he set aside two minutes in order to think of himself for the last time, and then for the last time to take a look around. . . . He was dying at the age of twenty-seven, healthy and strong. . . . Then when he had said farewell to his comrades, there came those two minutes which he had kept to think of himself; he had known beforehand what he would think about; he wanted just to imagine as quickly and vividly as possible how it all could be: he now existed and was alive, while after three minutes he would merely be *something*, someone or something, and so who? And where? All this he thought to resolve in those two minutes! Not far off was a church, and the top of its gilt roof gleamed in the bright sun. He remembered that he looked with horrible intensity at this roof and at the rays which flashed from it; he could not tear himself away from the rays; it seemed that these rays were to be his new nature, that after three minutes he somehow would merge with them. . . . The uncertainty and repugnance of this new thing which would be and even now was coming, were terrible; but he said that at that time nothing was more unbearable than the constant thought: "What if I were not to die! What if I should return to life — what an eternity! And all this would be mine! I then would turn every minute into an entire age, would lose nothing, would take careful count of every minute, would no longer waste a single thing!"

When compared with the letter to his brother, we find only one new theme distinguishing Prince Myshkin's narrative, the reflection as to what would be after death: "something" or "someone"? Nothingness or personal immortality?

The question remains undecided: ("All this he thought to resolve in those two minutes"). The immediate sensation speaks more readily of a pantheistic dissolution of the consciousness in cosmic life (merging with the rays), than of a continuation of personal life; and after death the soul remains chained to this world, no *transcensus* takes place; the condemned by all his thoughts and feelings is immersed in this earthly life and the idea of belonging to another world is for him "uncertainty and repugnance." At the last minute the condemned knows neither Christian repentance nor prayer. "A priest went about to each of them with a cross" — only passing reference is made to the "ritual." The name of Christ is not mentioned.

Prince Myshkin suggests that Adelaida Yepanchina draw the face of a condemned man a moment before the guillotine's fall. He mounts the last step of the scaffold "white as paper."

Then, when this weakness was beginning, the priest quickly, with a rapid gesture and in silence, suddenly raised the cross to his very lips, one of those little crosses, silver, Western style;[6] he raised it often, each minute. And as soon as the cross would touch his lips, he opened his eyes and again for several seconds seemed to come to

[6] The Western cross has four points; the Russian has two additional crossbars and, consequently, eight points.

life and his legs would move. He kissed the cross with greed, hastened to kiss it, as though hastening not to forget to lay aside provision for himself, *in case of need, but it is not likely that at that moment he was aware of anything religious.*

Through this visual image the horror of death, the agony of a soul is conveyed. Finally the entire remarkable scene is summarized by two symbols: the criminal's head and the cross. "Draw the scaffold," says Prince Myshkin, "so that only the very last step can be seen clearly in the foreground; the criminal has stepped onto it; his head, his face are as white as paper; the priest stretches out the cross; the former with greed extends his blue lips, and — *he knows everything*. . . . The cross and the head — there is the picture!"

What does this terrible "he knows everything" mean? What does the dying man know, greedily kissing the cross "in case of need"? That nonbeing awaits him and that after death there is no resurrection? Prince Myshkin's account is Dostoevsky's confession; in 1849, in the face of death, he was still a "child of nonbelief and doubt."

On Christmas Eve, just a few hours before departing for penal servitude, the writer was allowed to see his brother. A. Milyukov, who was present at the brothers' farewell, writes in his *Memoirs:* "Fyodor Mikhailovich was calm and comforted him [M. M.]. . . . 'Now, stop it, brother,' he said,

you know me, I'm not going to my funeral, you're not seeing me off to the grave — and in penal servitude there aren't wild beasts, but men, perhaps even better than I, perhaps more worthy than I. And we'll see each other again, I hope for that, I don't even doubt that we shall see each other. . . . And you write and, when I'm settled there, send books — I'll write which ones; why, we shall be allowed to read. . . . And I'll be released from penal servitude — I'll begin to write. During these months I have experienced much, have experienced much in my own self, and there ahead of me that which I will see and experience — this is what I'll write about. . . .

Five years later, writing to his brother from Omsk (February 22, 1854), Dostoevsky described his journey to Siberia:

Do you remember how we parted, my dear, cherished, my beloved? Right after you left me, the three of us, Durov, Yastrzhembsky, and I were taken to be put in irons. Just at twelve o'clock, that is exactly on Christmas Day, I put on shackles for the first time. They weighed about ten pounds and walking was extremely uncomfortable. Then they made us sit in open sledges, each separately, with a gendarme, and in four sledges, a sergeant-major in front, we set off out of Petersburg. My heart was heavy and somehow confused, uncertain from many diverse sensations. A kind of anxiety filled my heart and consequently it ached with bitter longing. But the fresh air revived me and since one usually feels a certain vitality and courage before every new step in life, I then was in effect quite calm and looked at Petersburg intently as we rode past the houses festively lighted and said good-bye to each house individually. We were driven past your apartment, and at Krayevsky's everything was lighted. You had told me that he was having a Christmas party, that the children and Emiliya Fyodorovna [M. M.'s wife] had gone there, and now at this house I became cruelly sad. I took my leave, as it were, of the dear children. . . . We were driven through the deserted countryside of Petersburg, Novgorod, Yaroslav provinces, etc. . . . I was frozen right through to my heart, and afterward could scarcely thaw myself in the warm rooms. But miraculously enough the journey thoroughly restored my health. . . . It was a sad moment when we crossed the Urals. The horses and covered sledges got stuck in the snowdrifts. There was a storm raging. We got out of the carts — it was night — and stood waiting while the carts were pulled out. All around there was snow, the storm. Here marked the boundary of Europe, ahead lay Siberia and our mysterious fate there, behind was all the past — it was sad and I was moved to tears. . . . The 11th of January we arrived in Tobolsk. . . . The exiles of the old days (that is, not they, but their wives) looked after us as after their own. What marvelous souls, tried by twenty-five years of affliction and self-sacrifice! We saw them only in passing, for we were strictly confined, but they sent us food, clothing, consoled and encouraged us. . . .

In the *Diary of a Writer* Dostoevsky relates how the wife of the Decembrist Fonvizin presented him with a little copy of the Gospels which during his four years of penal servitude he kept under his pillow. As to the Petrashevists' stay in Tobolsk, Yastrzhembsky's account has been preserved. When he, Durov, and Dostoevsky were sent to a narrow, dark, cold, and filthy cell, he fell into such despair that he decided to do away with himself. Dostoevsky saved him.

"Quite by accident and unexpectedly we were given a tallow candle, matches, and hot tea. Dostoevsky seems to have gotten hold of some excellent cigars. We spent a great part of the night in friendly conversation. Dostoevsky's sympathetic, kind voice, his tenderness and gentle feelings, even a number of his whimsical outbursts, thoroughly feminine, worked reassuringly upon me. I gave up all drastic decisions."

On January 23, 1850, Dostoevsky arrived at the penal colony in Omsk. His correspondence with his brother Mikhail was interrupted for a period of four years. Later he wrote to another brother Andrey: "And I consider those four years as a time in which I was *buried alive and closed in a coffin*. How horrible that time was I have not the strength to tell you, dear friend. It was unspeakable, interminable suffering because every hour, every minute weighed upon my soul like a stone."

His memories of these terrible years served as material for the novel *Notes from the House of Death* and for the epilogue to *Crime and Punishment*. The biographical data which we have at our disposal, corroborate the extraordinary truth and accuracy of these accounts. But the years that passed between the experience and the artistic reconstruction brought reconciliation and serenity with them. The motifs developed in the *Notes*: the savage conditions of the prison, the criminals' vile temperaments, their irreconcilable hatred toward the convict-nobleman and, in the darkness of this hell, the several radiant human images — were already noted in the letter written to his brother on February 22, 1854. But the letter's tone is different: in it are felt exhaustion, repugnance, even wrath.

Here is a description of the prisoners:

> They were coarse, ill-natured and exasperated people. Their hatred for the nobility exceeds all bounds and therefore they greeted us nobles hostilely and with malicious delight in our misery. They would have devoured us if given the chance. Consider, moreover, how much protection we had having to live, drink, eat and sleep with these people for several years, and when it was never even possible to complain of the innumerable affronts of every kind . . . 150 enemies never tired in persecuting us; it was amusing to them, a diversion, an occupation. . . . We were made to endure all the persecution and vindictiveness toward the entire class of nobility which to them formed the very breath of life. . . .

In the letter we likewise find prison conditions described with harsher strokes than in the *Notes*.

We lived in a heap, all together in one barrack. . . . All the floors were rotted through. The floor was covered with over an inch and a half of filth; one could slip and fall. . . . Six logs were made to heat the stove; there was no warmth, only unbearable fumes, and this for the entire winter. In the barracks the prisoners wash their laundry, and the whole small area is splashed with water. There is nowhere to turn around. From twilight until dawn no one is allowed outside to take care of his needs, for the barracks are locked, and a tub is set in the passage, and consequently the stench is unbearable. All the convicts stink like pigs, and they say that it is impossible not to act like pigs, so to say "man is only human. . . ." There are fleas, lice, and roaches by the bushels. . . . On fast days one is given a watery cabbage soup and almost nothing else. My stomach suffered unbearably, and several times I took ill. Consider whether it was possible to live without money, and if there had been no money, I should certainly have died, and no one, not one of the prisoners, could have endured such a life. . . . Add to all these pleasantries the almost complete impossibility of having books — what you got hold of, you had to read on the sly — the eternal animosity and quarreling around oneself, swearing, shouts, uproar, clamor, always being under guard, never alone, and this for four years without variation — really, one can be forgiven for saying that things were bad. . . .

In the letter, the plan of *Notes from the House of Death* is already outlined and the central idea expressed: *"these criminals are the most gifted, the strongest people of our entire nation."* Here is the place:

And in four years in prison I at last came to distinguish human beings among the thieves. Will you believe me: there are deep, strong, beautiful characters, and what a joy it was to discover gold beneath the rough, hard shell. And not one, not two, but several. Some it was impossible not to respect, others were decidedly beautiful. I taught one young Circassian (who was sent to penal servitude for armed robbery) the Russian language and how to read and write. [In the *Notes* this is the Daghestan Tartar Aley]. With what gratitude did he surround me. Another convict started to cry upon taking leave of me [In the *Notes* Sushilov]. I used to give him money, but was it much? On the other hand, his gratitude was immense. . . . Apropos: how many popular types, characters have I brought with me out of penal servitude! I have lived in the closest possible contact with them and consequently, it seems, know them pretty well. How many stories of vagrants and robbers and in general of every poor, wretched folk. It will suffice for entire volumes. *What a wonderful people.* Altogether no time has been lost to me if I have come to know not Russia, but the Russian people, well and so well as perhaps not many know them.

In the letter we find a complete program for *Notes from the House of Death:* the mode of life, temperaments, characters, "stories of vagrants and robbers," and the main idea: "These people were an extraordinary people." But it was only seven years later, in 1861, that Dostoevsky succeeded in realizing this proposed project. The writer's stay in prison gave rise to the legend that he was there subjected to corporal punishment. A party of convicts was demolishing a barge on the Irtysh; one of them, Rozhnovsky, dropped his ax in the river and was forced to plunge into the water. Dostoevsky and another prisoner were holding the rope by which he had lowered himself. Suddenly Krivtsov, the drunken and brutal governor of the colony, appeared and ordered them to let go of the rope. The prisoners did not obey and were punished with birch rods. Dostoevsky spent several weeks in the hospital; the prisoners thought that he had died — from this came his nickname "the corpse." Upon his return to the barracks, he fell upon the floor in an epileptic fit. The authenticity of this story is refuted by Doctor Yanovsky, A. Petrov, the Orthodox priest in Geneva, Baron Vrangel, and the writer's daughter, Lyubov Dostoevskaya. But one thing is absolutely certain: his first epileptic attacks took place in prison.

In a letter to his brother, July 30, 1854, he states: "I have already written to you regarding my sickness. Strange fits, like epilepsy, and all the same not epilepsy. . . . However, do me a favor and do not suppose that I am as melancholic and overly concerned about my health as I was in Petersburg during the last years. All that has completely passed, vanished without a trace." For a long time Dostoevsky did not suspect, and perhaps did not want to suspect that he had epilepsy. In the year 1857 a physician, Yermakov, presented him with the following certificate:

In 1850 for the first time he suffered an attack of the falling sickness (epilepsia) which manifested itself by an outcry, loss of consciousness, spasms of the extremities and face, foaming at the mouth, stertorous breathing, with small, rapid, abbreviated pulse. The fit lasted fifteen minutes. Thereupon followed general weakness and a return to consciousness. In 1853 this attack occurred a second time and since then has appeared at the end of every month.

The four years of penal servitude, four years of "unspeakable, interminable suffering," were the turning point in the writer's spiritual development. At Omsk prison began the "regeneration of his convictions." It was a long time in preparation and was not finally completed in penal servitude. The "old man" died slowly struggling torturously with the "new"; the "new" with uncertainty, with groping searched out its place. In the *Diary of a Writer* for 1873 Dostoevsky asserts that neither the scaffold nor penal servitude broke his convictions, that the thoughts and ideas which had possessed his spirit continued then as before to present themselves "as something purifying." But the underground work of criticism and reevaluation of the ideals of his youth was already taking place; by degrees his old "belief" was shattered, a new world-outlook imperceptibly was arising. In the *Diary* we read: "It would be very difficult for me to tell the story of the regeneration of my convictions. . . . The story of the regeneration of one's convictions — really can there in all the domain of literature be any story more full of absorbing and omnivorous interest? The story of the regeneration of one's convictions — why this is even first and foremost the story of their generation. Convictions are born in a man for the second time under his very gaze, at that age when he has sufficient experience and perception consciously to survey this *profound mystery of his soul.*"

The writer reveals the history of his soul not in philosophical terms, but in the artistic symbols of his great novels. All of them are acts of a single spiritual tragedy, the revelation of the "profound mystery of his soul." And in fact there is not in world literature a story more full of "absorbing interest."

Upon setting out for Siberia, Dostoevsky believed that, in changing his life, he "would be born again in a new form" (the letter of December 22, 1849). What took place in his soul during the four years of penal servitude? He did not have the strength to tell. "Well, how can I convey to you what is in my mind," he wrote his brother, "my ideas, all that I have lived through, of what I am convinced and what conclusions I have reached during all this time? I am not going to undertake it. Such a task is decidedly impossible. . . ." And after his description of life in the prison, he repeats: "What has happened to my soul, to my beliefs, to my mind and heart during these four years — I will not tell you. It is a long story." In human language there are no words to relate the terrible experience of a man buried alive. One can speak only by intimations and riddles. "The eternal concentration upon myself," he continues, "where I escaped from bitter reality, has yielded its fruits. I have now many *needs and hopes* about which I did not even think in the past. But these are all riddles and therefore, let us go on. . . ."

"Regeneration" began with a merciless judgment of his own self and of his entire past. In the barracks, in the "general heap," amidst the shouts and uproar of a "hundred and fifty enemies," the writer closed himself off in his "terrible solitude." Afterward he wrote regarding this period:

> I remember that all that time, despite my hundreds of companions, I lived in terrible solitude, and in the end, came to love this solitude. Alone in my heart I reexamined all my past life, sorted out everything to the last detail, carefully thought about my past, *judged myself* unyieldingly and sternly, and even at some times blessed fate for having sent me this solitude without which neither this judgment of myself nor this stern reexamination of my previous life would have taken place. And with what hopes did my heart then start to beat! I thought, I resolved, I swore to myself that in my future life there would be neither those errors nor those falls which had previously been made. . . . I waited, I bade fate to hurry, I wanted to put myself to the test once again in a new battle. . . . Freedom, a new life, *resurrection from the dead*. What a glorious moment!

In his soul there existed not only a judgment, but also a censure of the past, a rupture with it, liberation. Again he spoke of hope, of a new life. From his letter we learn about the negative expression of his inner activity (the overthrowal of the past), but we do not see its positive side. What new needs were born in his soul? And did his "resurrection from the dead" mean something more than being released from the "house of death"?

We find the answer to this question in a letter of Dostoevsky's to N. D. Fonvizina, who had given him the book of the Gospels in Tobolsk. Upon leaving prison he wrote:

> I have heard from many people that you are very religious, N. D. Not because you are religious, but because I myself have experienced and felt this keenly, I will tell you that in such moments one

thirsts like "parched grass" for faith and finds it precisely because truth shines in misfortune. I will tell you regarding myself that I am a child of the age, a child of nonbelief and doubt up till now and even (I know it) until my coffin closes. What terrible torments has this thirst to believe cost me and does still cost me, becoming the stronger in my soul, the more there is in me of contrary reasonings. And yet sometimes God sends me moments in which I am utterly at peace; in those moments I love and find that I am loved by others and in such moments I have constructed for myself a symbol of faith[7] in which everything is clear and holy for me. The symbol is very simple; here it is: to believe that there is nothing more beautiful, profounder, more sympathetic, more reasonable, more courageous and more perfect than Christ and not only is there nothing, but I tell myself with jealous love that never could there be. Moreover, if someone were to prove to me that Christ is outside the truth, then I would prefer to remain with Christ than with the truth.

This letter is a document of singular importance: it sheds light on the process of the "regeneration of his convictions." In penal servitude Dostoevsky judged himself. He, as it were, carried on a suit with that individual who had been his chief mentor, who had first persuaded him to his own belief — with Belinsky. We remember how the "passionate socialist" Belinsky initiated him into atheism, how in his presence he dethroned the "radiant personality of Christ." At that point the pupil accepted all his master's teaching however difficult it was for him to renounce the "most lustrous image of the God-man." When Belinsky would speak mockingly of Christ, "Dostoevsky's countenance used to change just as though he were on the verge of breaking into tears." In penal servitude he mentally continued his controversy with Belinsky. *He no longer accepted his teaching.* As yet he had nothing with which to refute the critic's atheistic argumentation, but his holy of holies — Christ's image — he would no longer surrender to him. The suit was brought to another plane; in opposition to the contentions of reason was posed the evidence of the heart. Dostoevsky was prepared to grant that Belinsky's arguments were irrefutable, that truth was on his side, but now *he did not even accept such a truth.* If Christ was not the truth, then he would be with Christ despite the truth.

And thus began the struggle between faith and reason in the writer's consciousness, thus arose the fundamental problem of his philosophy.

[7] The symbol of faith is equivalent to the Western term *the creed.*

But Dostoevsky's "symbol of faith" was far from the symbol of Nicea, and his religious thought still bore little resemblance to the faith of the Orthodox Church. He opposed to Belinsky's atheistic rationalism Christian humanism, not faith in the God-man Christ, but *love for Christ the man*. For him Christ was only the most beautiful, "sympathetic," and perfect of men. He even allowed that the One who said of Himself: "I am the truth," can be found to exist outside the truth; this premise is blasphemous to every believer. Here is the direction in which Dostoevsky's convictions were regenerated. In his misfortune, the thirst for faith became stronger; the quest for God was more tormenting; blissful moments of peace and love were sent to his rendered soul. And most important: the "radiant personality" of Christ entered the convict's life and began to occupy a central place in it — *for ever*. His encounter with Christ in the midst of robbers became a source of light, the beams of which overflowed through all his works after the time of penal servitude. Among them a special place is held by the epilogue to *Crime and Punishment*. Not only are the conditions in the jail where Raskolnikov languishes the same as those at Omsk prison, but even the hero's inner life completely reflects the experiences of the author himself.

Sonya informed them, among other things, that although he [Raskolnikov] seemed so intent upon himself and had, as it were, closed himself off from everyone, his attitude toward his new life was very direct and matter-of-fact. In the prison, in his surroundings, there was, of course, much that he did not notice, and did not want to notice. He lived somehow with his eyes cast down: it was repugnant and unbearable for him to look. But toward the end many things began to surprise him, and he somehow involuntarily began to notice that which formerly he had not even suspected. The most surprising thing of all, in general, was that terrible, that impassable chasm which lay between him and all these folk. It was as if he and they belonged to different races. They regarded him, and he them, with mistrust and hostility. . . . In the prison there were also exiled Poles, political prisoners. These simply considered all the rest as ignoramuses and churls and looked upon them with disdain; but Raskolnikov could not regard them this way: he saw clearly that in many respects these ignoramuses were far wiser than those very Poles! He himself was not liked and was avoided by all. Toward the end they even began to hate him. Why? He did not know. They scorned him, used to laugh at him, laughed at his crime — men who were much more guilty than he.

Both in the letter to his brother and in *The Notes from the House of Death*, the criminals' hatred is explained purely on a social plane: the muzhiks hate the gentleman-noble. In *Crime and Punishment* the motivation is deeper. "During the second week of Great Lent his [Raskolnikov's] turn came with the rest of the barrack to prepare himself to receive the sacrament. He went to the church and prayed together with the others. For some reason — he himself did not know why — one day a fight took place. Everyone at once fell upon him with fury: 'You're an atheist! You don't believe in God!' they shouted at him, 'We must kill you!' He had never spoken to them about God or about faith, but they wanted to kill him as an atheist."

We do not know whether such an encounter between Dostoevsky and the convicts ever in fact occurred. Even if it did not, if it is only an artistic symbol, its spiritual significance is not diminished. The people's hatred for a gentleman (in the letter: "a wonderful people"! In the *Notes*: "an extraordinary people") is explained *religiously*. The robbers believe in Christ and by this faith they are wiser than the non-believers. In Raskolnikov they instinctively sense an atheist and want to kill him. If the epilogue to *Crime and Punishment* has autobiographical value, the origin of Dostoevsky's cherished idea of Christ as the people's shrine becomes intelligible. Raskolnikov finishes saying that which was left not fully expressed in the letter of 1854 and in the *Notes from the House of Death*.

On February 15, 1854, the writer was released from the penal colony at Omsk.

V I I I

Exile · First Marriage
Uncle's Dream
The Village of Stepanchikovo

A week after being released from penal servitude Dostoevsky wrote to his brother: "It is clear in my mind. All my future and everything that I am going to do seems to be present before my eyes. I am content with my life." He wanted passionately to write; as to his material, "it will suffice for entire volumes." He hoped that in about six years he would be allowed to publish. "And now I will not write trash. You'll hear about me." His brother was requested several times to send books: "If you are able, send me the journals for this year, if only *Fatherland Notes*. But here is what is essential: I need (absolutely must have) historians, ancient (in French translation), and modern economists, and the Fathers of the Church. . . . Forward them without delay. . . ." And on another page: "So don't forget my books, beloved friend. Especially: historians, economists, *Fatherland Notes*, Fathers of the Church, and a history of the Church. . . . Realize, brother, that books — this is my life, nourishment, my future. . . ." And several lines later again: "Send me the Koran, Kant's *Critique de raison pure* . . . and without fail Hegel, especially Hegel's history of philosophy. My whole future is bound up with this. . . ." A month later again he asked for European historians, economists, the holy Fathers, and moreover, "Pisarev's physics and something on physiology." After the spiritual starvation of penal servitude Dostoevsky greedily immersed himself in books. The circle of his intellectual interests widened. Before his arrest, literature occupied him exclusively; he had read a few of the French socialists — in all two or three books. Now history and philosophy stood in first place. He strove to formulate a scientific basis for his new convictions, to confront economists with the holy fathers, to develop his own historiosophy. The critique of pure reason, the history of the

Church, and even physiology were indispensable to the foundation of his new world-outlook. But these extensive plans were not destined to be realized; the intended essays on politics and art were left unwritten. For three years all the writer's inner forces were absorbed by his first and tragic love.

Dostoevsky was enrolled as a private in the Seventh Line Battalion at Semipalatinsk. In this forlorn city there was a stone church, several mosques, and a barracks; the scant population consisted of civil servants, soldiers, and Tartar merchants. Beyond the city Kirghiz lived in their hide tents. The writer's service in the ranks was oppressive. "To be a soldier is no joke," he wrote to his brother, "a soldier's life with all its duties is not at all that easy for a man whose health is such and who is so unaccustomed to or, better to say, so totally ignorant of like pursuits. To gain this experience requires a great deal of work. I'm not grumbling; this is my cross and I have deserved it."

In the year 1854 a new district procurator, Baron Vrangel, arrived in Semipalatinsk from Petersburg. He knew Dostoevsky through his novel *Poor People* and brought him a package and letters. In his *Memoirs* he describes his first meeting with the writer: "When entering my room, Dostoevsky was extremely restrained. He had on a soldier's greatcoat with red stand-up collar and red epaulettes. Morose, with a sickly, pale face covered with freckles, he wore his light-blond hair cut short; in height he was taller than average. Staring intently at me with his intelligent grey-blue eyes, it seemed he was trying to peer into my soul." Soon they became friends; Dostoevsky used to spend all his evenings at Vrangel's. "Often when I returned home from work," the latter recalls, "There I would find Dostoevsky, who had arrived earlier than myself either from drill or from the regimental office in which he fulfilled various clerical jobs. Having undone his greatcoat, with a Turkish pipe in his mouth, he would stride about the room, often conversing with himself since something new was forever being born in his mind. I see him now just as in one of such moments: at that time he set upon the idea of writing *Uncle's Dream* and *The Village of Stepanchikovo*. He was in a wonderfully cheerful mood, was laughing and telling me of uncle's adventures, droning away at some excerpts from opera." Dostoevsky was very fond of reading Gogol and Victor Hugo; when he was in good spirits, he would declaim Pushkin; his favorite verses were: *Cleopatra's Feast*. During the summer he stayed with Vrangel at the latter's villa "Cossack Garden."

"I can clearly remember the image of Fyodor Mikhailovich helping me water a young sprout, in the sweat of his brow, having taken off his soldier's greatcoat, in a rose-colored chintz waistcoat that was faded from laundering; on his neck there invariably dangled a long, home-made chain of tiny azure beads which someone had given to him; on the chain was suspended a large, bulb-shaped silver watch." Some-times the friends went fishing and Dostoevsky, lying on the grass, would read aloud from Aksakov's *Notes on Angling Fish* and *Notes of a Hunter*. On warm evenings they would "stretch out on the grass" and, lying on their backs, would look at the myriads of stars which gleamed out of the blue depths of the sky. "Contemplating the grandeur of the Creator, the unknown, omnipotent Divine force produced upon us a kind of emotion, a consciousness of our nothingness, somehow hum-bled our spirit." Vrangel wrote to his father: "Fate has brought me together with a rare individual, both as to his heart and as to his in-tellectual qualities: this is our unfortunate young writer Dostoevsky. I am obliged to him greatly, and his words, advice, and ideas will strengthen me through my entire life. I work daily with him, and at present we are going to translate Hegel's philosophy and the *Psyche* of Carus. *He is an extremely pious individual,* sickly but of an iron will." In his *Memoirs* Vrangel speaks more in detail of his friend's "piety": "Dostoevsky and I talked very little about religion. He was *on the whole pious,* but rarely went to church and did not like priests, particu-larly Siberian ones. He used to talk about Christ with rapture. . . ." This fully corroborates our designating Dostoevsky's religiosity as *Christian humanism.* His rapturous love for the human image of Christ was still far from ecclesiastical Orthodoxy. The friends' project of a joint study of Hegel and Carus did not materialize. Vrangel was struck by Dostoevsky's "kindliness" and his indulgence toward people. "He used to find an excuse for the worst traits in a man's character, explain-ing everything as a want of education, the influence of surroundings, and even as nature and temperament. Everything that was oppressed, unhappy, afflicted, and poor found in him a special concern." All this is still the old Dostoevsky, the author of *Poor People,* the humanist and philanthrope. The inner upheaval had not yet occurred, the "crisis of humanism" was only in preparation.

Baron Vrangel introduced his friend into the homes of the Military Governor, General P. Spiridonov, the Battalion Commander Belikhov, and of Lieutenant Stepanov. In Semipalatinsk "society" Dostoevsky met his future wife Mariya Dmitriyevna Isayeva. Their romance was preceded by an initial affair to which the virtuous Vrangel makes reference guardedly. Dostoevsky had a pupil, the beautiful blonde Marina, daughter of an exiled Pole. When she turned seventeen, "she matured, blossomed out, grew pretty, and became extremely loose. She enlivened our house very much, would run all about, earnestly play the coquette, and made fervid advances toward her teacher." Her subsequent fate was pitiful: some eighteen-year-old youth seduced and abandoned her; thereafter she lived with a coachman, "a dirty Kirghiz"; finally married an old Cossack cornet and was unfaithful to him. Vrangel hints at Dostoevsky's captivation for this "loose" girl. "Later on," he writes, "when Dostoevsky was married, Marina more than once served as a cause of jealousy and discord between Mariya Dmitriyevna and Fyodor Mikhailovich, pursuing him with her coquetry." After this equivocal prologue there followed the drama: Dostoevsky fell passionately in love with Isayeva. He had a prophetic premonition of a turning point in his fate. Before his departure for Semipalatinsk, he wrote to N. Fonvizina: "I'm in a kind of expectation of something; I am, as it were, still quite sick now, and it seems to me that in a short, very short time something very decisive must happen to me, that I am drawing near to the crisis of my entire life, that I have, as it were, grown ripe for something, and that it will be something, perhaps calm and bright, perhaps terrible, but in any event, unavoidable. Otherwise my life will be a chance missed." His gift of clairvoyance did not deceive him — only, in the "unavoidable" that was approaching him, there was nothing "calm and bright."

"Mariya Dmitriyevna," writes Vrangel, "was about thirty years old. . . . A rather beautiful blonde of average height, very thin, with a passionate and exultant nature. Even at the time an ominous glow used to play on her pale face. She was well-read, fairly cultured, had an inquiring mind, was kindhearted and extraordinarily lively and impressionable." Her father, the son of a French émigré, Constant, was director of quarantine in Astrakhan. Mariya Dmitriyevna went to boarding school and had danced "with a shawl" at nobility balls. She married a teacher Aleksandr Isayev, had a son Pavel, and was deeply lonely and unhappy. A drunken husband, poverty, a miserable provincial life — such was the ardent dreamer's wretched fate. She attracted the enamored Dostoevsky, although she never responded to him with reciprocal love and considered him a "man without a future." Soon after the writer suffered a terrible blow: in May 1855 Isayev was transferred to Kuznetsk and he had to part with Mariya Dmitriyevna. Vrangel remembers that Dostoevsky "wept bitterly, sobbing like a child." The friends rode out on a moonlit May night to see the travelers off.

When the carriage disappeared, Dostoevsky remained standing as though rooted to the spot, silent, his head bowed; tears streamed down his cheeks. . . . We returned home at dawn. He did not go to bed — kept continually pacing up and down the room and saying something to himself. Exhausted by his inner agitation and the sleepless night, he set off to the adjacent encampment for drill exercises. When he returned, he lay down for the entire day, did not eat, did not drink, and only nervously smoked one pipe after another. . . . He lost even more weight, became despondent, irritable, wandered about like a specter. . . . Suddenly he became superstitious, visited fortune-tellers. . . .

Vrangel offered to arrange a rendezvous for him with Isayeva in Zmiyevo halfway between Semipalatinsk and Kuznetsk. But the friends waited there to no avail for Mariya Dmitriyevna; she did not come. A second meeting in this same city likewise did not take place; again Mariya Dmitriyevna was unable to come. Dostoevsky was tormented with jealousy. . . .

"It was frightful to look," recalls Vrangel, "at his gloomy disposition which told upon his health." Vrangel departed for Petersburg and Dostoevsky was left completely alone. In August Isayev died; Mariya Dmitriyevna was forced to go into debt in order to bury her husband. The writer implored Vrangel to send her money, but to do it "most delicately." "With an individual in debt," he wrote, "one has to act carefully; he is mistrustful." He now entertained the hope that Isayev's widow would consent to become his wife; he wrote her long ecstatic letters. She answered affectionately, but evasively. He felt that no doubt she would marry him if he had a "position" and money. Vrangel exerted himself in Petersburg; if only he were allowed to transfer to the civil service and permitted to publish, he could get married at once.

In autumn of 1855 Dostoevsky was promoted to noncommissioned officer; the new tsar's favor encouraged him and at the beginning of 1856 he informed his brother of his decision to get married: "My decision is taken and even if the earth should fall to pieces under me, I will carry it out. . . . Without that which is now for me the most important thing in life, I don't want to go on living. . . ." And he asked his brother to send him a hundred rubles. Meanwhile from Kuznetsk came alarming news: Mariya Dmitriyevna was troubled, desperate, constantly sick, was surrounded by old cronies who sought to arrange a match for her; in her letter there were "definitely fewer heartfelt words." Dostoevsky wrote to Vrangel (March 23, 1856) that he had "thunderous news." Mariya Dmitriyevna had received a proposal from "an elderly man, with good qualities, who is in the service and well-off," and she asked his advice as to what to do.

She adds that she loves me, that this is still only a conjecture and consideration. I was struck as if by a thunderbolt; I reeled, fainted, and wept all night. Now I am lying in my room. I can't get the idea out of my mind! I scarcely understand how I'm alive and what is said to me. Oh, Lord, do not grant *anyone this horrible, dreadful feeling!* Great is the joy of love, but the sufferings are so terrible that it would be better never to love. I swear to you that I fell into despair. I understood the possibility of an extraordinary act to which at another time I would never have been brought. . . . That same evening I wrote her a letter, a terrible, despairing one. The poor dear, my angel! She is ill as it is and I tortured her! Perhaps I have killed her with my letter. I said that I should die if I lost her. There were threats and endearments and abject pleas, I don't know what.

For many pages complaints, doubts, pleas are repeated; the words are inflamed, feverish, almost insane. Now he believes in her love: *"Elle m'aime, elle m'aime,* this I know, I see" — then he is torn by the thought that he is compromising her happiness; now he agrees to sacrifice himself, then he cries out: "To give her up is utterly impossible for me in any event. At my age love is not a caprice; it has lasted for two years. In ten months of separation not only has it not weakened, but it has grown to absurdity. I will perish if I lose my angel; either I will go out of my mind or into the Irtysh." Detailed plans thereupon follow as to "arrangements": transfer to the civil service in Barnaul, a loan of a thousand silver rubles from his uncle, hopes of the sovereign's clemency at the time of the coronation and, lastly, literary earnings. "I expect to write a novel even better than *Poor People.* Why, if I'm allowed to publish (and I do not believe, hear me, I do not believe that it will be impossible to obtain this), why, then, the rumor will go out, the book will provide me with money, reputation; it will attract the government's attention to me, and even my return will be hastened." The letter is replete with passion and despair. Reading it, you involuntarily believe that its author was prepared for anything, that he was on the brink of insanity or suicide. The feeling of reality was lost, the soul brought to a fiery pitch. For Dostoevsky, love was a "horrible and dreadful feeling."

His correspondence with Mariya Dmitriyevna became more and more dramatic. With ever greater frequency she mentioned a young school-teacher, Vergunov, a friend of her late husband's. Dostoevsky decided upon a desperate move: without informing the authorities he set off for Kuznetsk and upon his return from there wrote Vrangel: "I saw her! What a noble, what an angelic soul! She cried, kissed my hands, but she loves another. . . . The two days I spent were like I don't know what; it was bliss and torment — unbearable! At the end of the second day I left full of hope." Shortly thereafter she wrote him that she was "miserable, weeping" and loved Vergunov more than him. Dostoevsky persuaded himself that he had to save her from marrying this crude twenty-four-year-old Siberian, that in talking her out of this foolish step, he was solicitous only of her happiness. "I wrote a long letter jointly to both of them. I pointed out everything that can come from an ill-matched marriage. . . . She replied, ardently defending him, as though I had attacked him. And he, just like a stupid Kuznetskian, took it as a personal affront and insult to himself. He wrote me an abusive reply. . . . How this will end, I don't know, but she will ruin herself and my heart is sinking as a result of it. . . . I'm like a madman in the full sense of the word, this whole time."

"Dostoevskianism" appeared earlier than Dostoevsky's novels. It is hard to believe that Mariya Dmitriyevna did in fact exist, and was not invented by the author of *The Humiliated and Wronged*. Her hysterical sensitivity, her love for two men, the outbursts of jealousy, the dramatic explanations, the fateful decisions, the agony and torment — are thoroughly in Dostoevsky's style. When he arrived in Kuznetsk, she arranged a "scene for three" in the course of which Vergunov cried on Dostoevsky's chest, Dostoevsky wept at the feet of his beloved, while Mariya Dmitriyevna in tears conciliated the rivals. What a "situation" for a novel! . . . It seems that life imitated literature, reality anticipated fiction. The writer sacrificed himself: he interceded on behalf of Isayeva for the subsidy due her husband's service, for the appointment of her son to the cadet corps, for Vergunov's promotion to a better position. In Petersburg Vrangel must solicit for Mariya Dmitriyevna's preferred choice: "This is all for her, for her alone," Dostoevsky wrote him. "At least she won't be in poverty then. . . . If she is going to marry him, then let there at least be money. . . ."

On October 1, 1856, Dostoevsky was promoted a commissioned officer. Again hope was kindled: she could not marry Vergunov since the latter received only 300 rubles salary. "I love her to the point of madness," he wrote Vrangel. "The thought of her would have brought me to the grave or literally have driven me to suicide, had I not seen her. Only to see her, only to hear her! I'm an unhappy madman! Love in such form is a disease. I'm aware of this." In November he went to Kuznetsk; the wedding was set for "before shrovetide," but money was needed. "I have over a 1,000 rubles worth of copy," he informed Vrangel. "But if I'm not allowed to publish for yet another year — I'm lost. Then it is better not to live! Never in my life have I faced such a critical moment as now!" He borrowed 600 rubles from Kovrigin, an engineer in Omsk, and asked the same amount from his Moscow uncle Kumanin.

On February 6, 1857, Dostoevsky was married in Kuznetsk to Mariya Dmitriyevna Isayeva. Fate took pains that the denouement would correspond to the style of a novel. Frequently critics reproach the author of *The Devils* with a passion for tragic catastrophes. The catastrophe which culminated the novel that he did not write, but through which he lived, was more terrible than all his fictions: after the wedding, on the return journey from Kuznetsk, the young wife saw, with terror and repugnance, her husband yelling and struggling in an epileptic attack. Dostoevsky wrote his brother (March 9, 1857):

On the return journey I stopped in Barnaul at the home of a good acquaintance. There I was visited by misfortune; quite unexpectedly I was taken with a fit of epilepsia, which frightened my wife to death and filled me with melancholy and despondency. The doctor told me, contrary to all previous testimonies of doctors, that I had *real epilepsy* and in one of these seizures I must expect to be suffocated by a spasm of the throat and will die in this way and no other. . . . When I married I had complete faith in the doctors who had assured me that these were simply nervous attacks which might pass with a change in my way of life. If I had known for certain that I had real epilepsy, *I would not have gotten married*.

From this day until Mariya Dmitriyevna's very death, we do not find in Dostoevsky's vast correspondence a single word about her. The marriage lasted for seven years; during the final years they lived apart and the writer was in love with another woman. After his wife's death he wrote to Vrangel (March 31, 1865): "Oh, my friend, her love for me was boundless; I loved her too without measure, but we did not live happily. . . . She and I were decidedly unhappy together (due to her passionate, mistrustful, and morbidly capricious nature), but we could not stop loving one another. Indeed the more unhappy we were, the more we became attached to one another."

The writer's second wife, Anna Grigoryevna, corroborates: "Fyodor Mikhailovich deeply loved his first wife. In his life this was his first real sentiment. His youth was spent entirely in literary work. . . . His infatuation with Panayeva was too short-lived and does not count. This was a genuine, powerful feeling with all its joys and torments." Mariya Dmitriyevna's was a long and excruciatingly painful death from consumption. Dostoevsky passed the last days at her bedside. In the face of death everything that was onerous and painful was forgotten and forgiven; in his soul there remained only compassion. And his words about the deceased breathe magnanimity and love; Anna Grigoryevna repeats them scrupulously. The writer's daughter, Lyubov Dostoevskaya, speaks otherwise. However prejudiced her *Memoirs* are, nonetheless a portion of truth is contained in the "gossip" which she has communicated. "The eve of her wedding," she writes, "Mariya Dmitriyevna spent the night with her lover, an insignificant private tutor, a handsome man." This romance continued in Semipalatinsk; Vergunov accompanied her even to Russia. "At the very time that Dostoevsky in his calash was abandoning himself to reveries, at a distance of one post station behind him a britzka followed with the handsome teacher whom his wife used to convey everywhere after her like a little lapdog." Mariya Dmitriyevna had outbursts of hatred toward her husband. "In the dining room she would stop before a portrait of Dostoevsky, stare at it for a long time, shake her fist and shout: 'Convict, dishonorable convict.'" Perhaps the novelist's daughter is appending an effective closing scene to her father's romance; but then "double feelings" and love-hate were fully in the character of Mariya Dmitriyevna, hysterical and consumptive. "She and I were decidedly unhappy together," confessed Dostoevsky.

The story of the writer's unhappy marriage is concealed from us by a mystery. In one letter to Vrangel he said: "*Par ma jalousie incomparable* I drove her to despair." This was even before the wedding. What did Dostoevsky undergo if Mariya Dmitriyevna, having become his wife, was in fact unfaithful to him with Vergunov? The tragedy of jealousy later was depicted in his brilliant tale *The Eternal Husband.* What has been reflected in it: that which actually was, or only that which *could have been*? We do not know: Dostoevsky's heroes realize not only his personal fate, but also all the possibilities of that fate which remained unfulfilled.

In the first part of *Netochka Nezvanova* we find outlined the figure of an exultant dreamer who has coupled her life to a drunken husband. His meeting with the Isayev family enabled the writer to transform this sketch into a psychological portrait. Isayev, an inveterate drunkard and teacher who had lost his position, and his consumptive wife continue to live in the novel *Crime and Punishment* under the names of Marmeladov and Katerina Ivanovna. The drunken civil servant in the tavern tells about his wife and we recognize the features of the writer's first wife. "And know," he says,

> that my spouse was educated in an excellent institute for the daughters of the nobles of her province and at her commencement danced with a shawl in the presence of the governor and before other personages. . . . Yes, yes, a lady, ardent, proud, and unbending. She herself scrubs the floor and has to get along on black bread, but will not allow disrespect to herself. . . . She married her first husband for love. . . . She loved her husband excessively, but he took to cards, got into trouble with the authorities, and with that he died. And she was left after his death . . . in a far-off and savage district where I at that time happened also to be, and she had been left in such hopeless straits, that I, although I had seen many affairs of every sort, would not be capable of describing it. . . . You can judge to what degree her miseries had gone by the fact that she, cultured and educated and coming from a distinguished family, consented to be my wife. But she did! Crying and wailing and wringing her hands — she did! For there was nowhere to go. Do you understand, kind sir, what it means when there is no longer any place to go? No! That you still do not understand.

The first three years of exile (1854-1856) were taken up with his love for Mariya Dmitriyevna. Dostoevsky had many literary plans, but he could not write. "My dearest friend," he confessed to his brother, "I was in such turmoil during the past year, in such anguish and misery, that I positively could not work." "I could not write," he informed Maikov. "One circumstance, one event, which had long been delayed in my life and, at last, has visited me, captivated and engulfed me completely. I was happy and could not work. Later sorrow and grief visited me." And finally, just before the wedding itself, he answered Vrangel: "You write that I am too lazy to write; no, my friend, but relations with M. D. have taken up all my time during the last two years. At any rate, *I have lived, though I have suffered, yes, lived!*"

Meanwhile his thirst to write tormented him. He believed in his vocation. "More than ever I know," he wrote, "that it was not for nothing that I entered on this road, and that I will not cumber the earth to no purpose. I am convinced that I have talent and that I can write something good" (letter to Mikhail, January 13, 1856). In prison he gave thought to a long tale; in Semipalatinsk he "noted down some memories of his term in penal servitude" and "for fun began a comedy." He informed Maikov of this (January 1856). "My hero so pleased me that I abandoned the form of comedy despite the fact that it was getting on well, simply for the pleasure of following as far as possible the adventures of my new hero and of myself laughing at him. This hero is a bit like me. In short, I am writing a *comic novel*. . . ." This work, originally conceived in the form of a comedy, subsequently was given the title *The Village of Stepanchikovo*. With unyielding determination the exiled writer struggled for freedom. In order to prove his loyalty, he did violence to his talent and composed three patriotic odes. The first of these *On European Events in the Year 1854* was inspired by Pushkin's invective: *To the Calumniators of Russia*. The author branded the champions of Mohamet against Christ as the enemies of "Holy Russia," and predicted that from Russia would come the "rebirth of the ancient East."

> Dishonor to you, apostates of the Cross,
> Extinguishers of the Divine Light!
> But God is with us! Hurrah! Our task is holy,
> And for Christ, who is not glad to lay down his life!

The most rabid nationalism is founded on the religious mission of the Russian Empire. The poem was sent to Petersburg, but did not meet the approval of Dubelt and disappeared in the archives of the Third Section. Lack of success did not weaken the author's patriotic zeal. He wrote a second poem on the occasion of the Empress Aleksandra Fyodorovna's birthday, full of respectful, servile feelings toward the widow of Nikolai I. Of the emperor who had sent him to the scaffold and banished him to penal servitude, the repentant rebel speaks in a tone of prayerful eulogy:

> Is he no more who illumined us like the sun
> And opened our eyes through his immortal deeds?
> . . . .

And with a fiery sword, having risen up, a dreadful archangel,
He pointed out to us the age-long path of the future. . . .

The convict blesses his fate:

And in my heart I knew that tears are redemption,
That once again I am a Russian, and again a human being!

The poem was entrusted to General Hasfort, Commander of the Siberian Corps, who presented it to the Minister of War, calling his attention to the "warmth of patriotic sentiments." For these sentiments Dostoevsky was promoted to noncommissioned officer. Finally, in the spring of 1856, he composed a third poem dedicated to the coronation of Emperor Aleksandr II:

Our tsar goes to receive the crown;
Giving voice to a pure prayer,
Millions of Russians implore:
Bless, O Lord, the tsar!

The poem hastened its author's advance to the rank of officer. It would be possible to disregard these belabored verses and loyal sentiments which were calculated to secure an immediate "monarchial favor," if . . . they were not sincere. But Dostoevsky, while in penal servitude, did actually condemn his "revolt" and repent of the revolutionary enthusiasms of his youth. The struggle to liberate the peasants by way of an uprising, the going out onto the square with a red standard, the secret printing operation — all this now seemed to him a criminal mistake. On the political plane, the "regeneration of his convictions" was complete. The new world-outlook to which he would remain faithful all his life was already formed in the year 1854. The ecclesiastical-monarchical imperialism of the author of *The Diary of a Writer* is prefigured in the patriotic verses of 1854-1856. When Maikov informed him of a "new movement" in Russian society, Dostoevsky answered:

Russia, duty, honor! Yes! I have always been a true Russian — I tell you frankly. What then is new in this movement which has been disclosed around you, about which you write as of some kind of current? Yes! I share with you the idea that Russia will put an end to Europe and her destiny. This has long been clear to me. . . . I assure you that I, for example, am so much akin to everything Russian that even the convicts did not frighten me. They were the Russian people, my brothers in misfortune, and I had the happiness more than once to find generosity even in the soul of a robber, precisely because I was able to understand him; for I myself was a Russian!

During this same year he wrote to General Totleben, hero of the Sevastopol Campaign, asking him to intercede for his pardon: "I was guilty, I acknowledge this fully. I was convicted of intending (but not more) to act against the government; I was sentenced lawfully and justly. A long ordeal, hard and acutely painful, *has sobered* me and I have in many ways altered my thoughts. But at that time I was blind, believed in theories and utopias. . . . Thoughts, even convictions, change; a man himself changes too, and why suffer now for that which is no more, which in me has reverted to the complete opposite — suffer for former mistakes."

Penal servitude had "sobered" the utopian-dreamer; he offered a solemn repentance of the errors of his youth. He wanted to express his new convictions and planned an article on Russia, but he was afraid that the censors would not pass it. "I spoke to you about the article on Russia," he wrote to Vrangel in 1856, "but it turned out simply a political pamphlet. . . . It is unlikely that they would allow me to begin publishing with a pamphlet in spite of the most patriotic ideas. This essay has occupied a great deal of my time! But I discarded it . . . and therefore I have decided upon another article: *Letters on Art*. My article is the fruit of ten years' reflection. Several chapters will contain whole pages from the pamphlet. It is, properly, *about the role of Christianity in art*." But even this essay was set aside. If one remembers that the question of a Christian art was first posed in Russian literature by Gogol and that his *Correspondence with Friends* had appeared in 1847, then it is possible to conjecture that in the course of these ten years Dostoevsky had been reflecting upon Gogol's problem. The last strong impression which he carried away into penal servitude was Belinsky's letter in answer to Gogol; before his arrest he had read it aloud three times and in the solitude of prison he mentally continued the mystic Gogol's controversy with the socialist Belinsky about art, Christianity, and Russia. The image of the author of the *Correspondence* remained unrelentingly with him in penal servitude; for this persecution, Dostoevsky avenged himself on Gogol in *The Village of Stepanchikovo*.

The problem of art engrossed the writer through the whole period of his exile. In 1858, welcoming Mikhail Mikhailovich's intention to publish a newspaper, he again referred to his articles on art.

"I have a few literary essays of this sort in notes and outline: *about contemporary poets, about the statistical tendency of literature, about the uselessness of tendencies in art* — articles which are written heatedly and even pointedly — but on the whole, with a light touch." Dostoevsky frequently said "in notes" when referring to what he had only as an idea. In any case, none of these outlines or projects has come down to us.

He wanted to return to literature as brilliantly as he entered it; he must have a big success, a rehabilitation, recognition. All his subsequent fate depended on this. But with what would he return? With a political pamphlet, articles on art, a tale, a comic novel? The writer hesitated, and was afraid. His epileptic attacks grew more frequent; he was depressed. He wrote to his wife's sister, V. D. Constant: "You know, I have a kind of presentiment, an expectation, that soon I must die. . . . My assurance of an imminent death is completely cold-blooded. It seems that I have already experienced everything in this world and that nothing is left to which it is possible even to aspire." But the streak of despondency passed and again he struggled for freedom, made plans, chained himself to life. In 1857 he succeeded through Pleshcheyev's efforts to enter into correspondence with the publisher of the *Russian Messenger*, M. Katkov, who offered to print his new work and sent him an advance of 500 rubles. Mikhail Mikhailovich, in the name of his brother, promised a novel or a tale to the journal *The Russian Word* and took 500 rubles advance. Dostoevsky was forced to confess ashamedly that he had nothing ready. The novel on which he was working "with pleasure" had "expanded" to too great proportion and he had "put it aside in a drawer." He needed money urgently, but did not want to "spoil the idea which he had been considering for three years, for which he had gathered an enormous amount of material." Now he was writing a short tale, and having finished it, was "going to set about a novel of Petersburg life in the manner of *Poor People*." In the following letter to his brother there were guarantees that he had only laid the first novel aside, but had not abandoned it. "This novel is so dear to me, has so grown upon me, that I would not abandon it decisively for anything. To the contrary, I hope to make of it a chef d'oeuvre." And meantime he was working on a second novel. Several months later he wrote that he had also discarded this work: "I have laid aside writing the novel until my return to Russia. I did this out of necessity. The idea in it is happy enough, the character new, not as yet having appeared anywhere. But seeing that this character, most likely, is now in great fashion in Russia, in actual life . . . I am convinced that I would enrich my novel with new observations upon returning to Russia. . . ."

On July 19, 1858, he announced that he was writing two tales: one long one for the *Russian Messenger*, another somewhat shorter for the *Russian Word*. The "long tale" designates that work which earlier had been called a comic novel, now *The Village of Stepanchikovo*. The somewhat shorter tale is *Uncle's Dream*. The novel of life in Petersburg, which was started and then abandoned, is *The Humiliated and Wronged*. The advance was taken and spent, the manuscript deadlines drew near and the tales were still not finished. "The long tale that I am writing for Katkov [*The Village of Stepanchikovo*] displeases me, has become repugnant. But much has already been written; to discard it in order to begin another is impossible, and I have to repay my debts." *Uncle's Dream* also did not please him. . . . "I find it sad that once again I am forced to appear in public in such poor guise. . . . For the sake of money I am compelled *expressly to invent* tales. And how oppressive this all is! It's vile having to work as a penniless writer." The tale *Uncle's Dream* which Dostoevsky "tossed off in haste," was printed in the March issue of the *Russian Word* for 1859.

The author himself gave a harsh appraisal of this unsuccessful work in a letter to M. P. Fyodorov, who wanted to adapt it for the stage (in 1873). "I had not reread my tale *Uncle's Dream* for fifteen years. And now, having reread it, I find it bad. I wrote it in Siberia at a time soon after leaving penal servitude, solely for the purpose of again beginning my literary career and terribly afraid of the censors (as regards a former convict). And consequently I unwillingly wrote a trifling thing of dovelike gentleness and remarkable innocence. It would still be possible to make a little vaudeville out of it, but as to a comedy — there is little content, even in the figure of the prince — the only serious figure in the whole tale." In fact the "innocence" of this thing borders on childishness. Prince K., an old man, who has lapsed into idiocy, comes by chance, in the city of Mordasov, to the house of a provincial lioness, Mariya Aleksandrovna Moskalyova; this latter envisages marrying him to her daughter, the proud beauty Zina. Zina's admirer, Mozglyakov, impedes Mariya Aleksandrovna's plan by convincing the prince that he made the proposal in his sleep. All the ladies of Mordasov gather at Moskalyova's; a scandal occurs. The prince is taken to a hotel and he dies there.

This is a vaudeville hastily remade into a tale. We again meet with Dostoevsky's characteristic propensity for the *theatrical*. In the same way as *Another Man's Wife and the Husband under the Bed, Uncle's Dream* is dependent upon stage perspective. Dialogue occupies a prominent place in it; the descriptions remind one of stage-directions. "It is ten o'clock in the morning. We are in the home of Mariya Aleksandrovna, on Grand Street. . . . The furniture, which is quite clumsy, is predominantly the color red. . . . In the spaces between the windows are two mirrors. . . . Near the back wall stands a fine piano. . . . Mariya Aleksandrovna herself is seated by the fireplace in the best of humors and in a light-green dress. . . , etc." The story is made up of theatrically significant scenes and ends with a dramatic denouement in which all the personages participate. The composition of Dostoevsky's novels is closely connected with *theatrical technique*; in *Uncle's Dream* this connection is displayed with particular clarity. Stylistically the tale is written in the old manner of the period before penal servitude: the ironic pathos of Gogol's *Story about How Ivan Ivanovich Quarrelled with Ivan Nikiforovich* is parodied in *Uncle's Dream*. "Mariya Aleksandrovna Moskalyova is, of course, the first lady in Mordasov and of that there can be no doubt. She conducts herself as though *she does not stand in need of anything*, but, to the contrary, all and everyone *stand in need of her*. . . . She knows, for example, such capital and scandalous things about certain persons in Mordasov that were she to *relate* them, on a suitable occasion, and *prove* them as she knows how to prove them, there would be an *earthquake* in Mordasov *comparable to the one in Lisbon*." The author considered the figure of the prince the "only serious one in the whole tale." It is interesting as regards its subsequent fate in Dostoevsky's work. The old prince is completely artificial. "He seemed to be entirely put together out of kind of tidbits. No one knew when and where he had managed to disintegrate so." He wears a wig; his moustache, side-whiskers, and imperial are false. He powders and rouges himself, wears a corset; one leg is made of cork, his right eye is glass. He has squandered away his entire fortune and lives on an estate under the dominion of his housekeeper.

This "corpse on springs" is a caricature of the Russian European-gentleman and Westernizer. What a rich past he has: he has written vaudevilles and couplets, was on friendly footing with Lord Byron; in Germany he studied philosophy, became a member of a Masonic lodge, seriously intended to grant freedom to his Sidor, and now thinks of traveling abroad "in order more conveniently to keep his eye on the European enlightenment." The author characterizes the prince by the peculiarities of his speech. Lyubov Dostoevskaya and Baron Vrangel report that the writer loved to "perform him," imitating his intonations. The hero's effeminate gentility is shown through the prism of his expressions and puns. "A few syllables he pronounced with uncommon sweetness, particularly stressing the letter 'e.' 'Yes' with him somehow came out 'ye-es,' but only a touch more sweetly." He loves to insert French phrases: "C'est délicieux! C'est charmant! Mais quelle beauté! Vous me ravissez," and to make a show of *bons mots*. He concludes the story of his hydropathic cure with the sentence: "Thus it is that if I, in the end, had not taken ill, then I assure you, I would have been completely healthy." Such is the portrait of the Russian nobleman at the beginning of the century, who had "disintegrated." The prince is the spiritual father of another "Russian European," Stepan Trofimovich Verkhovensky (*The Devils*). The latter is also a "handsome man," formerly a *bon vivant;* he also studied in Germany and is full of "noble ideas," also "keeps an eye on the European enlightenment," and despises Russia. He has the same effeminate intonations, French expressions, and "nobleman's" manners. The prince's "disintegration" is transformed into the morbid apprehension and "cholerine" of Stepan Trofimovich.

Next to the prince stands Moskalyova, "the first lady in the city," imperious, ambitious, and flighty. Suddenly she hits upon the idea of marrying the old man to her daughter; in *The Devils* there is the same situation: "the first lady in the city," Varvara Petrovna Stavrogina, unexpectedly decides to give her ward Dasha to Stepan Trofimovich. The "proud beauty" Zina loves another, but submits to her mother's will; Dasha also loves another, and likewise does not oppose her benefactress' wish. Thus a thread extends from the unsuccessful farce *Uncle's Dream* to the novel-tragedy *The Devils*. But the entire tale is not written in the style of a farce: there is inserted an episode from sentimental melodrama which borders directly upon the third part of *Netochka Nezvanova*. Netochka's protectress, Aleksandra Mikhailovna, had a romance with a certain "dreamer." By chance Netochka finds his letter and reads: "We were not equal. I was unworthy of you. Once, it is now a long time ago, I had a dream something like this, and *I dreamed like a fool*. . . . You have been bitterly mistaken in me! Never, never could I raise myself to your level!" The novel remained unfinished; thus we do not even know who this friend of Aleksandra Mikhailovna was and why he was unworthy of her. In *Uncle's Dream* this theme is developed more clearly and with certain bluntness. Zina is loved by Vasya, a teacher in the district school, a sexton's son, a "scribbler of rhymes" in the *Library for Reading*. The lovers quarrel; in order to avenge himself upon Zina, Vasya exhibits a letter of hers and that very evening attempts to poison himself. He does not die, but falls sick with consumption. Before his death he begs Zina's forgiveness:

> I was not fit to live. . . . I'm an evil and shallow man. . . . Ah, my friend, my whole life was a *dream*. I have only *dreamed*, always *dreamed*, and have not lived. . . . I wasn't even a villain at that moment, but was simply a *worthless individual*. . . . I can't help feeling, Zinochka, that even then I didn't escape from sweet *romantic nonsense*. Even at that point I kept thinking: how beautiful it would be, that here I would be lying on my bed, dying of consumption, while you would be pining away, suffering, to think that you had driven me to consumption. . . . It was stupid, Zinochka, stupid, wasn't it?

Dostoevsky's last work before penal servitude, *A Little Hero*, was an affirmation of heroism, romanticism, "Schillerism." Since then nine years had passed. Faced with the terrible reality of the "House of Death," his romantic ideals crumbled in a heap. In *Uncle's Dream* the romantic *dreamer is entirely deposed*. How dissimilar do we find the poet Vasya, an "evil and shallow man," to the dreamer Ordynov in *The Landlady* or to the hero of *White Nights*! The author judged his youth sternly; that by which he used earlier to live was now "sweet romantic nonsense." The dreamer, torn away from life, was simply a *"worthless individual."* And so after his political repentance began his exposure of literary idols. Romanticism was condemned as moral corruption.

Having sent his tale *Uncle's Dream* to the *Russian Word*, Dostoevsky continued work on *The Village of Stepanchikovo*. On May 3, 1859, he wrote his brother:

> This novel, of course, has very great deficiencies and above all, perhaps, its length; but what I'm convinced of as of an axiom is that it also has at the same time great merits and that it is the *best of my works*. I've been writing it for two years (with an interruption in the middle for *Uncle's Dream*). The beginning and middle are set, the end I have been writing hurriedly. But here I have placed my soul,

my flesh and blood. I don't want to say that I've talked myself out in it entirely; that would be nonsense. There will still be much that I have to express. Besides there is little of the heart in the novel (that is, of the passionate element, as for example in *A Nest of Gentlefolk*), but there are in it two vast, typical characters which I have been creating and noting down for five years, which have been formed perfectly (in my opinion), characters that are completely Russian and until now poorly portrayed in Russian literature.

The *Russian Messenger* returned the novel because it could not agree to the author's stipulation (100 rubles a sheet).[A] The manuscript was given to *The Contemporary*, but Nekrasov did not like it. Dostoevsky was upset: "For God's sake," he wrote his brother, "be more gentle and delicate with them. You needn't give the impression that we're *sick at heart and afraid.* . . . But here, what I don't like: if we're forcing ourselves upon *Fatherland Notes*. The novel is being *spat upon* and it will be buried with coffinlike silence. Besides it's really *not effective.* . . . But, however, if *Fatherland Notes* will give 120 without difficulty, I'll agree." Finally, *The Village of Stepanchikovo* was bought by A. Krayevsky and appeared in the 127th issue of *Fatherland Notes* for 1859.

The novel *The Village of Stepanchikovo and its Inhabitants. From the Notes of an Unknown* is constructed according to the rules of classical comedy: after the exposition of the intrigue and the characters, the action develops in two dramatic situations, and after an effective catastrophe (the expulsion of Foma Opiskin) it concludes with a happy denouement ("Foma Fomich establishes general happiness"). The sole action is concentrated in one place and within a short segment of time (two days). The dialogues' expressiveness and the tension of the situations heighten the novel's *theatrical quality*.

Col. Rostanev's mother, a general's widow, has come with her pugdogs and cats to settle on her son's estate; immediately after her also arrived Foma Fomich Opiskin who had lived in her house as a hangeron. This pharisee and despot has brought both the general's lady and her son under the subjection of his influence. Rostanev is in love with his ward Nastenka whom Opiskin is pursuing. The novel ends with the hypocrite's shameful expulsion. Dostoevsky reproduces exactly the subject schema of Molière's *Tartuffe*.[B] Foma Fomich is the Russian

[A] At that time Turgenev was paid 400 rubles.
[B] N. Alekseyev, *O dramaticheskikh opytakh Dostoevskogo* (Regarding Dostoevsky's Dramatic Experiments), Odessa 1921.

Tartuffe, Rostanev is Orgon, his mother Mme Pernelle. Rostanev's nephew and Nastenka, who contend against the pharisee, correspond to Molière's Damis and Elmire. Cléante is transformed into the landowner Bakhcheyev, who helps unmask Foma and appears just before the catastrophe. The original comic design itself determines the novel's *dynamic structure*. Its content is Rostanev's struggle with Opiskin. Four chapters of the first part expound the causes and circumstances of the conflict and present the combatants' characteristics. The fifth chapter commences the firing between Rostanev's camp and that of Foma. The main hero, Opiskin, steps forward triumphantly only in the seventh chapter. The enemies' first encounter ends in Foma's complete victory; Rostanev humbly asks his forgiveness. From there, up until the fourth chapter in the second part, a "general encounter" is gradually being prepared. It begins with an attack by Foma and ends with Rostanev's counterattack. But the crafty pharisee turns his defeat into victory. In the denouement he steps forward as everyone's common benefactor. The tension of the conflict is increased by the slow development of the action and the unexpected explosions. They all enhance, and lead ultimately to, the final turmoil, the catastrophe.

This is the general principle of the dynamic structure of Dostoevsky's novels. In *The Village of Stepanchikovo* it is for the first time applied systematically. The exposition introduces the reader into the tense atmosphere of the work. The unreasonable Foma reigns without opposition. But a resistance is already growing against his tyranny. In the fourth chapter all the characters, with the exception of Opiskin, are presented in a big "ensemble scene." The inhabitants of the village of Stepanchikovo are gathered around the table for tea. The narrator exclaims: "Well, what odd creatures! It's *as though* they were gathered here on purpose!" We sense that a thunderstorm is approaching and we hear its first peals. The personages seem to be saturated with electric energy and in turn they "explode." The first to give way is Rostanev's daughter, Sashenka. "Horrid, horrid Foma Fomich," she cries, "I'll say it openly; I'm not afraid of anyone! He is stupid, capricious, dirty, base, a tyrant, a gossip-monger, a little liar. . . . And I would tear him to pieces, your Foma Fomich! I would challenge him to a duel, and there would kill him with two pistols." There is universal consternation. The General's lady falls into a faint. This is the *first scandal*. In the seventh chapter the valet Gavrila "explodes." Opiskin has forced him to study French vocabulary words. He cries to Foma: "You have become now a completely wicked man. . . . You, though by birth even a gen'ral's son, and yourself, maybe, are not far from being a gen'ral, but are so wicked as, that's to say, a real fury must be." This is the *second scandal*. The third is provoked by Rostanev's nephew. "'But he is drunk,' I said looking around in bewilderment. 'Who? Me?' shouted Foma in a voice not like his own. 'Yes, you!' — 'Drunk?' — 'Drunk!' . . . The General's lady seemed ready to faint, but judged it better to run after Foma."

The "general encounter" between Opiskin and Rostanev is even more dynamic. It is the name-day of Rostanev's son, Ilyusha. Everyone is gathered in Foma's room. Ilyusha is declaiming verses. And suddenly there is a *"scandal"*: Foma declares that he can no longer remain in the Colonel's house for the latter is immorally involved in an affair with his ward. "You have succeeded," he shouts, "in turning a hitherto most innocent girl into the most depraved of girls." Here, at last, the gentle Rostanev himself "explodes" and throws Opiskin out. "Uncle seized him by the shoulders, turned him round like a straw and violently threw him against the glass-door. . . . The impact was so strong that the half-closed doors themselves opened wide and Foma who had flown head over heels down the seven stone steps, was stretched out in the yard. Tiny bits of broken glass were scattered about near the bottom of the staircase." The stage effect of the "catastrophe" is underlined by a *thunderstorm*. The dramatic energy is discharged. A happy denouement is set forth. The "thunderstorm," its approach, its development and explosion — these are the symbols of the structure of Dostoevsky's novels.

The author boasted of the fact that in *The Village of Stepanchikovo* he had created "two vast, typical characters." These are Foma Fomich Opiskin and the "uncle" — Colonel Rostanev. The Russian Tartuffe — Opiskin — had been in government service somewhere, had suffered for truth, used to occupy himself with literature, with eloquent tears commented on various Christian virtues, would go to Liturgy and even to matins, at times used to predict the future, and in a skillful way condemned his neighbor. "Imagine," says the narrator, "the most insignificant, the most cowardly individual, an abortion of society, of no use to anyone, utterly worthless, completely vile, but immensely egotistic and moreover, decidedly not endowed with anything by which he could have in some way justified his morbidly sensitive vanity. I caution beforehand: Foma Fomich is the personification of the most boundless vanity, but . . . of an oppressed vanity, crushed by previous failures, one that began to fester long, long ago and ever since that time has given off envy and poison, at every encounter, at every other person's success." Yu. Tynyanov in his work *Dostoevsky and Gogol* convincingly showed this figure to be a *parody*. All of Dostoevsky's creative work in the period before his exile passed under the aegis of Gogol. He used to imitate him as a master, and struggled against him. He took an active part in Gogol's controversy with Belinsky, and the image of the author of *Correspondence with Friends* pursued him even in penal servitude. In *The Village of Stepanchikovo* the writer settles accounts with his "Gogolian period" and mercilessly avenges himself upon that which was the "authority of the thoughts" of his youth. Foma Fomich is a caricature of Gogol. He too is a man of letters, a preacher, an instructor of morality. Under his influence, in the epilogue of the novel, Nastenka begins to read the lives of the saints, and says with compunction that "ordinary good deeds are still not enough, that one ought to distribute everything to the poor and be content in poverty." Among his Moscow friends, Gogol found everywhere a quiet lodging, a servant girl, a table with his favorite foods. In Rostanev's home "complete comfort surrounds the great man." Everyone walks on tiptoe and whispers: "He is writing a work!" Foma develops the idea of two articles taken from Gogol's *Correspondence with Friends: The Russian Landowner* and *To the Man Occupying a Prominent Place*. His reflections on literature parody Gogol's essay: *The Subject for a Lyric Poet*. He preaches the salutary advantage of sufferings, quoting Gogol directly: "As for myself I will only say that misfortune is perhaps the mother of virtue. This was said, I believe, by Gogol, a frivolous writer, but who from time to time had some *meaty* thoughts."

All the devices of Gogol's preaching style are comically exaggerated. In his *Testament* Gogol wrote: "I choose that no memorial be erected over me." Foma exclaims: "Do not put up a *monument* to me! Do not put one up to me! I do not need *monuments*! Raise up a *monument* to me in your own hearts, and nothing more is needed!"

Gogol thought to save Russia by his preaching, dreamed of an ascetic feat, of a monastic cell. Foma Fomich also awaits a feat: "to write a most profoundly thoughtful composition of the soul-saving sort, which will give rise to a universal earthquake and all Russia will convulse. And when all Russia has convulsed, then he, Foma, scorning glory, will enter a monastery and day and night pray in the Kiev Caves for the happiness of the Fatherland."

In the *Correspondence with Friends* lofty pathos is joined to the most common expressions; such phrases, for example, are to be encountered: "Only in a stupid worldly noodle could such a stupid thought have taken shape." Foma's sermon is in the same mixed style; he declares: "*Only in a stupid worldly noodle* could the necessity of such absurd proprieties have been conceived."

Foma Opiskin is, in fact, a "vast, typical character." The immortal figure of the Russian Tartuffe has forever entered our literature, but it is painful to think that in creating it, the author decided so unjustly to abase his teacher Gogol. While ridiculing its human weaknesses and errors of style, he did not appreciate the enormous spiritual and social significance of the *Correspondence with Friends*. On the other hand, Dostoevsky was indebted to Gogol not only for the technique of his verbal art, but also for the basis of his religious world-outlook. Gogol's thoughts regarding the role of Christian art, the structuring of society on the ground of ecclesiastic communality, and the transfiguration of the world through the inner illumination of man were wholly assimilated by Dostoevsky.

The other "vast character," about which the author speaks, was left in a somewhat clouded state. Colonel Yegor Ilyich Rostanev is not a "character," but only the rough sketch of a "character." Before the final embodiment of this concept Dostoevsky had still to spend many years.

Rostanev is an epic hero: "tall and well-built with ruddy cheeks, with teeth white as ivory, with a long dark-blond moustache, with a loud, sonorous voice and a frank, hearty laugh." This is a man of refined delicacy, honorable and courageous; his goodness knows no limits. He considers all men angels and is ready to give away everything provided "all might be content and happy." His ardent and pure heart lives in enthusiasm. When his nephew expounds his humane ideas to him ("in the most fallen creature there still can exist the loftiest human sentiments") and in conclusion reads Nekrasov's verses:

When out of the darkness of error. . . ,

the uncle goes into ecstasy. " 'My dearest, my friend,' he said much affected, 'you understand me completely. . . . It's so, it's really so! Lord, why is it that man is wicked? Why am I so often wicked, when it's so fine, so splendid to be good!' " The uncle's enraptured monologue about the beauty of nature reminds one of Dmitry Karamazov's "hymn." "But just look, though," says Rostanev, "what a glorious spot we have here! What nature! What a picture! What a tree, just look at it; it's as big around as a man. What sap, what foliage! What sunshine! How after the storm everything has become joyous, has been washed clean! Why, one might think that even the trees understand, that they also feel for themselves and rejoice in life. . . . Wonderful, wonderful is the Creator!"

One recalls Dostoevsky's letter to his brother from Petropavlovsky Fortress: the seventeen trees in the small prison courtyard, the longing for green leaves, the exclamation "on voit le soleil." All the ecstasies of his heroes are bound to these tokens of nature.

In the figure of Rostanev, humble and pure of heart, one can see the author's first attempt to portray a "positively beautiful individual." It did not succeed; the uncle emerged as too colorless a personality and character. But in his soul there was already kindled the "cosmic rapture" of Dmitry Karamazov. Yet another line stretches out from *The Village of Stepanchikovo* to *The Brothers Karamazov*. It links the lackey Vidoplyasov with the lackey Smerdyakov. At its first embodiment one of the most ominous and tragic figures in Dostoevsky's world bears a comic character. But strangely, even in this farcical appearance it does not make one laugh.

Vidoplyasov was still a young man, well dressed for a servant, not worse than many a provincial fop. . . . *His face was pale and even livid;* he had a long, hooked nose, thin, unusually white, as though it were made of china. The *smile on his thin lips* expressed a certain melancholy and yet a refined melancholy. His large eyes, prominent and as though made of glass, had an extraordinarily dull expression and yet, for all that, gleamed with refinement. His thin, soft ears were stopped up with wadding, out of refinement. His long, fair, and sparse hair was set in curls and pomaded. His dainty hands were white, clean, and had all but been washed in rose water. He was short, *flabby, and weak,* and walked about somewhat in a cowering position.

Like Smerdyakov, he has also lived in Moscow, despises the country, writes verse — *The Lamentations Of Vidoplyasov* — has grasped upon a number of small ideas. "All the distinguished people used to say," he declares, "that I quite resemble a foreigner, preeminently in the features of my face." He conceives of culture as "refinement" and foppishness, like a lackey, becomes unbalanced as regards the sense of his own personal dignity, and wants to change his name to a more elegant one such as Oleandrov, Tyulpanov, Essbuketov.[1] Dostoevsky's

[1] *Vid* in Russian means aspect, look, appearance; *plyas* = dance; *oleandr* = oleander, rose bay; *tyulpan* = tulip; and *essbuket* (*bouquet*) was apparently written on bottles of scented pomade.

heroes are above all else characterized by their speech; all the unforgettable intonations of the moralist Smerdyakov are already present in the "lackeyish speech" of Vidoplyasov. "It is an unfounded name, sir," the latter argues. "Indeed it is, sir. It suggests all sorts of abomination. It is true, sir, that through my parents I have in that way had to suffer all my life, sir, inasmuch as I am destined by my name to receive many derisions and to endure many sorrows. . . ."

Vidoplyasov stands in awe of the *"philosopher"* Foma Fomich. The landowner Bakhcheyev says to Rostanev's nephew: "And at your uncle's, he alone [Foma] has driven the lackey Vidoplyasov almost to the point of insanity, *that learned fellow of yours!* That Vidoplyasov has lost his senses through Foma Fomich." Thus are marked the future relations between the lackey Smerdyakov and his "learned brother," the "philosopher" Ivan Karamazov. Let us note, lastly, in *The Village of Stepanchikovo* an allusion given in passing to a dramatic situation which in *The Brothers Karamazov* develops into the famous encounter scene between the two rivals, Grushenka and Katerina Ivanovna. In it the idyll of reconciliation culminates in a rift when Grushenka asks for "the young lady's little hand" . . . and does not kiss it. In *The Village of Stepanchikovo* the poor civil servant and willing buffoon Yezhevikin, upon becoming acquainted with Rostanev's nephew, also asks for his "little hand." "Laughter rang out . . . I was about to withdraw my hand — it seems that this was just what the old man was waiting for. 'But I only asked to shake it, little father, if only you will allow me, and not to kiss it. And now you thought that I meant to kiss it? No, father of mine, as for the present I still only want to shake it. . . . But treat me with consideration; I'm really not such a scoundrel as you think.' "[c]

Among the guests who have collected at Rostanev's country manor, "the most conspicuous of all was a certain very strange lady who was dressed richly and in extremely youthful fashion, although she was far from being young, at any rate, about thirty." This old maid, Tatyana Ivanovna, who has spent her entire life in the homes of benefactresses and has drained to the bottom the cup of humiliation, has just received a large inheritance and is unbalanced regarding the prospect

[c] Yezhevikin belongs to the family of "willing buffoons," the progenitor of which is Polzunkov in the story of the same name. Members of this family are: Marmeladov in *Crime and Punishment*, Lebedev in *The Idiot*, Lebyadkin in *The Devils*, and Fyodor Pavlovich Karamazov in *Brothers Karamazov*.

of suitors. A meek, daydreaming, magnanimous "half-wit," she awaits her fated-one; he will be the "ideal of beauty," "all possible perfection," an artist, a poet, or general's son.

"Her face was very lean, pale, and withered, but extraordinarily animated. A vivid flush appeared continually on her pale cheeks, almost at her every movement. . . . I, however, liked her eyes, light blue and gentle, and although around these eyes little wrinkles were already to be seen, nonetheless their regard was so open-hearted, so gay and kind, that somehow it was especially pleasant to meet with them."

The "half-wit" Tatyana Ivanovna is a first draft of the "holy fool" Marya Timofeyevna in *The Devils*. Mlle Lebyadkina is also about thirty years old. . . . "On her narrow and high forehead, in spite of her makeup, three long *wrinkles* stood out in sharp contour. . . . Sometime or other in her youth this face, which had grown thin, may even have been pretty. But her quiet, *affectionate* grey eyes were and are still now remarkable; a certain something dreamy and *sincere* shined in her peaceful, almost *joyful regard*." She also dreams about her fated-one, awaits for her Ivan the Tsarevich. Tatyana Ivanovna coquettishly throws a rose at the feet of Rostanev's nephew. Dostoevsky sensed that the rose was symbolically fitted to the image of this poor unbalanced woman. He saved it also for his "lame" heroine. Marya Timofeyevna comes to church with a rose in her hair.

The *Village of Stepanchikovo* was a relay on Dostoevsky's path. The Gogolian road had been traversed to its end; ahead opened up the perspective of the novel-tragedy.

In January 1858 the writer submitted a request to be allowed to retire and asked permission to return to Russia. The imperial order granting his discharge was received only in March 1859. He was not permitted to live in the capitals and as a place of residence he chose Tver. On July 2 he left Semipalatinsk. Dostoevsky describes his journey in a letter to his Company Commander A. Geibovich: "On the road I had two attacks and since that time it has let up. . . . The weather remained very favorable. Almost the entire journey the carriage did not break down (not once!); there was no delay in getting horses. . . . The forests of Perm are magnificent, and those of Vyatka, utter perfection. . . . One beautiful evening, about five o'clock in the afternoon, wandering in the foothills of the Urals, in the midst of a forest we came at last upon the border of Europe and Asia. An excellent post had been set up with inscriptions and near it in a hut was an old disabled soldier. We got out of the carriage, and I crossed myself because the Lord had finally brought me to see the 'promised land.' " He stayed in Kazan for ten days awaiting money from his brother. He went to the fair at Nizhny; visited the Sergius Monastery. "I had not been in it for 23 years. What architecture, what monuments, Byzantine halls, churches! The sacristy filled us with wonder." In Tver he rented an apartment and began to wait for his brother. Mikhail Mikhailovich arrived in September. "What joy there was. . . . We discussed a great many things. But what! how can one tell of such moments. He remained with me for about five days."

In Tver the writer longed for Petersburg. "Tver is the most hateful city on earth," he wrote his brother. He worked in confusion; planned a new novel "with an idea" and decided to spend a whole year writing it without hurrying. He proposed to redo the tale *The Double* and to publish his works in three volumes; he advised his brother "to run a risk and undertake some literary enterprise, a journal, for example." But his main wish was to return quickly to Petersburg. He wrote to Vrangel, Timashev, Dolgorukov, to the sovereign himself. At last permission was granted and in December 1859 Dostoevsky returned to the capital. He had left it exactly ten years before.

Notes from the House of Death

In his copy-book Dostoevsky set down his literary plans for the year 1860: "1) Mignon, 2) Spring Love, 3) The Double (revise), 4) Notes of a Convict (excerpts), 5) Apathy and Impressions." No drafts have been preserved on the theme of "Mignon," but the image of the heroine of Goethe's novel *Wilhelm Meister* remains invisibly present in the writer's work. From Tver he informed Mikhail Mikhailovich that he was contemplating "two big novels"; the latter answered him: "My dearest, perhaps I am wrong, but your two full novels will be something in the nature of Wilhelm Meister's *Lehrjahre*. Let them also be written as Wilhelm Meister was, in fragments, little by little, over a period of years. Then they will turn out as successful as Goethe's two novels." A rivalry with Goethe is felt in the *Humiliated and Wronged:* the litterateur, Ivan Petrovich, is no less related to the author's biography than is Wilhelm Meister to the life of Goethe himself; the figure of Nelly is inspired by that of Mignon. The idea of Goethe's novel — renunciation of personal happiness for the sake of serving one's neighbor — decidedly influenced the composition of *The Humiliated and Wronged.* The name of Mignon is encountered even later in Dostoevsky's copy-book; while working on *The Idiot* and *The Devils,* he did not abandon the thought of creating a "Russian Mignon." The revision of *The Double* was limited to several abridgments of the original text; from the excerpts of *Notes of a Convict* we have received an entire book: *Notes from the House of Death.* Not a trace of *Apathy and Impressions* has been preserved, but the plan of *Spring Love* has come down to us in several variants.

A rich prince is traveling with his dependent, a "writer." They stop in a provincial city where the prince acts the role of a "man with convictions"; he is surrounded by the servile respect of all society. He begins to pay suit to the fiancée of a certain wretched civil servant; this latter surrenders herself to him, believing that he will marry and save her from her betrothed, whom she despises. But the prince is afraid of hurting his career. The writer sacrifices himself and marries the disgraced girl. In this rough sketch already appear the features of the heroes of *The Humiliated and Wronged:* the prince is Alyosha, the writer Ivan Petrovich, the fiancée Natasha. The prince's "playing of the liberal" will be assumed by Alyosha Volkovsky; later this motif will be treated in *A Nasty Predicament.*

In the variants, these themes are noted: the civil servant's marriage to the "sins of the prince"; the offender is slapped; the marriage of the prince himself; enmity between the prince and the writer. All these are as yet unclear allusions to several situations in *The Devils* (Stepan Trofimovich suspects that they want to marry him to the "sins of Stavrogin"; Shatov's slap; Stavrogin's marriage; the enmity between Stavrogin and Shatov).

The idea of publishing a monthly journal came to Mikhail Mikhailovich Dostoevsky as early as 1858; Fyodor Mikhailovich's return to Petersburg hastened its realization. The year 1860 was for the Dostoevsky brothers full of the toils and drudgery of organizing the journal; a program was worked out, literary connections were established, contributors were chosen, material was gathered. Fyodor Mikhailovich, in the midst of all this concern regarding the journal, found time to work on two books: *Notes from the House of Death* and *The Humiliated and Wronged.*

This same year witnessed his short-lived passion for the actress Aleksandra Ivanovna Schubert. Dostoevsky's old friend, Doctor Stepan Dmitriyevich Yanovsky, had married the actress Schubert, whose father was a serf. Dostoevsky, a friend of the family, took part in the family drama. Schubert did not get along well with her husband, and left him to go to Moscow. The writer dreamed of turning out "a little comedy, though of one act" and of presenting it to the artist "as a sign of his most profound regard." He traveled to Moscow to comfort her and upon his return, tenderly asked her forgiveness "for foisting his friendship upon her." In his last letter he assures her that he is not in love with her, but these assurances are written in a gallantly amorous tone.

I speak to you frankly: I loved you very much and ardently up to the time when I myself told you that I was not in love with you, because

I value your good opinion, and, my God, how I grieved when it seemed that you had deprived me of your confidence. I blamed myself. Indeed, what torture that was! . . . I am so glad that I am convinced that I am not in love with you! This gives me the possibility of remaining still attached to you without fearing for my own heart. I know that I am attached disinterestedly. Farewell, my dove, with veneration and faith I kiss your dear mischievous little hand and squeeze it with all my heart.

The "veneration" is not fully consistent with the "mischievous hand"; the "disinterested attachment" seems too playfully gallant. Dostoevsky in the role of comforting his friend Yanovsky's wife calls to mind the writer Ivan Petrovich in the equivocal position of Natasha's comforter and friend of her fiancé Alyosha (*The Humiliated and Wronged*).

In Omsk jail the writer listened to the convict's speech and noted down precise expressions, sayings, folk elements. In a letter to his brother after his release from prison he wrote: "How many popular types, characters have I brought with me out of penal servitude! . . . How many stories of vagrants and robbers. . . . *It will suffice for entire volumes.*" In 1856 he informed A. Maikov: "At times when I have nothing to do, I write down some of the memories of my stay in penal servitude, which was extremely curious. By the way, there is little here that is purely personal." The notations were interrupted for three years. For his "return to literature" this theme appeared as dangerous to him; he wrote *Uncle's Dream* and *The Village of Stepanchikovo*. In the fall of 1859 at Tver he conceived the plan for a "little book." "*Notes from the House of Death*," he wrote his brother, "has now assumed in my mind a complete and definite plan. It will be a little book of about six or seven printed sheets. My personality will disappear from view. These are the notes of an unknown; but I vouch for their interest. That interest will be of the most capital sort. Here there will be the serious, the gloomy, and the humorous and *folk conversation with its particular penal servitude colorings* (I read you several of the expressions which I had written down on the *spot*), and the depiction of personalities unheard-of in literature, and the touching, and, finally, most important — my name. . . ."

Notes from the House of Death. A Novel in Two Parts was originally printed in the year 1860 in the newspaper *The Russian World*. The first chapters were reprinted in the Dostoevsky brothers' journal *Time* and the whole novel was published in it in the course of 1861 and 1862. A. Milyukov writes in his memoirs (*Literary Meetings and Acquaintances*):

> This work came out under circumstances that were quite favorable; the censorship at that time was animated by a breath of tolerance and in literature works appeared which until recently were still unthinkable in print. Although the novelty of the book, devoted exclusively to the mode of convict life, the somber canvas of all these stories about terrible evildoers and, lastly, the fact that the author himself was a political criminal who had just returned, somewhat disturbed the censor, yet this, notwithstanding, did not force Dostoevsky to deviate in anything from the truth, and *Notes from the House of Death* produced a startling impression. In the author they saw as it were a new Dante who had descended into hell, the more horrible in that it existed not in a poet's imagination, but in reality.

Dostoevsky rightly apprised the *factual* interest in his work: a former convict's story about that unknown and terrible world from which he had only recently returned acquired in the reader's eyes an historical authenticity. The writer continually underlines the character of a witness's testimony; he is, so to say, describing simply and exactly everything that he saw and heard himself. The fiction of the narrator-prisoner Aleksandr Petrovich Goryanchikov cannot deceive; everywhere is heard the voice of Dostoevsky, an eye-witness of the events. The second fiction — the absence of the "personal element" — is as conventional as the first. It is true the author presents himself in the role of a navigator who has opened up a new world and objectively describes its geography, people, manners, and customs. "Here was a peculiar world, not like anything else; here were its own peculiar laws, its own dress, its own manners and customs, and a living house of death, a life as nowhere else and a people set apart." But this description is not at all the communication of a learned traveler. Both the author's devices and his goal are different. "Objectivity" is only a means for augmenting the given impression; factual authenticity is considered as a foundation of artistic authenticity. The matter-of-fact and annalistic quality of the style heightens the illusion of documentation. With enormous skill Dostoevsky fashions out of his *personal* impressions, feelings, and evaluations the "peculiar world" of penal servitude, and artistically persuades us of its reality. At first glance it appears that the creator is not seen behind his creation; but having carefully examined the creation, we notice that it is all a revelation of its creator's personality.

Notes from the House of Death has an unusually adept structure. The description of prison life and of the convicts' temperaments, the robbers' histories, the characteristics of individual criminals, reflections regarding the psychology of crime, a picture of conditions in the jail, journalism, philosophy, and folklore — all this complex material is distributed freely, almost without order. Meanwhile all the details are calculated and the particulars subordinated to a general plan. The principle of composition in the *Notes* is not static, but *dynamic*. The author sketches in rapid strokes a broad picture: the fortress, the jail, the earthen rampart, barracks, the prison courtyard, work in the shops or on the banks of the Irtysh; the prisoners, their external appearance, occupations, manners; from the crowd of men that have been branded and put in chains, a few representative figures are called forth; the first morning in jail; conversation over tea; the carousing and drunkenness; evening — neighbors lying on their plank-beds: their histories; reflections on the "house of death" (chapters 1-4). These are the impressions on the first day of prison life. The story continues with the first month spent in jail; the theme of work on the Irtysh returns; new meetings and acquaintances are described; the most typical scenes of the convicts' life are depicted. Then the story of the first year is centered in several picturesque episodes: the bathhouse, the feast of Christmas, a theatrical, Easter. In the second part the events of the following years are summarized. The succession of time almost disappears. Such is the perspective of the narrative: the foreground (the first day) is brightly illumined and all the details are drawn precisely, the second plane (the first month) is more feebly lighted and presented in general strokes; and the further the planes recede, the broader is the generalization. The many-leveled composition corresponds to the design: the jail is immobile; it is the "house of death" frozen in perpetuity, but the author moves. He descends through the circles of hell. In the beginning he is an external observer, grasping only the most glaring and striking features; later he takes part in prison life; finally, he penetrates into the mysterious depths of this world, he perceives anew that which had been seen, reevaluates his first impressions, deepens his own conclusions. The return to themes that already have been treated is explained by the action from the periphery to the center, from the surface to the depths. The angle of vision gradually changes, and familiar pictures are illuminated each time in a new fashion.

The prison folk are characterized by their language. The mixture of colloquial speech from all the ends of Russia with the thieves' jargon is full of an original expressive power. It abounds with proverbs, sayings, aphorisms and pointed comparisons. The author indicates the people's love for verbal disputes, for ready-witted answers, for artistic invective. In jail abuse almost never ends in a fight; the prisoners find in it aesthetic pleasure of their own sort. Here is an example of such verbal combat:

"The wolf's got one song and you've picked it up! But then you're from Tula!"

"So let's suppose I am from Tula. In your Poltava you used to choke yourselves with dumplings."

"Go and lie! You yourselves, what did you eat! You ladled out cabbage soup with a bast-shoe."

"And now it's just like the devil feeds us with buckshot."

"To tell you the truth, brothers, I am a pampered fellow; from earliest childhood I was tried on prunes and dainty loaves. My own blood brothers have a shop in Moscow to this day. They haggle over the wind in Passerby Row; extremely rich merchants they are."

"Why, they might go hunting after you now instead of sable. . . ."

"But then, it's my head that's worth a lot, brothers, my head!"

"Even that head of his is not his own, but a gift of charity; it was given him in Tyumen for Christ's sake, when he came with the gang. . . ."

This vibrant and colorful speech bears witness to the acute sense of observation and somber humor of the morose and sarcastic prisoners.

The pictures of life in the prison are shocking in their grim strength. Dostoevsky plunges his scenes in an ominous darkness and suddenly, with a brilliant, ghastly light, he illumines several deformed, branded faces, shaven skulls, figures wearing the prison jacket one half of which is dark brown, the other gray. Known to all is the story of the prison theatricals in which the folk plays *Filatka and Miroshka* and *Kedril the Glutton* are performed; unforgettable are the accounts of the celebration of Christmas in the jail, of the "grievance" addressed by the criminals on their being served bad food, of two prisoners' escape, but as a real chef d'oeuvre of descriptive art there stands the portrayal of the bathhouse, "simply Dantean," in Turgenev's expression. The studied dryness of tone, the calm sketching of details intensify the impression.

When we opened the door to the bathhouse, I thought that we were entering hell. . . . Steam, blinding the eyes, soot, filth, crowding. . . . On the entire floor there wasn't a spot as big as your palm where prisoners were not sitting, squatted down, splashing themselves from their pails. . . . On the shelf about fifty birch switches were being raised and lowered at the same time; everyone used to whip himself to the point of intoxication. They increased the steam every minute. This was no longer heat; it was boiling fire. The whole place roared with shouting and laughter to the accompaniment of a hundred chains being dragged along the floor. . . . Filth poured down on all sides. Everyone was in a kind of intoxication, in a state of excitement; there were shrieks and cries. . . . The prisoners' shaven heads and their bodies, which were steamed crimson, looked more monstrous than ever. On a back which has been scorched with heat, usually the scars, received at some time or other from the blows of whips and sticks, show forth clearly so that now all these backs seemed freshly covered with wounds. Horrible scars! . . . The steam is increased, and it covers the entire bathhouse in a dense, hot cloud; everyone began to laugh, to shout. Out of the cloud of steam gleamed beaten backs, shaven heads, bent arms, legs. . . .

In contrast to this infernal orgy there is the moving description of the prisoners' preparation to receive the sacrament during Passion Week. Against the background of this "hellish" gloom shines the spring light of approaching Easter: "the prisoners prayed very earnestly, and each of them brought his poor kopeck to the church every time for a candle or to place in the church collection. 'Why, I too am a man,' perhaps he thought or felt as he gave it, 'before God, all are equal.' We took the sacrament at the early Liturgy. When the priest, with the chalice in his hands, read the words: 'But like the thief receive me,' almost everyone prostrated himself to the ground, the shackles resounding, apparently applying these words literally to himself."

This "depiction," this that had been "seen and heard" forms the exterior stratum of the *Notes*. A new, peculiar world had been opened before the writer's astonished gaze. But he is not confined by a description of its surface; he strives to enter it inwardly, to understand the "law" of this world, to penetrate its mystery. The concrete for him is only the envelopment of the spiritual, the image — the starting point of the movement of ideas; depiction resolves into interpretation. The dynamics of the structure are disclosed in the philosophical perception of the experience of the "house of death."

Life itself arranged for Dostoevsky the experiment from which his philosophy developed. His first impressions of penal servitude were terror, surprise, and despair; years were needed before he believed in this new reality and came to understand it. And now by degrees everything terrible, monstrous, and mysterious that surrounded him began to clear in his consciousness. He understood that "the whole significance of the word 'prisoner' denotes a man without a will" and that all the peculiarities of penal servitude are explained by one idea "the loss of freedom." It seemed he could have known this earlier; "however," remarks Dostoevsky, "reality yields a completely different impression than *learning and hearsay*." The author does not exaggerate the horrors of prison life: he did not find work in the shops too difficult; the food was tolerable; the authorities, with a few exceptions, were humane and well-disposed; in the jail one could occupy oneself with a chosen trade. "The prisoners, although they wore shackles, walked freely all over the jail, swore at one another, sang songs, worked for themselves, smoked pipes, even drank vodka, and at night some organized card-playing." It was possible to grow accustomed to the physical sufferings (the noise, smoke, the stench, the cold). The torture of penal servitude is not in this: *it is in restraint*. . . .

Having made this discovery, the writer returns to the characterization of his comrades in misfortune and deepens it. In the first chapter he had noted their passion for money, now (in the fifth chapter) he explains it. The prisoner is greedy for money, and through bloody sweat, amidst the greatest dangers, he earns a kopeck; but after long months of accumulation, in one hour he dissipates all his savings. Why? Because with a spree he buys that which he "values still one degree higher than money. And what is higher than money to a prisoner? Freedom or at least some dream of freedom. . . . He can persuade himself *if only for a time* that he has incomparably more liberty and power than it appears. . . . Finally, in all this carousing there is its own risk, that is, all this has at least some semblance of life, at least a remote *semblance of freedom*. And what will you not surrender for freedom?" Out of the yearning for freedom flow all the peculiarities of the convicts' character. The prisoners are great dreamers. That is why they are so somber and reserved, why they so fear to let themselves go and so hate chatterers and fun-makers. There is in them a certain convulsive restlessness, they never feel themselves at home in jail, they are burdened by the work because it is *compulsory*, they are hostile and quarrel among themselves since living together is *by force*.

"Among the prisoners," writes the author, "no regard of friendship was ever to be observed. I do not speak in general, this is already so much the more, but in particular, that some one prisoner might make friends with another. . . . This is a remarkable feature; *it does not happen this way in freedom*." Men deprived of liberty are oppressed, join in senseless arguments, work with aversion. But if they are allowed to manifest their initiative, they are at once transformed. "Tasks" in the workshops are always completed before time; at the theatricals the actors display a mass of invention and talent. On a holiday, having spruced themselves up, they feel that they are men like everyone else, they become attentively polite and friendly. And what joy and high spirits reign in the jail at the purchase of the bay horse! The prisoners understand their own responsibility for the general affair, haggle, examine the horses, just like "free men." The *motif of freedom* runs through the entire book; the whole structure is determined by this ideological design. At the end of the *Notes* there is a story of a wounded eagle which used to live in the prison courtyard. The prisoners set him free and for a long time gaze after him with their eyes. "'Look at 'im!' said one thoughtfully. 'Won't even look back!' added another. 'Not once, brothers, has he looked back; he's running off for himself!' 'And what did you think he would turn around to thank you?' observed a third. 'It's a well-known thing — freedom. He has smelled freedom!' 'Liberty, that is.' 'You can't even see him now, brothers.' 'What are you standing there for? March!' the escorts began to shout, and all in silence trudged off to work. . . ." The idea of the *Notes* is freedom, embodied in the symbol-image of the eagle.

The censorship committee was concerned by the description of several "licenses" that had a place in the Omsk jail: white bread, vodka, smoking. Dostoevsky sent two pages of "supplement" which did not go into any edition. This reflection summarizes the main idea of the book: there is no higher torment for a man than the loss of freedom. "What is bread! Bread is eaten in order to live, but here there is no life! Try, build a palace. Furnish it with marble, pictures, gold, birds of paradise, hanging gardens, every sort of thing . . . and enter it. Why, perhaps, you may never even have the desire to come out! Perhaps, as a matter of fact, you might not go out! Everything is to be had! The best is an enemy of the good. But suddenly a trifle! Your palace is enclosed by a fence, and you'll be told: everything is yours, delight in it! But only do not go one step away from here! And believe me at that same moment you'll want to be rid of your paradise and to step over beyond the fence. Moreover, all this magnificence, all this luxury will even foment your suffering. It will become offensive to you, precisely because of this splendor."

The author sets in opposition to liberty a "gilded cage." Soon the image of the "palace" will be imbued with a new idea content: every compulsory, rationalized organization of society, every utilitarian "paradise on earth" purchased at the price of freedom, be it Fourier's phalanstery or a communistic commune — all this is a "house of death," a palace enclosed by a fence. This idea is developed in *Winter Notes on Summer Impressions* and in *Notes from Underground*. The underground man dreams of "tossing off to hell" the "Crystal Palace" simply in order to *"live according to his own stupid will."* The dialectic of freedom is culminated by Dostoevsky in the *Legend of the Grand Inquisitor.*

In *Notes from the House of Death* the problem of freedom is naturally joined to the problem of personality. Outside of freedom there is no personality. As a result, the prisoners are so sullen and morbidly irritable; all their efforts are directed to the salvation of their own person, to the preservation of their human dignity. "The general tone was made up outwardly of a certain peculiar personal dignity with which almost every inmate of the jail was permeated." The prisoners are terribly haughty, boastful, easily offended, given to formalism; are concerned as to how to deport themselves externally. They are humiliated in their human dignity and uphold it with spite, distortion, obstinacy. The authorities' repugnance in their dealings can drive the most meek of them to crime. "The convict himself knows that he is a convict, an outcast, and knows his place before the authorities; but by no brands, by no shackles will you force him to forget *that he is a man.*" Some prisoner for long years lives quietly and peaceably and suddenly he will go on a spree, turn violent, even commit a serious crime. "The cause of this unexpected outburst is an anguished, convulsive manifestation of his personality, an instinctive longing for his own self, a desire to assert himself, his constrained personality which suddenly manifests itself and proceeds to the point of malice, to frenzy, to the eclipse of reason, to fits, to convulsions. . . . Here there is not a question of reason, here there are convulsions."

The upper stratum of the *Notes* is an *artistic description* of the facts; the middle is their psychological explanation with the help of the idea of freedom and of personality; the lower is a *metaphysical* investigation of good and evil in the soul of man.

Dostoevsky begins with a simplified division of the convicts into good and evil. "Everywhere," he writes, "there are bad people, and among them there are also good ones. Who knows, these people are, perhaps, by no means so very much worse than those *others* who remain there beyond the jail." Having expanded the circle of his investigation and conferred upon it a universal significance, the writer contrasts the good and the evil, the strong-willed and the gentle-hearted. "There are natures so innately beautiful," he says, "so richly endowed by God that even the mere thought that they could at some time or other change for the worse, seems impossible to you." Such is the young Tartar Aley. "His whole soul was expressed on his handsome, one could even say, beautiful face. His smile was so trusting, so childishly naive; his big black eyes were so soft, so affable that I always felt a special pleasure, even a comfort in my anguish and grief, when looking at him. . . . This was a strong and steadfast nature. . . . I got to know it well afterward. He was chaste as a young maiden." Dostoevsky taught him to read the Gospel in Russian. "I asked him whether he liked what he had read. He glanced up quickly and a blush appeared on his face. 'Ah, yes!' he answered, 'yes, Isa[1] is a holy prophet, Isa spoke the words of God. How good it is!' 'And what do you like best of all?' 'Where he says: forgive, love, don't hurt others, love even your enemies. Ah, how well he speaks!' " Aley is a man touched by grace, an *anima naturaliter christiana*.

Another figure, the old Schismatic,[2] is the first sketch of an elder in Dostoevsky. "This was a little, old, gray-haired man of about sixty. . . . There was something so peaceful and calm in his gaze that, I remember, I used to look with a certain special pleasure at his clear, bright eyes which were surrounded by tiny wrinkles like so many rays. . . . . Rarely have I met such a good, kind being in my life. . . . He

---

[1] The Tartar Aley means to say "Jesus."

[2] Cf. n. 5, Ch. IV. In 19th century Russia the Old Believers were subject to a more subtle and perhaps invidious persecution than the immolation of the late 17th and early 18th centuries. Pressures were constantly being applied by the government to induce them to convert to the established Church. The Old Believer in this passage belonged to a community from which several members had been received into the Orthodox faith. He violently adhered to his religious beliefs and as a sign of moral protest burned down an Orthodox church that was being constructed.

was gay, often laughed — a clear, gentle laugh in which there was much of childlike simplicity." The Old Believer from the *House of Death* belongs to the line of the pilgrim Makar Dolgoruky, Bishop Tikhon, and the elder Zosima.

Sirotkin is a kind-hearted and "good-looking lad," neat, gentle and pensive; kind-hearted and selfless is Sushilov, "a thoroughly shy, humble, even downtrodden individual whose nature it is to efface his personality everywhere." In all these people there is innate good, independent of education and surroundings, like a *gratia gratis data*.

In opposition to them stand the men of evil. Dostoevsky encountered them for the first time in penal servitude They attracted and terrified him by their mysteriousness. He long did not understand them. And that which, at last, he understood, was the most jolting revelation which penal servitude offered to him. These criminals did not know *repentance*. "In the course of several years I never once saw among them even the slightest sign of repentance, even the least disquieting thought about their crime. Why, it seems possible that in so many years one might have noticed at least something, seized upon, caught up in these hearts, be it only some passing hint which might have borne witness to an inner anguish, to suffering. *But there was none of this, positively none.*" How does one explain this lack of repentance? By ignorance, by moral stupidity, by want of development. The author casts aside "preconceived points of view." The prisoners were literate. "Probably more than half of them knew how to read and write. In what other place where the Russian people are gathered together in large masses, could you isolate a group of 250 persons, of whom half were literate?" Dostoevsky does not hesitate to make a daring, almost incredible assertion: these villains, murderers, criminals *were the best Russian people*. "How much youth has to no purpose been buried in these walls, how many great forces have perished here in vain. *Now it must all be said:* why these are, perhaps, the most gifted, the strongest people of our entire nation. But mighty forces have perished in vain. . . ."

So, the "preconceived" point of view concerning conscience and moral law does not explain anything. The best people, literate, gifted, strong, do not experience any pangs of conscience. The enigma of criminality is set before the writer. "The philosophy of crime," he concludes, "is a little more difficult than is supposed." So arises the theme of *Crime and Punishment*.

The question of conscience is more complicated than the proponents of optimistic morality think. The author investigates the mysterious nature of evil in the example of several "strong" personalities.

Take the convict Gazin. Dostoevsky says about him:

> This Gazin was a horrible creature. He produced on all a terrible, painful impression. It always seemed to me that nothing could be more savage, more monstrous than he. . . . I sometimes felt that I saw before me a huge, gigantic spider, the size of a man. . . . It was related that in the past he liked to cut up little children — solely for pleasure; he would lure the child somewhere to a suitable spot, at first would frighten, torture it and, having fully relished the terror and dismay of his little victim, would cut its throat, calmly, slowly, with enjoyment. . . . Meanwhile in prison he conducted himself very prudently. He was always quiet, did not quarrel with anyone and avoided a quarrel but, as it were, out of contempt for the others, *as it were, considering himself better than all the rest.* . . . Something arrogantly derisive and cruel was always on his face and in his smile.

Gazin is a demonic personality; his image is presented by the writer as the embodiment of pure evil, his violence toward children as a sign of demonic possession (Svidrigailov and Stavrogin). This evil force is symbolized in the image of the spider (Svidrigailov's "bathhouse with its spiders," the spiders of Versilov, Ippolit, Ivan Karamazov). Gazin expresses the destructive nature of evil — the principle of Ahriman. In another thief, Orlov, is shown evil's grandeur — the principle of Lucifer. Of this terrible miscreant Dostoevsky writes:

> I can say positively that never in my life have I met an individual so strong, of such an iron will. . . . *This was in reality a complete victory over the flesh.* It was evident that this man could exercise unlimited control over himself, holding every sort of torture and punishment in contempt, and did not fear anything on earth. . . . Moreover, I was struck at his strange haughtiness. I do not think there was any creature in the world that could have acted upon him simply by authority. . . . I tried to enter into conversation with him about his adventures, but when he realized that I was getting at his conscience and sought in him merely some sign of repentance, he looked at me with as much arrogant contempt as though I had become suddenly in his eyes a foolish little boy with whom it was

impossible to discuss things as with a grownup. His face even reflected something like pity toward me. After a minute he burst out laughing at me, a perfectly ingenuous laugh, devoid of any irony. . . . On the whole, he could not help despising me and certainly must have regarded me as a submissive, weak, pitiable creature and *inferior to him in all respects.*

Dostoevsky came upon a titanic personality, a superman for whom ordinary morality is pitiable childishness. Evil is by no means a damaging of the will, a weakness of character; to the contrary, in him it is a terrible power, a somber grandeur. Evil does not lie in the lower carnal nature's dominion over the higher spiritual faculties; the miscreant Orlov portrays a complete victory over the flesh. *Evil is a mystical reality and a demonic spirituality.*

Orlov proudly laughed at the naive moralist Dostoevsky and scorned the "weak individual" in him. In the novel *The Humiliated and Wronged* the villain, Prince Volkovsky, mocks the writer Ivan Petrovich's Schillerian nobility of soul. From the superman Orlov descend all of Dostoevsky's "strong personalities." Raskolnikov's problem is already in view. People are divided into the strong for whom "everything is permitted," and the weak for whom morality was devised. Raskolnikov, Stavrogin, Ivan Karamazov place themselves "beyond the confines of good and evil." This Nietzscheanism before Nietzsche Dostoevsky brought with him out of penal servitude.

Encounters with such people as Gazin and Orlov were a decisive event in the writer's spiritual life. In the face of this reality, his former convictions toppled in a heap like a house of cards. Rousseauism, humanism, utopianism — all were scattered in fragments. The philanthrope who not long before had been preaching mercy to those who had fallen and taught that "the humblest person is your brother," now called for the protection of society against "monsters and moral Quasimodoes." Describing the criminal A-v who "for the gratification of the very smallest and most whimsical of bodily pleasures was capable in the most cold-blooded manner of killing, butchering, in a word, of everything," the author exclaims: "No, a conflagration is better, pestilence and famine are better, than having such a man in society." This is the complete collapse of humanism: the disenchantment with good and the justification of penal servitude!

But the tragedy which the writer experienced in prison was still more profound. He spent four years surrounded by two hundred and fifty enemies who did not conceal their hatred for the nobility and "used to look with love upon their sufferings." When the terrible Gazin was preparing to smash the nobles' heads with a heavy bread-tray, the convicts waited in silence. "Not one cry against Gazin; so strong was their hatred for us." When the prisoners submitted their "grievance" to the authorities, they excluded the nobles from the common action. Dostoevsky was deeply offended and argued with the convict Petrov that they ought to allow him to participate in the grievance . . . "out of comradeship." "But . . . but in what way are you our comrade?" he asked with perplexity. And then the nobleman-prisoner at last realized: "I understood that they would never accept me into their company, however much I might be a convict, even if I were in for ever and a day, even if I were assigned to the Special Division."[3] The abyss between the higher classes and the simple people was more profound and impassable than it seemed to many democrats. The European-civilized nobleman was alien to the people; long and resolute sufferings were needed in order to merit their confidence. They — the representatives of all the corners of Russia — were robbers and enemies; they, for four years, without tiring, pursued him with their cruel hatred. He loved them and sought their love. In the vast majority they remained irreconcilable. He could have closed himself off in the feeling of his own righteousness and moral superiority, as did the exiled Poles. But he did not repeat after them the contemptible: "Je hais ces brigands!" He did not grow bitter and was not crushed. He performed the greatest act of Christian humility: he acknowledged that truth was on the side of his enemies, that they were an "extraordinary people," that in them was the soul of Russia. . . . In the utter hell of penal servitude the writer found that which forever after he was to venerate: the Russian people.

"The highest and most sharply characteristic trait of our people," he writes, "is this feeling of justice and the thirst for it. . . . It requires only taking off the exterior, superficial shell and looking at the kernel itself somewhat more attentively, somewhat more closely, without prejudice and one will see in the people such things as he had not guessed beforehand. Our wise men cannot teach the people much. I will even say positively, to the contrary, *they themselves have yet to learn from them.*" Dostoevsky the populist was born in penal servitude.

The day of his release arrived. "The shackles fell away. I lifted them

[3] The classification of prisoners who were sent to penal servitude for the most serious crimes and were subjected to the sternest measure.

up. I wanted to hold them in my hand, to gaze at them a last time. . . .
'Well, go with God! Go with God!' said the convicts in coarse, abrupt,
but as it were, somewhat pleased voices. Yes, go with God! Freedom,
a new life, resurrection from the dead. . . . What a glorious moment!"

In reality, a resurrection from the dead! The seed which had died in
the "house of death," sprouted and bore fruit: the brilliant novel-tragedies. The writer's experience of penal servitude constituted his spiritual ←
riches.

"Believe me," he wrote to his brother in 1856, "that having been in
as much turmoil as I, in the end you'll extract from life a little philosophy, a word which you can interpret as you like."

Dostoevsky's philosophy is "*extracted from life.*" He is an "existen-
tial philosopher," "Kierkegaard's double" according to Lev Shestov.[A]

[A] Léon Chestov, *Les révélations de la mort. Dostoïevsky – Tolstoï*, Paris 1923.
Léon Chestov, *Kierkegaard et la philosophie existentielle*, Paris 1936.

X

The Humiliated and Wronged

At the same time Dostoevsky was working on *Notes from the House of Death*, he wrote a full-length novel *The Humiliated and Wronged*. "I find myself in a thoroughly feverish state," he informed A. Schubert in 1860. "My novel is the cause of it all. I want to write it well, I feel that there is poetry in it, I know my whole literary career depends on its success." The novel was published in individual chapters with the appendage "to be continued" in the journal *Time* (January–July 1861). The same year it appeared in a separate edition. The novel enjoyed great success with the public. "It was almost universally read with pleasure," wrote Dobrolyubov, "it was all but universally spoken of with high praise." However, the reviewers received it harshly. The same Dobrolyubov considered it "below aesthetic criticism," and A. Grigoryev called its heroes dolls, manikins, walking texts. After Mikhail Mikhailovich Dostoevsky's death, Grigoryev's letter was published. The critic reproached the editor of *Time* for "driving the lofty talent of F. Dostoevsky like a relay-horse."

The writer came to the defense of his late brother and with amazing candor and humility told the story of the creation of *The Humiliated and Wronged*. Here is what he wrote in *Epoch* in 1864:

> If I wrote a feuilleton novel (which I fully admit), then it is I who am guilty of this and I alone. This is how I have written all my life, this is how I wrote everything that I have created except for the tale *Poor People* and several chapters of *The House of Death*. Very often it has happened in my literary life that the beginning of a chapter of a novel or tale was already at the printer's and the type was being set, while the conclusion rested still in my mind, but without fail it had to be written for tomorrow. Having grown accustomed to working this way, I acted in just this manner with *The Humiliated and Wronged*, but this time not compelled by any-

one, but in accord with my own will. The journal which we had started, the success of which was more dear than anything to me, needed a novel, and I proposed a novel in four parts. I myself convinced my brother that I had thought out the whole plan long ago (which was not so), that writing it would be easy for me, that the first part was already written, etc. Here I was not prompted by reasons of money. I fully acknowledge that in my novel many dolls are presented, and not people, that there are in it walking texts, and not characters which have been given an artistic form (for which, really, time was required and the maturing of ideas in the mind and the soul). At the precise moment that I was writing it, I, it is evident, in the heat of work, was not aware of this, but only perhaps had an inkling. But here is what I knew for certain when beginning to write: 1) though my novel might not even turn out, nonetheless there would be poetry in it, 2) that there would be two or three strong and fiery passages, 3) that the two most serious characters would be portrayed most faithfully and even artistically. This assurance was enough for me. A crude work emerged, but in it there are a half-hundred pages of which I am proud.

We do not share now either the harsh judgment of the critics or the writer's own humble review. Dostoevsky's novel-feuilleton must be recognized as one of the most successful examples of this literary genre. Its dependence on the melodramatic adventure novels of Frédéric Soulié, Eugène Sue, Victor Hugo, and Dickens is completely obvious, but into the old forms *the author has inserted a new psychological and ideological content.*

In *The Humiliated and Wronged* two plots are developed along parallel lines: the story of Natasha Ikhmeneva and that of Nelly. The main heroine is Natasha; her history occupies about two-thirds of the novel. The principles of composition are the same as in *The Village of Stepanchikovo*: a series of effective, dramatic scenes separated one from another by a brief explanation of the progressing events. The compact exposition leads us immediately into the action.

Nikolai Sergeyevich Ikhmenev served as the administrator of Prince Volkovsky's estates; the orphan Vanya was raised in his home. A childhood love bound the boy to Ikhmenev's daughter, Natasha. Vanya grows up and goes to study in Petersburg. The friends are separated for four years. Meanwhile the Prince sends his nineteen-year-old son Alyosha to the Ikhmenevs in the country, and the latter falls in love with Natasha. The Prince suspects his overseer of a calculated design, accuses him of defalcation. In order to bring the matter to court, Ikhmenev moves to Petersburg with his family. He is threatened by ruin and want. At this point the "past time" ends and the "present" begins. After four years Vanya is transformed into the writer Ivan Petrovich and plans to marry Natasha. Fame and love smile on him; but a year passes and the young author falls into poverty. Ikhmenev's case continues to drag on; Alyosha begins every day to frequent Natasha. The "information" offered by the narrator Ivan Petrovich introduces us to the complication of the action. In order to underline the melodramatic character of the situation, we will give each scene suitable titles and excerpt characteristic passages. The first scene we will call: "The daughter leaves her parents." Natasha decides against her father's will to join her beloved Alyosha. She has "sunken, pale cheeks, lips parched as in fever, and eyes flashing out from under their long lashes with a burning fire." . . . " 'Dear papa, you too bless . . . your daughter,' she brought out in a gasping voice and sank before him on her knees."

A half year passes. Prince Volkovsky attempts to break his son's relations with Natasha. He introduces him to a rich, eligible girl, Katya, and the young man is captivated by her. The second scene can be called: "The father curses his daughter." The offended Ikhmenev swears that he has long since forgotten Natasha, but by chance a medallion with her portrait falls from his pocket. His wife, Anna Andreyevna, exclaims: " 'My dearest, so you do love her still!' . . . But no sooner had he heard her cry than an insane fury gleamed in his eyes. He seized the medallion, threw it violently onto the floor and with frenzy began to trample it under his foot. 'For ever, for ever I curse you!' he shouted hoarsely, gasping for breath, 'for ever, for ever!' "

As a title corresponding to the third scene we have: "The Prince craftily asks Natasha's hand for his son." Natasha resolves to sacrifice herself and free Alyosha. The latter informs her that he has confessed everything to Katya and that she is sacrificing herself for the sake of Natasha's happiness. "Natasha, as it were overwhelmed by happiness, dropped her head on her breast and suddenly began softly to cry. Now Alyosha could no longer contain himself. He threw himself at her feet; he kissed her hands, her feet; he seemed frantic." This scene of triple self-sacrifice is worthily completed by Prince Volkovsky's magnanimous proposal to Natasha.

In the fourth scene: "Natasha unmasks the Prince." Several days pass. Alyosha grows more and more cold toward Natasha. Then she understands the Prince's clever intention and renounces all rights to Alyosha. The affronted girl boldly speaks the truth to the face of her offender: "You came here on Tuesday and contrived this betrothal. . . . What does it matter for you to deceive me? And what is an insult to some girl like me? Why, she's wretched, a run-away, cast off by her father, defenseless, she has disgraced herself, is immoral."

The fifth scene we entitle: "The rivals meet." Katya pays a visit to Natasha who gives up Alyosha to her. "Katya sat on the arm of Natasha's chair, not letting her out of her embrace, and began to kiss her hands. . . . Alyosha came in. Seeing them both in each other's arms and weeping, he fell in exhaustion and anguish on his knees before Katya and Natasha."

Finally, the sixth scene can be entitled: "The villain tears off his mask." Prince Volkovsky comes to Natasha, who is now forsaken and abused, offers her money and the protection of a depraved old man, Count N. Ivan Petrovich breaks into the room. "I spat in his face and with all my force struck him on the cheek. He was at the point of throwing himself upon me, but seeing that there were two of us, took to flight, having first seized from the table his parcel with the money. . . . I threw a rolling pin after him which I had picked up from the table in the kitchen. . . . Having run back into the room, I saw that the doctor was holding Natasha, who struggled and was tearing herself from his arms as though in convulsions."

A title suitable for the novel's epilogue would be: "Return of the prodigal daughter." Alyosha goes away with Katya. Natasha is reconciled with her parents. The abandoned fiancé consoles his unfortunate betrothed. The finale is poetically sad. . . . "Natasha and I went out into the garden. The day was hot, sparkling with light. . . . After a week they were going away. . . . Natasha turned a long, strange look upon me. . . . 'Vanya,' she said, 'why did I destroy your happiness?' And in her eyes I read: 'We might have been happy together forever.'"

As regards its composition and style, the main plot — the story of Natasha's ill-fated love — belongs *to the literary genre of sentimental melodrama*. The secondary plot — the story of Nelly — is constructed in accord with the pattern of Western European *mystery novels*. It is plunged in the mysterious, the enigmatic, and fantastic. A "very strange event" happens to Ivan Petrovich: on the street he meets an old man with a deathlike face, "having the appearance of a madman who had escaped from his keepers." He is accompanied by a dog, also "extraordinary." "There must without fail be something fantastic about it, bewitched!" thinks the narrator. "Its fate is by some mysterious, unknown ways bound to the fate of its master." The author does not hide the source of his inspiration. "I remember," he confesses, "the thought once struck me that the old man and the dog had somehow stepped out of a page of Hoffmann, illustrated by Gavarni, and were strolling about the wide world as walking advertisements for the edition." The prologue is enacted in the German Müller's confectioner's shop among virtuous and patriarchal Germans (Schultz, Krüger) who read the Frankfurt newspaper and delight in the "humor and shrewd observations" of the well-known German wit Saphir; the setting heightens the "Hoffmannesque" character of the adventure. The dog Azorka dies in the shop; after a few minutes the old man dies too. The narrator moves into his apartment. No less "strange" is the second occurrence. Five days after the old man's death, Ivan Petrovich, sick and depressed, hears the door to his room open and on the threshold appears a girl of about twelve or thirteen years, "thin, pale, with large black eyes and disheveled black hair." This is Nelly, the late Smith's granddaughter. Her outward appearance is marked by its "strangeness." "It would have been difficult to encounter a stranger, a more original creature," observes the narrator. "She had an enigmatic, mute, and fixed gaze." "Her pale, thin face had a kind of unnatural, sallow, bilious tinge." Ivan Petrovich succeeds in tracking down his mysterious visitor; he finds out that Nelly lives with Bubnova, an evil and drunken woman of the lower classes, who tortures her and is planning to sell her to a dissolute merchant. The narrator meets his former school companion Masloboyev, who "is not exactly a detective, but is engaged in several affairs, in part officially and in part on his own account." With his help he saves Nelly from dishonor. "Suddenly the door was violently thrown open, and Yelena [Nelly], pale, with dazed eyes, in a white muslin dress, crumpled and torn, with hair that had been carefully combed out, but was now tousled as in a struggle, burst into the room. She rushed straight to me and seized me round with her arms." After this prologue in the spirit of Hoffmann, complication of the intrigue follows in the manner of Eugène Sue. The innocent girl's adventures among the dregs of the capital, the poverty and vice, hide-outs and dens, the cruel, drunken old woman torturing her victim and the virtuous amateur detective who saves the heroine — all this recalls *The Mysteries of Paris*. Moreover, the author does not conceal it. Masloboyev, when telling Ivan Petro-vich the story of Nelly's mother, adds jokingly: "And here you thought I intended to reveal God knows what *mysteries of Paris* to you. One can see plainly that you're a novelist."

After the adventure plot, the style undergoes a new sharp break; there begins a psychological tale about a young, wounded heart, about the early awakening of love in a proud and passionate girl. The author returns to his theme of the development of a child's soul, to which the novel *Netochka Nezvanova* was dedicated. Netochka's first falling in love and the struggle of love and pride in the soul of Princess Katya are joined in the story of Nelly. Ivan Petrovich takes her into his own apartment. For a long time she is afraid and looks at him "with her long, fixed stare in which together with doubt and a wild curiosity there was still a certain strange pride." She rejects his help, wants to work as a laborer, tears to pieces the muslin dress she has on, weeps bitterly, and torments her protector. "No, I'd rather hire myself out as a servant," she declares. "They will scold me, but on purpose I'll say nothing. They'll beat me, and I'll continue to be silent. Let them beat me, I won't cry for anything. They will be sick with anger because I won't cry." But by degrees her fits of hatred and obduracy grow weaker. Love overcomes pride. "Nelly glanced at me quickly," says the narrator, "flushed, lowered her eyes and, advancing two steps to-ward me, suddenly threw both her arms round me and with her face pressed tightly, tightly against my bosom. . . . All her feeling, which for so long had been repressed, suddenly at once poured forth in an uncontrollable outburst — and I came to understand this strange stub-bornness of a heart, chastely secreting itself for the time . . . and all this until that inevitable outburst when the whole being would sud-denly forget and surrender itself to this necessity of love, gratitude, affection, tears."

The "wounded heart" has opened itself; Nelly has revealed her secret to Ivan Petrovich. She plagued him because she loved him, because out of pride she was avenging herself on him and on herself for her feeling. "This was a character," says the narrator, "strange, nervous, and passionate, but who had smothered her own impulses; sympa-thetic, but locked up in pride and inaccessibility." A character well known to us through Dostoevsky's great novels.

After Nelly's unexpected meeting with Prince Volkovsky, she suffers an epileptic fit and falls ill with burning fever. Upon recovering, she changes radically. There remains not even a trace of her former tenderness toward Ivan Petrovich. She becomes more and more sullen and irritable. "Her strange ways, her caprices, at times almost hatred for me," says the narrator, "all this continued up to the very day that she stopped living with me." In the end, she leaves him and goes out in the streets to beg. Ivan Petrovich understands nothing. "'And just what is this?' I wondered. 'Can it possibly be some unusual consequence of her sickness? Can it be that she is mad or going out of her mind?'"

But Natasha solves the riddle: "'You know, Vanya,' she said, 'having thought upon it, I am convinced that she loves you.' 'What? . . . How is it possible?' I asked in amazement. 'Yes, this is the beginning of love, of a woman's love.'"

The inception of womanly love and jealousy in a thirteen-year-old girl is portrayed with consummate art. The figure of Nelly is full of a strange, disquieting charm. There is in it more of life and poetry than in the sensitively deliberate Natasha. We have already noted the inner relationship between the novel *The Humiliated and Wronged* and the design of Goethe's *Wilhelm Meister*. Nelly is inspired by Mignon. In her we also find features of eroticism: big black eyes, black hair, a sallow complexion; she is half a foreigner, and although her grandfather was English, nonetheless her character displays a Southern passion and violence. Her happy childhood was spent abroad, and she loves to recall "the lakes and valleys of Italy, the flowers and trees, the village inhabitants, their costume and their sun-tanned faces and black eyes . . . the hot Southern city with its azure skies and azure sea. . . ."

The denouement of Nelly's story is first given in the ironic explanation of the detective Masloboyev, afterward in the pathetic narration of the heroine herself. Masloboyev succeeded in finding a trace of Nelly's mother. The daughter of the rich factory-owner, Jeremy Smith, was seduced and victimized by Prince Volkovsky. After long wanderings with her daughter abroad, she returns to Russia, succumbs to poverty, is taken ill with consumption. Smith does not wish to forgive his wayward daughter. Even his granddaughter's prayers do not move him. Finally Nelly brings him to her mother, but the latter is already dead. The author himself characterizes this story in the spirit of the French social novel of the "mysteries of a big city."

"This was a somber story," he writes, "one of those somber and tormenting stories which so frequently and imperceptibly, almost mysteriously unfold under the heavy Petersburg sky, in the dark, clandestine by-lanes of the vast city, amidst the flighty ebullition of life, dull-

witted egoism, conflicting interests, morose debauchery, hidden crimes
— amidst all this uttermost hell of a nonsensical and abnormal life. . . ."

The denouement is romantically sad. Ivan Petrovich asks Nelly to
tell Ikhmenev the story of her life in order to persuade him to forgive
Natasha. She understands that he is offering her as a sacrifice and
humbly consents. She passes her last days in the home of the Ikhmenevs, surrounded by everyone's love; she dies peacefully midst flowers
in the springtime. Just before her death she says to Ivan Petrovich:
"Vanya, when I die, marry Natasha." The enigma of her parentage is
disclosed: Nelly is the lawful daughter of Prince Volkovsky. She knew
this, but would not go to the Prince, and died unreconciled.

Nelly's story can be defined as a *psychological tale* inserted within
the frame of a *romantic melodrama*. The plots are constructed along
parallel lines: Natasha loves Alyosha who loves another (Katya), Nelly
loves Ivan Petrovich who loves another (Natasha). Natasha leaves her
father and her fiancé and goes away with Alyosha; the latter promises
to marry her and abandons her. Smith's daughter also leaves her father and fiancé and goes away with Prince Volkovsky who deserts
her. This repetition of the subject is a conscious device. The motif of
Nelly and her mother does not duplicate Natasha's motif, but accompanies it in a lower tonality.

Natasha and Nelly's stories are completely independent. They
could have constituted two separate tales. The author unites them
through the character of the narrator. The story of the novice writer
Ivan Petrovich restates the already familiar scheme of the tales *Poor
People* and *White Nights*. A virtuous hero disinterestedly loves a young
girl and sacrifices himself for the sake of her happiness. To his feeling
she responds with friendly attachment, but loves another. The author
renovates an old subject by infusing into it autobiographic content.
The hero is not an elderly civil servant like Makar Devushkin, not a
Petersburg dreamer like Nastenka's admirer, but *Dostoevsky himself
of the period of the forties*. Ivan Petrovich's story is the writer's personal confession, his memories of the drama which he experienced at
the outset of his literary career. Lyricism breaks into the novel-feuilleton, and an original alternation of styles results. Ivan Petrovich writes
a tale about a poor civil servant which meets with great success.

"B. [Belinsky] was delighted as a child," he tells us. After a year
nothing remains of his brilliant hopes. The young author lapses into
poverty and obscurity. His nerves are in disorder; he undergoes inexplicable anxiety, fits of mystical terror. He is forced to work as a day-

laborer for an "entrepreneur." His confessions to Natasha seem abstracted out of Dostoevsky's letters to his brother: "I'm still writing my novel," he says, "but it's difficult, it's not coming along well. The inspiration's dried up. I suppose I could write it off the top of my head, if you like, and it might turn out entertaining, but it's a pity to spoil a good idea. This is one of my favorites. And yet without fail it must be ready for the journal on time. I'm even thinking of putting the novel aside and inventing a tale quickly, in this way, something rather light and graceful, and without the slightest pessimistic note."

Ivan Petrovich describes his misfortunes without bitterness or anger. Having learned of the death of the critic B. (Belinsky), Ikhmenev remarks to the narrator: "Of course you used to say, Vanya, that he was a good man, generous, sympathetic, with feeling, with a heart. Well, so it is now, they are all like that, men with hearts, those sympathetic fellows of yours. They only know how to multiply their orphans." Even the mention of the hated "entrepreneur" Krayevsky affords a most gentle good humor. Ivan Petrovich is not the whole Dostoevsky, but only the Dostoevsky of the forties, the idealist and romantic, Belinsky's friend, the author of philanthropic tales. When the author was writing *The Humiliated and Wronged,* this stage of his spiritual development had long since passed. He was recreating himself such as he was in his youth, but he was recreating so as to judge and condemn. Ivan Petrovich is a pitiful failure; he suffers a complete breakdown both in literature and in life. He never finishes his novel; Natasha does not come back to him. He is writing his notes in a hospital while waiting for death. "Yes, it was a good idea of mine," he says. "Moreover, it is something to leave to the doctor's assistant; at least he will have my notes to stick round the windows when he puts in the winter frames."

The abundance of autobiographic material in Ivan Petrovich's story and the "personal tone" in which it is related would seem to indicate the author's intention to make him the hero of the novel. In point of fact, Dostoevsky's design is much more clever and malevolent. The romantic of the forties is not a hero, but only the *parody of a hero.* He stands in the foreground, but he is only the instrument of the intrigue. It is not he who arranges the characters' fate, but they who use him as a passive intermediary. He continually scurries about among them, bringing Natasha together with her parents, Katya with Natasha, the Ikhmenevs with Nelly. Through Masloboyev he uncovers Nelly's relationship to Prince Volkovsky; with Nelly's help he seeks the reconciliation of Natasha and her father. He does only what pertains to all, is attendant to everyone's affairs, transmits letters, carries out commissions. He runs "on errands," "on assignments," is a general helper, witness and adviser. But in the face of such exterior bustling, the pseudohero is interiorly passive; he does not render any influence on the development of the action. His sole deed, slapping Prince Volkovsky's face, is the forceless explosion of a weak individual.

Dostoevsky's notebooks attest to the importance which he set upon the question of the *narrative tone*. When contemplating a new novel, he asked himself first of all: how is the story to be told? In the author's name, omnipresent and all-seeing, or in the name of a narrator, a witness to the events? Will the narration be a dry recording of facts or the emotional account of a personally involved participant? The greatest hesitations are apparent in his work on *Crime and Punishment*. The original version was planned in the form of a criminal's confession. *The Gambler, A Raw Youth,* and *The Devils* make use of a narrator. In *The Idiot* the author himself relates, while in *The Brothers Karamazov* the fiction of the narrator-chronicler is almost imperceptible. Dostoevsky naturally gravitated toward the personal, lyric tone of a story, but could not always surmount the difficulties connected with it. The witness-informant was of no value as a hero; his function as informant inevitably relegated him to a secondary plane. This is how the problem is solved in *The Devils* where the narrator is an impersonal being, a simple inmate, one of the members of Stepan Trofimovich's circle. In *A Raw Youth* an attempt was made of joining together in one person a narrator and a hero. Arkady Dolgoruky tells about himself, his own life and his idea, but even he does not long hold fast to the hero's pedestal and, yielding place to Versilov and Akhmakova, descends imperceptibly to the role of a simple narrator. The unresolved contradiction between the tone of "recording" and that of "confession" is the most important peculiarity of Dostoevsky's stylistics.

In the novel *The Humiliated and Wronged* the love relationships unite not two, as is usual, but always three. Natasha stands between Alyosha and Ivan Petrovich. The one she loves, the other loves her. Ivan Petrovich finds himself between Nelly, who loves him, and Natasha, whom he loves. Natasha loves Alyosha, but he loves Katya. The triplicity of human interrelations is affirmed by Dostoevsky as a psychological law and expresses something very profound and mysterious in his art. In all his works the hero stands between two heroines or the heroine between two heroes.

In the tales of the period before penal servitude we saw: Varvara between Devushkin and the student Pokrovsky (*Poor People*), Katerina between Ordynov and Murin (*The Landlady*), Nastenka between the dreamer and her fiancé (*White Nights*), Aleksandra Mikhailovna between her husband and her beloved (*Netochka Nezvanova*). This same correlation is likewise repeated without change in the great novels. In *Crime and Punishment* we have before us the triangle: Svidrigailov–Dunya–Razumikhin. In *The Idiot* the triangles: Myshkin–Nastasya Filippovna–Rogozhin, and Nastasya Filippovna–Myshkin–Aglaya. In *A Raw Youth* Versilov is put between his wife and Akhmakova; in *The Devils* Stavrogin between Dasha and Liza, and Liza between Stavrogin and Mavriky Nikolayevich. Finally, in *The Brothers Karamazov* we find three triangles: Mitya between Grushenka and Katerina Ivanovna, Katerina Ivanovna between Mitya and Ivan, Grushenka between Mitya and Fyodor Pavlovich. Dostoevsky only refers to happy love, but always depicts unhappy love. The one who loves is not loved, and the one loved does not love. In his novels, love never suffices for itself, is not fulfilled between two; its ring is broken by a third. Triplicity bears witness to the *naturally tragic character of love in this world*, to its incurable wound.

If Ivan Petrovich is only the professed hero, then who is the real one? The composition of *The Humiliated and Wronged* recalls a casket with a double bottom. The secret drawer opens slowly and the structure's enigma is explained only in the finale. But up until then the reader is led to believe that the novel is not written about a hero, but about two heroines. The foreground is clearly illuminated; on the proscenium stand two girls, Natasha and Nelly, and two love dramas are presented. One can suppose that the author is returning to a situation indicated in *Netochka Nezvanova*: to the opposition of the "proud" and the "meek." But Natasha and Nelly are also pseudoheroines. For the time they only screen the main hero; behind the illuminated proscenium on which they act, there is a background plunged in mysterious twilight. From it by degrees Prince Volkovsky's figure is singled out, slowly it grows, and in the end overshadows all the characters of the action. The intensity of interest is sustained by this gradual shifting of planes.

The novel's real hero is Prince Volkovsky; all the action's hidden springs are in his hands, his evil will determines the fate of all the personages. He is absent from the first part; is spoken of only indirectly and enigmatically. The second part begins with his return; he wears a noble mask, but acts with deceit and cunning. In the third part, in the scene in the restaurant, he tears off his mask and steps forward in all his unsightliness. In the fourth, he disappears, but we learn of his complete triumph. This successive revelation of an enigmatic hero's personality is characteristic of the technique employed in Dostoevsky's novels. Likewise in *The Devils* Stavrogin is at first shown through rumor and gossip, then in action and, lastly, in "idea."

From the stories about the Prince we learn in the first part that he is the "beggarly offspring of an ancient line," was married to the daughter of a rich merchant–lease contractor whom he tormented to death; that he abandoned his son and served abroad "in one of the most important legations." Upon his return to Petersburg, he finds that his son is planning to get married to Ikhmenev's daughter, and prevents this from taking place. In the second part the Prince decides to marry Alyosha to the millionairess Katya.

In the third part, through the detective Masloboyev's investigations, it is disclosed that the Prince had deceived and victimized Smith's daughter and that Nelly is his legitimate daughter.

The Prince is the typical villain of melodrama, the indispensable appurtenance of an adventure novel–feuilleton. On his conscience lies the ruin of two wives, his daughter, the old man Smith, the destruction and disgrace of the Ikhmenev family, Natasha's shattered life. And at the end of the novel he triumphs, prospers, and prepares to marry a wealthy fourteen-year-old girl.

The Prince is the center of the action. In him all the mysteries find their solution. As the father of Nelly and Alyosha he serves to unite both plots. The composition of *The Humiliated and Wronged* is parallel in structure to the *Village of Stepanchikovo*. A villain under a mask of virtue enchants a good but weak individual, cunningly overpowers his will. In the earlier work we find Opiskin and Rostanev; here Prince Volkovsky and Alyosha. The "good" enter into struggle with the evil one. Before there were Rostanev's betrothed Nastenka and his friend, the narrator — now there are Alyosha's fiancée Natasha and the other narrator, Ivan Petrovich. Both then and now the evil individual's attack and the counterattack of the good end in the supposed disgrace of the villain. Opiskin is expelled, Volkovsky is struck a blow on the cheek. But in both novels the affair concludes with his complete triumph.

The Humiliated and Wronged stands at the threshold of the novel-tragedies. Studying its composition, we penetrate the very process of creating a new form. Before our eyes a new genre is fashioned, a new narrative style is evolved. The "novel-tragedy" is not of lofty descent. At its basis lies "boulevard literature": the adventure and the crime novel. Dostoevsky began his ascent from below, but he raises vulgar and second-rate literary forms to the summit of high art. The models of E. Sue and F. Soulié are filled with brilliant psychological and ideological content. The writer's "spiritual realism" is in the portrayal of the *life of ideas.* The adventure novel helped him to embody these ideas in a concrete form. It taught him the dramatism of action and the dynamics of structure. Thus "criminality" was converted into *Crime and Punishment* and *The Brothers Karamazov.*

The raising of the novel-feuilleton to the level of the psychological novel already begins in *The Humiliated and Wronged.* Into the framework of two melodramas—one sentimental, the other romantic—there is inserted a profound ideational design. The spiritual experience of penal servitude is translated into the language of artistic images. It can be called *the shattering of idealism.* Before penal servitude, Dostoevsky was an idealist, a utopian, a socialist, a humanist. All these "-isms" were descended from Rousseau's axiom: "man is by nature good." After penal servitude, belief in "natural goodness" was lost. All the heroes of *The Humiliated and Wronged,* except one, are good and virtuous, and this one easily vanquishes them. If "natural goodness" is impotent, then is it goodness? Is it perhaps that what seemed goodness in the daydreams of his youth is not goodness at all? Then one has to expose its lie, tear off its mask. It is not the "good" who judge the "evil" one, but the "evil" who judges and condemns the "good."

Of these the first is Prince Volkovsky's son, Alyosha. "A most charming boy, good-looking, delicate and nervous like a woman, but at the same time, merry and simple-hearted, with an open soul, one capable of the most noble sentiments, with a loving, upright, and grateful heart." But "he has no character" and a "complete lack of will." "He will do, if you like, even something bad, but it will be impossible to blame him for this bad conduct, and one can only pity him." "He was naive for his years and understood almost nothing of real life. Moreover, even at forty he would not have learned, it seems, anything of it. *Such individuals are as it were condemned to eternal adolescence."* Alyosha carries off Natasha from her relatives, wants to marry her, but does not imagine how and on what he will live with her. He prepares to write some tales, a novel on the theme of one of Scribe's comedies and all at once he laughs: "What a writer I'll turn out!" Afterward he promises to give music lessons, to sell his trifles. . . . He rents an "elegant" apartment for Natasha, but soon his money comes to an end. Natasha moves to a somewhat lesser apartment and begins to work. Alyosha cries that he despises himself, but continues to do nothing; betrays his betrothed with some Josephines and Minnas, returns to her with a guilty expression, and, having been set at ease, relates to her all the details of his adventures. He falls in love with Katya, but also loves Natasha. "We will, all three of us, love one another," he dreams. Breaking Natasha's heart, the "most charming boy" remains innocent. "Yes, and when," observes the narrator, "how, could this *innocent* have become guilty?" Alyosha is Rousseau's *homme de la nature,* an innocent before the Fall, a heart innately good, beyond moral will and the moral law.

The "idea" of Alyosha is concretized by the author; he leads his simple-hearted hero into a circle of idealistic utopians, which recalls the Petrashevsky circle. Alyosha's naive chatter suggests a bitter parody on the people of the forties. He becomes acquainted with two of the "enraptured girl" Katya's relatives, Lyovinka and Borenka. One is a student, the other is simply a young man. They have a circle: students, officers, artists, one writer; they meet together on Wednesdays. "These are all fresh young people," relates Alyosha.

They all possess a flaming love toward the whole of mankind. We all speak about our present, future, about the sciences, about literature, and speak so well, so directly and simply. . . . *And yet they call us utopians.* . . . We talk in general about everything that is directed toward progress, humanism, love; all this is spoken in relation to contemporary questions. We talk about the press, about the reforms that have been begun, about love for mankind, about contemporary public figures. . . . Consequently we all, under Bezmygin's leadership, have given our word to act honorably and straightforwardly all our lives. . . . I am enraptured by *lofty ideas.* Let them be erroneous, nonetheless their foundation is holy.

A. Bem has pointed out that Lyovinka and Borenka chanced into Dostoevsky's novel out of *Woe from Wit* (Levon and Borenka). They are transposed out of the English Club into Petrashevsky's circle. Alyosha plays the role of Repetilov.[1]

The "good" boy is hopelessly tossed about between two loves. He ends by going away to the country with Katya, assuring Natasha that without her he will die. He torments and is tormented, sins and repents, weeps and begins anew.

Alyosha's image is complex. On the social plane he is an uprooted aristocrat, the victim of an evil heredity and a debauched milieu. This is the source of his eternal immaturity, childishness, disengagement from reality. On the psychological plane here is an idealist-utopian in the spirit of Petrashevsky, a worshiper of all the "noble and beautiful." On the moral, *the incarnated impotence of natural goodness*, a man without character, without will and without personality. A "good heart" does not keep Alyosha from dissipation, perfidies, deceit, even treachery; in spite of all his sensitivity, he is a most fierce egoist.

In the person of Alyosha, Dostoevsky executes his "innocent" beautiful-soul of the forties. After the experience of penal servitude it appeared to him as unmitigated light-headedness — Khlestakovism and Repetilovitis.[2]

Still more of a parody is the portrayal of the romantic heroine, Nelly's mother. The story of this unfortunate girl whom the Prince wronged and then deserted is placed in the mouth of the amateur detective Masloboyev. The Prince carried Smith's daughter off with him to Paris, defrauded and abandoned her. She had a German fiancé who remained faithful to her in her misfortune. Masloboyev says about him: "An *ideal man* was in love with this beauty, *one of the Schiller brotherhood*, a poet, at the same time a merchant, a *young dreamer*, in a word, a regular German, one Pfefferkuchen." The most comical names are chosen for the German idealist: from Pfefferkuchen he is

---

[1] *Woe from Wit* (sometimes translated *The Trouble with Reason*), written 1823-1825 by Aleksandr Griboyedov, is one of the greatest Russian comedies. It combines the traditional comedy of manners and satire with realism and topical interest. Its plot deals with the "angry" idealist Chatsky's return to his native Moscow and his disillusionment with what he finds there. Repetilov is a monumental character sketch in the play, and a prototype of many of Dostoevsky's creations. He is a loquacious, thoroughly obnoxious individual who revels in his "progressive ideas" and his self-abasement. In the last act he invites Chatsky to a meeting of a "clandestine" society at the English Club where over champagne "loud and open" discussions are carried on about "what no one understands." Included among those who attend these sessions are the brothers Levon and Borenka, "marvelous lads."

[2] Notes on Khlestakov: Cf. n. 1, Ch. III; on Repetilov: Cf. above.

turned into Frauenmilch, then into Feuerbach, and finally, to Bruder-schaft. "Frauenmilch dragged along to Paris after her. . . . She cried all the time, and Pfefferkuchen whimpered, and many years passed like that. . . ." She had the Prince's written promise of marriage in her hands, but she was so "elevated" a being that instead of a "practi-cal application of the law to the affair," she confined herself to an "elevated and noble contempt" toward her seducer. "Bruderschaft also encouraged her and did not reason; *they read Schiller.* At last, Bruder-schaft sickened of something and died." Masloboyev mockingly charac-terizes the romantic heroine:

> The Smith woman was the craziest and most scatterbrained woman in the world. . . . Why, this is romanticism, this is all *astronomical foolishness* on the most wild and mad scale. Take one thing: from the very beginning she dreamed only of something *like a heaven on earth* and of angels, she fell in love without restraint, believed bound-lessly, and I am convinced, went out of her mind afterward not because she had been deceived in him, because he was capable of deceiving and abandoning her; but because her angel had turned into dirt, and had spit upon and degraded her. Her *romantic* and crazy soul did not sustain such a transformation.

With what ecstasy of destruction does the author ridicule his former holy of holies! With what malicious despair does he talk about his sacred dream — to bring down heaven on earth, to set up an earthly paradise! The "elevated" feelings of the "Smith woman" led not only to her own ruin, but also to the ruin of her daughter Nelly. The "most kind" Nikolai Sergeyevich Ikhmenev's "naive romanticism" is the cause of his downfall and shame. He belongs to those people who "if once they come to love someone (sometimes God knows what for), then surrender themselves to him with their whole soul, extending their devotion sometimes to the point of comedy." He had come to love the Prince and could not forgive him his wrongs; he initiated a lawsuit and lost it, cursed Natasha and forgave her. He does not understand anything in reality, "passes over from doubt to full enthusiastic faith." This is a grown-up child, helpless and weak-willed. Instead of man-like action, there is only ludicrous daydreaming.

The "sensitive heroines," Natasha and Katya, are no less impotent. They are marionettes in the Prince's hands; they do not know how to contend, but know only how fruitlessly to sacrifice themselves. Na-tasha suffers, declaims verse, walks about the room with her arms folded and passively looks on as Alyosha little by little grows cold toward her. But she can do nothing in order to restrain him, in order to defend her love. The "enraptured" Katya talks about lofty ideas, intends to donate a million for the common good, weeps on Natasha's bosom, but most calmly takes her fiancé from her. And with her, as with Alyosha, "goodness" screens the most unsightly egoism.

There remains the writer Ivan Petrovich, the author of a philanthropic tale, the representative of conscious good. Alyosha has not yet matured as to the moral law; Ivan Petrovich is its convinced bearer. He is a humanist and moralist. In him lives the Kantian imperative; he does good for the sake of good, sacrificing his own interests, placing himself at the service of others. Ivan Petrovich saves and takes charge of the orphan Nelly, admonishes and directs Alyosha onto the right path, fights with the villainous Prince, tries to secure Natasha's happiness. But what pitiful results! *Humanistic morality is just as powerless as natural goodness.* With the passing minutes Natasha comes to hate her self-denying friend. "My comfortings," remarks Ivan Petrovich, "used only to torment her; my questionings ever more and more annoyed, even angered her." After her farewell to Alyosha, Natasha turns round to her "comforter": "And it's you!" she cries. "You here again before me! What? Again you have come to comfort me. . . . Go away, I cannot see you! Away! Away!" In this same manner Nelly also from time to time responds to his disinterested solicitation: "she looked at him with hatred as though he were guilty of something in her regard."

Tragic is the spectacle of the impotence of "natural goodness": love, compassion, selflessness are not able to help one's neighbor. Evil is not overcome by good. At the end of the novel the Ikhmenevs are faced with a shattered life, Natasha with an incurable wound in her heart; Ivan Petrovich is spending his last days in a hospital, Nelly is lying in her grave. But the treacherous Alyosha enjoys a state of bliss with Katya, the villainous Prince prospers and is preparing to get married. A full triumph of evil. Why is this? *Can it be humanistic good is imaginary?* Thus Dostoevsky poses his fundamental ethical problem. Its resolution is in the novel-tragedies.

The author humbly acknowledged that in *The Humiliated and Wronged* "many dolls are presented, and not people," but he added that in this "crude work" there were "a half-hundred pages of which I am proud." To these pages without doubt belongs the remarkable nocturnal scene in the restaurant between the Prince and Ivan Petrovich. This is the first "philosophical conversation" in Dostoevsky's creative work, reminiscent of Versilov's conversation in the tavern with his son and Ivan Karamazov's *profession de foi* to Alyosha, also in a tavern. For the first time into the external action, the clash of events and battle of passions, there bursts forth in a fiery flood an inner action, a battle of ideas. *Judgment of the apparent good is entrusted to the villain.*

The "idea" of Prince Volkovsky's personality has its origin in the elderly and respectable civil servant Yulian Mastakovich, the sensualist who marries a young girl (the *Petersburg Chronicle* and *A Christmas Tree Party and a Wedding*). About the Prince, Masloboyev informs us: "He will marry next year. He selected his fiancée a whole year ago. At that time she was just fourteen years old, now she is already fifteen; it seems, she is still going around in pinafores, the poor little thing." The Prince himself confesses his love for perversity to Ivan Petrovich: "Out of boredom I began to make the acquaintance of pretty young girls. . . . I love importance, rank, a big hotel, a huge stake at cards (I'm awfully fond of cards). But mainly — women, and women in all forms. I even love clandestine, obscure perversity, the stranger and more original, *even tinged with a little filth for variety.*" However, the voluptuary Yulian Mastakovich is an innocent child by comparison with the Prince. In Volkovsky comes to life the terrible man-spider Gazin who used licentiously to cut up little children (*Notes from the House of Death*). Ivan Petrovich observes that the Prince "found a certain pleasure, a certain, perhaps, even sensuality in his own insolence, in this effrontery, in this cynicism, with which he was, at last, tearing off his mask before another." The comparison with a spider is repeated: "He produced on me," says the narrator, "the impression of some kind of reptile, of an enormous spider which I would terribly have liked to squash." In the Prince there is the same fascination of power as in the fearless robber Orlov. He is a strong personality standing beyond the moral law. "I have never had pangs of conscience in anything," he proudly declares.

In Dostoevsky's world, Prince Volkovsky has a large posterity: in one line emanate from him the "sensualists" (Svidrigailov, Fyodor Pavlovich Karamazov, and the countless "old men": the Totskys, Yepanchins, Sokolskys, and others). In another, the "supermen"

(Raskolnikov, Kirilov, Ivan Karamazov). Both these lines are joined in Stavrogin. Volkovsky's portrait greatly resembles that of Stavrogin. Both their faces are handsome, but are repulsive masks.

The regular oval of his somewhat swarthy face, his excellent teeth, his small and thinnish lips, beautifully outlined, his straight, rather long nose, his high forehead on which not even the tiniest wrinkle could be discerned, his grey, rather large eyes — all this made up an almost handsome man, and yet his face was not pleasant. This face repelled one, and precisely because its expression was as though not its own but always affected, deliberate, borrowed. . . . Studying it more attentively, you began to suspect under the outer mask something evil, cunning, and to the highest degree egotistical. . . .

The Prince invites Ivan Petrovich to supper in a restaurant, and his half-drunken chatter turns into a cruel settlement with idealism. He mocks the jilted fiancé's spirit of self-sacrifice. "Why, Alyosha has carried off your fiancée," he says, "why I know this, and you, *like some Schiller or other*, are crucifying yourself for them, wait upon them, and act almost as their errand-boy. . . . Why, this is just some nasty little play at magnanimous feelings. . . . And worst of all: it's shameful! shameful!" He scorns his son: "I am, in the end, so very bored by all this innocence, all these *pastorals* of Alyosha's, all this *Schillerism*, all the loftiness in this damnable intrigue with this Natasha. . . ." He does not believe in any goodness. He is just the same as everyone else; only the others keep silent, while he speaks: "If it were possible for each of us to describe all his hidden secrets, but in such a way that he would not be afraid to reveal not only that which he fears to tell his best friends, but even that which occasionally he fears to confess to himself, why then such a stench would rise up on the earth that we all should necessarily suffocate. . . . You accuse me of vice, depravity, immorality — while I, perhaps, am only guilty of being more open than others, and that's all."

To the humanistic lie regarding man's natural sinlessness there is opposed the religious truth of original sin. The utopian idyll ended in the *House of Death. The religious tragedy has begun.*

"At the basis of all human virtues," asserts the Prince, "lies the most profound egoism. And the more a deed is virtuous, the more of egoism there is there. . . ." And what remains for a man to do who is sick from all this "vulgar loftiness"? One thing only: to grimace and stick out his tongue. The Prince continues: "One of the most piquant delights for me has always been to adapt myself at first to this style, to enter this tone, to encourage *some eternally young Schiller,* and then suddenly, all at once, to dumbfound him! Suddenly to raise my mask before him and distort my enraptured face *into a grimace, to stick my tongue out at him,* and precisely at that moment when he least of all expects this surprise." This was the reason that he invited Ivan Petrovich to the restaurant to provide himself the pleasure of "spitting a little on this whole business and of spitting right before his eyes." The Prince's "idea" is illustrated by his anecdote about the mad Parisian functionary who used to throw a broad cloak over his nude body and "with an important, majestic mien" walk out onto the street. Upon meeting a passerby, he "would open his cloak and display himself in all his 'straightforwardness.' " This image is the symbol of humanistic goodness: nakedness under an ostentatious cloak.

Prince Volkovsky rises in revolt, but yet innocently, like a little boy; he makes grimaces and sticks out his tongue. The "gentleman" from the *Notes from Underground* acts more daringly; he not only shows his tongue to the "crystal edifice," to this humanistic paradise on earth, but he proposes to "send it all off to hell." Dostoevsky is one of the greatest spiritual rebels in world history.

After his nocturnal conversation with the Prince the narrator goes away in indignation. He is "astounded," he cannot "describe his own anger." But if he had reflected upon the words of this "reptile" whom he would have liked to squash, perhaps he would have recognized that there was much truth in them. The novel which he himself is narrating, as it were, designedly confirms the Prince's theory about egoism. Are not Alyosha and Katya in fact egoists; is not Natasha an egoist, purchasing her happiness with her parents' unhappiness and the suffering of her fiancé? Is not the "most kind" old Ikhmenev an egoist, intending to challenge the Prince to a duel and in that way to destroy Natasha, so as to satisfy his own vengeance? Yes, and all the "humiliated and wronged" are egoists precisely in their humiliation and suffering. The author explains his paradox by the example of Nelly and her mother. Ivan Petrovich surrounds the poor orphan with protection and care, but she runs away from him and begs for alms. The narrator remarks: "She had been wronged, her wound could not heal, and she, as though on purpose, was trying to irritate her wound. Just as if she herself took pleasure in her pain, *this egoism of suffering,* if it can so be expressed." At the novel's denouement we learn that Nelly's mother was legally married to Prince Volkovsky, possessed an official document, and could have saved herself and her daughter from poverty and ruin. But she sacrificed both herself and her daughter solely in order to enjoy to the end her proud suffering. The Prince confesses that he did not return her father's stolen money to her since he reasoned that "by returning the money to her, he would, perhaps, make her even unhappy." "I would have taken from her the *pleasure* of being miserable entirely because of me," he says, "and of cursing me for it all her life. Believe me, my friend, in unhappiness of such kind there is even a certain lofty rapture, to feel oneself completely right and magnanimous and to have the full right to call one's offender a scoundrel. This rapture of malice is met with *in Schilleresque natures,* as is evident. Perhaps afterward she had nothing to eat, but I am convinced that she was happy." In suffering there is egoism, a rapture of malice, contempt toward the persecutor, pleasure in shame, vengeance against an unjust fate, delight in one's own nobility, a defiance of the world. The "humiliated and wronged" are really not so unhappy; there are subtle pleasures known to them which they would not exchange for any well-being.

Thus Dostoevsky demolishes the "natural" morality of atheistic humanism.

X I

The Journal *Time* (1861-1863)
Winter Notes on Summer Impressions
His Intimacy with A. Suslova

In the autumn of 1860 Dostoevsky prepared an announcement regarding the publication of a new journal *Time*. In this manifesto he spoke of the "enormous change taking place in Russia." The Petrine reform had reached its ultimate limits. A new epoch was coming in. "We have, at last, become convinced that we too are a distinct nationality, in the highest degree original, and that our task is to create our own new form, one native, proper to ourselves, taken from our *soil*, taken from our national spirit and from national principles." Peter's reform was necessary, but it cost too dearly: it separated the educated class from the people. The new journal would fight for "the reconciliation of civilization with the national principle"; its motto would be: "union no matter what price, regardless of any sacrifice, and as soon as possible!" And the announcement ended with the inspired prophecy: "We foresee, and foresee with reverence, that the character of our future activity must be to the highest degree *universal to mankind;* that the Russian idea perhaps will be the synthesis of all those ideas which Europe is with such obstinacy, with such courage, developing in its separate nationalities; that perhaps all that is hostile in these ideas will find its reconciliation and furthest development in the Russian national spirit."

Time wanted to create a new social current occupying a middle position between Westernism and Slavophilism. For the first time there sounds the fundamental idea of Dostoevsky's journalism of the seventies: the Russian idea is the reconciliation of all European ideas, the Russian ideal is universal to mankind.

Into the bitter conflict of the Westernizers and Slavophiles the new journal entered as a "nonpartisan of either camp" — an ambiguous and dangerous stance. It advocated the cause of reconciliation, but soon had to submit to bombarding from both sides and to contend on two fronts. In the very first issue (January 1861) the editor declared: "The public has understood that with Westernism we are stubbornly stretching a foreign caftan upon ourselves in spite of the fact that it has long been bursting at every seam, and that with Slavophilism we are sharing the poetic illusion of reconstructing Russia according to an ideal view of its ancient manner of life, a view that has been set down in place of a genuine understanding of Russia, some kind of ballet decor, pretty, but false and abstract. . . . But now we want to live and to act and not to fancy." The positions of the Westernizers and the Slavophiles were marked by their clarity: the first were materialists, liberals, cosmopolitans; the second, Orthodox, conservatives, nationalists. *Time's* position was disconcerting in its vagueness: the "union of civilization with the national principle," the "reconciliation of ideas" seemed hazy notions.

But the journal attracted readers through its literary content. Mikhail Mikhailovich Dostoevsky served as official editor; Fyodor Mikhailovich managed the artistic and critical section. In the first issue *The Humiliated and Wronged* was published; after it followed *Notes from the House of Death,* the works of Ostrovsky, Nekrasov, Turgenev, and Shchedrin. Dostoevsky was not adverse even to "sensations"; he ran a translation of *The Crimes of Lacenaire* and extracts from *The Memoirs of Casanova.* For the first number he wrote a feuilleton *Petersburg Dreams in Verse and Prose,* one of the most poetic of his creations. He succeeded in attracting as contributors two gifted young critics, Apollon Grigoryev and N. N. Strakhov. Thus the group of those "rooted in the soil"[1] was formed. N. Strakhov in his memoirs sketched Dostoevsky as he was during the epoch of *Time.* "He wore only a moustache in those days and in spite of his enormous forehead and most beautiful eyes, had a thoroughly soldierlike appearance, i.e., the facial characteristics of a common peasant." He used to express himself almost in a whisper, but when he was inspired, would talk loudly. He idolized Pushkin and loved to read "Just now on the places thawed by

---

[1] *Pochvennost* is one of the most difficult terms in Russian to translate. It is a coinage from the Russian *pochva* (soil, earth). I have translated it "(being) rooted in the soil," and its opposite, *bespochvennost* as "uprooted from the soil." Its adherents, Dostoevsky, Grigoryev and Strakhov, sought to construct a "Christian philosophy" on the basis of man's "organic collectivity" (*sobornost*) and his "immediate" relation to the "soil." An excellent discussion of the *pochvenniki* and their concepts is to be found in Zenkovsky's *A History of Russian Philosophy,* I, 400-432, Columbia University Press, 1953.

spring" and "As in the warm spring season."[2] At three o'clock in the afternoon the contributors usually met in the editorial office; before dinner they used to take a walk; in the evening between six and seven Dostoevsky frequently visited Strakhov; at twelve he would sit down to work and would write until five or six in the morning, sustaining himself with tea. He slept until two o'clock in the afternoon. This was the way he worked all his life. The very process of writing was tormenting to him. "It has always been more pleasant for me to ponder my compositions," says his alter ego, Ivan Petrovich, in *The Humiliated and Wronged*, "and to dream how they will be written, than actually to write them and, truly, this has not been from laziness. Why then?" This question is answered by N. Strakhov: "An inner labor constantly engaged him, the growth and movement of ideas were taking place and it was always difficult for him to tear away from this labor so as to write. Remaining seemingly idle, he was, in effect, working without rest. . . . His thoughts were teeming; incessantly new images were produced, plans for new compositions, and old plans expanded and developed." During the two years spent working on the journal *Time* Dostoevsky, according to his own admission, wrote up to a hundred printed sheets. The cost of this terrible exertion is witnessed in the notebooks of 1862-1863: "Epileptic attacks: 1 April — strong; 1 August — weak; 7 November — medium; 7 January — strong; 2 March — medium." "However," wrote Dostoevsky, "the success of the journal which we had started was more dear than anything to me," and success was attained. The editor of *Time* and the author of the sensational *Notes from the House of Death* was satisfied. "My name is worth a million," he declared proudly to Strakhov.

From January to November 1861 Dostoevsky published in *Time* a series of articles on Russian literature in which he attempted to clarify the ideology of the new movement. European civilization used to answer the needs of the Russian "soil," but now it "has already completed its circle with us; we have already outlived it all; have received from it all that was suitable and are freely returning to our native soil." The author was full of joyful hopes. "The new Russ is even now gradually groping about, is even now gradually becoming conscious of itself. . . ." He relates the "tale of our development": how there arose a consciousness in Russian society, how analysis penetrated it, how self-accusa-

---

[2] "Just now on the places thawed by spring" is the third line of a lyric poem beginning: "Cold winds still blow" (*Yeshchyo duyut kholodnye vetry*) written in 1828. The second: "As in the warm spring season" is from the *Folk-Tale about a She-Bear*, ca. 1830.

tion and self-condemnation were born; he recalls the ecstatic veneration of George Sand, the founding of the "natural school," Russian Byronism, the appearance of the "two demons" Gogol and Lermontov, the conception of the "literature of exposure."

"No, we have long been investigating everything carefully, analyzing everything, we pose riddles to ourselves, are anxious and tormented by the solutions. . . . You see, we also have lived and experienced much. . . ."

Dostoevsky sums up the totals for the Petrine period of Russian life and affirms its spiritual importance. This is his first attempt at a *philosophy of Russian culture*. Russia's apprenticeship is ended, he thinks, she has matured to her own original idea: *the complete universality of man*. "Yes, we believe that the Russian nation is an extraordinary phenomenon in the history of all mankind. . . . And it is terrifying to what degree the Russian man is free in spirit. . . ." In the year of the emancipation of the serfs, the writer prophesied for Russia "a new activity, unknown in history." He regarded the future optimistically: the intelligentsia would bring to the people its education, while the people "with love will value the educated class as its teachers and instructors, will acknowledge us its genuine friends, will value us not as hirelings, but shepherds. . . ."

Seized by the idyllic attitude of the first days of the reforms, the ex-convict forgot the terrible experience of Omsk prison; the abyss between the civilized class and the people no longer seemed so profound to him: reconciliation was near at hand.

The historiosophy of the *Diary of a Writer* is already elaborated in the articles of 1861. For twenty years the author "lived out" the ideas of the Pushkin speech. "Pushkin's colossal significance" lies in his being the embodiment of the Russian spirit, the Russian ideal. "The appearance of Pushkin," Dostoevsky wrote in *Time*, "is proof that the tree of civilization has already ripened to bearing fruits, and these its fruits are not rotten, but magnificent golden fruits. In him we understood that the Russian ideal is *complete integrity, complete reconciliation, complete universality*." Pushkin is the justification of Peter's deed, the meaning of the Petersburg period of our history, of our "European captivity." He is for us "the beginning of everything that we now have." The Russian man saw himself in Onegin: "he still does not know what to do, does not even know what to respect, although he is firmly convinced that there is something which one must respect and love."

Dostoevsky polemized both with the Westernizers and with the Slavophiles, but in the beginning his sympathies were on the side of the former. He was irritated by Konstantin Aksakov's contemptuous haughty tone, by the formalism and intolerance of the newspaper *The Day*. The Slavophiles had a rare capacity to understand nothing in contemporary reality. Their ideal consisted in "the panorama of Moscow from Sparrow Hills, the fanciful representation of Moscow life in the middle of the seventeenth century, the siege of Kazan and the Monastery, and other panoramas represented in the French taste by Karamzin." Westernism "all the same was more real than Slavophilism." In an article *Literary Hysterics*, directed against Katkov's *Russian Messenger*, Dostoevsky hotly defended the "uprooted Westernizers." Yes, they had no soil, their activity was false and life fantastic. But really could one laugh and ridicule this Russian tragedy? Did it not bear witness to a strained life? "Blessed is he," exclaims the author, "who even in a misshapen appearance is capable of seeing its historically serious aspect; and really is the man in error necessarily a scoundrel? And sometimes precisely the more misshapen life appears, the more convulsive, the more deformed, the more *incessant* is this manifestation, the more it means life wants to declare itself at whatever price — while you say there isn't even life. Here there is anguish, suffering, and yet what does this mean to you?" Keeping sharply aloof from the Slavophile *The Day* and Katkov's *Russian Messenger*, *Time* maintained friendly relations with the radical *Contemporary;* Nekrasov and Shchedrin were contributors on it. *The Contemporary* acclaimed the novel *The Humiliated and Wronged* and even ran a laudatory tribute to *Time*. The government considered the Dostoevsky brothers' journal in opposition and dangerous.

But friendship with the "Westernizers" did not last. N. Strakhov and other contributors of *Time* more and more openly manifested their hostility toward Nekrasov's group. At first Dostoevsky curbed their polemic heat, would add numerous "notes from the editor" to their articles, but soon he himself was caught up in the fight. Defense of the "Westernizers" reverted into an embittered polemic against the "nihilists." Dostoevsky's hopes for a moving reconciliation of the intelligentsia with the people were replaced by alarm before the approaching revolution. In 1861 the "students' story" shattered all his idyllic dreams. The students rose in rebellion. The university was closed; arrests and perquisitions were begun; students were placed in Petropavlovsky Fortress; on the streets a crowd cheered them. The truce between *Time* and *The Contemporary* came to an end; a venomous and merciless battle began.

It confined itself at first to the realm of art. Dostoevsky attacked Dobrolyubov and his utilitarian theory. One cannot impose various designs upon art and prescribe laws; it has "its own integral, organic life," it answers man's innate need of beauty "without which, perhaps, he might not want to live on earth." When man is in discord with reality, in conflict, i.e., when he is living most of all, the thirst for beauty and harmony appears in him with its greatest force. Art is useful here because it pours in energy, sustains the forces, strengthens our feeling of life. "Art is always contemporary and real, never has it existed otherwise and, most important, it is unable to exist otherwise." This is an important *profession de foi* of Dostoevsky the artist; he defends the autonomy of art, deriving its usefulness from an *aesthetic need* without which man "perhaps might not want to live on earth." The author upholds the spiritual nobility of man which is degraded by the utilitarians. "Man accepts beauty without any conditions and so, simply because it is beauty, and with veneration he bows down before it, not asking why it is useful and what one can buy with it." Beauty is more useful than the simply useful, for it is the ultimate goal of being. On this height, the way of art meets with the way of religion. The idea of beauty is mystically deepened in the great novels and is crowned by the prophecy: "Beauty will save the world."

Strakhov relates that from the year 1861 *The Contemporary* began to act "like some sort of committee of public safety" and systematically engaged in literary executions: Pogodin, Sluchevsky, Kostomarov, the Slavophiles were "annihilated"; finally, Turgenev's novel *Fathers and Children* was destroyed. Strakhov, under the pseudonym of "The Pigtail," came forward to its defense. Then *The Contemporary* attacked *Time* (an article *Concerning the Spirit of* "Time," April 1862). The polemic was cut short by Chernyshevsky's arrest. Revolutionary ferment was growing each month; proclamations were diffused with threats "to inundate the streets with blood and not leave a stone upon a stone." In May 1862 fires were started in Petersburg; for two weeks whole quarters were burning. In June *The Contemporary* was closed for eight months.

In the summer of 1862 Dostoevsky went abroad for the first time. The dream of his entire life was at last realized; he would see Europe, the "land of holy wonders"! The year before he wrote to Ya. P. Polonsky in Italy:

You are a lucky man! How many times since my very childhood have I dreamed of visiting Italy! When I was still reading the novels of Radcliffe, at the age of eight, various Alfonsos, Catarinas, and Lucias ate their way into my mind. . . . Then came Shakespeare, Verona, Romeo and Juliet, the devil knows what enchantment there was! And instead of Italy I landed in Semipalatinsk, and before that in the House of Death. Can it be that now I will not succeed in traveling through Europe while there still is some strength and ardor and poetry left?

And here, at last, he had "freed himself."

In *Winter Notes on Summer Impressions* he recounts: "I was in Berlin, in Dresden, in Wiesbaden, in Baden-Baden, in Cologne, in Paris, in London, in Lucerne, in Geneva, in Genoa, in Florence, in Milan, in Venice, in Vienna, and in some of these places twice — and all this I toured in just about two and a half months." His itinerary was planned beforehand; he was not in a condition to select his stops. He wanted "to view everything, absolutely everything." "Lord, how much I expected for myself from this trip! So what if I do not examine anything in detail, I thought, instead, I've seen everything, have visited everywhere; instead, out of all these precious things there will be formed some sort of whole, some sort of general panorama. All the 'land of holy wonders' will present itself to me at once, in a bird's-eye view, like the promised land in perspective from a mountain top."

In Berlin he stayed a total of only twenty-four hours and the city produced "a most sour impression" upon him. "I noticed immediately, at first glance, that Berlin is to an unbelievable degree like Petersburg"; for that reason he quickly "slipped off" to Dresden, "cherishing the most profound conviction in my soul that one had especially to accustom oneself to Germans and that unless one did so, it would be exceedingly difficult to stand them in large masses."

In Dresden he "suddenly felt that there was nothing more repugnant than the Dresden type of women." In Cologne the cathedral did not please him, but a month later, seeing it a second time, he wanted "to beg its forgiveness on his knees." Entering France, he suffered his first encounter with the "European spirit." At the frontier station of Erquelines four strange travelers boarded the coach; they were without luggage, in threadbare frock coats, dirty linen, and bright neckties. The faces of each were similar, wrinkled, and self-satisfied. The Russian traveler learned with astonishment that these were "police-spies." In Paris at the Hôtel des Empereurs the landlady noted down all his characteristics in detail. "Oh, monsieur, this is indispensable," she exclaimed, and Dostoevsky was dumbfounded by the "colossal regulation" of this "most virtuous city in all the wide world." He wrote to Strakhov: "Paris is the most boring city and if there were not very many really extraordinary things in it, then, truly, one could die of boredom. The French, with God as my judge, are enough to make a man nauseated. . . . A Frenchman is quiet, honorable, well-mannered, but insincere, and with him money is everything. No ideal. . . . You will not believe how loneliness is encompassing my soul here. An oppressive, heavy feeling." From Paris he went to London for eight days, viewed the International Exposition, frequently met with Herzen. London astonished him. In the *Winter Notes on Summer Impressions* he writes:

What broad, overwhelming canvases! This city, bustling day and night, and boundless like the sea, the screeching and howling of machines, these railways laid above the houses (and soon even under the houses), this boldness of enterprise, this seeming disorder which, in actuality, is bourgeois order of the highest degree, this polluted Thames, this air steeped in coal dust, these splendid squares and parks, these terrible corners like Whitechapel, with its half-hungry and naked population, the City with its millions and worldwide commerce, the Crystal Palace, the International Exposition. . . . Yes, the Exposition is astonishing!

Having returned to Paris, Dostoevsky went from there to Geneva where he met N. Strakhov. Together they set out for Lucerne, then across Mont-Cenis to Genoa. From Genoa they went by boat to Leghorn, from there to Florence. Strakhov informs us that Dostoevsky was bored in the Uffizi, compared the Arno to the Fontanka, and with passion read Hugo's new novel *Les Misérables*.

In September they both returned to Russia. Neither in his letters nor in the *Notes* does the writer mention Italy, about which he so ardently dreamed from early childhood. In Europe a total disappointment awaited him — the "land of holy wonders" proved to be a cemetery.

The November issue of *Time* ran Dostoevsky's short story *A Nasty Predicament*. The rosy hopes of the reform's first days had been dissipated. The emancipation of the serfs, for the sake of which the writer "had entered upon revolution" and for which he had paid with ten years' exile, did not afford him joy for long. The "festival of reconciliation" between the people and the intelligentsia had shortly before still inspired his journalism; now he took revenge upon himself for his incorrigible "romantic dreaming" and ridiculed his naiveté. In place of a hymn to the epoch of great reforms, he wrote a violent satire against it. The reform had not succeeded; in place of it there has ensued a "nasty predicament."

In the government officials of the new reign he recognized all those same features of the utopians of the forties, only suddenly having put faith in their parliamentarian talents. In the person of his hero, the Actual Councilor of State Ivan Ilyich Pralinsky,[A] he sketches a murderous caricature of them. Ivan Ilyich is a general, still young, loves to talk and "to assume parliamentary poses." In moments of despondency he calls himself a "parleur" and "phrase-maker." "But reconstructed Russia presented him all at once with great hopes. He all at once began to speak eloquently and to speak on the latest themes." He is a "poet at heart" and his favorite subject is humaneness. "Humaneness is the chief thing," he exclaims, "humaneness with our inferiors, remembering that they too are men. Humanity will save everything and bring out everything. . . . Humaneness, I say, can serve, so to speak, as the cornerstone of the coming reforms and in general to the renovation of things." The author of *Poor People* and *The Humiliated and Wronged*, whose humane reputation had been asserted by Belinsky and Dobrolyubov, does not find sarcasms strong enough with which to make fun of the reformers' "philanthropy." He would like, as did his hero, Prince Volkovsky, "to spit a little on this whole business." Not long before, he was writing in *Time* about how the people would receive their "shepherds" with love. In *A Nasty Predicament* this prediction is parodied.

Pralinsky proposes the following syllogism: "I am humane, consequently, I am loved; therefore, people feel trust in me. Trust is felt, therefore, they have faith; they have faith, therefore, they love . . . , i.e., no — I want to say if they have faith then they will believe also in the reform, will understand, so to speak, the very essence of the affair, so to speak, *they will embrace one another in a moral sense.*"

Chance helps His Excellency verify in fact the validity of his idea. Returning on foot from his visit, he hears music in a certain decrepit,

[A] Pralinsky from "praline." The sweet name underlines the hero's sweetness.

one-storied little house. He learns that his subordinate Pseldonimov, "a civil servant with a salary of ten rubles a month," is getting married, and decides to undertake an action "patriarchal, lofty and moral": to delight this poor fellow with a visit. "My action will revive nobility in them," sweetly muses the general. "And indeed I will raise up the humiliated man morally; I will restore him to my very self. . . . They are already mine: I am their father, they my children. . . ."

Pralinsky's appearance at the lowly wedding at first causes consternation, but quickly the guests surmise that he, "it seems, well . . . is a little under the influence" and begin to conduct themselves disrespectfully. In confusion, the general keeps on emptying his champagne glass. A student cries in his face like a cock, a collaborator of the satirical journal *The Firebrand*[B] flings pellets of bread at him. Pralinsky feels that he is drunk, wants to leave, but remains for supper and delivers a toast.

" 'I have already said, ladies and gentlemen, that Russia . . . Yes, namely Russia . . . in a word, you understand what I want to say. . . . Russia is experiencing, according to my most profound conviction, hu- humaneness.' 'Hu- humaneness!' rang out at the other end of the table — 'Hu-hu!' 'Tyu-tyu!' "

A scandal erupts, and the collaborator of *The Firebrand* "exposes" the humane general. The latter fares very badly and is laid upon the marriage bed; all night he suffers with a stomach disorder. The young couple settle themselves on a feather-bed placed between two chairs; the chairs give way and they drop down with a crash. Pseldonimov's family happiness and his service career are forever ruined. Coming to himself on the following morning, Pralinsky does not leave his house for eight days. "There were moments when he was almost thinking of being tonsured in a monastery. . . . He imagined to himself peaceful subterranean chanting, an open coffin, life in a solitary cell, forests and caves." With this biting stroke the "humanist's" portrait is concluded. The short story is written in the style of Shchedrin's most violent exposures. This is a crude farce, but not divested of comic force. For the universally acknowledged preacher of philanthropy, humaneness has now turned into "hu- humaneness, hu-hu, tyu-tyu!"

In the February and March issues of *Time* for 1863 there appeared *Winter Notes on Summer Impressions*. This remarkable attempt at

[B] The satirical journal *Spark* is parodied.

philosophical journalism is written in the form of letters to friends about the 1862 journey abroad. Dostoevsky calls the sentimental traveler Karamzin to mind and begins his notes completely in Karamzin's style: "See how many months you have now been urging me, my friends, to hasten to describe my foreign impressions to you, not suspecting that by your request you place me simply at an impasse." Having reminded the readers of the sentimental tradition of *Letters of a Russian Traveler,* the author only intensifies the impression of contrast; there is nothing more opposed to Karamzinian sentimentalism than the savage irony of the *Winter Notes.* Dostoevsky's critics, especially the foreign ones, reproach him for the prejudice and haste of his evaluation of European culture; he remained in Europe just two and a half months, in Paris less than a month, in London eight days. When did he have the time to penetrate the Parisian bourgeois' psychology, to study the conditions of the London proletariat? This misunderstanding is provoked by the exceptional originality of the *Notes'* literary form. The author pretends that he is describing his "impressions," but this is only the device of a publicist who is creating a new and cutting form of the historico-philosophical treatise. Dostoevsky came to Europe with a preconceived idea and only "verified" it by his foreign impressions; reality fully bore out his theoretical construction.

If one regards the *Winter Notes* as a travel journal, then one is forced to admit that in all world literature a stranger "description of a journey" does not exist. Strakhov tells in his memoirs:

> Fyodor Mikhailovich was not a great master of the art of traveling. He was not occupied particularly by nature, or by historical monuments, or works of art, with the exception perhaps of the greatest; all his attention was directed *toward people,* and he used to seize upon only their nature and characters, and perhaps a general impression of street life. He ardently began explaining to me that he detested the usual, routine manner of visiting the various celebrated places with a guide-book in hand. . . .

Strange are the *Notes on Impressions* in which there is not mentioned one monument of art, one church, one landscape, except perhaps the panorama of London streets; in which Italy and Switzerland are passed over in silence, and Paris is presented through several encounters with the "bourgeois." But Dostoevsky was not hunting for picturesque impressions; he grasped the "idea" of Europe and, in accord with a few indications, unriddled the mystery of the European man.

The writer's philosophical essay is devoted to two themes: the first of them is Russia and the West, the second Europe's destruction. Reflecting in his railway coach upon the fate of his native land, the author is astounded by our "captivation" with the West. "Why, everything, unquestionably almost everything that we have — of development, science, art, civil-mindedness, humanity, everything, everything, why it comes from there — from that same land of holy wonders! Why our entire life, even from very childhood itself, has been set up along European lines. . . ." And he asks: why is this so? "Why does Europe have upon us, whoever we might be, such a powerful, magic, compelling impact?" And how have we succeeded in resisting this pressure and not "being transformed decisively into Europeans?" What then has saved us from the loss of national character? . . . "Why it is truly sad and ludicrous to think that if there had been no Arina Rodionovna, Pushkin's nurse, then, we should perhaps have had no Pushkin. . . . And Pushkin, wasn't he a real Russian? He, a gentleman's son, saw into Pugachyov and fathomed Pugachyov's soul. He, an aristocrat, embraced Belkin in his soul. . . .[3] *Why this was a prophet and herald.*"

No, Russia was not transformed into Europe, has not forfeited its originality; "there is a kind of chemical fusion of the human spirit and one's native land"; one cannot tear oneself away from it. In the 18th century, when no one doubted the holiness of European apron-strings, when Russian noblemen scrambled into silk stockings, perukes, and hung little swords on, this European civilization was only a phantasmagoria. The steppe landowners continued to live according to tradition, did not scorn the muzhiks, and were intelligible to them. The Russian de Rohans and Montbazons dealt with their domestic serfs as before, managed their families patriarchally, in the stable flogged their small landowning neighbors as formerly. The "Europe, which had been attested and summoned," at that time lived along amazingly well with the Russian past.

[3] Pugachyov, an illiterate Cossack, declaring himself to be Emperor Peter III, led the famous peasant uprising against the forces of Catherine the Great. His troops ravaged and destroyed whole areas of southeast Russia, the Volga and Ural districts. He was finally captured and executed in 1775. Pushkin wrote a monumental two-volume *History of the Pugachyov Rebellion* and Pugachyov appears as a character in his novel *The Captain's Daughter.* Ivan Petrovich Belkin is the fictional narrator of his *Belkin's Tales.* The portrait of this provincial landowner is completely charming in its simplicity, candor, and ingenuousness.

But now it is not so. "Now we are fully Europeans and matured." The author comes down upon the Russian Europeans, the "greenhouse" progressives, and civilizers. The polemics with the Westernizers and nihilists, begun in the journal *Time*, are carried over to the *Notes*. "We ourselves are so excellent, so wonderful, such Europeans, that even the people are nauseated looking at us. . . . How haughtily we solve questions, and what questions they are: that there is no soil, the people do not exist, nationality — this is only an established system of taxation; the soul is a *tabula rasa*. . . ." Later a direct thrust is aimed against *The Contemporary* which had "executed" Turgenev for his novel *Fathers and Children*. "With what serene self-satisfaction we wreaked vengeance upon, for example, Turgenev for having made bold not to be content with our majestic personalities. . . ." But the "exposition of exposers" ends on an optimistic note. The author believes that in Russia there are not only the "sergeant-majors of civilization and European petty tyrants," that a young individual has already been born, that this new Chatsky[4] will soon make his appearance, "but now not in hysterics, as at Famusov's ball. but *as a conqueror, proud, powerful, gentle, and loving*." It is especially necessary to underline this belief of Dostoevsky inasmuch as it will lie at the base of his ultimate creative work. Quests for a new "positively beautiful individual" inspire his great novels; he searched for him in the nobility, in the people, in the spiritual ranks. Prince Myshkin and Alyosha in different ways embody the writer's dream of the coming Russia.

His reflections on Russia and the West bring the author to a conclusion: Europe has helped us in our national development, but now we have matured to an independent life and European civilization is not only no longer useful to us, but it is harmful. Even in the West itself it has become corrupt, and from development has turned into a "hindrance to development." The second part of the *Winter Notes* — the destruction of Europe — is devoted to proving this affirmation.

In London the former convict did not fear meeting with the political emigré Herzen in spite of the fact that the editor of *The Bell* was under the surveillance of Russian police. At this period he was spiritually close to Herzen who at that time was writing his *Endings and Beginnings*. Like those "rooted in the soil," Herzen believed in Russia's lofty historical vocation, found the embryos of a new social structure in the peasant commune and the workers' artel, felt in Russian literature the spirit of a great people. Strakhov observes that the *Winter Notes on*

4 Chatsky: cf. n. 1, Ch. X.

Summer Impressions reflect Herzen's influence. The author of *Endings and Beginnings* without doubt strengthened Dostoevsky's conviction in the destruction of the West. Here is what he was writing at that time: "All the civilized world is entering upon bourgeoisdom, and its avant-garde has already arrived there. Bourgeoisdom is the ideal toward which Europe is aspiring, is raising itself from its lowest points. . . . Yes, dearest friend, it is time to come to the calm and humble acknowledgement that *bourgeoisdom is the definitive form of European civilization*, its majority, its *état adulte*."

Europe's decay is shown by Dostoevsky with amazing force in the tableau of the two cities, Paris and London. In the first, there is bourgeoisdom congealed in its self-satisfied well-being; in the second, bourgeois order in all its demonic majesty. The author calls Paris the most moral and the most virtuous city; in it everything is reasonable, defined, regulated. Everyone has convinced himself that he is content and completely happy, and they have become petrified in the "stillness of order." The bourgeois wants to persuade himself that the ideal has been attained and that Paris is an absolute earthly paradise.

Bourgeois well-being is depicted in fine parody: "If one beholds the great courtyard of the Palais-Royal at evening, then one must without fail shed a tear of emotion. Countless husbands are strolling arm in arm with their countless spouses; round about frolic their charming and well-behaved children. A little fountain gurgles and the monotonous lapping of its jets is reminiscent of something calm, quiet, eternal, constant, Heidelbergian. . . ."

"All Frenchmen have an amazingly noble air." At the theatre the public loves a melodrama in which "the more lofty characteristics and lofty lessons are proposed." The hero necessarily must be disinterested in money — curse in nasty words and spit on a million — but at the end of the play, nonetheless, a million he receives "in the guise of a reward for virtue."

Despite his unspeakable nobility, there is in the nature of the bourgeois much servility and innate spying, but his main characteristic trait — this is eloquence. "His love of eloquence is inextinguishable and with the years flames up ever more and more." To this end six liberal deputies are maintained in the legislative body. They are completely useless, but when they speak, the mouths of all France water. Even the invalid, showing the tombs in the Panthéon, becomes intoxicated with his own rote eloquence.

In opposition to the bourgeois paradise of Paris stands the capitalistic hell of London. The tone changes sharply; ironic delight is replaced by gloomy and vehement pathos. "This is a kind of biblical picture, something about Babylon, some prophecy out of the Apocalypse, coming to pass before your eyes." The sensation of an approaching end, which had been hidden away in Paris under hypocritical well-being, in London bursts forth into the open. Dostoevsky was inspired by the Apocalypse, a book with which all his work is mystically joined. Like the prophet of Patmos, he saw in London a Babylonian whore — in the ebullition of the huge city, a sacrifice to Baal. "On Saturday nights a half-million workers, male and female, together with their children, flood the entire city like a sea. . . . Clusters of gas lamps burn in the butcher shops and restaurants, brightly illuminating the streets. . . . The people crowd in the open taverns and in the streets. Here they eat and drink. The beer-houses are adorned like palaces. . . . They all quickly hasten to get drunk to the point of insensibility. . . ."

In the Hay Market "at night public women flock by the thousands. . . . At every step there are magnificent coffee-houses, adorned with mirrors and gold. . . . The crowd doesn't have enough room on the sidewalks and pours over onto the street. All of them thirst for prey and throw themselves with shameless cynicism onto the first passerby." Dostoevsky remembered a girl of dazzling beauty drinking gin in the Casino with some gentleman, and in the crowd on the street a little girl of about six years, filthy, emaciated and bruised, with an expression of hopeless despair on her face. "In general, cheerful subjects," he concludes.

The International Exposition, the "Crystal Palace" astound the Russian traveler; for some reason he finds it terrifying. "You sense the terrible force which has united all these countless people, having come from all the world, into a *single herd*. This is the full triumph of Baal, the ultimate organization of an anthill." The author here touches upon his most profound idea regarding the Antichrist's earthly kingdom; criticism of the bourgeois order in the spirit of Herzen suddenly grows into an apocalyptic vision. The capitalistic regime is the kingdom of Baal, the demon to whom human sacrifices are brought. It is he who has frightened people into a herd; it is he who has erected the gigantic anthill. "But if you saw how proud is that mighty spirit who created this colossal setting and how proudly convinced this spirit is of its victory and of its triumph, then you would shudder for its pride, obstinacy, and blindness, but you would shudder also for those over whom this proud spirit hovers and reigns."

The "Crystal Palace" of the Exposition is transformed in the *Notes from Underground* into the "crystal palace" of socialism; the proud and powerful spirit will be called by name in the *Brothers Karamazov*. This is the Antichrist, the Grand Inquisitor. In the brilliant prophetic images of the *Winter Notes* are sown the grains of Dostoevsky's greatest religious insights. In the kingdom of Baal the human spirit is overwhelmed, subordinated, seeks salvation in gin and debauchery. An apocalyptic image transfixes the soul: "You sense, looking at all these pariahs of society, that still for a long time the prophecy will not come to pass for them, that still for a long time they will not be given palm branches and white robes, and that for a long time yet they will be imploring the throne of the All Highest: 'How long, O Lord. . . .'"

After the visions of the Parisian "paradise" and the London "hell" there is an historico-philosophical explanation. The French Revolution did not succeed: liberty has fallen only to the man with a million; equality has acquired an offensive significance, while fraternity has not been attained, because in the West there exists no fraternal principle. For want of brotherhood, the socialists are attempting to create it by reason and calculation. The result is the same anthill as is had in capitalism. They drive a man into phalansteries, but he resists and declares that "his own will is better." These few strokes indicate the basic theme of *Notes from Underground*.

But if the personal principle, the "self-determination in one's own I," has hindered the formation of brotherhood in the West, then does salvation perhaps lie in impersonalism? Dostoevsky answers this question with an inspired definition of brotherhood which has become the catechism of all contemporary Orthodox sociology. The relationships between individuality and the collective, the difference between the atheistic commune and Christian communality, the personalistic character of the future social order founded on love and freedom — all this is already contained in this reasoning of our greatest thinker. "Is salvation to be found in impersonality?" asks Dostoevsky.

To the contrary, to the contrary, I say; not only is it not necessary to be impersonal, but precisely one must become *individual*, even in a degree much higher than that which is now established in the West. Understand me: voluntary, fully conscious self-sacrifice, free of any outside constraint, of one's entire self for the benefit of all is, in my opinion, a mark of the highest development of individuality, of its highest power, its highest self-mastery, the highest freedom of one's own will. Voluntarily to lay down one's life for all, to go upon the cross, onto the stake for all, is possible only in the most developed stage of personality. . . . In what would brotherhood consist, if we were to transpose it into rational, conscious language? In that each distinct personality itself, without constraint, without any advantage for itself, would say to society: "We are only strong all together; take all of me. . . . I will annihilate myself, I will merge with complete indifference, if only this brotherhood of yours may thrive and endure. . . ." And the brotherhood, to the contrary, should say: "You are giving us too much. . . . Take everything from us also. With all our forces we will strive unfailingly to assure you as much personal freedom as possible, as much self-revelation as possible. . . . We are brothers, we are all your brothers, and there are many of us and we are strong; so be fully calm and bold, fear nothing and rely on us."

And Dostoevsky believed that there was in the nature of the Russian man a need for brotherhood, that instead of European "anthills" — capitalistic and socialistic — our native land would first produce a fraternal communality. This is his prophecy about Russia.

The *Winter Notes on Summer Impressions* introduce us to the realm of Dostoevsky's philosophical constructions; they are opened by the *Notes from Underground* and culminated in the *Legend of the Grand Inquisitor,* the loftiest creations of Russian thought and Russian art.

In the year 1863 the Polish uprising broke out. A burst of patriotism mounted through society; revolutionary activity weakened. The government displayed a marked turn toward reaction. In the April issue of *Time* Strakhov ran an article *The Fatal Question,* in which he argued that to contend against the Poles by means of exterior force was not enough, that victory over them had to be justified morally. The article was abstract, vague, but thoroughly patriotic. Nonetheless it was taken as revolutionary and *Time* was closed.

In the spring Mariya Dmitriyevna's sickness grew sharply worse; she could no longer endure the Petersburg climate and Dostoevsky took her away to Vladimir. Having returned to Petersburg, he suffered "a serious and fairly prolonged illness" (a letter to Turgenev in June 1863).

Katkov and Iv. Aksakov busied themselves in an effort to restore *Time.* The writer begged Turgenev to wait a little with the publication of his tale *Phantoms,* which had been promised to the suppressed journal, and added: "We have *some* hope that our journal has only been suspended temporarily."

In the summer he went abroad for the second time. There he lived through a profound personal drama, his liaison with Suslova.

After the works of L. Grossman and Dolinin and the publication of Suslova's *Diary,* the figure of this "fatal woman" is comparatively well known to us. Apollinariya Prokofyevna Suslova, the daughter of one of Count Sheremetev's former serfs, was a typical woman of the sixties. She read Herzen, Proudhon, was interested in social questions, and advocated the emancipation of women. She wrote tendentious short stories (*Nowhere, Until the Wedding, By One's Own Road*) and was published in *Time.* In the autumn of 1861 she sent Dostoevsky, a "naive, poetic letter." The writer fell passionately in love with this twenty-year-old contributor. Suslova became his mistress, but from the very first days was troubled by this affair. In August 1863 she left for Paris, and from there wrote him a cruel letter: "I could have written you that I used to blush at our former relations, but there should be nothing new for you in that, for I never concealed it and how many times wanted to put an end to things before my departure abroad." She was expecting an exalted love, but encountered passion. In another letter there is the malicious irony: "You behaved like a serious, industrious man who also does not forget to enjoy himself on the ground that a certain great doctor or philosopher has maintained that it is necessary for one's health to get drunk once a month." Perhaps Dostoevsky was, in fact, guilty in respect to this young "intellectual"; consumed by passion and sensuality he abused her as a person. Her love turned into hate and she took revenge upon him with subtle cruelty. We have already said that the writer's first love — for Mariya Dmitriyevna Isayeva — seems like a story transposed into life from the pages of one of Dostoevsky's novels. That which has come to be called "Dostoevskianism" — was as a whole contained in the destiny of his future wife. In his intimacy with Suslova reality again anticipated fiction. The lovers' trip abroad reminds one of a dramatic situation extracted from *The Gambler* or *The Idiot.*

Suslova set out alone; Dostoevsky, detained by the closing of *Time,* arranged a rendezvous with her in Paris. On the way to France he stopped for four days in Wiesbaden and played roulette. This was the beginning of the writer's long and tragic passion for the game of chance. The two passions — for Suslova and for roulette — were interwoven indissolubly and mysteriously. His brother Mikhail wrote him in September 1863: "I don't understand how it's possible to gamble while traveling with a woman whom you love." Dostoevsky did understand this: love and gambling were a dual defiance of fate, a giddiness "on the brink of the abyss." He attempted to recount this afterwards in the novel *The Gambler*.

In Wiesbaden he began by winning 10,400 francs. "I then came home," he wrote his wife's sister, "and shut them up in a bag and intended to leave Wiesbaden the next day, without returning again to the tables; but I got carried away and dropped half my winnings." Part of the money he kept for himself; part he sent to his wife and brother. The madness of the game had already seized him: "I really do know the *secret*; it's terribly silly and simple and consists in restraining oneself at every moment, no matter what the phases of the game, and not becoming heated. This is the whole thing, and *to lose with this is simply impossible*."

Meanwhile, in Paris Suslova was living with a Spaniard, a medical student named Salvador, who had a "proud and self-confidently bold face and down on his lip." He soon abandoned her, she pursued, wanted to shoot him. At that point (August 26) Dostoevsky arrived. A dramatic explanation took place between them; Suslova first recorded this scene in her diary, and afterwards reworked it into a short story *The Stranger and Her Own*. The situation of the writer's courtship was repeated, his journey to Kuznetsk, where Mariya Dmitriyevna announced to him that she loved Vergunov. The rejected lover consoled, persuaded, assumed the role of friend and brother. The plot of *The Humiliated and Wronged* (Ivan Petrovich–Natasha–Alyosha) again was embodied in reality. From Paris they went away together to Baden-Baden. Suslova notes in her *Diary:* "The trip with Fyodor Mikhailovich has been quite amusing. While obtaining visas for our passports, he had a row in the Papal embassy. All along the way he kept speaking in verse. Finally, here where we had difficulty finding two rooms with two beds, he signed the register '*officier*' at which we laughed a great deal. He is constantly playing roulette and generally is very carefree."

One can judge the inner torture which the writer endured through his "fraternal" relations with Suslova, by the agonizing nocturnal scene recorded in her diary. The action of this "chapter out of one of Dostoevsky's novels" took place in Baden-Baden.

At about 10 o'clock we drank tea; upon finishing it, since I was tired that day, I lay down and asked F. M. to sit down closer to me. I felt good; I took his hand and held it for a long time in my own. He said that he was happy sitting like that. Suddenly he unexpectedly got up, was about to leave, but stumbled over my shoes, which were lying beside the bed, and in the very same manner quickly turned round and sat down. "Where did you want to go?" I asked. "I wanted to close the window." "Well close it, if you like." "No, it's not necessary. You don't know what happened to me just now," he said with a strange expression. "What?" I looked at his face; it was very agitated. "I just wanted to kiss your foot." "Ah, whatever for," I said in great confusion, almost in terror, and tucked in my feet. "The desire just came upon me and I decided to kiss it." Then he asked me if I wanted to sleep, but I said no, that I felt like sitting a little longer with him. Thinking of going to sleep and undressing, I asked him if the maid would come to take away the tea? He declared she would not. Then he looked at me in such a way that I felt uncomfortable; I told him so. "And I feel uncomfortable," he said with a strange smile. I hid my face in the pillow. Then I again asked whether the maid would come and again he declared that she would not. "Well, then go to your room. I want to sleep," I said. "In a minute," he said, but remained for some time. Then he kissed me very passionately and finally began to light a candle for himself. My candle was going out. "You won't have a light," he said. "No, I will; there's a whole candle." "But that's mine." "I still have another." "You always find answers," he said with a smile, and went out. He did not close his door and soon came in again on the pretext of shutting my window. He walked up to me and advised me to undress. "I'll get undressed," I said, pretending only to be waiting for him to leave. He once again left and once more came back under some pretext, after which he really went away and closed his door.

Suslova was not affecting naiveté; she reveled in the struggle and the danger. She engaged in the amorous duel calculatingly and with cunning. The lovers were worthy enemies of one another.

In Baden-Baden Dostoevsky lost his last penny. He confessed to his brother that he believed in his system, wanted to win a lot of money "for himself, for him, for his wife, for writing a novel." In the first quarter of an hour he won 600 francs. "This goaded me on. Suddenly I began to lose and could no longer restrain myself and lost every last penny." In the hotel he and Suslova trembled every moment lest they be presented with the bill, "and they had not a kopeck — scandal, the police . . . unpleasantness! His watch was in pawn in Geneva." "Regarding the details of my journey in general," he continued, "I'll tell you by word of mouth. Many different incidents, but terribly boring, in spite of A. P. [Apollinariya Prokofyevna]."

In Baden-Baden Dostoevsky met Turgenev. Outwardly, relations between the two writers were friendly, but in a letter to his brother he betrays in a word his deeply hidden animosity.

> In Baden-Baden I saw Turgenev. I visited him twice and he also visited me. Turgenev did not see A. P. I hid her. He is melancholic, although already improved with the help of Baden. Is living with his daughter. He told me all about his moral torments and doubts, philosophical doubts, which have passed over into life. *He's a bit of a fop.* I didn't conceal from him the fact that I was gambling. He gave me *Phantoms* to read, but I didn't read it because of the roulette, and so returned it unread.

One might conjecture that Dostoevsky, having lost everything, borrowed a small sum of money from Turgenev and for many years could not repay the debt. For this humiliation he never forgave the "Baden bourgeois" (as Turgenev used to call himself). If this supposition is correct, then the two writers' meeting in Baden in September 1863 can be considered the beginning of open hostility between them. Mikhail Mikhailovich answered his brother with a despairing letter:

> What a pity that you didn't take Turgenev's *Phantoms.* You've made such a mistake, I cannot even tell you. . . . Do you know what Turgenev means for us *at this point?* In any event, I must have a journal, otherwise I'll be ruined. I have debts, and will rot in debtors' prison. And my family? If it is possible, stop off at Baden on the way back and get the tale from him. Whatever our journal might be called, to begin with a tale of Turgenev's — why this is success.

Dostoevsky was frightened and from Turin (October 18, 1863) wrote Turgenev a forcibly amiable letter: "I write you candidly: your tale *Phantoms,* and specifically its appearance in the November issue, means a colossal amount to us. I already resolved in Petersburg to come to Baden (but not for the reason for which I came), but in order to see one another and to talk with you. And you know that: there was much I had to say to you and to hear from you. Yet somehow this did not materialize for us. And in addition there arose this damned 'revolt of the passions' [i.e., roulette]."

From Baden the strange voyagers traveled through Turin to Rome. Again there was a complete lack of funds. The writer implored Strakhov to borrow 300 rubles from Boborykin, the editor of *Library for Reading*, as an advance on a future short story; if the latter refused, to appeal to Nekrasov. At the end of the letter he wrote that he had been diligently studying the Slavophiles and adduced an extraordinarily. pertinent evaluation of them: "The Slavophiles, it is clear, have said a *new word.* . . . But there is a certain striking *aristocratic satiety* in their resolution of social questions."

Dostoevsky's trip with Suslova lasted two months. At the end of October they separated; he returned to Russia, she remained abroad. The affair was ended; there still remained the epilogue — a painful meeting in Wiesbaden in 1865. But Dostoevsky did not stop loving his tormentor. After many years her every letter threw him into deep agitation — his second wife Anna Grigoryevna bears witness to this. In 1865, in a letter to Suslova's sister, Nadezhda Prokofyevna, the writer speaks openly of his "fatal love."

Apollinariya is a great egoist. Her egoism and self-love are colossal. She demands everything from people, all perfections, does not excuse a single imperfection in consideration of other good qualities, but she absolves herself from the very least obligations toward people. She upbraids me to this day with being unworthy of her love, complains and reproaches me continually, whereas it was she who greeted me in Paris in '63 with the phrase: "You've come a little too late," i.e., that she had fallen in love with someone else, while two weeks before she had still been writing passionately that she loved me. . . . I love her still, love her very much, but I now might wish that I did not love her. She *is not worthy* of such love. . . . She has always treated me with off-handed contempt. . . . She does not admit equality in our relationship. Why, she knows that I still love her. *Then why does she torment me?*

The answer to this pitiable question is Suslova's diary. She avenged herself upon Dostoevsky for some terrible affront — real or imaginary. "They talk to me about Fyodor Mikhailovich — I simply *hate* him. . . .

When I recall what I was two years ago, I start to *hate* D. He was the first to kill my faith. . . . Now I feel and see clearly that I cannot love, cannot find happiness in the delight of love, because a man's caresses will remind me of *abuse and suffering*." We are unable to penetrate the ultimate mystery of this love-hate of Dostoevsky and Suslova.

In the year 1880, a year before the writer's death, Suslova, at forty years of age, married the twenty-four-year-old journalist V. V. Rozanov; six years later she left him, having fallen in love with a young Jew, Goldovsky. Rozanov implored her to come back; she answered: "Thousands of husbands find themselves in your position and do not howl — men are not dogs." For twenty years, out of malicious obstinacy, she refused to grant him a divorce.

To Rozanov we owe the picturesque portrait of "Suslikha" — the "infernal woman."[5]

I met Suslikha for the first time at the home of my pupil A. M. Shcheglova. . . . All in black, without collars and cuffs (mourning for her brother), with traces of a former (remarkable) beauty, she was a "Russian legitimist." With the glance of an experienced coquette she understood that she had 'struck" me; she talked coldly, tranquilly. And in a word, a thorough . . . "Catherine de Medici." In fact she resembled Catherine de Medici. With indifference she might have committed a crime, might have killed too, indifferently; might have shot into the Huguenots out of a window on St. Bartholemy's Night, directly with vehemence. Generally speaking, Suslikha really was splendid; I know that people were completely conquered, captivated by her. I have not seen another such Russian woman. She was *by the style of her soul* completely Russian, but if a Russian, then an Old Believer of the "sea-shore assent," or still better — a "Flagellant's Mother of God."

[5] *Suslikha* is a female Siberian marmot.

X I I

The Journal *Epoch*
Notes from Underground

In Russia Dostoevsky found his wife dying. He brought her from Vladimir to Moscow and did not leave her until her very death. The sick woman's condition was terrible. "Mariya Dmitriyevna," he informed his wife's sister, "has death constantly on her mind; she is melancholy and beginning to despair. Such moments are very difficult for her. Her nerves are extremely frayed. Her chest is bad and she has withered away like a matchstick. Horror! It's painful and dreadful to see."

The next year, 1864, proved tragic in Dostoevsky's life. The business of reestablishing the journal moved on slowly. Mikhail Mikhailovich devised new names: *Truth, Affair;* the censorship rejected them. Finally, after great delay, permission was granted to publish *Epoch.* The subscription was not opened in time; announcement of the new journal appeared in the *St. Petersburg Gazette* only on January 31, 1864. The January issue came out in March; its exterior appearance threw the writer into despair: an ugly cover, cheap paper, poor type, a mass of misprints. The editor had no money; the printing office was working on credit; the contributors had not been paid. When a year later *Epoch* discontinued its unfortunate existence, it turned out that the brothers had wasted on it all of the inheritance they received upon the death of Uncle Kumanin (about 20,000 rubles) and there remained debts of 15,000. For the first issue Turgenev sent his *Phantoms.* Dostoevsky extolled this work to its author. "In my opinion," he wrote, "there is an excess of reality in *Phantoms.* This reality is the anguish of a developed and conscious being, living in our time, a well-discerned anguish. All of *Phantoms* is filled with this anguish. This is a 'chord which sounds in the mist.'" But he informed his brother of his sincere judgment: "In my opinion, it [*Phantoms*] contains a lot of trash:

something nasty, morbid, senile, disbelieving out of impotence, in a word, all of Turgenev with his convictions." The amiable letters and compliments were pretense. The "knight of mournful figure" had not forgiven his affronter. With the years his hatred of the European Turgenev's "nasty" disbelief continually grew.

The writer took a fervid part in the destiny of *Epoch*; he advised his brother to establish a critical section in the journal under the title *Literary Chronicle*, promised him a "magnificent" article on the theoreticism and fantasticism of *The Contemporary*'s theoreticians and another about Kostomarov, set about writing a review of Chernyshevsky's *What's to be Done?*, Pisemsky's *The Troubled Sea* — and wrote nothing. On February 9 he confessed: "I won't hide from you that my writing has been going poorly. . . ." In lieu of a critical essay on Chernyshevsky, he proposed the tale *Notes from Underground* — his artistic answer to the novel *What's to be Done?* The writer worked on this "strange" composition in torment and despair, sitting at his dying wife's bedside. "Suddenly I became displeased with the tale. . . . The whole story is rubbish, and it is not ready yet." Mikhail Mikhailovich urged him on; *Epoch*'s affairs were progressing badly. Dostoevsky forced himself to undertake it anew: "Sat down to work, to the tale. I am trying to get it off my shoulders as soon as possible. . . . In its tone, it is too strange, and *the tone is bitter and savage*, could offend; consequently, it's necessary that poetry soften and support everything."

The first part of *Notes from Underground* was published in the January–February issue of *Epoch* for 1864. The second part was written with even greater difficulty: "My sundry afflictions are now so oppressive," he complains to his brother,

that I don't even want to mention them. My wife is dying, *literally*. Each day there is a moment when we expect her death. Her sufferings are terrible and are reflected on me because. . . . Then writing is not a mechanical work and nonetheless I am writing and writing. . . . Sometimes I fancy that it will be rubbish, but still I write with passion; I don't know what will emerge. . . . Here is something more: I'm afraid that my wife's death will be soon, and then *necessarily* there'll be an interruption in my work. If it were not for this interruption, then, of course, I would finish.

All the horror of the "underground," which encompasses us during a reading of the tale *Apropos of the Wet Snow*, is already contained in the writer's fears; there would *necessarily* be an interruption in the work for he would have to bury his wife. On April 9 he entreated his brother not to demand an installment from him for the March issue: "I repeat, Misha, I'm so worn out, so pressed by circumstances, I am now in such a tormenting situation, that I can't answer, in time of work, even for my physical powers. . . . I don't know what will come out, perhaps trash, but then I personally am relying on it [the tale] strongly. It'll be a forceful and candid thing; it will be the truth. Though it even be bad, well let it, but it will produce an effect, I know. And perhaps, it will be very good!" Several days later he announced that there would be three chapters in the second part. "The second chapter is in chaos, the third is still not begun, but I am putting the final touch to the first. . . . You understand what a *transition* is in music? It's just the same thing here. In the first chapter, seemingly, there is gibberish; then suddenly this chatter in the last two discourses is resolved by an unexpected catastrophe." In the printed edition this original composition was not preserved; the tale *Apropos of the Wet Snow* is divided not into three big, but into ten little chapters. It was published in the April number of *Epoch*. Thus, in haste, misfortune, and despair one of Dostoevsky's most brilliant works was created.

———

Notes from Underground is a "strange" work. Everything in it is striking: the structure, style, the subject. The first part consists of the underground man's confession in which the most profound problems of philosophy are examined. As for strength and daring of thought, Dostoevsky yields neither to Nietzsche nor Kierkegaard. He is near to them in spirit, he is "of their kin." The second part is the tale *Apropos of the Wet Snow*. The underground man, having explained his *credo*, relates his memoirs. The tie between the philosophical considerations and the shameful "anecdotes" from the hero's life seems utterly artificial. Only in the end is their organic unity disclosed.

In the works of the period prior to his exile, "idealistic dreaming" was the writer's central theme; he devoted many inspired pages to the dreamer's psychology, the aesthetic value of fantasy, and a moral condemnation of that illusory life which is "horror and tragedy." The underground is the natural culmination of "dreaming." The dreamer-romantic of the forties has in the sixties been transformed into a cynic-"paradoxalist." For forty years he has remained seated in his corner, like a mouse in the underground, and now he gets the desire to recount what he has experienced and thought in his angry solitude. The underground man's social and historical condition is defined by the same marks which earlier characterized the dreamer's state. This is "one of the representatives of a generation still living," i.e., an intellectual of the "Petersburg period of Russian history," poisoned by European culture, divorced from the soil and the people; an historical type who "not only can, but also must exist in our society." He is the product of a milieu, a bookish education, and an "abstract" civilization; not a living man, but a *stillborn universal man.* The author imputes to him the crime which earlier he had imputed to the dreamer: a betrayal of *living life.* ". . . We all have lost the habit of *life.* . . . We have lost the habit even to such an extent that at times we feel a certain loathing toward actual *living life.* . . . Why, we have come nearly to looking upon actual living life as a toil, almost as an obligation. . . . Why, we do not even know where *that which has life, is living* now, and what such a thing is, what name it bears." To the stillborn, who "for a long time have been born not of living fathers," to the homunculi out of test tubes, there is always opposed that same foggy-mystical ideal of "living life." Its content is not revealed: why, "we do not even know where that which has life is living." The significance of this mystery is lost. And so, the underground man is defined as an historical type and ascribed to the past: "one of the characters of recent times." But the historical mask is easily removed; the hero is not only in the past, but also in the present, not only "I" but also "we." The author steadily emerges beyond the confines of the personality of the Russian intellectual and limitlessly broadens his framework. The underground man proves to be a "man of the 19th century" — "a decent man who can talk only about himself," "a conscious individual" in general. He ventures to expound his own thoughts in the name of "every intelligent man," and, finally, *simply of man.*

Consequently, the underground man's paradoxes are not the whims of some half-mad eccentric, but a new revelation *of man about man.* The consciousness of the angry mouse, crushed in the underground, proves to be *human consciousness in general.*

We are hitting upon the enigma of consciousness. A man becomes a man if he possesses consciousness. Without consciousness man is an animal. But consciousness arises only out of conflict with reality, from a breach with the world. Consciousness must pass through isolation and solitude; it is *pain*. On the other hand — solitary consciousness does not exist; it is always joined with all mankind, it is *organically collective*. In this tormenting contradiction is the tragedy of personality. The "acutely developed personality" thrusts itself back from the world, desperately upholds its self-legitimacy and at the same time is attracted to people, understands its dependence upon them. All the relations between personality and the world, in Dostoevsky, are permeated by a fatal dichotomy. His heroes always love while hating, and hate while loving; his romantics are cynical, while his cynics are full of exultation. The author suggests the idea of duality to the reader in the stylistic devices of the first part of the *Notes*. This is not logical argumentation, addressed toward reason, but a direct hypnotic suggestion by voice and intonations. We perceive almost physiologically the underground man's division through the unsightliness of his style, the disharmony of syntax, the irritating brokenness of his speech. All Dostoevsky's heroes are characterized by their language, but the verbal portrait of the man from underground is the most expressive.[A]

Most of all, one is astounded by the contrast between the confession's exterior and inner form. This is a monologue in which each sentence constitutes a dialogue. The hero asserts that he is writing exclusively for himself, that he does not need any readers, yet meanwhile his every word is directed toward another, is calculated upon an impression. He despises this other, ridicules him, abuses him, but at the same time curries his favor, exculpates himself, argues and persuades. Cries of complete independence of another's opinion alternate with the most piteous efforts to win the enemy's regard.

The "underground" begins with the words: "I am a sick man. . . . I am a spiteful man. I'm an unattractive man. I think my liver is diseased." After the very first sentence: "I am a sick man," there are a series of dots and a glancing round at the reader. As it were, the narrator has already observed a compassionate smile and taken offense. The reader will still think that he requires his pity. Wherefore, there is the impudent: "I am a spiteful man. I'm an unattractive man." Then he continues willfully: "I'm not being treated and have never been treated, although I respect medicine and doctors." And again there is a look around: does he not now appear naive to the reader? In order to correct the impression, there follows the elegant pleasantry: "Besides, I'm still extremely superstitious, well, if only so far

[A] M. M. Bakhtin, *Problemy tvorchestva Dostoevskogo* (Problems of Dostoevsky's Creative Work), Leningrad 1929.

as to respect medicine." And again the apprehension: what if he seems reactionary to the enlightened reader? This leads to a new unsuccessful pleasantry in parentheses: "(I'm well educated enough not to be superstitious, but I am superstitious.)" But the reader can ask, then why he is not being treated? His answer must be shocking: "No, sir, I don't want to be cured out of malice." The reader shrugs his shoulders in confusion. This assumed reaction already provokes the narrator and he responds insolently: "Here you, to be sure, do not deign to understand this. Well, sir, but I understand it." And, running ahead, he anticipates the objection: "I, *of course*, won't be able to explain to you whom precisely I will irk in this case by my malice; I know *perfectly well* that I won't in any way 'sully' the doctors by the fact that I'm not consulting them; I *know better than everyone* that by all this I'll injure only myself and no one else." You were thinking to catch me, and here I caught you. I, it turns out, knew all your arguments better than you. But all the same. I am not being treated, so it is "from malice." You are surprised. Well, be surprised. That's just what I wanted. What's to be done; I'm already such a paradoxalist.

And so it is in each sentence. The polemics with an imaginary enemy, one cunning and venomous, are conducted in a strained, passionate tone. There are constant reservations, self-justifications, and refutations of another, presumed opinion. "Doesn't it seem to you, gentlemen, that now I am repenting before you?" Or: "Doubtlessly, you are thinking, gentlemen, that I want to make you laugh?" All these glances about ought to attest to a thorough indifference toward the reader, but they prove, to the contrary, a servile dependence upon him. Here is the source of all the narrator's growing irritability and rage. . . . In order to free himself from the power of another's consciousness, he attempts to besmut and distort his own reflection in this mirror; he tells dreadful things about himself, exaggerates his "unseemliness," cynically ridicules everything "noble and beautiful" in him. This is the self-defense of despair. The image, which will be impressed on another's consciousness, will be a mask unlike him. He is hidden beneath it, he is free, he has escaped from witnesses and again disappeared underground. Lastly, even after the most resolute affirmations there always remains a loophole: to deny one's words or completely to alter their meaning. "I swear to you, gentlemen, that I do not believe a single, not one single little word of what I have now scribbled down! *That is, I also believe it*, if you like, but at the same time, for some unknown reason, I feel and suspect that I'm lying like a shoemaker."

Such is the unending circle through which the sick consciousness is revolved. Indifference toward the hostile world and a shameful dependence upon it — this is a mouse's scurrying about, a *perpetuum mobile*.

The underground man is not only split in two, but is also without character; he has not been able to become anything; "not evil, nor good, nor an infamous scoundrel, nor honorable, nor a hero, nor an insect!" And this is because "the man of the 19th century must and is morally obliged to be a creature preferably without character; and the man with character, the doer, a creature preferably narrow minded." Consciousness is a sickness, leading to inertia, i.e., to a "conscious sitting-with-arms-folded." Thus Dostoevsky poses the problem of contemporary *Hamletism*. Consciousness kills feeling, corrupts the will, paralyzes action. "I exercise myself in thinking, and consequently with me every primary cause immediately draws after it another still more primary, and so on, into infinity." The causal chain extends to an ugly infinity, and in this perspective, every truth is not absolute, every good is relative. For the new Hamlet there remains one occupation: "intentional pouring water through a sieve." From consciousness comes inertia, from inertia there is boredom. Not acting, not living, man out of boredom begins to "compose life": insults, events, romances. The underground existence becomes fantasy; this is a game in front of a mirror. The man suffers, rejoices, is angry and, as it were, with complete sincerity. But each sensation is reflected in the mirror of consciousness; in the actor there sits a spectator who appraises his art. The underground man turns a prostitute's soul with noble speeches; he talks ardently, sincerely, goes as far as a "throat-spasm," and at the same time not for a minute does he forget that all this is a game. He gives Liza his address, but is terribly afraid that she will come. The voice of the on-looker says in him: "And again, again to put on this dishonorable, lying mask." The voice of the actor objects: "Why dishonorable? What dishonorable? I was speaking sincerely yesterday. I remember, there was then genuine feeling in me. . . ." But such is the nature of self-consciousness: to break everything down into "yes" and "no"; what "directness and sincerity" can there be in a game before a mirror?

Consciousness opposes itself to the world. It is alone, against it is everything. As a result it feels itself brought to bay, persecuted; hence the morbid sensitivity of the underground man, his self-love, vanity, suspicions. Like a harassed mouse, he hides in his hole and from distasteful reality escapes into fancy. The breach in his personality yet increases. On the one hand, there is vicious, petty debauchery; on the other, lofty dreams. "It is amazing that these influxes of 'everything beautiful and noble' used to come in me during periods of dissipation, and just when I found myself at the very bottom, used to come so, in separate little spurts, as it were, reminding me of themselves, but not putting an end, however, to the debauchery by their appearance. They rather, as it were, seemed to enliven it by contrast." Duality is experienced as a contradiction and suffering, becomes the matter of "tormenting inner analysis," but out of suffering there suddenly grows a "decisive pleasure."

Here is this remarkable passage: "I came to the point of feeling a sort of secret, abnormal, mean enjoyment in returning home to my corner on some most foul Petersburg night and being acutely aware that now even today I had again committed a repulsive deed, that that which has been done, can never again be reversed, and inwardly, secretly, gnawing, gnawing myself for this with my teeth, plaguing and consuming myself to the point that the bitterness would be turned, at last, into a kind of shameful, accursed sweetness, and, finally, into a decisive, serious pleasure! Yes, into pleasure, into pleasure! I insist on that." This paradoxical assertion is one of Dostoevsky's real psychological disclosures. In consciousness there occurs *a substitution of the aesthetic plane for the ethical plane*. Degradation is a torture, but a "too clear awareness" of degradation can afford pleasure. Looking into a mirror, it is possible to forget about *what* is reflected and to lose oneself in *how* it is reflected. The aesthetic experiencing of a sensation makes its embodiment in life superfluous. To dream about a feat is easier than accomplishing it. The underground man's need for love is completely satisfied by "ready established forms, stolen from poets and novelists." "There was so much of it, of this love, that afterward the need to apply it in reality was not even felt; that would have been a superfluous luxury."

His investigation of consciousness brings the author to a conclusion regarding its perversity. "I swear to you, gentlemen, that to be overly conscious — this is a sickness, a real, out-and-out sickness." And nevertheless it is better to be "an acutely conscious mouse" than a "so-called direct man and agent." It is better to be an abnormal man than a normal animal. The source of consciousness is suffering, but man will not renounce suffering just as he will not renounce his *humanity.* Thus in the *Notes the sick consciousness is revealed to us as a human tragedy.*

After the analysis of consciousness there follows a "critique of pure reason." The ill-disposed readers, with whom the underground man is polemizing, begin to acquire concrete features. They are the positivists from *The Contemporary* and the *Russian Word.* These are the utilitarians and the rationalists like Chernyshevsky. Dostoevsky is defending man from the inhuman philosophy of necessity. With a boldness not inferior to that of Nietzsche and Kierkegaard, he rises up against the "stone wall" of impossibility. Reason sees the greatest wisdom in bowing down to necessity; can one really argue with the laws of nature, the conclusions of the natural sciences and the axioms of mathematics? Hegel's "world reason" very placidly crushes individual persons under the wheels of its triumphal chariot; the poisoning of Socrates and Galileo's burning do not affect it in the least. To reason's declaration: "it is impossible," the underground man answers defyingly: "I don't want to" and "I don't like it." "Lord God," he cries, "and what do I care for the laws of nature and arithmetic, when for some reason these laws and twice two is four displease me? Of course, I will not break through such a wall with my forehead if I really have not the strength to knock it down, but I am also not going to be reconciled to it simply because it is a stone wall, and I don't have enough strength."

This recalls the lamentations of Job contesting with God. The thrusts against the laws of reason are clothed in a blindingly paradoxical form. The underground man does not deliberate, but mocks and "sticks out his tongue." "Twice two is four, after all, is a truly insufferable thing," he declares. "Twice two is four, why this, in my opinion, is simply an effrontery, sir. Twice two is four looks like a fop, stands across your road, arms akimbo, and spits. I am agreed that twice two is four is an excellent thing; but if we are to give everything its due, then twice two is five is also sometimes a very charming little thing."

The formula twice two is four is the victory of necessity and death. To believe in the ultimate future triumph of reason means to bury man in advance. When a list of all "reasonable" courses of action will be composed and all "reasonable" desires are calculated beforehand, then man will no longer have free will. The will will merge with intellect, and man will be converted into an organ stop or a piano key. Fortunately, this dream of the rationalists is not destined to be fulfilled, for intellect is not everything in a man, but only a part, whereas the will is the "manifestation of his entire life." The narrator most emphatically asserts that man is an *irrational* being whose chief aim is to preserve his humanity, i.e., free will.

The "critique of pure reason" turns into a polemic with utilitarianism. Blows are directed against Chernyshevsky and his novel *What's to be Done?*[B] The underground man is brought to frenzy by the positivists' base teaching about man. In the novel *What's to be Done?* he resented Lopukhov's idle spoutings that *advantage* is the solitary cause of human actions. "Now you engage in nasty affairs," says Lopukhov, "because your circumstances require it, but give you another milieu, and you would gladly become harmless, even useful, because you do not want to do evil *for no gain*, and *if it's advantageous to you*, then you can do what is pleasing — even act honorably and nobly, if it's so necessary. . . . Then the evil will see that they cannot be evil, and the evil will become good. Why, they have been evil only because it was to their detriment to be good." This degrading teaching concerning a prime mover of mankind — egoism, the crude bookkeeping of advantages and calculations, the infantile optimism in the comprehension of evil — excites an overflow of bile in the underground man.

"Oh, tell me," he cries,

who was it first declared, who first proclaimed, that man only does *vile things* because he does not know his own real interests, and that if he were to be enlightened, to have his eyes opened to his real, normal interests, then man would at once cease doing vile things, would at once become good and noble, precisely because he would see his own personal advantage in good; and we all know that no man can act deliberately against his personal advantage; consequently, so to say, through necessity he would begin doing good? Oh, the babe! Oh, the pure, innocent child!

The underground man understands that this seemingly innocent optimistic theory is deadly for man. A creature entirely determined by "rationally understood advantage" — is no longer a man, but an automaton, a machine, a "stop." And with fiery indignation and vehement pathos, he throws himself upon the calumniators. The humanity in man is *his free will*. The underground man comes forward to the defense of the "most advantageous advantage" for man—his unrestricted

---

[B] V. Komarovich, "Mirovaya garmoniya" *Dostoevskogo* (Dostoevsky's "World Harmony"). *Ateney*, 1-2, 1924.

and free volition. He suggests taking a look at world history. The spectacle is majestic, varied, uniform, but in any case not reasonable. Wise men have always taught man to live morally, while he has continued "out of sheer ingratitude" to do vicious things and to mix "his own pernicious, fantastic element" into everything. "It is just his fantastic dreams, his most vulgar stupidity that he will wish to retain, simply in order to affirm to his own self that men are still men, and not piano keys." Even if it be proved to him mathematically that he is a key, even then he will not be brought to reason, "will contrive destruction and chaos, will contrive sufferings of all sorts and will still insist on his own point! He will let go a curse through the world . . . and, perhaps, by his curse alone, he'll attain his end, i.e., really to convince himself that he is a man and not a piano key!" And if the chaos and curse be calculated beforehand—"man, in that event, will intentionally go mad so as to be rid of intellect and gain his point!"

Man can come to desire what is not advantageous in order *to have the right* to desire; this is the most advantageous because "it preserves for us that which is most important and most precious, i.e., our personality and our individuality."

This inspired defense of personality is summarized in a paradoxically incisive affirmation: "One's own unrestricted and free volition, one's own caprice, however wild it may be, one's own fancy, provoked at times although even to the point of madness — here this all is the *most advantageous advantage.*"

The author does not stop before the astonishing conclusion: "Man is in need of a purely independent desire, *whatever this independence may cost and to whatever it may lead.*"

The whole meaning of human existence, the whole meaning of human history lies in the self-assertion of the *irrational will* ("wild caprice, mad fancy"). The world process does not have any goal; progress does not exist; mankind is by no means striving after prosperity and order. It loves to construct and be happy, but perhaps it enjoys destruction and suffering not a bit less. Man is eternally condemned to go somewhere, but he has no desire at all to arrive there; he suspects that the end, once attained, is something in the nature of a mathematical formula, i.e., death. Consequently, he upholds his independence, *"to whatever it may lead,"* opens a road *"to wherever it may be."* The underground man ends his investigations of the will with the taunt: "In a word, man is structured comically; there is obviously a joke contained in all this." The paradoxalist scoffs at the *tragedy of the will* which has been opened before him.

Utopian socialism dreams of an earthly paradise, of universal prosperity. All these lofty idylls are begotten by its childishly naive understanding of man. At one time even Dostoevsky himself believed in all this "astronomical romantic foolishness" about the sinless *homme de la nature et de la verité*. Penal servitude cured him of his "Schillerism." Now he knows that man is an "immoral" creature, "phenomenally ungrateful," capable of contriving chaos and destruction for the sake of his most wild caprice. Chernyshevsky projected the founding of an ideal society on the basis of the rational agreement of wills, acting out of utilitarianism. The underground man again exclaims: "Oh, the babe! Oh, the pure, innocent child!" In what test tube did you manufacture these rational and utilitarian homunculi? In what chicken coop did you take some domestic animal for a man? One can imagine the transport of malice with which the paradoxalist read the poetic dream of the virtuous Vera Pavlovna, the heroine of *What's to be Done?*

A building, a huge building, as no single one is today. It stands among fields and meadows, gardens and groves. . . . The gardens are lemon and orange trees, peaches and apricots. But this building — what is it, what is its architecture? Now not one exists like it. Cast-iron and glass, cast-iron and glass only. No, not only: this is but the building's shell, this is its exterior wall. But there inside, there's already an actual house, a most immense house. It's covered by this cast-iron-crystal building as by a sheath; it forms broad galleries around it on all the floors. . . . This is an *immense crystal house.* . . . For everyone there's eternal spring and summer, eternal joy. . . . All are singing and celebrating.

In this earthly paradise of Chernyshevsky's it is not difficult to recognize Fourier's phalanstery; it must have reminded Dostoevsky of the "crystal palace" at the London International Exposition — the ultimate ideal of human organization on earth. Here the underground man no longer restrains himself and quite unceremoniously he answers Vera Pavlovna:

You believe in a crystal building, that can never be destroyed, i.e., in such a one at which it would be impossible either to stick out one's tongue on the sly or to show a fico in one's pocket. Well, and I perhaps for just that same reason fear this building, because it is crystal and can never be destroyed, and because it would be impossible even furtively to stick out one's tongue at it. Do you see: if instead of a palace, it were a chicken coop and it were raining, I perhaps would also creep into the chicken coop so as not to get wet, but *nonetheless I would not take the chicken coop for a palace.*

After the chicken coop another striking image is given of the "socialist paradise": a *tenement house*. "I will not accept as the crown of my desires a tenement house with flats for the poor on a lease of a thousand years and, if need be, with the dental surgeon Wagenheim's signboard hanging outside."

Finally, the third image is an *anthill*: "Man, perhaps, loves only to erect a building, and not to live in it, consigning it afterwards *aux animaux domestiques*, such as: ants, sheep, and so forth, and so forth. Now ants are of a completely different taste. They have a single marvelous edifice of that same type that can never be destroyed — the anthill."

A chicken coop, a tenement house, an anthill — the three indelible stigmas Dostoevsky imposed on the "crystal palace" of socialist collectivism. If the earthly paradise is bought at the price of transforming mankind into a herd of *animaux domestiques*, then to hell with "all this good sense."

"Why, I, for example, would not in the least be surprised," continues the underground man, "if suddenly for no apparent reason, in the midst of this future universal good sense, some gentleman or other with an ignoble or, better to say, with a reactionary and jeering countenance were to rise up, were to set his arms akimbo and say to us all: 'And what, gentlemen, hadn't we better kick over all this good sense and send it flying at last into the dust solely so as to toss all these logarithms off to hell and begin again ourselves to live according to our own stupid will?'"

The underground man's confession is the philosophical preface to the cycle of the great novels. Before Dostoevsky's work is disclosed to us as a vast five-act tragedy (*Crime and Punishment, The Idiot, The Devils, A Raw Youth*, and *The Brothers Karamazov*), *Notes from Underground* introduces us to the *philosophy of tragedy*. In the bilious and "unsightly" chatter of the paradoxalist the Russian philosopher's greatest insights are expressed. Through the sharpened edge of analysis the sickness of consciousness is uncovered, its inertia and dichotomy, its inner tragedy. The struggle against reason and necessity leads to impotent "weeping and gnashing" — *to the tragedy of Nietzsche and Kierkegaard.* Investigation of the irrational blind will, being cast about in void *self-formation,* reveals the *tragedy* of personality and freedom. Finally, the critique of socialism concludes with an assertion of the *tragedy of historical process,* purposeless and bloody, and the *tragedy of world evil,* which cannot be cured by any socialistic "earthly paradise." In this sense *Notes from Underground* is the greatest *attempt at a philosophy of tragedy* in world literature. The malicious despair and intrepid cynicism of the underground man unmasks all the idols, all the "sublimating frauds," all the "noble and beautiful," all the comforting illusions and salutary fictions, everything by which man has enclosed himself from the "dark abyss." Man is on the brink of a precipice — here is the *paysage* of tragedy. The author leads us through terror and destruction, but does he bring us to mystical purification, to a catharsis? Is it possible that "sitting with arms folded" and "intentional pouring water through a sieve" are the final word in his skeptic philosophy? To consider the *Notes* as an expression of "metaphysical despair" would mean not to observe what is *most important* in their design. The force of the underground man's revolt stems not from indifference and doubt, but from a passionate, exalted faith. He contends so vehemently with falsehood because a new truth has been opened for him. He still cannot find a *word* for it and is forced to speak in hints and circumlocutions. The underground man, "this acutely conscious mouse" — is nonetheless better than the tedious *homme de la nature et de la verité*; the underground is nonetheless better than the socialist anthill. But the paradoxalist believes that the underground is not the consummation and not the end. "And so, long live the underground!" he exclaims and immediately makes a reservation: "Ah! But indeed even here I'm lying! I am lying because I myself know, as twice two, that the underground is not at all better, but *something different, totally different for which I am thirsting, but which I can in no way find.*" What words and with what genuine sorrow they are uttered! And in fact he put out his tongue at the "crystal building" and showed a fico in his pocket only because it was not a "crystal building" at all, but an ordinary chicken coop. This was the reason he grew so angry because the "crystal building" was his most sacred dream, his most passionate faith. And instead of a palace he was offered a "tenement house with flats"! "But what's to be done if I've taken it into my head that if one must live, better that it be in a *mansion*. This is my wish, this is my desire. You will eradicate it only when you change my desires. Well, change them, allure me with something else, give me another *ideal*. But meanwhile I still won't accept a chicken coop for a palace. . . . *Perhaps the thing I took offense at was that of all your buildings there hasn't yet been one at which it might even be possible not to stick out one's tongue!*"

And the underground man, the individualist and egocentric, says this, hurling a challenge at the universe: "Is the world to crumble to pieces, or here am I to be deprived of my tea? I will say that the world may crumble so long as I always drink my tea!" But how is the world to crumble, when just now he has been dreaming about the "crystal palace" — the earthly paradise! Why, he consciously slanders himself, masking his love and faith beneath cynicism. If he also hides in the underground, it is because his love is abused and his faith not justified. The underground man is a *disenchanted idealist and a humanist put to shame*. He only alludes to his new faith. But these allusions are revealed to us in the light of one of Dostoevsky's letters to his brother regarding the publication of *Underground* in *Epoch*. "I must also complain about my article," he writes.

The misprints are terrible, and it would have been better not to print the next to last chapter at all (the most important one, where the essential thought is expressed), than to print it as it is, i.e., with sentences torn out and full of self-contradictions. But what can be done now! Those swines of censors — where I mocked at everything and sometimes *blasphemed for form's sake* — that's let pass, but where from all this I deduced the *need of faith and Christ* — that is suppressed.

The "next to last chapter," the tenth — which, in the form abridged by the censor, runs only a page and a half — is deemed by the author "the most important." It was from it that we quoted the passage about the real "crystal building" at which it would be possible not to stick out one's tongue. And so, the dream of a genuine earthly paradise is the central idea of the *Notes*. The mockery and blasphemy are only "for form's sake," for the heightening of contrast, to lend as much reinforcement as possible to the negative argumentation. In answer to it there had to appear a religious affirmation: "the need of faith and Christ." One can conjecture that at the base of the structuring of an "earthly paradise" the author would have placed that profound idea of brotherhood which he had contemplated in the *Winter Notes on Summer Impressions*. The union of personality with the communal would be justified religiously: by faith in Christ.

The censor distorted the design, but, strange as it might be, the author never reestablished the original text in subsequent editions. Dostoevsky's "philosophy of tragedy" has remained without its mystical consummation.

In the perspective of such a design the *Notes'* metaphysical significance becomes apparent to us. Dostoevsky is not investigating that abstract "universal man" contrived by Jean-Jacques Rousseau, whom he derisively calls the *homme de la nature et de la verité,* but the concrete man of the 19th century in all his moral "unsightliness." He is talking not about the "normal" consciousness which exists only in the bookish theories of humanists, but about the real consciousness of the civilized European. This consciousness is split in two, distorted, sick. Translating this definition into religious terms, we will say: Dostoevsky is analyzing the *sinful consciousness of fallen man.* In this lies the unparalleled originality of his *religious philosophy.*

In opposition to the innocent *homme de la nature* of humanism there stands the sinful man from underground; there is revealed the terrible spectacle of evil in the soul of man. By means of "negative argumentation," so characteristic of the writer, the fundamental lie of humanism is refuted: that it is possible to reeducate man through reason and advantage. Dostoevsky objects: 'No, evil is not overcome by education, but by a miracle. What is impossible to man, is possible to God. Not reeducation, but *resurrection*.' Here is the reason for the "need of faith and Christ."

The second part of the *Notes,* the tale *Apropos of the Wet Snow,* is joined to the first stylistically. The underground man's confession is an inner dialogue, a polemic, a struggle against an imaginary enemy. In the tale the inner dialogue becomes external, the fight is transferred from the sphere of ideas into the plane of life, the imaginary enemies are embodied in real ones: colleagues in the service, his obnoxious servant Apollon, his former school companions, at the head of whom stands the officer Zverkov, a dull, self-centered "normal man." The paradoxalist creeps out of his underground into the light of day, encounters the hostile world and, in conflict with it, suffers a shameful defeat. This practical experience completes the "tragedy of the solitary consciousness."

In the *Humiliated and Wronged* Prince Volkovsky reveals "a secret of nature" to Ivan Petrovich: if each of us would describe all his hidden filth, then "such a stench would rise up on the earth that we all should necessarily suffocate." Here this very same idea engages the underground man. He says: "Every man has memories of things such as he would not tell to all, but only perhaps to his friends. . . . There are also other things . . . which a man is afraid to reveal even to himself and every decent man has a number of such things stored away. I.e., one could even say: *the more decent he is, the more he has of them.*" The sinner is placed in opposition to the *homme de la nature,* the confession of the underground man to Rousseau's confession. "Rousseau, for example, certainly lied about himself in his confession and even lied intentionally out of vanity." Rousseau related all his villainies, but he concluded by acknowledging himself "the best of men." The underground man wants to find out: "whether it is possible to be completely open if only with one's own self and not fear the *whole truth?*" His confession has a religious significance; this is the repentance of a sinner. He is writing it down since it will appear more solemn on paper. . . . *"There will be a greater judgment upon one's self."*

And he judges himself mercilessly. He is "a coward and a slave"; he has a monstrous intolerance and aversion toward people; in the chancery he despises and hates all his fellow clerks. He leads a dissipated life "in seclusion, at night, secretly, timorously, sordidly, with shame," and in his corner escapes into everything "beautiful and noble," imagining himself a hero and benefactor of mankind.

Having grown estranged through bitter solitude, he longs to return to "living life," to approach people. Three of his school comrades are arranging a farewell dinner for a fourth, the officer Zverkov, who is leaving for the Caucasus. He always despised them and knew that they did not like him, and nevertheless "out of malice" he imposes himself upon their company, dines with them at the Hôtel de Paris, insults Zverkov and undergoes intolerable humiliations. He is a superfluous and unwanted guest at their banquet. They all are sitting together on a divan and engaging in friendly conversation; he *alone* strides about the room, rejected and angry. "I had the patience to walk like this right in front of them from eight till eleven o'clock, in one and the same place, from the table to the stove and from the stove back toward the table. . . . No one could possibly have degraded himself more infamously and more voluntarily, and I fully, fully understood this, and all the same, continued to pace from the table to the stove and back." This piercing image of the everlasting solitude of man among men grows into a symbol of world misfortune. "The time is out of joint," man's brotherhood has disintegrated. . . . The company, somewhat tipsy, sets out for a house of pleasure. In despair the underground man also follows along. "Either they will go down on their knees, clasp my legs, and by begging, obtain my friendship, or . . . or I will give Zverkov a slap in the face." His hatred is from rejected love, from his outraged dream of brotherhood. But he knows that these lofty aspirations are "a mirage, a cheap mirage, disgusting, romantic, and fantastic," and that the affair will end not with embraces, but in a fight. "Yes, and let them beat me now. . . . Let them! Let them! That's what I came for. Their mutton heads will be forced, at last, to see the *tragic* in all this!"

The tragedy of human communality — here is the theme of the tale *Apropos of the Wet Snow*. It is developed in two aspects: upon the tragedy of friendship follows the still more profound tragedy of love.

After the night spent with the prostitute Liza, the underground man "turns her soul upside down" with his noble pathos. He represents to her the horror of her life, draws an idyllic picture of the family, of love for a husband and child. Liza is overwhelmed and torn by confusion; for a long time she weeps bitterly, hiding her face in the pillow. The hero speaks with ardor and sincerely, but all this is a "game." He knows that the underground has already killed his every capacity for living life, that all his feelings are a "mirage" and self-deception, that he is doomed to the most shameful impotence. And from the awareness his tenderness toward Liza reverts to hatred. He runs about the room and curses: "It's like that, the damned romanticism of all these *pure hearts!* Oh, the obscenity, oh, the stupidity, oh, the poverty of these wretched sentimental souls!"

Love, goodness, purity arouse a demonic enmity in the doomed sinner; for his own sin he takes vengeance upon the just. Liza comes; she has left the "bawdy house" for good; love has transformed her. She surrenders her heart trustingly and modestly to her "savior." But instead of a "savior" she meets a malicious and dirty avenger who profanes her by his diabolic lust. "She guessed that the outburst of my passion had been simply revenge, a fresh humiliation for her, and that to my recent, most causeless hatred was now added a *personal* hatred, *born of envy.* . . ." The underground man completes his hideous revenge with a final "villainous act"; he shoves money into the hand of his deathly pale victim. . . .

So ends the dreamer-romantic who for forty years has sat in the underground. The "noble and beautiful" does not elevate, but corrupts; "natural good" turns into demonic evil. It is useless to preach the justification of the humiliated and restoration of the fallen, and the disillusioned philanthrope's love reverts to frenzied hate. The story of Liza is a parody on the romantic theme of the corrupted woman's salvation through love. Nekrasov's humane verses serve as an epigraph to it:

> When out of the darkness of error,
> By an ardent word of persuasion
> I rescued your fallen soul,
> And filled with profound torment,
> Wringing your hands, you cursed
> The vice which had enveloped you. . . .

The author interrupts the quotation with a mocking "Etc., etc., etc."

The tragedy of the underground man's love is the shattering of all romantic ethics. "Natural love" is as impotent as "natural good." This is one of the fundamental ideas of Dostoevsky's world outlook. It is most pointedly expressed in the *Diary of a Writer* for 1876: "Moreover, I assert," writes the author, "that the consciousness of our own utter inability to help or to bring, if only some, benefit or relief to suffering mankind, while at the same time remaining completely convinced of this suffering, can even *transform the love of mankind in your heart into hatred for it.*"

Notes from Underground is a turning point in Dostoevsky's creative work. Fallen Adam is cursed and condemned, and it is impossible to save him through human powers. But out of the "shadow of death" there is revealed a way to God, the "need of faith and Christ." The tragic philosophy is a religious philosophy.

On April 15, 1864, Dostoevsky wrote to his brother from Moscow: "Just now, at 7 o'clock in the evening, Mariya Dmitriyevna passed away, and wished you all a long and happy life (her words). Remember her with a kind word. She suffered so much during this time, that I don't know who could refuse to be reconciled with her."

On April 16 he recorded in his notebook:

Masha is lying on the table. Will I see Masha again? To love a person as one's own self, as Christ commanded, is impossible. On earth the law of personality binds us; the *I* stands in the way. . . . Christ was able, but Christ was eternal, from all ages the ideal toward which man strives and according to the law of nature must strive. After Christ's appearance, it became clear that the highest development of personality must attain to that point where man annihilates his own "I," surrenders it completely to all and everyone without division or reserve. . . . And this is the greatest happiness. . . . This is Christ's paradise. . . . And so, on earth man strives toward an ideal contrary to his nature. When man has not fulfilled the law of striving toward the ideal, i.e., has not *by love* offered his "I" in sacrifice to people or to another being (*Masha and I*), he experiences suffering and has called this condition sin.

Self-sacrifice, as the highest development of personality, was already affirmed in *Winter Notes on Summer Impressions*. Now this law is illumined religiously as a commandment of Christ, and is founded on His personality as the "ideal of mankind." But the spiritual law is confronted by the natural law — the nature of personality. From their struggle result suffering and sin. This is not a rational inference but a vital experience, born of the seven tragic years spent with his late wife (*Masha and I*). "Man," he continues, "must uninterruptedly experience suffering, which is balanced by the paradisaical enjoyment of fulfilling the commandment, i.e., as a sacrifice." At his wife's coffin Dostoevsky remembered suffering and sin, but also the "paradisaical enjoyment of sacrifice." Before the face of death the thought of a meeting beyond the grave directed his heart to Christ.

Having buried his wife and returned to Petersburg, the writer plunged into work on *Epoch*. The polemics with the nihilists which were begun in *Notes from Underground*, became pronounced in his journalistic essays.

At the beginning of 1864 a split occurred between *The Contemporary* and *The Russian Word*. Shchedrin in *The Contemporary* ridiculed the nihilists; the *Russian Word* accused *The Contemporary* of being reactionary, and Pisarev took up arms against Shchedrin. With regard to this dispute Dostoevsky wrote a venomous article: *Mister Shchedrin or the Split in the Nihilists. An Excerpt from the Novel* "Shchedrodarov." Shchedrodarov joins *The Contemporary* as one of the coeditors and its program is read to him. In it he is instructed that for the happiness of mankind "most important of all there need be a belly, in other words a stomach," that "the anthill is the very highest ideal of social organization," etc. The refutations of utilitarian socialism, already known to us, are completed with an exposure of the nihilists as being uprooted and theorizing. "You are going against *life*. It is not we who must impose laws upon *life*, but study life, draw our own laws out of *life* itself. You are theoreticians." The idea of being rooted in the soil is indissolubly joined in the author to an understanding of "living life," which passes as a leitmotif through all his works. This is his irrefutable argument, his ultimate self-evidence. Dostoevsky the journalist found some precise and biting formulas, was able to deal unexpected and cruel blows: "You are abstracted," he says to the nihilists. "You are shadows, you are nothing. From nothing nothing will come. You are foreign ideas. You are a dream. You are standing not on the soil, but on air. *Out from under you it glimmers*."

With this magnificent aphorism the exposition ends. Mankind's happiness, founded on the belly's repletion, suggests the Grand Inquisitor's words concerning bread. His polemics against the nihilists of the sixties would later help Dostoevsky solve the mystery of the Grand Inquisitor — the Antichrist.

The Contemporary replied to the article on Shchedrin with articles of shocking vulgarity: *The Triumph of Claptrappers; To the Martins: A Message to the Head Martin, Mister Dostoevsky.* An "Outside Satirist" made fun of the falling sickness of the coeditor of *Epoch.* Dostoevsky answered with *A Necessary Declaration:* "I understand that it is possible to laugh at some sick person's illness, i.e., I don't understand it at all, but I know that an individual who has arrived at a certain development can do it out of revenge, in a fit of already violent anger. . . . The 'outside satirist' . . . also knows, perhaps, how and when I contracted the illness. . . ."

All his life the writer hated the "exposers" with whom he had fought in the sixties. Caricatures of them are met in many of his works. In *Crime and Punishment* there appears a drunken writer who threatens to "make an exposure." He is beaten and driven out. In *The Devils* a crowd of similar litterateurs visit the salon of Varvara Petrovna Stavrogina in Petersburg. She signs a protest against an "unseemly behavior," but shortly after she too is exposed of "unseemly behavior." In *The Idiot* the author turns to autobiographical material for Keller's expository rhymes. In the year 1863 *The Contemporary* ran the following epigram in the *Whistle*:

> Fedya did not pray to God,
> Swell, he thought, just so!
> Forever he did loaf and loaf,
> And fell into a scrap!
> Once carelessly did he
> With Gogol's "Greatcoat" toy,
> And with ordinary dawdling
> Crammed away the time . . . etc.

Keller composes the verses against Prince Myshkin:

> For five years Lyova did
> With Schneider's greatcoat toy,
> And with ordinary dawdling
> Crammed away the time.
> Returning in tight gaiters,
> A million took as heir;
> He prays to God in Russian,
> And stole from students poor.

Lastly, in "The Brothers Karamazov" the type of the nihilist-"exposer" finds its artistic culmination in the image of Rakitin.

Apollon Grigoryev accused Mikhail Dostoevsky of "driving the lofty talent of his brother like a relay-horse." He was profoundly wrong. Dostoevsky had the temperament and talent of a publicist; journalistic work accustomed him to observe "current reality" attentively, to divine the "tenor of the times." All his novels are charged with elements of sensational journalism: the newspaper chronicle, the *faits-divers*, comments on criminal trials, references to articles, veiled or open polemics and stylistic parodies and caricatures. Not only are Russia's spiritual life and social movements reflected in his creative work, but the most trivial "late scoop" as well. The great novelist never ceased being a professional journalist.[c]

The death of his brother followed upon that of his wife; on July 10, 1864, Mikhail Mikhailovich died. Dostoevsky resolved to continue

[c] V. S. Dorovatovskaya-Lyubimova, *Dostoevsky i shestidesyatniki* (Dostoevsky and the Generation of the Sixties). The Collection *Dostoevsky*. Moscow 1928.

Epoch, took upon himself the publishing aspect, invited A. Poretsky to be editor, asked Turgenev and Ostrovsky to remain as contributors. He worked with despairing energy, published two issues a month. But a new blow overtook him: his closest collaborator and supporter Ap. Grigoryev died. In spite of the publisher's superhuman efforts, the journal's level sharply declined, the subscription fell off, cash at hand diminished, their relations with other Petersburg journals became ever more hostile. . . . In June 1865 *Epoch* terminated its existence.

In the final, February issue of *Epoch* there was published an original and clever satire of Dostoevsky's, directed against the social temper of the sixties. It is called *The Crocodile, an Extraordinary Happening or What Passed in the Passage: A true tale of how a gentleman of a certain age and of certain appearance was swallowed alive by the crocodile in the Passage, whole without leftovers, and what came of this.*[1] The civil servant Ivan Matveyevich sets out with his wife and a friend to the Passage where a German is exhibiting a crocodile for a quarter of a ruble. He tickles the animal with his glove and it devours him "whole without leftovers." The civil servant settles himself comfortably in the "crocodile's insides" and dreams of a brilliant career. He will devise a new theory of economic relations and give lectures on natural history; his wife will open a salon which will be frequented by scholars, poets, philosophers, foreign mineralogists, government personages.

The author describes the impression produced by this extraordinary happening on the civil servant's authorities, on the public and the press. The "fashionable notions" of the sixties are shown in the distorted mirror of caricature and parody. When the devoured civil servant's wife screams hysterically: "Tear him apart! Tear 'im apart!," there immediately appears at the entrance of the "crocodilery" "a figure with moustaches, a beard, and a cap in his hands" who pronounces: "Such a reactionary wish, madam, doesn't do honor to your development and is conditioned by a lack of phosphorus in your brain. You'll be promptly hissed in the chronicle of progress and in our satirical pamphlets. . . ." Ivan Matveyevich's colleague, Timofey Semyono-

---

[1] The pun here, which I have translated "What Passed in the Passage," is in Russian *passazh v Passazhe*. The first *passazh* is a colloquialism for an unexpected happening, a strange turn of events. The second means a covered gallery with shops and merchandise on both sides, leading out onto parallel streets. There was a famous Passage in Petersburg.

vich, feels that tearing the crocodile apart would not be "progressive," inasmuch as it is the property of a visiting foreigner, and one knows that "the economic principle is above all else, sir." Russia needs industry and a bourgeoisie, she "must give foreign companies the opportunity of buying up our lands in little chunks," and therefore it is preferable to leave the prisoner in the crocodile's entrails and consider him as though officially sent there "to investigate the facts on the spot." There then ensues a magnificent parody on the *Petersburg Leaflet*, "a newspaper without any particular tendency, and so only generally humane," and on *The Hair*, a masked allusion to Krayevsky's *The Voice*.[2] The first newspaper delights in a pompous and solemn style: "Yesterday in our capital, vast and embellished with sumptuous buildings, uncommon rumors were diffused." The reporter recounts with pathos how "a well-known gourmand of higher society" ate alive, bit by bit, an entire crocodile, and fervidly recommends acclimating these "interesting foreigners" in Russia. In opposition, *The Hair* responds to the "shocking fact and indecent event" with a demolishing expository feuilleton. It laments the unfortunate crocodile and "directs the attention of its readers to the barbarous treatment of domestic animals."

The author contrives the most unbelievable happening in order to intensify the comic effect of society's relationship to it. The crude inanity of the progressives and economists of the period emerges before us in all its poverty. As to form, Dostoevsky's *literary grotesque* measures up to Gogol; the "extraordinary happening" in the Passage is genetically allied to the hero's incredible adventure in *The Nose*. The author never conceals his borrowings; in the preface to the journal text, which has disappeared from subsequent editions, we read: "I consider it my duty to state that if perchance this all is a lie, and not the truth, then a more incredible lie has not until now appeared in our literature, except perhaps that occurrence, familiar to everyone, when one fine morning a certain Major Kovalyov's own nose ran off from his face and then went walking about in a uniform and a plumed hat in the Tauride Garden and along Nevsky."

Shortly after publication of *The Crocodile* a notice came out in the newspaper *The Voice* which accused Dostoevsky of lampooning Chernyshevsky who at that time was in prison. This cunning slander was the more dangerous to the writer in that the hero of his short story actually did recall the author of *What's To Be Done?* The civil servant, having been swallowed by the crocodile, proclaims "out of its insides":

[2] *Volos* = hair; *golos*, voice.

"Only now can I dream at leisure of ameliorating the fate of all mankind. . . . Doubtlessly, I will invent my own new theory of new economic relations and shall boast about it. . . . I will refute everything and be a new Fourier." This tirade contains an obvious parody on Chernyshevsky's *What's to be Done?* where "ameliorating the fate of all mankind," "new economic relations and the natural sciences" are also discussed. The civil servant has a "squeaky voice," eyeglasses, a good-looking wife; his ideas are "bookish, originated in some corner." "One has only," he says, "to isolate oneself somewhere in a far-off corner or be it, fall into a crocodile, to shut one's eyes and immediately you will devise a whole paradise for all mankind." In his journal articles Dostoevsky had reproached the nihilists for being uprooted and theoretical. Now he has found an expressive image for this disengagement from life: "crocodile entrails." Lastly, the epithet "prisoner," applied by the author to his ill-starred hero, can be understood as a reference to Chernyshevsky's prison confinement. Was Dostoevsky capable of such mean vengeance upon his helpless enemy? He defended himself with indignation against this suspicion. In the *Diary of a Writer* for 1873 he writes disconcertedly:

And so the presumption was made that I, myself a former exile and convict, rejoiced in the exile of another "unfortunate"; moreover — wrote on this occasion a joyful pasquil. But where now is the proof of this? In the allegory? But bring me what you will . . . *Notes of a Madman,* the ode *God, Yury Miloslavsky,* the verses of Fet — what you will — and I undertake to extract for you immediately from the first ten lines you designate, that here precisely is an allegory on the Franco-Prussian War or a pasquil against the actor Gorbunov, in a word, on anyone you please, on anyone you insist. . . .

In spite of all these clever explications the suspicion of "unbefitting conduct" weighed upon the author of *Crocodile* through his entire life.

After the death of his wife and his brother, Dostoevsky found himself endlessly alone. He sought female love, attempted to get married. G. Prokhorov has succeeded in uncovering a certain "abortive romance"[D] in which the writer was involved at the end of 1864 and the beginning of 1865. Its heroine was Marfa Brown (Panina), a woman

[D] G. Prokhorov, *Nerazvernuvshiysya roman F. M. Dostoevskogo* (F. M. Dostoevsky's Abortive Romance), *Zvenya*, VI, 1936.

of lower class; who had traveled throughout Europe and for a long time lived in England. In Petersburg she became acquainted with P. Gorsky, a contributor to *Time* and *Epoch*, and became his lover. One of her letters to Dostoevsky from Petropavlovsk hospital has come down to us. From it we conclude that the editor of *Epoch* was very disposed toward her, proposed that she translate English for his journal, helped her in her complicated relations with Gorsky, and visited her at the time of her illness. Marfa Brown intended to go from the hospital straight to Dostoevsky's, and with striking candor writes him:

In any case, whether I succeed or not in satisfying you from a physical standpoint and whether between us there will materialize that spiritual harmony upon which the continuation of our acquaintance depends, nonetheless, believe me that I'll always remain grateful to you for having, if only for a moment or for some time, considered me worthy of your friendship and your good-will. . . . At the present moment, it's really all the same to me whether your relationship toward me is of long or short duration; but, I swear to you, incomparably more than material gain I value the fact that you've not been repelled by the *fallen side* of my personality, that you've placed me higher than what I'm worth in my own opinion. . . .
We know nothing more about this affair.

Dostoevsky's other infatuation was of greater significance. In 1865 he proposed to Anna Vasilyevna Korvin-Krukovskaya, a beautiful and romantic girl who wrote tales, was mad about courtly novels, dreamed of becoming an actress or going into a monastery. Her nature was very gifted, searching, restless; she passed directly from mysticism in the spirit of Thomas à Kempis to revolution and nihilism. She did not love Dostoevsky and his courting was to no avail. Later the writer told his second wife Anna Grigoryevna:

Anna Vasilyevna is one of the best women whom I have met in my life. She is exceptionally intelligent, cultivated, educated in literature, and she has a fine, good heart. This is a girl of high moral qualities, but her convictions are diametrically opposed to mine, and she cannot give way in them; she is too straightforward. It is not at all likely, for that reason, that our marriage could have been happy. I gave her back her promise and with all my soul I wish that she meet a man who shares her views, and that she might be happy with him.

Only half of Dostoevsky's desire was fulfilled: Kurvin-Krukovskaya did marry a man who shared her ideas, the communard Jaclard, but her life with him was full of adventures and misfortunes. Anna Vasilyevna's sister, the future celebrated mathematician Sofya Kovalevskaya, confesses in her memoirs that she was in love with Dostoevsky. The writer did not notice the fourteen-year-old girl's love.

After Mikhail Mikhailovich's death, debts of 25,000 rubles remained; printing the last six issues of *Epoch* cost another 18,000. Dostoevsky assumed responsibility for his late brother's debts and pledged to support his widow and four children. After the failure of *Epoch* he was decisively ruined; debtors' prison threatened him. The writer asked Ye. P. Kovalevsky to grant him a subsidy of 600 rubles from the Literary Fund; he entreated Krayevsky to advance him 3,000 on a novel, and as security for this sum offered the rights to all his works. Krayevsky refused. Then there appeared a book dealer, F. T. Stellovsky, a literary speculator, who exploited Pisemsky and Glinka.[3] For 3,000 rubles, Dostoevsky sold him the right to publish all his works in three volumes and committed himself to write a new novel by November 1, 1866. If the manuscript was not delivered to the publisher before December 1, all the writer's existing and *future* works would become the exclusive property of Stellovsky. Dostoevsky agreed to this "indenturing contract" and received only an insignificant part of the agreed sum; the remainder was paid out to him in promissory notes signed by the editor of *Epoch*, which the book dealer had been able to obtain for a trifle.

In March 1865 Dostoevsky wrote to his old friend Baron Vrangel: "And now I've suddenly been left alone and things have become simply terrible for me. My whole life is broken in two. . . . Oh, my friend, I'd readily go back to penal servitude for as many years, just to pay off my debts and feel free again. Now I'll start writing a novel

[3] Aleksey Pisemsky (1820-1881) is closer in the spirit of his writings to the French naturalists than any of the Russian realists. His portraits, magnificent in their way, are gloomy and cynical. In Russian letters he has few rivals for his depiction of human baseness. His most important works are the novel *A Thousand Souls* and the tragedy *A Hard Lot*.

Mikhail Ivanovich Glinka (1804-1857) may be considered the first major Russian composer. On the basis of his studies in Italy, Germany, and France, he first applied European techniques to the traditional music of Russia. Among his compositions are the two operas *A Life for the Tsar* (1836) and *Ruslan and Lyudmila* (1842).

with a stick over my head, i.e., from need, in haste. . . . And mean-while, it always appears to me that I'm really just beginning to live. Funny, isn't it? A cat's vitality!"

From his creditors, the confiscation of his belongings and debtors' prison, the writer fled abroad with 175 rubles in his pocket.

XIII

Crime and Punishment

Dostoevsky arrived in Wiesbaden toward the end of July 1865, and within five days gambled away all his money. Once again he asked Turgenev for a loan; the latter sent him 50 thalers. He besought Milyukov to sell his next story to one of the journals and send him three hundred rubles. But neither *The Contemporary* nor *The Library for Reading* nor *Fatherland Notes* would agree to such a proposition. He sent two letters to Vrangel and received no answer. He wrote Herzen and was refused. During the early part of August, Suslova arrived in Wiesbaden, also without money. Their living together in a wretched hotel did not continue for long. After her departure Dostoevsky wrote her in Paris (August 22):

> You had just left, and on the following day, early in the morning, the people here at the hotel informed me that they'd been instructed not to give me dinner, tea, or coffee. I went to clear up the misunderstanding, and the fat German proprietor informed me that I did not "deserve" any dinner and that he would send me only tea. And so since yesterday I've not eaten dinner, and am living only on tea. And even the tea they serve is abominable — without a kettle. They don't clean my clothes or my boots; don't come when I ring; and all the servants treat me with unspeakable, quite typically German, contempt. The German knows no greater crime than to be without money and not to pay one's bills promptly.

In closing, he asked Suslova to send him some money.

He hardly emerged from his room and from morning till evening he wrote. He complained that at the hotel he was not given a candle for the night. In this cramped hovel, without money, without food, without light, "burning with some kind of inner fever" (a letter to Vrangel), in haste and despair, he worked on *Crime and Punishment*.

During these somber days at Wiesbaden only one person came to his aid, a Russian Orthodox priest, I. A. Yanyshev. At last, salvation arrived. Vrangel returned, after a leave of absence, to Copenhagen where he was stationed, and found there two desperate letters from Dostoevsky. He sent him some money and invited him to come to Copenhagen on his way back to Russia. The writer passed ten days at the home of his old friend from Semipalatinsk, and on the tenth of October returned to Petersburg. His third trip abroad lasted two and a half months.

When Dostoevsky left Russia, he had plans for a novel in mind. As early as June 8, 1865, in the course of a letter requesting money, he offered his new work to A. Krayevsky: "My novel is called *The Drunks* and will deal with the current problem of drunkenness. Not only is the question analyzed, but I am also exposing all its ramifications, especially pictures of families, the upbringing of children in this atmosphere, and so forth, and so forth. It will run no less than about 20 sheets, but perhaps even more." In Wiesbaden this project was succeeded by another. "I had hoped to dispatch one task [*The Drunks*] quickly enough," he wrote Katkov, "but I got carried away with another work (the one I'm writing now) and don't regret it a bit." And he goes on to sketch the contents of *Crime and Punishment*. We should not imagine, however, that this plan was entirely new to Dostoevsky and that it originated in Wiesbaden. We have one statement from the author which allows us to conclude that he developed the idea of the novel while in exile. In October 1859 he wrote to his brother from Tver:

> Don't you remember I talked to you about a *confession* — a novel that I wanted to write when all had been finished, saying that I would still have a lot to live through. Well, in fact I've definitely decided to write it now without delay. . . . It'll be, first of all, effective, passionate; and secondly, all my heart and soul will be put into this novel. I thought of it when serving my sentence, lying on a bed of wooden planks, *in an oppressing moment of melancholy and self-dissolution*. . . . The *Confession* will advance my name once and for all.

Crime and Punishment, which was initially conceived in the form of Raskolnikov's confession, arose out of Dostoevsky's spiritual experience during the years of penal servitude. It was there that for the first time he encountered "strong personalities" standing beyond the moral law; there that he began to "reevaluate his norm of values." The theoretician-murderer's tragic figure was born "in an oppressing moment of melancholy and self-dissolution." But in 1859 this plan had not yet been realized. The project's "gestation" was to continue for six more years. On the other hand, work in Wiesbaden progressed very rapidly.

In September 1865 there already existed a detailed outline of the tale. The writer suggested it in the letter to Katkov. This invaluable document permits us to look at the work through the author's own eyes, to grasp his central idea. "This is," he wrote, "the psychological account of a crime. The action is contemporary, taking place in the present year. A young man, expelled from the student body of the university, of lower-class origins and living in utter poverty, through thoughtlessness, through an infirmity of notions, having come under the influence of some of those strange, 'incomplete' ideas which go floating about in the air, has decided to break out of his loathsome situation in one stroke. He has decided to kill a certain old woman, the widow of a titular councilor, who lends out money at interest. The old woman is stupid, hard of hearing, sickly, and greedy. She demands a Jew's percentage, is malicious, and tears other people's lives to pieces, harassing her own younger sister like a factory worker. 'She is not fit for anything,' 'What does she live for?' 'Is she of use to anyone at all?' etc. These questions thoroughly disconcert the young man. He decides to kill her, to rob her of everything in order to bring happiness to his mother, who is living in the provinces; to save his sister, who lives with some landowners as a paid companion, from the lascivious claims of the head of this landowning family — claims which are threatening her with ruin; to finish his studies; to go abroad; and then for the remainder of his entire life to be honorable, upright, steadfast in fulfilling 'his humane debt to mankind,' which will, of course, 'expiate his crime,' if in fact the term crime can be applied to this act directed against an old woman, deaf, stupid, evil, and ailing, who herself does not know why she continues living on this earth and who after a month, perhaps, would die anyway of her own accord. Despite the fact that crimes of this nature are terribly difficult to perpetrate — i.e., some traces, clues, and so forth are almost always quite grossly evident and an enormous amount is left to chance, which almost always betrays the guilty party — it happens that in an absolutely fortuitous fashion he succeeds in accomplishing his undertaking both quickly and successfully. He passes almost a month after that before the final catastrophe. No one is suspicious of him, nor can they be. And so it is here that the whole psychological process of the crime unfolds. Insoluble questions confront the murderer; unsuspected and unanticipated feelings torment his heart. Divine truth and justice, the earthly law, claim their rights, and he ends by being *compelled* to give himself up. Compelled so that even if he perish in penal servitude, nonetheless he might once again be united to men. The feeling that he is separated and cut off from mankind, which he experienced immediately upon the completion of the crime, has tortured him. The law of justice and human nature have taken their hold. . . . The criminal himself decides to accept suffering in order to atone for his deed. But then I find it difficult to elucidate my thought fully. In my story there is, moreover, a hint of the idea that the criminal is much less daunted by the established legal punishment for a crime than lawgivers think, partly because *he himself experiences a moral need for it.* I have observed this even in the most undeveloped people, in the most crude circumstances. I wanted to express this idea particularly in a developed individual of the new generation so that the thought might be more clearly and concretely seen. Several incidents which have occurred quite recently have convinced me that *my subject* is not at all eccentric. Especially that the murderer is an intellectually developed young man who even has good inclinations. Last year in Moscow I was told (this is actually true) about a certain student expelled from the University after the incident with the Moscow students, that he decided to break into a post office and kill the postman. In our papers there are still many traces of this unusual infirmity of notions which is materializing into terrible deeds. (That seminarian who killed a girl in a barn after an agreement with her, and whom they arrested an hour later at lunch, and so forth.) In a word, I feel convinced that my subject is justified in part by contemporary life. . . ."

One can draw several important conclusions from this letter to Katkov. *Crime and Punishment* was originally designed as a *short tale* "in five or six printed sheets." The author envisioned its theme as something completely independent of *The Drunks.* It was only later that the story of the Marmeladov family (*The Drunks*) was introduced into Raskolnikov's narrative. From the very moment of its conception this plan to portray a "theoretician-murderer" was divided into two distinct parts: the crime and its causes, and the effects of the crime upon the criminal's soul. The author sees the first part as an *introduction* to the second, the main part. The tale is called "the psychological account of a crime," but in fact, this account begins only after the murder has been committed. "And so it is here that *the whole psychological process of the crime* unfolds." These two aspects of the idea will be reflected in the final text by the double title (*Crime and Punishment*) and by the peculiarities of its composition: of the novel's six parts — *one* is devoted to the crime itself and *five* to how the criminal struggles to free himself of it. According to the original design, the second part is related to the author's experience in penal servitude. In *Notes from the House of Death* Dostoevsky already expressed his belief that legal punishment has little effect. The idea that the criminal himself suffers a moral need for punishment is corroborated by reference to the former convict's *personal* observations. But this plan to submit a crime to psychological study and analysis, which arose while serving his sentence, actually materialized only in 1865 after his ruthless literary polemics with the nihilists. It is this which helped the author formulate the actual motivation for the crime, i.e., to outline the plan for the first part. The murderer is an "individual of the new generation" who has surrendered to "those incomplete ideas which go floating about in the air." The hero is not a vulgar criminal, but "an intellectually developed young man who even has good inclinations." If such a person "is thoroughly disconcerted" by the influence of nihilistic ideas, then one can appreciate how corrosive these ideas were, how "infirm" were the "notions" that pervaded the sixties. The genesis of this new work is apparent: the first part continues the fight against nihilism and is immediately linked to *Notes from Underground*; while the second part embodies that idea, first conceived in Siberia, which had been fostered over so many years.

What were the "incomplete ideas" that so captivated Raskolnikov? We find the answer in the letter to Katkov. The impoverished student decides to kill the old money-lender because she is "*not fit* for anything," is "*of no use* to anyone at all." On the other hand, her murder will be very *useful* to him: he will save his mother and sister, finish his education, will travel abroad. Raskolnikov is seduced by *a utilitarian morality* which derives all man's conduct from the principle of *practical usefulness*. The precursors of this new moral code failed to take any account of its complete immorality. Chernyshevsky and his disciples continued to consider themselves humanists and to dream about the happiness of all mankind. And this is also true in the case of Raskolnikov. Once he has committed this "practically useful" crime, he intends "then for the remainder of his entire life to be honorable, up-

right, steadfast in fulfilling 'his humane debt to mankind.'" Dostoevsky in his novel set about unmasking this blatant lie of "humane
utilitarianism" and showing that the *economic principle* *does not
lead to universal prosperity, but rather to mutual annihilation.*

In our final text of the novel this initial concept is most clearly expressed in the dialogue between Raskolnikov and Luzhin (the fifth
chapter of the second part). The author entrusts the defense of progress "in the name of science and economic justice" to the corrupt
businessman and "capitalist" Luzhin. He preaches: "Science says: love
only yourself before all others, for everything in the world is based
upon personal interest. . . . Economic justice adds that the more private enterprises that we have properly arranged in society, the firmer
are its foundations and the better the common good is established in it
as well. . . ." Later the conversation touches upon the murder of the
money-lender and Luzhin expresses his indignation at the growing
immorality of society. "'And what are you getting excited about?'
Raskolnikov suddenly interrupted, 'It happened in accord with your
theory.' 'What do you mean, in accord with my theory?' 'But take
what you were preaching a short while ago to its ultimate conclusions,
and it will come out *that you can cut people's throats.*"

Thus Raskolnikov's story completes Dostoevsky's fight with the generation of the sixties. Crime is only the "theory of practical egoism
pursued to its *ultimate conclusions.*" In the final printed text, however, the center of ideas is rudely shifted. The author's original polemic
design recedes to a secondary plane and yields its primary importance
to a new idea, that of the *strong personality.* The result is the two
planes of motivation so characteristic of *Crime and Punishment.*

Dostoevsky worked on the outline of his tale in Wiesbaden, on the
boat from Copenhagen to Petersburg, and in Petersburg itself. At first
he was completely satisfied with his progress. On September 28, 1865,
he wrote to Vrangel: "And then the *tale* which I'm now writing will
perhaps be better than anything I've ever written, if they'll only give
me enough time to finish it." In Petersburg, however, the tale imperceptibly swelled into a large novel. The author decided to sacrifice
everything that had already been written and start again from the beginning. He informed Vrangel of this abrupt change in his work: "This
is my novel for *The Russian Messenger.* It's a big novel, in six parts. I
had much of it written and ready by the end of November. *I burned
it all.* Now I can confess it. I wasn't pleased with it myself. *A new form,*
a *new plan* captivated me and so I began over again. I'm working day

and night, and for all that I'm not working very much. A novel is a work of poetry. In order to write it, one must have tranquility of spirit and of impression. But my creditors torment me, i.e., they're threatening to send me to jail."

Work on the new plan progressed simultaneously with the novel's publication in *The Russian Messenger*. Though the first part appeared in the January issue, the general composition of the novel was still not completely clear to the author himself. The success of the first three parts did much to rally his spirit. In April 1866 he wrote to the priest I. Yanyshev: "I should note that my novel has turned out extraordinarily well and has enhanced my reputation as a writer. My whole future depends upon my finishing it successfully." The fourth chapter of the fourth part — when Raskolnikov goes to see Sonya and she reads the Gospel to him — greatly embarrassed the scrupulous editors of *The Russian Messenger* and they refused to print it. Dostoevsky had to rewrite it, separating "the bad from the good," and to prove that there was nothing immoral in it. He wrote to N. Lyubimov: "I have absolutely and utterly separated the *bad* and the *good* and now it will be totally impossible to confuse them and to make improper use of them. . . . I have carried out all of your instructions. Everything is disentangled, circumscribed, and clear. Quite another tonality has been given to the reading of the Gospel. . . ."

Dostoevsky informed A. P. Milyukov of his run-in with Katkov and Lyubimov:

I myself am afraid to say anything about this chapter. I wrote it in a state of genuine inspiration, but perhaps it is worthless. But they're not concerned with its literary value, rather they are afraid that it might be immoral. In this respect I was right; there was nothing in it against morality and it even went too far in the other direction. But they see something else, and what's more, they see traces of *nihilism*. Lyubimov announced *resolutely* that it had to be rewritten. I took it, and this revision of such a long chapter has cost me, at the very least, three new chapters, if I'm to judge by the labor and anguish that I spent. But I revised and gave it back. But here's the last straw! I haven't seen Lyubimov since then and have no idea whether they're satisfied with the revision or whether they themselves will decide to rewrite the whole thing over again!

When sending the corrected chapter to his editors, the writer implored: "And now I *most earnestly* entreat you: *for the sake of Christ* let everything stand as it is now." But Katkov was still not content. He proceeded to cross out a whole series of lines "regarding the character and behavior of Sonya."

In the novel's most mystical scene, built upon the narration of the miracle in the Gospel, the well-meaning editors saw immorality and nihilism! And even now we still have no idea as to the original tonality of the reading from the Gospel. Dostoevsky never reinstated the earlier version even in later editions.

Dostoevsky passed the summer of 1866 in the village of Lyublino, near Moscow, at the home of his sister, Vera Mikhailovna Ivanova. Dr. A. P. Ivanov's family reminds us of the Zakhlebinin household in the short story *The Eternal Husband*. The Zakhlebinins' summer house serves as a sort of gathering-place for the gay, carefree young people of the vicinity, "the girls who are spending the summer in neighboring cottages." Among them one's attention is immediately drawn to that "clever and sharp-witted" young lady, Marya Nikitishna, "who is always bantering someone and is, by the way, quiet intelligent." Anna Grigoryevna informs us that Dostoevsky drew the portrait of this gay prankster with Mariya Sergeyevna Ivanchina-Pisareva as his model. The young people play at proverbs and catch; one of the young ladies sings romances on the piano; a theatre is set up in the garden. In the evening, around the samovar, there are lively conversations and disputes. The Zakhlebinins' life at their summer home gives us an idea of the writer's life with the Ivanov family in Lyublino. N. von Vogt, a student at the Institute of Land-Surveying, relates in his memoirs that Dostoevsky used to take part in the games, played the role of the king's ghost in a parody on Hamlet, was very fun-loving and "was almost always singing something to himself." While at Lyublino, Dostoevsky heard a romance based on the words of Heine, *Du hast Diamanten und Perlen*. In the fifth part of *Crime and Punishment* Katerina Ivanovna Marmeladova sings it on the street.

But the writer had not come to the country in order to rest; he had the most "eccentric" plans for the summer. He had pledged, according to the agreement with Stellovsky, to deliver a large, yet unpublished novel to the latter by the first of November. "I want to do an unprecedented and eccentric thing," he wrote to A. V. Korvin-Krukovskaya on July 17, "to write 30 printed sheets within the space of four months, forming two separate novels, of which I will write one in the morning and the other in the evening, and to finish them by a fixed deadline. Do you know, my dear Anna Vasilyevna, that even now such

eccentric and extraordinary things utterly delight me. I simply don't
fit into the category of staid and conventional people. . . . I'm convinced that not a single one of our writers, either living or dead, has
ever written under conditions comparable to those under which I *invariably* write. The very thought would be enough to kill Turgenev."
But this "extraordinary thing" was not realized in Lyublino. The writer
spent his time there working on the fifth part of *Crime and Punishment*
and only succeeded in giving some thought to the novel for Stellovsky.
A month before the deadline not one line of the new novel had been
written. A. Milyukov recounts in his memoirs that it was he who rescued Dostoevsky by advising him to turn to the help of a stenographer.
Olkhin, the director of a secretarial school, recommended his best pupil
to the writer. On October 4, 1866, Dostoevsky began to dictate *The
Gambler* to his future wife, Anna Grigoryevna Snitkina. The story was
finished by October 31, and he returned to *Crime and Punishment*.
The sixth and final part was written in November. The novel was
printed in *The Russian Messenger* in the course of 1866.

We are in possession of three notebooks with rough drafts and notations for *Crime and Punishment*.[A] They are spread over a period
between September 1865 and February 1866. It is difficult to reestab-
lish the precise chronological sequence of the notes since the author
made notations in different books simultaneously, interspersing them
with calculations as to how much he should realize from the edition,
with entries of his pressing debts and of addresses, with sketches of
persons and buildings and words written out in calligraphic form:
Napoléon, Julius Caesar, Rachel.

Theoretically one can divide the writing of the novel into two distinct periods: the first extends from September to the end of November
1865. At this time the author was still working on the *tale* the plan of
which he had proposed in his letter to Katkov. In it the narration is
presented in the first person, i.e., the hero himself relates the story. The
second period continues from December 1865 to December 1866. This
is the novel in which the author himself is the narrator.

The "tale" was envisioned in the form of a criminal's confession.
Here is a sketch from one of the notebooks:

[A] Central Archives, *Iz Arkhiva F. M. Doestoevskogo. Prestuplenie i nakazanie.
Neizdannye materialy.* (From the Archives of F. M. Dostoevsky, *Crime and Punishment.* Unpublished Materials.) Prepared for printing by I. N. Glivenko. Mos-
cow-Leningrad 1931.

I'm on trial and will tell everything. I'll write down everything. I am writing for myself, but let others and all my judges read it as well. This is a confession, a full confession. I will conceal nothing. About five days before today I was walking about like a madman. I will never say that at that time I was actually mad, and I don't want to justify myself by this lie. . . . I was in full possession of my mind. . . . It came to the point that I was even falling off into a kind of oblivion. . . . Everything, everything was sucked up into my plan. . . . And I was simply drawn (even) somehow mechanically drawn, to carry it out with greater haste and decide everything.

But as the work progressed, Dostoevsky's design became more complicated. The material which he had intended for his novel *The Drunks* was now infused into the "confession." The form which he had contemplated using, now proved to be too narrow a frame for the new psychological and intellectual contents. Traces of his unrelenting hesitations regarding the narration's form are to be found reflected in the notebooks. Dostoevsky writes:

> *I am the narrator, and not he.* And if it is a confession, then in that case I'm going to have to explain everything too much, *down to every last possible detail.* So that at every instant of the story everything might be clear. N. B. *To be taken into account.* As to a confession, it will not be candid at various points and it will be difficult to imagine for what possible reason it has been written. But *the author is the narrator.* Too much naiveté and truthfulness are needed. Imagine the author to be an omniscient being, one incapable of error, who is presenting one of the members of the new generation for everyone to see.

Being thoroughly immersed in his "fixed idea" and cut off from the reality of the world, the murderer would not be a suitable narrator. It is not his role to expound the complicated facts of an involved plot, to describe and evaluate the people who surround him. Dostoevsky decided upon a "new form" — the author would be the narrator, and he destroyed the original text of the "tale." This took place in November 1865 (the letter to Vrangel). However a large segment of this manuscript which he cast into the fire has been preserved for us in the notebooks. There are many passages of the "confession" which have simply been incorporated into the novel with the necessary substitution of the third person for the first and with minor stylistic emendations. Thus in the final text we find Raskolnikov's nightmare depicted: "Dusk had finally settled when he was awakened by a terrible scream. My God, who's screaming like that! In all his life he had never observed and heard such unnatural sounds, such howling, wailing, grinding, tears, thrashing, and swearing. He couldn't even conceive of such brutality, of such frenzy. He got up in terror and sat on his bed."

In the "confession" the corresponding passage reads: "Dusk had finally settled when a terrible scream woke me, and at dusk it is usually almost completely dark in my room. I opened my eyes. My God! Who's screaming like that. In all my life I had never heard such unnatural sounds, such howling, grinding, tears, swearing, and thrashing. I couldn't even conceive of such brutality, of such frenzy. I got up in terror and sat on the couch."

For a long time the fundamental idea of the novel continued to puzzle its author. In his sketchbooks he is constantly returning to the question: why did Raskolnikov commit the murder? And his answers are varied. We feel it possible to relate this complicated motivation to two basic ideas. The first of these corresponds to the original plan for the *tale* and is expounded in the letter to Katkov. It borders upon the concept of Rastignac in Balzac's novel *Père Goriot*: may not a man do something which in itself is a small evil, for the sake of accomplishing a great good; may he not kill one insignificant and pernicious being in order to bring happiness to many worthy people who otherwise are going to perish? Does a noble end justify illicit means? Can a man through his own will set aright the ways of Providence? In accord with this idea Raskolnikov imagines himself to be a magnanimous idealist, a humanist thirsting to bring happiness to all mankind. His heart which is noble and compassionate, is pierced by the spectacle of human suffering. In the past, at the cost of great personal sacrifice, he had tried many times to help the "humiliated and wronged." But the idealist arrives at the realization that he is utterly powerless when confronted with world evil. Humility and sacrifice are fruitless; good is completely ineffectual. Good people are continually perishing, while evil ones flourish. And then, in despair, he decides to "transgress" the moral law. This dialectic leads him to his crime: he kills a human being for love of humanity; he perpetrates evil for love of good. In the notebooks we find the "idea of Rastignac" developed at great length. Raskolnikov says: "By my very nature I cannot simply stand by and allow a miscreant to bring some poor, defenseless being to ruin. I will inter-fere. I want to interfere. And that is why I want power. . . ." "I am seizing power, I'm securing force — whether it be money or sheer might — not for evil. I bear happiness. Oh, why isn't everyone happy? A pic-ture of the golden age. It's already borne in minds and hearts. How can one not want to have it come about!" The author has imparted to the murderer his own dream about the "golden age"! And in another place: "His prayer upon coming back from the Marmeladovs. (briefly) Lord! If this attempt upon an old woman who is blind, stupid, not really needed by anyone, is a sin, considering the fact that I wanted to devote myself, then blame and convict me. I have judged myself exact-ingly; this is not vain pride. . . . And then after I have become noble, the benefactor of all, a citizen, I will repent (*he prayed to Christ*, lay down)."

Raskolnikov seeks power not because of his vanity; he consecrates himself to the service of mankind. He realizes that his act is a sin, and knowingly he takes it upon himself. He prays to Christ, and believes in repentance and expiation. "Poor mother, my poor sister," he says, "I wanted this for you. If there is a sin here, I resolved to take it upon myself, but only so that you might be happy." The author is fascinated by the acute paradox that lies in murder for the sake of others, in the desire for might and money in the name of complete altruism. Raskol-nikov is not the executioner but the victim. He has shed another's blood, but he would have been capable of shedding his own as well. "To Sonya: 'Love! And is it possible that I do not love, if I have de-cided to take such a horrible thing upon myself? So what that it's some-one else's blood and not my own? *And would I not give all my blood if it were necessary?*' He stopped and reflected. 'Before God Who sees me and before my conscience, talking with myself here, I say: I would give it.'"

This extraordinary entry gives us the definitive formula for the *idea of murder motivated by love.* Faced with such a conception of the hero, *Crime and Punishment* ought to have been transformed into *Crime and Expiation.* Raskolnikov who believes in God, who prays to Christ, but who has gone astray because of his love, must be saved. The author presents an outline that suggests a fortuitous denouement. "This very crime itself gives rise to his moral evolution, to the possi-bility of such questions as formerly would never have entered his mind. In the last chapter while he is serving his sentence of penal servitude, he remarks that without this crime he would never have realized such questions, desires, feelings, needs, aspirations, and development." In this way the crime becomes the source of his moral rebirth and leads to the criminal's spiritual restoration. Expiation can begin even before he is sent to the penal colony.

In one rough draft the following plan is indicated: after his confession to Sonya, Raskolnikov wanders about the streets. "A whirlwind. *A vision of Christ.*" Christ Himself comes to save the sinner who has repented. After this mystical encounter the hero chances upon a fire. "At the fire he accomplished resounding deeds (he saved someone from death). He arrives home all scorched. His mother, his sister are at his bedside. He makes his peace with everyone. His joy, the joyous evening. 'Now the only thing that matters is that you will expiate everything by heroism, you will redeem everything' (the words of Sonya)." Traces of this plan have come down to us even in the final printed text: the vision of Christ has been replaced by the reading of the Gospel with Sonya; the episode with the fire and "heroism" is transferred back to the past. At the trial Raskolnikov's landlady testified that "when earlier they were living in another house, at Five Corners, there was a fire at night and her lodger pulled two small children out of one of the apartments which had already caught fire, and was then badly burned." Finally the repentant criminal kisses the ground and goes to give himself up. "Sonya and love have conquered!"

But the author was not content with the "idea of Rastignac" and the image of the altruistic murderer. He penetrates the criminal's soul and discovers there even greater depths. Behind the idea that a noble heart has gone astray there lies hidden another idea, majestic and terrible. For the purposes of a schema one could call it *"the idea of Napoleon."* Raskolnikov divides mankind into two unequal parts: the majority — this is a "trembling creature" whose role is to obey; and the minority, composed of those people "who have power," who stand above the law (Napoleon). His committing the murder had no bearing at all upon love for mankind; he killed to find out "whether he was a louse or a man." The idea of Rastignac and that of Napoleon, in spite of their exterior resemblance (the transgression of the moral law), inwardly are diametrically opposed. According to the first, Raskolnikov's deed is an error executed in the name of the most noble intentions; according to the second, it is an objective crime, a revolt against the divine order of the world, the self-exaltation of the strong personality. In the first design, the murderer is a humanist and a Christian who acknowledges his sin and redeems it by repentance and suffering; in the second, he is an atheist, a *demonic personality*, not bound by conscience, who is incapable of repentance and rebirth.

The "idea of Napoleon" took hold of Dostoevsky. Parallel to the motif of love for mankind, he developed the motif of hate and contempt for them. Raskolnikov says: "How vile men are! Are they worth bowing down before and asking forgiveness? No, no, I will keep silent. . . . But with what *contempt*. How base, how vile men are. No: to gather them into one's arm, and then to do good for them. . . . Is it possible to love them? Is it possible to suffer for them? *Hatred for mankind*." The strong individual wishes power and only power. It is irrelevant what use he makes of this power; it does not matter whether he will turn it to man's good or to evil. There is only one thing that is important: *power for power's sake*. Humane motives are a lie and a deceit; truth is the metaphysical will to might. The murderer declares to Sonya: " 'Whatever I may be, whatever then I may do, whether I benefit mankind or I suck the living juices from it like a spider — this is my own affair. I know that I want to *dominate*, and that is enough. . . .' 'In what does happiness lie then?' said Sonya. 'Happiness is *power*,' he said." Another variant of this conversation with Sonya: "He says: 'To rule over them.' All this meanness and baseness on every side only angers him. *An utter contempt for people. Pride.* He informs Sonya of his contempt for people. He does not wish to stoop to argue with her." The pride of the man-godhead is underlined in the following note: "To Sonya: 'But I had to take the first step. I must have power. I cannot . . . *I want everything that I see to be different than it is.* Up till now that was all I needed. I even committed murder. After that *more is needed*. . . . I myself want to act. I don't know how far I will go. I don't want to submit myself to anyone.' " A man sets himself in place of God and wants to reorder all of creation. Murder is only the beginning of the revolt; "after that more is needed." It is impossible to say to what measure of evil he will go. His demonic path is only indicated by the author: "How base men are. *Dream about a new crime*." Dostoevsky halted before this abyss; Raskolnikov will not commit new crimes. But how will it all end? The fortuitous denouement which was suited to the "idea of Rastignac," is of course out of the question. The demonic personality cannot come to repentance and rebirth; it is doomed to perdition. Dostoevsky noted: *"Finale of the novel. Raskolnikov goes to shoot himself."* The hero's suicide was to have taken place immediately after Marmeladov's death. "Marmeladov's death. A bullet in the forehead."

The writer found himself faced with an insoluble dilemma: two opposing ideas were contending for his hero's fate. He could see two possible solutions to his problem: either to sacrifice one for the sake of the other or find some synthesis which would encompass both. It seems that for some time he was inclined to follow the first alternative. One entry reads: "The main anatomy of the novel: after the sickness and so on, it is of the utmost importance to direct the course of affairs onto a real climax and do away with this vagueness, i.e., *explain the murder in one manner or another* and establish his character and attitudes clearly. . . . Conflict with reality and the logical outcome of the law of nature and of duty." In other words, the author intended to discard the "idea of Napoleon" and bring his hero to a spiritual rebirth. . . . But this would have entailed impoverishing and simplifying the design. Dostoevsky chose the more difficult way out: to employ both ideas, to join them in a single soul, to portray the hero's conscience in its tragic duality. This almost impossible task was ingeniously realized in the novel. Originally, the murderer's true character was to be disclosed after Marmeladov's death at Razumikhin's soirée. At the requiem service[1] for the civil servant who was run down by horses, Raskolnikov experiences an influx of remorse and contrition, but it is followed by new affirmations of self: "He goes to Razumikhin's. The soirée. He arrives, having experienced contrition, and there follows *demonic pride*. Completely on the defense." In another variation, Marmeladov's death only serves to intensify his awareness of his own righteousness: "He went to Marmeladov's requiem service. . . . Shaken, confirmed, and proud, he goes to the soirée at Razumikhin's. *Devil-like pride*." Exposing the hero as a demon ought to be an effective *coup de maître*. "So here there is a *coup de maître*. At first there was apprehension, then fear and terror, and his character was not completely unmasked, and here suddenly his whole character unveiled itself in all its *demonic force* and all the reasons and motives for the crime become understandable. . . . The full import of this must come out at Razumikhin's soirée in his *satanic pride*." "The soirée at Razumikhin's (*terrible pride*). . . . In the novel the concept of *exorbitant pride*, of arrogance and contempt for this society is expressed in his image. His idea: to seize power over this society. Despotism is his

[1] A *Panikhida* is a service of prayer for the repose of the departed's soul (not a Divine Liturgy or "mass") held on the third, ninth, and fortieth days after death. It is also customary to celebrate *panikhidi* on the anniversaries of the departed's birth-day, name-day and death-day.

characteristic trait. To express all this at Razumikhin's soirée." Pride (demonic, devil-like, satanic) is insistently underlined. Love for mankind proves to be only a mask; contempt and despotism lie hidden beneath it. In view of such a conception, the proposed finale with the fire and the hero's surrendering himself to the police takes on quite another sense. Raskolnikov is punishing himself because of his weakness and cowardliness, but he does not repent. He turns himself over to the authorities out of *contempt*. "Pride, his arrogance and conviction of his own guiltlessness continually go *crescendo* and suddenly at its strongest phase, after the fire, he goes to give himself up." The most terrible thing of all is that this demonic force does not disroot his humanism. Under the psychological stratum an even deeper layer is uncovered — a metaphysical one. And before this profundity the psychological level is exposed as a false mask. *Raskolnikov is a demon embodied in a humanist.*

The "demon's" path leads to perdition, the way of the humanist who has sinned and then repented, brings salvation. But what of the path of the demon who is embodied in a humanist, of the man in whom "two opposing characters" are merged (Razumikhin's words regarding Raskolnikov)? The rough drafts testify to the difficulty the author experienced in arriving at a suitable denouement. The "vision of Christ" and his heroism at the fire had to be discarded; Svidrigailov, and not Raskolnikov fell heir to the solution of suicide. An exterior denouement still remained: his giving himself up to the authorities, the trial, his deportation to the penal colony; but this did not suffice for an interior, spiritual denouement. Raskolnikov did not repent and did not "rise" again to a new life. There is only a promise of his resurrection in the concluding words of the epilogue: the criminal is still young; the miracle-working force of life will sustain him. This "philosophy of life" which in the novel is expressed by Porfiry Petrovich had already been indicated in the rough drafts. "But now it's life that I want; [I thirst for] life and I will live," exclaims the murderer. "Suddenly morose desolation and infinite pride and the struggle that life might not completely perish, but *that there will be life*." After much hesitation the author finally arrived at this compromise as a solution. The murderer has not yet been saved, but he can be saved if he will completely give himself up to a spontaneous, irrational love of life. Naturally this is not yet faith; it is only the way to it. Dostoevsky wrote down his thoughts on the meaning of suffering. "The *idea of the novel*, the Orthodox outlook: in what does Orthodoxy lie. There is no happiness in comfort; happiness is purchased at the price of suffering. . . . Man is not born for happiness. Man earns happiness, and this always through suffering. There is no injustice here, for the *calling and consciousness of life* are arrived at by experience pro and contra and one must draw this experience upon one's self (by suffering, such is the law of our planet); but this immediate consciousness, which is felt as a living process, is a joy of such great intensity that one can pay for it by years of suffering." This concept of suffering as the source of consciousness had already been expressed in *Notes from Underground*. Suffering is the law of our planet. The man who accepts life, of his own will chooses suffering and in this "calling of life" he realizes intense joy. Raskolnikov is too immersed in life to perish from his demonic idea. By the whole "living process" he is bound to life's mystical force. The denouement of *Crime and Punishment* is founded upon this idea. It is interesting that the author considered it an "Orthodox outlook."

In the rough drafts we find several variations of Raskolnikov's romance with Sonya. After Marmeladov's death Sonya goes to visit Raskolnikov; then she writes him one or two letters. "Her letter possesses high artistic qualities." He is rude and cold to her. He offends her, but afterward goes and confesses his crime to her. When he is taken ill, he lies in her apartment; then later he runs away. At first the writer was tempted by a rather effective plan: the hero spiritually dies as a result of the old woman's murder; through Sonya's love he rises again to a new life. This is expressed symbolically by the contrast: "Marmeladov's death, the requiem service, his funeral, and then the begetting of new life — the love of Raskolnikov and Sonya." "His romance with Marmeladova begins at the ultimate limits of humiliation and despair. . . . Life ends on one side and begins on another. On one side the funeral and curses; on the other, resurrection." It seems that the author intended to write a scene in which the hero would declare his love to Sonya. Raskolnikov says to her: "You are now my sovereign and my fate, my life — everything." Or elsewhere: "He kneels before Sonya. 'I love you.' She says to him: 'Turn yourself over to the law.' 'Therefore, you don't love me?' he says. She is silent." In another variant the declaration takes place after he has given himself up. "She says to him then: 'We could not tell each other that we were in love until you had given yourself up.' "

The focal point of the novel's composition is the group scene at Marmeladov's funeral dinner[2] during the course of which Luzhin insults Sonya. The notebooks show that the author attached enormous significance to this motif wherein an unfortunate and humiliated girl is wronged. He sought a complete parallelism between his hero's and his heroine's fate. And so, just as Raskolnikov, Sonya now must *personally* stand before a choice. "Now, my lady, here's what," he says to her, "if suddenly you were given the right to decide all this: whether this man or those people could go on living — i.e., whether Luzhin could live and continue to pursue his loathsome activities, or whether Katerina Ivanovna must die — then what would you decide? Which of them would die?" Raskolnikov has already asked himself a similar question: who is to die — he, his sister Dunya, his mother, or the old money-lender? And he answered it: the old woman must die. Sonya answers differently: "Why, I cannot know the ways of Divine Providence. . . . And who has placed me here to judge who may live and who may not live." But in her very refusal to judge she judges and condemns the "theoretician-murderer."

In order that the contrast between these two solutions might receive its utmost dramatic import, Sonya had to be placed in Raskolnikov's position. Her beloved family is threatened by ruin just as was the poor student's family. Will she commit a crime in order to save it? The author has been assiduously arranging various possibilities wherein Sonya is to be confronted with insult and abuse. To begin with, Raskolnikov's mother insults her: "His mother in the first place blames Marmeladova for everything; she interrogates and *insults* her." Then his sister and Razumikhin start: "His sister becomes Sonya's archenemy. She turns Razumikhin against her in order to have him *insult* her, and when afterward Razumikhin began to side with Sonya, she quarrels with him. But then she goes to explain herself to Sonya. At first she *insults* her and then throws herself at her feet." Finally Dostoevsky decides to have Luzhin (or Lyzhin) offend her; but the "insult" motif is not the same here as appears in the final text. "Lyzhin must (at Lebezyatnikov's) be taken aback by Sonya . . . He *insults* Sonya on the street with Lebezyatnikov (his bitterness toward Sonya is not even intelligible. 'I will twist you round my little finger yet'). Sonya runs away from him. Finally it comes out that he has fallen madly in love with Sonya (nature)."

In incorporating this sequence of Sonya's humiliation at the hands

---

[2] After the burial service a funeral meal is held in memory of the departed. Among the foods traditionally served is a mixture of rice, raisins, honey.

of Lyzhin, the author has successfully resolved the problem of the novel's composition. Sonya's and Raskolnikov's paths have become parallel. One might conjecture that Luzhin was originally conceived of as a *pendant* to Raskolnikov. He is also a "strong personality," convinced that crime is admissible. "The 'fiancé' [Luzhin] expounds to him at length a theory in accord with which one could commit murder. N.B. He even talks about the death of the old woman: 'of course, it is permissible' according to the fiancé's theory. 'Do it once, but then put an end to it.'" Dostoevsky finally discarded this conception as an unnecessary duplication of the hero's own thought. He did, however, attempt to embody in the character of Luzhin another variation of the "strong personality"—that of the theoretician-miser. "There is avarice in Luzhin. In his miserliness there is something of Pushkin's covetous baron.[3] He worshiped money, for all things will perish, but *money* will not perish. 'I,' said he, 'am of low birth and I want without fail to be on the top rung of the ladder and *lord it over* others.'" As a consequence, the idea of "acquiring force" would be portrayed under two aspects: *power through crime* (Raskolnikov) and *power through money* (Luzhin). As it develops, the figure of Raskolnikov assimilates the second aspect as well. According to the original plan at Razumikhin's soirée the hero was to argue that "it is absolutely vital that from the very beginning one have some secured funds (5 thousand) in order to establish solid footing. Without that you will be forever cringing, fawning, saying yes to everything. (A picture of what one can do with it, develop one's forces and *stand up for one's freedom*.)" In the printed text the theme of money is very screened and subdued. The idea of crime for the sake of crime succeeds in dislodging the motif of robbery and aggrandizement. "Napoleon" has triumphed over the "Covetous Knight." But the embryo of this earlier design has been preserved in Raskolnikov's dialogue with the servant-girl Nastasya. The former student does not want to give lessons for a kopeck apiece. Nastasya asks: "And what do you want to get all your fortune in one fell swoop?" He looked at her strangely. "'Yes, *all my fortune*,' he answered firmly after a short silence." Having surrendered to the main hero his idea of dominating with the help of money, Luzhin is reduced to the role of a shrewd businessman who preaches a theory of egoism and the "economic principle."

In the course of work on the novel, Sonya's image undergoes a great

[3] Once again a reference to Pushkin's *Little Tragedy, The Covetous Knight.*

many modifications. In the rough drafts she is presented as a philosopher, a moralist, the bearer of the "Russian idea." We listen to her speech with surprise: " 'Like Christ the Russian people have always suffered,' says Sonya. . . . Arithmetic comes to nought, but spontaneous faith saves. Everything has been confused. One does not know in what to believe; one does not know on what to take a stand. 'Believe in the beauty of the Russian element' (Sonya). . . . 'One can be great even in humility,' says Sonya — she proves it, that is." In the novel reasonings about life and about the meaning of suffering pass from Sonya to Porfiry Petrovich. In the final printed text we find Sonya struggling with Raskolnikov not through ideas and sermons, but by her deeds and example. She does not reason and does not moralize, but believes and loves. "She is terribly bashful . . . always gentle and there is absolutely no irony in her. She is always serious and calm." These are the traits of character that are particularly developed in the novel.

The notebooks disclose to us the process of the novel's creation. But now we come to the published work. Here is an entire world, vast and complete in itself. It is governed by its own peculiar laws; lives by its own mysterious life. This new reality, which has been created by the genius of a great artist, is *real* because it discloses the very essence of being, but it is not *realistic* because it does not reproduce our reality. Perhaps no writer in all world literature has ever possessed such an extraordinary vision of the world and such a forceful gift to embody this into art as did Dostoevsky. The destinies of his incredible heroes are unimaginable; the circumstances of their lives are exceptional; their passions and thoughts mysterious. The naive consciousness tries to struggle with "Dostoevskianism." This is a "sick," "cruel" talent; his heroes are pathological types, criminals, degenerates, madmen. But it is impossible to contend with Dostoevsky. He immediately seizes possession not only of the reader's imagination, but of his whole being. He impregnates him with his own ecstatic ebullience; subjects him to the rhythm of his own breathing; he transforms him psychologically. Dostoevsky's influence exercises an hypnotic power. His world evolved slowly over a period of twenty years — from *Poor People* to *Crime and Punishment*. It was only in this latter novel that it acquired its ultimate structure as *a distinct spiritual reality*. This is the first of the five novel-tragedies, or to be more precise, *the first act of a great tragedy in five acts*.

The author observes all the unities of classical tragedy: those of place, time, and action. The story of Raskolnikov is set in Petersburg. The most fantastic city on earth gives birth to this fantastic hero. In the world of Dostoevsky, place and surroundings are mystically in harmony with his characters. They do not form a neutral expanse, but rather are spiritual symbols. Raskolnikov, like Hermann in Pushkin's *The Queen of Spades,* is a "Petersburg type." Where but in this sullen and mysterious city could the impoverished student's "unseemly dream" suddenly take shape? In *A Raw Youth* Dostoevsky writes: "It strikes me on such a morning in Petersburg, damp, humid, and foggy, the wild dream of some Hermann out of Pushkin's *Queen of Spades* (a colossal figure, extraordinary, from head to foot a Petersburg type — a type out of the Petersburg period) must be intensified to an even greater degree." Raskolnikov is Hermann's spiritual brother. He too dreams about Napoleon, thirsts for power, and kills an old lady. In his revolt "the Petersburg period of Russian history" reaches its final culmination.

In the course of the novel there are several brief descriptions of the city. They remind one of stage directions. However, in these few incisive strokes the author has succeeded in conveying to us a "spiritual *paysage.*" On a clear summer day Raskolnikov stands on Nikolayevsky Bridge and intently stares at "this truly magnificent panorama." "For some inexplicable reason a cold chill always came over him when he gazed at this magnificent panorama. In this splendid tableau he sensed a mute and deaf spirit." The soul of Petersburg is Raskolnikov's soul: in it we find the same grandeur and the same coldness. The hero "wonders at his sullen and mysterious impression and puts off finding an explanation for it." The novel is devoted to explaining this mystery of Raskolnikov, of Petersburg, of Russia. Petersburg is as vague and ambiguous as the human consciousness to which it has given birth. On one side we see the majestic Neva in whose sky-blue waters the golden cupola of St. Isaac's Cathedral casts its reflection, a "magnificent panorama," a "splendid tableau"; on the other side we find the Hay Market with its narrow streets and blind alleys, the dwelling-place of poverty, a loathsome and ugly sight. This is also the picture of Raskolnikov: "He is remarkably handsome, with exquisite dark eyes, hair that is dark chestnut; he is taller than average, slender and well-built." A dreamer, romantic, a lofty and proud spirit, a noble and strong personality. But this "excellent individual" has his own Hay Market, his dirty underground: the "thought" that he entertains of murder and robbery. The hero's disgusting and base crime has the slums, the basements, the taverns and dens of the capital as its accomplice. It would almost seem that the poisonous vapors that rise from this great city, its contaminated and feverish breath, have penetrated the impoverished student's brain and there given birth to this thought of murder. Drunkenness, poverty, vice, hatred, villainy, debauchery — all of Petersburg's murky depths — direct the murderer to his victim's house. The crime's surroundings, the section and house in which the money-lender lives, provoke as much "disgust" in the hero as his "unseemly dream" itself. Now he goes "to make an experimental trial." "A terrible heat had settled upon the street; and then there was the closeness, the bustle of the crowd, plaster all about, scaffolding, bricks, dust, and that stench which is so peculiar to summer. The unbearable stench that was emitted from the taverns, which were particularly numerous in that part of the city, and the drunks, whom one encountered at every step, served to complete the picture's *revolting* and miserable tonality. For an instant a feeling of *most profound disgust* illumined the young man's refined features. . . ." The house in which the old woman lives, on one side looks out upon the canal: "The entire house consisted of undersized flats and all kinds of tradespeople lived there — tailors, locksmiths, cooks, Germans of various sorts, girls who made their living through their own devices, petty bureaucrats, and so forth. The people coming in and leaving also scurried under these two gates."

After his "experiment" Raskolnikov cries out: "My God! how disgusting this all is." He is submersed in "a feeling of boundless disgust." The Hay Market with its girls, drunks and "tradespeople" and the idea of the crime are but two aspects of a single moral state. Another example of this incorporation of spirit and spiritualization of matter is to be found in the description of Raskolnikov's room: "It was a very small garret, about six paces in length, and had the most miserable appearance with its yellowish, dusty paper peeling off all the walls, and so low that a man who was even moderately tall, just found it impossible, and you always had the feeling that you were going to bang your head against the ceiling." The former student sleeps on a "clumsy, large sofa which was upholstered in chintz, usually without undressing, without sheets, covering himself with his dilapidated student's overcoat." The author compares this "yellow garret" to a cupboard, a trunk, and a coffin.

This is the material wrapping of Raskolnikov's "idea." His room is an ascetic monk's cell. He has locked himself up in his corner, in his "underground"; he has lain down in a "coffin" and he thinks. All his life has been passed in thought; the exterior world, people, reality — these have ceased to exist. He dreams of wealth though he is completely disinterested; he dreams of a practical deed though he is a theorist. He does not need either food or clothing because he is an immaterial spirit, *the pure consciousness of self*. He is a continuation of that mental process about which "the man from underground" told us. The violent idea of the crime could be born only in a narrow, low garret such as this. His thinking eats away at the old morality and decomposes the psycho-physical unity of man. Raskolnikov must pass through *ascesis*; he must dematerialize himself in order to feel the demonic power within him and rise in revolt against God. The "yellow garret" is the symbol of a devil-like, jaundiced divorce from mankind. In Dostoevsky the world of nature and of things does not have its own independent existence; it is humanized and spiritualized to its ultimate limits. Surroundings are always shown through the refraction of consciousness as its function. The room where a man lives is the landscape of his soul.

The description of the old money-lender's flat likewise has "psychological" import: the dark, narrow staircase, the fourth floor, the small bell that sounds with such a faint ring, the door which is only opened the slightest crack, the dark vestibule partitioned off by a screen, and finally the room "with its yellow wallpaper, geraniums, and muslin curtains on the windows." "The furniture which was all very old and of yellow wood, consisted of a sofa with a huge arched wooden back, a roundish table of oval form in front of the sofa, a dressing-table with a mirror set against the wall between two windows, some chairs along the walls and two or three penny-pictures in yellow frames, depicting young German maidens with birds in their hands — that was all the furniture there was. In one corner a lamp was burning before a small icon. Everything was very clean, and the furniture and floor were highly polished. Everything was glistening." At once the hero translates his impression into the language of psychology: "It's in the houses of spiteful, old widows that one finds such cleanliness." What is most striking is how *impersonal* these surroundings are, the absence of soul and life in this order, the crude bourgeois banality of the "young German maidens" and the hypocritical piety of the icon-lamp.

Raskolnikov's garret is a coffin; the old woman's flat is the neat web of a spider; Sonya's room is an ill-formed barn. "Sonya's room seemed to resemble a barn. Its shape was that of an extremely irregular quadrangle, and this accorded it a somewhat ill-formed appearance. A wall with three windows which looked out upon the canal, cut across the room somewhat slantwise so that one corner which converged in a dreadfully acute angle, ran off inward, while the other corner was now too ungainly obtuse. . . . There was scarcely any furniture at all in this whole big room. . . . The yellow-colored wallpaper, messy and worn, had turned black in all corners. . . ." Sonya's mangled fate is symbolized by this deserted room with its ill-formed corners. Raskolnikov who has divorced himself from the world, occupies a narrow coffin; Sonya who has turned toward the world, has a "large room with three windows." Svidrigailov remarks to Raskolnikov enigmatically: "All men need air, air, air." The theoretician-murderer suffocates himself in his coffin, in a vacuous expanse of thought. He goes to Sonya in her spacious barn with three windows to breathe the *earth's air*.

Whenever Dostoevsky fixes upon an urban landscape, he invariably introduces "taverns" and public houses. Beneath the shouts of the drunken patrons, midst the smoke and bedlam, his heroes carry on keen ideological disputes, make confessions and decide "ultimate questions." The baseness of these surroundings is pushed to the very point beyond which one passes into a strange piercing lyricism. That which is disgusting and distorted suddenly opens upon itself and reveals unknown beauty. Raskolnikov makes his way down a flight of stairs from the street level to a cellar.

Just at that moment two drunks were emerging from the doors, and with supporting and abusing one another, they clambered up onto the street. . . . Then right behind them a whole troop came out — about five men with one girl and a concertina. . . . The proprietor of the establishment had on a full Russian coat and a terribly grease-stained black satin waistcoat, no tie, and his whole face looked as though it had been smeared with oil just like an iron lock. A boy of about fourteen was working behind the counter, and then there was another boy, younger, who did the serving if anything was wanted. Sliced cucumbers, black biscuits, and fish cut into small pieces were lying on the counter; all of this gave out a foul odor. The atmosphere was so close that it was insufferable even to sit there, and everything was so permeated with the smell of wine that it seems conceivable that one could get drunk in five minutes merely on the air itself.

This tavern forms the world of Marmeladov, the "drunken" civil servant. In the midst of these surroundings that reek of wine, that resound with the laughter and cursing of drunks, he relates his pitiable history to Raskolnikov. It is interrupted by the sounds of a hurdy-gurdy and the "cracked little voice of a seven-year-old child" singing "The Little Farm." The hurdy-gurdy serves to intensify the pathos of the story of Christ receiving drunkards into His Kingdom. "And He will stretch forth His hands to us and we'll fall down . . . and will begin to cry . . . and we'll understand all things! Then we'll understand all things! . . . And everybody will understand . . . and Katerina Ivanovna. . . . Even she'll understand . . . Lord, Thy Kingdom come!"

In force of its religious intensity, this confession of the drunkard in the tavern is surpassed only by the scene in which the adulteress and thief together read from the Gospel. Dostoevsky's lyricism always rises *de profundis*.

Morose Petersburg, the dark streets, the back alleys, canals, channels, and bridges, the many-storied houses in which poverty dwells, the saloons, the taverns below street level, the police stations, the embankments and islands — this is the landscape of *Crime and Punishment*. The reader does not encounter a single "artistic description" or "beauty of nature." Rather he is presented with a formal entry of the "setting of the action" and the businesslike directions of a stage producer. And yet in face of this, the whole novel is diffused with the air of Petersburg, is illumined by its light. The soul of the city is embodied in Raskolnikov. It resounds in him like the melancholy strain of the street-organ. "I love," he says, "when they sing to the accompaniment of hurdy-gurdy on a cold, dark, damp evening in autumn, above all when it's damp, and all the passersby have pale green, sickly faces, or better yet when a wet snow is falling, straight down, without a wind — you know what I mean? and the gas-lamps on the street shine through it. . . ."

Wet snow, street lamps, a hurdy-gurdy — the whole of Petersburg is contained in these magic words. . . .

In their spiritual existence Dostoevsky's heroes are little dependent upon the seasons and changes of weather. Meteorological conditions are rarely indicated in his novels. However, when they do occur, they always mark the transcription of a spiritual state. Natural phenomena, just as the *paysage*, exist only in man and for man. Raskolnikov commits his crime "in the beginning of July, when it was extraordinarily hot." He wanders about the city. "As he was passing over a bridge, silently and calmly he gazed at the Neva, at the *brilliant setting of the brilliant red sun."* When after the crime, the murderer goes to the station house, the sun blinds him:

An unbearable heat had again settled upon the street; in the course of all these days not a drop of rain had fallen. Again there was the dust, bricks, and plaster, again the stench from the little shops and taverns, again one met drunks at every step. . . . The *sun* shone brightly into his eyes so that they began to ache when he looked, and he felt his head spinning round and round — the usual sensation of a man sick with fever when he suddenly goes out into the street on a bright sunny day.

Raskolnikov is a nocturnal being. His small room is almost always kept dark. He is a proud spirit of darkness, and the shadows of gloom have engendered his dream of power. Life on earth, illuminated as it is by the sun, is alien to him; he is cut off from the "consciousness of day." But now the "idea" serves to press the theoretician into action; he has to emerge out of the twilight of abstract thought and enter into life, has to confront reality. The light of day dazes him as it would a night bird. Out of the cold of abstraction he finds himself thrown into the Petersburg summer — hot, stinking, oppressive. His nervous irritability becomes intensified; the embryo of his sickness begins to mature. The sun unmasks his helplessness and weakness. "He is not even capable of murder." He commits blunder after blunder, and as a moth is drawn to a candle, he flies into the nets of Porfiry Petrovich. In Dostoevsky, the sun is a symbol of "living life" which triumphs over the stillborn theory. Raskolnikov enters the old woman's room and finds it brightly illuminated by the setting sun. A terrible thought flashes across his mind: "And so the sun will be shining like this *then* too!" We feel that the criminal's horror when faced with the sun, already portends his ultimate destruction.

Raskolnikov is betrayed by daylight; night absorbs his double Svidrigailov in its dark bosom. The man who has outraged the inviolability of Mother-Earth and severed his ties with the human family, annihilates personality within himself and falls under the power of impersonal cosmic forces. The final night before his suicide Svidrigailov wanders through deserted streets in the midst of a storm and driving rain. The spirit of nonbeing which has become embodied in him discerns a "fateful heritage" in this revolt of the elements. His moral chaos merges with the chaos of nature. The description of this stormy night is the apex of Dostoevsky's "mystical realism."

Up till ten o'clock Svidrigailov stops in at "various taverns and filthy holes"; listens to a street-organ in some amusement park. "The evening was close and depressing. About ten o'clock terrible storm-clouds were to be seen gathering from all sides. A clap of thunder struck, and rain gushed forth in torrents like a waterfall. The water did not fall in drops, but whole streams of it lashed out onto the ground. Every moment there was a flash of lightning, and one could count up to five during the duration of each red glow." At midnight he goes over to the Petersburg side and takes a room in a filthy wooden hotel, but even this little cubicle does not shield him from the raging elements. They pursue him. " 'There must be some kind of garden under the window,' he thought. 'The trees are making a noise. How I dislike the sound of trees at night when it's stormy and dark. A nasty feeling!' " Rain, dampness, water fill him with intolerable disgust. "I have never in my life liked water, even in a landscape." He is tormented by a nightmare: a young girl, whom he has abused, has drowned herself and lies in a coffin surrounded by flowers. He throws open the window: "The wind burst violently into his narrow room and covered his face with what seemed like hoar frost. . . . In the midst of the darkness and the night the firing of a cannon resounded, behind it — another. . . . 'Ah, the signal! The water is rising,' he thought."

The drowned girl's image breaks over him like an inundation. The defiler becomes the victim of water's vengeance. Svidrigailov kills himself in a humid fog on a dirty street that is lined with wet trees: "A dense milky fog lay over the city. Svidrigailov walked along the slippery dirty wooden pavement in the direction of the Little Neva. He began vaguely to imagine the waters of the Little Neva which had swollen during the night, Petrovsky Island, the wet paths, the wet grass, wet trees and bushes." He stops before a house with a tower, and pulls the trigger.

———

The "unity of time" is as rigidly observed in the novel-tragedy as "unity of place." In Dostoevsky's world, time is not measured by the same standards as in our reality. His heroes do not live in mathematical time, but in "real duration" (the durée réelle of Bergson). At one point, time is extended without limit; at another, it is contracted; then it almost vanishes completely. Given their dependence upon the heroes' spiritual exertion, segments of time comprise a greater or lesser number of events. In the course of exposition, time tends to unfold slowly; as the activity rises, the action is quickened, and before the catastrophe it is transformed into a whirlwind. Just as with space, it is humanized and spiritualized to an ultimate degree: *it is a function of human consciousness.* In outlining his plan for *Crime and Punishment* the writer informed Katkov that Raskolnikov "passes almost a month after that [the crime] before the final catastrophe." According to the printed text the interval becomes even more condensed. One finds it difficult to believe that all the intricate and diversified action of the novel takes place within the compass of two weeks. Raskolnikov's story is entered upon *ex abrupto:* "in the beginning of July, when it was extraordinarily hot, toward evening." The author offers an exact account of the days. On the first day, the hero makes an "experimental trial" and becomes acquainted with Marmeladov. On the second, he receives a letter from his mother, wanders about the city and in the Hay Market finds out by chance that the old woman will be alone tomorrow at seven in the evening. On the third day, he commits the murder. With that the first part ends; it embraces the events of three days — the preparation and perpetration of the crime. In the course of the second part, Raskolnikov loses his awareness of time. He falls sick and lies in a coma. "Sometimes he had the feeling that he had been lying there now for a month, other times that everything had taken place that very day." On the fourth day, the hero once again enters reality. The rhythm of time is abruptly accelerated; the events of the third and fourth parts all take place within the limits of two days. Before the denouement the hero is removed from the temporal order a second time. "Raskolnikov now experienced a strange interlude. It was as though a mist had fallen in front of him and closed him off in irredeemable and oppressive solitude. . . . He was absolutely convinced that he was making mistakes then in regard to many things, for example, in the dates and time of certain events." The world loses its objectivity; the temporal and causal bond grows dim in the criminal's consciousness. He no longer exists within the framework of order established in the world. His apathy "like the sickly indifferent state of some dying men" is the beginning of nonbeing.

This contrast between those instances in which the author fixes and determines time precisely and those lapses into a nontemporal order, serves as a subtle artistic device. Raskolnikov, the thinker and theoretician, lives beyond time; Raskolnikov, the agent, enters into time. His crime is the dividing point between idea and reality, and it is set in time in a most exact and detailed fashion.

The novel-tragedy's composition is determined by the third unity of classical tragedy, the unity of action. *Crime and Punishment* is the story of one idea, one man, one fate. All the personages and events are ordered about Raskolnikov. He is the dynamic center: it is from him that the beams go forth and diverge, and their reflections return to him. Out of the novel's forty scenes he takes part in thirty-seven. The two secondary plots, the story of the Marmeladov family and that of Raskolnikov's sister Dunya, have no independent meaning in themselves. They form part of the hero's fate; they are the embodiment of his contesting ideas. The idea that good is utterly powerless and that suffering is absurd is realized in the family of the drunken civil servant. Out of its bosom the image of Sonya rises up. She is the hero's good angel. Dunya similarly embodies her brother's belief that sacrifice is purposeless. She also rises out of the bosom of a family (the Raskolnikovs, mother and daughter), and she draws with her Svidrigailov who is mystically bound to the hero as his angel of evil. The battle between good and evil that is waged within the murderer's soul, is substantialized in the opposition of these two personalities, Sonya and Svidrigailov. Raskolnikov's consciousness reveals itself in three aspects. He is placed before us like a figure out of a mediaeval mystery-play, standing between a good and an evil angel. When Sonya becomes distinguished from the Marmeladov family and enters into personal relations with the hero, the compositional function of this plot comes to an end. It reaches its culmination earlier than Raskolnikov's own story and anticipates the central denouement in its effective double catastrophe (Marmeladov's death at the end of the second part and that of Katerina Ivanovna at the end of the fifth part). Dunya's history also has a double catastrophe (the rupture with Luzhin and the conflict with Svidrigailov). The streams of all three plots are joined only once: at the funeral dinner for Marmeladov, Dunya's former fiancé, Luzhin, insults Sonya and Raskolnikov defends her (the end of the fifth part). In the sixth part the secondary plots are exhausted: the Marmeladov spouses are dead, and Dunya marries Razumikhin. The hero is left with his two mystical companions, Sonya and Svidrigailov.

The principle of the composition is threefold: there is one central plot and two collateral ones. In the course of the main intrigue there is only one external event (the murder) and a long chain of interior events (reflections and perceptions of the external act). In the collateral themes there is an accumulation of exterior happenings that are stormy, effective, and dramatic: Marmeladov is crushed by horses; Katerina Ivanovna, half out of her mind, sings on the street and vomits forth blood; Luzhin accuses Sonya of stealing; Dunya attempts to shoot Svidrigailov. The principal intrigue is tragic; the accessory ones, melodramatic. The central theme ends in a catastrophe; the collateral plots often resolve themselves in what is only the parody of a catastrophe, a scandal: Dunya's rupture with Luzhin; the funeral meal for Marmeladov.

Raskolnikov is not only the compositional, but the spiritual center of the novel as well. The tragedy springs up in his soul and the external action only serves to reveal his moral conflicts. He must pass through an excruciatingly painful split in his very being, must "weigh in his mind everything pro and contra," in order to arrive at an understanding of himself. He is an enigma even to himself; he does not know his own dimensions and limits. He cast a glance into the depths of his "ego" and his head began to spin round before this bottomless abyss. He tests himself, performs an experiment, asks: who am I? What am I capable of? What do I have the right to do? Is my strength great? At the center of all Dostoevsky's novels there stands a man who is striving to resolve the enigma of his personality (Raskolnikov, Prince Myshkin, Stavrogin, Versilov, Ivan Karamazov). In this sense the writer's artistic creation constitutes a unique process and quest for *self-knowledge*. On the surface this process is psychological, but beneath this exterior plane the questions disclose themselves as having fundamental ontological import: the image of God in man, the personality's immortality, freedom, sin. The man who seeks to unravel the meaning of his very being becomes an object of study to those who are about him. Dostoevsky's characters are inborn psychologists and seers. They scrutinize the hero with insatiable rapacity as Porfiry Petrovich scrutinizes Raskolnikov. He is an enigma to them as well, and they never tire of seeking to puzzle it out. Each one of them uncovers some unexpected element, and in his own way throws light upon some new feature. The process of self-examination is complemented by the process of perceptive discernment on the part of others. Raskolnikov is characterized by his mother, his sister, Razumikhin, Porfiry, Sonya, Svidrigailov, Zametov, by almost all the dramatis personae. In exactly the same way all the characters in *The Devils* strive to unriddle the mystery of Stavrogin. Dostoevsky's heroes are spiritual, are pure consciousness. They are tragically divided, but they strive to be reunited with themselves. They struggle and contend against one another while at the same time remain open to a communal synthesis.

In this process of self-examination the personality reveals itself as mighty in the scope of its design ("the image of God") and powerless in actuality (in sin). Its likeness to God lies in its freedom, but this very freedom gives rise to evil as well. "Here the devil struggles with God, and the field of battle is the human heart," says Mitya Karamazov.

A true knowledge of self lies in the acceptance of this struggle, in the resolution of good and evil within the framework of life. This is why Dostoevsky's novels are "novel-tragedies."

Crime and Punishment is a tragedy in five acts with a prologue and an epilogue. The *prologue* (the first part) depicts the preparation and perpetration of the crime. The hero is enveloped in mystery. The impoverished student is afraid of his landlady; we find him in a state of illness that "resembles hypochondria." He goes to a money-lender to pawn his silver watch, and talks about a certain "venture." "I want to undertake a *venture* of those proportions, and yet at the same time I am frightened by nonsense such as this! . . . Am I really capable of *it*?" The word "murder" is not spoken. "My God!" Raskolnikov cries out as he is leaving the money-lender's apartment, "how disgusting *this* all is! . . . Is it really possible that *such an appalling thing* could have entered my mind! . . . Above all it's filthy, obscene, vile, vile!" This "unseemly dream," which for a whole month has filled his being as he sat deliberating in his corner, now provokes within him spasms of revulsion. And so on the very first pages of the novel we find the hero in a state of intense conflict. He does not believe that he is in fact capable of carrying out the "venture." This idea of his is purely theoretical. "I've learned to spout nonsense as I lie whole days and nights in my corner and think. . . . So, I'm amusing myself for the sake of fantasy — toys." The dreamer abhors his own practical inability; the romantic is aesthetically repulsed by the "vileness" of murder. This dichotomy within the hero's consciousness is the beginning of his self-knowledge. Two motifs are struck in the tavern scene with Marmeladov, the endlessness of human sorrow and the inefficacy of sacrifice (Sonya). His mother's letter presses the hero to face some decision. His own sister is preparing to sacrifice herself, having sold her life to the contemptible businessman Luzhin. She is stepping out onto Sonya's road. "Sonechka, Sonechka Marmeladova, eternal Sonechka, so long as the world stands!" Raskolnikov exclaims. And this sacrifice is being made for him. Can he accept it? And if he refuses to accept it, what then awaits him? Poverty, hunger, destruction?

"Or should one renounce life completely," he says, "and docilely accept one's fate as is, once and for all, and stifle everything in oneself having renounced any *right to act, to live and to love?*" The dilemma is posed in its most acute form. Christian morality preaches humility and sacrifice, but Raskolnikov has lost his faith. He is an atheistic humanist; for him the old norms of truth and justice have become lies. He is convinced that humility and sacrifice ultimately lead only to ruin. And what does one do — accept this destruction? Is it possible that man has no *right to life?* It is immoral to transgress the old moral law, but is bringing oneself to ruin and destruction moral? "All this present anguish was engendered in him a very long time ago. It matured and became concentrated, taking the form of *a terrible, violent, and fantastic question.*"

His mother's letter is the turning point in the hero's fate. Up until now he had been lying on his sofa resolving abstract questions; now life itself demands that he take immediate action. The dreamer is caught unawares. For a month he has been amusing himself with his "fantastic idea"; "now it appeared suddenly not as a dream at all, but under a new, frightening, and as yet completely foreign aspect, and he suddenly *became conscious* of this himself. . . . His head began to pound and everything grew dark before his eyes." A new level of consciousness has been reached: the idea is beginning to take on substance. Nonetheless, the hero cannot reformulate his entire being in one stroke. Reason embraces the new "idea," but "nature" continues to live within the framework of the old moral order. Little by little the abstract dream seizes possession of his consciousness. "Nature" struggles with it in desperation, is horrified, strives not to believe, pretends that it does not know it. In order to weaken its resistance, the author introduces the motif of sickness. The hero's pathological condition is repeatedly underlined: after the murder he lies for four days in a state of nervous delirium and this illness perdures through the end of the novel. Thus by his very example Raskolnikov proves the reasonableness of his theory. Did he not maintain in an article entitled *About Crime* that "the act of committing a crime is always accompanied by sickness"? Only illness can ultimately succeed in demolishing the disillusioned romantic's "nature," in overcoming the aesthete's revulsion when faced with the "vileness" of murder. In the end "nature" declares open warfare upon the "unseemly dream." All of Raskolnikov's compassion, all his anguish and horror when confronted with world-evil find expression in his nightmare about the horse. Mikolka beats the nag about the eyes with a shaft, and then finishes it with a crowbar. The hero sees himself as a child. "He begins to cry. His heart rises within him; tears come streaming down. . . . Letting out a scream he forces his way through the crowd over to Roan. He clasps his arms around its dead, blood-soaked head and kisses it, kisses it on the eyes, on the lips." This cruel deed fills him with mystical terror. He sees murder for the first time not as an algebraic symbol, but as blood that has been poured forth, and he is appalled. He too will kill a creature, just as Mikolka did . . . blood will flow — sticky, warm blood. Raskolnikov renounces his plan. . . . "Lord! Why, even if I have the choice, I will not do such a thing. Lord, show me the way that I'm to follow — I renounce this accursed dream of mine." This nightmare that brought him back to childhood, resurrects his childhood faith, and the atheist turns and appeals to God. He had grown up in a religious family. "Remember, my precious," his mother writes him, "how when you were a child, when your father was still alive, you used to mouth your prayers at my knees, and how we were all happy then." "Nature" rejects the poison that is in its system — the thought of crime. Raskolnikov exalts in his deliverance: "Freedom! Freedom! He was now free from that spell, from that sorcery, the fascination, from the temptation." But this victory on the side of good does not perdure for long. The idea has already penetrated his subconscious, and after this final outburst of rebellion it becomes his driving force, his *destiny*. The hero no longer exercises control over his life; he is drawn forward. Mysterious occurrences steadily lead the murderer to his victim. By pure chance he comes upon the Hay Market, and there by chance he learns that tomorrow at seven o'clock the old woman will be alone. "His initial feeling of surprise turned to horror. He did not decide anything rationally, and he absolutely could not reason, but with all his being suddenly felt that he no longer had either freedom to reason or to will."

On the day of the murder he acts mechanically: "As though someone were leading him by the hand and dragging him along irresistibly, blindly, with unnatural force, without objections. Just as though he had fallen like a piece of cloth into the wheel of a machine and it was beginning to draw him into the apparatus." By willing a murder, man betrays himself to the powers of dark necessity. He is stripped of his freedom and acts with the automatism of a person walking in sleep. Everything takes place unexpectedly and by chance: he takes the ax not from the kitchen as he had planned, but from the porter's lodge; he accidentally kills Lizaveta; forgets to lock the door; he has no idea of how to commit the robbery. "It was as though he were in a delirium. . . . He forgot himself. He was not asleep, but in a state of oblivion." The prologue ends with the murder. As yet neither the hero nor the readers know the real reason for the crime.

The *first act of the tragedy* (the second part) portrays the crime's immediate effects upon the criminal's soul. It deals a terrible spiritual blow to Raskolnikov. He comes down with a nervous attack and fever. He is close to madness and wants to kill himself. "What, can it really have begun already? Can *my retribution be this close* already?" He tries to pray and laughs at himself. Laughter gives way to despair. He is summoned to the police bureau because of a debt that he has not paid his landlady. He concludes that his crime has been discovered and prepares to throw himself on his knees and confess everything. In the office his nerves fail and he falls into a faint. This is a fatal moment in his destiny: the murderer attracts the attention of the clerk Zametov and this latter tells the prosecuting magistrate Porfiry Petrovich about the strange student. The counteraction against Raskolnikov is set in motion as a result of this fainting spell, this serves to fasten the first thread of the net in which the magistrate eventually envelops him. The criminal is betrayed by "nature."

In the storm of feelings and sensations that have engulfed the murderer, one begins to predominate. "A dismal sensation of acutely painful, infinite *solitude and alienation* became consciously apparent in his soul." He awaited the punishment with which the pangs of conscience would afflict him; there was none. There was, however, something else: a mystical awareness of his estrangement from the human family. The murderer has stepped beyond something more than the moral law: *the very basis of the spiritual world itself.* After he has buried the stolen articles under a stone, he suddenly asks himself a question: "If in fact this whole thing was done with a purpose and not just frivolously, if you really had a definite and set *design*, then why didn't you look and see how much money there was?" The humanist-dreamer has suffered defeat. He displayed his utter helplessness in action; he grew frightened, committed blunders, lost his head. If in fact he had killed the old woman in order to rob her, then why is he not interested in the stolen goods? Or the deed was perpetrated "frivolously," and the humanistic motivation served only as a pretext. This *crisis* within his conscience is underlined by his illness and loss of memory which lasts over a period of three days. When the hero finally comes to himself, the old man, the sensitive "friend of humanity," has already died in him. Raskolnikov is aware of his infinite solitude and is not overwhelmed by it. He "cut himself off from all and everything as with a pair of scissors." He finds people unbearable. "'Let me be, let me be, all of you,' Raskolnikov cried out in a rage, 'And will you leave me alone, once and for all, you tormentors? I'm not afraid of you! Get away from me! I want to be alone, alone, alone, alone.'" Thus a new consciousness is born — the consciousness of a strong personality, fiendishly proud and solitary. His fear, his faint-heartedness, the sickness have passed. The hero senses a terrible energy that has been aroused within him; he feels that they are suspicious of him, that they are following him, and with ravishing glee he throws himself into the battle. Upon meeting Zametov in a tavern, he casts an insolent challenge at him: ". . . And what if it was I who killed the old woman and Lizaveta?" He experiences "a wild, hysterical sensation in which, nonetheless, there was an element of unbearable delight." He goes to the old woman's house, enters her apartment, tries the little bell, asks about the blood. As he is leaving, he informs the porter of his name and address. This new, forceful spirit which has begun to burn within him, overcomes his body. The opposition of "nature" is broken. The bold fighter remembers his fears and specters with contempt. "So there *is* life!" he exclaims, "My life didn't end along with the old woman's! Grant her the Kingdom of Heaven. And then that's enough, my good lady; it's time you went to your repose! Now the kingdom of reason and light has come! and . . . and will and strength. . . . And we'll see now! We'll try our strength now!" he adds arrogantly as though adverting to some dark force and defying it. The tragic hero throws down a challenge to fate. The new *strong individual* is endowed with "animal-like cunning," unheard-of boldness, a will to live, and diabolical pride.

The *second act* (part three) relates the course of the strong individual's struggle. The author intensifies our new impression of the hero by means of various indirect characterizations. Razumikhin remarks about his comrade: "I know Rodion: morose, somber, *haughty and proud.* . . . Sometimes . . . cold and *insensible* to the point of being inhuman. Really, it's just as if there were *two* opposing characters in him which alternately replace one another. . . . *He sets a terribly high value upon himself,* and not completely without reason. . . . *He doesn't love any-one,* and never will." Pulkheriya Aleksandrovna describes the fantastic plan her son had of marrying his landlady's consumptive daughter. "Do you think," she adds, "my tears, my supplications, illness, my death perhaps from grief, our poverty would have stopped him then? *He would have stepped most calmly over all obstacles.*" Thus Raskolnikov's "second character" is revealed to us as being diametrically opposed to the first. We see that he has deceived himself in saying that he was going to sin for the sake of his mother's happiness; why, he "would have stepped most calmly over" her very death in order to satisfy a simple caprice.

The hero recognizes the fact that Porfiry suspects him, and proceeds to challenge him. He cannot bear inactivity and uncertainty. He is impatient to "try his strength." During the course of his first meeting with the prosecuting magistrate, he expounds his theory of "exceptional people." "The exceptional man has the right . . . that is, not a legally established right, but he himself has the right to permit his conscience to step over . . . certain obstacles." Razumikhin perceives the terrible essence of this theory: "What's original in these ideas," he says, "is that ultimately you are allowing a man to shed blood in accord with the design of his conscience. . . . Why, this license to shed blood according to your conscience . . . it's, it's, in my opinion, more terrible than an official authorization to shed blood, a legal one." What is terrible is that Raskolnikov's theory does not merely negate Christian morality, it goes further; it sets another, an anti-Christian code of morality in its stead. The "strong individual" is not without conscience: he has *his own conscience which authorizes the shedding of blood.* The proud demon is sad in his lonely grandeur. "It seems to me," Raskolnikov says, "truly great people experience an immense sadness while on earth." The whole tragedy of man-godhood is expressed in these few words.

And suddenly the hero founders; after this first encounter Raskolnikov undergoes an utter humiliation. An artisan comes to him, and in a "quiet, but clear and distinct voice" says: "murderer." Who is this man and what did he see? Does it mean that there is evidence against him? Does it mean that he was not ever capable of committing murder? "And how could I, knowing myself, *having misgivings about myself,* have dared take up an ax and soil myself with blood. . . ." No, he is not a strong individual. "I was in a hurry to step beyond. . . . I didn't do away with a human being; I did away with a principle! It was the principle that I did away with, and I didn't get to step beyond. I remained on the other side. . . ." The very fact that he has misgivings about himself and does not believe in his strength, attests to his shameful weakness. No, he is not a Napoleon, but an "aesthetic louse," "even more foul and disgusting than the louse that he has killed." "Oh, the vulgar banality! Oh, the baseness! Oh, how I understand the 'prophet' with his scimitar, on his steed: Allah commands, and you obey — 'trembling creature'!" This crisis culminates in a terrible dream. Raskolnikov takes up an ax and strikes the old woman across her skull; but she inclines her head forward and "breaks out in a quiet, hardly audible laugh." The victim laughs at her murderer: she is alive. He strikes again and again; she laughs more heartily. *It is impossible to kill her: she is immortal.* And yet it was not so long ago that Raskolnikov mockingly bid her final farewell: "That's enough, my good lady; it's time you went to your repose!" Now all the people around him are like corpses, while the dead woman continues to live. He has cut himself off from the living "as with a pair of scissors," but it is impossible for him to be separated from her: they are joined together forever . . . by blood.

The *third act* of the tragedy (part four) carries Raskolnikov's struggle to its ultimate climax. The hero has apparently triumphed, but his victory is only veiled defeat. He awakes from his terrible dream; there standing before him is Svidrigailov, the man who has wronged his sister. Raskolnikov is tragically divided: there are "two opposing characters" within him. The "strong individual" convulsively struggles against the humanist, torturously frees himself from "principles" and "ideals." Svidrigailov is exactly the same as Raskolnikov, but he has already succeeded in completely "curing himself" of all moral prejudices. He is the embodiment of one possible resolution of the hero's fate. There exists a metaphysical similitude between them. "We have a certain point in common," says Svidrigailov, "We are *berries from the same tree.*" They both follow along the same path, but Svidrigailov is more free and bold than Raskolnikov and pursues it to its very end. The student "has stepped beyond," "has authorized the shedding of blood in accord with his own conscience," but for all that he continues to uphold "humanism," "justice," "what is noble and beautiful."

Svidrigailov tells Raskolnikov that eternity strikes him as a country bathhouse: "covered with soot and with spiders crawling along all the corners." The latter asks in disgust: "And really, really, you see nothing more comforting, more just than that?" Svidrigailov answers with derision: is it for him, a murderer, to talk about justice! Can he preach morality! What hypocrisy! Why won't he hand over 10,000 to Dunya from the man who has humiliated her? Why, "the end justifies the means"! Raskolnikov has abolished the old morality, and yet he still clings to beauty, honor and all the rest of humanistic rubbish. Svidrigailov is more consistent: good and evil are merely relative concepts; everything is permitted — all things are one and the same. What is left is universal boredom and vulgar banality. And he is bored. He has amused himself in whatever ways he could: he was a card-sharper, spent some time in prison, sold himself to his late wife for 30,000. Perhaps he will take a flight in a balloon or set off on an expedition to the North Pole. He has visions, the shreds of other worlds, but what crude banalities! Svidrigailov's boredom is not psychological, but rather metaphysical. The ultimates merge together; good and evil are indistinguishable — a deformed infinity, indifference, absurdity. Svidrigailov is not a simple villain: generously he lets Dunya go, he contributes money, helps the Marmeladovs. He tests his freedom in evil and finds that it has no limit. For a time he is engaged by his passion for Dunya. He shoots himself out of boredom. The superman can find nothing to do in the midst of people. His strength finds no outlet, and so it becomes self-destructive.

Svidrigailov is a sensualist. There are terrible crimes upon his conscience: his wife's murder, the suicide of his servant Filipp and of the fourteen-year-old girl whom he wronged. He loves the most filthy debauchery, but his conscience is at peace and he has a "fresh complexion." He is placed next to Raskolnikov to serve as his dark and somber double. He is born of the hero's nightmare; he emerges out of his dream. The hero asks Razumikhin: "You actually saw him — saw him clearly? Hm . . . in that case. But then you know, it struck me . . . it all seemed to me that perhaps this was just a fantasy. . . ." In exactly the same way after his nightmare, Ivan Karamazov asks Alyosha if he has seen his visitor. Svidrigailov is Raskolnikov's "devil."

This meeting with his double marks a new stage in the hero's consciousness. Being convinced of his defeat ("Not a Napoleon, but a louse") he begins to lose his sense of reality. He lives in a state of delirium, is no longer capable of distinguishing dream from reality (Svidrigailov's appearance). Precipitously the action moves on to its denouement.

In opposition to this scene with Svidrigailov stands the scene with Sonya; the evil angel is counterbalanced by the good angel, the "bathhouse with its spiders" by the resurrection of Lazarus. Svidrigailov showed Raskolnikov that the demonic way leads only to the boredom of nonbeing. Sonya points out another way and discloses the image of Him who said: "I am the way." The murderer can be saved only by a *miracle*, and Sonya passionately prays for a miracle. As in the case of the conversation with Svidrigailov, the dialogue with Sonya proceeds to soar to metaphysical heights. Sonya answers the hero's arguments about the absurdity of sacrifice, the futility of compassion, and the inevitability of ruin and destruction, *by her faith in a miracle.* "God, God will not permit anything so awful." " 'But it is possible that this God doesn't even exist,' Raskolnikov answered with a certain malicious pleasure." Suddenly he asks Sonya to read to him from the Gospels "about Lazarus." She believes that "even he, he — though he is blinded and does not believe — now he too will hear, he too will believe, yes, yes, immediately, now." The reading is over. Raskolnikov has received an answer to his mute question: "What is it she's waiting for, a miracle? Yes, it must be. *But really isn't this a sign of insanity?*" The miracle did not take place. The murderer's faith was not restored, and he only concluded that Sonya was mad: she actually believes in the resurrection of a corpse that has been dead for four days!

He calls Sonya "a great sinner"; she is as guilty of damning her soul as he. "You have ruined a life . . . your own (it's the very same thing)."

These terrible five words in parentheses (*it's the very same thing*) are filled with malice and a fiendish lie. To lay down one's life for one's friends is *the very same thing* as destroying the life of one's neighbor! In horror Sonya asks: "And what — and what should one do?" "What should one do?" answers the demon, "*Wreck and demolish* what one has to, once and for all, that's what; and then take the suffering upon yourself. What? You don't understand? You'll understand later. *Freedom and power*, but mainly, power! Over every trembling creature and over the whole anthill!" The reading of the Gospel occasions an outburst of diabolic pride. Ruin and destruction are set in opposition to the Resurrection ("wreck and demolish what one has to"); love of power stands and defies humility; the figure of the man-god opposes the image of the God-man.

The criminal's pride leads him to challenge Porfiry Petrovich to a second encounter. He demands that "an interrogation take place in accord with legal form." The magistrate analyzes in detail his conduct after the murder, enumerates his blunders, and shows that "psychologically he will not run away." The hero's hatred mounts with each minute. At last he can endure it no longer. "'You're lying about everything,' Raskolnikov began to shout, 'you're lying, you damned punchinello. . . . You're lying and mocking me so that I will give myself away!" And suddenly we are confronted with an unexpected peripeteia. Porfiry had intended to expose the murderer on the basis of the artisan's testimony, but instead Mikolka the painter comes and confesses that it was he who killed the old woman. Raskolnikov laughs at the evidence that the magistrate had wanted to produce, at his "psychology that cuts both ways." "Now we will still go on struggling with one another!" he exclaims proudly.

The *fourth act* (part five) marks a slowing in the action before the culmination of the catastrophe. Its major section is devoted to the scene in which the characters gather for Marmeladov's funeral dinner. In the course of this second meeting with Sonya, the strong individual arrives at the final stage of his self-knowledge. With scorn he rejects as "rubbish" the idea that the crime was committed out of humanistic motivations. "Nonsense! I simply committed murder! *I committed murder for myself, for myself alone*," Raskolnikov declares. He performed an experiment; he was resolving the enigma of his own personality. "I had to *find out*, and find out quickly whether I was merely a louse just like everybody else, or whether I was a *man*. Would I be able to step beyond, or not? Was I a trembling creature, or did I possess the right?" He nurtures the greatest possible contempt for the human "herd." This "trembling creature" must be made to submit to the iron rod. The strong individual rises in revolt against the order of the world. . . . "Suddenly it struck me as clear as the sun how strange it is that up till now not a single man has ever dared or does dare, just casting aside all this absurd rubbish, to take everything quite simply by the tail and send it flying to hell. I . . . I wanted to have this daring and I committed murder." Raskolnikov continues the revolt begun by the man from underground ("and hadn't we better send all this good sense flying . . . to hell") and prepares the way for the Grand Inquisitor's despotism. A morality of force leads to a philosophy of violence. The superman is revealed as the Prince of this world — the Antichrist. Raskolnikov summarizes disdainfully: "I wanted to turn myself into a Napoleon, and for that purpose I even committed murder." He concedes his mistake: the man who doubts his right to seize power, does not have any such right, and consequently he too is a "louse" just like everyone else. "Was it really the old woman that I killed? I killed myself." Sonya says: "God has struck you down; He has handed you over to the devil." The murderer actually accepts this explanation: "Why, I myself am aware of the fact that the *devil* has been pulling me along. . . . And it was the devil that murdered the old woman; I didn't do it." Oh, now it makes no difference to him who is guilty of his defeat — the devil or God. Since it is clear that he is only a "louse," why not admit that someone was amusing himself at his expense? Sonya tells him to kiss the ground, to give himself up, "to accept suffering and through it to redeem himself." He does not believe in suffering or in redemption. Sonya's love conjures up "bitter hatred" in him. He will give himself up because he is "a coward and a wretch," but he will never submit himself to humiliation and repent. Once again pride flares up within him: "Perhaps I still am a man and not a louse, and I've been too quick to condemn myself. I will still continue to struggle." He does not reject his theory of strength and power. "Sonya understood that this somber catechism had become his faith and law."

The *fifth act* (the sixth part) presents the catastrophe. The author depicts the parallel ruin of the two "strong individuals" — Raskolnikov and Svidrigailov. The murderer has a premonition of his end: he is in a state of semidelirium, wanders about the streets without purpose, sits down in a tavern, then falls asleep somewhere in the bushes. . . . "The lack of air in all this congestion began to suffocate him." Porfiry Petrovich's arrival resolves this tension. The magistrate analyzes the whole "psychological process of the crime" and gives him an historic definition. "Here we find a fantastic, gloomy business, *a contemporary affair, an incident of our own times,* sir, when the human heart has grown troubled, when the phrase is quoted that 'blood refreshes.' . . . Here we have bookish dreams, sir, here *a heart that has been exasperated by theories.*" As though struggling for air, Raskolnikov asks: "So . . . who then . . . committed the murder?" "Porfiry Petrovich started back in his chair just as though this were completely unexpected and he was astonished at the question. 'What — who committed the murder?' he pronounced, as though not believing his ears. 'But *you* committed the murder, Rodion Romanovich! It was you who committed the murder, sir.' "

After the "strong personality" has been defeated, it is then exposed. Svidrigailov follows in Porfiry Petrovich's place. The latter has pointed out Raskolnikov's theoretical mistake ("a bookish dream"); the former discloses his moral hypocrisy. "No, I'm talking about the fact," he says, "that you go on moaning and moaning now. *Every moment one sees the Schiller in you.* . . . And if you really feel that one shouldn't stand by a door and eavesdrop, but that it is all right to crack open old women's skulls with whatever happens to fall into your hands, for one's own pleasure, then you'd better hurry and set out for somewhere in America! I understand what questions you have on your mind — moral ones, right? The questions that face the citizen and the human being? Well, you just set them aside. Of what interest are they to you now? Ha! Ha! Because you're still a citizen and a human being? And if so, then you shouldn't have butted into this affair. One shouldn't undertake anything that is not for one's own advantage."

Svidrigailov, Raskolnikov's double, laughs at him, just as Ivan Karamazov's double, the devil, amuses himself with him. They both embody a strong individual's doubt in himself. Now the hero is faced with only two possibilities: either to shoot himself or give himself up. He does not have enough strength of will to commit suicide, and so he surrenders to the authorities. This is not a sign of penitence but of pusillanimity: for him punishment is an "unnecessary shame" and "senseless suffering." He reflects contemptuously: "And how can it have come about that in the end I . . . will be humbled, will be humbled through my conviction?"

Raskolnikov goes to Sonya in a state of irritation and gloom, and asks for a cross: "This symbolizes the fact that I'm taking the cross upon myself, ha! ha!" His laugh is blasphemous and shows his hatred for Sonya, who is sending him to this disgraceful end. . . . Remembering her words: "Bow down to the people," he falls upon his knees in the street, but he cannot confess: "I have murdered." He goes into the police station, and comes out again. He sees Sonya standing in the courtyard, and once again goes into the building and at last declares: "It was I who killed the old widow and her sister Lizaveta with an ax and then robbed them."

Raskolnikov's tragedy ends with an *epilogue*. The criminal has now spent a year and a half in penal servitude. Sonya has followed him to Siberia, but nonetheless he "tortures her by his contemptuous and rude manner." Has he changed? No, he is the same — solitary, morose, proud. "He examined himself thoroughly and severely and his obdurate conscience could find no particularly terrible fault in his past, except perhaps a simple *blunder* which might have happened to anyone. . . . *He did not repent of his crime.*"

" 'Well, why is it that my act seems so unseemly to them?' he used to say to himself, 'Because it was evil? What does the word "evil" mean? *My conscience is at peace.*' " In the words "My conscience is at peace," the final truth about Raskolnikov is suddenly revealed. He is in fact a superman. He has not been defeated; it is he who has conquered. He wanted to try out his strength and found that there were no limits to it. He wanted "to transgress" and he transgressed. He wanted to show that the moral law had no relevance for him, that he stood beyond the confines of good and evil, and now — his conscience is at peace. He has not been ruined because "his rupture with mankind has proved a source of torment" for him — oh no, he loves his proud solitude; or because "his nerves did not hold out," "nature surrendered" — all that is nonsense. His strength would have been sufficient. It is not without reason that Porfiry Petrovich considered him a "bold fighter," and Svidrigailov said to him: "You yourself are a thorough-going cynic. You have, at any rate, enormous stuff in you. You can recognize a great deal, a great deal, *but then you can accomplish much as well.*" Nor has he been ruined because of the fact that Porfiry caught him in his "psychology that cut both ways." He is not cowered even by Porfiry. It is only while serving his sentence that he comes to understand the reason for his downfall. "He was ashamed precisely because he, Raskolnikov, had come to his ruin so blindly, desperately, onerously, and stupidly, *through some decree of blind fate.*" This last feature crowns his majestic image. None of his adversaries is worthy of the strong individual; he has but one single enemy — fate. *Raskolnikov has been brought to destruction like a tragic hero in battle with blind Destiny.* But how could the author present this bold truth about the new man to the readers of Katkov's well-meaning journal in the 1860's? He had to cover it by throwing an innocent veil over it. He did this, however, hurriedly, carelessly, "just before the final curtain." While the hero is in the labor camp, just after recovering from his illness, he casts himself at Sonya's feet . . . and he begins to love: "Their sick and pale faces already shone with the dawn of a renewed future, *of a total resurrection into a new life.* They had been resurrected by love." "But," the author adds discreetly, "this begins a new story. . . ." The novel ends with a vague anticipation of the hero's "renewal." It is promised, but it is not shown. We know Raskolnikov too well to believe this "pious lie."

Crime and Punishment resuscitates the art of ancient tragedy in the form of a contemporary novel. Raskolnikov's story is a new embodiment of the myth of Prometheus' revolt and the tragic hero's destruction in the course of his struggle with Fate. But Dostoevsky, the great Christian writer, adds an infinitely more profound dimension to the metaphysical significance of the myth. It is to the Russian people themselves that the author consigns the role of passing final judgment upon the "strong individual." On one occasion "everyone at once fell upon him with fury. 'You're an atheist! You don't believe in God!' they shouted at him. 'We must kill you!' "

This judgment, as it is expressed by the people, conveys the *religious idea* of the novel. Raskolnikov's "heart has grown troubled"; he has stopped believing in God. For Dostoevsky, atheism reverts invariably to the deification of man. If there is no God, then I myself am God. The "strong individual" sought to free himself from God — and he has succeeded. His freedom proved to be infinite. But in this infinity ruin awaited him. Freedom from God shows itself as sheer demonism; renunciation of Christ, as *slavery to Fate*. After having traced the course of atheistic freedom, the author leads us to the religious basis of his world-outlook: *there is no freedom other than freedom in Christ; he who does not believe in Christ stands subject to the power of Destiny.*

X I V

The Gambler
Second Marriage · Life Abroad
(1866-1868)

The short novel *The Gambler* was first conceived in the year 1863 in the form of a story. The author wrote to Strakhov from Rome:

At present I have nothing ready. But a fortuitous enough (in my own judgment) plan for a short story has been worked out. Most of it has been noted down on scraps of paper. . . . The subject of the story is as follows: a certain type of Russian abroad. Note: Russians abroad were a big topic in the journals this summer. All this will be reflected in my story. And also in general it will reflect the contemporary moment (as much as possible, of course) of our inner life. I'm taking a straightforward nature, of a man, nonetheless, much developed, but in every regard still immature, who has lost faith and *does not dare not believe,* revolting against the authorities and fearing them. He reassures himself with the thought that there is nothing for him to do in Russia and consequently there is bitter criticism of people in Russia summoning back our Russians living abroad. But the chief thing is that all his vital juices, forces, impetuosity, daring have gone into roulette. He is a gambler and not a mere gambler, just as the Covetous Knight is not a mere miser. (This is by no means to compare myself with Pushkin. I'm speaking only for clarity.) He is a poet in his own way, but the point is that he himself is ashamed of this poetry, for he deeply feels its baseness, although the necessity of risk also ennobles him in his own eyes. The whole story is the story of how for the third year he's been playing roulette in gambling houses. . . . If the *House of Death* attracted the public's attention as a portrayal of convicts whom no one had portrayed *graphically* before house of death, then this story will without fail attract attention as a first-hand and most detailed portrayal of roulette gambling. . . . The thing, perhaps, is really not at all bad. Why, the *House of Death* was equally curious. And this is a description of its own kind of hell, of its own kind of prison "bathhouse"; I want and will endeavor to make a picture.

Dostoevsky's first concern was to seize the "contemporary moment," to reply to the critical issue ("Russians abroad"); then to grasp the features of the man of the epoch, the representative of a definite social outlook (the man "still immature," prepared to rebel, yet who "does not dare not believe," a man for whom "there is nothing to do in Russia" and whose forces are lost in the "poetry" of a game of chance). In this sequence Dostoevsky's concepts arise: from the apprehension of the "idea" of the present historical moment to its embodiment in a personality. But this ideational-psychological plan was not realized. The novel was dictated hurriedly, improvised in twenty-seven days, and of the original scheme only the "first-hand portrayal of roulette gambling" was preserved.

The author relied on the effect of the subject's novelty and compared the "hell of roulette" to the hell of the House of Death. There was great exaggeration in this: the character of the casinos and the gamblers' experiences could not form the content of an entire novel. Therefore the motif of the "poetry of gambling" is augmented by a new motif: love–hate. Autobiographical material is introduced: memories of the journey abroad with Apollinariya Suslova. The heroine of the novel, Polina, inherits both her name and her passionate, ambitious character. About the dual theme of love and gambling grows up a complicated tragi-comical plot.

A ruined general, Zagoryansky, living with his family in Roulettenburg, falls in love with a Frenchwoman, the adventuress Mlle Blanche; Polina is his stepdaughter; the narrator-gambler, his children's tutor. The enigmatic heroine is surrounded by foreign admirers: the French marquis des Grieux and an Englishman, Mr. Astley. The general awaits his Moscow grandmother's inheritance in order to pay off his creditor des Grieux and marry Mlle Blanche. But instead of a telegram anouncing her death, "la baboulinka" herself, an invalid, but powerful and obstinate, seventy-five-year-old lady arrives at Roulettenburg. Within several days she loses 100,000 and causes havoc in the general's family. Des Grieux no longer aspires to Polina's hand, Mlle Blanche forsakes the enamored general. The narrator wins 200,000, becomes, quite unexpectedly even to himself, Mlle Blanche's lover and, having squandered this money with her in Paris, continues to roam about gambling casinos. The grandmother dies, the general marries Mlle Blanche, Polina recovers from a long illness in Mr. Astley's family.

In *The Gambler* the exterior action — picturesque, varied, dramatic — predominates over the interior. The depiction of characters and analysis of their feelings yields place to the narration of effective and unexpected events. The narrator afterward recalls his life in Roulettenburg as a "whirlwind that swept him up in its vortex." "At times I keep thinking," he writes, "that I am still spinning round in that whirlwind and at any moment again this storm will rush by, sweep me up in passing on its wing, and I will again be tossed out of order and a sense of measure, and begin to spin, spin, spin. . . ." This is how the author defines the *dynamic* character of his work: it is a whirlwind, a storm, a vortex; the moment of crisis when a man dashes out of the habitual rut, loses his sense of measure. A few days determine the fate of all the dramatis personae. "All this was something strange, unseemly, and even tragic," says the narrator. One can imagine that in *The Gambler* Dostoevsky is parodying his own style: all the action verges toward a catastrophe.

The narrator, the young nobleman Aleksey Ivanovich, is seized by two feelings: love for General Zagoryansky's daughter Polina and passion for roulette. Ordinarily an enigmatic hero is placed at the center of Dostoevsky's novels; in *The Gambler* stands an enigmatic heroine. Aleksey Ivanovich declares that "he would like to penetrate Polina's secrets"; he does not know whether she loves or hates him; is troubled by her mysterious relations with des Grieux and with Mr. Astley; with passionate exertion he unriddles the enigma of the proud and imperious beauty. The depiction of the hero's love-hate for Polina bears the mark of the author's personal confessions; Suslova's diary helps us separate reality from fiction. Like Polina, Suslova was in love with a contemptible foreign student Salvador who also promised to marry and then abandoned her. Dostoevsky was tormented by jealousy as Aleksey Ivanovich, likewise found himself in shameful bondage to his beloved. In the name of his hero he portrays his own personal love tragedy.

"It is true," confesses the narrator,

it had been easier for me during those two weeks' absence than now on the day of my return, although on the journey I also felt anguished like a madman, dreamed like one asphyxiated, and even in my sleep each moment saw her before me. Once (it was in Switzerland), having dozed off in my carriage, it seems, I began to speak aloud with Polina, which made all the passengers sitting with me laugh. And once again I set myself the question: do I love her? And once again I was unable to answer it, i.e., better to say, I told myself for the hundredth time over that I *hated* her. Yes, she was hateful to me. There have been moments (and always just at the end of our conversations), that I would have given half my life to strangle her. I swear, if it were possible slowly to plunge a sharp knife into her breast, then, I feel I would have set about it with pleasure. And meanwhile I swear by all that's holy, if on the Schlangenberg, on the fashionable *pointe*, she really had said to me: "Throw yourself off," then I would straightway have jumped and even with pleasure. All this she understands wonderfully and the thought that I realize quite positively and distinctly how utterly she is beyond me, that thought, I am sure, affords her uncommon pleasure. . . . It seems to me, up till now she's looked upon me as that ancient empress who began to undress in front of her slave because she didn't consider him a man. . . . She knows that I love her desperately, allows me even to speak of my passion, and, of course, she couldn't express her contempt for me more than by permitting me to speak unhindered and uncensored of my love.

Let us recall Suslova's account of the journey with Dostoevsky "on fraternal bases," of the painful night in Wiesbaden when she actually almost undressed before him and enjoyed his humiliation; let us remember how skillfully she aroused his passion in order then to thrust him aside with scorn — and we will understand the "slave's" dream of driving a knife into the "empress." But the rejected lover was ashamed not only of his slavery and humiliation, he was tormented that in this ignominy he was experiencing a keen pleasure hitherto unknown to him.

Aleksey Ivanovich admits to his sovereign: "Well, yes, yes, serving as your slave is a pleasure to me. There is, there is pleasure in the ultimate degree of abasement and nothingness! The devil knows, perhaps it is also in the knout when the knout is laid upon one's back and tears the flesh into little pieces. . . ." The repugnant sweetness of falling and disgrace, the sensuality of self-degradation is one of the themes of *Notes from Underground*. In his liaison with Suslova, the demonic force of eros was disclosed to the writer and it clearly illuminated the dark and filthy underground of the soul. In man's heart "the devil struggles with God." The erotic theme in Dostoevsky's work rises from his tragic love-hate. *The Gambler* is its first artistic embodiment. From Polina come the "fatal women" of his novels: Nastasya Filippovna, Aglaya, Katerina Ivanovna, Grushenka.

Passion borders on madness, is aligned with obsessive images: the rustle of a dress, the narrow outline of a foot. "Upstairs in my garret," says Aleksey Ivanovich, "I have only to remember and imagine the rustle of your dress and I'm ready to bite off my hands." In the same way the sensualist Svidrigailov in *Crime and Punishment* is driven out of his mind by one rustle of Dunya's dress. "The outline of her foot is rather narrow and long, tormenting. *Exactly that, tormenting,*" continues the narrator.

Passion is not at all the worship of beauty, the respect of personality; it is irrational, demonic, and destructive. This is a dark affliction, murderous and suicidal. The hero with cynical candor "declares his love" to Polina.

I haven't a single human thought on my mind. For a long time now I don't know what is happening on earth, neither in Russia, nor here. . . . I see only you everywhere, and am indifferent to all the rest. Why and how I love you — I don't know. Do you know that perhaps you're not at all pretty? Imagine, I don't even know if you're pretty or not, *even your face?* Your heart certainly isn't good, your mind not noble, that can well be. . . . Do you know that some day I will kill you. I'll do it not because I'll stop loving you or will be jealous, but I will simply kill you because *I sometimes long to devour you.* . . . Do you know an unbelievable thing: I love you more each day, and indeed this is almost impossible. . . . Savage, limitless power, if only over a fly, why this is also pleasure of its kind. Man is a despot by nature and loves to be a tormentor.

Passion, as the yearning for power over another, can *most naturally* lead to murder. The voluptuous spider devours his victim; thus the theme of Rogozhin–Nastasya Filippovna is indicated.

To Aleksey Ivanovich's proposal to jump off the summit of the Schlangenberg, Polina mockingly responds with a command to tease an important German baron. By substituting tragedy with farce she underlines her contempt for the victim. After her rupture with des Grieux, the "tormentress" comes into the narrator's room — she needs 50,000 in order to repay a debt to the Frenchman. Aleksey Ivanovich runs to the gambling house and wins 200,000. Polina does not take the money. "You're giving too much," she says. "Des Grieux's mistress isn't worth 50,000 francs. . . . I hate you." With hatred she surrenders herself to him, but in the morning frantically she hurls the money into his face and runs away to Mr. Astley. Why? What is this, revenge for an insult? Disbelief in his love? Abused vanity? In the epilogue Mr. Astley reveals Polina's secret to the gambler: she loved him and loves him till now. This unexpected acknowledgment ends the "story of a certain love-hate." But the whirlwind encompassing the hero is not alone passion for Polina. He also knows another "vertigo of destruction" — the passion for gambling. Mikhail Mikhailovich Dostoevsky was astonished that his brother traveling with a woman he loved could be so passionately captivated by roulette But for the writer, love and gambling were mysteriously connected. The twofold challenge to fate, a dual struggle to death itself, captivated the desperate gambler. The intoxication of risk, the atmosphere of the gambling casinos, the greedy crowd surrounding the roulette tables, the heaps of gold, the croupier's cries, the tapping of the little sphere rolling through the notches, the loud palpitation of heart, the foreboding of ruin and hope for "resurrection" — all this base and painful "poetry of gambling" wholly possessed his soul. In *The Gambler* the "hell of roulette" is described in detail, the gamblers' psychology is depicted, fantastic winnings and losses are related. In the name of the hero-gambler the gambler-author tells: "With what trembling, with what faintness of heart I hear the croupier's cry: *'trente et un, rouge, impair et passe,'* or *'quatre, noir, pair et manque!'* With what greed I look at the gambling table along which are strewn louis d'or, friedrichs d'or, and thalers, at the little columns of gold when they are scattered from the croupier's shovel into piles glowing like fire, or at columns of silver a yard high lying stacked round the wheel. Even while approaching the gambling hall, two rooms away, as soon as I begin to hear the clinking of money being poured out, I almost go into convulsions." With what a fevered lyric tone this tirade is written! But most important — it is not a thirst for gain, not a dream of a million, but the sensation of risk, the intoxication of a challenge.

Once the hero lost everything and suddenly in his vest pocket discovered a last gulden. "Then, it appears, I shall have something for dinner!" he thought, but turned back and placed it on manque. "It's true," he adds, "there is *something peculiar* in the sensation, when one is in a foreign country, far from home, from friends, and not knowing whether you'll have anything to eat that day — you put down your last gulden, your very, very last!"

Dostoevsky loved this sensation, loved the *intensity* of the experience, independent of its psychological content. What spasms clenched his throat when he lost his last gulden in a foreign land, a spasm of horror, of despair, or of unendurable pleasure?

In the novel *The Gambler* there are several expressive, masterfully sketched portraits. The Moscow grandmother, Antonida Vasilyevna Tarasevicheva, "alert, vehement, self-satisfied, erect, shouting loudly, imperatively, and scolding everyone," calls to mind Khlyostova of *Woe from Wit* and Akhrosimova in *War and Peace*. The extravagant, capricious, but good and magnanimous old lady loses a 100,000 recklessly, distributes rubles to beggars, tenderly loves the "haughty" Polina, patronizes the poor teacher Aleksey Ivanovich, despises foreigners, making exception only for the Englishman, Mr. Astley. The author was extremely successful with the figure of Mlle Blanche, the French adventuress, greedy for money, calculating, naively cynical, and good-natured. The Germans are described with unhidden contempt. At the table, around the losing grandmother, fawn three wretched Poles, petty swindlers, and parasites, who "hover close to the pani's stacks," flatter, attend, and steal from the distraught old woman. This is a first draft of the scene with the Poles in *Brothers Karamazov*. Of all the foreigners only the Englishman is portrayed with sympathy. Mr. Astley is an eccentric, timid, taciturn, and virtuous. He is secretly in love with Polina, saves her after the catastrophe, gives money to the grandmother, helps the teacher, and all this he does simply, peevishly, without rhetoric. Set in opposition to the awkward and angular Englishman is the brilliant, gallant Frenchman des Grieux, a scoundrel and rogue, arrayed in his "elegant national form. . . ." "The Frenchman's national form," remarks the narrator, "was structured into an elegant form while we were still bears. The Revolution took over from the nobility. Now the most vulgar little Frenchman can have manners, deportment, expressions, and even thoughts of thoroughly elegant form, not having to participate in this form with his own initiative, or soul, or heart; all this has been acquired by inheritance. As for themselves, they can be more inane than the most inane and viler than the most vile." To European form there is opposed Russian formlessness; to German order and French elegance, Russian unseemliness and impetuosity.

The German accumulates for fifty or seventy years and after five, six generations, a Rothschild emerges. The Frenchwoman Mlle Blanche lends gamblers money at interest, calculatingly sells herself to rich admirers, and after a few years she will have a fortune of a million francs. Russians strive to get rich quickly and easily. Mr. Astley proposes that roulette was devised especially for Russians. They are avaricious and prodigal, unrestrained in their passions, and rabid speculators. The narrator ponders over "Russian unseemliness." "Russians are too richly and variously endowed to discover an appropriate form for themselves right away. Here it's a matter of form. For the most part we Russians are so richly endowed that for an appropriate form we need *genius*."

Russian capabilities perish fruitlessly (the fate of Aleksey Ivanovich) in debauchery, passions, chance; senselessly young forces are dissipated. Russia does not have stable traditions, established forms. When will the Russian chaos cease, the Russian cosmos be created? When will there appear a "positively beautiful" Russian "individual"? These thoughts bring the writer to the theme of his next novel *The Idiot*.

The Gambler is a brilliant improvisation; in it are all the merits and faults of this genre. It is composed of heterogeneous material; the author's personal recollections are interwoven into an inventive plot. The effect of the subject's novelty (the kingdom of roulette) is utilized, and in conclusion the question of a *new Russian form* is posed.

Dostoevsky dictated the novel *The Gambler* to the young stenographer Anna Grigoryevna Snitkina. It was fated that the writer's future wife should be first to hear the tale of his love for Polina Suslova.

In her memoirs, Anna Grigoryevna describes their first session of stenography: "He obviously was irritated and could not collect his thoughts. Now he would ask me my name and immediately forget it, then commence walking about the room, would walk for a long time, as if having forgotten my presence." After dictating a few sentences, Dostoevsky asked Anna Grigoryevna to come in the evening. Their work together began. "I got myself ready," she continues, "and Fyodor Mikhailovich commenced walking about the room rather rapidly, on a diagonal from the door to the stove; moreover, coming up to it, without fail, he knocked on it twice. . . . Once, finding himself in a singularly agitated frame of mind, Fyodor Mikhailovich told me that at the present moment he was standing on a boundary and that there were three roads presented to him: either to go to the East, to Constantinople and Jerusalem, and perhaps remain there forever; or to go abroad and plunge his whole soul into roulette gambling, which was so absorbing to him; or, finally, to marry a second time."

On October 29 the last installment of *The Gambler* was dictated. Dostoevsky informed N. A. Lyubimov: "The 31st of October I finished and yesterday delivered my novel in 10 sheets, in accord with the contract, to Stellovsky. These 10 sheets I began and finished in one month. Now I'm starting the ending of *Crime and Punishment.*" *The Gambler* was published in the complete collection of works, Stellovsky's edition, 1867. The writer set about dictating the final part of *Crime and Punishment* to his assistant.

On November 8 Dostoevsky proposed to Anna Grigoryevna. He related his plan for a new novel taken from an artist's life. "A harsh childhood. The early loss of his beloved father, certain fatal circumstances (a serious illness) which tore the artist from life and his beloved art for tens of years. Then there was a return to life (recovery), a meeting with a woman whom he came to love, torments falling to him through this love, the death of his wife and people near to him (a favorite sister), poverty, debts. According to his words, the hero was a prematurely aged man, suffering from an incurable disease (paralysis of the arm), morose, suspicious; it is true, with a tender heart, but unable to express his feelings; an artist, perhaps, even talented, but a failure, not having once in his life succeeded in embodying his ideas in those forms about which he dreamed and always tormented by this. . . . The heroine (Anya) was meek, smart, good, full of life, and possessed great tact in her relations with people. . . .

" 'And is your heroine good-looking?'

" 'Not a beauty, of course, but not at all bad — I love her face.'

". . . The artist met Anya in artistic circles, and the more often he saw her, the more he liked her, the more strongly he became convinced that with her he could find happiness. . . .

" 'Put yourself in her place for a minute,' said Fyodor Mikhailovich in a trembling voice. 'Imagine that I am this artist, that I'm confessing my love to you and ask you to be my wife, tell me what would you answer?'

" 'I would answer that I love you and shall all my life.' "

Dostoevsky's first letter to his fiancée (December 9, 1866) begins with the salutation: "My dear Anya, my darling on her name-day," and ends with the words: "Endlessly loving you and endlessly believing in you, all yours F. D. You are my entire future, and hope, and faith, and happiness, and bliss — everything."

Anna Grigoryevna's mother was a Swede from Finland. From her she inherited grey eyes, her calm positive character, and a sense of personal dignity. She was sincerely religious, even somewhat superstitious, economical, precise, and limited. She did not deceive the writer's trust — all her life she was his devoted wife, self-denying collaborator, passionate admirer. Anna Grigoryevna comprehended little of her husband's ideas, did not share in his spiritual life, but stood as a faithful guardian at the door of his study. To her he owed the relative well-being of the final years of his life, the domestic comfort, the orderly existence. She quietly endured everything, forgave, comforted, worried, supervised, managed the household, raised the children, transcribed his novels, took care of the budget and correspondence, set aside money for a rainy day. She lived only by him and for him; after his death she devoted herself to the cult of his memory.

Dostoevsky's intention to marry was met hostilely by the family of his late brother Mikhail Mikhailovich and the writer's stepson Pavel Isayev. Anna Grigoryevna very dramatically describes her first encounters with the relations. The wedding took place on February 15, 1867. Dostoevsky was twenty-five years older than his bride.

Inviting N. N. Strakhov to the wedding, the writer adds: "I have grown so unsocial after the last year of hermitic life and have been dulled by the 44 printed sheets which I've written in one year, that it was extraordinarily difficult for me even to write this note."

Dostoevsky's second wife was forced to live through the same horror which, ten years before, his first wife Mariya Dmitriyevna experienced; after the wedding, as a result of excitement and the champagne, in one day Fyodor Mikhailovich had two epileptic attacks. "To my extraordinary grief," recalls Anna Grigoryevna, "the fit was repeated an hour after the first, and that time with such force that for more than two hours F. M., by now conscious, screamed from pain at the top of his voice; that was something horrible. Hearing his cries and moans unrelenting with the hours, seeing his face distorted by suffering, completely unlike his own, his eyes madly fixed, not at all understanding his disconnected speech, I was almost persuaded that my dear, beloved husband was going out of his mind." The doctor advised the sick man to go abroad for treatment. He succeeded in getting 2,000 rubles from Katkov as an advance on a future novel not yet begun. But this sum was spent in payment of the most pressing debts and to help the relatives. Then Anna Grigoryevna decided to pawn all her dowry (furniture, dishes) and on this money the young couple went abroad (April 14, 1867). Dostoevsky really intended to be treated; he felt dangerously ill. . . . "You know how I left and for what reasons," he wrote to Maikov from Geneva, "to save not only my health, but even my life. The attacks had begun to recur every week, and to feel and clearly recognize that this was a nervous and *cerebral* disorder was unbearable. My reason was, actually, disturbed — this is the truth; I felt this, and the disorder of my nerves brought me to moments of frenzy."

The Dostoevskys settled in Dresden. The writer as usual worked at night, rose at eleven in the morning, at two met his wife at a picture gallery; they would have dinner at three in a restaurant, then go for a walk in the park and listen to music; at nine o'clock they used to return home, drink tea; and Fyodor Mikhailovich would sit down to work. Anna Grigoryevna in her stenographic scrawl punctually noted down her impressions in her diary; descriptions of historic monuments and famous paintings alternate with the restaurant's menu and an account of purchases.

Dostoevsky was full of hopes and inspiration; he experienced a vast spiritual uplift, was delighted by the spring, loved to listen to Beethoven's symphonies and devoutly looked at the Sistine Madonna. He was mysteriously drawn to Claude Lorrain's landscape, *Acis and Galatea*; the fantastic *paysage*, illuminated by the setting sun, became mystically joined in his imagination with the dream of a golden age. Later, Stavrogin in *The Devils* and Versilov in *A Raw Youth* talk about it as a symbol of earthly paradise. But the author's honeymoon ended with a catastrophe. The idyllic life in Dresden began to tire him; he grew irritable, became angry at German order, was homesick for Russia; struggled with a temptation and hesitated to confess it to his young wife. Finally he revealed his plan to her: they needed money and the only way to acquire it was to go to Homburg to play roulette. On May 16 Dostoevsky set out. He wrote his wife that it was shameful and repugnant to him. God had sent him a beautiful pure angel, and he had cast her aside. . . . In another letter there are new assurances of love: "You usually see me, Anya, sullen, gloomy and capricious; this is only the exterior, such as I always was, broken and corrupted by fate; inwardly it is different, believe me, believe me!"

In a third letter he informed her that he had lost everything, sold his watch, and then won again; and once more he talks about his onerous character: "Even face to face when we are together, I am uncommunicative, morose, and entirely lack the gift of expressing myself completely. *I don't have form, gesture.* My late brother Misha often reproached me poignantly for this. . . . I prayed for you at night with tears, could not restrain myself. . . ." On May 21st there were new losses and a request to send 20 imperials for the trip home. Anna Grigoryevna was frightened by the letter's desperate tone and worried about her husband's health. He answered: "My health is excellent. This nervous disorder, which you fear in me, is only physical, mechanical. Surely it is not a moral disturbance. *And moreover my nature requires this; that's how I'm made.*"

This is an important acknowledgment: lack of money, solicitude about tomorrow were only pretexts. Dostoevsky loved gambling for the sake of gambling, loved its baseness, its terror, its sweet torture. His nature needed this — extreme sensations, the struggle with fate, the foretaste of ruin. Anna Grigoryevna sent money and went to the station to meet her husband. He did not come; he had lost everything and had not the wherewithal to return. He asked her once again to send money for the fare. "My angel," he wrote, "don't think for a moment that I might also lose this. Don't abuse me now to such a degree! Don't have such a low opinion of me. *Why, I too am a man!* Why, there is something human also in me!"

Finally, on May 27 the gambler returned, sullen, preoccupied: he himself was to blame for his failures; he played haphazardly, without a system, wagering only an insignificant sum. If one played coldly and deliberately, there was no possibility of losing. But to achieve this one had to settle in a city where there was roulette, for example, in Baden-Baden. On July 3, having received 500 rubles from Katkov, Dostoevsky and his wife traveled to Baden. Anna Grigoryevna passed the oppressing days in a hotel room. "F. M.," she recalls, "used to return from roulette pale, exhausted, barely keeping on his feet, would ask me for money (he entrusted all the money to me), leave, and after a half-hour return still more disconcerted, for money, and this up until the time he had lost everything we had with us. When there was nothing with which to go to the tables and there was nowhere to obtain money, F. M. used sometimes to be so overwhelmed that he began to weep, got down on his knees before me, imploring me to forgive him for tormenting me with his behavior, would go into extreme despair."

The half-mad, feverish existence continued about a month. Everything was lost. Dostoevsky pawned his wedding ring and won 4,000 francs. Three days later he pawned his wife's earrings and lost. Upon returning from the game, he swore that he would not play any more and, covering his face with his hands, cried like a child. The following morning he again played and pawned his fur coat and his wife's coat; the hotel was not paid for; they subsisted on tea alone. Goncharov lent him three pieces of gold, Katkov sent another 500 rubles. Again roulette and again losses. With difficulty he escaped at last out of "accursed" Baden and traveled to Geneva with a sum of 70 francs. Describing his stay in Baden to Maikov, the writer adds a remarkable sentence: "And worst of all is that *my nature is base and too passionate:* everywhere and in everything I go to the ultimate limit, *all my life I have crossed beyond the frontier.*" In creating his heroes, Dostoevsky realized his own self. The investigation of freedom, the "acquiring of strength" — is the philosophical projection of his personal experience. "All his life" he "crossed beyond the frontier"; they "*transgress.*" Raskolnikov, Versilov, Stavrogin, Ivan Karamazov are fighters, rebels, criminals, tragic heroes, stand "at the ultimate limit," at the brink of the precipice.

But the turmoil of gambling and the horror of poverty did not hinder the writer's intense spiritual labor. He took stock of his thoughts about Russia and the West, about Russian Europeanism, about Christianity and socialism. After his polemics with *The Contemporary* and the clash with Shchedrin and Chernyshevsky, the writer returned to the sources of Russian nihilism and planned an essay on Belinsky. He reworked and rewrote it about five times, and remained unsatisfied; his relations to his teacher and friend, who had turned into his bitter enemy, were contradictory and complex. And so this article never did appear in print.

In Baden-Baden Dostoevsky's final breach with Turgenev took place. It was a long time in coming, even from the forties. The meeting with Turgenev in Baden was providential. Dostoevsky had conceived a novel about the new Russia, was realizing himself as a Russian and Christian, and he needed an enemy, a living concrete personality with whom one could engage in controversy. All his work is an inner polemic, manifest or hidden. For the creation of a positive ideal he had to thrust aside a negative reality. His genius is revealed only in struggle. Its nature is *dialectic.* And here it was destined that Turgenev become the symbol of Russian evil, the embodiment of national and

religious apostasy. In conflict with the author of *Smoke* Dostoevsky's
world-outlook was crystallized.[A]

In the letter to Maikov (August 28, 1867) the writer expounds his
conversation with Turgenev in detail. This is a brilliant dramatic dialogue which seems extracted from a novel.

I went to him in the morning, at 12 o'clock, and found him at lunch.
I'll tell you frankly: even before this I didn't like the man personally.
Most unpleasant of all is that I still owe him 50 thalers from 1857
[1863?], from Wiesbaden (and have not returned them yet!). Also I
don't like his aristocratic, pharisaic embrace when he advances to
kiss you, but presents his cheek. Terrible, as though he were some
general.

Dostoevsky accused Turgenev of *atheism, hatred for Russia, and
worship of the West*. Here is the first accusation:

And these people boast, moreover, that they're atheists! He declared
to me that he's a decided atheist. But, my God! Deism gave us
Christ, i.e., such a sublime representation of man that it's impossible
to understand it without veneration and impossible not to believe
that this is an eternal ideal of mankind. And what have these here
— the Turgenevs, Herzens, Utins, Chernyshevskys — offered to us?
In place of the most lofty Divine beauty, on which they spit, all of
them are so vilely egocentric, so unashamedly irritable, so thought-
lessly proud, that it is simply incomprehensible what they hope for
and who will come after them?

For Dostoevsky, at the center of the world stands Christ, the meaning and goal of mankind's history. The negation of this "eternal ideal"
is tantamount to the destruction of the cosmos and the murder of man.
The second accusation is of Russophobia.

His book *Smoke* exasperated me. He himself said that the main
thought, the fundamental point of his book, is contained in the sentence: "If Russia were to collapse, then there would be no loss, no
disquietude among mankind." He declared to me that this is his
basic conviction about Russia. I found him terribly exasperated by
the failure of *Smoke*. He reviled Russia and Russians unseemingly,

[A] Yu. Nikolsky, *Turgenev i Dostoevsky. Istoriya odnoi vrazhdy* (Turgenev and
Dostoevsky. The Story of an Enmity), Sofia 1921.

terribly. But here what I noticed: all these petty liberals and pro-gressives — preeminently the schools who still follow Belinsky — find their first pleasure and satisfaction in reviling Russia. The difference is that Chernyshevsky's followers simply revile Russia and wish its downfall (preeminently its downfall). But these offshoots add that they *love Russia*. . . .

. . . Turgenev said that he was writing a long article on all the Russophiles and Slavophiles. I advised him for convenience to order a telescope from Paris. "What for?" he asked. "It's a great distance from here," I answered. "Train your telescope on Russia and exam-ine us, or else really it'll be difficult to see distinctly." He became terribly annoyed.

Turgenev, actually, nurtured a complicated, divided feeling toward his country. Potugin in *Smoke* says that he loves and hates "his dear, foul, precious native land," and adds: "Our little Mother Orthodox Russ could collapse into the depths of Tartarus and not one tack, not one small pin would be disturbed by our cherished land; everything would remain most calmly in its place, because even the samovar, and bast-shoes, and the shaft-yoke, and the knout — these our celebrated products — were not invented by us."

Dostoevsky with his morbid and jealous love for Russia snatched out of Turgenev's Catullan formula "I hate and love" only the first part "I hate." He did not want to discern his "I love," the mystical bond of his work with the Russian spirit and tongue, with the Russian people and nature. In his ruthless critique of Russia, Turgenev was a Russian inas-much as he considered that the Russian people "do not spare their personal weaknesses." Blinded by hatred, Dostoevsky forgot that the "petty liberal" who had written *Smoke* was likewise the author of *A Sportsman's Notebook* and *A Nest of Gentlefolk*.

Lastly, the third accusation is of Westernism. "He said that we ought to crawl before the Germans, that there is one common and inevitable road for all — this is civilization — and that all attempts at Russism and independence are swinery and foolishness." Leaving, Dostoevsky, somehow without meaning to, apropos of nothing, came out with all that three months of the Germans had accumulated in his soul. "Do you know what cheats and swindlers one meets with here? Truly the common people here are much worse and more dishonest than ours, and that they are stupider, there is no doubt." "Turgenev turned pale (literally, I'm exaggerating nothing, nothing) and said to me: 'Speaking like that, you affront me personally. You must know that I have settled here for good, that I consider myself a German and not a Russian, and take pride in it.' I answered: 'Though I read *Smoke* and have talked with you for an entire hour, nonetheless I in no way expected you to say this, and therefore forgive me for having insulted you.' "

Brought up on German literature and philosophy, Turgenev considered Germany his second homeland. He possessed a strongly developed sense of gratitude. In the preface to the German edition of *Fathers and Children* he wrote: "I am obliged to Germany in too many things." Underlining his thankfulness to his "zweites Vaterland," he loved to call himself the "Baden bourgeois." But who of the generation of the forties might not repeat these grateful words? And were not really even the Slavophiles themselves educated on Schelling and Hegel?

The writer concludes his letter: "Perhaps you will find unpleasant that malicious joy with which I have described Turgenev to you and how we abused each other. But, by God, I can't help it: *his convictions insulted me too deeply.*" This "insult" served as a reagent for Dostoevsky's "convictions." Opposing himself to Turgenev, the atheist, cosmopolitan, and Westernizer, he was constructing his own Christian and national-Russian world-outlook. But at the base of the discord between the two writers lies a more profound metaphysical irreconcilability. Turgenev was a fatalist lacking in will and saw history as an impersonal, predetermined process. Dostoevsky affirmed freedom of will and the power of the personality. Turgenev wrote: "Is there God? I don't know. But now I do know the law of causality. Twice two is four." Dostoevsky, on the other hand, with a frenzy of despair fought against the law of necessity and by a volitional act "acquired" faith in God. At the end of his life Turgenev arrived at "la résignation, la hideuse résignation"; Dostoevsky, at the "sublime ideal of mankind," Christ.

Their dispute was not a simple literary quarrel: in it is expressed *the tragedy of the Russian self-consciousness.*

In Geneva Dostoevsky visited the "Congress of Peace" and listened to Bakunin's speech. For the first time in his life he saw the real leaders of socialism and world revolution. He was astonished by the poverty of their thoughts: from the tribune, before an audience of five thousand, they openly preached atheism, the abolition of large governments and private property. "But mainly — fire and the sword, and after that, as everything will be destroyed, then, in their opinion, there also will be peace" [a letter to Sofya Aleksandrovna Ivanova]. From Turgenev's Westernism it was not far to Bakunin's socialism. The idealistic romanticism of the forties led to atheistic materialism, liberalism to destruction by fire and sword. Dostoevsky, at last, clearly saw the enemy's face; the idea of "Shigalyovism" rose from his impressions of the Geneva congress of 1867. Now he knew with whom to fight and ardently began to work on plans for a novel. "I arrived at Geneva with ideas in my head," he wrote Maikov. "I have a novel and if God helps, it will come out a big thing and, perhaps, not bad. I love it terribly and will write it with pleasure and excitement." The first drafts are dated August 16, 1867. But work advanced slowly. The Geneva climate reacted on his nerves, Switzerland exasperated him with its self-satisfied banality. At the beginning of October the writer went to Saxon-les-Bains, played roulette and, as usual, lost; in November another trip and more losses. He pawned his ring and overcoat and begged his wife to send 50 francs for the trip back. "My holy angel, Anya," he wrote her, "understand that I'm speaking seriously, that another life is beginning; you will see me, finally, down to work."

Having returned from Saxon-les-Bains, he reread his notes for the novel and sorted out the good and bad. On December 4 he began to "contemplate" a new novel. So the year 1867 ended for Dostoevsky, the year of his marriage, life abroad, roulette, and tormenting work on *The Idiot*.

In 1868 the writing of the novel continued. From the writer's correspondence with Maikov we can watch the gradual development of his new convictions. The criticism of liberalism was sharpened. Dostoevsky followed Russian literature and journalism with repugnance; all this was "baseness and abomination." The Russian liberal was the deep-rooted and conscious enemy of Russia, an inveterate retrograde. "This is the formerly so-called 'cultured society,' a collection of all who have renounced Russia, not having understood it, and become Gallicized — here this is the Russian liberal, and that means, a retrograde." Opposed to Europe were the Russian people who are "immeasurably higher, nobler, more honest, more naive, more capable and filled with another most lofty Christian thought which Europe does not understand with its decayed Catholicism and stupidly self-contradictory Lutheranism." Nationalism was founded on Russia's religious mission.

"A great renovation is being prepared for the whole world through Russian thought (which is intimately linked with Orthodoxy, you are right) and this will be achieved in some hundred years — *here is my passionate faith.*" Russia was conceived as a *Christian monarchy*, resting on the mutual love of the monarch and the people. "Here abroad," writes Dostoevsky, "I have decidedly become, for Russia, a *thorough monarchist*. If anyone among us has done anything, then, of course, it is only he (the tsar). Our people have given and continue to give its love to every tsar and finally trust in him alone. For the people this is a mystery, a priesthood, an anointing." From populism, the loving veneration before the moral qualities of the Russian people, Dostoevsky passed to faith in the Russian idea. Maikov had suggested that the Russian idea was intimately joined with Orthodoxy. The Slavophiles helped him discover it as the idea of an *Orthodox empire.* Dostoevsky united with the Slavophile nationalists of the late formation (like Iv. Aksakov, Maikov, Danilevsky) and his Russian idea became at once aggressive. "In order that this great work be accomplished," he declared, "it is necessary that the *political right* and preeminence of the Great Russian race be exercised decisively and now incontestably over all the Slavic world." And from pan-Slavism it was not far at all to militarism: "I would terribly like," he confesses, "to see political railroads (Smolensk, Kievan) erected most quickly, yes most quickly, *and that there also be new arms very soon."* Russia would bear its image of Christ to the world, but it would bear it on the bayonets of "new arms." The ideology of the *Diary of a Writer* was worked out in the correspondence with Maikov. To the end of his life Dostoevsky could not draw himself out of the tragic contradictions of his Christian imperialism.

Reflections on East and West, on Russia's mission and her national politics went parallel with the development of his religious experience, the intensification of his mystical feeling. Faith in Russia and faith in immortality are two mysterious elements of the writer's soul. He believed in God not because he believed in Russia (like Shatov in *The Devils*), no, the "consciousness he has of being a Russian" was a purely religious manifestation. When his sister Vera Mikhailovna Ivanova's husband died, he wrote her: "Indeed, you believe in a future life, Verochka, just as all of you do; not one of you is infected by rotten and foolish atheism. . . . Never lose hope of meeting together and believe that the future life is a necessity, and not only a consolation." To the deceased's daughter, his niece Sonya, he wrote about the same thing: "Dear Sonya, can you really not believe in the continuation of life and above all, in a progressive and infinite in consciousness, and in the general union of all. But know that *le mieux n'est trouvé que pour le meilleur!* This is a great thought. *Let us make ourselves worthy of better worlds, resurrection, and not death in inferior worlds.* Believe!"

On January 11 the writer sent the first part of *The Idiot* off to Katkov. He was working in a cold room without removing his winter overcoat; complained of poverty, indigence, sickness, exile. On February 22 a daughter Sofiya was born to him. Anna Grigoryevna recalls: "In the intervals of suffering I asked first the midwife, then the *garde malade* to find out what my husband was doing. They informed me that he was on his knees and praying, then that he was sitting in deep meditation, covering his face with his hands." The confinement cost a lot of money; Katkov's advances were spent. Dostoevsky went a third time to Saxon-les-Bains. He lost, pawned his ring and begged his wife to send him the last hundred francs: "Oh, my angel," he wrote her, "I love you endlessly, but I'm destined by fate to torment all those whom I love! . . . Don't consider my request for 100 francs mad. I'm not mad! And also don't consider it depraved; I won't act meanly, won't deceive, won't go to gamble. . . ." On the same evening, he wrote a second letter; he had lost the money received from pawning his ring, but this "base occurrence" inspired him with a "wonderful, excellent thought which [would] serve decisively for [their] common salvation." "Yes, my dearest," he adds, "I believe that perhaps God in His infinite mercy, did this for me, *a reprobate and spider, a petty gambler*, having taught me and saved me from gambling, and consequently, also you and Sonya, us all for our entire future. . . ." The "excellent thought" consisted of asking Katkov for a new advance of 300 rubles, going over to Vevey where the climate was better, of finishing the novel and moving down to Italy. . . . But instead of "common salvation" a terrible grief was awaiting the writer. On May 12 little Sonya passed away. The father vented his pain in a letter to Maikov. It is impossible to read these tormenting lines without being deeply affected.

My Sonya has died, three days ago we buried her. . . . Oh, Apollon Nikolayevich, say, say my love for my first baby was comical, say I expressed myself ridiculously about her in many letters to many people who had congratulated me. For them I was only comical; to you, *to you* I'm not afraid to write. This little three-month-old creature, so poor, so tiny, was already a person and a character for me. She was beginning to know me, to love, and smile when I came near. When with my comical voice I used to sing songs to her, she liked to listen to them. She didn't cry and didn't frown when I kissed her; she used to stop crying when I came near. And now they say to me in consolation that I'll have other children. But where is Sonya? Where is this little personality for whom, I say boldly, I would accept the cross's agony if only she might be alive.

Of the whole Bible Dostoevsky loved the book of Job most of all. He himself was a Job, contesting with God about truth and justice. And the Lord inflicted him, as Job, with the greatest tests of faith. No one so undauntedly struggled with God as the author of *The Legend of the Grand Inquisitor,* no one so daringly questioned Him about the righteousness of the world's order and no one, perhaps, so loved Him. But the Old Testament saint was comforted when new children were born to him and forgot about the dead. Job-Dostoevsky could not do this. The human soul is more precious than the whole universe; what "world harmony" can recompense for the loss of one, be it the littlest and poorest individual? What "earthly paradise" will calm the father's heart whose baby is dead? *"But where is Sonya?"*

Out of the writer's personal grief arose Ivan Karamazov's revolt; "world harmony" flew into fragments because of one "child's little tear." Dostoevsky saw the *person* of his three-month-old daughter, unique, irreplaceable, eternal. And the revelation of *personality* set before him with astonishing force the question of personal resurrection (the theme of *Brothers Karamazov*).

The orphaned couple settled in Vevey. Anna Grigoryevna cried during the nights and woke up from terrible nightmares; the writer worked frenziedly on *The Idiot,* which tired him to aversion. He learned that his letters were being intercepted by the police, that a secret surveillance had been established on him; his longing for Russia mounted to hysterics. In September 1868 the Dostoevskys moved to Italy; at first they lived in Milan, then in Florence. The writer's inner state improved; he visited churches and museums, was enraptured by the paintings of his favorite artist Raphael, read Russian newspapers and journals in the library. All of 1868 was spent working on *The Idiot.*

X V

The Idiot

In August 1867 Dostoevsky wrote to Maikov from Geneva: "I have a novel," but at the same time confessed that "there isn't much yet down in black and white." In October he informed him: "I'm throwing myself full force into the novel, headfirst, staking everything on one card; what will be, will be." Work on the first draft continued until December 4; we find curious details about it in another letter to Maikov (dated January 12, 1868, new style): "Having taken so much money in advance from *The Russian Messenger* (horror: 4,500 rubles), I really hoped at the beginning of the year that poetry would not desert me, that poetic thought would flash upon me and unfold artistically by the end of the year and that I would succeed in satisfying everyone. This seemed all the more likely to me, as always in my mind and in my soul many embryos of artistic thoughts flash and become manifest. But indeed they just flash; and a full embodiment is needed, which always takes place unexpectedly and suddenly, but it is impossible to calculate when precisely it will take place; and then having once received the full image in one's heart, you can proceed to its artistic execution. Then it is possible to calculate without a mistake. . . ."

These self-observations of the writer are corroborated by the notebooks: the idea of the work was born at once in a multitude of concepts ("artistic thoughts"), which contended among themselves; dozens of plans, variants, drafts of the plot, and sketches of the characters rushed to realization. The notebooks—they are a fused mass, fiery whirlwinds. Finally, in a moment of inspiration the *embodiment* (the "full image") was attained: the idea subjugated the material to itself. The further work ("its artistic execution") flowed along quickly: at night the writer sketched the scenario of the novel, and in the morning Anna Grigoryevna wrote out his half-improvisations in shorthand.

Let us return to the letter to Maikov: "Well sir, all summer and all autumn I formed various thoughts (some were very ingenious), but a degree of experience always gave me a presentiment of the falsehood or difficulty or immaturity of such and such an idea. Finally I settled on one and began to work, wrote a great deal, but *December 4th (foreign style) I tossed the lot to the devil*. I assure you that the novel could have been mediocre; but it became unbelievably repugnant to me precisely because it was mediocre, and not positively good. . . . I didn't need this. . . ." Notes of this rejected version have been preserved in the sketchbooks No. 3 and No. 11.[A]

In the first, the author wrote from September 14 to October 27; in the second from October 29 to November 30. On the first page of notebook No. 3 the name Mignon is met. Let us remember that the list of literary projects for the year 1860 already included that name. It is possible that the new novel was conceived by the writer as the story of a Russian Mignon. The idea concretizes: on the second page in the margins opposite the name Mignon is written "Olga Umetskaya," and two pages further on the notation: "The story of Mignon is exactly the same as the story of Olga Umetskaya." Dostoevsky was interested in the new Russian courts and attentively followed trial proceedings. He was very struck by the Umetsky case and he wrote to Maikov: "I so long to return to Russia. Then I wouldn't have to leave the Umetsky case without saying my word, I would publish it." Anna Grigoryevna writes: "I remember that in the winter of 1867 F. M. was interested in the details of the Umetsky trial, which had raised a great tumult at that time. He was interested to the point that he intended to make the heroine of the trial, Olga Umetskaya [in the original plan], the heroine of his new novel."

The Umetsky case was tried in September 1867 in Kashira. The parents were charged with torturing their children. Their fifteen-year-old daughter Olga, driven to despair by their cruel treatment, attempted to set fire to the manor. "She was a blonde of medium height with ruddy face and blue eyes. The expression of her face is childishly shy and concentrated. She speaks softly, is confused and blushes." The image of Goethe's Mignon was joined with the figure of the incendiary Umetskaya. The criminal trial became the starting point of the novel. The writer intended to write the story of a Russian family in order to show by its "unsightliness" the decomposition of the Russian "cultured class."

[A] *Iz arkhiva F. M. Dostoevskogo. Idiot. Neizdannye materyaly* (*From the Archives of F. M. Dostoevsky. The Idiot. Unpublished Materials*). Ed. P. N. Sakulin and N. F. Belchikov. Gosizdat. Moscow, 1931.

In the first version we see a "ruined landowning family (of established name)" who have suddenly appeared in Petersburg. The father is returning from roaming about abroad without any means. . . . "As long," observes the author, "as these people had money, then if they weren't *intelligent*, at least, they were representative. . . . But without money they fall quickly." The abject landowner goes as far as stealing money. His wife is "a person worthy of respect and noble, but without sense." Their elder son is handsome, pampered by the mother, "with pretension to originality"; the daughter earns a living by giving piano lessons, she has a fiancé, an officer, who lends out money on security. In the novel, the family of General Ivolgin develops from this landowning family: the general who is reduced to thievery, his wife, son Ganechka, daughter Varya, and her fiancé, the usurer Ptitsyn.

Their other son is an *idiot*; he was to be the novel's hero. In the family lives a foster-child, Mignon, alias Olga Umetskaya. The roles are indicated: an uncle, "a usurer with poetry," and a "young person" *Héro* (the heroine), with whom the handsome son falls in love. Such is the original list of main characters. In the notebooks, work is concentrated on the construction of a complicated plot and an explanation of the hero's personality.

The "idiot" of the first version is directly opposed in character to Prince Myshkin. This is a proud personality, the spiritual brother of Raskolnikov. The author notes: "The *idiot* received the reputation of an idiot from his mother, who hates him. He feeds the family, yet it is thought that he does nothing. *He has epileptic and nervous fits.* Didn't finish his studies. The idiot's passions are strong, his need of love burning, *his pride excessive;* out of *pride* he wants to master himself and conquer himself. Finds pleasure in humiliation. Those who don't know him, laugh at him, those who do, begin to fear." And so the hero is a strong personality who is humiliated: out of pride he hides his feelings, "conquers himself." A position is found for him in a chancery; for three days he goes and transcribes papers, but the affair ends with a scandal: "He quarreled and left; he was tempted, in that everybody trembles before the director, right there to spit in his puss. . . ."

But the proud individual's pretended humility did not satisfy the author; he introduced the motif of *fortune* (the idea of Prokharchin, Raskolnikov, Arkady Dolgoruky).

A great deal of money falls into the idiot's hands. He is accused of theft and driven out of the house; he is friends with the adopted child

Mignon. "The idiot talks, feels, and looks like a master. Fortune. Mignon hides and watches the money. He and Mignon day and night on the streets of Petersburg. For three days they roam about. . . . In the rain, in the cold, at night they discuss gold, riches."

The "selfness" of the strong personality, the proud affirmation of his own "I" must manifest itself in love. . . . The "idiot" is in love with the cousin of his sister's fiancé. "This love is both love and the highest satisfaction of pride and vanity; this is the ultimate degree of ego, this is its kingdom. . . ." "His love is strange: it is purely an immediate feeling, without any reflections. He does not dream and doesn't calculate, for example, whether she'll be his wife, whether this is possible, etc. It is enough for him to love. . . . Finally, he begins not to notice reality. . . . Pride leads him even to the point that he does not notice that she doesn't pay any attention to him: 'I don't care, why I love for myself.' The ultimate manifestation of pride and egoism. . . . She instinctively does not believe his love, and consequently also doesn't pay any attention to it. In essence, if she doesn't understand, she then somehow feels that this is limitless selfness and that he needs her in order to reinforce his personal self-definition."

The idea of the covetous knight ("fortune") is combined with the idea of love-egoism. In this variant the "idiot" comes near to the hero of the story The Meek One.

In the following plan, the motif of oppression and humiliation returns: "Oppressed. He is ashamed of everyone and everything, of his secret sensations, is wild, oppressed. He acts basely from viciousness and thinks that it should be so. In pride he seeks a way out and salvation. He ends by performing a divine act. . . ." But the theme of "oppression" did not please the author; he criticizes himself. "If he's simply oppressed—there'll be nothing but one who is oppressed. An old theme, worn out, and everything important and the new idea of the novel will be lost. But proceed in this way—1) oppressed, and 2) show what sort of man was oppressed. In the first place, oppressed, in the second, the immediate thirst for life and self-definition in self-pleasure. . . . He has transformed pride itself into poetry and brought pleasure to its apotheosis. Love thrusts him for the first time onto a new road. But love for a long time contends with pride and, finally, itself is turned into pride. This wild pride captivates Héro (although she also sees that, given the occasion and in his ultimate development, he is ready even for crime). . . . N. B. and chiefly: it is necessary that the reader and all the characters of the novel understand that he is capable of *killing Héro,* and that all wait for him to kill her. . . . And, lastly, *third*—the immediate force of development leads him finally to a view and a way."

The theme of "selfness" is developed: love-egoism can drive a man to murder his beloved. In this plan the "idiot" is close to Parfyon Rogozhin. The author ascribes to him the *possibility* of that crime which Nastasya Filippovna's lover commits. The way of salvation is indicated for the proud personality. The "idiot" possesses a vital force, asserting itself in the thirst for pleasure, an immediate force which sustains him through all his falls and leads him "to a way." The "Karamazov" elemental vitality saves him from ruin. We again meet with Dostoevsky's mystical naturalism, with his faith in the natural grace of life. But it still remains unclear how life "will save" the hero, with what "divine act" he will end.

A new thought occurred to him: to begin the novel from the place at which *Crime and Punishment* was concluded, to fulfill the promise given there to depict the "resurrection" of the strong personality. The writer notes down: "He could have evolved into a monstrosity, *but love saves him.* He is permeated by a most profound compassion and pardons mistakes. In exchange he acquires a high moral sense in development and accomplishes an heroic exploit." In the following plan this idea takes form. The idiot's "villainy" is underlined. "*The definite plan of the novel. Plan on Iago.* With the character of the idiot—Iago. But finishes in a divine way. Renounces, etc. He slandered everyone, intrigued regarding all, got his way, took money and the fiancée, renounced everything." An effective plan: a villain who finishes in a divine way. The idiot's new characteristics are: an *exceptional* man; stealthy, cold, envious, vindictive, like Shakespeare's Iago. His "passion is like steel, a cold razor, the maddest of the mad." He burns his finger in order to demonstrate his power to the heroine; a cunning intriguer, he steals the legitimate son's fiancée from him. And suddenly—a full regeneration and resurrection. . . . How does it take place? Love for Héro did not seem a sufficient reason to the author; he complicated it with a new motif. Wronged by the idiot, the legitimate son overcomes him by his meekness and total forgiveness. An intrigue is indicated in which it is already possible to view a misty outline of the plot of the novel *The Idiot.* The hero is a natural son. "Traveled with the son (legitimate). They became friends. The natural son knows that this is the son. The son has only heard of the existence of a bastard. Timid and somber at the meeting with the general's family. An incident: he knocked his head. Hid himself. Disappeared. Everyone: what a strange fellow he is. Son: yes, but he didn't appear stupid to me. He's strange, it's true. A real holy-fool."[1] We recognize here the meeting of Myshkin with Rogozhin in the train, the prince's appearance in the family of General Yepanchin, his awkwardness and strangeness ("He knocked his head, hid himself"—but in the final version, broke a vase). The hero's main trait has been found: *he is a holy-fool!* But under the holy-folly there is still concealed a proud personality, a "villain." The theme of righteousness has risen, but it is still attributed to the legitimate son. In this way the future Ganya Ivolgin fulfills the functions of the future Prince Myshkin, while Prince Myshkin is still not separated from Rogozhin ("maddest of mad passions").

"Though the idiot has slandered the son, yet strangely, the son is simpleminded (Fedya) and by his simplemindedness enchants the idiot more and more. In the end, by his so meekly forgiving him. The idiot falls in love with the son, though he also laughs at himself."

Thus are marked out the relations between Myshkin (the son) and Rogozhin (the idiot). With difficulty Dostoevsky opened up a road for himself in the labyrinth of complicated variants.

Toward the end of October 1867 the scheme of the plot was determined. At the center stood *Héro* (the future Nastasya Filippovna); for her there compete: the uncle (the future Totsky), the idiot (the future Prince Myshkin), the uncle's son (the future Rogozhin), Ganechka (here his name appears for the first time) and the general (the future Yepanchin). The author notes this important stage in his work: "Remark. Well, here now is a new road; where will it lead?" The hero is still not embodied in a "full image." What is his idea? How does one show him as a representative of the contemporary generation? There follows a series of notes, making the idiot's personality more precise historically and philosophically. His idea is *force without faith, power without application.* "The whole novel is the struggle of love with hate." The author writes: "A young specimen, a man in the process of formation. . . . The main thought of the novel: so much power, so much passion in the contemporary generation and they don't believe in anything. Unlimited idealism with unlimited sen-

---

[1] "Holy-fools" or "holy-fools in Christ" (in Russian *yurodivye*) are a category of Eastern saints who, in order to vanquish spiritual pride and concern for human esteem, voluntarily feign imbecility as an heroic feat or exploit (*podvig*) and expose themselves to humiliations. Frequently "holy-fools" have been endowed with the gift of prophecy and have been the voice of justice and truth. Westerners are perhaps most familiar with this image through the character of the "fool" in *Boris Godunov.*

sualism. . . . Ergo, the entire problem is that such a colossal and anguishing nature (inclined to love and revenge) needs life, passion, a task, and corresponding aim. . . . From childhood it needed more beauty, more beautiful sensations, more encompassing love, more education. But now: thirst for beauty and an ideal and at the same time no faith in it, or faith, but there is no love for it. Even the devils believe and tremble." This plan is continued in notebook No. 11. And so, the idiot is a representative of the "contemporary generation," a *great, idle power,* exhausting itself in inactivity. From boredom he "contrives all this slop, all this vaudeville." The Russian man does not have either family or historical traditions; his thirst for beauty is not satisfied, he does evil in order to "dispel ennui." The idea of the novel is illuminated religiously: the tragedy of the young generation is in its *disbelief.* After the pragmatic schema there is outlined the psychological schema. "At first: 1) vengeance and self-love (vengeance not for anything, he himself acknowledges this, and this is a trait). Then: 2) furious and unmerciful passion. 3) Higher love and renovation."

A day later the author noted down, "No good. The principal thought about the idiot isn't coming out." In reality, there is nothing new in this "superfluous man"; the hero, anguishing and idle, contriving a "vaudeville" out of boredom, is a banal romantic type. How will his "unmerciful passion" be transformed into "higher love"? How to show his "colossal nature"? How to save this new Pechorin?[2]

Notebook No. 11 is filled with variants which go still further away from the theme of Prince Myshkin, and approach the theme of Stavrogin. Dostoevsky was absorbed by the tragic fate of the "strong individual." The action is developed in the direction of the plot of *The Devils.* The idiot is a demonic personality. Like Stavrogin, "he is morbidly proud to such a degree that he cannot not consider himself a god, and at the same time he so lacks self-esteem (he so clearly analyzes himself), that he cannot not intensely despise himself endlessly and to the point of falsehood." "He arrives apathetic, purposeless enough, filled with inner grief. A Christian and at the same time does not believe." "In his development and from the surrounding milieu he has drawn all these poisons and principles which have entered his blood." "A terribly proud and tragic figure." "He is actually noble, perhaps, even

[2] Pechorin is the central character in Lermontov's novel *Hero of Our Time* (1840). He is the type of the romantic-realist hero, misunderstood, suffering from acute boredom, who is unable to channel his positive, creative energies, remains superfluous, self-centered, and ultimately destructive. The figure of Pechorin exercised enormous literary influence upon the following generations.

great and in a real way proud, but is not able to restrain himself, to be in a real way great and proud, although he also fully recognizes genuine pride and greatness." " 'You will end with either a great crime or a great exploit!' the son says to him. 'God grant it!' he answers quite seriously. 'But, undoubtedly, with nothing. . . .' " The theme of "humiliation and villainy" is discarded: the author imperceptibly passes to a completely different idea—the problem of greatness. The great personality, noble, heroic, falls into evil; greatness passes over into fiendish pride, unassuaged love into hatred, ungratified thirst for activity into malice. The strong personality stands at a cross-roads: either an heroic exploit ("to die for all on the cross") or a crime ("I will hold everyone under foot in chains"). But more truly, like Stavrogin, he will accomplish nothing. . . . At first Dostoevsky wanted to show the greatness of his hero only in his love for Héro; then he felt that passion alone was not enough, and devised the motif of a *secret marriage*. The hero was married off to a girl who had had a child. It was thought that he would not suspect her sin, but he knew that a child was being kept hidden, and went with Umetskaya and caressed it. . . . "At first he ran after and attracted Héro, then renounced Héro, because he came to love his wife with *lofty compassion*. But torments her." "Condemns himself of injustice, and the fact that he married out of compassion, out of a lofty feeling, even this he does not regard as of any value to himself." From the confused variants it is possible to distinguish the scheme of the plot of *The Devils*. The idiot is Stavrogin, his wife is Marya Timofeyevna, *Héro* is Liza. And nonetheless several new traits connect the hero with Prince Myshkin: "He is the Uncle's legitimate, but not acknowledged son. Idiot. Married him at the Umetskys. Then the Uncle sent him to Switzerland." "The idiot captivates all by his childish naiveté." Finally, an important note: "He is a *prince*. Idiot. Everything on vengeance. A humiliated creature. The prince is a holy-fool (he with the children)." Myshkin's image is overwhelmed by the image of Stavrogin, but in our eyes there begins its slow liberation. The holy-fool–prince, surrounded by children, is the germ of a new conception, the birth of a new hero.

The last plan is dedicated to the unfolding of this new design. The theme of *The Devils* begins to fade, that of *The Idiot* returns. The holy-fool–just-man in desperate struggle overcomes the demon who has seduced him—Stavrogin. "The character of the idiot. An eccentric, marked by peculiarities. . . . He will sometimes suddenly begin to lecture everyone about future bliss. . . . A son rejected from childhood, the idiot has acquired a passion for children. There are children with him everywhere. The idiot and the woman in childbirth. Went to a 12-year-old boy to ask pardon. . . . Chiefly — the character of his relationship to children. . . . The idiot with children. First conversation (And we thought that you were so boring!), about Fyodor Ivanovich, about Mont-Blanc, about Switzerland, about the story of a certain teacher and a boy, about the existence of God, and finally, about a ward-fiancée, of her future position, reconciles her with the children. An alliance is concluded. . . . An entire flock has collected about the holy-fool. For example: he has somewhere or other on Peterburgskaya a boy. . . . He goes to him (all for the children). . . . Necessary: exhibit the idiot's character masterfully. In the 3rd part of *The Idiot*—children's nursery and a room for women (women's toil). Some of them sleeping in and others coming every day."

We recognize Prince Myshkin surrounded by the school children in Switzerland and reconciling them with the unfortunate Marie. In the final text of the novel, the "children's theme" is ascribed to the past; from the children surrounding the Prince only Kolya Ivolgin remains; the projected shelter and workshop was abandoned. The "union" with the children and the creation of a brotherhood was laid aside until *The Brothers Karamazov*. There another friend of children—Alyosha Karamazov—realizes the idea of Myshkin. In the last notes appear motifs that are familiar to us through the novel: the slap given the idiot and Holbein's painting. "If the idiot came, then without fail a slap in the face. . . . Up until the slap itself everyone laughs at the idiot and he is held in terrible disdain."

In the second part of the novel, Rogozhin shows Myshkin a copy of the Basel *Crucifixion of Christ* by Holbein, and the latter exclaims: "Why, some people's very faith could be shattered by this painting!" In notebook No. 11 the holy-fool Umetskaya reflects upon the crucifixion. She "was absorbed in reading the Gospel, and in madness preaches: 'Death on the cross disconcerts reason. But he has overcome reason too.' 'What is this—a miracle?' 'Of course, a miracle, but, besides. . . .' 'What?' 'There was, besides, a terrible cry,' 'What sort of cry?' 'Eloï! Eloï!' 'Then this is the eclipse.' . . . 'I don't know, but it is a terrible cry.' " . . . "The story of the Basel Holbein of Christ. . . ." in the novel Prince Myshkin tells about a peasant who slit his friend's throat while uttering a prayer. In the *Moscow Gazette* of November 5, 1867, Dostoevsky had read about the case of a peasant Balabanov who had killed the artisan Suslov. They were drinking and taking a bite together, and Suslov showed the other his silver watch. "When Suslov prepared to set up the samovar, Balabanov took a kitchen knife from the table, approached Suslov, and, with the words: 'Bless, O Lord; forgive me for Christ's sake,' slit his throat." Balabanov was a peasant of Yaroslav Province, *Myshkin* district. Such is the origin of Prince Myshkin's surname.[3]

The eleventh notebook ends with the remark (November 30, 1867): "Detailed arrangement of the plan and *begin* work in the evening." On December 4 everything was "tossed to the devil." Was it not because for the author Prince Myshkin's birth was an unexpected, miraculous event which at a stroke destroyed all his previous work? The new hero required a new novel, the old plans proved useless. In a moment of illumination the writer suddenly *saw* the idea which until then had only flashed uncertainly before him. *He must depict a beautiful individual.*[4] Till now he had been developing a *dynamic* concept according to which the image of God was not a gift given to man but a task which he had to accomplish; at the price of terrible trials, sufferings and struggle, perhaps even through sin and crime, the strong personality was to uncover in himself the image of God, and attain sanctity. He did not succeed with this conception: with torment verging on despair, he exerted himself to "formulate a beautiful individual." But the Christian mystery of salvation was replaced by the tragedy of fate. The more profoundly he penetrated the mystery of human "selfness," the more uncertain and misty this ascent *ad astra* appeared to him. The strong personality was demonic: rising to the consciousness of his divinity, he revolts against God. Before this open abyss Dostoevsky stopped. Stavrogin's line was sharply broken off.

There remained a *static* conception: a personality already born "beautiful": the image of God would gleam in it from the beginning, like a *gratia gratis data.* Set in opposition to the strong individual without grace, *earning* sanctity in the sweat of his brow, is the grace-filled image of the innate just-man.

Having on the fourth of December rejected the plans of notebooks No. 3 and No. 11, in two weeks Dostoevsky planned a new novel. Let us return to the letter to Maikov of January 12, 1868:

Well, what was I to do? Why, it was the 4th of December (And I had taken money in advance from Katkov and promised the novel for the January issue!) After that (since my entire future depended

---

[3] It might also be noted that in Russian *mysh* means "mouse."
[4] *Prekrasny* means morally beautiful, excellent.

on it), I began to wrestle with the creation of a *new novel*. I thought from the 4th to the 18th of December (new style) inclusive. On the average, I think, there emerged about six plans (not less) daily. My head was turned into a mill. How I didn't go mad, I don't understand. Finally, on December 18th, I sat down to write my new novel; on January 5th (new style), I sent off five chapters of the first part (about 5 sheets) to the editors with the assurance that on January 10th (n. style) I would send out the remaining two chapters of the first part. Yesterday, the 11th, I sent out these two chapters and so have sent off the entire first part—about 6 to 6½ printed sheets. On the whole I simply don't know myself what sort of thing I've sent. But as far as I can have an opinion—a thing not very pretty and by no means effective. For a long time now a certain idea has tormented me, but I've been afraid to make a novel out of it, because the thought is too difficult and I'm not ready for it, although the thought is most tempting and I love it. This idea is —*to portray a wholly beautiful individual.* There can be, in my opinion, nothing more difficult than this, in our age especially. . . . This idea has issued even before in some artistic form, but indeed only *in part*—and the whole is necessary. Only my desperate situation compelled me to use this premature thought. I took the kind of risk one takes at roulette: "perhaps, it will develop under my pen." This is unforgivable. . . . The whole thing presents itself to me under the aspect of the *hero*. This is the way it's been set up. I am obliged to construct an image. Will it develop under my pen?

And so, the "beautiful individual" was born prematurely almost against the author's will: if it were not for his "desperate situation," he would not have "risked" putting this "premature thought" as the foundation of the novel. And, actually, the image of Prince Myshkin bears traces of *not being fully embodied.*

Further on, Dostoevsky relates that four heroes have appeared in his novel. "Of them," he continues, "two are strongly delineated in my *soul* [probably, Rogozhin and Nastasya Filippovna], one has still not been completely delineated [apparently, Aglaya] and the fourth, i.e., the main, i.e., my primary hero [Myshkin]—*is extraordinarily weak.* Perhaps he does not sit weakly in my heart, but he is terribly difficult."

This confession after the conclusion of the first part is astounding! The prince still remained "weakly delineated," and his ultimate fate was unclear to the author. His figure developed in the process of writing. Almost up until the very end of the novel his final secret was impenetrable to his creator. All the great writer's genius is in his relation to his heroes as authentic living personalities. His creative act is involved in the mystery of birth: a son's personality is not clear even to his father.

Dostoevsky concludes the letter: "The first part is, in the main, only a simple introduction. One thing is necessary: that it excite curiosity, if only some, for what follows. . . . In the second part, everything must be established definitely (but it will still be far from being explained). . . . *The novel is called 'The Idiot.'*"

The author's concern regarding interest is very characteristic. The reader's curiosity must be aroused from the very beginning and maintained until the end. Characters and events at first are strongly "delineated," then "established definitely," but enigma surrounds them until the very finale, and the mystery is "explained" only at the denouement. Such is the ordinary technique in the construction of Dostoevsky's novels. The author was not at all assured of himself. "The first part, in my opinion, is weak," he confesses in the middle of the letter, and at the end declares: "Perhaps even the first part is not bad." With such harshness he judges one of his greatest creations.

On the day following the letter to Maikov he wrote to his niece, S. A. Ivanova (1/13 January 1868). The idea of the "beautiful individual" is here defined *religiously:*

The main thought of the novel is to depict a *positively beautiful individual.* There is nothing more difficult than this on earth and especially at present. All writers, not only ours, but even all Europeans, who but undertook the depiction of the *positively* beautiful, have always had to give up. Because this task is immeasurable. The beautiful is an ideal, but neither our ideal nor that of civilized Europe has been in the least perfected. On earth there is only one positively beautiful person—Christ, so that the appearance of this immeasurably, infinitely beautiful person is, of course, an infinite miracle in itself. (The entire Gospel of John is in this sense: it finds the whole miracle in the *incarnation* alone, in the manifestation of the beautiful alone.) But I have gone on too long. I will mention only that of the beautiful characters in Christian literature the most finished is Don Quixote; but he is beautiful simply because at the same time he is also comic. Dickens' Pickwick (an infinitely weaker conception, but nonetheless vast) is likewise comic, and because of that alone captivates us. Compassion appears toward the beautiful that is mocked and does not know its own value, and, consequently, sympathy appears in the readers. This arousing of compassion is the secret of humor. Jean Valjean is also a powerful attempt, but he excites sympathy through his terrible misfortune and the injustice of society toward him. I have nothing comparable, decidedly nothing, and therefore I'm terribly afraid that it will be a positive failure. . . . The second part, to which I'm sitting down today, I will finish in a month (I have worked this way my entire life). It seems to me that it'll be somewhat stronger and more capital than the first.

The depiction of a "positively beautiful individual" is a prodigious task. Art can approach it, but not solve it, for the beautiful individual is a saint. Sanctity is not a literary theme. In order to create the image of a saint, one has to be a saint oneself. Sanctity is a miracle; the writer cannot be a miracle-worker. Christ only is holy, but a novel about Christ is impossible. Dostoevsky was facing the problem of religious art which tormented poor Gogol to death. He sought predecessors in world literature: he recalled Dickens with his Pickwick, Victor Hugo (Jean Valjean), and especially the brilliant creator of Don Quixote, Cervantes. The new novel would be written like a *Russian Don Quixote* of its kind. The mournful figure of the knight without fear and reproach bends over the cradle of Prince Myshkin.

The writer began to ponder the second part on January 1/13, 1868. The first notation in notebook No. 10 is dated March 7. During January and February he wrote and sent off to the *Russian Messenger* 11½ printed sheets. On March 2 he informed Maikov: "I've still not begun the 3rd part of the novel [in the final edition, the second] which I gave my word of honor to deliver to the editors by April 1st, our style; last night the whole plan of the 3rd and 4th parts was radically changed (for the third time now); the disorder of my nerves has increased and the number and violence of my fits—in a word, this is my situation."

Maikov encouraged him with the news that the beginning of the novel was successful; the writer implored him to communicate to him as soon as possible his opinion about the finale of the second (in our text, the first) part, i.e., about the soirée at Nastasya Filippovna's home. "This finale," he adds, "I wrote with inspiration, and it cost me two fits in a row. . . . As for *The Idiot*, I am so afraid, so afraid, that you cannot imagine. Even a kind of unnatural fear. It's never been like this before." Almost a month went by; Dostoevsky was absorbed in family cares (the birth of his daughter) and wrote "not a single line." On April 9 he complained to Maikov: "I work and nothing gets accomplished. I only tear it up. I'm in the most terrible depression; nothing will emerge. . . . The day before yesterday I had a very strong attack. But yesterday I nonetheless wrote in a state not unlike madness. Nothing comes out."

In May his daughter Sonya died; the unhappy father wrote S. A. Ivanova from Vevey: "In spite of all my grief, this entire month I have sat day and night at my novel (and how I cursed work, how unpleasant and repugnant it was to write!) and wrote very little. . . . Until now, the second part still drags on." It was finished and printed in the July issue of the *Russian Messenger*.

The third part was no less agonizing to write. "I'm discontent with the novel to the point of aversion," the author informed Maikov (August 2, 1868). "I've striven desperately to work and have not been able: my soul is indisposed. Now I will make my last efforts on the third part. If I set my novel right, I'll recover myself, if not then I'm ruined." Three months later he wrote S. A. Ivanova from Milan: "In two months the year ends, and of the four parts of the novel that I'm writing, a total of three are finished, while the fourth, the longest, is still not even begun. Lastly (and my main concern) is that this fourth part and its conclusion is the most important thing in my novel, i.e., the whole novel was almost both written and conceived for the novel's denouement."

The catastrophe (Nastasya Filippovna's murder by Rogozhin) is the most important thing in the novel: the action is carried toward it in a broad torrent that continually accelerates; the composition becomes intelligible only from the denouement; it is directed to a goal. The idea of *The Idiot* became finally clear to the author only in his work on the fourth part. He wrote Maikov (October 26): "Now, when I see everything, as in a mirror, I'm bitterly convinced that never before in my literary life have I had a single poetic thought that was better and richer than that which has now become clear to me in a most detailed plan for the fourth part." The entire world acknowledges now that the finale of *The Idiot* is one of the summits of the great writer's art; he himself thought otherwise. "And here the idea of *The Idiot* has almost foundered," he wrote to Maikov.

Despite all his exertions, the novel was not finished in 1868 and its last chapters were despatched as a supplement to the February issue of *The Russian Messenger* for 1869. On January 25 the writer informed S. A. Ivanova: "Now it [*The Idiot*] is finished, at last! The last chapters I wrote day and night with anguish and the most terrible anxiety. . . . I am not pleased with the novel; it didn't express even one tenth part of what I wanted to express, although nonetheless I don't deny it and even now love my miscarried thought."

The notes to the second, third, and fourth parts of *The Idiot* have come down to us in sketchbook No. 10. The notations from March 7 to the middle of July 1868 relate to the second part; those from September 8 and 15 relate to the third; those from November 7 and 10, to the fourth.

Work progressed along two lines, compositional and psychological. On May 12 the plan was outlined: "The prince remained absent 3 months. He has a lunch, meeting of the rivals. Nastasya Filippovna says: 'I'm a princess.' She runs away from the prince and kills herself. Aglaya marries the prince or the prince dies." But right away another variant: Nastasya Filippovna is not a princess. However, after an insulting scene with Aglaya, she decides to marry the prince; then leaves him for a bordello and marries Rogozhin. He cuts her throat. The prince marries Aglaya. There is a remark in parentheses: "He almost wanted, dies." The author found it very difficult to contrive a suitable role for Aglaya; first he writes down: "Rogozhin falls in love with Aglaya," then he indicates an intrigue between Aglaya and Ganya and adds: "The character of Ganya develops, in keeping with passion, to colossal seriousness." If Rogozhin falls in love with Aglaya, it is possible to connect her more closely with the catastrophe. "Aglaya is the principal reason that Rogozhin killed N. F." If Ganya loves her, then one can construct a new dramatic effect on this. The prince wants to marry her, "she assents to everything and, in order to take revenge, runs away with Ganya on the eve of the wedding." Finally, the general schema is indicated: "In the novel three loves: 1) passionate-immediate love—Rogozhin; 2) love from vanity—Ganya; and 3) Christian love—the prince."

The rejected variants appear to us now as less artistic than the final text. We are hypnotized by the realness of its embodiment; but before the creator's eyes there crowded together innumerable *possibilities* of his heroes' fates, demanding embodiment and defending their right to life. He by no means chose the most artistic of them, but it became artistic because he chose it. In this freedom of choice is the secret of art.

The unfolding of Prince Myshkin's image went parallel to work on the composition. The author concentrated all his attention on his strange hero, attentively examined his character. The prince continued to remain an enigma for him.

A thought came to him: but, perhaps, enigma was the prince's "nature"? Perhaps it was not necessary to unpuzzle him? "Should I not develop the prince's character enigmatically *through the whole novel,* now and then defining details (more fantastic and questioning, arousing curiosity), and suddenly explain his character in the end?" "And might not the prince be presented as a continuous sphinx? . . . N. B. *the prince as Sphinx.*" But faced with the hero's continuous enigma, the religious idea of the novel grew dim. Dostoevsky returned to the old plan of the eleventh notebook: the prince is a child and surrounded by children. "How to make the hero's character sympathetic to readers? If Don Quixote and Pickwick, as virtuous types, are sympathetic to the reader and have succeeded, it is because they are comical. . . . The hero of the novel, the prince, if not comical, then possesses another sympathetic trait—*he is innocent.*" The prince is innocent as a child and believes in the Kingdom of God on earth. His "idea" is connected with the dream of the "golden age." This is attested by the remark: "Every blade of grass, every step, Christ, the prince's inspired speech (Don Quixote and the acorn)." Don Quixote delivers his famous speech about utopia holding an acorn in his hand; the Russian Don Quixote, Myshkin, comes to people preaching the Kingdom of God on earth. And he is surrounded by children, the "sons of the Kingdom." A curious plan is indicated: the prince has a double life, one with adults, another, the real one—with children. "He has institutions and schools." "In Petersburg he has something like a club. . . ." "The prince has a children's club clandestinely." The prince's "secret" is explained only in the finale. "Should the novel not end with a confession?" Dostoevsky wrote down. "Develop his relations with the children this way: at first, when the story is more concerned with Aglaya, with Ganya, with N. F., with the intrigues, etc., might mention not be made slightly, and *almost enigmatically* of the prince's relations with children, with Kolya, etc.? Should the club not be mentioned, but after having been alluded to in remote rumors, could one not present the club suddenly and the prince in the midst of it like a tsar, in such fashion in the 5th or 6th part of the novel?" "They begin to form the children's club in the third and fourth parts." "All the questions, both the prince's personal ones (in which the children take a passionate interest) and general ones, are resolved in it, and there is much in this that is touching and naive." "N. B. Through the children Rogozhin confesses to the crime he has committed." "The prince tells the children about Christopher Columbus and that it is necessary for an intelligent man to be really a great man in order to prevail even against common sense."

The design is dazzling and daring. Not a dream about paradise, but paradise already realized on earth in the brotherhood of children; the Kingdom of Heaven existing in reality next to the earthly kingdom! On the one side, the children's club—on the other, the dark world of the Yepanchins, Ivolgins, and Rogozhins; the prince's gospel (his speeches and sermons) is realized in action: the children judge the affairs of "this world," transform it by their influence (Rogozhin confesses his crime). But this is no longer a novel, but a mystery; not art, but theurgy. The teacher, surrounded by disciples and bearing to the world the gospel of the Kingdom of God, is not the prince, but Christ!

Dostoevsky thought his idea out to the end. On one page of the rough notebook we read the slowly, calligraphically formed words: "The humble igumen Zosima. Basil the Great, Gregory the Theologian, John Chrysostom; the Gospel of John the Theologian." And after these in large letters is written: "N. B. Prince Christ." After profound reflection (the names mechanically inscribed)—a sudden decision. But how would he show Christ's image in the prince? The author made several notations: "Theory of practical Christianity." "About faith. Christ's temptation. Compassion is all of Christianity." "The prince forgives everything." "Christian love—the prince." "Considers himself inferior and worse than all. Sees the thoughts of those around him through and through." "Decidedly always ready to blame himself." And, lastly, the most important note: "*Humility is the most terrible force which can exist in the world!*" Compassion, universal forgiveness, love, humility, wisdom—such are the traits of the prince-Christ. Before the immensity of the task Dostoevsky halted. In the final text the prince's "divine character" has disappeared; his "justness" has been screened by human weaknesses. The writer overcame his temptation to write a "novel about Christ."

The hero's character was now revealed in three directions: enigma, innocence, sanctity. And nonetheless the author remained unsatisfied. The prince has developed into a great spiritual force, but how is it to be manifested? Could it be only in the love intrigue among Nastasya Filippovna, Rogozhin, Aglaya, and Ganya? He has outgrown this narrow world. "In order to present the character of the idiot more fascinatingly (more sympathetically), I must also think up some field of action for him." And the author imagines: the prince's sphere is Russia; he becomes acquainted with the Russian people, prepares for a vast activity, and suddenly dies. There follows a series of rough outlines: "Begins to love the Russian people to the point of passion." "The action of Russia on the prince. How much and in what way he has changed." "Russia acts on him by degrees. His beginning to see clearly." "The prince returns, overwhelmed by the immensity of his new impressions of Russia, of anxieties, ideas, of his condition, and what to do." "The main problem: the character of the idiot. Unravel him. Here is the thought of the novel: how is Russia reflected? Everything that might have worked out in the prince, has been extinguished in the grave. . . . But. . . . For that *the novel needs a plot*." It was possible to show the prince, a social activist and populist, only from afar, but not to portray him. Otherwise, it would amount to projecting a new plot, to writing a new novel. And the author doomed his hero to a premature death. In the final text of the novel traces of this original Russophile design have been preserved.

An examination of the outlines convinces us that the design of *The Idiot* is as much *personalist* as the design of *Crime and Punishment*. Both there and here the center of the novel is the personality. The writer's work on the plans consisted principally of explaining the main hero's *character*.

The concept of *The Idiot* grows organically out of that of *Crime and Punishment*. Raskolnikov lost his faith, his "heart was muddled," and he wanted to "transgress" the moral law. In the example of the crime of a man of the new generation, the author has shown the crisis of 19th century Russian consciousness. Raskolnikov is completely Russian, a "type of the Petersburg period," but that which takes place in his soul is not a personal or a national phenomenon: in it is reflected the condition of the entire world. The tragedy of contemporary humanity is disclosed in its full force in Russia, a country of the greatest extremes and contradictions. The Russian spirit, not fettered by tradition and boundlessly free, experiences the world drama most intensely. Here is why Dostoevsky's novel-tragedies, in spite of all their national singularity, have universal significance. But in *Crime and Punishment* the crisis of consciousness is concentrated in one soul, which has plunged out of the old world-order. In *The Idiot* all the dramatis personae are drawn into this crisis, all belong to a perishing world. The "positively beautiful individual," Prince Myshkin, alone stands opposed to the "dark forces" and perishes while struggling with them. In *Crime and Punishment* only Raskolnikov and his double, Svidrigailov, are infected by the terrible infirmity; the rest, evidently, are still healthy. In *The Idiot* the baneful contagion has embraced everyone, all the souls are ulcerous, all the foundations are unstable, all the wellsprings are poisoned. The world of the novel *The Idiot* is more terrible and more tragic than the world of *Crime and Punishment*. People rush about in a fever, talk in delirium, groan, and gnash their teeth. The two novels are two stages of the same illness: in the first the illness is in germ; in the second, in full development. We know with what agitation Dostoevsky watched all that happened in Russia from abroad, how somberly he looked at reality, how he attempted to find in the legal chronicles threatening signs of a near end.[5] The papers complained of the decline of morality, the increase of crimes, robberies, and murders. But at the same time, never did he so believe in the coming renovation of the perishing world, in the salvation of mankind by the image of the Russian Christ. The contradiction between despair and hope, disbelief and faith was embodied in *The Idiot*. The novel is constructed on the jolting contrast of darkness and light, death and resurrection.

In the sixties the writer's pessimism and optimism appeared morbidly exaggerated, the novel was not understood and almost unnoticed; the old world stood, apparently, solid and unshakable; the process of destruction, about which Dostoevsky spoke, was taking place in the dark depths of consciousness. Only now, in our catastrophic epoch, are we beginning to understand his prophecy.

The hero of the novel is Prince Myshkin; similar to Raskolnikov, he stands at the center as the compositional core and spiritual meaning of the action; he is present everywhere, participates in everything, is related to everything. The author describes and characterizes him many times; the dramatis personae continually talk about him, judge him, condemn, or extol. And he himself continually confesses to us. Yet, at the same time, Myshkin eludes us. By no direct characteristic

[5] The *legal chronicle* was a section printed in Russian newspapers that gave an account of hearings, testimonies, and trial proceedings.

can we grasp his *essence*. One has only to tear him away from the world in which he lives, to consider him *separately*, and at once his image becomes obscure. In effect, alone, separately, he does not even exist. He lives not in space, but in the souls of the people surrounding him, as their love, dream, ideal, or as their hatred, envy, malice. The nimbus, encircling him, is woven of the rays which issue from their eyes, from their hearts. His light arises in their darkness, and it is seen only because around it is darkness. The image of the prince is not sketched and not sculptured—it is *chiaroscuro*. Dostoevsky's art lies in the Rembrandt-like illumination of his novels.

But what then is this "world of darkness"? The drunkard and rogue Lebedev interprets the Apocalypse: "We are living at the time of the third horse, the black one," he says, "and the horseman who has a balance in his hand, since everything in the present age goes by measure and contract, and all men seek nothing but their own rights: 'a measure of wheat for a denarius or three measures of barley for a denarius. . . .' And behind him follows the pale horse, and that one whose name is death, and hell follows him. . . ." The author puts the apocalyptic vision into the mouth of a buffoon and by this contrast underlines its terrible meaning. The world finds itself under the sign of the horseman with the balance in his hand; having renounced God, people have come to worship the golden calf, all spiritual values have disappeared before the power of money. Lebedev is ridiculed; he, it is said, holds that the "star Woodworm" in the Apocalypse is the network of railroads which have extended over Europe! He exclaims: "Not the railroads, no, sir! Strictly, the railroads alone won't pollute the fountains of life, but all this in the whole, sir, is accursed, this tendency of our last centuries, in its general, scientific, and practical entirety, is perhaps really accursed." The contemporary state of the world with its industry, scientific techniques, and capitalism is under a curse, and Lebedev, calling himself the "professor of the Antichrist," predicts ruin: behind the black horse appears the pale horse, his name is death.

We enter into a world of money, millionaires, capitalists, businessmen, usurers, and greedy adventurers. General Yepanchin used to hold shares in government leases, has an important voice in sound stock companies, "is reputed a man with big money"; he owns two houses in Petersburg, an "estate with revenues," and a factory. This is the new type of Russian dignitary-capitalist. His former colleague, the retired General Ivolgin, lives in poverty; his wife rents out rooms to lodgers; his daughter, Varya is preparing to marry a solid young man Ptitsyn, although it is also known that "he is especially engaged in making money, by lending it at a very high interest on more or less good security"; his son Ganya sets as his goal accumulating a fortune, irrespective of all obstacles. He is in the service of General Yepanchin and is not indifferent to his daughter Aglaya. But it is proposed that he marry the notorious old Totsky's former mistress, Nastasya Filippovna; he is promised 75,000 for this and he agrees. The first part of the novel is constructed on an involved intrigue at the center of which is money. The new man, Ganya, is greedy, avaricious, selfish, and unprincipled. Before all else he needs "capital." Deciding to marry "another man's sins," he is at the same time afraid of losing the rich, eligible Aglaya, and begs her to give him hope. The latter rejects him with scorn: "He has a filthy soul," she says to Prince Myshkin, "he knows and does not make up his mind, he knows and nonethreless asks for guarantees. He is not capable of marrying on faith." Nastasya Filippovna, wronged by her purchase-sale, appears in the wretched apartment of her fiancé and cruelly humiliates him. At that moment, the young merchant, Rogozhin, breaks in with the intention of buying Ganya's betrothed from him. He shouts at his rival: "Why, show you three silver rubles, take them now out of my pocket, so you'd crawl on all fours as far as Vasilyevsky[6] after them—that's the sort you are. I've come here now only to buy you off for money. I said I'll do it, and I'll do it."

After this unseemly scene, Ganya reveals his "idea" to the prince. Money will give him strength. He will accumulate. "I'll begin straight off with capital: in fifteen years they will say: 'There goes Ivolgin, the king of the Jews!' . . . Having acquired money, you know, I will be an original man in the highest degree. The vilest and most hateful thing about money is that it even gives talents. . . . Why does Yepanchin affront me like that? Simply because I'm too insignificant. Well, sir, but then. . . ."

The man of the new generation yearns for might and finds it in money. The accumulation of wealth, as one of the most terrible temptations, is a constant theme of Dostoevsky's: the idea of the "Covetous Knight," Rothschild, the "king of the Jews" haunted the author. It is noted in *Mister Prokharchin* and *Crime and Punishment*, is developed in *The Gambler* and *A Raw Youth*.

In the novel, "The Idiot," we see the fatal power of money over the human soul. All the heroes are seized with a passion for profit, all of

---

[6] Vasilyevsky Island, a section of St. Petersburg, situated between the Neva and the Little Neva, opposite the Senate. The Bourse or Stock Exchange was located on it.

them are either usurers (like Ptitsyn, Lebedev, the captain's widow Terentyeva), or thieves, or adventurers. Ganya's idea is modified by his surroundings. Ptitsyn lends out money soundly on interest and knows his limit: to obtain two or three homes with an income; General Ivolgin borrows from everyone and ends by stealing; the lodger Ferdyshchenko, upon becoming acquainted with the prince, unexpectedly asks him: "Do you have money?" And having received a 25 ruble note from him, for a long time examines it from all sides, and returns it. "I came to warn you," he declares, "in the first place, not to lend me money, because without fail I'll ask you." This comic episode underlines the universal, terrible enchantment with money. The theme of money is reinforced by the reflections of the characters themselves. Ganya says to the prince, "Here there are terribly few honest people, none more honest than Ptitsyn." His thirteen-year-old brother Kolya philosophizes about the same thing: having made friends with the prince, he shares his thoughts with him. His child's soul is already offended by his parents' unsightliness, by the immorality of society. "There are terribly few honest people here," he observes, "so there's really no one at all to respect. . . . And have you observed, prince, in our age all are adventurers! And especially among us in Russia, in our beloved fatherland. And how it came about in this way, I don't understand. It seems, once how solidly it stood, but what is it now? . . . Parents are the first to go back on their word and are themselves ashamed of their old morals. See there, in Moscow, a parent was trying to persuade his son to stop *at nothing* to get money: it was reported in the papers. . . . They're all money grubbers, all, to a man." Kolya alludes to the murder of Danilov and connects avarice with crime. In his words the basic idea of the novel is already intimated.

The first part concludes with the reception at Nastasya Filippovna's. The motif of money is introduced in Ferdyshchenko's story about his basest action: he stole three rubles from acquaintances; they accused a servant of the theft and discharged her. Neither then nor afterward did he feel any pangs of conscience. And the narrator concludes: "Here it seems to me that there are many more thieves than nonthieves in the world and that there doesn't even exist a man so honest that he's never stolen anything, at least once in his life." By this ignoble, buffoonish confession, the effect of the catastrophe is prepared. Rogozhin arrives to buy Nastasya Filippovna: in his hands is a "big bundle of paper, wrapped firmly and compactly in *The Exchange Gazette* and tied round and round and twice across with string like that which is used to tie sugar loaves." At first he offers 18,000, then goes up to 40, and, finally, reaches 100. In the tragic auction, the bundle—the 100,000 —plays the main role.

Nastasya Filippovna releases Ganya from his word and disgraces him. The motif of covetousness is connected with the motif of criminality. The service of mammon leads to homicide. "No, now I believe," she says, "that such a man would kill for money! Why, they've all been excited by such greed nowadays, are so obsessed by gold, that they seem to have gone mad. He's only a child, and already he clamors to become a money-lender. Or a man will wind silk round his razor, tighten it, then sneak up gently from behind and cut his friend's throat like a sheep's, as I read not long ago." Nastasya Filippovna is citing the affair of the merchant Mazurin, who killed the jeweler Kalmykov. Once again the legal chronicle bursts in on the novel. The author constructed his apocalyptic vision of the world on the facts of the "current moment." The heroine flings the bundle with the 100,000 into the fire and hurls a challenge to Ganya: draw the money out of the fire and it's yours. The effect of this scene consists in the contrast between the hostess' disinterestedness and her guest's greed. She challenges not only Ganya but the whole "damned" world which adores the golden calf. A tumult take places: Lebedev "moans and scrambles into the fireplace"; Ferdyshchenko offers "to snatch out only 1,000 with his teeth"; Ganya falls into a faint. Even the prince enters into this bacchanal of gold: he offers his hand to the heroine, declaring that he has received an inheritance, that he is also a millionaire.

In the second part there appears a company of extortioners: Burdovsky alleges that he is the illegitimate son of Pavlishchev, Prince Myshkin's benefactor, and contrives a suit against him in order to secure a tidy little sum. His friend, Keller, places in the newspaper an "expository" and hideously slanderous article about the prince. Lebedev says about these young people that they "have gone further than the nihilists." The apocalyptic theme is developed in the indignant monologue of Lizaveta Prokofyevna Yepanchina: the kingdom of the golden calf is the vestibule of the kingdom of death. "In fact the end of everything has come," she shouts. "Now it's all been explained to me! Why, this stammerer, won't he murder someone" (she points to Burdovsky), "well, I'll wager that he'll murder someone! He won't, if you like, take your money, your 10,000 but at night he'll come and murder you, yes, and take it out of your cash box. He'll take it with a clear conscience! . . . Phoo, everything is turned upside down with them, they've all gone topsy-turvy. . . . Madmen! Vain creatures! *They don't believe in God, don't believe in Christ!* And indeed, vanity and pride have so eaten you up, that it'll end by your devouring one another—this I predict to you. And isn't this nonsense and chaos and isn't it unseemliness?"

In the words of General Yepanchin's wife is expressed the author's inviolable idea: the moral crisis experienced by 19th century mankind was a *religious crisis*. Faith in Christ is extinguished, night is dropping onto the world; it will perish in the bloody chaos of a universal world-war. Yelizaveta Prokofyevna's terrible prophecy is "scientifically" summed up by the *raisonneur* Yevgeny Pavlovich. But his cold-blooded diagnosis of the age's sickness is, perhaps, still more terrible than the general's wife's violent indignation. "Everything that I've heard," he says, "boils down, in my opinion, to the theory of the triumph of right, before everything, and setting everything aside, even to the exclusion of everything else, and even perhaps before an investigation of what that right consists in? From this position one can easily jump to the right of force, i.e., to the right of the individual fist and personal caprice, as indeed has very often happened in the world. Proudhon arrived at the right of force. In the American war many of the most advanced liberals declared themselves on the side of the plantation owners on the ground that Negroes were Negroes, inferior to the white race, and consequently the right of force was behind the whites. . . . I only wanted to observe that from the *right of force it is not far to the right of tigers and crocodiles and even to Danilov and Gorsky.*" This prophecy has been fulfilled literally: the people of the twentieth century know by experience what the right of force and the right of tigers and crocodiles is. . . .

Such is the picture of the world disclosed in *The Idiot*. The idea that lack of faith inevitably leads to murder is embodied in the novel's action: all the heroes are murderers, either in actuality or potentially. Atheistic mankind stands under the sign of death.

On what is Dostoevsky's Apocalypse based? Is it not on morbid fancy? He was passionately indignant when the critics called his novel fantastic, and asserted that he was more of a realist than they. Threatening signs of the "troubled times" approaching the world were already inscribed in "contemporary reality"; it was necessary only that one know how to interpret them. The author scrutinized the most minute facts, news releases, the chronicle of events, reports of trial proceedings, and prided himself that he had grasped the most elusive "currents of the moment." When *Crime and Punishment* was published, there appeared in the newspapers accounts of the student Danilov's case. On January 14, 1866, Danilov had killed and robbed the money-lender Popov and his maid. The poor student lived by giving lessons, was intelligent and well educated, was noted for his steady and placid character: he had a "handsome appearance, large black expressive eyes and long thick hair thrown back." At the time of the trial a convict Glazkov suddenly testified that it was not Danilov, but he who had killed the usurer; soon after, however, he retracted his statement, "confessing that Danilov had prompted him." Dostoevsky was astonished; reality was imitating fiction with amazing exactness. Danilov's case reproduced the plot of *Crime and Punishment*; even the false confession of Glazkov corresponded to Nikolka's false self-accusation in the novel. His "realism" was triumphing. "Oh, my friend," he wrote to Maikov, "I have completely different understandings of reality and realism than our realists and critics. My idealism is more real than theirs. Their realism does not know how to explain a hundredth part of the real facts that have actually taken place. But we by our idealism *have even prophesied facts.* It has happened."

In Dostoevsky's art, the greatest flights of fancy are joined with a painstaking study of facts. He always began his ascent from the low grounds of everyday reality. His novels are saturated with the chronicle of events.

The plot of *The Idiot* is closely connected with the criminal trials of the sixties. The very concept of the novel originated with his impression of the Umetsky affair. In the final text, not one detail of this family drama has been preserved. The "furious, proud" Mignon-Umetskaya is only the distant prototype of Nastasya Filippovna. The Umetsky trial was the ferment which stirred the author's creative thought into action, but was dissolved almost without trace in the process of his work. Two other murder cases—Mazurin's and Gorsky's—determined the composition of the novel. Dostoevsky acknowledged to S. Ivanova that the whole novel was almost both written and conceived *"for its denouement."* The denouement is Rogozhin's murder of Nastasya Filippovna; consequently in it lies the meaning of the novel. The idea of the "murderousness" of the fallen world is realized in the hero's "act of murder." The figure of the murderer-millionaire originated under the influence of the merchant Mazurin's trial.

In November 1867 the writer read in the newspapers the judicial inquiry into Mazurin's murder of the jeweler Kalmykov. The murderer belonged to a rich merchant family well known in Moscow. Like Rogozhin he had inherited a fortune of two million from his father, lived with his mother in her home which was on a populated commercial street. (Rogozhin lives at the corner of Gorokhovaya and Sadovaya, Mazurin—at the corner of Myasnitskaya and Zlatoustinsky Lane.) In this house he committed the murder and in it hid his victim. "For a long time strange rumors had been circulating" round the Mazurin home; in Rogozhin's home "everything is, as it were, kept hidden and concealed." Mazurin, like Rogozhin, killed on a hot June day with a new knife bought for household use, covered the corps with oilcloth, and placed around it bottles of Zhdanov disinfectant. He, like Rogozhin, was sentenced to fifteen years' penal servitude. Nastasya Filippovna alludes to this murder; she had read about it that very day when Rogozhin entered her life: on Wednesday, November 27, 1867. So exactly does the author date this event.

But the image of Rogozhin is psychologically connected with still another criminal, the schoolboy Vitold Gorsky. Prince Myshkin has a presentiment that his brother-in-the-cross will raise his hand against him; in anguish he wanders through the city, and suddenly remembers Gorsky: this image of the murderer is mysteriously joined in his imagination with Rogozhin and Lebedev's nephew. The same evening Rogozhin takes up a knife against him. In *The Voice* of March 10, 1868, Dostoevsky read about the trial of Gorsky, a student, of noble family. Gorsky killed six people in the home of the merchant Zhemarin. "He has a sharp character, a will exceeding youthful development, he is a Catholic, but according to his talk doesn't believe in anything." He testified that he murdered with the intention of committing theft.[B]

The characters in *The Idiot* continually refer to the Zhemarins' murder. The atmosphere of the novel is poisoned by emanations of blood. An oppressive expectation, a growing certitude is created. Death is really present, seeks an executioner of his decrees, and finds him in Rogozhin. He is chosen because in him the forces of the fallen world attain their greatest tension: the curse of money especially weighs upon him. Rogozhin emerges from the dark merchant world in which, from generation to generation, money has been accumulated. In the

[B] V. Dorovatovskaya-Lyubimova. *"Idiot" Dostoevskogo i ugolovnaya khronika ego vremeni (Dostoevsky's Idiot and the Legal Chronicle of his Time)*. Pechat i revolyutsiya 1938, III.

somber house on Gorokhovaya, his grandfather and father, with in-domitable passion and fanatic tenacity, acquired a fortune. Lebedev says of Rogozhin's father: "But you see, the deceased would drive a man into the next world for ten rubles, let alone for ten thousand." Greed bordering on crime also characterizes Parfyon's brother Semyon. Rogozhin relates: "At night, my brother cut the solid gold tassels off the brocade pall on my parent's coffin: 'No use wasting 'em,' he says, 'cost a fortune they do.' And now for that he can go to Siberia if I'd like, 'cause it is a sacrilege." The Rogozhin kingdom of darkness is surrounded by sinister mystery: his house on Gorokhovaya is "big, somber, three storied, without any architecture, of a dirty-green color . . . with thick walls and extraordinarily few windows." This house is a symbol: it has its own soul, lives its own nocturnal life. "Both outside and inside somehow it is inhospitable and cold, every-thing is, as it were, kept hidden and concealed." And the author adds: "The architectural combination of lines has, of course, its own secret." This is a monastery or prison, a dwelling for misers and fanat-ics. The exterior of the house is described more in detail than the out-ward appearance of Rogozhin himself, for the hero has still not torn himself away from his patrimonial bosom; he is joined by blood with his family and its age-old traditions. The prince examines a portrait of Parfyon's father: "a wrinkled, yellow face, a suspicious, stealthy, and mournful gaze." He is struck by the son's spiritual similarity to his father: if passion for Nastasya Filippovna had not taken hold of Rogo-zhin, he "would have become exactly like his father," "would have set-tled down silently alone in this house with an obedient and submissive wife, would have been harsh and sparing of words, trusting no man, yes, and simply not needing to and only making money silently and drearily." Parfyon is of a race of people who have one passion, driven inward, who have one idea, stubborn and proud. Only his passion has changed direction—it has turned not on money, but on a woman. But really is this human love? Rogozhin needs to have power, to dominate, to satisfy his egotistical greed. He will not relent and will not stop before obstacles: his nuptial night with Nastasya Filippovna will end with murder. In the kingdom of mammon, love becomes hatred, the union of lovers—mutual destruction. Nastasya Filippovna unriddles the mystery of the Rogozhin house. She writes to Aglaya: "He has a somber, gloomy house and it contains secrets. I'm convinced that he has, kept hidden in a chest, a razor wound round with silk, like that Moscow murderer. He also lived in the same house with his mother and wrapped his razor in silk, in order to slit someone's throat. All the while I was with them in the house, I felt that somewhere or other under a plank there was a dead man hidden—by his father, perhaps— and covered with oilcloth like that Moscow man and surrounded in the same way with bottles of Zhdanov disinfectant. I could even show you the corner. . . ."

Rogozhin's father perhaps did not kill anyone, but was capable of murder. The passion for gain is in its essence murderous. Nastasya Filippovna recalls Mazurin's crime and predicts her own destruction.

The action of the novel is directed toward the catastrophe. In the first scene Prince Myshkin and Rogozhin meet by chance in a railway compartment and talk about Nastasya Filippovna; in the final scene they are again together and again talk about her over her corpse. From the first meeting to the last, there is an enormous interval, the entire action of the novel, comprising about six hundred pages. The farther apart the poles become, the stronger and more dazzling is the electric discharge between them. Throughout the entire novel the tension grows without stopping. It culminates in an effect unique in world literature: the two rivals' nocturnal vigil over the corpse of the murdered woman.

The state of excited expectation is created by the device of *anticipation and foreknowledge*. Prince Myshkin has only learned about Rogozhin's passion for Nastasya Filippovna, and to Ganya's question whether the latter will marry her, answers assuredly: "Why, what do you mean, I think he could marry her even tomorrow; he might marry her and in a week perhaps murder her." Likewise, Nastasya Filippovna does not doubt that Rogozhin will cause her ruin; she foresees even the circumstances of her death. Finally, the murderer himself continually has a presentiment of his *inevitable course of action*. And in this sense, Rogozhin is Raskolnikov's spiritual brother: he also is a tragic hero, having fallen into the power of fate; he too struggles with it and perishes in the struggle. In him lives the ominous heritage of his ancestors, their demonic passion and possession. He issues from the bosom of the "world of darkness" and serves that "great and awesome spirit" about which Lebedev prophesies. Rogozhin kills because "the devil has been a murderer from time immemorial." His crime is explained on several planes, socio-historical, psychological, moral. But the prince reduces all this motivation to one cause—*religious*. In Rogozhin's home hangs a copy of Holbein's *Crucifixion*; he tells the prince that he loves to look at it. " 'At this painting!' abruptly cried the prince, struck by a sudden thought, 'at this painting, why some people's very faith could be shattered by this painting!' 'That's what's taking place,' suddenly Rogozhin affirmed unexpectedly." The thought of his brother-in-the-cross pursues the prince in his semi-delirious wandering about the streets. He reflects: "Rogozhin is not only a passionate soul; he is moreover a fighter; *he wants to restore his lost faith by force.* He has an agonizing need of it now." And these words complete the sketch of the "fighter's" tragic image. Rogozhin has lost his faith and fate leads him to murder; he resists: *he wants to believe and cannot.* The murderer is not only an executioner, but also a victim: he is consumed by his own fire. God and the devil contend for his soul; exchanging crosses with the prince, he raises a knife against him; after surrendering Nastasya Filippovna to him, he kills her.

Mystically connected with Rogozhin is one of the members of Burdovsky's "company," the seventeen-year-old youth Ippolit Terentyev. He is in the final stage of consumption and has two or three weeks yet to live. At the prince's villa in Pavlovsk, before a large group of people, Ippolit reads his confession: *My Necessary Explanation,* with the epigraph: "Après moi le déluge." This independent tale is in its form directly related to *Notes from Underground.* Ippolit, also an underground man, has closed himself off in his corner, separated himself from his family and comrades and become immersed in contemplating the dirty brick wall of the house opposite. "Meyer's wall" has shut him off from the entire world. He has done a lot of thinking while studying its stains. And now, before his death, he wants to reveal his thoughts to people. Ippolit is not an atheist; however, his faith is not Christian, but *philosophical.* He conceives of the divinity in the form of Hegel's world reason, erecting "universal harmony as a whole" on the destruction of millions of living beings; he admits providence, but does not understand its inhuman laws, and therefore concludes: "No, better let's leave religion alone." And he is right: the rational deism of the philosophers is concerned with universal harmony and completely uninterested in particular events. What does it care about the death of a consumptive adolescent? Is it possible that World Reason is going to violate its laws for the sake of some insignificant fly? Such a God Ippolit can neither understand nor accept and "leaves religion alone." He does not even refer to faith in Christ: to the individual of the new generation the Savior's divinity and His resurrection seem prejudices long outlived. And here he is left alone in the midst of a devastated world over which reigns an indifferent and merciless creator of the "laws of nature" and "iron necessity." Dostoevsky takes in its purest guise and in its most acute form the dechristianized consciousness of the cultured man of the 19th century. Ippolit is young, upright, passionate, and candid. He fears neither proprieties nor hypocritical conventions, but wants to speak the truth. This is the truth of a man condemned to death. If one objects that his is a special case, that he has consumption and must die soon, he will retort that the datelines here are without differentiation, and that everyone finds himself in his position. If Christ did not rise and death has not been vanquished, all living things are condemned to death, precisely as he is.

Death is the sole king and master on earth, death is the resolution of the mystery of the world. Rogozhin, looking at Holbein's painting, lost his faith; Ippolit was at Rogozhin's and also saw this picture. And death appeared before him in all its mystical terror. The Savior, taken down from the cross, is depicted as a corpse: looking at His body, already touched by corruption, it is impossible to believe in its resurrection. Ippolit writes: "Here one instinctively reflects that if death is so horrible and its laws so mighty, then how can they be overcome? How can they be overcome when even He did not conquer them, He who conquered nature during His lifetime? Looking at this picture, nature appears in the guise of some immense, implacable, and dumb beast or to put it more accurately, much more accurately, though also strangely, in the guise of some huge machine of the latest construction that has senselessly seized, dismembered, and swallowed up, impassively and without feeling, a great and priceless being, such a being, which alone was worth all of nature and all her laws, all the earth, which was created perhaps solely for the appearance of this being!" Such ardent love for the human countenance of the Savior and such terrible disbelief in His divinity! Nature "swallowed up" Christ. He did not conquer death—all this is accepted as an evident truth, nor is it even subject to doubt. And then the whole world becomes the prey of the "dumb beast," unfeeling and senseless. Mankind has lost its faith in the resurrection and gone mad with terror before the beast. "I remember," Ippolit continues, "that someone led me, as it were, by the hand, with a candle in his hands, showed me some enormous and repulsive tarantula, and began assuring me that this was that same *dark, impassive and all-powerful creature.*" Out of the image of the tarantula develops Ippolit's nightmare: into his room crawls a "horrible animal, a kind of monster." "It was like a scorpion, but was not a scorpion, rather it was more disgusting and much more horrible and it seemed, precisely because of the fact that such animals do not exist in nature, that it had appeared *expressly* to me and in this itself was contained some kind of mystery. . . ." Norma—an enormous Newfoundland—stops dead before the reptile: in her fright there is something mystical: she also "felt that in the beast there was something ominous and some kind of mystery." Norma cracks the scorpion with her teeth, but it stings her.

In Ippolit's mysterious dream, this is the symbol of man's struggle with evil. Evil cannot be conquered by human forces. Ippolit's thoughts about death are inspired by Rogozhin. In *his* house he saw Holbein's picture: *his* phantom compelled the consumptive to decide to commit suicide. Ippolit imagines that Rogozhin entered his room at night, sat down on a chair, and for a long time was silent. Finally, "he moved away the hand on which he was leaning, straightened up, and began to open his lips, almost preparing to laugh": this is Rogozhin's nocturnal face, his mystical image. Before us is not the young merchant-millionaire who has fallen in love with a Camille and is recklessly spending 100,000 for her; Ippolit sees the embodiment of the evil spirit, somber and derisive, destroying and being destroyed. The dream about the tarantula and Rogozhin's phantom merge for Ippolit into one apparition. "It is impossible to go on living," he writes, "when life assumes such strange forms that insult me. This apparition degraded me. I'm not capable of submitting to a *dark power* which takes the form of a tarantula." So arose Ippolit's "ultimate conviction" to kill himself. If death is the law of nature, then every good deed is senseless, then everything is immaterial—even crime. "What if it occurred to me now to kill anyone I wanted or even ten people at once . . . then what a quandary the court would face while judging me?" But Ippolit prefers rather to kill himself. Thus is shown the spiritual bond between Rogozhin and Ippolit. The suicide can become a murderer and the reverse. "I hinted to him [Rogozhin]," the adolescent recalls, "that in spite of all the difference between us and all the contrasts, *les extrémités se touchent* . . . so that perhaps even he was by no means so far from my 'ultimate conviction' as it seemed." Psychologically they are opposite: Ippolit is a consumptive youth, torn away from life, an abstract thinker. Rogozhin lives a "full, spontaneous life," is possessed by passion and jealousy. But metaphysically the murderer and the suicide are blood brothers: both are victims of disbelief and accomplices of death. Rogozhin has a dirty-green house-prison; Ippolit, Meyer's dirty wall; both are prisoners of the beast—death.

In Dostoevsky's work, Ippolit's confession holds an important place: it unites the man from underground's revolt with the revolt of Ivan Karamazov.

Our journeying along the ways of the "world of darkness" is ended. We have investigated its dual structure, empirical and metaphysical. On the empirical plane, before us was unfolded a picture of Petersburg society at the end of the sixties (more precisely at the end of 1867 and the beginning of the year 1868), and the history of several Russian families (the Yepanchins, Ivolgins, Lebedevs, Rogozhins). In this is the socio-historical meaning of the novel. On the metaphysical plane, *The Idiot* is an apocalyptic vision of the world standing under the sign of the black horse and a prophecy of its nearing end (the pale horse). Over mankind, which has fallen away from Christ, the "great and awesome spirit" rules, and will rule "until the end of time which is still unknown to us."

Dostoevsky's art is symbolic, like every great art. His "mystical realism" penetrates the veil of appearances to the "essence of things." The writer's dual sight creates a particular perspective and the special illumination of his novels. These two planes are more precisely manifest in the development of the personality of the main hero, Prince Myshkin.

Let us examine first his empirical image. "A young man of about 26 or 27, a little taller than average height, with very fair, thick hair, with sunken cheeks and a rather thin, pointed, almost white beard. His eyes were large, blue, and attentive: in their gaze there was something gentle, but heavy, something of that strange expression by which some people can at first glance divine epilepsy in the subject."

He is the last of the ancient family of Princes Myshkin, early was left an orphan, was raised in the country, and in childhood suffered a grave nervous illness. A rich friend of his father, Pavlishchev, placed him in Doctor Schneider's sanatorium in Switzerland and the "idiot" spent four years there.

Upon recovering, he decided to return to Russia where none of his family remained, except a distant relation—the wife of General

Yepanchin. We become acquainted with him in the compartment of a train on the Petersburg-Warsaw railway, approaching Petersburg. He is dressed like a foreigner. "He had on a fairly full and heavy cloak without sleeves and with an enormous hood, exactly like travelers often use in winter, somewhere far abroad—in Switzerland or, for example, in northern Italy." In his hands there is a "light bundle of old faded foulard," on his feet "thick-soled shoes with gaiters." The description concludes with the author's remark: "all quite un-Russian." He does not know anyone in Russia. Yepanchina is "just barely related" to him; he does not even have a place to stay. He is a stranger in his homeland. General Yepanchin's valet asks him: "You've grown disaccustomed to our ways?" The prince answers: "That's true. Do you believe, I'm amazed at myself, I haven't forgotten how to speak Russian." The motif of complete unfamiliarity with Russia is repeated in the prince's conversation with Yepanchin. "It's been over four years since I've been in Russia; and when I left, I was scarcely in my right mind. And then I didn't know anything, but now it's even worse." And further: "In fact, General, I know practically nothing of either the customs here, or generally, how people live here. . . ." The prince's social character is precisely defined: he is a Russian nobleman of the "Petersburg period," a European, torn away from the soil and from the people. He is part of the numerous family of "uprooted intellectuals" that includes Ordynov in *The Landlady*, the prince in *Uncle's Dream*, Alyosha Volkovsky in *The Humiliated and Wronged*, Versilov in *A Raw Youth*, and Stepan Trofimovich Verkhovensky in *The Devils*. These people live in a fantastic world (its symbol: Myshkin's Swiss sanatorium) and, chancing into our reality, feel themselves superfluous and helpless. They lack form and a sense of measure. "I don't have gesture," complains the prince. "I always have the wrong gesture, and this provokes laughter and degrades the idea. Nor is there a sense of measure, and this is the main thing." *Strangers*—they seem *eccentric*, inexperienced—they appear ludicrous. The prince's ingenuous avowals incite Rogozhin's and Lebedev's laughter, General Yepanchin's patronizing smile, the ironic remarks of his daughters. The prince is comic in his awkwardness, does not know how to bear himself in society, shatters an expensive vase. He is amazingly naive and impractical. The laws of social life were not written for him; he seems to have "tumbled down from the moon"; in the people around him he arouses curiosity, wonder, sometimes indignation. He is considered now stupid, now crafty, but most frequently of all an idiot or a holy-fool. The prince recognizes his estrangement and is tormented by it. "Now I'm going to see *people;* with people perhaps I'll be bored and oppressed." And actually in our world he is troubled and melancholy. At the concert in Pavlovsk, sitting beside the girl he loves, he dreams about flight: "He longed to go away somewhere, to disappear from here completely. . . . And let them, let them now forget all about him. Oh, this was even necessary, even better, if they hadn't known him at all, and this whole vision were only a dream." Being torn away from the soil denotes estrangement from people, withdrawal from life, and abstractness. The prince recalls how in Switzerland he had stretched out his arms to the brilliant sky and wept. "What tormented him was that he was completely a stranger to all this."

The theme of estrangement is extended: the prince is a stranger not only to people, but also to nature, to the whole world. His social definition is completed by new psychological content; the prince is not only a Russian nobleman who has been torn away from the soil, but also a *dreamer*, living in a fantastic world, who has lost his tie with "living life." The raisonneur, Yevgeny Pavlovich, at the end of the novel accuses the prince of *lying;* he *invented* his love for Nastasya Filippovna, he *imagined* that he had to marry her. "The fundamental cause of all that has happened," he explains, "has been due to the enormous, overflowing mass of intellectual convictions which you have till now taken for real, natural, and spontaneous convictions." The prince read many books about Russia in Switzerland, hurried to his native land and, upon arriving plunged into "activity": to save a wronged beauty. Yevgeny Pavlovich means to say that the prince was captivated by the "feminine question," imagined himself a hero of George Sand or Dumas and busied himself with the *rehabilitation* of a fallen woman, which had been fashionable since the time of the *Dame aux camélias.* All this resulted from nervous impressionability and intellectual enthusiasm. Thus practical reason judges and condemns the "unfortunate idiot." This is a visionary, a dreamer, who suffers complete defeat upon encountering reality. Prince Myshkin belongs to that race of dreamers which filled Dostoevsky's work in the period before penal servitude, and which, after his exile, gave rise to the "man from underground" and Raskolnikov. We recognize familiar traits: abstractness, fantasy, eccentricity, solitude, . . . But in *The Idiot,* to the old there is added a new element. The prince not only analyzes his infirmity, but yearns for a cure. He returns to Russia in order to discover the soil, to reunite himself with the people, to return to the sources of living life. And in this lies his difference from all the "dreamers" who precede him. For six months he roams about Russia and returns to Petersburg "under the very strong impression of all that had so overwhelmed him in Russ." He had conversed with an intellectual-atheist about religion, heard about a peasant who had cut his friend's throat, while saying: "Lord, forgive me for the sake of Christ," had seen a drunken soldier who for twenty kopecks sold him the cross he wore on his neck, had met a young peasant woman who had devoutly crossed herself when her child, whom she was still nursing, smiled at her for the first time—and suddenly he understood that *the essence of religious feeling has nothing to do with any reasoning or any atheism.* He owes this revelation to the Russian people. "But the main thing," he concludes, "is that you will notice this most clearly and most quickly in the Russian heart." The prince has come to believe in the Russian Christ, has found the soil and yearns for activity. "There is something to do, Parfyon!" he says enrapturedly to Rogozhin. "There is something to do in our Russian world, believe me!" Contact with his native land transforms Myshkin into a mystical populist. He constructs an entire religious philosophy, which he ardently expounds at the Yepanchins' soirée. The stammering "idiot" unexpectedly turns into an eloquent preacher, fanatically asserting that "Catholicism is not Christian faith," that it preaches the Antichrist and begets atheism and socialism. To the contagion that is spreading from the atheistic West, Russia must oppose the authentic image of Christ. "Oh, we need to resist," the prince exclaims, "and right now, now! We must in order that our Christ, whom we have preserved and whom they do not even know, may shine forth in resistance to the West." The prince's Slavophilism evolves into the idea of *Russian Orthodox messianism.* "Show the Russian man in the future the renewal of all mankind and its resurrection, perhaps, by Russian thought alone, by the Russian God and Christ, and you will see what a mighty and upright, wise and meek giant will grow before the astonished world." In this inspired sermon there is much national pride.

The author puts himself in the place of his meek and foolish hero and expounds his own credo to us. No less autobiographic are the prince's conclusions that Russian liberalism is a retrograde phenomenon, that Russian literature is "not at all Russian, except perhaps Lomonosov, Pushkin, and Gogol." All these thoughts are almost literally transferred into the novel from Dostoevsky's correspondence with Maikov. The prince's sermon is heightened by his direct harangue to the "upper class." Great is its sin before Russia (Westernism), great is its treason against the Russian people (being torn away from the soil), but really cannot the "cultured stratum" repent and be reunited with the "Russian element"? Before the face of the approaching Antichrist, will the best people understand their responsibility, their historical mission? Concern for the fate of the nobility and faith in its resurrection sound in the prince's words. We hear the agitated and passionate voice of Dostoevsky himself: "I fear for you, for you all and for all of us together. Why, I myself am a prince, of ancient lineage, and am sitting with princes. I'm speaking in order to save all of us, in order that our class may not disappear to no avail, in darkness, without having realized anything, abusing everything, and having lost everything. Why should we disappear and cede our place to others, when it is possible to remain in the fore and be leaders? Let us be in the fore, and we will also be the leaders. Let us become servants in order to lead others."

Such is Prince Myshkin's *empirical* image: we have examined and have recognized it. The prince is an artistic self-portrait of Dostoevsky himself, his story is *the writer's spiritual biography*. A dismal, joyless childhood, a dream-filled "fantastic" youth, an oppressive nervous ailment, epileptic attacks, four years passed outside of life (with Dostoevsky, the four years at Omsk; with Myshkin, the four years in the Swiss sanatorium). Both for the author and for his hero this "prison period" was a time of intense spiritual labor, a preparation for the cognition of Russia. Then for both there is a return to his native land, a "regeneration of convictions," a reunion with the people, and meeting with the Russian Christ. The deciding event in the writer's spiritual life was the minutes spent on the scaffold in anticipation of the death penalty. The novel's plot did not allow him to lead his hero onto the scaffold. But he put in his mouth a detailed account of this event, compelled him to relive all the particulars of the ominous ceremony. In the romance with Nastasya Filippovna have been reflected the writer's memories of his love for the "fatal woman," Apollinariya Suslova. Finally, he made the prince the bearer of his new Slavophile-populist ideas from the period of his journeys abroad 1866 to 1870.

Dostoevsky's novels are the history of his soul; the interior is projected in the exterior, in myths and symbols (the characters, plots, composition). His personal consciousness is revealed in its *universality*.

Let us turn now to Prince Myshkin's *metaphysical image*. Into the "world of darkness" comes a man "not of this world," into the chaos

· 369 ·

and unseemliness enters a *"positively beautiful individual."* He is not
an active fighter contending in the struggle with evil forces, not a tragic
hero challenging fate to combat; he does not judge and does not accuse, but his very appearance provokes a tragic conflict. One personality is set in opposition to the entire world; on this contrast is founded
the *dynamic* structure of the novel. The inner law of personality
shows itself directly opposed to the law of the world of darkness.

Into the kingdom of human greed, pride, hatred, and sensuousness
comes a man longing to give up his soul for his neighbor, divested not
only of self-love but of a feeling of personal dignity, disinterested, humble, compassionate, and chaste. In the train compartment his chance
fellow travelers—Rogozhin and Lebedev—laugh at the "holy-fool": he
does not understand their derision and laughs together with them.
Yepanchin drives him away, the prince is not affronted and "having
gaily burst into laughter," prepares to leave; Aglaya and Adelaida
call him an ass: "the prince began to laugh together with them." When
he is abused, he always blames himself and justifies his offender. Ganya
shouts at him in frenzy: "damned idiot"; the prince calmly explains to
him that "formerly he was in fact almost an idiot, but now he has long
since recovered, and therefore it is a little unpleasant for him when he
is called an idiot to his face." When Ganya slaps him, he covers his face
with his hands and in a breaking voice says: "Oh, how you will feel
ashamed of your behavior!" With endless humility the prince submits
to Aglaya's despotic haughtiness; Rogozhin's hatred and jealousy he
answers with fraternal love; Nastasya Filippovna's distraught pride he
calms with compassion. Everyone asserts himself, he belittles himself;
everyone bows down before money, he arrives with a meager bundle
and without a cent in his pocket; coming into an inheritance, he distributes money to his enemies and offenders. Everyone is possessed by
the idea of his own right, he knows only his obligations and his guilt
before all. The "world of darkness" is the kingdom of falsehood: the
prince is truthful and ingenuous to the point of naiveté.

And this meek individual, sickly and helpless as a child, engenders
a whirlwind of passions and events around him. His weakness becomes a terrible force. The "prince's law" cannot exist with the law
of the fallen world, their collision is inevitable, their tragic struggle predestined. People, who have lost God, have forfeited reality: they live
amidst phantoms and fictions. Their relations and mores are based on
conventions. The prince is truth bursting into a world of falsehood.
People are attracted to him as to light, and are repulsed from him as

from an enemy. "Humility is a terrible force," he says. The higher reality repels the lower, truth kills falsehood. The meek prince by his existence alone shakes the foundations of the sinful world. With their passions, vices, and weaknesses, Rogozhin, Ivolgin, Lebedev cannot, while loving, not hate him. The collision of the two worlds is anticipated by a comic misunderstanding. In General Yepanchin's anteroom the prince has a conversation with the valet, not as a visitor with a lackey, but as a human being with a human being: "It would seem," remarks the author, "that the prince's conversation was the most ordinary; but the more ordinary it was, the more absurd it also became in the present instance, and the experienced valet could not but feel that what was completely decent between a *man* and a man was completely improper for a guest and a *man.*"

The prince knows man and does not know man in quotation marks. And consequently the imprint of "foolishness" lies on all his conduct. The valet "for some reason or other liked the prince, in his own way, of course. But from another point of view, he aroused in him a decided and churlish indignation." And everyone has the same dual relationship to him—attraction and repulsion, love-hate. The "world of darkness" rises up against the individual who does not live according to its law. The novel-tragedy depicts the story of this struggle, ending with the destruction of the "beautiful man."

The "murderous life" of the devil's kingdom is realized in Rogozhin's murder. The prince at his very first appearance declares "Thou shalt not kill." In Yepanchin's antechamber he tells the valet about a certain Legros' execution in Lyons and concludes, "It is written: 'Thou shalt not kill,' so because he committed murder, is he also to be killed? *No, this isn't possible.* . . . Christ himself spoke of such torture and of this agony. No, one cannot treat a human being like this." He repeats the same story in the Yepanchins' parlor, adding to it another tale—about a man who was led up onto the scaffold and was pardoned. It seems that the prince knows through personal experience what death is. In expectation of the penalty the condemned experiences not physical fear of the end, but a mystical terror before an unknown future. The man-killing devil tempts the soul with a vision of the abyss of nonbeing. . . . "No this isn't possible." On the empirical plane, these philosophical conversations in the anteroom and the salon, immediately upon his return from Switzerland, are more than improbable. On the metaphysical, we see in them the complication of the action, the beginning of conflict, and the axis of the composition. Despite the prince's "Thou shalt not kill," Rogozhin will kill, and the prince will be his moral accomplice. The novel is built on the antithesis between the prince's law: *"No, this isn't possible"* and the law of the "world of darkness": *"Everything is permitted."*

The hero brings people not only an injunction, but also a gospel. By his personality, by his existence, he unmasks falsehood; destroying, he wants to build. Adelaida Yepanchina mockingly remarks to him: "This is all philosophy: you're a philosopher and have come to instruct us." "You, perhaps, are right," smiled the prince, "I really am, if you like, a philosopher, and who knows, maybe actually I have a notion of instructing. . . . That may be, indeed, that may be." After the conversation about the man condemned to death, Aglaya asks mockingly: "That is, you think that you'll live more wisely than everyone?" The prince answers "with a calm and timid smile": "Yes, this thought has occurred to me sometimes."

The "idiot" proves to be a philosopher, the holy-fool prepares to instruct! The rupture of the two planes, the empirical and metaphysical, is sharply underlined. On the one the prince is a ridiculous simpleton, on the other a wise man and preacher. In our "dark world" he wanders gropingly; he is lost and helpless in a choral dance of phantoms, but he has an "essential mind"—a vision of genuine reality. In the third part of the novel Aglaya instinctively grasps the "idiot's" duality. "If they do say about you," she declares, "that your mind . . . that is, that you're sometimes afflicted in your mind, then it is unjust: I've decided that and have argued about it, because though you really are mentally afflicted (you, of course, won't be angry at this, I'm speaking *from a higher point*), yet on the other hand, your *essential mind* is better than any of them have, it's something that they've never even dreamed of, because there are two minds, one that is essential and one not essential. Isn't that so? It is, isn't it?" With his *essential mind* the prince rises *to mystical contemplation of the world in God.* But this happiness is purchased at the price of great suffering. The prince has experienced in his soul all the torture and anguish of the fallen Adam. An orphan, not knowing his family and having no parentage, a pitiful idiot, sent to Switzerland for treatment through the kindness of a benefactor, he in exile, in a lonely little mountain village, tasted all the bitterness of a foreign country, loneliness, abandonment. And for him, as for Adam expelled from paradise, the earth brought forth thistles and thorns, and he, like Adam sat at the closed gates of paradise and wept. "He remembered how he had stretched out his arms to that bright infinite blue and wept. What tormented him was that he was completely a *stranger to all* this. What was this banquet, what was this great everlasting holiday to which there was no end and to which he had long, always been drawn, since his very childhood, and in which he could never take part. . . . And everything has its path and everything knows its path, goes forth with a song and arrives with a song; only he knows nothing, understands nothing, neither men nor sounds, *a stranger to everything and an outcast*."

And here, when in tears he was tormented in the "shadow of death," his soul was illuminated by a great light: *a vision of paradise* visited him. That which he did not know and did not understand with his "not essential mind," was unexpectedly revealed to his essential mind—his mystical contemplation.

An instant later, foam at his mouth, he writhed in convulsions: an epileptic attack was beginning. Dostoevsky bestowed upon his beloved hero that which was most intimate and holy in him: his ecstasy and his epilepsy. But what is the spiritual value of that "unbearable second" of bliss? Can one credit a pathological state? Prince Myshkin answers for the author:

> What if it is a disease? What does it matter that it is an abnormal tension, if the actual result, if the moment of sensation, remembered and examined afterwards in health, proves to be harmony, beauty in the highest degree, gives an unheard of and an undivined feeling of completeness, measure, reconciliation, and an ecstatic, prayerful fusion with the very highest synthesis of life? . . . . This moment in itself was worth the whole of life.

The prince tells Rogozhin in Moscow: "At that moment somehow I seem to understand the extraordinary saying that *there shall be no more time*. . . . Probably this is that same second in which there was not enough time for the water to spill out of the epileptic Mohamet's overturned pitcher, though he had time in that very same second to survey all the habitations of Allah." The prince knows world harmony *through experience*, was really in the habitations of Allah, in paradise. Dostoevsky and his hero in their ecstasy beheld the divine foundation of the world, Sophia, that "fire of things" which kindles the soul forever. In this blinding light evil and sin disappeared like smoke. The "higher existence" overcame the inferior. The mystical experience was profound, authentic but incomplete, and in this incompletion lies the tragedy both of the writer and his hero.

Prince Myshkin brings people his "philosophy," his ecstatic world-sensation. His words sound solemnly: *"Now I'm going to see people."* What will he teach them? And again, only Aglaya guesses his secret. She compares the prince to Pushkin's "poor knight" who believed in his ideal and blindly surrendered his whole life to it. . . . "There, in these verses," she adds, "it is not said exactly what the 'poor knight's' ideal consisted of, but it is apparent that it was some shining image, an 'image of pure beauty.'" Aglaya concludes: "The 'poor knight' is that same Don Quixote, but only serious and not comic." This clearsightedness of love penetrates the very essence of the prince's nature. He arrives in the dark world with a shining vision of paradise: bewitched by the primeval "image of pure beauty," he does not perceive and does not want to perceive the distortions and perversions of the image. Here are his strength and weakness. He looks at the filthy cow-maid Aldonsa and sees in her the beautiful princess Dulcinea; and he is right: in the most fallen being, the image of God is incorruptible. But he is wrong not to notice Aldonsa: she is an inferior reality, but nonetheless *reality*. The prince believes that if all people would live by their "essential mind," they would at once find themselves in paradise; they have only to desire it and they would see the divine foundation of the world. In other words, to the "holy simpleton," the prince, as with Don Quixote, a foretaste of paradise has been given, but the way to it has not been indicated. Both preach ecstasy, but really, can ecstasy be taught? The prince convinces unseemly and evil people that they are beautiful and good, persuades the unfortunate that they are happy, looks at the world lying in evil and sees only the "image of pure beauty." At the Yepanchins' soirée Myshkin becomes inspired: "Listen," he exclaims, "in fact, can one really be unhappy? Oh, what do my grief and misfortune matter, if I have it in my power to be happy? You know, I don't understand how it's possible to go past a tree and not be happy seeing it. To speak with a man and not be happy that you love him. Oh, only I don't know how to express it . . . but how many things there are at every step, things so beautiful, which even the most hopeless man finds beautiful? Look at a child, look at God's sunrise, look at the grass, how it grows, look into eyes which gaze at you and love you."

These are some of the most magical words written by Dostoevsky. The prince's ecstasy ends in a fit. Aglaya succeeds in catching him in her arms and with horror hears the wild shriek of "the spirit that tore and cast down" the unfortunate man.

The prince does not perceive evil because he is not involved in it: he is *innocent*. He has the soul of a child. Professor Schneider in Switzerland said that "he was a complete child, that he was utterly a child, that he was like an adult only in stature and face, but in development, soul, character, and perhaps even mind—he was not an adult and so he would remain." He "does not like to be with adults, with people, with grownups, because he does not know how; with people he feels bored and oppressed." The acknowledgment is astounding; the prince opposes himself not only to adults, but also to *people in general*: he is not fully a man and therefore among people he feels oppressed; he passionately yearns to enter human life and cannot. The *prince is a being of another aeon—before the Fall*: he has a different destiny. Consequently, there is in his image a terrible transparency and elusiveness. The fact of his *not being fully incarnated* is connected with his asexuality: "Because of my inherent disease, I have no knowledge at all of women. . . . I can't marry anyone." It seems that he does not tread upon the earth, but hovers over it like a bodiless spirit in ineffectual pity for sinful men; he is tormented and commiserates but cannot help. Sinless himself, he does not understand that sin requires redemption and that the cross of Golgotha is inscribed in the history of the world. The prince's tragic failure is sharply defined by the spokesman of "practical reason" Yevgeny Pavlovich: "Dear prince," he says, *"paradise on earth is not easily bestowed:* but you, however, somewhat rely on paradise: paradise is a difficult thing, prince, much more difficult than it seems to your excellent heart." But the prince has the experience of organizing an earthly paradise: in the Swiss village he succeeded in creating around himself and the unfortunate consumptive girl Marie a brotherhood of children, founded on love. And this Swiss idyll he attempts to transfer into the world of darkness. In Myshkin's childlike dream is all the tragedy of utopianism. The prince does not understand that for fallen humanity the gates of primeval paradise have been barred forever, that its path goes not back to lost innocence, but forward to the transfiguration of the world.

From the Swiss "paradise" the prince falls into the "hell of Petersburg." Nastasya Filippovna, Rogozhin, Ganya, Aglaya, Lebedev writhe and groan in the dark blaze of passions. Myshkin tells them that the world is beautiful and that life is happiness. He torments them with compassion and lacerates them with love. He wants to save but destroys and is destroyed himself. In Dostoevsky's novels, ideas are embodied in people and dialectic is transformed into tragic conflict. Objections are raised against the prince's "thesis" by his friends-enemies—Ippolit and Rogozhin. Ippolit is as superfluous a guest at the feast as the prince, but he also passionately loves life and God's beautiful world. "That which matters is life, life alone," he asserts, "the process of discovering it, continual and eternal, and not at all its actual discovery." The prince preaches salvation through ecstatic love of life. Ippolit objects: And death? Will love really save me from death? I've got consumption and in two weeks I must die. How will the prince console me? And Ippolit comes to hate his friend. The prince's "mystical naturalism" is mercilessly denounced by the boy condemned to death. "The prince," he says, "in his Christian proofs will undoubtedly reach the happy conclusion that in the main it is even better that you die (Christians such as he always come to this idea—it is their favorite hobbyhorse)." Thus the prince's "Christianity" is unmasked. His other opponent Rogozhin refutes his teaching not by ideas, but by life. Through his love the prince wants to save Nastasya Filippovna. Rogozhin also loves her, is prepared to give up his life for her, but ends by killing her. The prince, like a child, does not know that in the fallen world the bright force of love is captivated by the dark element of eros, is tragically divided in two and distorted. Asexual, he does not understand the horror of sex, the murderousness of sensuality. He wants to save the world through faith and love and by deeds of love. Ippolit and Rogozhin contradict him: neither life nor love save: *they themselves stand in need of salvation.*

The religious drama of salvation and perdition is embodied in the *myth-plot* of the novel: the prince's struggle with Rogozhin for the soul of Nastasya Filippovna.

Here also we must distinguish two planes. *On the empirical plane* Nastasya Filippovna is a "proud beauty" and a "wronged heart." In her figure merge two lines of female characters of which one ("the proud beauty") stems from *Netochka Nezvanova* (young princess Katya), and the other (the "wronged heart") from *Poor People* (Varenka). She is closest to Dunya in *Crime and Punishment* and Polina in *The Gambler*. At seven years of age, the heroine was orphaned and was brought up in the village of the rich landowner Totsky; when she was seventeen years old, he made her his mistress. Four years later she moves, and establishes herself in Petersburg. The timid and melancholy young girl is transformed into a dazzling beauty, into an "extraordinary and unexpected being," possessed by pride, revenge, and contemptible hatred for her "benefactor." Totsky, intending to marry General Yepanchin's daughter Aleksandra, wants to give his former mistress in marriage to Ganya Ivolgin. Nastasya Filippovna learns that the latter is selling himself for 75,000, and with indignation rejects him. At this moment Rogozhin and Myshkin enter her life. One wants to buy her love for 100,000, the other offers his hand to her. Nastasya Filippovna darts about between them like a harassed beast. She yearns for salvation, but does not doubt her own destruction. Is it for her, Totsky's concubine, to dream about happiness with the prince? Is it for her, "Rogozhin's," to be a princess? She becomes intoxicated with shame and is consumed with pride; at the church, in her wedding gown, she runs away from Myshkin and with resignation submits to Rogozhin's knife. It is this melodramatic story of an innocent sinner and repenting Camille, written in the spirit of the fashionable French idea of *"la rehabilitation de la chair"* (Saint-Simon, George Sand) that Dostoevsky made the cover of his religious myth.

On the metaphysical plane his heroine is the "image of pure beauty," seduced by the "prince of this world" and waiting in her dungeon for a liberator. The soul of the world, the beautiful Psyche—existing in the bosom of the divinity, on the boundary of time—fell away from God. Having grown proud because of her likeness to God, she employed her freedom for evil and affirmed herself in "selfness." And together with her the whole world fell under the law of sin and death; "every flesh languishes and groans." From her former existence outside of time, Psyche has preserved memories of the "sounds of heaven"[7] and a feeling of fatal, irreparable guilt. The evil spirit that seduced her excites pride and a consciousness of guilt in the exile and through this drives her to destruction.

And here a man comes to her with tidings about her heavenly homeland. He too has been in the "shade of the gardens of paradise," he saw her there in the "image of pure beauty" and in spite of her earthly degradation, recognizes his other-worldly friend. By stages the author dexterously prepares the meeting of his heroes. At first the prince hears about Nastasya Filippovna, then three times he contemplates her portrait. " 'So this is Nastasya Filippovna?' he uttered, looking attentively and curiously at the portrait: 'Wonderfully beautiful!' he added immediately, with *warmth*. On the portrait was depicted a 'woman

---

[7] References throughout this section are to Lermontov's famous poem *The Angel*. It depicts an angel flying down through the midnight sky with a young soul in its arms. On its way the angel sings of innocence, paradise, and God. Then when the soul is left in this world of sorrow and tears, it remembers and longs for that heavenly sound.

of really *extraordinary beauty.'* " At first glance the prince recognizes
only the *beauty* of Psyche, at the second he observes her torture in
this world. "A remarkable face," he says, "a cheerful face, but she
has *suffered terribly*, hasn't she? Her eyes tell one that, here these
two cheek bones, the two points under her eyes. It is a *proud* face
terribly proud. . . . " At the third, "he draws the portrait to his lips
and kisses it."

Finally there comes the meeting. The prince is shaken: mingled with
his rapture is mystical terror. This is she, Psyche! "And how did you recognize that it was me?" Nastasya Filippovna questions him, "Where have
you seen me before? *How is it, in fact, it seems as though I have seen
him somewhere?* And permit me to ask why just now you were astounded out there? What is there so astounding about me?" The
prince answers confusedly that he recognized her from her portrait, that
she was as he had imagined her. . . . "I also seem to have seen you
somewhere." "Where, where?" "I have surely seen your eyes somewhere . . . but that can't be! . . . It's nonsense. . . . I've never been
here before. Perhaps, in a dream. . . ."

Thus takes place the mystical meeting of the two exiles from paradise. Vaguely they remember their heavenly homeland . . . as "in a
dream."

Nastasya Filippovna is prepared to destroy herself: she leaves
Totsky, breaks with Ganya, and wants to go away with Rogozhin.
The prince rushes to save her—he offers her his hand and assures her
that "she is not guilty of anything." "You are proud, Nastasya Filippovna," he says to her, "but perhaps you are so unhappy now that you
consider yourself actually guilty. . . . I saw your portrait a short while
ago and recognized a face that I knew. I felt at once *as though you
had already called me.* . . ." Mysterious words: the prince recognized
Psyche, heard her summons, guessed her longing to be liberated.
He painfully wants to save her, but does not know how. He thinks
that by the magic words "you are not guilty," he will shatter the
fetters of the evil that has enmeshed her. But she knows her fall, and
the prince's reminding of her lost purity only lacerates her. She yearns
for the redemption of her sin, and he talks about sinlessness after she
has fallen. And Nastasya Filippovna goes away with Rogozhin. "And
now I want to amuse myself, why, I'm a streetwalker."

The prince loves to say "beauty will save the world." And here he
has found that beauty. Its fate on earth is tragic: it is profaned, de-

graded, possessed by demonism, excites impure and evil feelings: vanity (in Ganya), sensualism (in Totsky and Yepanchin), sensual passion (in Rogozhin). Amidst the whirlwinds that she excites, her countenance becomes dark and is disfigured. The heavenly bride becomes an earthly woman and responds to the prince's compassionate fraternal love with an earthly erotic love. Rogozhin is forced to explain to his innocent rival: "And indeed can it be, prince, you still haven't grasped what's really going on here? . . . She's in love with somebody else—here, understand that. *Just as I love her now,* so she loves somebody else now. And that other man, do you know who? It's you! That you didn't know, did you?"

The prince's love does not save, but destroys; having come to love him, Nastasya Filippovna condemns herself, a "streetwalker," and consciously goes to her death. The prince knows that she is perishing *on account of him,* but endeavors to convince himself that it is not so, that "maybe God will even bring them together." He laments her as an "unfortunate demented," but loves another, Aglaya. Nevertheless, when this rival insults Nastasya Filippovna, the prince cannot bear her "desperate, frenzied face" and imploringly says to Aglaya: "Really, is this possible! You see she's so unhappy!"

Now Nastasya Filippovna can no longer be mistaken: the prince's pity is not love and it never was love. From their wedding ceremony, she runs away with Rogozhin and the latter kills her. This is why the murderer leads the prince up to her deathbed—the two together keep vigil over the dead woman's body; they are accomplices: they have both killed her by their "love."

Psyche awaited a liberator: the prince deceived her: she took his ineffectual pity for saving love. That same myth is employed by the author in *The Devils* and *Brothers Karamazov.* In the former novel, the motif of a liberator's imposture is sharply underlined: the captivated bride (Marya Timofeyevna) awaits her fated one. Stavrogin deceives her and she guesses that he is not Ivan the Tsarevich, but a pretender and shouts at him: "Grishka Otrepyev—anathema!" Her mysterious guilt is symbolized by her physical defect (she is "lame"). In *Brothers Karamazov* Grushenka holds the place of Nastasya Filippovna, Mitya–Rogozhin's, Alyosha–Prince Myshkin's, Liza Khokhlakova–Aglaya's. Alyosha's compassionate love helps, Mitya's passion does not destroy. But this is a different spiritual plane, a different mystical experience. Its symbol is not the "children's paradise" of

Prince Myshkin, but the Elder Zosima's monastic cell. In opposition to the secular just-man's dreamlike Christianity is set the "Orthodox" faith of the monk and holy ascetic.

We know from Dostoevsky's letters and rough drafts that the image of Aglaya was more weakly delineated in his imagination than any of the others, that he had great difficulty assigning her her proper place in the composition of the novel. In fact, the figure of the proud, willful girl never did receive its ultimate artistic embodiment.

In his sketchbook, there is an enigmatic notation: "Beauty will save the world—two examples of beauty." We might conjecture that the author wanted to contrast two images of beauty in the novel, and show their different fates in the sinful world. Nastasya Filippovna, beauty in degradation; Aglaya, beauty in innocence. Nastasya Filippovna, "a woman of extraordinary beauty"; Aglaya, "an uncontested beauty." The mysterious force of beauty is present in both of them. As she scrutinizes the portrait of Nastasya Filippovna, Adelaida Yepanchina exclaims: "Such beauty is a force. With such beauty, it is possible to turn the world upside-down." Prince Myshkin describes the faces of the Yepanchin sisters, but refuses to talk about Aglaya. "It is difficult to judge beauty," he explains. "I am still not prepared to. Beauty is an enigma."

Thus, according to the author's design, the idea of beauty is embodied in the two images of his heroines. The prince believes that beauty will save the world. Tragic experience shows him the reverse. In a world of evil, *it is necessary to save beauty*. With Nastasya Filippovna, the feeling of guilt flares into enraptured pride, and is transformed into sensuous ruin. With Aglaya, innocence passes over into capricious self-will and unbridled ambition. The one revels in her shame; the other, in her purity. The first avenges herself for Totsky's abuse; the second, for her love of the "idiot." But Aglaya's pride is only a variation on the theme of Nastasya Filippovna, and her rival's beauty eclipses her own. She is condemned to play a supporting role. There is a tragic grandeur in Nastasya Filippovna's rage; in Aglaya's capricious escapades, there is only childish irascibility. The former perishes out of her love for the prince; the latter marries an emigré Polish count "with a dark and ambiguous background" and falls under the influence of some Catholic priest.

The image of "the positively beautiful individual" did not attain its complete embodiment in the novel *The Idiot*. But Dostoevsky did not renounce the "immeasurable" task. The pilgrim Makar Dolgoruky in *A Raw Youth*, Bishop Tikhon in *The Devils*, the Elder Zosima and Alyosha in *Brothers Karamazov*—all bear witness to the author's incessant efforts to achieve "the miracle of embodying beauty."

XVI

Florence and Dresden
The Eternal Husband and
The Life of a Great Sinner

In January 1869 Dostoevsky wrote his niece, S. A. Ivanova, from Florence:

> In three months we will have been abroad two years. In my opinion, it's worse than being exiled in Siberia. I'm speaking seriously and without exaggeration. If here one finds such a sun and sky, and there are such *wonders of art*, unheard of and unimaginable, quite literally, as you have here in Florence, then in Siberia, when I came out of prison, there were other merits which do not exist here, and especially—Russians and the motherland, without which I cannot live.

The last words are also spoken "seriously" and without exaggeration: the writer was genuinely homesick for Russia, and all his letters are full of tormented complaints about his banishment. He was distressed by *The Idiot*'s failure. "I feel," he wrote to Strakhov, "that, compared with *Crime and Punishment, The Idiot*'s effect on the public has been weaker. And consequently all my *amour-propre* is now aroused: I would like to produce this effect." Reflecting upon the fate of his last novel, he expresses an opinion on his own creative work —an acknowledgment extremely valuable to us. "I have my particular view on reality (in art)," he wrote,

> and that which the majority call almost fantastic and exceptional, for me sometimes constitutes the very essence of the real. Commonplace phenomena and a conventional view of them is, in my opinion, no longer realism, but even the contrary. . . . Truly is not my fantastic "idiot" reality, and yet the most ordinary! Yes, precisely now such characters must exist in our strata of society that are torn away from the land—strata that in reality become fantastic.

In this way Dostoevsky defended himself from the attacks of his opponents: his novels are fantastic because Russia was fantastic, reality itself was fantastic; his realism was more profound than the realism of Goncharov and Turgenev with the "baseness of their outlook on reality." Of all the Russian writers only Lev Tolstoy, who "has succeeded in saying something of his own," interested him. He read *War and Peace* with enthusiasm, although Strakhov's rapture seemed exaggerated to him. "You ask in your letter," he wrote the critic, "what I'm reading. Well, I've been reading Voltaire and Diderot all winter. This, of course, has brought me both profit and pleasure."

Voltaire's *Candide*, in which Pangloss's optimism is so cleverly satirized, helped Dostoevsky in his struggle with utopianism. His "rebels" rise up against the reasonableness and justice of world history, and in their criticism are heard echoes of Voltaire's sarcasms. A year before *The Brothers Karamazov* the writer noted in his copybook: "Momento. For the whole of my life. Write the Russian *Candide*." In Ivan Karamazov's philosophy, Russian Voltaireanism finds its culmination.

Anna Grigoryevna's pregnancy forced the Dostoevskys to quit Italy, where they were completely alone, and seek asylum in a Slavic country. They went to Prague, but did not find a single lodging free there; reluctantly they returned to a city they already knew—Dresden. In September 1869 a daughter, Lyubov, was born. The writer complained of his complete lack of funds: "How can I write," he asked Maikov,

when I'm hungry, when in order to get two thalers for the telegram, I pawned my trousers? Well, the hell with me and my hunger. But after all, she is feeding a child, what if she *herself* goes to pawn her last warm woolen petticoat. And this is the second day now we've had snow (I'm not lying, check the papers!); why, she can catch cold. . . . And after this they demand from me artistry, the purity of poetry, without strain, without stifling, and they point to Turgenev! Let them look at the conditions in which I am working!

Dostoevsky wrote the tale *The Eternal Husband* for the journal *Dawn* and with difficulty obtained an advance of 100 rubles from the editors. He was planning a long novel, or more precisely, a series of novels and set about writing with passion. "I rise at one in the afternoon," he informed S. A. Ivanova (December 14, 1869),

because I work during the night, and otherwise I can't fall asleep at night. I work from three to five. I take a walk for a half-hour, to the post office, and from the post office return home through the

Royal Garden—always one and the same route. At home we have dinner. At seven o'clock I go out again for a walk and again home through the Royal Garden. At home I drink tea and at 10:30 sit down to work. I work till five o'clock in the morning. Then I lie down and, as soon as it strikes 6 o'clock, I fall immediately asleep.

The plan of *The Life of a Great Sinner* was interrupted by that of *The Devils*. The writer was oppressed by the thought that he was torn away from Russia. He wrote to Maikov (March 25, 1870):

Abroad I will really fall behind—not the age, not the knowledge of what's going on among us (to be sure, I know this better than you, for *every day* I read *three Russian newspapers* through to the last line, and receive two journals)—but I will fall behind *the living stream of life*:—not the idea, but its flesh—and oh, how this influences artistic work. . . .

He must return to Russia at any price whatsoever: only in the homeland would he be able to write *The Life*. "Here is still another thing," he confessed to S. A. Ivanova: "I long terribly, almost irresistibly, to travel to the East before returning to Russia; i.e., to Constantinople, Athens, the Archipelago, Syria, Jerusalem, and Athos. . . . Supposing there'd be no reason to regret the money spent: I could write a book about the trip to Jerusalem, which would reimburse everything, and such books sell well. I speak from experience."

The Franco-Prussian War began. Dostoevsky wrote with repugnance of the Germans who plundered and tortured like a horde of Huns. In the reading room every evening he saw German professors, doctors, and students who demanded the bombardment of Paris. He spoke with contempt about the "young Germany" and asserted that a nation that had proclaimed the right of the sword, blood, and violence was condemned to destruction.

The tragic year 1870 came to an end. Dostoevsky informed Maikov (December 30, 1870):

Yes, by all means I want to come, and will return in spring for sure. Here I find myself in such a hideous state of mind that I almost cannot write. It's a horror to me how difficult it is to write. I feverishly watch the events, both at home and here, and have seen much of life during these four years. I've lived powerfully, though in isolation. What God will send further, I will accept without complaint.

. . . But if you only knew what a genuine repugnance, nearly hatred, Europe has aroused in me during these four years.

His epileptic attacks were accompanied by periods of "extraordinary anguish" and unbearable mystical terror. "I've been ailing for some time," he wrote to Strakhov (March 18, 1871), "but I have been chiefly tormented after a fit of epilepsy. When the attacks have not occurred for a long time and suddenly break out, then an extraordinary, moral anguish results. I come to despair. Formerly this depression continued about three days after the fit, but now up to seven, up to eight days, although the fits themselves occur much less frequently in Dresden than anywhere else. . . ."

Anna Grigoryevna bore her third pregnancy with difficulty: she grew thin, was nervous, did not sleep at night. Her husband's condition troubled her, and she resorted to an extreme means—she proposed that he go to Wiesbaden to play roulette.

Dostoevsky lost everything, and at night in despair ran in search of a Russian priest. On the dark unfamiliar street he found a temple that he took for an Orthodox church; he wanted to go in, but it turned out to be a synagogue. At midnight he wrote to his wife: "Now this fantasy has ended forever. . . . Moreover, I have, as it were, been wholly reborn morally (I say this both to you and to God). . . . Don't think I'm mad, Anya, my guardian angel. A great thing has happened to me. The hideous fantasy that tormented me for almost ten years has vanished. Anya, trust that our resurrection has drawn near, and believe that from now on I'll attain my goal and will bring you happiness." Actually, he underwent some sort of mystical experience. From that day, Dostoevsky never gambled again in his life. The "fantasy" had disappeared instantly and for good.

The writer's last impression of Europe was a confirmation and justification of his Christian world-view: the people who had been preaching paradise on earth ended in the Paris Commune. Reality hastened to prepare material for the author of *The Devils*. On May 18, 1871, he wrote to Strakhov: ". . . But consider the Paris Commune. . . . In essence, it's all the same Rousseau and the dream of recreating the world anew through reason and experience (positivism). They desire the happiness of man and stop at Rousseau's definition of the word 'happiness,' i.e., at fantasy, not even justified by experience. The conflagration of Paris is a monstrosity. 'It didn't succeed, so perish the world, for the Commune is above the happiness of the world and France.' However, to them (yes, and to many), this delirium does not seem a monstrosity, but, on the contrary, *beauty*. And so *the aesthetic idea has become muddled in the new humanity*. In the West they have lost Christ (through the fault of Catholicism), and therefore the West is collapsing, solely because of this. The ideal has been altered, and how clear this is!"

Shigalyov and Pyotr Verkhovensky in *The Devils* are people who have passed through the experience of the Paris Commune.

In July 1871 Dostoevsky received an advance of 1,000 rubles from the *Russian Messenger* and returned with his family to Russia. Before their departure from Dresden, fearing a search at the Russian border, he burned the manuscripts of *The Idiot*, *The Eternal Husband*, and the first variant of *The Devils*. On the ninth of July he arrived in Petersburg; on the sixteenth of July a son, Fyodor, was born to him. Dostoevsky's "European exile" lasted more than four years (April 14, 1867–July 9, 1871).

Anna Grigoryevna informs us in her memoirs: "Strakhov pressed my husband to become a contributor to *Dawn*. Fyodor Mikhailovich agreed to this with pleasure, but only when he had finished his novel, *The Idiot*, with which he was having such difficulty and which very much dissatisfied him."

Having finished the novel, he wrote to Strakhov: "I have a story, very short, about two printed sheets. . . . I was thinking of writing this story four years ago, in the year of my brother's death, in response to the words of Ap. Grigoryev, who praised my *Notes from Underground* and said to me at the time: 'This is how you must write.' But this is not *Notes from Underground;* this is completely different in form, although its substance is the same, my usual substance; if only you, Nikolai Nikolayevich, will acknowledge that I as a writer have some particular substance."

From the little story grew a tale of eleven printed sheets with the title *The Eternal Husband*. As always his first enthusiasm changed into dissatisfaction and, finally, aversion. The writer complained of the heat in Florence, of his attacks, and lack of funds. "Can you imagine what penal labor this has been," he wrote to S. A. Ivanova, "Even more so as I began to hate this obnoxious tale from the very beginning."

The Eternal Husband was printed in the first two issues of *Dawn* for 1870. Sofya Kovalevskaya informs us in her memoirs that in 1866 Dosto-

evsky once narrated to their family a scene from a novel that he had
thought up in his youth (the author himself wrote to Strakhov that
the idea of his story arose in the year of his brother's death, i.e., in
1865). Kovalevskaya relates the content of this scene:

The hero, a middle-aged landowner with a good and thorough
education, has lived abroad, reads good books, buys paintings and
engravings. In his youth he led a dissolute life, but later became more
serious, devotes himself to his wife and children, and enjoys universal esteem. One morning he wakes up, the sun is shining through the
window of his bedroom; everything around him is clean, beautiful,
and comfortable. And he feels himself clean and worthy of respect.
A sensation of satisfaction and peace flows through his entire body.
Like a true sybarite, he delays getting up in order that he might
enjoy a little longer the agreeable state of his general physical pleasure. Finding himself between dream and waking, he relives in his
memory various pleasant moments of his last journey abroad. He sees
again the enchanting thread of light that falls on the bare shoulders
of St. Cecilia in the Munich gallery. And he again recalls a clever
phrase from a book he read not long ago "about beauty and the
harmony of the world!"

Suddenly, just at the very highest point of his agreeable imaginings
and reminiscences, he feels a certain disagreeable inner ache, a
gloomy memory. So it happens with people who have an old wound
from which the bullet has not been removed: several minutes earlier
they were not in pain at all—and suddenly the old wound begins to
smart, smarts and smarts. The landowner begins to ponder: what
does this mean? He is in no way sick, he has no concerns, and meanwhile, what is pressing his heart ever more and more intensely? At
last, he begins to surmise that it is a certain memory there; he makes
an effort, exerts his memory, and suddenly actually recalls, and moreover so vividly and realistically, that his whole being experiences a
repugnance as though it had taken place yesterday, not twenty years
ago. And in the course of all this time, in the course of twenty years,
it had not disturbed him in the least. He recalls how once, after a
night spent in dissipation, drawn along by his drunken companions,
he had violated a little ten-year-old girl.

And Sofya Kovalevskaya recalls that with a cry of horror her mother
interrupted the narrator.

This scene is turned into the exposition of *The Eternal Husband*.
The motif of a wronged girl, indicated in *Crime and Punishment*

(Svidrigailov), is developed in *The Devils* (Stavrogin's confession). The story *The Eternal Husband* is constructed with extraordinary art. In respect to form this is perhaps Dostoevsky's most accomplished work. The writer always recognized that he lacked a "sense of measure," that the composition of his novels was not harmonious. "I just don't know how," he confessed to Strakhov; "to this day I have not learned to master my means. A multitude of separate novels and tales are compressed together into one, so that there is neither measure nor harmony. . . ." One can conjecture that in *The Eternal Husband* Dostoevsky set himself a formal task and resolved it brilliantly. The structure of the tale is striking in its severity, the proportion of its parts, unity of plan, and symmetry of episodes. The action falls harmoniously into three parts, of which the first—the prehistory—is concerned with the past (Velchaninov's liaison with Trusotsky's wife in the city of T.); the second takes place in Petersburg (Velchaninov's dueling with Trusotsky); the third—the epilogue—at the station of one of the southern railways (Velchaninov's meeting with Trusotsky's second wife). The central part, in its turn, is divided into three periods, each of which occupies five chapters. The composition satisfies all of the rules of classical poetics (exposition, complication, rising action, culmination, catastrophe, denouement, epilogue); the episodes are apportioned according to a strict plan, the details seem to be measured out in advance. "Harmony" and a "sense of measure" triumph. This time the writer fully "mastered his means." *The Eternal Husband* is a chef-d'oeuvre of Russian narrative art.

The action of the story expresses the eternal husband's tragic conflict with the "eternal lover." Between the fashionable-society Don Juan Velchaninov and the provincial civil servant Trusotsky lies an abyss. The author underlines their contrast—social, psychological, spiritual. They are antipodes, essentially repulsing one another. After their very first meeting we have a presentiment of the inevitability of their collision and struggle to the death. The motif of mutual repulsion is developed with increasing intensity. But parallel to it, gradually arises and grows a contrary motif of mutual attraction. The rivals and mortal enemies are mysteriously alike; they have a common fate; on the spiritual plane they form a pair and supplement each other. They cannot tolerate each other, but they are also unable to exist without each other. Their hatred is love: these are two convicts fettered to one chain. Velchaninov—a "man who has lived much and broadly," of a most fashionable upbringing—toward the age of thirty-nine suddenly feels that he is growing old and takes sick with acute hypochondria. A lawsuit over an estate suffers a bad reverse; he remains for the summer in Petersburg, and the white nights, the dust, and stifling heat irritate his nerves still more. His "snobbish impudent self-confidence," his ability to please women, his gaiety and flippancy turn into anguish and moroseness. In his eyes appear melancholy and cynicism; he begins to like solitude and to reflect upon "higher causes." At night, during periods of insomnia, thoughts and sensations divide him. "Suddenly and God knows why" he recalls events from his remote past and memories that are still "scathing." He sees before him a little old civil servant whom he had offended for the sake of a successful pun; the wife of a school teacher whom he slandered "solely for a joke," a girl of the lower middle class with whom he "himself not knowing why" had begotten a child. All these pranks seem to him now to be actual crimes, but at the same time he knows that "all these tears of repentance are fruitless and that he will never change."

Velchaninov is represented to us in a state of inner crisis, of peculiar moral illness. It begins in the form of anguish, vague and without cause; then gradually it materializes in the image of "a stranger with crape on his hat." The feeling of guilt is mysteriously connected with this gentleman in mourning. Velchaninov remembers that he met him on the street about two weeks ago and felt a purposeless animosity. At their second meeting he spits from "pointless aversion." After the third, he begins obsessively to think about him. After the fourth, his animosity becomes madness: "By God, I'll smash him to pieces. It's only too bad that I don't carry a cane! I'll buy a cane!" At last, upon meeting the stranger for the fifth time in a restaurant, he shouts at him: "Hey, you! With the crape on your hat! You're hiding now! Stop: who are you?" The gentleman runs away in confusion, and the hero, astonished, asks himself: "And what if he's not actually pestering me, but I'm pursuing him, and the whole farce lies in this?" The same night he has a dream: a crowd of people accuse him of a crime that he committed; among them is a certain strange man whom at one time he very much loved and from whom he now awaits sentence or acquittal. But the man keeps quiet, and Velchaninov begins to beat him with infuriation and "limitless pleasure." Suddenly three sonorous strokes of a little bell are heard. The hero wakes up, raises the curtain on the window, and on the pavement opposite sees the "gentleman with the crape." Several minutes later Pavel Pavlovich Trusotsky comes into his room. Thus Velchaninov slowly realizes his mysterious connection with his "friend-enemy." Repulsion, animosity, aversion, frenzy, a yearning for murder grow simultaneously with attraction. He cannot not think about this "rascal." He is bewitched by the stranger: "Here I'm at it again." He is vexed: "Again I'm thinking about him. And what the hell do I care about the look in his eyes? Can't I live without this gallows-bird!" Trusotsky rises out of Velchaninov's nightmare like a fantasy of his diseased conscience, like his incarnated sin. Dostoevsky enters into the dark and still unexplored region of the metapsychic communion of the human consciousness. Ten years ago the hero chanced upon the city T., often visited the civil servant Trusotsky's home, and became the lover of his wife Natalya Vasilyevna. This liaison continued for an entire year. Natalya Vasilyevna, a dissolute and cold woman, possessed the "gift of enslaving and dominating." When she grew tired of Velchaninov, she discarded him like an "old, worn-out shoe," and took a somewhat younger lover. She held her husband in submission: he adored her, noticed nothing, and was happy. Pavel Pavlovich proved himself the classical example of the "eternal husband": "he was only a husband and nothing more."

Trusotsky informs Velchaninov of the death of his wife; he came to Petersburg with his daughter Liza who had been born eight months after Velchaninov's departure from T. Pavel Pavlovich has taken to drink, leads a dissipated life, and torments the unfortunate girl. Velchaninov surmises that Liza is his daughter and places her in a family of his friends. The center of our attention gradually is shifted from the lover onto the "eternal husband." Trusotsky is surrounded by enigma: at first timid and deferential, he becomes ever more unconstrained, derisive, and insolent. He does not reveal his secret until the end and only at the denouement do we understand his strange conduct. He tells Velchaninov that he found his wife's correspondence with another of her lovers, Bagautov: the hero does not remember having himself written a single letter to Natalya Vasilyevna, and constantly asks himself: does the husband know about his liaison with the deceased, or not? He is convinced that Liza is his daughter, but even here Trusotsky cunningly sustains his doubts. The lover wants an open, honorable struggle; the husband dissimulates in buffoonery, in mocking assurances of devotion, in ambiguous outpourings of sentiment. He forces the lover to drink champagne with him and clamors to kiss him.

Everything appears doubled, is confused, shaken, sways, tosses in

Trusotsky: he embodies in himself the "dichotomy" of the hero's thoughts. "I need him, this man!" exclaims Velchaninov. "I must unriddle him, and then too decide. Here we have a duel." And he feels that his destiny is bound up with its solution. Trusotsky is a venomous fog, having risen from the depth of his own soul and threatening to poison him. If he unriddles him—the sorcery will disappear and he will recover. The conflict takes on a tragic character, this is a struggle for life. Trusotsky, tittering and whimpering, revolves around Velchaninov like a petty demon, envelops him in a net of insinuations, of spiteful jests, painful grimaces, and malicious winks. The lover is in the power of this "buffoon" and "madman" and he has by his own sin created this painful tie. Liza's death appears to him as a deliverance: it seems that, having lost his daughter whom he had come to love ardently, he "will be quits" with his adversary. With this the first part concludes. This is not the end, but only a respite before a new, more violent skirmish between the enemies.

Trusotsky wishes to marry a fifteen-year-old girl and implores Velchaninov to meet his fiancée. They go to the Zakhlebinins' villa, and amidst the company of young people the lover agilely assumes his habitual role of a worldly charmer and conqueror of hearts. The fiancée confides her secret to him: she hates Trusotsky and loves a young nihilist. In rage the "eternal husband" carries off his rival and the witness of his shame. Finally, the catastrophe erupts. Velchaninov has an attack of liver bile; Trusotsky touchingly nurses him, and at night attempts to cut his throat. On the following day he departs, after having sent to his rival an old letter of Natalya Vasilyevna's. And so, he knew that Velchaninov was his wife's lover. The "husband's" riddle is solved; he is disarmed—his evil charms have lost their power, and he disappears, like the dream out of which he arose. The "lover" is saved. The crisis of conscience has passed, and he is recovering. "A feeling of extraordinary, immense joy seized him," concludes the author. "Something had ended, had resolved, a sort of horrible anguish had gone away and dissipated completely. . . . He recognized clearly that he had escaped a terrible danger." Trusotsky had attempted to slit his throat with a razor, but had only wounded his hand. They "were quits."

In the epilogue, two years later, at a station on a southern railroad, Velchaninov meets Trusotsky for the last time. He is accompanied by his wife Lipochka, a provincial lady vulgarly and tastelessly dressed, and a friend of the house, a young lancer Mitenka. The "eternal husband" remains true to his life's role.

In this ingenious story Dostoevsky discovered laws of the spiritual world hitherto unknown. Human souls are joined by mysterious threads: one consciousness, like a magnetic field, attracts another, opposite and complementary to it. Trusotsky, the "eternal husband," is indissolubly fettered to Velchaninov, the "eternal lover." Their opposition is based on similarity: both of them are held in a woman's captivity. The lover Don Juan is threatened by the danger of enslavement: he can be debased to the state of an "eternal husband." Conversely, the "eternal husband" is an unsuccessful Don Juan: he envies the lover as an ideal he cannot attain. Velchaninov sees Trusotsky and shudders with hatred and aversion, but meanwhile is unable to tear himself away from his repulsive image. He recognizes himself in this distorted mirror. In the same way, Raskolnikov is bewitched by Svidrigailov, Stavrogin by Pyotr Verkhovensky, Ivan Karamazov by Smerdyakov. Shameful and comic is the role of the "eternal husband": his adoration of his wife, blindness, and friendship with her lover. But really is not the role of the "eternal lover" shameful? Velchaninov, enchanting the young girls at the Zakhlebinins' villa by singing passionate romances and conquering the heart of the provincial Lipochka, abases himself no less than Trusotsky. Both the husband and the lover are equally chained to a woman and in this slavery of passion lose their personalities. At bottom, their fate is identical. Don Juan hates the eternal husband as a threat to himself, the eternal husband takes revenge upon Don Juan for the failure of his own life. In Dostoevsky the idea of Don Juanism develops dialectically, disintegrating into opposites, and polarizing in the extremes of the "eternal husband" and the "eternal lover."

When the duel has ended and the husband's personality is decisively unriddled by the lover, Velchaninov states the characteristics of his opponent. How could such a moral monster, "such a Quasimodo" be formed? And here he resolves: "This Quasimodo from T.," he reflects, "was more than stupid and noble enough to fall in love with his wife's lover. . . . He esteemed me for nine years, honored my memory, and remembered my 'dictums.' But did he love me yesterday when he professed his love and said, 'Let's settle our accounts'? Yes, *it was from malice that he loved me*—this love is the strongest." Trusotsky's hatred arises out of offended love, a noble trust deluded is changed into hateful malice.

Velchaninov continues:

> But why it could be, but why, it surely was so, that I made a colossal impression on him in T.—just that, colossal and gratifying, and it is precisely with *such a Schiller* in the form of a Quasimodo that this could happen. . . . It would be curious to know exactly how I impressed him. Actually, perhaps by my fresh gloves and knowing how to put them on. Quasimodos love aesthetics, oh, they love them. . . . Hm! he came here in order to "embrace me and to shed tears. . . ." That is, he came to kill me, and thought that he was coming "to embrace and shed tears." But what if I had wept with him, maybe he would in fact have forgiven me, because he wanted terribly to forgive! Oh, how glad he was when he forced me to kiss him. Only he didn't know then how it would end: would he embrace me or cut my throat. *The most monstrous monster—is the monster with noble feelings: I know this by personal experience.*

The idea of the mystical connection between the two Don Juans is completed in the finale with concrete psychological content. Trusotsky is defined as a *disenchanted romantic* (Schiller) and an embittered dreamer. For twenty years he did not divine that his dissolute wife was having lovers, for nine years he honored and esteemed Velchaninov: in what blindness, in what a fantastic world this naive man lived! In this being torn away from life, a "dichotomy of thoughts and sensations" arises, loftiness becomes "Schillerism," worth turns into monstrosity. The man-milksop, the weak and impersonal "eternal husband" with the soul of a romantic is a comic and pitiable figure. "The most monstrous monster—is the monster with noble feelings." The theme of "dreaming," passing through all of Dostoevsky's work (especially in the period prior to Siberia), reaches its culmination in *The Eternal Husband*. The "Quasimodo" with the soul of a Schiller has the underground man's psychology. The lover in frenzy shouts at the husband "Be -e off with your *underground* rubbish, you are yourself *underground* rubbish."

But toward the end of the conflict Velchaninov makes an unexpected and strange discovery: he himself is the same "underground man" as his opponent. *And in this they are joined;* with all their diversity, they are alike in a fatal manner. In each of them, the monstrous image of the other is reflected, as in a mirror. Velchaninov confesses to Pavel

Pavlovich: "Both of us are depraved, *underground*, hateful men." Really, does not the lover suffer from the same inner division as the husband, does he not also recognize all the abomination of his filthy and empty life, understanding at the same time that these "tears of repentance" are completely senseless? Thus the theme of Don Juanism is interwoven with the theme of the "underground" and the mystical connection of human consciousness is disclosed on two planes.

Dostoevsky was right, informing Strakhov that the "substance" of his story was the same as in *Notes from Underground.* "My usual substance," he added. What this "substance" consists of we now know: Dostoevsky's works are *the history of human consciousness in its tragic duality.*

At the end of 1868, in a period of tormenting work on the last part of *The Idiot,* Dostoevsky conceived a new "huge novel." He informed Maikov (December 11, 1868): "Here I have in mind now a huge novel, the name of it is *Atheism* (for God's sake, this is between us), but before beginning it, I must read through almost an entire library of atheists, Catholics, and Orthodox. . . . I have my character: a Russian, one of our society and on in years, not very educated, but not uneducated either, not without rank, suddenly, well on in his years, loses his faith in God. All his life he has been concerned only with his career, has never done anything unconventional, and until he is 45, has not distinguished himself in any way. (The solution is psychological: profound sentiment; a man and a Russian.) The loss of faith in God has a colossal effect on him (properly the action in the novel, the circumstances are many). He moves about among the new generation, among atheists, among the Slavs and Europeans, among Russian fanatics and hermits, among priests; and, incidently, strongly bites at the bait of a Jesuit propagandist, a Pole; from him descends into the abyss of a sect of flagellants; and at the end attains both Christ and the Russian land, the Russian Christ and the Russian God. But for me it comes to this: write this last novel, even if it kills me—I will express myself completely. . . ."

The concept of the "last novel" is religious; having lost his faith, a Russian in his searchings becomes acquainted with all the varieties of religious experience (atheists, Slavophiles, Westernizers, fanatics, monks, Orthodox priests, Catholic Jesuits, flagellants) and, finally, attains the "Russian Christ." *Atheism* was never written, but its idea was realized in various refractions in *The Devils, A Raw Youth* and *Broth-*

ers Karamazov. Near to the hero of *Atheism* are the "God-seekers" who have lost their faith, Stavrogin and Versilov, and Alyosha Karamazov, who has attained the Russian Christ.

On January 25, 1869, the writer informed S. A. Ivanova: "The theme is 'Atheism.' (This is not an exposure of contemporary convictions, this is something else and a genuine poem). . . . Two or three characters have been terribly well composed in my mind, among others a Catholic priest-enthusiast (somewhat like *St. François Xavier*). . . . If I don't write this, then it will begin to torment me. . . ."

The rough drafts of *Atheism* are very scanty. The hero's personality is scarcely indicated: he is a money-lender, one of Dostoevsky's numerous exponents of the idea of the "Covetous Knight." Suddenly he undergoes a spiritual change. "It's impossible to live this way, but where is one to go?" He decides to reform. "Self-education requires stubborn effort. . . . Terrible effort is needed, for I am a passionate usurer and love gold," he says. And the author adds: "He has been possessed by the idea of self-mastery. . . . The thought of progressive self-perfection through deeds of heroic sanctity astounds him (he has no faith); he wants to attain perfection (undertakes heroic deeds and falls at once). Self-perfection little by little. Then you will love nature and find God." He secretly does good deeds. The basic lines of the plot are indicated: the thief Kulishov kills either the hero's father or his wife. He assumes the blame himself. "The money-lender says to his fiancée: I'll abandon my property and go to be tried by suffering, for I'm not an atheist, but believe. She answers him: if you go, I too will go with you. Then he, not believing in any reward if he goes (for he is an atheist), resolves to part with his property differently, i.e., to shoot himself. Being convicted of his wife's death saves him, and he goes to suffer, | to Siberia with joy."

Thus the finale is indicated: salvation through heroic deeds, the attainment of faith through suffering; the usurer's fate remotely suggests the fate of Mitya Karamazov. In the rough drafts of *Atheism* are met: the murderer Kulishov, who in the notebooks for *The Life of a Great Sinner* will turn into Kulikov, and in *The Devils* into Fedka, the convict; the cripple (a hunchback) and the captain (Kulishov murders them) are prototypes of Marya Timofeyevna and Captain Lebyadkin in *The Devils*; and, finally, the prince, the beautiful woman, and the protégée are the future Stavrogin, Liza, and Dasha.

The plan was not developed beyond this primitive stage. The author was absorbed in other work and did not return to his idea until the end

of the year 1869. In December there arose a new project, more grandiose, and it engulfed the preceding plan. The idea of *Atheism* was
absorbed in the idea of *The Life of a Great Sinner*. On December 14,
1869, Dostoevsky wrote to S. A. Ivanova:

> I intend something much more important for it [*The Russian Mes-
> senger*]. This is a novel of which the first section will be printed in
> the *Russian Messenger*. The whole thing will be finished perhaps
> in five years and will be broken up into three tales, distinct from one
> another. This novel is all my expectation and all the hope of my life
> —not only in a monetary respect. This is my greatest idea which only
> now, in the last two years, has expressed itself within me. But in or-
> der to write it, I mustn't hurry. I don't want to spoil it. This idea is
> everything for which I have lived. Meanwhile, on the other hand, in
> order to write this novel, I will have to be in Russia. For example,
> the second half of this first tale takes place in a monastery. I need
> not only to see one (I've seen many), but also to live in a monas-
> tery. . . .

Three months later he informed Strakhov that he had had the idea
of his new novel for three years, that it was possible to write the first
section abroad, since the action was to begin many years ago; that the
novel would be at least of the same dimension as Tolstoy's novel, and
would consist of five separate novels. "The general title, otherwise, will
be *The Life of a Great Sinner* with a special title for each section," he
added.

Finally, in a letter to Maikov (March 25, 1870) the writer expounded
a detailed plan of the *Life*. . . .

> The first tale I intend for Kashpirov [i.e., for *Dawn*]: here the action
> will still belong to the forties. *The main question, which will be
> dealt with through all the parts, is the very one which has tormented
> me consciously or unconsciously throughout my entire life—the
> existence of God.* The hero in the course of his life is now an atheist,
> now a believer, then a fanatic and sectarian, then an atheist again.
> The second tale will take place all in a monastery. On this second
> tale I have set all my *hopes.* Perhaps it'll be said at last that not
> everything I have written is nonsense. I will confess to you alone,
> Apollon Nikolayevich: in the second tale I want to introduce Tikhon
> Zadonsky as the principal figure[1]—of course, under a different name,

---

[1] St. Tikhon Zadonsky (Timofey Sokolov) was born 1724 into a very poor rural
family in the province of Novgorod. Educated at the seminary, he early displayed
great virtue and intellectual accomplishments. He was appointed suffragan Bishop
of Novgorod in 1761 and Bishop of Voronezh in 1763. As prelate he worked tire-

but also a bishop who will be living in a monastery in retirement.

A 13-year-old boy, who has taken part in committing a crime, intelligent and depraved (I know this type, our educated circle), the future hero of the novel, is put into the monastery by his parents to be instructed. This young wolf and child-nihilist meets Tikhon. (You surely know the character and the whole person of Tikhon.) There in the same monastery I shall place Chaadayev[2] (under another name, of course). Why shouldn't Chaadayev have been confined to a monastery for a year? Suppose that Chaadayev, after writing his first essay, for which the doctors used to examine him every week, grew impatient and published abroad, for example, a brochure in French; it could very easily have happened then that for this he would have been sent off to live in a monastery for a year. Others too can come to visit Chaadayev. Belinsky, for example, Granovsky,[3] Pushkin even (of course I don't really have Chaadayev, but in the novel I'm only taking this type). In the monastery is also Pavel Prussky,[4] as well as Golubov, and the monk Parfeny. (In this world I'm an expert and know the Russian monastery from childhood.) But most important of all is Tikhon and the boy. . . . Now, don't talk about Tikhon. Perhaps I will portray a majestic, *positive*, holy figure. This is not Kostanzhoglo[5] and not the German (I've for-

---

lessly for social justice, education, and morality, but finally, because of a nervous ailment, he asked permission to retire and spent the rest of his life in the monastery of Zadonsk. He was a remarkable preacher and writer, combining in his spiritual way aspects of Western evangelism and devotion to the crucified Savior. His veneration as a saint grew rapidly and he was formally canonized by the Church in 1860.

[2] Pyotr Yakovlevich Chaadayev (1794-1856) was one of the most influential philosophical and intellectual figures of the early decades of the 19th century. The son of a wealthy landowner, he attended Moscow University and served in the Napoleonic campaigns. Abroad he became acquainted with Schelling and was very much influenced by his thought. In 1829 Chaadayev undertook writing his *Philosophical Letters* (in French). His philosophical system was strongly neo-Platonic, influenced by later Christian thought and German Idealism. He conceived of the world as a unity through Christianity, or more exactly as attaining unity through Roman Catholicism. His first *Philosophical Letter* violently criticized Russia and its role historically and culturally. Upon its publication in 1836, he was declared insane by Nikolai I and placed under house arrest and the surveillance of a doctor.

[3] Timofey Granovsky (1813-1855), noted professor of history at Moscow University, a Westernizer, friend of Herzen and Belinsky, and one of the leaders of the idealist movement of the forties. His public lectures (1843-1846) mark an epoch in the history of Russian intellectual thought.

[4] Prussky=the Prussian.

[5] Kostanzhoglo is the ideal landowner in the second part of Gogol's *Dead Souls*; the German in Goncharov's *Oblomov* is Stolz. Both are embodiments of industry, practicality, and efficiency.

Lavretsky is the weak hero, a Slavophile and idealist, of Turgenev's *Nest of* gotten his name) in Oblomov. How are we to know: perhaps, Tikhon is precisely the Russian *positive* type that our literature is seeking, and not Lavrovsky, not Chichikov, not Rakhmetov, etc. It's true, I will create nothing, I will only present the real Tikhon whom long ago I took to my heart with enthusiasm. But I will consider even this, if it succeeds, as an important achievement for myself. The first tale, though, is the hero's childhood; naturally they are not children in the scene; it is a romance.

The idea of spiritual sufferings and the comparative examination of all religious beliefs, expressed in the plan of *Atheism*, becomes concrete in the *Life*. In the monastery there are: a Russian saint, Tikhon Zadonsky, a child-nihilist, the Westernizers Chaadayev and Granovsky, the atheist Belinsky, the monk Parfeny, and the former Old-Believers Pavel Prussky and Golubov.

In the forties Pavel Prussky founded a schismatic monastery near Gumbinnen, but ended by converting to the Orthodox faith. Konstantin Yefimovich Golubov was his disciple, the editor of an Old-Believer journal *Truth*, which was published in Johannesburg. This former schismatic, a peasant and self-taught philosopher, also joined the Church and defended Russia's need for autocracy united with the Orthodox faith. The monk Parfeny, tonsured in a Mount Athos monastery, wrote many works against the schism. Dostoevsky was deeply impressed by his book *The Narrative of Parfeny, a tonsured monk of Holy Mount-Athos, about his wanderings through Russia, Moldavia, Turkey and the H. Land*. It influenced the stylistic formulation of the Elder Zosima's sermons in <u>Brothers Karamazov</u>. From it also was borrowed the scene of the holy-fool Semyon Yakovlevich in *The Devils*.

Notes from *The Life of a Great Sinner* have been preserved in sketchbook No. 2: the first entry is dated September 8/20, 1869. The author outlined the grandiose plan of the novel in the form of five tales: three of them in twenty printed sheets and two in forty. He noted down: "20 childhood, 20 the monastery, 40 before exile, 20 the female and Satan, 40 heroic exploits." The first tale *Childhood* is divided into four acts: 1) Early Childhood; 2) The Family, Souchard,

---

Gentlefolk. Chichikov is the central character in Gogol's *Dead Souls*. He is a marvelous scoundrel and rogue, the acme of ambitious, vulgar banality. Rakhmetov is the utilitarian hero of Chernyshevsky's *What's to be Done?*

Flight, and Kulikov; 3) Chermak-Examination; 4) The Country and Katya, Debauchery with Albert. The plan of this tale is worked out in detail; the second tale, *The Monastery* and the third, *Before Exile* are indicated in their general features: the fourth and fifth have been left only as projects. Out of the scattered and disorderly notes appears the following schema of *Childhood*:

The first act. The landowner Alfonsky's illegitimate son in early childhood is sent by his parents to the country and entrusted to some "old people." Vulgarity and depravity surround him there. In the evenings guests come; they drink, express themselves cynically, haggle over women. The child is offended by the adults' "unsightliness." He early begins to reflect. "It astonishes him that all these people (the grown-ups) really believe in their rubbish, and are much more stupid and insignificant than outwardly they seem." He develops a disrespect toward those surrounding him, but not yet out of understanding, "but solely from contempt toward them." He withdraws into himself and reads a lot. "He used to know the entire Bible." He is absorbed in reading novels and lives in dreams. The proud and solitary boy has a strange friendship with a lame girl, Katya. He exacts submission and worship from her. He says to her: "I myself am God," and forces her to adore him. "What does he talk about with the lame girl? About all his dreams. When I'm big, I will marry you." He dreams of becoming rich: the cripple keeps his secret: he dominates her and "is given to beating her." But now Katya disappears. The boy finds her half-frozen and saves her. Here for the first time love awakens in him and he kisses her. "He never behaved tenderly with the cripple until the time when he carried her in his arms." The following entry speaks of the hero's religious consciousness: "First confession. Is there a God? Pity and repulsion and the eternal question about God." Finally, the old couple die: he is eleven years old, Katya ten. They move to Alfonsky's house in Moscow.

The second act. In the family the boy is at once given to understand that he is illegitimate. His brother Misha steals something; Alfonskaya accuses the bastard and his father whips him. He declares: "I don't consider you my father!" and moves into the servants' quarters; he pretends to be an imbecile and suffers everyone's contempt. He is placed in Souchard's boarding school; there he passes two years. "In the city and in the boarding school he astonishes everyone by his brutality. They call him a monster and he conducts himself like a monster. A passionate desire to amaze everyone with his impudent pranks. . . .

He began to accumulate money with an unclear idea, but this idea continually asserted itself and was made clear to him by the ultimate course of events. The principal impetus was moving to Alfonsky's." Further on there is noted the Alfonskys' family drama: the father has a mistress, the lackey Osip Kulikov's sister; his stepmother also has a lover, her former fiancé. The boy understands everything and is involved in the intrigue.

Living among the servants, he makes friends with the lackey Kulikov, who had been taken into the master's home to entertain his owners with his stories and amusing character. But Alfonsky flogs Kulikov's brother to death, and turns the other over to the military authorities. The lackey runs away, and with him both the hero and his crippled friend. Kulikov kills Orlov, a soldier who has deserted, and the boy finds that he acted as his accomplice. "A fact which produces a shocking effect on him and somewhat confuses him so that he feels the natural need to withdraw into himself and reflect in order to fix his goal on some object or other. He resolves nonetheless on money. As yet he doesn't think about God." "After Kulikov he is, as it were, submissive, both in his family and the boarding school." "He is unsociable and uncommunicative, moreover he cannot be otherwise, remembering and knowing such horror behind him and looking at all the other children, for example, as something completely alien to himself and from which he has been torn far off to the side, to evil or to good—blood sometimes torments him." Alfonsky, because of his insolent behavior, is killed by his peasants in the country. The boy enters Chermak's gymnasium.

The third act. There are several brief notations. "About the classical education at Chermak's." "Development, reading. Is terribly captivated by something. By Hamlet, for example. Inhabitants of the moon. He is isolated from everyone not only in this, but by his dream of power and of immoderate superiority over everyone. He is knocked off this height by the sciences, poetry, etc. On the examination he distinguished himself unexpectedly—he had wanted to appear an idiot. But he profoundly despises himself for not having held out and having distinguished himself. The pure ideal of the free individual flashes before him sometimes. . . ."

The fourth act. During the summer a woman doctor in the country falls in love with the hero. "Presents herself to him in some kind of radiance. A passionate desire to dirty himself, to sully himself in her eyes and not to please." Having returned to Moscow, he strikes up with his school companion Lambert, who introduces him to debauchery. "Lambert revels in it and finds nothing greater. National flightiness. And he enters into debauchery, though with an irresistible desire, also with fear. The futility, filth, and absurdity of dissipation astound him." He and Lambert commit a new crime: they tear off a star from the crown of an icon and hide themselves, but when Lambert begins to scoff at religion, he beats him; he is surprised by this in that he considers himself an atheist. After "hellish dissipation" with Lambert, crimes, and sacrileges, he goes and gives himself up "with bitterness," seeing that he still does not know in the name of what he is doing this. On this, *Childhood*, the first part of the *Life*, ends.

The author summarizes the idea of his work. "The main thing. The significance of the first part. His hesitations, instability of purpose, instinctive consciousness of superiority, power, and strength. Search for a point of firm support. But in any case, an exceptional man." There follow very curious reflections about the *style* of the tale. "The first N. B. *The tone* (the story is a *Life*, i.e., though the author narrates, it is concise, is not stinting of explanations, but presents them in scenes. Here harmony is needed). The dryness of the story sometimes borders on *Gil Blas*. At passages that are effective and scenic, write as though there was nothing to value in this at all. But the dominating idea of the *Life*, so that it might be evident, i.e., without explaining the entire dominating idea in words and always leaving it in enigma, that the reader might always see that the idea is pious, that the *Life* is a thing so important that it was worth while starting from his childhood years. . . . The future man is continually in view and on a pedestal."

The second part of the *Life*, the tale *The Monastery*, is represented by a few notations concerning the personality of Tikhon. The bishop, living in the monastery in retirement, takes the child-criminal under his protection, opens a new world to him, one of love and "living life." "Tikhon's vivid stories about life and earthly joy, about family, father, mother, brothers. . . . Tikhon's extraordinarily naive, and therefore moving, stories about his sins against the domestics, concerning pride, vanity, derisions ('I would have done this all so differently now,' says Tikhon)." "Tikhon's story of his first love, about children: living as a monk is inferior, it is necessary and better to have children, when you have a vocation." "About beetles and about the universal joy of living life, inspired stories of Tikhon." "About the bear." "God grant a good night to us and to all the beasts (read thoroughly the description of animals in Humboldt, Buffon, and the Russians)." "What is Satan about?" "This alone is touching that he has come in contact with the boy." "Friendship with the boy who allows himself to torment Tikhon with his pranks." Parting with his little friend, the bishop "blesses him for his sin and for his regeneration" and preaches humility to him ("How mighty humility is").

We can judge the contents of the third part of the *Life*—the tale *Before Exile*—from the following brief plan, "The Main Thought" (May 3/15, 1870). Dostoevsky wrote: "After the monastery and Tikhon, the great sinner goes out again into the world with the idea of becoming *the greatest of men.* . . . He conducts himself in this fashion: he is the proudest of all the proud and behaves toward people with the greatest arrogance. At the same time there is a vagueness regarding the forms of his future greatness, that quite coincides with his youth. But (and this is the main thing) *through Tikhon* he mastered the idea that in order to conquer the whole world, one must conquer only oneself . . . he has not chosen his career, and has no time: he earnestly begins to look after himself." The idea of amassing riches contests within him with a yearning for education. "Suddenly, youth and dissipation, heroic exploits, and terrible villainy. Self-rejection. Insane pride. From pride becomes an ascetic-hermit and pilgrim. Journey through Russia. A romance, love, yearning for humility (rich canvas). Sin and regeneration. An extraordinary man. Ends by establishing his own foundling home and becomes a Haas.[A] Everything brightens. He dies, confessing his crime." After great errors and searching, the hero is saved. Blessed by grace, he discovers God and is united to "living life."

In this huge design Dostoevsky wanted to "express himself completely." The novel, of the same dimension as Tolstoy's *War and Peace*, artistically was to resolve the question that had tormented him throughout his entire life, the question of God's existence. The *Life* was conceived as a *theodicy*: the image of the "positively beautiful individual" that had pursued the author in his work on *The Idiot* was revealed in the *Life* in both its aspects, dynamic and static. The majestic figure of Saint Tikhon (the static conception) was opposed by the figure of one who was becoming just (the dynamic conception). But the religious poem, which the writer considered his main work and almost the meaning of his whole life, was not realized. The *Life* was left a depository of disorderly accumulated materials. However, the project did not disappear without a trace; it invisibly continued to live in the writer's subsequent creative work. The author drew on the store of

---

[A] The Moscow doctor and philanthropist.

ideas and subject matter in the *Life* for *The Devils, A Raw Youth,* and *Brothers Karamazov.*

The hero of the *Life* transmits many of his characteristics to Stavrogin, the hero of *The Devils.* The latter has the same "inordinate pride," the same "heroic exploits and terrible villainies," the same "strength of will," and demonic grandeur. From the *Life, The Devils* inherits both the cripple and Bishop Tikhon. The novel *A Raw Youth* is still more closely connected with the *Life.* Arkady Dolgoruky is an illegitimate son, in childhood cast out of the family and living among strangers. He also has the "idea of Rothschild": he too studies at "Touchard's," is friends with the debauched Frenchman Lambert, and takes a heated part in his parents' family drama. In Alfonsky, the hero's father, it is possible to see the pre-image of Versilov; in his mistress, the pre-image of Akhmakova. Tikhon's "vivid stories" are changed into the benevolent conversations of the pilgrim Makar Dolgoruky. Finally, the idea of the *Life* shapes the design of *Brothers Karamazov.* The Elder Zosima's teaching about the universal joy of life develops Tikhon's thoughts; Alyosha's friendship with Liza Khokhlakova recalls the friendship of the hero of the *Life* with the lame Katya. The youth of the "great sinner" is ideologically connected with Ivan Karamazov's youth. The hero of the *Life* has "infinite dreams, that extend to overthrowing God and establishing himself in His place. . . ." Ivan inherits from him his idea of man-godhood. Finally, Osip Kulikov, the lackey-murderer, implicating the boy in his own crime, is related to Ivan's lackey-murderer and "accomplice"—Smerdyakov.

Dostoevsky's majestic conception *The Life of a Great Sinner* is the spiritual center of his work: like a subterranean spring, it nourished his great novels of the seventies and the eighties with its waters.

XVII

Work on the Novel
The Devils

The history of the origin and development of the concept of *The Devils* is extraordinarily complicated. Dostoevsky lived through a genuine creative tragedy, the significance of which can only be conjectured. At the end of 1868 *The Idiot* was finished. The public received it coldly. The writer himself was profoundly dissatisfied with his work: his first attempt to create the figure of a "positively beautiful individual" had ended in failure. From his exile abroad he avidly scrutinized Russia, read through three Russian newspapers daily, was terribly afraid of losing contact with the "stream of life" and passionately believed in the birth of the new Russian man. Life in the West sharpened his hatred of Europe and his love for the homeland. The Russian "God and Christ" was sharply set in opposition to the Catholic West, which had lost the image of Christ. The Franco-Prussian War and the Paris Commune convinced him that the struggle between the European Antichrist and the Russian Christ was near and unavoidable. Was Russia ready for this conflict? Did she understand the danger of the European poisons—positivism, atheism, socialism? Had she yet brought forth a new man, united with the soil, the people, Orthodoxy? For Dostoevsky these questions were not philosophy, but life. He saw the history of the world in the light of the Apocalypse, in images of the final struggle between God and the devil, and ecstatically believed in Russia's religious calling. But faith must be justified by reality, the prophet's vision united with the artist's realism. Dostoevsky was a personalist, he felt an idea only through personality. If the new Russian idea had already been conceived—the new Russian man must also be born. He existed, one had only to find him. In the July-August issue of the *Russian Messenger* for 1868 the writer read about a former Old Believer Golubov, who had joined the Orthodox faith, and wrote to Maikov (December 11, 1868): "And do you know who these new Russian men are? Look at this muzhik, a former schismatic with Pavel Prussky. He is not the type of the future Russian man, but he is, of course, already one of the future Russian men."

And in the same letter he discussed the plan of his novel *Atheism*, the hero of which, after long religious sufferings, "at the end attains both Christ and the Russian land, the Russian Christ and the Russian God." It is possible to speculate that the concept of *Atheism* rose under the impression of Golubov's "person." A year later *Atheism* grew into a massive "poem," *The Life of a Great Sinner*. Golubov was consigned to the second plane: he appears episodically in the tale *The Monastery*, together with Pavel Prussky and the monk Parfeny, and takes part in a religious dispute. Bishop Tikhon inherited his idea: not the former Old Believer Golubov, but an Orthodox saint, Tikhon Zadonsky, justified the religious mission of Russia. The writer wanted to portray this "majestic figure" in his novel, and was certain that now he would not be reproached that his hero was "invented" or "fantastic." Captivated by this design, he worked assiduously on the plan for the *Life* (December 1869). And suddenly, at the same time, another concept occurred to him, out of which, after long reworking, grew the novel *The Devils*. We have the testimony of the author himself "Speaking *most precisely*, the tale (novel, if you like) that I thought up for *The Russian Messenger* [i.e., *The Devils*] was already begun at the end of last year [1869]" (letter to Strakhov of December 2, 1870). Moreover, the first notes to *The Devils* in notebook No. 1-10 must be dated December 1869. How can one explain this *simultaneous* appearance of two different plans? We suppose that in the author's original presentation they successfully supplemented one another. In the first project the idea of the "positively beautiful individual" was embodied in the image of Tikhon Zadonsky. But a saint of the 18th century could not serve as an example of the "new Russian man." The series of novels in the *Life*, which was estimated at five years of work, was much too far removed from the contemporary: the action of the first tale *Childhood* took place in the forties. The second project tempted the writer because of its topical character: it involved real persons and events of the "current moment." In October 1869 Ivan Gregoryevich Snitkin, Anna Grigoryevna's brother, arrived in Dresden. A student at the Petrine Agricultural Academy, Snitkin told Dostoevsky about his school companion Ivanov. Here is what Anna Grigoryevna writes in her memoirs:

Fyodor Mikhailovich, who used to read various foreign newspapers (there was much printed in them that did not appear in Russian ones), came to the conclusion that in a short time there would be political disturbances at the Petrine Agricultural Academy. Fearing that my brother, because of his youth and lack of character, might take an active part in them, my husband prevailed upon my mother to invite her son to visit with us in Dresden. . . . Fyodor Mikhailovich, who was always sympathetic toward my brother, took an interest in his studies, his acquaintances, and in general the condition and attitude of the student world. My brother used to talk in detail and with enthusiasm. Now the thought occurred to Fyodor Mikhailovich to portray the political movement of that time in one of his tales and to take as one of his principal heroes the student Ivanov [under the name of Shatov], who was afterward murdered by Nechayev. My brother described the student Ivanov as an intelligent man, distinguished by his firm character, who in a radical way had changed his former convictions. And how deeply my husband was shocked when later he learned from the papers about the student Ivanov's murder.

The murder of Ivanov occurred November 21, 1869. In it were involved Nechayev, the students Uspensky and Kuznetsov, and the writer Pryzhov. Ivanov had belonged to Nechayev's circle, but broke with it, being unwilling to submit to its authority and "hinting even that he would leave the society and form a new society of his own." He was killed in the Petrine Academy park, and his body was thrown in an icehole in the pond.

Dostoevsky had had a presentiment that there would be political agitation at the Academy—and Ivanov's murder shocked him as the realization of his prediction. Consequently, he still had not lost the feeling of Russian reality. Ivan Gregoryevich's stories about Ivanov and his murder by Nechayev inspired Dostoevsky to write a "novel-pamphlet." Ivanov, having repudiated the revolution, merged with Golubov, who had renounced the schism. Golubov-Ivanov was set in opposition to the nihilist Nechayev. The writer was attracted by this new concept. He wrote to Maikov (February 12, 1870): "I set down a rich idea. Like *Crime and Punishment*, but even nearer to reality, even more urgent, and directly concerned with the most important contemporary question." He informed Strakhov that he "viewed the thought with delight" and vouched for the "novelty of the thought and the originality of the device." He rejoiced that he had at last found a "contemporary theme," and asked him to send Stankevich's booklet on Granovsky. He "needed" it "like air." "Material absolutely indispensable for my work," he added, "material that I can in no way do without." Having outlined the characteristics of Verkhovensky-Granovsky, he wanted to concretize them, to enrich them with factual material. The eternal concern of the "realist" Dostoevsky.

But having paid tribute to the contemporary, the writer hoped to return to his main theme—the *Life*. On March 24, 1870, he wrote to Strakhov that the "piece" in the *Russian Messenger* would be finished soon, that he had strong hopes for it, "however, not from the artistic, but from the tendentious side." "Let it turn out only a *pamphlet*; but I will express myself." On the following day he wrote to Maikov: "What I'm writing is a tendentious piece, I want to speak out rather more forcefully. Here the nihilists and the Westernizers will begin howling about me that I'm a *retrograde!* Well, the hell with them, but I'll say everything to the last word!" And in the same letter he gave a detailed plan of the *Life*. This is an important stage in the history of the creation of *The Devils*. The author was convinced that the "pamphlet" would not divert him long from his work on the "poem"; that in about three months he would finish it and, after resting for a month, would again return to the *Life*. He believed that these heterogeneous plans could not interfere with one another: the *Life*—the culmination of all his literary activity—was a majestic religious poem; *The Devils* was a tendentious piece, a pamphlet, without pretensions to artistry.

"Sometimes, *in my opinion*, it is necessary to moderate the tone," he declared to Strakhov, "to take the whip into your hands and not defend yourself, but yourself to attack, much more brutally." In such a frame of mind *The Devils* was conceived. The author was ready to sacrifice artistry for the sake of exposure. But his hope to treat the two themes along parallel lines was not realized. The novel-pamphlet expanded and engulfed all the writer's forces. In May 1870 he informed S. A. Ivanova that the *Life* had been laid aside until his return to Russia, and that *The Devils* would comprise not twelve printed sheets, but twenty-five. ("I am condensing into about 25 sheets what ought at least to have taken 50 sheets.")

And so, from December 1869 to May 1870 the projects of the *Life* and *The Devils* existed side by side: the first, as the principal, "artistic" theme; the second, as a collateral, "tendentious" theme. In May *The Devils* supplanted the *Life*, absorbing part of its material. Until July the tormented planning of the novel continued, tendentiousness contended with artistry; the tone had not been found, the main hero was disappointing. The plot did not fit together, the idea was still obscure. In July a series of oppressive attacks tore the writer away from work for an entire month. Upon his recovery, he reread his outlines and began to despair. On August 11 he noted down: "The novel has been definitely weeded out (terrible!)."

Several of the author's remarks have come down to us regarding this creative drama. In August Dostoevsky wrote to Kashpirov, the editor of *The Dawn*, "Since the beginning of the year I've been working on a novel for the *Russian Messenger*. I thought for sure that it would be finished by the end of summer. . . . I had already written up to 15 sheets. Throughout the entire course of the work the novel had gone slowly and toward the end it became repugnant. . . . Then my fits recurred about a month ago. Having taken up my work again, after my illness, about three weeks ago, I saw that I could not write, wanted to tear up the novel. For two weeks I was in a very oppressed state and about ten days ago I finally recognized the weak point of all that I had written. Now I have decided resolutely: to destroy all that has been written and to revise the novel radically, and only a part of what has been written will go into the new text, but also in a radical revision. . . ." On August 17 he remarked about the same thing to S. A. Ivanova: "Two weeks ago, upon undertaking my work again, I suddenly saw all at once where I had been faltering and where I had made a mistake; at this point, through inspiration, a new plan for the novel presented itself in complete harmony. It was necessary to change everything radically; not reflecting in the least, I struck out all that had been written (up to about 15 sheets, roughly speaking) and began anew from the 1st page. All the work of an entire year has been destroyed. Oh, Sonechka! if you but knew how difficult it is to be a writer, that is, to undergo this lot." With his niece, Dostoevsky was more open and lyrical: he did not hide his tragic relation to the event.

But why did this creative revolution take place? What was the author's original mistake? We find the answer to this question in a letter the writer sent to Strakhov (October 9, 1870): "Never has anything cost me so much labor. In the beginning, i.e., even at the end of last year, I looked at this piece as forced, as contrived, looked down upon it. Then a genuine inspiration visited me—and suddenly I came to love the thing, lay hold of it with both hands, willingly set about cancelling out what had been written. Then in the summer again a change: another new character came forward claiming to be the real *hero of the novel*, so that the former hero (a curious character, but really not deserving the name of hero) was relegated to the second plane. The new hero captivated me to such an extent that I again undertook a revision."

At first the novel progressed slowly, like a topical "piece," a "pamphlet," then "inspiration visited": *The Life* was put aside, *The Devils* developed into a full novel—first revision; during the summer a new hero stepped forward and a second revision took place. But who then was this new hero and whom did he supplant?

From a letter to Katkov (October 8, 1870) we conclude that the "creative revolution" was provoked by the unexpected appearance of *Stavrogin*, which diminished the importance of the former hero, *Pyotr Verkhovensky*. "One of the most important events in my story," wrote Dostoevsky,

will be Ivanov's murder by Nechayev, which is well known in Moscow. I hasten to add a reservation: I do not know and never have known either Nechayev or Ivanov, or the circumstances of this murder, except from the newspapers. And even if I had, I would not have begun copying them. I'm only taking the accomplished fact. My fantasy can in the highest degree differ from the reality that took place, and my Pyotr Verkhovensky may in no way resemble Nechayev, but it seems to me that in my astonished mind imagination has created that character, that type, which corresponds to this crime. Without doubt, it is not useless to present such a person: but he alone would not have tempted me. In my opinion, these deplorable monstrosities are unworthy of literature. To my personal amazement, this character developed in my hands into a half-comic character, and consequently, despite the fact that the event occupies one of the most prominent places in the novel, it is nonetheless only an accessory and circumstance in the action of another personage who might really be called the main character of the novel.... This other character (Nikolai Stavrogin) is also a somber character, also a villain, but it seems to me that this character is *tragic,* although many, to be sure, will say upon reading: "What is this?" I turned to the poem about this character because for too long now I have wanted to portray him. I will feel very, very sad if I don't succeed with him. It will be still more sad if I hear the criticism that the character is stilted. *I have taken him from my heart.*

Dostoevsky did not reveal to the editor of the *Russian Messenger* the drama that he had experienced. He proudly declared that Pyotr Verkhovensky was a deplorable monstrosity, unworthy of literature: that he alone would not have tempted him to write the novel. In reality, the drama consisted precisely in the fact that the author was originally tempted by the idea of a novel-pamphlet with the main hero Nechayev-Verkhovensky. In this was his "mistake," and on account of this he had to destroy "the work of an entire year." In the new version, Pyotr Verkhovensky was assigned to the secondary plane, as a half-comic character, and at the center was placed the genuinely tragic hero—Stavrogin. The author actually "took him from his heart." Outlines for the figure of this demonic personage were already met in the rough drafts for *Crime and Punishment;* his traits are delineated in the notebooks to the *Idiot* and in the notations for *The Life of a Great Sinner.* Stavrogin is the magnificent culmination of the writer's reflections over many years on the fate of the "strong personality."

The crisis in August 1870 ended the tragic contention of *The Life* and *The Devils.* The novel-pamphlet vanquished the "poem," but this victory proved illusory: the hero of *The Life* supplanted the hero of *The Devils* and relegated to a secondary plane the topical plot—Nechayev's murder of Ivanov. "Tendentiousness" was converted into an accessory; Stavrogin's fate became the main theme. The novel's philosophic and artistic significance grew immediately. Originally, the idea had been developed *dramatically* through the opposition of the believing Russian Golubov-Ivanov and the nihilist, Nechayev, torn away from the soil; now it was *tragically* revealed in the encounter of the atheist Stavrogin and the saint Tikhon Zadonsky. Political activity and social sedition were shown as the natural consequences of the religious idea's having become "muddled." Stavrogin, entering *The Devils* out of *The Life,* also brought with him his ideational adversary—Tikhon. Sending the first half of the first part of the novel to Katkov (October 8, 1870), the author informed him: "But not all my characters will be somber: some will also be radiant. . . . For the first time I want to touch upon one category of characters, still rarely dealt with in literature. As the ideal of such a type, I am taking Tikhon Zadonsky. My character is also a prelate living in retirement in a monastery. I confront him with the hero of my novel, and bring them together for a time. I'm very much afraid: I've never tried this; but I know something of this world."

The birth pangs of the new idea continued for an entire year; for an entire year the writer only "discarded and modified"; for weeks he "stopped working from the beginning, and wrote from the end"; he continually "lost the tone." "I have written such heaps of paper," he confessed to Strakhov, "that I've lost even a system for referring to what has been noted down. I have altered the whole plan no less than ten times and have written the entire first part anew." But here an idea was born in a flow of inspiration: "At last everything was created at a stroke and now cannot be changed." The religious thought was embodied in the Gospel image of the Gadarene man possessed by devils. The novel's title appeared: *The Devils*. The first act of the creative tragedy was ended. The author understood what forces had invisibly ripened in his soul and yearned for embodiment. Now he had mastered them, had perceived his religious task. With the assurance of a conqueror he informed Maikov of the idea of his work:

The facts have shown us that the malady which has afflicted civilized Russians was much stronger than we ourselves imagined, and that the affair did not end with Belinsky, Krayevsky, etc. But here we have what the Evangelist Luke bears witness to. Exactly the same thing has taken place among us. The devils went out of the Russian man and entered into a herd of swine, i.e., into the Nechayevs and Serno-Solovyeviches and others. These have drowned or will drown surely, and the healed man, from whom the devils went out, is seated at the feet of Jesus. So it must have been. Russia has vomited up this filth which poisoned her, and now, of course, in those scoundrels who were vomited up there has remained nothing Russian. But observe, my dear friend: he who loses his people and nationality, loses also the faith of his fathers and God. . . . And another strength may be our own faith in our personality, in the holiness of our vocation. The whole vocation of Russia is contained in Orthodoxy, in the *light from the East,* which will stream to mankind who is blinded in the West, having lost Christ. . . . Well, if you want to know, this is precisely the theme of my novel. *It is called "The Devils."*

The second act of the tragedy began: the struggle for the salvation of the "strong personality." The "light from the East" must overcome the fiends' darkness: Stavrogin, having unexpectedly been transformed into the main hero, grew into a symbolic image of possessed Russia, which, having been healed, was seated at the feet of Christ. The rough drafts reveal to us Dostoevsky's desperate fight and his tragic defeat. Stavrogin was not saved: a terrible black cloud hung over the destiny of Russia. . . . Echoes of this drama are heard in a letter to S. A. Ivanova: "I have been writing my novel and have been totally unable to cope with it. I'm turning out decided trash, but to discard it is impossible because I like the thought too much!" He wrote to Maikov about his fear and despair: "God, how I was afraid and still am. . . . And for what follows I'm simply in despair, will I set it right. . . . Again I repeat: I have fears, like a scared mouse. The *idea* tempted me and I came to love it terribly, but will I succeed with it—here's the problem." On July 9, 1871, Dostoevsky returned to Petersburg. The printing of the novel was held up for an entire year. The third and fourth parts came out only at the end of 1872.

The preparatory materials for *The Devils*[A] (notebooks Nos. 1, 2, 3, and 4) have come down to us in their entirety. We see the great creator of souls in the process of his superhuman labor. There is no spectacle more pathetic than that limbo in which Dostoevsky's heroes were engendered, fashioned, and developed. Their fate before birth was full of instability, trials, and catastrophes; it is perhaps still more dramatic than their life in the novel.

Of all the characters in *The Devils*, Shatov was formulated first. In subject he is related to the student I. Ivanov, the member of Nechayev's group "The People's Retribution." In the first outline of the novel (December 1869), he is portrayed, under the name of "the teacher," as an ideational enemy of the nihilists. The connection of this original plan with the Nechayev affair is quite evident. "At the count's the bailiff is a nihilist, and there is a den of nihilists. The nihilists make the teacher a proposal. . . . (Proclamations). Nechayev appears for a moment, to kill the teacher (?) (He is killed on the way?)." An important place is reserved in the plot for "the teacher." He is of a "humble and timid character. . . ." "Terribly distracted and strange. Partly a nihilist . . . The teacher repeatedly shows extraordinary strength of character, daring, courage. The fire. Slap in the face."

"In the course of the novel, the teacher continually grows more and more in beauty. He begins from the ridiculous and ends as a complete *ideal of beauty*. The role of a Christian. . . ." The plot was constructed around him. An "important lady" has a son—the prince A. B. and a protégée. The prince, a "passionate, proud, and disorderly man," has

A *Zapisnye tetrady F. M. Dostoevskogo* (*F. M. Dostoevsky's Notebooks*). Commentaries by N. I. Ignatova and Ye. N. Konshina. Akademiya. 1935.

foolishly entered upon a liaison with the protégée. She becomes pregnant. The "important lady" is horrified. She gets the idea of marrying the teacher "to her son's sins," and offers him 15,000. He goes to the protégée and wins her confidence. "She even begins to speak openly with him, about Christ, about God, and about the sciences. She listens. 'You are a good man!' But suddenly begins to cry. Timidly he explains his thought: 'If it had been without 15,000? Why have you kept silent?—I love you.'" Finally, she comes to say: "And I love you." The prince envies the teacher. "For a long time there has been verbal swordplay between the prince and the teacher, and envy and hatred lay in the relations between them." "Neighbors have also returned from abroad. The daughter is a beauty and rich heiress."

Such are the first hazy contours of characters we already know. The "important lady" is the future Varvara Petrovna Stavrogina; the protégée—Dasha; the beauty—Liza Tushina; the Prince—Stavrogin; Nechayev—Pyotr Verkhovensky. The love intrigue among the prince, the protégée, and the teacher would afterward fall into two independent episodes: Varvara Petrovna's project—to marry Stepan Trofimovich Verkhovensky "to her son's sins," and the return of Shatov's wife after Stavrogin has made her pregnant. The dramatic situations are noted: the slap in the face, the duel with no shot fired, and the conflagration.

In the final rough drafts the teacher is given the name of *Shaposhnikov*. Probably he inherited this surname from the Old Believer Bishop Shaposhnikov, who died in 1868; it is possible that by this the author wanted to underline his hero's ideational tie with the Old Believers.

Shaposhnikov, a former student, took part in the disorders. "A type of one who has roots." He says that "no one knows himself in Russ." "Russia has been overlooked." "We cannot know our own singularity and cannot regard the West independently. . . . Peter the Great wanted Europeans without fail by ukase, and got Europeans 150 years later, on the condition that they had torn themselves away from their own people and had not become attached to others, because all the latter are nationalistic, and we deny nationality at its root, but want to be pan-Europeans, and there simply are no such pan-Europeans." The future Shatov is characterized as being rooted in the soil and a nationalist; his ideological image grew up at once through all the revisions and restructurings of the novel he retained his essential traits. His relations with the future Pyotr Verkhovensky ("the student") are very close to the relations that existed between Nechayev and his victim—Ivanov. "The student asks Sh. to take part. The latter had the stupidity to go to their meetings. He raised objections. Said too much. The St. reproves him for having said too much. Sh. answers hotly that he considers himself in no way bound. The St. gets a band of three ready to kill Sh. They kill him." Soon Shaposhnikov is turned into *Shatov*.[1] This name is symbolic; the former nihilist, having become rooted in the soil, yearns for faith, but still totters, "wavers." He himself bears the sin of Russia. In notebook No. 3 a speech of the prince is outlined: "Among us one doesn't believe in himself, and it's even impossible to, because there is nothing to believe in. This *wavering*'s been going on for all of two centuries. All our reforms, beginning with Peter, have consisted solely in that he took a stone that was lying solidly, and contrived to set it on its edge; we too are standing and balancing on this point. The wind'll blow and we will fly away." It is this "wavering" that the newly-baked, "rooted" Shatov expresses. His nationalism is set in opposition to the cosmopolitanism of the Nechayev clique. But he is unable to contend religiously with the nihilists: he himself is still only searching for faith. Consequently in the original design this struggle was entrusted to the former schismatic Golubov. The Prince (the future Stavrogin) "has altered his convictions." He becomes a skeptic, scrutinizes people mistrustfully. "Looks to Sh. and to Golubov to be strengthened in his convictions. Looks also to Nechayev. Listens even to Granovsky [the future Stepan Trofimovich]." As a result, it turns out that he is strengthened in Golubov's ideal, and rejects all the rest. "Golubov's ideas are humility and self-mastery and that God and the kingdom of heaven are inside us in self-mastery, and freedom is there too. He did not expect to meet Golubov. Upon meeting him, he is astounded; is terrified, and submits to him willingly."

Golubov was conceived as an exponent of the idea of Orthodoxy, as a genuine Russian, a believer. An enormous role was intended for him in the novel: he was to have astounded Stavrogin and restored his faith. Through Golubov the hero was to attain resurrection and salvation. "*The Prince at Golubov's*: 'I'm doing the first thing (among those torn away from the soil)—I believe.' *Golubov*: 'And the last thing! This is the first and the last. Nothing more is needed, everything lies in this alone!' "

. . . "Golubov says: 'More humility is needed; consider yourself as nothing, then you'll be saved and you will attain peace.' " The author outlines a synopsis of Golubov's speech. This is one of the most important documents we have concerning Dostoevsky's religious world-view.

[1] shatat'sya=to waver, totter.

Golubov says: Paradise is in the world. It exists even now and the world is created perfectly. Everything in the world is pleasure—if it is normal and legitimate, not otherwise, only under this condition. God created both the world and the law, and created yet another miracle—he showed us the law through Christ, for example, in life and in a formula. Consequently, unhappiness results solely from abnormality, from not observing the law. For example, marriage is paradise and completely true, if the spouses love only one another and are united by mutual love in their children. With the slightest deviation from the law, marriage at once turns into unhappiness. . . . Deviations can be terribly varied, but they all depend on a lack of self-discipline. The man having ten children and without means considers himself unfortunate, for he doesn't know how to master his lustful desires and degrades himself to the point that he groans from the least privation. Self-mastery consists of discipline, the discipline of the Church. . . . You say, a slave is not free. But Christ says that a slave can be free in the highest degree, while being a slave. . . . Believe me, if everyone should rise to the height of self-mastery, there would be no unhappy marriages, no hungry children.

One might think that these reflections were written not by Dostoevsky, but by Tolstoy: the rationalism and moralism of the sermon on self-mastery is so astounding, the teaching about paradise on earth is permeated with such naturalism.

For Golubov, Christ is only an "example" and formula, the Church is only discipline, salvation is only the fulfillment of the law! The tragic dichotomy of Dostoevsky the mystic did not disappear up to the very end of his life: with inspiration he taught that all Christianity is reduced to faith in the divinity of Jesus Christ, and at the same time admitted some kind of "normal," "legalistic" institution of paradise on earth by means of purely human "self-mastery."

And so originally Golubov carried on the religious controversy with the nihilists; he opposed Nechayev–Pyotr Verkhovensky. Shatov was to have come forward as his disciple, developing his religious idea on the plane of Russian national messianism. Under March 29, 1870, appears the note: *"Without Golubov"* and twice *"Golubov isn't needed."* This reversal is explained by the rapid and steady growth of the main hero —Stavrogin. The author observes: "And so, all the pathos of the novel is in the prince, he is the hero. All the rest move around him, like a kaleidoscope. *He replaces even Golubov.* Of immense stature." The

functions of the dramatis personae are changed: now it is not Golubov who "astounds" the prince-Stavrogin, and not Shatov who preaches
to him about the vocation of Russia, but the reverse: the prince "inflames Shatov to the point of enthusiasm, but he himself does not believe." In the final text, Stavrogin's sermons are relegated to the past;
Golubov's religious heritage is divided among Shatov, Stavrogin, Bishop
Tikhon, and Kirilov ("the earthly paradise"). In the notebooks, Shatov's
ideology was developed with greater breadth and daring than in the
novel. His inspired words about Christ belong to the writer's loftiest
creations.

"You, negators of God and Christ," says Shatov, "haven't even
thought how everything in the world would become filthy and sinful
without Christ. You judge Christ and laugh at God, but yourselves, for
example, what models do you present; how petty, depraved, greedy,
and vain you are. Setting aside Christ, you are removing the inaccessible ideal of beauty and good from mankind. In its place, what do you
propose that is of equal force?"

Granovsky [St. T. Verkhovensky]: "Let's suppose, one can still argue
about this; yet what prevents you, without believing in Christ as God,
from looking upon him as the ideal of perfection and moral beauty?"

Shatov: "Not believing at the same time that the Word became flesh,
that is, that the idea has appeared in the flesh, and consequently, it is
not impossible and is accessible to all mankind? And really, can mankind dispense with this consoling thought? Why, Christ came in order
that mankind might realize that the nature of the human spirit can be
manifest in such a heavenly luster, actually and in the flesh, and not
only in a dream or as an ideal, and that this is both natural and
possible. The followers of Christ, having deified this luminous flesh,
began to bear witness in the most cruel tortures what happiness it is
to bear this flesh in oneself, to imitate the perfection of this image and to
believe in it in the flesh. Through these the earth has been justified.
Others, seeing what happiness this flesh gives, as soon as a man
begins to unite himself to it and in fact resemble its beauty, wondered,
were astonished; and it ended by their wishing to taste this happiness
themselves, by becoming Christians, and now rejoicing in their tortures. This is precisely the very essence, that the Word in fact 'became
flesh.' In this lies the whole of faith and all the comfort of mankind,
which it will never renounce, but you want to deprive it precisely of
this. Besides, you will succeed only if you show man something
better than Christ. Show something then!"

In the final text Shatov was transferred to the second plane: his ideational richness passed over to Stavrogin. Such is the history of his "pre-existence." His way goes from the student Ivanov through the Old Believer Golubov to Stavrogin's *"wavering"* disciple.

Immediately after Shatov, the immortal figure of *Stepan Trofimovich Verkhovensky* arose. Nihilist-sons are immediately linked by the author with idealist-fathers. The years of the forties were morally responsible for the sixties. In the beginning of February 1870 Dostoevsky outlined the brilliant characteristics of the "great poet who was never at a loss for words." In the notebook, Stepan Trofimovich still bears the name of the famous Moscow professor-historian Timofei Nikolayevich Granovsky. This is a "pure and ideal Westernizer with all his beauties." "Characteristic traits: throughout his life, aimlessness and lack of resolution in his opinions and his sentiments, which formerly constituted suffering, but has now been transformed *into second nature.*" "He used to be a famous name (two-three articles, one study, a journey through Spain, observations on the Crimean War in manuscript which passed from hand to hand and resulted in his being persecuted). Unconsciously he places himself on a pedestal, like relics which one comes to venerate, he loves this." "Loves to write mournful letters. Shed tears here, there." "Loves champagne." "Leave me God and art. I yield up Christ to you." The author treats his hero with ironic sympathy. However ridiculous Stepan Trofimovich is, nonetheless he is really a poet. "*Dies irae.* The golden age, Greek gods." Verkhovensky is not a portrait of Granovsky, but a synthetic image of the Russian idealist of the forties. Certain of his traits were borrowed by the author from V. P. Botkin (*Journey through Spain*), from B. N. Chicherin (*Observations on the Crimean War* alludes to Chicherin's essay *The Eastern Question from the Russian Point of View*), from A. I. Herzen ("he arranged his monetary affairs well" and "cries over all his wives") and even from Belinsky. The image of the "ideal Westernizer" presented itself to Dostoevsky all at once, at full height. Through all the revisions of the novel he kept his own aesthetic *credo* intact. According to the original plan, he was to have given lectures on the Madonna, and to reason that "without Shakespeare mankind must not live and, it seems, mankind simply could not live." Ideologically, his personality is no less consistent than the personality of Shatov, "rooted in the soil."

The image of *Pyotr Stepanovich Verkhovensky* is directly related to the personality of the revolutionary S. G. Nechayev, the founder of the society "The People's Retribution," the organizer of the student

Ivanov's political murder and the author of *The Catechism of a Revolutionary*. A fanatic, ascetic, and despot, Nechayev possessed an enormous strength of will and exacted blind submission from his followers. After Ivanov's murder he fled abroad, for three years collaborated with Bakunin, but was turned over to the Russian government; and died in Petropavlovsky Fortress. Psychologically, Verkhovensky is little like Nechayev. The author was drawing not a portrait, but a caricature of the revolutionary. There is a somber and cold grandeur in the personality of Nechayev; in the image of Pyotr Verkhovensky, comic and mean traits are underlined. Out of the sinister demon, Dostoevsky made a tittering and troublesome "petty devil." Besides, the author of the novel-pamphlet did not even intend to reproduce reality. "My Pyotr Verkhovensky," he acknowledged, "may in no way resemble Nechayev." The hero is characterized not psychologically, but ideologically, as the exponent of the idea of atheistic nihilism. In the plan of the novel-pamphlet his role was much more significant than in the printed edition. The action was built on the struggle of "the new Russian man" (Golubov-Shatov) with nihilism. Pyotr Verkhovensky stood at the center of the intrigue as an *anti-hero*. In the very first drafts he inherited Nechayev's name, organization of "five," dissemination of proclamations, his revolutionary propaganda among the workers, and the murder of Shatov. The author elaborates his psychological characteristics: "At the beginning the student is very meek and taciturn, so that his father even makes fun of him (he didn't invent gunpowder). But suddenly a quarrel with the father . . . a bold quarrel. 'The old woman and so forth.' The *'student'* is simple, direct, wants to rebuild the world. To undermine it with counterfeit money and rumors—by whatever might chance. . . ." "The student is not stupid, but what hinders him are mainly his scorn and nihilistic haughtiness toward people. Doesn't want to know reality. (Anecdote, by hearsay, that the factory workers duped him, and he left convinced, *à la française*, that there would be barricades.) He doesn't even pose the question of nobility and baseness, like the other nihilists. He has other matters to attend to and is not concerned by subtleties. He says, one must act." Here is a sample of his conversations with Shatov.

Nechayev: In proclamations against the government the more one lies, the more honest it is. This is a device of Herzen's.

Shatov: And of the Jesuits.

Nechayev: The Jesuits are an extraordinarily intelligent order, and there is, if you want, truth in their approach. You won't succeed otherwise in our world.

The Princess (with ardor): I've always thought that.

Shatov: If you think, you won't come to any conclusions, so decide without thinking, like an ox—here's your despicable program.

The pathos of destruction is energetically expressed in a dialogue between Stepan Trofimovich and his son. The father says: "Aren't you thoughtless, and what responsibility are you taking upon yourself for the streams of blood which you wish to shed? It is difficult to build. You are demolishing because that is easiest of all." Pyotr Verkhovensky answers: "No responsibility, we are simply holding up our heads. The people will create the future society after the universal destruction, and the sooner the better."

Stepan Trofimovich: . . . The people, if they are carried away by the insurrection and marauding, then will also be appeased at once, will build something quite different, but in their own way and, I daresay, even much worse.

Pyotr Verkhovensky: Let them; but it's still good that one world will perish. Another will come, though with its errors too, built by the people, but without doubt a little bit better. When the mistakes are seen, we or our followers will overthrow it again, and so on, until the time when our program will be accepted as a whole. But even at the first experiment we will have already attained our goal by the fact alone that the principle of the ax and of revolution shall be admitted.

Stepan Trofimovich: But if you don't know for sure that your program is right, how do you take the crime of destruction upon your conscience?

Pyotr Verkhovensky: We believe that our program is right and that everyone, upon accepting it, will be happy. Here is why we are resolved on blood, because happiness will be bought with blood.

Stepan Trofimovich: And what if it will not be bought, what then?

Pyotr Verkhovensky: We are certain that it will be bought, and this is enough for us.

This political dialogue is worthy of the best pages of *The Devils.* Verkhovensky is presented as a theoretician of anarchy; he has *an original catastrophic evolutionism.* History moves from one destruction to another, and each new world is "a little bit better" than the preceding one. At the end of the series of destructions comes "universal happiness"—earthly paradise. In notebook No. 3, the numerous remarks are united in two sections: "About what Nechayev wanted" and "Nechayev's view on the course of interior politics." This program of anarchism, amazing in the keenness of its formulations, is worthy of separate investigation. The author sharply underlines that his hero is not a socialist, but an anarchist. "Nechayev is not a socialist," he writes, "but a rebel; in his ideal there is insurrection and destruction, and then *whatever might come.*" The twelve points of his program are expounded with extraordinary concreteness. Here, for example, is the tenth point: "The augmenting of villainies, crimes, and suicides to jolt the popular spirit, to provoke disbelief in the stability of the order, and to incite mobility in the Stenka Razin[2] part of the folk population. The augmenting of vices and dissipation, wine; the distribution of money." And Nechayev concludes: "A year, or less, of such an order and all the elements will be ready for the great Russian revolt. Three provinces will break out at once. Everyone will begin to destroy one another, *traditions will not be spared.* Fortunes and wealth will collapse, and then after a year of revolt, immediately introduce a socialist republic, communism, and socialism. . . . If they will not consent—again, they will be massacred, and *so much the better.* . . ." "Nechayev's principle, his *new word,* is that, finally, it is necessary to incite a revolt; but so that it might be real, the more sedition and disorder, blood and ruin, fire and the destruction of tradition there is—the better. It's no concern to me what will ensue: the main thing is that what exists be jolted, shaken loose, and broken." Such declarations can appear as a malicious caricature of the Russian revolutionary movement; but the fantasy of the tendentious author proved prophetic. The notes about Nechayev were composed in May, and probably June, 1871 (the sole date in the notebook is May 13, 1871), and the accounts of the Nechayevists' trial began to appear in the *Government Messenger* only on July 1. Consequently, Dostoevsky could not have known the "common rules of the organization," composed by Nechayev and read at the trial. But meanwhile, the points of his hero's program which the writer formulated were repeated literally in this instruction. In the chapter *The Relationship of the Society to the People* the real Nechayev writes:

With all its forces and means it will promote the development of

---

[2] In the late 1660's, Stenka Razin, a Cossack leader, organized a ruthless popular uprising. For several years they terrorized Astrakhan and the whole Volga region with pillaging, murder and destruction. Although not formally directed against the government, its social consequences were vast.

those misfortunes and those evils which must at last rouse the people out of forbearance and compel them to a general uprising. . . . Our business is terrible, complete, universal, and merciless destruction. Consequently, approaching the people, before all else we must unite ourselves with those elements of the people's life which have never ceased to protest in fact against everything that is connected with the government. We will unite with the savage world of robbers, these true and only revolutionaries in Russia. To assemble this world into one indestructible, all-shattering force—here is our entire organization, conspiracy, task.

Pyotr Verkhovensky fulfills with literal exactness all Nechayev's rules in the novel; his obedient tool is Fedka, the convict. Nechayev's "five" was founded on complicity in crime, espionage, slander, and despotism. In the same way, Pyotr Verkhovensky organizes his five. "The association," he declares, "can act by violence, lies, deceit, murder, slander, and theft, so long as it still has not seized control and is struggling. And moreover, it can act this way afterward." Nechayev was handed over to the Russian government as a criminal offender, on October 19, 1872, and the third part of *The Devils* appeared in the November and December issues of *The Russian Messenger* for 1872. Dostoevsky's novel-pamphlet proved to be acutely topical. It was genuine clairvoyance and prophecy.

According to the original design, Pyotr Verkhovensky proclaimed the teaching of equality which in the novel has passed over to Shigalyov. He said that one must "concern oneself with perfect equality, and for this, the first thing was to lower the level of education, sciences and talents." Persons with higher abilities, even people too strong physically or very beautiful are to be expelled from society. "No columns, no art, no music, for this all corrupts. The necessary only is necessary. Here is the motto of the earthly sphere, and the necessary is always attainable." The idea of the physical modification of man's nature also belonged originally to him; in the final text this was given to Kirilov. The objection is made to Verkhovensky that his future people will devour one another. "So much the better!" he takes up. "That is the very highest goal. For they will devour one another only up to a certain point—for afterward they will be changed altogether, their nature will change, and man through long practice will organically adapt himself to the association, *and each will be for all and all for each.* Here it is primarily necessary to alter man's nature physically. Here it is quite necessary in order that personality might be changed into herd spirit. . . ."

And so Pyotr Verkhovensky was conceived by the author as the *philosopher of anarchism*. Only unimportant traces of this ingenious design have been preserved in the novel. The hero was divested of almost all his ideational riches. After the "creative revolution," in August 1870, Dostoevsky radically reconstructed the novel. Unexpectedly, Stavrogin stepped forward as the main hero and became a character of "immense stature." The former hero Pyotr Verkhovensky yielded to him and was reduced to the role of his disciple and lackey. All the grandiose and tragic passes over to Stavrogin; Verkhovensky, by contrast, is painted *in comic tones*. In the middle of August 1870 the writer began to revise his characteristics. "Meanwhile," he noted down, "in the city, in the manner of *Khlestakov*, St. T-ch's son. Miserable, vulgar, and nasty. Nechayev's and Telyatnikov's quarrel in the tavern, or in this genre. He frustrates St. T-ch's marriage, promotes the slander; little *comical* scandals, just as before, only a *Khlestakovian* way out." But the author felt that he would not ultimately succeed in transforming Verkhovensky into Khlestakov. He remarked: "In doubt about Nechayev." And finally, he reverted to the device of enigma. "Nechayev has two roles. I, the chronicler, do not know the second at all and do not present it (I don't know, for example, what he had to do with Liputin, with Shatov, and do not talk about it; but I know about the sessions, and do refer to those)." A special tone of narration was created for Pyotr Verkhovensky: he remains in the shadow, an enigmatic semidarkness—and from the imprecision of contours, his figure acquires a new terrifying expressiveness. The author explains this artistic device: "The whole atmosphere and all of Nechayev's movement lies in the fact that at first nothing at all is evident to the reader except certain foolish and strange characteristic traits. Don't do as other novelists, that is, from the very beginning blast forth about him, that here this is an unusual individual. On the contrary, conceal and disclose him only gradually, by strong artistic features (for example by the difference between his intellect and craftiness and his thorough ignorance of reality)." So, in the final text, Pyotr Verkhovensky is transformed into an enigmatic hero.

The surname Verkhovensky is as symbolic as the surname Shatov. The author noted regarding Stepan Trofimovich: "Through the entire novel Granovsky continually exchanges caustic remarks with his son about *pre-eminence*."[3]

---

[3] verkhovenstvo=pre-eminence, supremacy, sovereignty.

Shigalyov became distinguished from Pyotr Verkhovensky when the latter was transformed into the "Khlestakov of the revolution." In the notebooks his image is indicated schematically. . . . "N. B. Shigalyov— his own system. Shigalyov comes to a point—and stops. Cites an example—the Commune. Nechayev corrects him—destruction for the sake of destruction, and there what you please. The prince then asks Nechayev: 'Are you saying this to them in fun?' *Nechayev*: 'No, I'm serious. But you thought that it was a joke?' *Prince*: 'No, I thought that it was serious, because it's as funny as it is serious.' "

Pyotr Verkhovensky shouts at Shigalyov: "But do you know, you can pay up, Mr. Fourier." Shigalyov answers: "And what, you will kill me and it'll end, nonetheless, by your adopting my system. And moreover, permit me to remark to you that I'm not Fourier. I beg you not to confuse me with that sweet and abstracted milk-sop." This conscious anachronism of the author's is very curious. Nechayev, becoming comic, begins to resemble Petrashevsky and sees in Shigalyov "Mr. Fourier."

In this way the author indicates the ideational connection between the Nechayevists and the Petrashevists. It finds its full expression in the *Diary of a Writer* for 1873. In the essay *One of the Contemporary Falsehoods* Dostoevsky writes: "How do you know that the Petrashavists could not have become the Nechayevists, that is, have set themselves on Nechayev's very path, in such an instance, were things to have taken a similar turn? . . . But permit me to speak concerning myself only: probably I could never have become a *Nechayev*, but a *Nechayevist*, this I do not vouch; it is possible, I too could have become one . . . in the days of my youth." Here was why with such passionate indignation Dostoevsky "drove out the devils": he, a former Petrashevist, was responsible for Verkhovensky's principle of destruction and Shigalyov's equalization. The Russian tragedy was his personal tragedy.

The figure of the atheist and suicide *Kirilov* appeared very late (not earlier than the summer of 1871). At first he was an "engineer," Pyotr Verkhovensky's agent, sent by him from Switzerland with secret instructions. The author gave him the name of Tikhon Zadonsky—in the world *Kirilov*. In this symbolic rapprochement of the atheist with the saint is the key to Kirilov's disbelief. He kills himself, since he cannot endure the thought that there is no God; his atheism is engendered by an enraptured love of God and the despair of divine abandonment.

Kirilov believes, but does not know that he believes. The schema of his philosophy is outlined:

"If God does not exist, then there is a new era. But it is absolutely certain that people will devour one another. In such case, God is indispensable. But since He does not exist, then God is indispensable to deceive people. In this case, I don't want to live. Happiness with deceit is not necessary, it's better to blow everything to smithereens. *Pyotr S-ch:* No, better only one's self!" And in another draft: "The matter lies precisely in that God really doesn't exist. *It is for this reason that I'm shooting myself. If God doesn't exist, I don't want to remain in this world. Christ died on the cross with the thought of God."*

These notes leave us no doubt: the reason for Kirilov's suicide is his love for God, whom he denies. The motif of man-godhood is expressed with significantly less force in the final text. Dostoevsky had a special tender feeling toward his unfortunate hero. In notations for the final part of *The Devils,* he outlined the plan of a "preface." "In Kirilov is the people's idea to sacrifice oneself at once for the truth . . . to sacrifice oneself and everything for the truth—here is the national trait of the generation. Bless it, God, and send it an understanding of the truth! For the whole question consists in that—what to consider as the truth. This is why the novel was written."

In the printed text of *The Devils* the chapter *At Tikhon's* was omitted. It has been preserved only in the proofs. The "positively beautiful individual," Bishop Tikhon, was not destined to enter the framework of the novel. His exclusion violates the equilibrium of the composition and distorts the novel's ideational perspective. Tikhon was to have stood in opposition to Stavrogin, as Shatov opposes Pyotr Verkhovensky. The conflict, which had arisen between the man rooted in the soil and the nihilist, was to have been developed in the atheist's and the saint's dispute about God. Tikhon's encounter with Stavrogin was intended by the author as the culmination point of the novel. Katkov omitted the chapter *At Tikhon's* and the religious idea of the novel remained incompletely expressed. In the copybooks we find curious notations regarding the conversation in the monastery. The motivation of Stavrogin's coming is varied. He appears either to affront the bishop, or to question what the latter believes, or to read his confession, or, finally, in order to confess to him his violent, passionate love for a certain woman. "I've received news," he says, "that she will come. I will not oppose her: a single thought is hurling me into the madness of passion." So, the chapter *At Tikhon's* was originally to have prepared Stavrogin's scene with Liza at Skvoreshniki. Tikhon, coming into *The Devils* out of *The Life*, retained his meek and gracious image. "On the earth one must be happy." His reflections about the next life would afterward pass to the Elder Zosima. Here is what Tikhon preaches: "I am a dreamer. I imagine it in this fashion: the soul will roam and will see all its sin, and not as now, but *all of it*—and will see that God opens His embrace to it; having taken all this into consideration, it will be troubled and itself demand its full punishment, and will begin to search for it, but it is answered by love—and in this is its hell. The consciousness of unfulfilled love must be more terrible than anything and it is in just that that hell consists. What did I give you?—eternal happiness. And what did you create? eternal unhappiness. . . . The soul will recognize that each is responsible for all. . . . Man will see, in the clearest way possible, that everything, absolutely *everything* in the world and in his earthly life has depended entirely on him alone. Everything that has happened and about which he didn't even know, could, through Christ's example, be full of his love alone." Tikhon likewise inherited Golubov's ideas. He says "directly" to the prince (Stavrogin): "The soil is lacking. A foreign education. Love the people, their holy faith. Love them to enthusiasm."

The prince replies: I also love what is foreign. I love science, art.

Tikhon: As a guest, and not as a master in his own home. You love science, then why didn't you become a man of science? You love universal mankind—but do you believe in it? Do you believe in God and Christ?

Another notation:

Tikhon: You don't know anything holy! If only you would revere something as holy.

The prince: What for?

Tikhon: If you have said what for, that means you are simply not ready. This occurs not *what* for, but *as it is.* It contains its own recompense. It draws irresistibly, for it is harmony. If you don't feel the need and don't love anything, then, of course you are incapable.

Stavrogin was to have burst out in frenzy:

A spasmodic, unseemly diatribe about how everything must be blown to smithereens. I hate everything. . . . Goes out (immediately after the fit, as though feeling ashamed).

Tikhon: And I almost thought you would stay. Don't you want a little coffee? To please me.

The prince: I never drink coffee at this time, but with you I'll drink a cup, you are a very respected man.

This humoristic trait did not go into the final text. The author concludes: "Tikhon—the main thought. The unique freedom is conquering oneself." This is very close to Golubov's theory of "self-mastery."

In the novel *The Devils* a kind of fate pursued the positive heroes. Golubov disappeared, Shatov declines in ideational importance and withdrew into the shadows; in accord with Katkov's will Tikhon was excluded. The entire proscenium is occupied by Stavrogin, he is *everything* and has no opponents. He contends with himself, with his demon, and overcomes him, destroying himself. The story of his pre-existence in the author's imagination is full of tragic, absorbing interest. When in the original mist, the fiery glimpse of his spirit flashed, the struggle of the creator with his creation began. Stavrogin, like Proteus, took diverse forms, hid himself under all possible masks, but never lost the untamable force of his own "ego." In his proud self-will he defended his freedom and did not obey his creator. One gets the impression that having appeared, he went his own way, not concerning himself with the task and purposes of the author. He led his own painful, mysterious life and it is difficult to believe that his personality is only a literary fiction.

In the very earliest drafts the prince (Stavrogin) is shown as a Russian aristocrat who suddenly understands the whole meaninglessness of his own existence. A strong individual, richly endowed and sincere, he lives turbulently through a severe moral crisis and fitfully seeks a way out: "The prince was a most dissipated individual and haughty aristocrat. He recommended himself as a desperate enemy of the emancipation of the peasants and their oppressor." "Present the prince in the novel, as an enemy of nihilism and liberalism and a haughty aristocrat." And suddenly the thought strikes him: it is impossible to live this way any longer. "He turns aside from everyone, becomes a skeptic, looks distrustfully at people and their convictions"; judges himself harshly and comes to the conclusion that he is nothing. On March 15, 1870, Dostoevsky outlined his characteristics: "The prince is a man who finds that he is bored. The fruit of the Russian age. He *arrogantly* knows how to stand by himself, i.e., how to detach himself from noblemen, and from Westernizers, and from the nihilists, and from Golubov, but the question remains for him. What is he himself? The answer for him: *nothing*. He has enough intellect to acknowledge that he in fact is not a Russian. He ends by reasoning that he *doesn't find it neces-* *sary to be a Russian,* but when the absurdity of what he has said is proven to him, he evades by asserting that he is by himself." The author summarizes: "Present a man who has become aware that he lacks the soil." But this acknowledgement did not suffice for building the hero's personality. "Nothing" and "oneself"—was a deadlock; the author promptly corners himself: "The prince is a lofty nature and to be nothing does not satisfy and torments him. What will the torment of a nobleman divorced from the soil lead to? Can he renew himself or must he perish?" The writer tries both possibilities: "The prince—an indifferent role . . . does not have special ideas. . . . He feels only repugnance toward contemporary people with whom he has decided to break. An immediate repugnance because he has already comprehended that he is torn away from the soil. But he has no ideas. 'I opened my eyes and saw too much and could not endure our being without the soil. Our entire generation has proven insignificant and unnecessary.'" And after these remarks, the words underlined: "*The prince shot himself.*" But parallel there is indicated another variant—the prince's salvation. He meets Golubov and the Old Believer's idea about Russia's religious vocation inspires him. "Upon meeting him [Golubov], [the prince] is astounded; is terrified, and submits to him willingly." His conception changes radically: he is now not "nothing," not "an indifferent role," but "*a man with an idea.*" "The idea seizes him and possesses him, embodying itself in him, passing over into his nature, always with suffering and anxiety, and once having become established in his nature, exacting a ready application in action." The hero is removed from the deadlock, becomes dynamic, and throws himself into the fight. He is placed at the center of the action, becomes involved in the Nechayev affair, discovers Shatov's murderers, carries on a dual love intrigue with the "beauty" (Liza) and the protégée (Dasha). The author outlined a new plan: "The prince arrived, having now resolved everything, all his misgivings. *He is a new man.* . . . With furious energy inside, he expresses himself little, looks derisively and skeptically like a man who already possesses the ultimate solution and idea. . . . He has come to correct his mistakes in the city, injustices, etc. Becomes reconciled with the offended, suffers a slap in the face. Defends blasphemy, discovers the murderers and, at last, announces solemnly to the protégée that henceforth he is a Russian. He prays to the icons, etc." And the author concludes: "In such fashion, it turns out that the prince is a romantic and enigmatic character . . . *a new man."*

Rereading the notes related to this design, we feel how passionately the author was attracted by this thought, how dear the image of the new Russian man was to him. "The main idea, then," he wrote, "(i.e., *the pathos of the novel*) is that the prince and the protégée are *new people,* who have overcome the temptation and resolved to begin a new, restored life. . . . The prince has a strong character and an obstinate, but impressionable, melancholy, timid soul." However, the writer understood the extraordinary difficulty of such a task. "Problem: to embellish and create this pair—the prince and the protégée. *Here exactly is the crux.* The prince prepares to become a justice of the peace. More poetry." In these words: "Here exactly is the crux" are expressed all the author's doubts and hesitations. What will this new man do? Where will he go? What activity can be devised for him? Various possibilities are indicated. The prince humbles himself and is content with work that is modest, but useful for Russia. He says to the protégée: "I am a simple and plain man, but we will be good and worthy people. And now I know my strengths." Or the prince imposes a severe religious test on himself: repentance and self-mastery. Here are his words to Dasha: "I will not be a new man. I'm too unoriginal, but I have found, at last, a few precious ideas and am keeping to them. But before every rebirth and resurrection—self-mastery. And therefore I need you, you will save me by your gentleness. . . . Before, I used to condemn nihilism and was its embittered enemy, but now I see that it is we who are more guilty than anyone, and worse than all, we the nobles, who have been torn away from the soil, and therefore we, we must be reborn before all others: we are the chief corruption, on us lies the principal curse, and from us everything has flowed."

The image of the prince—a severe ascetic, desiring to embody in life Golubov's idea of self-mastery, engrossed the writer: "The prince is honest, cruel, has taken a decision, hates contemporary order. . . . Irony, defense in the form of attack. Hatred. A pure character. New form of boyar. Terribly proud. Honest people must save themselves quickly and begin a new race. To be new men, begin revision with one's own self. I am not a genius, but nonetheless I have conceived a new thing, no one in Russ has thought of besides me: *self-correction."* In this phase of work on the novel the future demon-Stavrogin very closely resembled the austere Christian–Old Believer Golubov. The prince became the exponent of his idea and supplanted Golubov in the pages of the novel.

However, the author was not quite certain that modest, but useful activity, "poverty and toil," suited the ardent and lofty spirit of his hero. He projected a more heroic future for him: "Wants to become a peasant and a schismatic. . . . A monk. . . ." And suddenly, all hopes for Stavrogin's salvation were completely shattered. Some sort of mysterious catastrophe took place in his fate. It is as though the repenting sinner, Golubov's disciple, the austere Christian and preacher of self-correction, derisively removed his mask. Yes, he employed lofty words, delivered pious sermons, *but he did not believe any of this.* That fascinating and terrible Stavrogin, whom we know from the novel, was born in his real guise March 29, 1870. Here is this remarkable note:

"It turns out this way, that the main hero of the novel is the prince. He joins Shatov, inflames him to the point of enthusiasm, *but he himself does not believe.* Observes everything and remains indifferent even to the murder of Sh., which he knows about. N. B. It remains a problem: was he really speaking seriously with Sh. and was he himself inflamed. . . . Shot himself. Letter to her: forgive me. Perhaps I really am mad." We feel that on the day of this notation Dostoevsky understood that his hero's fate obeyed its own law, which its creator was not empowered to change. Nikolai Stavrogin entered Dostoevsky's world not as a Christian on the way to salvation, but as *a tragic mask,* doomed from eternity to destruction. He *knows* that he lacks the soil, *knows* that the only salvation is in Christ, *knows* that without faith he will perish—and *does not believe.* He acknowledges the existence of God and the necessity of religion intellectually, but his heart is not with God but with the devil. This duality of consciousness is more strongly underlined in the rough notes than in the printed text. The contrast between the prince's Christian ideas and complete disbelief is tragically heightened in them. In inspired monologues the prince develops the author's most profound thoughts about faith and disbelief; all this brilliant dialectic did not go into the novel. The prince says to Shatov: "Strength is in the moral idea. The moral idea is in Christ. In the West, Christ has been distorted and diminished. It is the kingdom of the Antichrist. We have Orthodoxy. As a consequence we are the bearers of a clear understanding of Christ and a new idea for the resurrection of the world. . . . If faith and Orthodoxy were shaken in the people, then they would immediately begin to disintegrate. . . . Now the question: who then can believe? Does anyone (of the Pan-Slavs, or even the Slavophiles) believe, and finally, even the question: *is it possible to believe?* And if not, then what does it mean to shout about the Russian people's strength in Orthodoxy? This, consequently, is the only question of the times. There the *disintegration*, atheism, began earlier; with us, later, but it will begin certainly with the entrenchment of atheism. And if this is inevitable, one must even wish that the sooner it happens, the better. (The prince suddenly remarks that he agrees with Nechayev that it is best to burn everything.) . . . It emerges, consequently, that the whole matter lies in the pressing question: can one believe, being civilized, i.e. a European, i.e. believe absolutely in the divinity of the Son of God, Jesus Christ? (for all faith consists only of this). . . . You see: either everything is contained in faith, or nothing is; we recognize the importance of the salvation of the world through Orthodoxy. And so the whole question is, can one believe in Orthodoxy? If one can, then everything is saved; if not, then better to burn. . . . But if Orthodoxy is impossible for the enlightened man (and in a hundred years half of Russia will be enlightened), then consequently, all this is hocus-pocus and Russia's whole strength is provisional. . . . Is it possible to believe seriously and in earnest? Here is *everything*, the burden of life for the Russian people and their entire mission and existence to come. But if it is not possible, it is by no means so unforgivable if one should insist that it is best to burn everything. Both exigencies are quite identically philanthropic. Slow suffering and death or quick suffering and death; the quick is of course even more philanthropic. *And so, here lies the enigma. . . .*"

The tragic dilemma is pointed out with merciless logic: either to believe, or to "burn everything." In all world literature the question of whether it is possible for the civilized man of the 19th century to believe is not stated with such undaunted candor as in this rough draft of *The Devils*. The salvation of Russia, the salvation of the world, the fate of all mankind is contained in this one question: do you believe? And Shatov poses it to Stavrogin: "Tell me frankly," he asks, "really, really don't you believe?" The latter answers: "I'll be courteous and answer you: *no, I don't believe.*"

Stavrogin performs heroic acts: when Shatov slaps him in the face he submits, he announces his marriage to the cripple, he confesses to Tikhon, but his efforts are fruitless: *he does not believe.*

The action of the novel is constructed on this enigmatic dichotomy of the main hero. Stavrogin is a mystery which all the dramatis personae attempt to solve. "It is curious," remarks the author, "that he could understand the nature of Russia so profoundly, when he explained it and by this inflamed Shatov, but what is still more curious and *incomprehensible* is that he did not, in reality, believe any of it." And further: "The prince came more and more frequently to Shatov at night, Shatov grew more and more inflamed, his eyes used to glow. The prince's eyes burned too with a terrible fire. And strangely, with each visit, the more and more he *was transformed into an enigma for Shatov!*" And it was not only the essence of Russ that Stavrogin was able to understand, but the mystical depths of Christianity. He says to Shatov, regarding Christ's teaching: "But there there is no doctrine, there you have only fortuitous words, but the main thing is Christ's image from which every doctrine emanates. From Christ comes the thought that the chief gain and purpose of mankind is the result of morality once acquired. . . . Christ's morality is contained in two words: this is the idea that the salvation of personality lies in the voluntary and willful renunciation of it, provided that it serve others. But the main thing is not in the formula, but in the personality that is attained; refute the personality of Christ, the ideal incarnate—really, is this possible? It is not the morality of Christ, nor Christ's teaching that will save the world, but precisely faith that the Word became flesh. . . . Because only with this faith do we attain worship, that ecstasy which most attracts us to Him directly. With less ecstasy, mankind perhaps would certainly be led astray, at first into heresy, and at the end into atheism and into *troglodytism*, and would disappear, rot away."

The stronger the contrast is between the prince's "religious ecstasy" and his cold disbelief, the more tense the action of the novel. Dostoevsky intended to reinforce the opposition of his hero's two countenances in an effective final scene. Stavrogin discloses the nihilists' conspiracy, uncovers the murderers, establishes peace in the disordered city, and after a solemn thanksgiving service he delivers a speech: "We will bear to the world the sole thing that we can give, and at the same time, the only thing necessary. Orthodoxy, the just and glorious, eternal confession of Christ, and a full, moral renewal through His name. And an Elijah and an Enoch will go forth from us in order to struggle with the Antichrist, that is, with the spirit of the West. . . . Hurrah for the future!" And immediately after this the notation: "Leaves for Petersburg and hangs himself at Skvoreshniki. *This is important.*" The struggle for the hero's salvation was ended. Stavrogin decided his own fate. He was not a Christian, not the new Russian man, but a *pretender*. In August 1870 Dostoevsky destroyed the whole original draft and reconstructed the novel in accord with his new conception of Stavrogin's personality. His *demonism* was advanced onto the first plane. On August 16 the author wrote down: "The prince is a somber, passionate, *demonic*, disorderly character without any measure, with a sublime question which comes down to: to be or not to be? To live, or to destroy oneself?" And further: "N. B. Everything is contained in Stavrogin's character. . . . *Stavrogin is everything.*"

The new version was sharply distinguished from the old. Vast religio-philosophical material was excluded. The pretender's sermons were set aside—he is plunged in mysterious silence. His conversations with Shatov and Kirilov are relegated to the past. The religious concept of the novel was radically impoverished. The main issue—the question of faith and disbelief—is screened behind the complicated embellishment of the intrigue. All the author's original plans were upset. The diabolically fascinating figure of Stavrogin appeared, matured, and "declared its own will"; it "captivated" the writer, mocked his good intentions, and subverted his ideological designs.

X V I I I

The Devils

Dostoevsky was the creator of a new narrative form, the novel-tragedy.
In *Crime and Punishment* and in *The Idiot* it was elaborated and developed, in *The Devils* it attained its perfection. *The Devils* is one of the
greatest artistic works in world literature. In notebook No. 3 the writer
himself defines the genre he had created. "I don't describe the city,"
states the chronicler,

> the setting, mores, people, functions, the relationships and the curi-
> ous vacillations in these relationships of our provincial capital's
> strictly private life. . . . I also have no time to be expressly occupied
> with a *picture* of our little corner. I consider myself a chronicler of
> one curious, private *event*, that took place among us suddenly, unex-
> pectedly, in recent times, and plunged us all into bewilderment. It
> goes without saying, since the affair took place not in heaven, but
> rather among us, that it is just impossible for me not to concern my-
> self sometimes in a purely pictorial fashion with the mores aspect of
> life in our province; but I caution that I will do this only insofar as
> it will be required by the most urgent necessity. I will not begin
> to occupy myself especially with the descriptive part of our contem-
> porary manners.

Dostoevsky's novel is not the description of a city, not a portrayal of
manners: the "descriptive part," the conditions of life, do not engage
him. He is a chronicler of events that are unexpected, sudden, amazing. His art is contrary to the poetics of Tolstoy, Turgenev, Goncharov: against the *statics* of descriptions and history he advances the *dynamics* of events—movement, action, struggle. He had "no time" to
paint with words or to narrate customs in epic style; he was himself
seized by a whirlwind and carried along with the rushing current of
happenings. In one of his letters to Maikov we find the remarkable
sentence: "Being more a *poet* than an *artist*, I have perpetually adopted

themes beyond my own powers." The writer was sincerely convinced that his novels lacked sufficient artistry, justified himself by his oppressive working conditions, and humbly acknowledged himself inferior to such artists as Turgenev and Lev Tolstoy. This low opinion of his works is explained by the limitations of his poetics. For Dostoevsky, artistry was identical with *descriptiveness*, "the ability to paint," and he understood that he did not compare in this area with the masters of "the tableau." But he did not guess that his artistry was completely different, not comparable with the former and perhaps superior to it. To the principle of descriptiveness he opposed the principle of *expressiveness* (that which he called poetry); to the epic—the drama, to contemplation—inspiration. Descriptive art reproduces a natural given: it is directed to the sense of measure and harmony, to the Apollonian principle in men; its summit lies in impassionate, aesthetic contemplation; expressive art tears itself away from nature and creates a myth about man: it calls upon our will and questions our liberty; it is Dionysian and its summit is tragic inspiration. The first is passive and natural, the second active and personal; we admire one, participate in the other. One glorifies necessity, the other affirms freedom; one is *static*, the other *dynamic*.

All the peculiarities of the structure and technique of Dostoevsky's novels are explained by the principle of artistic expressiveness. He knows only man, his world and his fate. The hero's personality appears as the axis of composition; around it the dramatis personae are distributed and the plot is constructed. Raskolnikov stands at the center of *Crime and Punishment*; at the center of *The Idiot*—Prince Myshkin. This centralization attains its limit in *The Devils*. In the notebook we have already met the notation: "*The prince [Stavrogin] is everything*." And in fact, the whole novel is the fate of Stavrogin alone, everything is about him and everything is for him. The exposition is devoted to the story of Stepan Trofimovich Verkhovensky—the hero's tutor and ideational father; the spiritual roots of the atheist of the sixties are immerged in the "romantic dreaming" of the forties. Therefore, Verkhovensky enters Stavrogin's biography. Next to his father in spirit is set his mother in the flesh—Varvara Petrovna, who is intimately bound by twenty years of friendship to her "hanger-on." Four women are grouped around the hero—Liza Tushina, Dasha, Marya Timofeyevna, and Shatov's wife: all of them, like mirrors, reflect various images of the charming demon. The women are a part of the Russian Don Juan's tragic fate; in them lies his possibility of salvation and the threat of ruin. With respect to the "eternal feminine" he commits his greatest crime (Matryosha) and his loftiest action (his marriage to the cripple): he awaits resurrection through a woman's love (Liza) and before death comes running to a woman's maternal compassion (Dasha). The stages of the wanderer Stavrogin's life are marked by women's names; his ideational trials are symbolized by his amorous deceptions. His ruin becomes inevitable when love is finally extinguished in his heart (the farewell with Liza at Skvoreshniki). Following the first concentric circle—four women—comes a second—four men: Shatov, Kirilov, Pyotr Verkhovensky, and Shigalyov. The image of Don Juan is replaced by the image of Faust—the seeker, eternally dissatisfied and rebellious. Stavrogin is their teacher, their leader, and master. They all live by his life; they are his ideas, which have received independent existence. The hero's complex and contradictory personality generates the Orthodox nationalist Shatov, and the man-god Kirilov, and the revolutionary Pyotr Verkhovensky, and the fanatic Shigalyov. Both the mistresses and the disciples who are in love with their master—all these are only Stavrogin, only his consciousness, dissolving into insurmountable contradictions, struggling with the demon's temptations.

The third concentric circle is composed of secondary personages from Pyotr Verkhovensky's "society": petty devils, let go upon the earth by "the great and terrible spirit of negation": the Virginskys, Liputin, Lebyadkin, Erkel, Lyamshin, and several of the "inhabitants" of the provincial capital.[1] Finally, the governor Von Lembke and the great writer Karmazinov are linked to the main hero through the Drozdov family: Liza Tushina is the daughter of General Drozdov's widow, Karmazinov is her relative. By means of this centralized composition an extraordinary unity of action and proportionality of parts are attained. The radii from all the circles lead to the center; the currents of energy run through the whole organism of the novel, throwing all its parts into action. Shocks and explosions, taking place in the depth of the hero's consciousness, transmit vibrations from one circle to another: the waves dilate and grow, tension seizes a few people at first, then small groups, and finally, the whole city. Stavrogin's inner struggle be-

---

[1] The *guberniya* (government, or as I have translated it, province) was the basic administrative and territorial unit in Russia from the beginning of the 18th century until 1929-1930. In 1775 Catherine the Great divided the country into fifty *gubernii* (provinces), each with 300,000–400,000 inhabitants, to be administered by a governor. The *gubernsky gorod*, the "provincial capital," or literally "governmental city," was the political center and the main city in a *province*.

comes a general movement, is embodied in conspiracies, revolts, fires, murders, and suicides. Thus ideas are transformed into passions, passions into men, men express themselves in events. The internal and exterior are indivisible. The dissolution of personality, riot in the provincial capital, the spiritual crisis that Russia was experiencing, the world's entry into a catastrophic period of its history—such are the dilating circles of *The Devils'* symbolism. Stavrogin's personality is universal to the world and all mankind.

The second particularity of Dostoevsky's expressive art is its *dramatism*. *The Devils* is a theatre of tragic and tragi-comic masks. After the exposition—a short account of past events and the characteristics of the main personages (Stepan Trofimovich Verkhovensky, Varvara Petrovna Stavrogina, her son Nikolai Vsevolodovich, her protégée Dasha, the Drozdov and Von Lembke families)—there follows the complication: Stavrogina's plan to marry Stepan Trofimovich to Dasha; it consists of two dramatic dialogues (Stavrogina-Dasha and Stavrogina–Stepan Trofimovich). Old Verkhovensky's forced suit is connected with the mysterious love relations that have arisen abroad among Stavrogin, Liza Tushina, and Dasha. In the following chapters a third love intrigue is noted: Stavrogin–Marya Timofeyevna; Liputin tells the story of the cripple, Liza becomes passionately interested in her, Shatov defends her: Kirilov protects her from the beatings of Captain Lebyadkin. Finally, a fourth love intrigue is referred to in passing: Stavrogin–Shatov's wife. Thus around Stepan Trofimovich's courting the knot of the intrigue is complicated and entangled. Four female figures appear about Stavrogin; they are accompanied by new dramatis personae: Dasha is joined with her suitor Stepan Trofimovich and her brother Shatov; Liza Tushina, with her fiancé Mavriky Nikolayevich; Marya Timofeyevna, with her brother Lebyadkin and protectors Shatov and Kirilov; Mariya Shatova, with her husband. Dostoevsky's human world is constructed like a complicated inter-communion and moral pan-unity. The complication leads us to an effective ensemble scene: the "significant day" Sunday arrives. All the leading characters meet "by chance" in Varvara Petrovna's drawing room. Such fatal "chances" are the law in Dostoevsky's world. He transforms this convention of theatrical technique into a psychological necessity. His people are drawn to one another by love-hatred; we follow their approach and have a presentiment of the unavoidability of conflict. The orbits of these planets are calculated beforehand and the points of intersection are determined. With each moment our tension grows, we await the collision, fear it, and hurry it on by our impatience. The author torments us by delaying the tempo before the explosion (retardation) forces us to rise through all the degrees of expectation (gradation), deludes in false denouements (peripeteia), and finally jolts us with the catastrophe. This is the device of his *dynamic composition.*

The "significant day" begins with Varvara Petrovna's meeting the cripple in church; she takes her home and Marya Timofeyevna's "secret" provokes a long series of dramatic explanations, scandals, explosions. The widow of General Drozdov accuses Varvara Petrovna, Dasha clears herself before her benefactress, Lebyadkin hints at his sister's abuse. Suddenly Stavrogin and Pyotr Verkhovensky return from abroad; the first declares that Marya Timofeyevna is not his wife and respectfully leads her away; the latter unmasks the slanderer Lebyadkin and disgraces his father. Varvara Petrovna drives Stepan Trofimovich from her house, Shatov strikes Stavrogin in the face, Liza has a fit of hysterics. All these dramatic, unexpected, and extraordinary events are concentrated in one scene. The highest point of tension is Shatov's slap; it is prepared by the preceding conflicts. The dramatic energy is discharged and the current of action is ramified. After the mass scene there are a series of dialogue scenes, after the "significant day" is Stavrogin's "night." Eight days pass; the chronicler resumes his story from Monday evening "because," he declares, "in fact, a 'new scandal' began with that evening." The first catastrophe was the "denouement of the past and the complication of what was to come." The cripple's secret has not been disclosed and becomes the source of new happenings. Stavrogin converses with those "who have embodied his ideas"; each successive conversation is more dramatic than the one preceding: after the dialogue with Pyotr Verkhovensky he visits Kirilov, Shatov, Lebyadkin, and Marya Timofeyevna. Shatov's slap is the first burden that he assumes; his decision to announce publicly that he is married to the cripple is the second burden. The scene ends tragically: Marya Timofeyevna shouts in the hero's face: "Grishka Otrepyev—anathema!" and Stavrogin in a frenzy tosses money to Fedka the convict. The next dramatic moment is Stavrogin's duel with Gaganov. And his third burden proves a failure and a lie. The hero is removed to the second plane and yields place to his double, Pyotr Verkhovensky. The tone of the narration changes—it becomes more tranquil and slower; the framework expands: into the novel pours social life, "states of mind," the political evil of the day. Pyotr Verkhovensky exhibits an indefatigable activity: he makes a fool of the governor, becomes the favorite of the governor's wife, arranges the meetings of a secret society, sows alarming rumors, scatters proclamations, and agitates among the workers.

The next big ensemble scene is devoted to a session of "ours." This is a chef d'oeuvre of political satire, built on sharp tragi-comical contrasts. Shigalyov's initial speech, jarring in its somber energy, follows caricatured discussions among a girl student, a high-school pupil, and a major. The mass scene *At Ours* corresponds to the mass scene in Varvara Petrovna's drawing room; the first is a family tragedy, the second a social satire; both are concentrated around Stavrogin and his duality is reflected in their contrast. The hero's tragedy attains its culmination point in the scene *At Tikhon's*: his intent to publish his confession is the fourth and last burden that he wants to assume. The failure of this false repentance deals him the final, mortal blow. From this moment the action is broken: instead of rising, it falls, and is borne ever more rapidly to its denouement. The third part of the novel is devoted to the catastrophe, or more accurately, to a series of catastrophes, constituting a denouement of exceptional force. At a public fête for the benefit of governesses, Lebyadkin, Karmazinov, Stepan Trofimovich, and a certain maniac come forward; after these uproarious scandals follows the grandiose scandal at the ball and "quadrille of literature." All this culminates in the conflagration of the section across the river and riot. After the "political" catastrophe come personal ones: almost all the heroes of the novel perish: Marya Timofeyevna and Lebyadkin are killed by Fedka the convict; Liza Tushina perishes near their burning house; Fomka kills Fedka, Pyotr Verkhovensky kills Shatov; Kirilov and Stavrogin end in suicide; Stepan Trofimovich dies at an inn; Von Lembke goes out of his mind. The novel-tragedy divides into three acts: the complication is given in the form of a "false catastrophe" (the gathering at Varvara Petrovna's, 1st part); the culmination (*At Tikhon's*) is prepared by the second ensemble scene (*At Ours*, 2nd part), the denouement is introduced by the third mass scene (*The Fête*) and falls into a series of separate catastrophes (3rd part). The huge world of the novel, populated by a multitude of people and surcharged with a mass of events, is organized with brilliant art. Every episode is justified, every detail calculated; the disposition and sequence of the scenes are determined by the unity of the design. This world is possessed by a single impulse, animated by a single idea; *it is dynamic, and rushes toward its goal.*

The third characteristic of Dostoevsky's expressive art is its interest. The novel's action must captivate the reader, excite his curiosity. The author draws us into the world of his invention, demands our participation and collaboration. The reader's activity is sustained through the enigmatic, strange, unusual and unexpected nature of the events. The chronicler anticipates and reinforces the impression by his personal evaluations, conjectures, and hints. The complication of the novel (Stepan Trofimovich's courting) is introduced by the narrator's following remark: "Did he have a presentment that evening of what a *colossal* trial was being prepared for him in the immediate future?" The events abroad in which Stavrogin, Dasha, and Liza took part are surrounded by mystery. Varvara Petrovna endeavors to grasp their significance, but, the chronicler adds: "Something remained there she *did not understand or know.*" Nor is this ambiguity explained: the chronicler poses suppositions and loses himself in conjecture; our interest is aroused. Marya Timofeyevna's story is presented in distorted reflections: the malicious gossip Liputin and the drunken scapegrace Lebyadkin give their accounts. The secret's explanation leads to a new involvement; relations between Stavrogin and the cripple are explained by Pyotr Verkhovensky; a fresh lie is imposed onto the former deceptions. The chronicler is perplexed as to why Liza shows such interest in Shatov. "There was in all this," he acknowledges, "an enormous amount that was *unclear.* Here something was understood." Riddles are piled on riddles. The chronicler meets Mlle Lebyadkina; the mysteriousness of the setting astounds him. "Listen, Shatov," he says, "what can I now conclude from all this?" "Eh, conclude what you want," the latter answers. And the narrator enigmatically remarks: "An incredible thought became more and more fixed in my imagination." We are prepared for the improbability of the subsequent revelations. The "significant day," ending in Shatov's slapping Stavrogin, is introduced by the remark: "This was a day of surprises; a day of the denouement of the past and the complication of what was to come, of shrill explanations and *still worse entanglement.*" Stavrogin's respectful, chivalric attitude toward the cripple is incomprehensible, Liza's hysterical excitement is mysterious, Shatov's act remains an enigma. The chronicler underlines this effect by the remark: "But *sud-*

denly here an incident occurred that *no one could have expected.*"
In the second part, Pyotr Verkhovensky's whole behavior is confusing
in its duplicity and strangeness. He mortally hates Stavrogin and at
the same time loves him and kisses his hand. From this dark
being a shadow extends at first onto his immediate surroundings, then
onto his secret society, and finally over the whole city. The conspiracy
spreads, the action of the entire novel is slowly plunged in ominous
gloom. Against its background flashes the glow of the fire across the
river; the knife of Fedka the convict gleams as he kills Lebyadkin;
Pyotr Verkhovensky's shot resounds as it strikes down Shatov.

Enigma is Dostoevsky's favorite device; the explanation of one
secret draws after it the appearance of another: the continuous
explanations lead to "still worse entanglement." We are involved
in a complicated net of events and involuntarily become prosecutors
and detectives. In his notebook Dostoevsky writes about the "peculiar
tone of the story." "The tone" he remarks in the margins, "lies in
not explaining Nechayev [Pyotr Verkhovensky] or the prince [Stav-
rogin]. . . . *Suppress him* (Nechayev) and reveal him only little by little
in strong artistic traits." The prince is characterized as an "enigmatic
and romantic" personage. On this conscious device is built an effect
of contrasting illumination: amidst the precisely outlined and clearly
illuminated characters, the main heroes are surrounded by a mysterious
shadow; their features are fluid, their contours indistinguishable. And
this adds a peculiar, painful expressiveness to the novel's two "demons";
the emptiness of nonbeing shines through their fantastic features. . . .
Spirits of negation and destruction—they cannot be ultimately explained or portrayed. Dostoevsky's mastery is in the gradation of
shadows, in the light contrasts, and in dual illumination.

The concentration of action around the personality of the main hero,
the dramatism of the construction, and the enigma of tone—these
are the three properties of "expressive art." The novel-tragedy is
saturated with dramatic energy, contains countless potentials of struggle and conflict. Not only is the whole tragic, but also each of its cells.
All the dramatis personae, who take part in the common tragedy,
simultaneously experience their own personal tragedies. The plots
involved in one Dostoevsky novel would be sufficient for ten ordinary
"descriptive novels." Let us attempt, out of the counterpoint of *The
Devils*, to distinguish the basic motifs of the "personal tragedies."

Stepan Trofimovich Verkhovensky, with whose history the action of the novel begins and ends, belongs to the writer's greatest creations. The breath and warmth of life is in the image of this pure idealist of the forties. He lives so immediately and naturally on the pages of the novel that he seems independent of the author's own will. Each sentence of his and every act strike us as being inwardly true. With good-natured humor, Dostoevsky pursues the exploits of his "fifty-year-old infant," chaffs at his weaknesses, drolly apes his "gentlemanly" intonations, but decidedly delights in him. The figure of Stepan Trofimovich testifies to the author's extraordinary gift of humor. Verkhovensky was a "most excellent individual," "most intelligent, and gifted." He belonged to a pleiad of celebrated names in the forties; studied in Germany, distinguished himself in a chair at the university, wrote a study on the "causes of the uncommon moral nobility of some certain knights" and a poem resembling the second part of *Faust*. But his brilliant career was "cut off by a whirlwind of circumstances" and he ended up in the provincial capital, living as a "hanger-on" in the home of his despotic friend and benefactress—Varvara Petrovna Stavrogina. The idealist was reduced to cards and champagne, fell regularly into "civic distress," that is into melancholy, which invariably ended in fits of cholerine. But he was sustained by the "pleasant dream of his beautiful civic attitude." For twenty years he had stood before Russia as an "embodied reproach," and he entered upon the role of one persecuted and exiled. He was married twice: the first time to some "frivolous young girl," by whom he had a son Pyotr. This "fruit of his first, joyful, and still undarkened love" was brought up somewhere in a remote region. His second wife was a German: the marriage appeared, evidently, to be the consequence of his enthusiasm for German idealist philosophy. But the knight-romantic's chief love was his twenty-year-long platonic feeling for Varvara Petrovna, composed of habit, vanity, egoism, and the most lofty and sincere attachment.

The idealist lives by a "higher thought," the idea of eternal beauty; he is a genuine poet; he is familiar with inspiration and a presentiment of world harmony. Dostoevsky entrusts to Verkhovensky his most sacred ideas. But his aestheticism in theory is transformed in practice into unsightly amoralism. Stepan Trofimovich can ecstatically preach the happiness of all mankind and gamble away his serf Fedka at cards. The uprootedness of romantic daydreaming is exposed by the author in biting parody. Verkhovensky writes to Varvara Petrovna from Berlin: "And we have almost Athenian evenings, but only in their delicacy and refinement; everything is noble, a great deal of music, Spanish airs, the dream of all mankind's regeneration, the idea of eternal beauty, the Sistine Madonna, light with interspersions of darkness." There is a discord between dream and reality which sometimes brings the knight of the severe lady to nervous outbursts and he gloomily declares: "*Je suis un . . .* simple parasite, *et rien de plus,*" or: "*Je suis un . . .* man thrust against the wall." This discord is turned into conflict with the arrival of his son Pyotr. Stepan Trofimovich clashes with the nihilists, among whom the first is his *cher* Petrusha. He reads *What's to be Done?* and enters into the battle. Indignation, civil sentiment, and daring kindle in the enervated and weakened aesthete. Verkhovensky boldly states that "shoes are inferior to Pushkin and very much so," and fearlessly comes forward before the unruly audience at the "fête." It is precisely to him, this weak and insignificant character, that Dostoevsky gives the right to unmask the young generation. The author forgives his hero all his falls and sins on account of his chivalrous loyalty to the idea of eternal beauty, for his being imbued with a "higher thought." "Yes, but do you understand," Stepan Trofimovich shouts at his son, "do you understand that if the guillotine is primary for you and that with such enthusiasm, then it is only because the easiest thing is to chop off heads, but having an idea is the most difficult of all. These carts, and how does one say it: 'the rumble of carts, bringing bread to mankind,' are more useful than the Sistine Madonna, or however they say it—is *une bêtise dans ce genre.*" Stepan Trofimovich's words echo Lebedev's prophecy in *The Idiot* and prepare for the "temptation of bread's" final exposure in *The Legend of the Grand Inquisitor.*

At the fête Verkhovensky addresses the nihilists in solemn and inspired words: " 'But I proclaim that Shakespeare and Raphael are superior to the emancipation of the serfs, superior to nationality, superior to socialism, superior to the youthful generation, superior to chemistry, superior to almost all mankind, for they are already the fruit, the real fruit of all mankind, and perhaps the greatest fruit that can possibly exist! A form of beauty has already been attained: were it not attained, I, perhaps, would not consent to live. . . . It is possible for mankind to live without bread; only without beauty is it impossible, for then there will be nothing left to do on earth. The whole secret is here, all of history is here! . . . I will not relent! . . . ,' he cried absurdly in conclusion and banged his fist with all his force upon the table." The "idealist's" tragi-comical speech contains the main idea of the novel and the author's most sacred trust. The former ideal of beauty has become muddled in mankind, and "troubled times" have begun for it. Dostoevsky always held that society is directed by aesthetic principles and that the contemporrary crisis was at root a crisis of *aesthetic consciousness*. Stepan Trofimovich's "absurd coming forward" at the fête is his spiritual triumph and practical defeat. The lecturer is hissed and jeered. He puts on his traveling coat, takes his cane, and leaves Varvara Petrovna's house. He will die as he lived, a "Russian wanderer," a homeless spiritual vagabond, a "superfluous man." The tragedy of the uprooted romantic is symbolized by this last journey along the high road. At an inn Verkhovensky meets a book-hawker Sofya Matveyevna and she reads him the Gospel story about the healing of the possessed Gadarene. The somber and terrible novel-pamphlet concludes with a luminous prophecy for Russia. "These devils," pronounces Stepan Trofimovich in great agitation, "these are all the ulcers, all the miasmata, all the impurity, all the devils and imps that had accumulated in our great and dear patient, in our Russia, for ages, for ages. *Oui, cette Russie que j'aimais toujours*. But a great thought and great freedom will overshadow her from on high, all these devils, all this impurity, will go out of her just as with that man possessed. . . . But the patient will be healed and will 'sit down at the feet of Jesus,' and everyone will look with amazement. My dear, *vous comprendrez après*, but now this troubles me very much. . . ." After his prophecy about Russia—the last words of Stepan Trofimovich are devoted to the great idea of immortality. The free-thinker, who had felt himself a pagan, in the likeness of the great Goethe, discovers in death the pledge of eternal life. The aesthetic idea of the novel is crowned by a triumphant, mystical assurance. "My immortality," the dying man says firmly, "is necessary if only because God will not wish to do injustice and completely extinguish the fire of love for Him, once it has been kindled in my heart. And what is more dear than love? *Love is higher than existence*, love is the crown of existence and then how is it possible that existence should not submit to it? If I have come to love Him and rejoiced in my love, is it possible that He should extinguish both me and my joy and turn us into nothingness? If God exists, then I too am immortal! *Voilà ma profession de foi!*" So the *tragedy of the aesthetic consciousness* ends religiously.

A "great, eternal, infinite thought" raises up the old-womanish parasite to the height of mystical contemplation. The idealist of the forties confessed his responsibility for the nihilists of the sixties; he condemned himself to ruin with the devils who had entered into the herd of swine. And by this act of repentance he cleansed himself and shone forth in an immortal idea—in beauty saving the world. Verkhovensky's inner drama is depicted through "sharp artistic traits" with increasing dramatism: the courting of Dasha, the conflict with Varvara Petrovna, the collision and struggle with his son, his final journey and enlightened death at the inn—such are the pathetic acts of this "personal tragedy."

Into the framework of Stepan Trofimovich's story is set the main action of the novel—Nikolai Vsevolodovich Stavrogin's spiritual tragedy. We become acquainted with the hero a few weeks before his suicide, see him in the last critical period of his life. Stavrogin enters the world of the novel, like a living corpse, hoping for resurrection and not believing in its possibility. His tense spiritual life is ascribed to the past and is shown in the refractions of several human consciousnesses: Shatov, Kirilov, Shigalyov embody stages of his religious searchings.

Of all these embodiments *Shatov* is the most vital: the image of the idolized teacher Stavrogin is peculiarly refracted in this disciple's ardent soul. With Shatov ideational duality is transformed into personal tragedy. Dostoevsky makes him the herald of his own religious-national credo and introduces extensive autobiographical material into his story: so, for example, Shatov's joyful excitement at Marie's delivery reproduces exactly the author's experiences at the birth of his first child. Shatov was born Varvara Petrovna's serf, was Stepan Trofimovich's pupil, studied at the university and was expelled after a certain student incident; he married a poor governess, roamed for a long time about Europe; then radically he altered his socialistic convictions and rushed to the opposite extreme. "He was clumsy, fair, disheveled, short in stature, with broad shoulders, thick lips . . . with a knitted brow, with an impatient, obstinately downcast glance, as though he were ashamed of something." The hero resembles the author not only in his convictions, but also outward appearance. When Stavrogin in an affectionate voice tells Marya Timofeyevna that he is not her "husband, nor father, nor fiancé," Shatov "suddenly drew back his long, heavy arm and with all his might struck him on the cheek. Nikolai Vsevolodovich staggered violently in his place." The cause of this unexpected act is explained in the famous nocturnal scene between the teacher who has betrayed his idea and the disciple in revolt. Shatov expounds to Stavrogin the latter's thought regarding the religious vocation of Russia. It might seem that the long philosophical deliberation should delay the narration's quick tempo. In fact, the reverse occurs: Shatov's ideological conversation with Stavrogin is the highest point of dramatic tension. Dostoevsky knew how to *dramatize thoughts*. In his works ideas are melted in the fire of passion, transformed into powerful energies that live, collide, struggle, explode, destroy, or save. The author characterizes Shatov as "one of those ideal Russian beings who will suddenly be struck by some strong idea and at once will be positively obsessed by it, sometimes forever. They never have the strength to cope with it, but will believe in it passionately and so their whole lives pass afterward as though in the last agonies beneath a stone that has fallen on them and already half-crushed them." Shatov does not reflect, but shrinks under the stone of an idea that has fallen on him; does not philosophize, but screams and groans. The premises lead him not to a logical conclusion, but to a question of life and death. But it is not for Shatov alone that a "strong idea" becomes a personal tragic fate; all Dostoevsky's heroes tempestuously and dramatically *experience* their ideas. Stavrogin says to Kirilov that he "*has felt* a completely new thought." The latter asks him, "You've felt a new thought? That's good." Dostoevsky's people *feel* thoughts. Ideological material served the writer as a potent means of artistic expressiveness. After being slapped, Stavrogin goes to the man who insulted him: the latter has waited for him for an entire week in ague, in fever. He says that he hit him for his "fall," for his "lie"; Stavrogin informs him that he intends in the near future publicly to announce his marriage to the cripple. Shatov asks him to grant him ten minutes. "We are two beings and have met in infinity . . . for the last time in this world. Drop your tone and speak like a human being. . . ." "His ecstasy approached delirium." After Shatov's inspired monologue about the Russian people, the "only God-bearing people," Stavrogin asks coldly: "I wanted simply to know: do you yourself believe in God or not?" "I believe in Russia, I believe in her Orthodoxy. I believe in the body of Christ. . . . I believe that the new Coming will take place in Russia. . . . I believe. . . ." Shatov began to stammer in ecstasy. "But in God? in God?" "I . . . I will believe in God."

This dialogue is the culminating point of Shatov's tragedy: the exponent of the Russian messianic idea does not believe in God! The dichotomy between faith and disbelief destines him to ruin. The somber scene of the murder in the Skvoreshniki park is prepared by a peripeteia—his wife's arrival and the birth of a child. Shatov has not seen Marie for three years: she abandoned him after two weeks of married life in Geneva. But he loves her, as before, with devotion and rapture. She gives birth to a child whose father is Stavrogin. It does not even enter the husband's mind that his wife has betrayed him; the whole night he exerts himself, borrows money, brings a midwife, attends to the patient. A new joyous life begins for him. After the delivery, he says to Virginskaya: "'Rejoice, Arina Prokhorovna. . . . This is a great joy. . . . The mystery of the coming of a new creature is a great and incomprehensible mystery.' Shatov muttered incoherently—dazed and enraptured. As it were, something was turning over in his head and pouring out of his soul apart from his own will. 'There were two and suddenly there's a third individual, a new, new spirit, whole, complete, such as human hands cannot fashion; a new thought and new love, it's even strange . . . and there is nothing greater on earth.'" Marie, irritated, is suddenly assuaged and kisses her husband. "Shatov now cried like a little boy, then said God knows what. . . . He talked to her about how they would begin to live 'anew and forever,' about the existence of God, about all being good." In the love for his wife and in the mystery of the birth of a new being he finds faith and rises from the dead. At this moment Erkel comes for him and takes him away to the park at Skvoreshniki. There he is killed. The transition from birth to death, from the light of resurrection to the darkness of destruction, is jolting in its mystical terror. The pathetic tension of this scene almost exceeds human strength. Before the story of the murder, Dostoevsky gives a detailed description of the Skvoreshniki park. The *paysage*, introduced in this scene of great tragic depth, becomes a powerful resonator, heightening the dramatic force of the events. With Dostoevsky, the *paysage* appears only in moments of catastrophe, when delaying the tempo reinforces the tension. In *Crime and Punishment*, Svidrigailov's final night before his suicide is described; in *The Idiot*, we are presented with Rogozhin's house in which the murder of Nastasya Filippovna takes place. Mute nature receives a tongue in moments fatal for man; her symbolic speech accompanies the groans of the dying, the murderers' cries, and the raving of those going out of their minds. In those moments the unity of cosmic life is mysteriously disclosed.

This is the description of the place of Shatov's murder. "It was a very *gloomy* place, at the end of the vast Stavrogin park. . . . Here an old prohibited forest began: huge, age-old pines stood like *gloomy* and vague spots in the *gloom*. It was so dark that it was almost impossible to see one another at two paces. . . . For some unknown reason, at some unrecorded date, a certain rather absurd grotto had been built there out of the rough unhewn stones. The table and benches inside the grotto had long ago decayed and crumbled. About two hundred paces to the right was the bank of the park's third pond. These three ponds, beginning at the house, stretched one after another, more than two-thirds of a mile, to the very end of the park. It was hard to imagine that any noise, cry or even shot could reach the inhabitants of the deserted Stavrogin house."

Pyotr Verkhovensky "firmly and accurately" shoots Shatov point-blank: "They set down the lantern, swung the corpse, and threw it into the water. A dull and prolonged sound was heard." Thus "the prophet of Russian messianism perishes."

The tragedy of another of Stavrogin's disciples—*Kirilov's*—is parallel and contrasting to the tragedy of Shatov. He is also a man of one idea and contracts beneath the stone which has crushed him; likewise is torn from the soil, blind to real life; is also a fanatic and ascetic whose thought has been transformed into will and passion. His story is related by the author with no less artistic inspiration than the story of his ideological fellow companion and adversary. Kirilov is a young structural engineer. "Well-built and lean, with dark hair, somewhat muddy complexion, and black lusterless eyes, he seemed a little melancholy and confused, spoke disconnectedly and somehow ungrammatically." For four years he remained abroad, in solitude: shut off in his idea, as in an impregnable fortress; completely within himself, in his silence; he has lusterless eyes and impeded speech. Thus "sharp traits" reveal to us the abstractedness of a nature that has fallen out of intercourse with men. Kirilov is a human symbol of *subjective idealism*.

His tragedy lies in his fatal dichotomy of mind and heart. With his mind he arrives at the negation of God and the necessity of suicide; with his heart he passionately loves life and pities people. Just like Shatov, he is mysteriously connected with Marya Timofeyevna (also lives in the same house with her), protects her from her drunken brother, fusses over children, takes an ardent part in the fate of Shatov's wife. He has a loving, tender heart and a "childlike laugh." Out of respect for his landlady he lights an icon-lamp. He does not sleep at night, incessantly drinks tea, walks about the room and thinks. Pyotr Verkhovensky says mockingly to him: "I know that you haven't devoured an idea, but an idea has devoured you." In Kirilov's "idea" one should distinguish two heterogeneous parts: a mystical premise and a logical conclusion. The first we already know from the novel *The Idiot*; Kirilov in part literally repeats, in part develops Prince Myshkin's "mystical experience." His account of the "moments of eternal harmony" coincides exactly with the description of the idiot's ecstasies. "Do you have moments of eternal harmony?" he asks Shatov. . . . "There are seconds, only five or six of them come at a time, and suddenly you feel the presence of eternal harmony, perfectly attained. This is nothing earthly, I don't say that it's from heaven, but that man in his earthly form can't endure it. One has to be physically changed or die. It's a clear and indisputable feeling. As it were, suddenly you perceive all nature and suddenly say: 'Yes, this's true!' God, when He was creating the world, at the end of every day of creation said: 'Yes, this is true, this is good!' . . . What's most terrifying is that it's so horribly clear and such joy. If it lasted more than five seconds, then the soul couldn't hold out, and must perish. In these five seconds I live through a lifetime and would give up my whole life for them, for they're worth it. To endure ten seconds, one would have to be changed physically." Shatov says to Kirilov: "Beware of falling sickness," and recalls the epileptic Mahomet. In these words, the connection between the visions of Myshkin and Kirilov is definitely established. Both of them are ecstatics and visionaries. At the basis of their perception of world harmony lies the real personal experience of the epileptic Dostoevsky. The second of unendurable bliss, experienced before his attacks of epilepsy, was the source of his religious world-sensation. The spiritual value of this experience is indisputable: in it is given a foretaste of future bliss, the light of the coming Kingdom of God on earth. For an instant eternity opens to the spectator, and the future merges with the present. He is crushed by the reality and evidence of this new plane of existence. "Most terrifying," says Kirilov, "is that it is so horribly clear." But this clarity seduces the visionary: he takes what is to come for the present, is convinced that world harmony has already been attained, and that earth has become paradise: he sees the divine foundation of the world and does not notice that "the world lies in evil." One can call this flaw of the religious consciousness *mystical naturalism*. Kirilov, like Myshkin, passionately loves life and the world.

Once again we meet in Dostoevsky the invariable symbol of cosmic beauty—the leaf of a tree. "Have you ever seen a leaf, a leaf from a tree?" Kirilov asks Stavrogin. "I saw a yellow one, somewhat green, not long ago; it had rotted underneath about the edges. It was carried by the wind. When I was ten, I used to close my eyes on purpose in the winter, and imagine a leaf, bright, green, with little veins and the sun was shining. . . ." In Petropavlovsky Fortress, the writer longed for green leaves; Ivan Karamazov speaks of sticky little leaves. The visionary sees that the world is beautiful and all people are happy. There is no evil, all men are good. "Everything is good," declares Kirilov. "Man is unhappy because he doesn't know that he's happy; for that reason alone. This is everything, everything! . . . That mother-in-law will die, and the girl will remain—everything is good, I suddenly discovered it." Stavrogin asks: "And someone will die of hunger, and someone will affront and dishonor the girl—is this good?" "It is," answers Kirilov. "Everything is good, everything!" But from the same mystical premise Myshkin and Kirilov draw different conclusions. Prince Myshkin is a moralist: he believes that it is possible to teach people to be good, to persuade them that they are beautiful, to transform their dark and evil lives into paradisal bliss. His magnanimous attempt fails and he perishes. Kirilov's thought is more resolute and daring. The truth of the heart and that of the mind clash in his consciousness and "it is impossible to live with two such thoughts." His heart in a rapture of ecstasy knows that life is paradise; his sober mind understands that "life is pain and fear." Where then is the way out of this contradiction? Kirilov finds it in the idea of *man-godhood.* The present state of mankind is temporary and must be overcome. "Man and the earth will change physically," time will be no more and no future eternal life will follow, but an eternal one here below. But for this to happen, it is necessary to stamp out falsehood and deceit, which have turned the earthly paradise into a "devils' vaudeville." This deceit is God. "All man did was to invent God so as to live without killing himself." Man is afraid of death and the mystery beyond the grave—and to this fear has given the name of God. Fear must be conquered, and then the idea of God will be extinguished in mankind. "There will be freedom when it is possible not to care whether one lives or one doesn't." Kirilov decides to kill himself simply to free mankind from God, Who is "the pain of the fear of death." This act of the greatest self-volition will produce a change in the history of mankind. "One, the one who is first, must certainly kill himself, otherwise who'll begin and prove this? But I declare my self-will and am bound to believe that I don't believe. Only this will save mankind, and in the next generation will transform them physically; for in his present physical condition, as far as I can see, it is impossible for man to be without his former God. . . . I am killing myself to show my defiance and terrible new freedom." Man, having killed God and attained a terrible freedom, will himself become God. "If there is no God, then I am God. . . . If God exists, then all is His will, and I can do nothing against His will. If He doesn't, then it's all my will and I'm bound to express my self-will. . . . I'm bound to shoot myself, because the highest point of my self-will—is to kill own self. . . . For the first time in world history I alone have not wanted to invent God."

Kirilov's idea is summarized by the author in five short overpowering remarks. Kirilov says to Stavrogin: "He who teaches that all are good will end the world." Stavrogin objects: "He who taught it was crucified." *Kirilov*: "He'll come and his name will be the man-god." *Stavrogin*: "The God-man?" *Kirilov*: "The man-god, that's the difference." In fact, the whole astonishing difference is in this transposition. The beginning is placed at the end, and Christ is supplanted by the Antichrist. The paradox in Kirilov's idea is that with iron logic he draws an atheistic deduction from a mystical premise. His consciousness of the divinity of the world leads him to the denial of its Creator. But this denial is only the reverse side of an insatiable love for God. "God has tormented me throughout my entire life," confesses this atheist. His heart cannot live without God, but his mind cannot admit the existence of God. "God is necessary, and therefore *must be*, but I know there is no God and *there cannot be*—it is impossible to live with two such thoughts." His consciousness is thus tragically divided. On one hand there is the murder of God, a declaration of his self-will, the demonic dream of the man-god; on the other—the despair and moral anguish of a believing heart, powerless to overcome the disbelief of reason. Kirilov kills himself not only to destroy the idea of God, but also because without God he cannot live. He says regarding people who have lost their faith: "I've always been amazed that they just go on living."

Pyotr Verkhovensky takes advantage of Kirilov's decision and forces him to assume the responsibility for Shatov's murder. The religious tragedy of the man struggling with God is concluded by the scene of his suicide, almost unbearable in its horror. Kirilov's "man-godhood" is the most ingenious creation of Dostoevsky the philosopher and artist.

Two opposed states of consciousness, which coexisted in Stavrogin, were embodied in his disciples' personalities and were experienced by them as personal tragedies. Shatov and Kirilov are two moments in the dialectic of his spirit. Shatov says to Stavrogin: "At the very time that you planted the idea of God and country in my heart, at the same time, perhaps even on the same days, you were

poisoning the heart of this unfortunate, this maniac Kirilov with venom.
. . . You filled him with lies and slander and drove his reason to frenzy."

Shatov and Kirilov are Stavrogin's spiritual descendants; *Pyotr Verkhovensky* is his abortion. He remains on a lower plane of existence, sunk in chaotic matter: the former are spirits, he is a petty devil; the first are heroes of a tragedy, he is a personage out of a tragi-comical farce. The author confessed that Verkhovensky turned out a comic character *unexpectedly*. The somber villain's change into a buffoon forced the writer to simplify his characteristics and to transfer his ideological baggage to another character—Shigalyov. But, despite this reduction of the revolutionary's image, his spiritual connection with the ideologist Kirilov was nonetheless preserved. Verkhovensky says to Kirilov: "You know that, in your place, I would kill someone else to show my self-will, and not myself. You could have become useful. I'll tell you whom, if you are not frightened. . . . We can come to terms." The latter retorts: "Killing another would be the lowest point of my self-will, and this is just like you. I'm not you: I want the highest point, and will kill myself." If there is no God, man has a terrible freedom. On this the atheists Kirilov and Verkhovensky agree; but they "express self-will" in different ways. Kirilov chooses the higher point—and kills himself; Verkhovensky, the lowest—and kills others. Stavrogin calls Kirilov "magnanimous"; he directs the thrust of his idea against his own breast and perishes in man-godlike grandeur. Verkhovensky translates the notion of self-will into the language of political action. "Everything is permitted" is for him turned into the right to employ falsehood, deceit, crime, and destruction. From the atheistic premise he deduces a theory of political amoralism. For Dostoevsky, socialism and revolution are the natural outcome of atheism. Verkhovensky's traits are described in harsh caricature: he is a "political cheat and intriguer, a scoundrel and false mind," in Kirilov's opinion; Shatov calls him a "bug, an ignoramus, a simpleton, who understands nothing in Russia." Abroad, Verkhovensky had declared ties with the "Internationale"; in Russia, he organizes secret societies, diffuses proclamations, sows sedition, and is preparing an uprising. He is a buffoon, gossip, slanderer, traitor; maliciously he derides his father; drives the governor, Von Lembke, to insanity, secretly plots Lebyadkin's murder; and shoots Shatov. He is a typical villain of melodrama. But out from under the crudely painted mask another face appears for one instant, and we suddenly understand that Verkhovensky, playing the banal role of an intriguer, is cautiously guarding his own secret. Stavrogin says enigmatically about him, "Verkhovensky is an enthusiast. There is a point where he ceases to be a buffoon and turns into a being who is . . . half-mad." He touches upon this point in the ingenious scene *Ivan the Tsarevich*. The intriguer and swindler is suddenly transformed into an inspired poet. With fiery rapture he delivers a half-crazed speech about sedition, with passionate love he entreats Stavrogin; these lyrics of destruction catch one's breath. " 'Stavrogin, you're a handsome man!' screamed Pyotr Stepanovich almost in transport, 'do you know that you're handsome! What's most precious is that you sometimes don't know it. . . . *I love beauty*. I'm a nihilist, but love beauty. Really can nihilists not love beauty? Only they don't love idols, well, but I love an idol! You are my idol! I, I need precisely such a man as you. I know no one, except you. You are my leader, you're my sun, and I am your worm.' He suddenly kissed him on the hand. . . . 'Mad!' whispered Stavrogin."

After the hymn to beauty follows a hymn to destruction: "Listen, we first will spread sedition. . . . I've already told you: we will permeate the very people. . . . We'll spread drunkenness, gossip, denunciations; we'll resort to unheard-of debauchery; we'll stifle every genius in childhood. . . . We will proclaim destruction. . . . We must, we must exercise our bones a little. . . . We will spread fires. . . . We'll spread legends. . . . Here every mangy little group will be useful. Well sir, and the riot will start! There'll be such an upheaval as the world has never seen. Russ will be enveloped in darkness, the earth will begin to cry for its old gods. . . . Well, right then we will bring forward. . . whom?" Stavrogin repeats: "Whom?" *Verkhovensky*: "Ivan the Tsarevich." "Whom-m?" "Ivan the Tsarevich: you, you!" No, Verkhovensky is not simply a "villain of melodrama," not merely a "petty devil" of nihilism—he has "holy madness," frenzy "on the brink of the gloomy abyss," demonic inspiration, the idea of universal destruction. With his lips speaks the powerful and awesome spirit of nonbeing. Nihilism, anarchism, atheism are phantoms rising out of the metaphysical abyss *"nothing."*

And once again in this dialogue the last word belongs to aesthetics. The world is beauty, creation is beauty, God is beauty; but chaos, destruction, and nonbeing can also appear as beauty. Both ideals of beauty—the ideal of the Madonna and the ideal of Sodom are contained in man's heart; opposite poles converge. With contempt Stavrogin repudiates the "mad" Verkhovensky. No, he is not "Ivan the

Tsarevich." The latter in rage cries to him: "Wretched, profligate, degenerate little aristocrat!" The concept of "world-upheaval" is aborted into a pitiful riot in the provincial capital. Verkhovensky disappears: he is a "worm" and without his "leader," his "sun," he is doomed to impotence. In this failure is contained the germ of his personal tragedy.

In the course of work on the novel, out of the figure of Pyotr Verkhovensky Dostoevsky formulated his complementary image—*Shigalyov*. Behind the "petty devil," tittering, bustling, and poking about, stands a heavy, clumsy, and sullen demon. Verkhovensky is the giddy Khlestakov of the revolution, Shigalyov is his ponderous Sobakevich. This theoretician of destruction is characterized by his *ears*. "I was struck," says the chronicler, "most of all by his ears, of unnatural size, long, wide, fat, somehow singularly prominent. He produced an inauspicious impression on me." During the session "At Ours" Shigalyov intends to read a notebook filled with extraordinarily fine writing. He is the creator of a new system of "organizing the world." It is true, the system is still not complete and is contradictory, but nonetheless "there can be no other solution of the social formula." His great disclosure concludes with the following sentence: "*Starting out from limitless freedom, I end with limitless despotism.*" One-tenth of mankind receives freedom of personality and limitless right over the remaining nine-tenths who are transformed into a herd. Then the earthly paradise will be founded. Shigalyov's system is the logical continuation of Raskolnikov's idea; it will be realized in practice by the "Grand Inquisitor." The "long-eared" theoretician's thought passes as a whole into the legend composed by Ivan Karamazov.

In his "hymn to destruction" Pyotr Verkhovensky is inspired by the theory of Shigalyov, of this "new Fourier." He makes a lyric improvisation out of the scientific treatise. The learned sociologist and the "half-mad" poet complement one another in their worship of the ideal of satanic beauty.

The tragic motifs of Shatov, Kirilov, Pyotr Verkhovensky and Shigalyov, like rivers flowing into the sea, converge into the main theme of the novel: the tragedy of Stavrogin. The image of the "fascinating demon" is created with inconceivable art. Stavrogin appears at first at a distance, in obscure outline: the chronicler relies on hearsay to narrate his childhood and youth (the distant past); then briefly describes his short stay in the provincial capital three years ago (the recent past);

and, finally, expounds the events of the last month (the present). A temporal perspective is created: the hero slowly draws near to us, becoming ever more visible and defined.

The eight-year-old boy's tutor was Stepan Trofimovich; he aroused the first sensation of "holy anguish" in him, woke him at night in order to vent his own feelings. "They used to throw themselves into one another's embraces, and wept." At the lycée the youth was "sickly and pale, strangely quiet and melancholy." Then he entered military service, frequented higher society—and suddenly he began madly to carouse, fought twice in duels, was reduced to the ranks, distinguished himself, was promoted an officer, and resigned from the service. Then he hit upon the dregs of Petersburg; passed days and nights in disreputable places. Such is his remote past.

Three years ago he came to the provincial capital. The narrator was struck by his outward appearance. "The most elegant gentleman of all whom I ever chanced to meet, extraordinarily well-dressed, with manners that only a man accustomed to the most refined surroundings could possess." He was unusually handsome, but his beauty repelled one. . . . "His hair was somehow intensely black, his light eyes somehow peculiarly calm and clear, his complexion somehow peculiarly delicate and white, the color in his cheeks somehow too bright and pure, his teeth like pearls, and his lips like coral—it would seem a picture of beauty but at the same time, he was also, in a way, repulsive. It was said that his face suggested a mask." Stavrogin's secret is imprinted upon his face, consists in the enigmatic combination of the two words: "*repulsive beauty*." Suddenly, the taciturn and unassuming gentleman commits several incredible acts: he seizes Gaganov, an elderly member of the club, by the nose, publicly kisses the civil servant Liputin's wife on the lips, bites the ear of the governor—and does all this pensively, out of boredom, and "without the least repentance." Stavrogin's exploits end in an attack of cerebral fever. Upon recovering, he departs. To the enigma of his face corresponds the enigma of his behavior. No one in the city considers him mad. For three years "Prince Harry," as Stepan Trofimovich calls him, travels. Something takes place in Paris with Liza Tushina and Dasha; the obscurity around him intensifies. At this point the recent past concludes and we enter the present. Stavrogin once again appears in the city and the chronicler describes his outward appearance a second time:

"Just as four years ago, when I first met him, so now, I was astounded upon first seeing him. . . . One thing struck me; before, though I

considered him handsome, his face nonetheless was like a mask. . . .
But now, I don't know why, from the very first glance he impressed
me as being quite incontestably handsome, so that one could no longer
say that his face was like a mask. Wasn't it because he was a
little paler than before and, it seemed, had lost some weight?
Or was it, perhaps, that some sort of *new thought* now shined in his
eyes?" He kisses his mother's hand with an indulgent smile and in an
"affectionate, melodic voice" says to Marya Timofeyevna: "You should-
n't be here." Extraordinary tenderness shines in his eyes; he respectfully
leads the cripple away and returns "gay and peaceful." "Good-na-
turedly and jokingly" he talks about his chivalry, tenderly embraces his
mother, he addresses himself to Liza "with a most innocent and sincere
air." The narrator adds: "I will observe that he was extraordinarily
modest and polite, but that apart from his politeness, had a thoroughly indifferent demeanor, even listless." It seems that this comedy
is beginning to bore him; under his official smile "is felt impatience and
even irritation." Before the episode of the slap, the chronicler inserts
the remark: "During those fits of *blind fury*, which seized him
sometimes, he nonetheless could maintain complete control over himself." Shatov strikes him in the face; Stavrogin "kept silent, looked at
Shatov, and turned pale as his shirt. But strangely enough, the look in
his eyes seemed to die out. Ten seconds later, his eyes looked cold, and
—I am convinced that I'm not lying—calm. . . . Shatov was the first to
drop his eyes, and evidently because he was forced to drop them."

Such is our first acquaintance with the hero; he is shown, but not
explained; we see him (his face, figure, movements, gestures), follow his strange actions, but do not understand him. The other dramatis personae attempt to explain him: the narrator, Varvara Petrovna,
Liputin, Lebyadkin, Pyotr Verkhovensky, but their conjectures only
lead us into error. This device of "presentation" is Dostoevsky's artistic
discovery. The effect is attained: Stavrogin astounds us. We fall under
the fascination of his extraordinary personality, we are captivated by
his *beauty, power, and mystery*.

In the second part (*Night*) the terrible spectacle of the hero's *deathlike quality* is by degrees disclosed to us. He is asleep, sitting in an
armchair in his study: Varvara Petrovna enters and is astonished that
her son "could sleep that way, sitting so straight and so *motionless*:
it was almost impossible to perceive even his breathing. His face was
pale and harsh, but completely *immovable*, as though *congealed;* his
eyebrows were somewhat drawn together and frowning; he positively

resembled a *lifeless waxen figure*. . . . If Varvara Petrovna had remained another three minutes, then she surely could not have borne the stifling sensation of this *lethargic immobility* and would have awakened him." With contemptuous indifference the hero talks with Pyotr Verkhovensky, Kirilov, and Shatov. The latter cries ecstatically to him: "You, you, Stavrogin, how could you have recourse to such a shameless, untalented, flunkeyish absurdity. Is this the *exploit* of Nikolai Stavrogin?" But the latter does not understand why "everyone forces some kind of banner upon him." Shatov passionately unmasks him: in Petersburg Stavrogin moved in a brutish sensuous society, had corrupted children, married the cripple "through a passion for cruelty, through passion for remorse of conscience." "Kiss the earth," he shouts at him, "pour forth tears, beg absolution," and advises him "to attain God by toiling like a muzhik." Stavrogin listens attentively, "as though he really had met something new and serious, which was worth considering." Leaving, he promises to visit Tikhon.

The mystery of the hero's marriage is disclosed in his dialogue with Lebyadkin; deciding publicly to announce his marriage to the lame girl, Stavrogin says: "I married your sister when the whim hit me, *after a drunken dinner*, because of a bet over a bottle of wine."

Every new scene heightens our impression of the hero's duality. In Varvara Petrovna's salon his exasperation and cold indifference are hardly noticed under his mask of social amiability; in the scene with the cripple his "official civility" and extraordinary capacity to control himself betray him. Entering, Stavrogin stops at the door and obstinately, with disgust, examines his wife's face; recollecting himself, he goes up to her "with the most courteous and affectionate smile." But Marya Timofeyevna calls him a pretender and proudly declares: "I am my prince's wife, I'm not afraid of your knife!" Then he pushes her away with all his strength and flees, repeating with insatiable malice "A knife! A knife!" On the bridge he is met by Fedka the convict and he tosses him some money, as though agreeing to the Lebyadkin murder.

After the encounters with Shatov and with Marya Timofeyevna there follows a third clash—the duel with Gaganov. Stavrogin fires into the air and declares to his opponent: "I give you my word that I in no way intended to insult you. I fired high because I *don't want* to kill anyone else." But this magnanimous gesture affronts Gaganov still more. After the duel the hero irritably asks his second Kirilov: "Why do I have to endure what no one endures, to assume burdens that no one can support?" Kirilov answers: "'I thought you yourself were seeking a burden.' 'I seek a burden?' 'Yes.' 'You've seen this?' 'Yes.' 'It's so obvious?' 'Yes.' Stavrogin had a very troubled look, was *almost astounded*."

On this ends the third act of Stavrogin's tragedy. His secret is by degrees disclosed before us. We know already the strange contradictions of his nature, its fatal dichotomy. Superhuman power and impotence, a yearning for faith and disbelief, the search for a "burden" and complete spiritual necrosis. In the scene with Dasha this duality is deepened metaphysically. Stavrogin sees apparitions: a devil visits him. Subsequent editions have omitted this passage, in connection with the deletion of the chapter *At Tikhon's*. In the journal version Stavrogin tells Dasha about his devil. "'Now there will begin a series of his visits. Yesterday he was stupid and impudent. He is a dull-witted seminarian, the self-contentment of the sixties, a lackey in thought, lackey in surroundings, in soul, in development, remaining fully convinced of the invincibility of his own beauty. . . . Nothing could be more hateful. . . . I was furious that my personal devil could appear in such a wretched mask. Never before has he come this way. Besides, I remained silent, on purpose! I not only was silent, I was immovable. He grew terribly furious on this account, and I was very happy that he was furious. I am even happy now. . . . Oh, no, I don't believe in him, don't worry,' he smiled. 'As yet, I don't believe. I know that this is myself under different forms; *I appear double* and talk with myself. But nonetheless he grew very furious; for he would terribly like to be an independent devil and for me actually to believe in him. He laughed yesterday and assured me that atheism doesn't prevent this.'

"'The moment that you believe in him, you are lost! God, even this man wants to do without me!' Dasha cried out with pain in her heart.

"'Do you know his theme yesterday? All night he asserted that I am juggling, am seeking burdens and insurmountable tasks, and do not believe in them myself.'

"He suddenly burst out laughing and this was terribly absurd. Darya Pavlovna shuddered and recoiled from him.

"'There were terribly many devils yesterday!' he shrieked, guffawing —'terribly many! They clambered out of all the swamps!'"

The theme of the "devils" passes as a leitmotif through Stavrogin's biography. Now his turpidity and "lethargic immobility" at the beginning of the second part are clear to us. Varvara Petrovna finds her son in a state of demonic trance; he wants to provoke his devil by silence and immobility. The motif of apparitions connects this scene with the chapter *At Tikhon's*: Stavrogin confesses to the prelate that he suffers from hallucinations and sarcastically asks:

" 'But can one believe in the devil, without believing in God at all?' 'Oh, one certainly can, very often and at one and the same time,' Tikhon raised his eyes and also smiled."

Stavrogin—according to the original design—was to reform the possessed man of Gadara into whom a legion of devils had entered. Out of him, as out of an infected wellspring, the poison of disbelief had been discharged onto Russia; from him came all the devils and imps, whirling round her in a snowstorm of sedition. The deletion of the chapter *At Tikhon's* and the abridgment of the journal text distorted the symbolism and metaphysical significance of the novel. Dostoevsky could not reconcile himself with this sacrifice. He transferred the motif of "apparitions" and conversations with the devil into the novel *The Brothers Karamazov*. Stavrogin's devil was turned into Ivan Karamazov's devil. The hero of *The Devils* calls him a self-contented seminarian—a man of the sixties, a lackey in thought. "Oh, what a demon this is!" he exclaims. "He is simply a nasty, little, scrofulous imp with a cold in his head, one of those who have miscarried." This outline helped the author re-create the image of the devil-parasite in *The Brothers Karamazov*.

After the third act, Stavrogin's tragedy is transferred to the second plane; we see him rarely and in passing. He tells Liza of his marriage to Marya Timofeyevna indifferently and somehow cursorily; with squeamish repugnance he withdraws from Pyotr Verkhovensky's intrigues and conspiracies. The fourth act of the tragedy is the chapter *At Tikhon's*. In the proofs, it followed the eighth chapter of the second part: *Ivan the Tsarevich*. As is known, Katkov absolutely refused to print it: Dostoevsky went to confer with him in Moscow, and promised to redo it. Here is what he wrote to S. A. Ivanova (February 4, 1872):

Upon leaving Moscow, I thought that correcting the rejected chapter of the novel, as the editors want, still would not be, God knows, so difficult. But when I set about the task, it turned out that it was impossible to amend anything, really to make any changes, the slightest. And at a time that I was going about to my creditors, I contrived four plans—for the most part while sitting in cabs—and was tormented for almost three weeks which to adopt. I ended by discarding them all and thought up a new variant, i.e., *preserving the essence of the matter*, I altered the text as much as would satisfy the editors' modesty, and in this sense will send them an ultimatum. If they don't agree, then I really don't know what to do.

But this redaction was also turned down by Katkov. The novel appeared in *The Russian Messenger* without the chapter *At Tikhon's*. In the following editions of the novel the author did not include it. It was published only in 1923 in two editions—the original (*Moscow*) and the one that was rewritten (*Petersburg*). In the first, Stavrogin's crime (violating a young girl) is portrayed as a real fact; in the second, the confession is called "a morbid product, an affair of the devil." It is possible that Stavrogin invented this whole happening out of "a passion for the pangs of remorse" and consciously calumniated himself.

The omitted chapter is the culmination of Stavrogin's tragedy and Dostoevsky's loftiest artistic creation. The struggle of faith with disbelief, which grows through the duration of the whole novel, here attains its most extreme tension. The opposition of the two ideas is embodied in the encounter of two personalities—the atheist Stavrogin and the mystic Tikhon. The enigmatic hero's secret is revealed and the resolution, which we have so long awaited with anxiety and excitement, strikes us in its unexpectedness. Stavrogin irritably and mockingly tells Tikhon about his hallucinations: he, of course, does not believe in the apparitions and realizes that it is a disease. Tikhon answers seriously: "Devils do exist beyond doubt, but the understanding of them can be greatly varied." Then Stavrogin loses his self-possession and betrays himself. With diabolic pride he declares to Tikhon: "I will tell you seriously and insolently: I believe in the devil, I believe *canonically*, in a personal one, not in an allegory, and I have no need to inquire of anyone; this is the whole thing."

Yes, this is the whole thing: Stavrogin canonically believes in the devil, without believing in God; the proud and strong spirit, God-like in his grandeur, has renounced the Creator and closed himself off in selfness. He desired to be by himself—"to express his self-will." "If there is no God, I am God," said Kirilov. Stavrogin has realized this:

he is God in his unlimited power and freedom. But in the experience of man-godhood the strong personality finds not triumph, but defeat. His power is purposeless, for there is no point of its application, his freedom is empty since it is the freedom of indifference. Stavrogin is a lie and slave to the "father of lies"—the devil. The god-like personality is split into two countenances; there appears a double—"a nasty, little imp, one of those who have miscarried"; free belief in God is necessarily replaced by faith in the devil. Stavrogin falls into demonic possession, practical satanism. It is his "credo": "I believe canonically in the devil." Opposed to it is Tikhon's confession of faith. To the apostate's question whether he believes in God: Tikhon answers, "I believe, . . . And let me not be ashamed of Your Cross, Lord. . . ."[A]

Two forces, the greatest in the world—faith and disbelief, God and the devil—have clashed. This instant of blinding luster has been prepared by the whole action of the novel; for this instant it was also written.

Dasha predicted to Stavrogin: "The moment you believe in your demon, you are lost." He believed and boldly declared this. And he knows that hereafter he is doomed. But still he does not admit that he is vanquished, seeks salvation, not believing in it; he gives Tikhon his confession to read. The author explains: "The basic thought of the document is a strange, sincere need of punishment, need of a cross, of all the people's chastisement. And meanwhile this need of a cross is nonetheless in a man who does not believe in the cross." The confession tells about his rape of the young girl Matryosha and of her suicide. The transgressor did not experience any repentance and here for the first time in his life understood his "man-godhood." Having denied God, he has put himself beyond God's law—in limitless freedom. "I don't know and don't feel evil and good, and not only have I lost the sensation, but I know that there is no evil or good (and this I have found agreeable), but only a certain prejudice: I can be free from every prejudice, but if I attain this freedom, then I am lost." Freedom beyond the confines of good and evil is pure demonism. Later on there is related the vision of the golden age and the Fall (its symbol: a tiny, reddish spider). With minor changes, this entire account is transposed into Versilov's dream in A Raw Youth. Tikhon calls the hero to humility and faith: he will be saved, if he overcomes his pride. And

[A] Stavrogin (from the Greek σταυρός—cross) is mystically linked with the cross. He seeks the cross, not believing in it, breaks the crucifix, lying on the table in Tikhon's room. The bishop exorcises the apostate with the words: "And let me not be ashamed of Your Cross, Lord."

suddenly, filled with inspiration, the prelate prophesies: "No, not after its publication, but even before publication, a day, an hour, perhaps, before the great step, you'll rush to a new crime, as a way out, and will commit it solely to avoid the publication of these pages on which now you insist." In frenzy Stavrogin pronounces "damned psychologist," and runs out of the monastery.

Dostoevsky called Christ the "everlasting ideal of beauty." The man-god, revolting against the God-man, strives to substitute one ideal of beauty with another. Stavrogin is a handsome man, but his beauty recalls a mask. He is a refined gentleman, his fascination is irresistible, his movements and gestures are full of elegance; but in all this there is something repulsive. In the scene with Tikhon his false, deceitful beauty is unmasked: Tikhon is struck not only by the "dreadfulness" of the confession's matter, but also by the disharmony of its style. "But is it not possible to make some corrections in the document?" he asks Stavrogin. "Why?" the latter is perplexed. "I wrote it sincerely." "*It might be somewhat in the manner.*" The style of the confession in its verbal slovenliness reflects the spiritual decomposition of its author. The prelate surprises Stavrogin with his remark about the "document." The latter expected horror, confusion, indignation. Tikhon appraises the confession aesthetically: it is not beautiful. He fears that its "ugliness will kill it" and that the proud sinner will not be able to bear his readers' *laughter*. The Antichrist's "beauty" is illusory. Spiritual vision uncovers its unseemliness. Stavrogin's secret is disclosed: he is "a lie and the father of lies." Everything in him is a lie—his beauty, his strength, his yearning for an heroic feat, his grandeur. The "confession" is shameful and unseemly; it contains the disgusting rape of a pitiable young girl.

"Its ugliness will kill it," predicts Tikhon. This takes place quickly. In our eyes Stavrogin is already dead—Tikhon has torn from the pretender the pompous mantle of Ivan the Tsarevich, the mask of demonic beauty.

After his exposure in the monastery follows the exposure at Skvoreshniki. The man-god proved to be an imp with a cold; the victorious Don Juan an impotent lover and worthy of scorn. Having forebodings of his ruin, he clings to Liza's love; he does not love her and knows this, but nonetheless accepts her sacrifice and draws her after him to death. After the night spent with him at Skvoreshniki, Liza understands, as earlier Marya Timofeyevna did, that her prince is a "pretender." "I must confess to you," she says, "ever since those days in Switzerland—I've been convinced that you have something horrible, filthy and bloody on your conscience, and at the same time, something which casts you *in a terribly ridiculous light.* . . . I will laugh at you for the rest of my life." The devil's fraudulent grandeur provokes laughter. His pretension to an heroic exploit is *comical.* Liza only repeats the words of Tikhon. Then comes the fifth act of the tragedy, the catastrophe. Stavrogin kills himself. "The citizen of the canton of Uri was hanging there behind the door. On the little table lay a scrap of paper with the penciled words: 'Don't accuse anyone, I did it myself. . . .'" The ugliness of his death—suicide—is the last diabolic grimace of the so-called man-god. The "strong personality's" defeat takes place on the plane of life, metaphysics, and aesthetics. Against the "everlasting ideal of Christ" is posed the aesthetic mirage of the Antichrist.

While working on *The Idiot,* the author confessed that the whole novel had been written for the sake of the last scene (Nastasya Filippovna's murder). One can generalize this assertion: all Dostoevsky's novels were written for the sake of the catastrophe. This is the law of the new "expressive art" that he created. Only upon arriving at the finale do we understand the composition's perfection and the inexhaustible depth of its design. Reading the novel, we continually move forward, scale a mountain; from the summit of the catastrophe we see the whole *paysage* of the novel spread out as on one's palm. The riddles are explained, the mysteries are disclosed. From Stavrogin's letter before his death we learn the ultimate reality about him. "I have tried my strength everywhere," he writes. "When I tried it for my own sake and for display, it seemed limitless, as it has before throughout my life. . . . But what to apply this strength to—this is what I've never seen, do not see even now. I am still able, as I always was in the past, to desire to do something good, and derive pleasure from this; at the same time, I desire something evil, and also feel pleasure. . . . Only negation has poured out of me, without any generosity and without any strength."

Now, from the heights of the finale, we survey the hero's whole life; his tragedy is the *agony of the superman.* Great gifts were given to Stavrogin. He was destined for a lofty vocation, but he once betrayed his holy-of-holies and renounced God. Spiritual death befell the apostate during life. He knows that a terrible punishment has already begun and that his soul is decomposing. The stench of his spiritual decay forces him to make convulsive efforts to save himself. He as-

· 462 ·

sumes "intolerable burdens," seeks an heroic exploit, yearns for penance and the people's chastisement. He comes to the provincial capital with a new idea: with the decision to publicize his marriage to the cripple, but upon meeting his wife unexpectedly at his mother's, he solemnly denies her in order not to repulse Liza Tushina. His magnanimous feeling toward Marya Timofeyevna struggles with his sensuous dream of Liza: everything is divided and evil is just as attractive as good. Shatov takes revenge upon the hero for his treason and strikes him in the face. The proud individual suffers the insult—this is his first feat; but even it is equivocal; in his action Stavrogin displays not humility, but excessive strength; not repentance, but a new self-elevation. He goes to Shatov and warns him of his danger; but even this good act is fruitless, since it is motivated by cold arrogance, and not by love. "I am sorry that I can't love you, Shatov," he says to him. And knowing about Pyotr Verkhovensky's plan, he does not prevent him from killing Shatov. Good once more is diverted by evil; moral responsibility for the betrayed disciple's death falls upon his master. His second feat—his intention of announcing his marriage to the cripple—leads to her murder. Marya Timofeyevna curses her betrayer; Stavrogin knows about Fedka the convict's plan and ambiguously encourages him (gives him money). The third exploit—he fired into the air during his duel with Gaganov—is turned into a new and still more cruel affront to his opponent. The fourth—his intention to publish his confession—is exposed by Tikhon as a demonic temptation, and leads to his final abjuration of God (Stavrogin's Antichrist credo). There is no penitence for the demonic superman, he is not capable of humble faith, not fit for a religious feat. Only a miracle can save him. Not believing in a miracle, he grasps at it; but after the night spent with Liza at Skvoreshniki, the "pretender's" final lie is disclosed. Love has long since dried up in his dead heart. Sensuous impulse does not save him and destroys the unfortunate girl. His last attempt at salvation is turned into a new, terrible crime.

The four "exploits"—the four misdeeds—are the four acts of the man-god's tragedy. The fifth act is his suicide. The "living corpse" sunders his illusory existence. The powerful spirit of negation, the metaphysically sterile will, the great strength without application return to nonbeing.

Stavrogin is Dostoevsky's greatest artistic creation. In the family of "strong individuals" (Prince Volkovsky, Raskolnikov, Svidrigailov, Ippolit, Kirilov, Versilov, Ivan Karamazov) he is the strongest; the image of "limitless strength." This is the man of a new aeon, this is the man-god about whom Kirilov dreamed and by comparison with whom Nietzsche's superman seems only a shadow. This is the coming Antichrist, the prince of this world, the terrible prophecy about the cosmic catastrophe drawing near to mankind. Dostoevsky speaks about the ultimate metaphysical mysteries in the language of myths.[B]

The union of the "handsome" Stavrogin with the lame half-wit Marya Timofeyevna is the symbol of a sort of surrealistic reality. She is the soul of the world, the "eternal feminine," Mother Earth. She is oppressed in captivity, awaiting her liberator. Her beauty is obscured, for having sinned, she has fallen to vanity and corruption. Her guilt in relation to her beautiful bridegroom is suggested by her physical defect. In spite of her original sin, she is faithful to her betrothed and waits for him. But her fiancé has denied her, has been seduced by his god-like freedom, and has fallen away from God. The bride recognizes, and does not recognize him: she is both wife and not a wife to him. He is both a prince and Grishka Otrepyev—a pretender. A former angelic radiance, a new demonic darkness are terribly confounded in him. His betrayal brings ruin both to her and to himself: she becomes the devils' spoil, profaning the holy shrine of Mother Earth (its symbol: the episode of the desecration of the icon of the Mother of God); he dies a "second death during life" and his dead mask is used by the devils who have settled in him. The myth of Mother Earth is Dostoevsky's most profound vision. His characters who struggle with God are always guilty of abusing this holy shrine. Sonya begs Raskolnikov to kiss the earth that the latter has profaned. Shatov implores Stavrogin to do the same thing. The soul of the world is oppressed in the captivity of Marya Timofeyevna's passions, in Nastasya Filippovna's hysterics, in Grushenka's ecstasy. In this perception of world tragedy, Dostoevsky is close to Goethe. Marya Timofeyevna calls Gretchen to mind; she also sings a simple folk song, dreams about a child, and prays God that her beloved might remain faithful to his mystical calling. Stavrogin is a Russian Faust, but a Faust who is not saved, but who perishes; Pyotr Verkhovensky is Mephistopheles.

Marya Timofeyevna is the writer's most impenetrable creation. She is depicted most realistically: the feeble-minded, mistreated sister of Captain Lebyadkin, a girl of about thirty, with an emaciated face and

---

[B] See W. Iwanow. *Dostoewsky. Tragödie. Mythos. Mystik.* Tübingen. 1932. [This remarkable book is translated: *Freedom and the Tragic Life. A Study in Dostoevsky.* The Noonday Press, 1957, New York.]

quiet, kindly gray eyes; a cripple and holy-fool; but at the same time all these qualifications: outward appearance, costume, circumstances, social position—appear fantastic. Under them glimmers another reality, a different mystical plane of being. Marya Timofeyevna is the beautiful maiden, the bride of folk tales. On the table before her is an old pack of cards, a rustic mirror and a worn-out copy of a song book. She also speaks "in fairy-tales"; lives in her memories of the monastery, of the mother superior, the Athos monks, of the holy-fool Lizaveta the Blessed, of the old women and pilgrims. To her is given the gift of foreknowledge and vision. The author consigns to his poor half-wit the greatest spiritual treasure: the secret of Mother Earth. Marya Timofeyevna recalls: "And at that time, whispers to me a certain old woman, coming out of the church—she lived with us as penance for her prophesying: 'The Mother of God, what is she, do you think?' 'The great Mother,' I answer, 'the hope of the human race.' 'That's right,' she says, *'The Mother of God is the great Mother Moist Earth* and great joy is contained in that for man. And every earthly anguish, and every earthly tear is a great joy for us! And when you water the earth beneath you a foot deep with your tears, then you will rejoice over everything. And you no longer,' she says, 'will have any, any sorrow; such,' she says, 'is the prophecy.' . . . I would sometimes go to the shore by the lake; on one side is our monastery, on the other—our mountain with a peak, so they call it Peak Mountain. I used to climb this mountain, I would turn my face toward the east, fall down to the earth, weep, weep and I don't remember how long I wept, and I didn't remember then and I didn't know anything then."

The divine principle of the world—Sophia—is revealed in the symbols of the Virgin Mother of God and the Mother Earth. Dostoevsky had a genuine Sophiac experience: in his ecstasy was revealed to him the "fire of things." Marya Timofeyevna's joyful lamentation, Alyosha Karamazov's tears of emotion, the elder Zosima's teaching about ecstasy are different forms of one adoration. The mystical cult of the earth lies at the base of the writer's teaching about being rooted in the soil and populism: the holy earth and the people–God-bearers are not ideas of reason, but the object of passionate faith.

The Devils was conceived as a vast icon diptych: in opposition to the dark panel was set a light one; in opposition to the demonic personality—a "positively beautiful individual." The Christian ideal of beauty is embodied in Bishop Tikhon, whose image Dostoevsky had "long ago taken to his heart with enthusiasm." By the deletion of the chapter *At Tikhon's* this concept was destroyed and only the dark panel of the diptych remained: the picture of hell, of universal ruin, of the raging of the demonic snowstorm. (As an epigraph, the author took Pushkin's verses: "The devil, it seems, has led us into a field, and whirls about us on every side.")

The "majestic" figure of the prelate is presented delicately and with reverence. The author acknowledged that he was "terribly afraid," and this task was beyond his powers. But in the uncertainty of the sketch and the portrayal's ascetic severity is felt a vast reserved force. Tikhon is the antithesis of Stavrogin: the strong individual is opposed by the weak, the proud by the humble, the wise of this age by a holy-fool. Tikhon is a "tall and lean man, about 55 years old, in a simple cassock and seemed, as it were, somewhat sickly, with a vague smile and a strange, as though timid, glance." The father archimandrite censures him for a "negligent life and all but heresy." . . . "Whether through weakness of character or through absent-mindedness that was unpardonable and inappropriate to his dignity, he could not inspire any special respect toward himself, even in the monastery." The monks passed over him in silence, "as it were, wanted to conceal some weakness of his, perhaps, holy-folly." He has "a chronic rheumatic ailment in his legs and at times sort of nervous spasms."

To Stavrogin's "magnificence" Tikhon opposes his poverty: sickliness, weakness, helplessness, and holy-folly. He speaks with his visitor, timidly and with confusion, "bashfully casting his eyes down with a certain altogether unnecessary smile." The guest ironically instructs him: " 'You, reverend Father Tikhon. . . . I've heard from others, you are of no value as an adviser. . . . You are strongly criticized here. It is said you have only to see something sincere and humble in a sinner, immediately you go into ecstasy, and humble yourself, and begin to run after him and ingratiate yourself.' 'Of course, it is true that I don't know how to approach people. I have always felt this my great deficiency,' uttered Tikhon with a sigh and so simple-heartedly that Stavrogin looked at him with a smile."

Tikhon does not preach humility to the proud man—he is himself incarnated humility. But under his holy-folly is hidden spiritual wisdom, the gift of clairvoyance and prophecy. He is afraid to offend the sinner, attempts to express himself softly, is confused and asks forgiveness. But the reading of the confession produces a repulsive impression on him and "decisive indignation" is heard in his voice. He prudently and carefully touches upon his guest's weak spot: there is nothing heroic in his confession—*it is ugly and ridiculous.* Pronouncing the death sentence over the man-god, the prelate suddenly remembers himself and entreats him not to despair of his salvation. " 'Oh, don't believe that you will not conquer!' he exclaimed, suddenly remembering himself, but almost in rapture. . . . 'It has always turned out that the most shameful cross has become a great glory and a great power. . . .' " "If you believe that you can forgive yourself and seek to attain this forgiveness by your own suffering then you already believe in everything. . . . And Christ will forgive you." If the sinner acknowledges his sin and is tormented by it, he has already returned to God. "God will forgive you for your disbelief, for in truth you honor the Holy Spirit, without knowing Him. . . . For there are no words in the human tongue, nor thought, to express all the ways and purposes of the Lamb, 'until His ways are revealed unto us.' Who will embrace Him who cannot be embraced, who will understand Him who is *everything,* who is infinite." But Stavrogin does not know either humility, or repentance; his confession is a new challenge to God and man, a new outburst of diabolic pride. The words of the "damned psychologist" provoke insatiable malice in him. Tikhon sees that he is doomed. "Tikhon stood before him, his palms pressed together and thrust forward, and a painful spasm, it seemed as though from intense fright, passed momentarily over his face. 'I see . . . I suddenly see clearly that you have never, poor lost youth, stood so close to a new and more terrible crime, as at this moment.' "

Unfathomable humility, bashful tenderness, foolish wisdom and reserved ecstasy are not only indicated ideationally, but also artistically portrayed in Tikhon. His spiritual treasure he will share with the pilgrim Makar Ivanovich Dolgoruky in *A Raw Youth* and with the elder Zosima in *Brothers Karamazov.*

Yet the prelate's dominant trait is not moral, but *aesthetic.* Tikhon is a spirit-bearing just-man, illuminated by the beauty of the Holy Spirit. The man-god's handsome mask falls to dust in the rays of the true beauty of the spirit. The aesthetic side is underlined in his features and setting. Stavrogin's decomposing style is opposed by his lofty, severe archaicized language. The one has verbal formlessness; the other, the purity of Church form. In Tikhon's cell are: "three elegant things: a very rich comfortable armchair, a big writing desk of excellent finish, an elegant carved bookcase"; a little table, a what-not, an expensive Bukhara, engravings of "secular subjects"; in the library together with spiritual book are novels and theatrical works.

Dostoevsky's verbal mastery deserves special analysis. *The Devils* is constructed on the most subtle stylistic effects. Every character is immersed in his own verbal element and by comparing and opposing the dramatis personae the author is able to draw complicated patterns in the texture of his narrative. To reinforce their expressiveness, the colorless, neutral background of a "chronicle" is selected. An impersonal narrator describes the events in an exact and dry official tone. Each personage is registered in his "chronicle" by his peculiar speech patterns, through the uniqueness of his diction. Thus Stepan Trofimovich is characterized by his French-Russian speech, "gentlemanly" intonations, and elegant puns. Before his death he says to the book-hawker Sofya Matveyevna: "*L'Evangile, voyez-vous, désormais nous le prêcherons ensemble* and I will be delighted to sell your beautiful booklets. Yes, I feel that this, I daresay, is an idea, *quelque chose de très nouveau dans ce genre.* The people are religious, *c'est admis;* but they still do not know the Gospel. . . . I will expound it to them." This entire monologue is a chef d'oeuvre of psychological stylistics.

The monomaniac and fanatic Kirilov, who has broken with human intercourse, is defined by his strange, agrammatical speech. He talks in a sort of abstract, universal *Volapük.* Here is how he expresses himself: "If I inadvertently made several points to you, and you caught them up, then as you wish. But you don't have the right, because I never speak to anyone. I despise talking. . . . If I have a conviction that is clear for me . . . but you've done this stupidly. I don't deliberate about those points where it's all been concluded. . . ."

Marya Timofeyevna is shown in the fairy-tale illumination of her folk-monastic speech; Bishop Tikhon in his magnificent, severe Church-Orthodox language; Shatov in the fiery inspiration of a prophet; Pyotr Verkhovensky in the disconnected, intentionally coarse and vulgar remarks of his "nihilistic style"; Lebyadkin in the drunken lyrics of a barroom poet; Shigalyov in the dull heaviness of scientific jargon; Stavrogin in the formlessness and artificiality of his "universal tongue." The clash and interweaving of these verbal styles and rhythms form the complicated counterpoint of the novel's stylistics. The author makes continual use of the devices of parody and caricature. Newspaper phraseology helped him to verbally characterize his nihilists; literary works served as material for his sharp, caustic parodies. His old hostility toward Turgenev inspired the writer to take cruel revenge upon the author of *Smoke.* Dostoevsky portrays the "Baden bourgeois" under the guise of the "great writer" Karmazinov. He spitefully makes fun of his appearance, "shrieky and lisping voice," manner of "advancing to kiss one and presenting his cheek"; he parodies his conversation with him in Baden-Baden and ascribes to him the following "Germanophile" declaration: "This now is the seventh year I've resided in Karlsruhe. And last year when the city council proposed laying a new drainage-pipe, then I felt in my heart that this Karlsruhe drainage question was more pleasing and dear to me than all the questions concerning my dear fatherland, throughout all the time of the so-called local reforms." After this caricature of the "great writer's" personality there follows a brilliant and murderous parody of *Enough* and *Phantoms*. Karmazinov at the "Fête" reads his tale *Merci*. "Mr. Karmazinov, with an affected air and intonation, announced that he 'at first had not agreed to read on any account.' (It was quite necessary to announce this!) 'There are,' he said, 'some lines which sound so deeply from the heart, that it is impossible to utter them aloud, so that such holy things cannot be brought before the public.' (Well, why then did he bring them?); 'But since he had been entreated to do so, he was doing so, and as he was, moreover, laying down his pen forever and had sworn never to write anything again, now so be it, he had written this final piece: and since he had sworn never on any inducement to read anything in public, now so be it, he would read this last essay to the public etc., etc., all in this genre."

The parody on Turgenev's *Phantoms* is a chef d'oeuvre of literary caricature. With all the clarity of hatred Dostoevsky observes the wordy lyrics and pretentious fantasies of his enemy. His senile, romantic, pessimistic philosophy is satirized with extraordinary malice and verity. "Thirty-seven years ago when, you recollect, in Germany, we were sitting under an agate-tree, you said to me: 'Why love? Look, ochra is growing all around and I love you, but the ochra will cease to grow, and I shall stop loving!' Then the fog whirled up, Hoffmann appeared, a water-nymph whistled a tune from Chopin, and suddenly out of the fog, in a laurel wreath, over the roofs of Rome appeared Aneus Marcius. 'A shiver of rapture ran down our spines, and we parted for ever.'"

In Baden Turgenev had insulted the Russian patriot and believing Christian in Dostoevsky. In the novel *The Devils*, he took fierce revenge upon his foe. The caricature of Turgenev (Karmazinov) is no less artistically perfect than the caricature of Gogol (Foma Opiskin).

X I X

The Epoch of *The Citizen* ·
The Diary of a Writer for 1873

On June 9, 1871, Dostoevsky returned to Petersburg. His voluntary four-year exile was ended. Abroad he had longed for Russia; in Russia he felt that he was a stranger, dreamed of journeying to the East, prepared to write a book about Greece, Athos, the Holy Land. On July 10 a son, Fyodor, was born to him. The disconsolate life of a poor litterateur began: the harassment of creditors, discord with his relatives, moving from apartment to apartment. Anna Grigoryevna discovered that her possessions had been sold; the writer learned that his stepson, Pavel Isayev, had disposed of his entire library. In the summer of 1872 Dostoevsky, escaping from his creditors and relatives, moved to Staraya Russa. There began a streak of misfortunes: the writer's daughter Lyubov broke her arm, and the father took her to Petersburg for an operation. Anna Grigoryevna's sister, Svatkovskaya, died; her mother was dangerously ill. She herself was suffering from a tormenting illness (an abscess in her throat). The writer was anxious: "I find living unbearably tedious," he wrote his wife. "If it were not for Fedya, then perhaps I would go mad. What a gypsy life, tormenting, utterly dismal, without the least joy, but only worry, only worry. . . ." His homeland greeted him coldly: the novel *The Devils* was not successful. The liberal critics turned on the "retrograde" and announced that the talent of the author of *Poor People* had completely foundered. And he believed their criticism and did not suspect that his work was one of genius; from the smallest failure he grew downcast and his spirits fell. In January 1873 Dostoevsky accepted Prince Meshchersky's offer to edit his newspaper *The Citizen*.

Here is how this event is depicted in Prince Meshchersky's memoirs. After the former editor, Gradovsky, had left, the paper's situation was critical.

And at this difficult moment, on one of the Wednesdays when we were talking about this question over a cup of tea, I never will forget with what a good-natured and at the same time inspired countenance, F. M. Dostoevsky turned round to me and said: "Would you like me to be the editor?" At first, we thought that he was joking, but then came a moment of serious joy, for it appeared that Dostoevsky had reached this decision out of sympathy with the aims of the publication. Moreover, Dostoevsky's resolution had its own spiritual beauty. Dostoevsky was—despite the fact that he was Dostoevsky—poor; he knew that my personal and editorial means were limited and therefore told me that he wished for himself only the most necessary honorarium to cover the costs of living, he himself designated 3,000 r. a year and payment for each line he contributed. . . .

The writer became the head of a conservative organ to which Maikov, Filippov, and Strakhov contributed. Soon he began to feel that he had fallen into "bondage": he had to give all his time to the paper; to come to terms with the contributors, read their articles, to correct proofs, to carry on an enormous correspondence and to edit the style of Meshchersky's untalented and vulgar writing. At first he spared the publisher's amour-propre; loaded his articles with praise and wrote them anew; extolled the idea and delicately objected to the "sharpness of tone." But Meshchersky aspired to the role of an ideational leader and the editor began to have clashes with his apparent partisan. Dostoevsky had to spend forty-eight hours in the guardhouse for running an article about the "Kirghiz delegates in St. Petersburg," in which the words of the Sovereign were cited; he had not been informed that speeches of members of the Imperial family could not be printed without the Minister of the Court's permission. The writer took advantage of his unexpected rest to enjoy rereading Hugo's *Les Misérables*. Another disagreeable incident occurred on account of a very well-meaning article apropos of the famine in Samara province. "For its reprehensible tendency" the censor forbade retail sale of *The Citizen* for a month and a half. In the middle of January 1873 a storm nearly burst out once again: the newspaper again ran a story concerning the "highest individuals" without leave of the Minister of the Court. Finally, because of an article about Russian Germans, the Minister of Internal Affairs issued a warning to the journal. Dostoevsky was oppressed by the tiresome and fruitless work. He wrote to M. P. Pogodin (February 26, 1873): "Images of tales and novels are teeming in my mind and formed in my heart. I think of them, make notes, every day add new features to the plan which I have set down and then see that all my time is taken up with the journal, that I am no longer able to write, and I come to remorse and despair. . . . Nonetheless, struggling is a good thing. The present struggle is material for future peace. . . . Sometimes I definitely think that I made a great foolish mistake in taking over *The Citizen*."

In a letter to his wife during the summer of 1873 the writer describes his nightmares in detail. The importunate images that pursued him are related to death and the sufferings of children; from his subconscious they passed into creative imagination; in his works we constantly encounter scenes where children are tortured. This "cruelty" flowed out of the depths of his "night consciousness," out of some old wound that never healed. . . . "I'm seriously afraid of falling ill," he informed his wife. . . .

During the night of Saturday to Sunday, among my nightmares I dreamt that Fedya had climbed up onto the window-sill and had fallen from the fourth floor. Just as he flew by, tumbling downward, I closed my eyes with my hands and began to cry in despair: "Good-bye, Fedya!" and then woke up. Write me as quickly as possible whether something didn't happen to him between Saturday and Sunday; I believe in second sight all the more since this is a fact and will not be at ease until I receive your letter. . . . Today, from Sunday to Monday, I dreamt that Lilya [his daughter Lyubov] was an orphan and met with some tormentress and the latter whipped her with rods, big ones, the kind used for soldiers, so that I found her breathing her last and she kept saying: "Mommy! Mommy!" This dream will almost drive me out of my mind today.

Ivan Karamazov tears us unmercifully with his stories about the torturers of children: he is tormented and torments; the author attempted to free himself from his personal, unbearable agony in artistic images. He suffered through the "little tear of a child" in his nightmares.

Relations with Meshchersky grew tense: the editor stopped printing his foolish spoutings; the self-enamored writer became angry: "This morning," wrote Dostoevsky to his wife (July 20, 1873), "I received all at once a telegram and two letters from the prince concerning the inclusion of his article. His letter seemed utterly rude to me. Today I'll answer him so sharply that in the future he will give up trying to dictate precepts to me."

In addition to his work of editing, the writer composed a literary journalistic section under the title *Diary of a Writer*. In the autumn of 1873 instead of the *Diary* he undertook the political review of foreign events. He was not prepared and not competent in this area and being obliged regularly to write political surveys turned into an intolerable burden for him. In November 1873 a bitter clash took place between the publisher and the editor. Meshchersky in one of his articles recommended that the government organize student hostels in order to supervise the students. Dostoevsky vigorously protested. "The seven lines about supervision," he wrote to Meshchersky, "or, as you express it, about the government's *labor* of supervision, I have rejected radically. I have the reputation of a man of letters and besides that children. I do not intend to ruin myself. Moreover, your thought is profoundly opposed to my convictions and troubles my heart."

Dostoevsky's conservatism was peculiar; the former Petrashevist and convict could not follow along with the reactionary Meshchersky. Hatred for socialism and his Slavophile dream of a Christian empire led the writer into the extreme right camp. He appeared to be in his enemies' arena. What a tragi-comical misunderstanding was this collaboration of the greatest spiritual revolutionary and the publisher of *The Citizen!*

From the beginning of 1874, Dostoevsky did not run a single line under his own name. On March 19 he resigned his editorship "for reasons of poor health."

Dostoevsky's first meeting with K. P. Pobedonostsev occurred during his association with *The Citizen*; the forceful and strange personality of the future over-procurator of the Synod[1] entered his life and occupied an important place in it. The famous ecclesiastical dictator's influence on the author of *Brothers Karamazov* is still insufficiently explained: without doubt, it was very significant. Pobedonostsev came to the editorial offices of *The Citizen* and, not having found the writer, asked that he come to his home. Dostoevsky spent an entire evening with him. "He talked all the time," he informed his wife, "told me a great deal, and

[1] In 1721 Peter the Great issued his famous *Spiritual Regulation* which abolished the Patriarchate and in effect undermined much of the Church's practical and social force. Based upon Protestant ecclesiastical structure, and contrary to Orthodox canonical tradition, it established a Holy Synod to govern the Church. This body was composed of twelve members, bishops and heads of monasteries, and its regular meetings were attended by a layman, the Over-Procurator, who represented the Emperor and exercised considerable power in Church affairs. Constantin Pobedonostsev held this important post from 1880 to 1905. This "grey eminence" was extremely reactionary and his influence on the course of Russian policies during the reigns of Aleksandr III and Nikolai II were to have decisive negative effects upon the future of the Monarchy.

pressed me to come again today. If I should be sick, then let him know and he himself will come and visit me. He wrapped me up in a traveling rug and since there was no one in the empty apartment except for a servant girl, then, in spite of the servant's having run out into the ante-room, he escorted me, with a candle in his hands, down three dark flights of stairs to the very entrance."

In creating a special section in *The Citizen* with the title *The Diary of a Writer*, Dostoevsky realized his old dream about a new form of philosophical-literary journalism. He strove for a direct intercourse with the reader: he converses with him, argues, shares his impressions, invites objections, tells about his past, considers current events, talks about politics, literature, the theatre; polemicizes with his opponents, cites happenings from the legal chronicle, introduces the reader into his intimate world, into the circle of his literary projects and philosophical ideas. He created an extraordinarily free, flexible, and lyric form, half-confession, half-diary. In the first issue of *The Citizen* for 1873 he writes: "My position is undefined in the highest degree. But I will talk with myself and for my personal pleasure in the form of this diary, and let things come out as they may. What will I talk about? About everything that strikes me or forces me to think."

Several articles in *The Diary of a Writer* are devoted to memoirs. The author sketches brilliant portraits of the men of the forties. Here is Herzen: "Always, everywhere, and throughout his whole life he was above all, a *gentilhomme russe et citoyen du monde*, simply a product of the former serfdom which he hated and from which he was descended not through his father alone, but precisely through his rupture with his native land and with its ideals." Here is Belinsky: "an enraptured personality without restraint" and "a completely happy man, who possessed wonderful peace of conscience." In the article *One of the Contemporary Falsehoods* the author tells the story of his own enthusiasm for utopian socialism and establishes a connection between the Petrashevists and the Nechayevists. In the article *Something Personal* he talks of Chernyshevsky with profound respect and reports his conversation with him apropos of the proclamations *To the Young Generation*.

Of the journalistic essays, two are particularly interesting: *The Milieu* and *Vlas*. The first is related to the question of the new Russian courts.[2] Dostoevsky was frightened by the false humanism of their ver-

[2] Aleksandr II, in 1864, promulgated his judicial reforms which included the improvement of court procedure, the introduction of the jury system and justices of the peace, and the organization of lawyers into a formal bar.

dicts. Jurors were inclined to acquit criminals, appealing to the "influence of their milieu." This doctrine, in his opinion, was directly opposed to Christianity which, having proclaimed mercy toward the sinner, considers it, however, a man's moral duty to struggle with his environment, sets the limit where environment ends and duty begins. "*Making man responsible, Christianity in that itself also acknowledges his freedom.*"

The author continues his fight for personality and freedom begun in *Notes from Underground.* He defends the dignity of man against the determinism of utilitarian philosophy and religiously proves the idea of responsibility. "It is necessary to state the truth," he writes, "and to call evil, evil . . . Let us go into the courtroom with the thought that we too are guilty; this distress of the heart, which nowadays everyone fears so much will be our punishment." In the Russian people there is an unexpressed, unconscious idea: it is manifested in their calling crime—misfortune and the criminal—an unfortunate. The acknowledgment of common guilt, of "universal iniquity" is directly in opposition to the doctrine of environment. The people pity the sinner, but do not exculpate his sin; in penal servitude not one of the convicts felt that he was innocent, no one considered his punishment unmerited. Russians instinctively sense the great religious value of suffering as a purification.

In the article *Vlas,* the writer relates an extraordinary story of the people's mores, told to him by a certain "elder." A muzhik once crawled in on his knees and confessed his terrible sin to this monk, a "spiritual counselor." "Several of us fellows got together in the village," he said, "and started arguing among us: who would outdo the others in daring? Because of pride, I challenged them all. Another fellow took me aside and said to me, face to face, 'Swear by your salvation in the next world that you'll do just what I tell you.' I swore. 'Now soon it'll be Lent,' he says, 'start fasting to receive the sacrament. When you go to communion, take communion, but don't swallow it. You step back, take it out with your hand, and save it. And then I'll tell you what to do.' And I did it. Straight from the church he led me into a kitchen garden. He took a pole, drove it into the ground, and says, 'Put it there!' I put it on the pole. 'Now,' he says, 'get a gun.' I brought one. 'Load it.' I loaded it. 'Lift it and fire.' I lifted my arm and took aim. And now just as I was going to shoot, suddenly I see before me a cross and on it the Crucified. Then I fell down with the gun, and became unconscious." The elder imposed a terrible penance on the sinner "even

· 475 ·

beyond human strength, reasoning the more, the better. He himself had come crawling after suffering. . . ." The "extraordinary" episode inspired Dostoevsky to investigate the ultimate secrets of the people's soul; this psychological sketch belongs to his most brilliant creations. The *very possibility*, he thinks, of such a dispute in a Russian village is striking. In this boldness is manifest an "oblivion of all measure in everything, a need to strike over the brink, a need for the fainting sensation of approaching a precipice and half-leaning over it to steal a glance into the abyss itself. . . . This is a need of negation in a man, sometimes most believing and venerating, a negation of everything, of the most sacred thing in one's heart, of one's highest ideal, of all that is sacred to one's people." The impetuosity with which the Russian hastens to reveal himself in good or evil is astounding. . . . "Be it love, or liquor, debauchery, self-love, envy—in all these many a Russian will surrender himself almost without restraint, is prepared to break with everything, to renounce everything: family, customs, God." A fatal element of self-negation and self-destruction is peculiar to the people. . . . No one has ever perceived it with such force as Dostoevsky. He was the first to expose Russia's tragic face and foretell the ruin approaching her. The people's soul is antinomic: to the pathos of destruction and the ecstasy of ruin is opposed a yearning for salvation and repentance. . . . "I think the most important, most fundamental spiritual quest of the Russian people is their need of suffering, perpetual and insatiate suffering, everywhere and in all things. . . . The Russian people, as it were, delight in their suffering. . . . It is said the Russian people know the Gospel poorly, do not know the basic principles of faith. Of course, this is so, but they do know Christ and bear Him in their hearts from time immemorial. . . . Perhaps the sole love of the Russian people is Christ and they love His image in their own way, i.e., to the limit of suffering. . . . And here, to flout such a popular sanctity, thereby to tear oneself from the whole land, to destroy one's self forever and ever by negation and pride for only one moment of triumph—the Russian Mephistopheles could not have conceived anything more daring!" All that the writer says about the Russian people applies above all to himself. He himself "crossed over the brink in everything," knew the terrible dichotomy between faith and nonbelief, himself bore his insatiable love for Christ through the furnace of negation. Penetrating the people's soul, he found in it a reflection of his own person, plunging into the depths of his own spirit, he met there the spirit of the people. *Dostoevsky's soul is the soul of Russia.*

The *Diary of a Writer* for 1873 includes a short story entitled *Bobok.* The *danses macabres* of the Middle Ages, romanticism's "horror novels," the terrible stories of Edgar Poe pale before the inexpressible horror of this "literary joke." Dostoevsky often reflected "how everything on earth would become sinful and filthy without Christ" and here he depicts the decomposition of atheistic humanity, while still alive, in a shocking scene of conversations among the dead, who lie rotting in their graves. A half-mad litterateur strolls about a cemetery. It is October. A grey, dry day. "About fifteen corpses arrived together. Palls of different prices, there were even two catafalques. . . . I walked up and down among the graves. Different grades. The third grade costs thirty rubles and is decent and not so expensive. . . . I peeped into the graves—horrible: water and what water! Absolutely green and, well, what can one say. The grave diggers were continually bailing it out with a scoop. . . . I don't like to read epitaphs; they're always the same. On a slab beside me lay a half-eaten sandwich—stupid and out of place."

A summary of impressions, two details: green water in the graves and a half-eaten sandwich on a slab—this is all. But, indeed, the most unbridled fantasy could not create a more piercing sensation of mystical terror. Suddenly the narrator hears a conversation among the dead: "I hear—the sounds are muffled, as if the mouths are covered with pillows: and for all that, they are audible and very near." A major-general is playing vint with a court-councilor. An irritated lady belonging to higher society is disturbed that a merchant is buried next to her. " 'Little mother Avdotya Ignatyevna,' the shopkeeper suddenly cried out, 'my dear lady, tell me then, setting aside your anger, why am I going through these trials, or's something else taking place?'—'Ah, he's at it again, I even had a presentiment, 'cause I scented the spirit from him, his spirit, and it's he who's tossing around!'—'I'm not tossing around, little mother, and there's no peculiar smell from me, because I've still got our complete body, I've quite conserved myself, but now you, little lady, have already begun to taint—since your smell is really unbearable, even for this here place. I keep silent only out of politeness.' " "The mystery of death!" pronounces the merchant. On this contrast between the "mystery of death" and the hideous vulgarity of the chatter beyond the grave, impregnated with its putrefaction, is constructed the effect of the cemetery farce.

The conversation among the dead turns to ticklish themes—about a certain Katish, who is "of good family, educated, and a monster, a monster to the nth degree." A privy councilor, losing his breath, stammers: "For a long . . . for a long time now, I've been entertaining the vision of a little blonde . . . about fifteen years of age . . . and in just such a setting." Baron Klinevich prepares "to arrange himself for the best and gaily pass the remaining time." The lasciviousness after death adds to the vulgar banality and completes the picture of moral corruption. Through the words of the "homespun" cemetery philosopher Platon Nikolayevich the author discloses the religious significance of his *danse macabre.*

"The body here [in the grave] is once more revived, the residues of life are concentrated, but only in consciousness. This continues another two or three months . . . sometimes even a half-year. There is here, for example, one fellow, who has almost completely decomposed, but once every six weeks or so, he still will suddenly mutter one word, senseless, of course, about some bobok: 'Bobok, bobok'—but this means that in him too life continues to glow as an imperceptible spark. . . . Here the stench that we perceive is a moral one—hee! hee! A stench emanating from the soul, so that we might succeed in two or three months to come to our senses, and this is, so to speak, the ultimate mercy." Dostoevsky expresses his tormenting alarm about atheistic humanity in nauseating, repulsive images. All these privy councilors, major-generals, barons, and illustrious ladies, all these vulgar individuals and debauchees possess immortal souls. What fate awaits them beyond the grave? In what infernal darkness will their immortal spirit live? Is their salvation possible? The Lord according to His mercy gives them a time for repentance even after death—are they capable of "coming to their senses"? The author, stifling in the corpses' stench dooms his "dead souls" to perdition. He is terrible in his pitiless justice. The "gay deceased" use their last days of existence to organize a diabolic orgy. One of them says: "I suggest that we all pass these two months as pleasantly as possible and to that end arrange everything on different bases. Ladies and gentlemen! I suggest that we be ashamed of nothing. It is impossible to live on earth without lying, for life and falsehood are synonyms; well, here we will not lie just for fun. . . . Up there all this was tied with rotten strings. Off with the strings and let's live these two months in the most shameless truth: *let's be nude and bare ourselves.*" " 'Let's bare ourselves, let's bare ourselves!' they began to shout at the top of their voices. 'I want terribly, terribly to bare myself!' shrieked Avdotya Ignatyevna." This "let's be nude and bare ourselves" reveals satanic depths before us. All

Dostoevsky's demonic heroes are drawn to an ultimate exposure, to metaphysical shamelessness. Prince Volkovsky, in the *Humiliated and Wronged*, sensuously dreams of a confession from which a stench would rise up through the whole earth. Svidrigailov, in *Crime and Punishment*, is cynically candid with Raskolnikov and enjoys his disgust. Ippolit in *The Idiot* is not ashamed to "bare himself" publicly before his indignant audience. Nastasya Filippovna's guests relate their most base actions with relish. In *The Devils*, Stavrogin flings his confession into Bishop Tikhon's face as a diabolic challenge to divine law and divine truth. "Let's bare ourselves and be naked" is the limit of satanic negation and destruction: before the face of the cosmos the abyss of nonbeing reveals its obscene nudity with a shameless laugh. *The void opens up with a burst of laughter: "Hell is full of mirth."*

"Bobok" is the most terrible of Dostoevsky's metaphysical visions. The atheistic world is decomposing while still alive. The putrefaction of souls is more horrible than the corruption of bodies.

Another literary work, included in the *Diary* of 1873, is called *Little Pictures*. Its very first lines: "Summer, vacations, dust and heat, heat and dust" transport us into the atmosphere of the novel *Crime and Punishment*. Sultry, dusty Petersburg in summer is the unforgettable landscape of Raskolnikov's crime. The author's imagination was captivated by the "morose city," which is mystically joined with all his creative work. In the sketch he strolls along Nevsky Prospect, reflects on "the characterless and impersonal" architecture of the Russian capital, drops into the amusement establishments and "tavern gardens," mixes with the Sunday crowd of workers and is struck by the concentrated gloom of the people walking by. But, as always, his main attention is directed to the children. Since the time of *The Idiot* he had dreamt of writing about children; *The Diary of a Writer* is full of observations and notes about children. So, little by little, material for the "children's episodes" in *Brothers Karamazov* was collected. In *Little Pictures* he describes an artisan, dressed in his holiday clothes, a German frock coat, who is leading his son by the hand. "It is a boy slightly over two years, very weak, very pale." The writer already has in mind a pitiful tale about a widowed father and an orphaned child.

"I love," he writes, "while roaming through the streets, to look attentively at some completely unknown passersby, to study their faces and conjecture who are they, how they live, what their occupation is." The suddenness of his creative penetration and the concreteness of his fiction are astonishing: Dostoevsky instantly creates the setting, mores, the events, the characters of a little drama. He concludes with the ironic remark that from this entire history "it is impossible to draw anything instructive." The morose city is Petersburg and the children playing on its gloomy streets are pale, undernourished, and anemic. But how the author loves these poor little children with their sad faces and crooked legs! The "children's theme," culminating Ivan Karamazov's revolt, is one of Dostoevsky's "great lyric themes." Its tone of pathos is already advanced in *Little Pictures*. "My God," suddenly exclaims the author, "a child is like a flower, like a little leaf set on a tree in spring; it needs light, air, liberty, fresh food, and here, instead of these—a stuffy basement with some kvas or cabbage smell, a terrible stench at night, unhealthy food, cockroaches and fleas, humidity, dampness dripping from the walls, and outside—dust, bricks, lime." All these crowds of sickly, deprived children would merge afterward into one image, that of the innocent little martyr Ilyusha Snegiryov.

The surveys of foreign events that Dostoevsky ran in *The Citizen* were devoted to reflections on the fate of Europe. At the center of his observations stood France, and he was troubled by the legitimist movement on behalf of Count Chambord. He felt that the entire future evolution of world history depended on France's role: "This nation of genius," he writes, "which has succeeded to the ancient world and for 15 centuries stood at the head of the Latin races of Europe and in the last centuries has had an incontestable, prime influence on all the races of Europe, almost a century ago lost this vital force that moved and nourished her for so many hundreds of years. This vital force consisted in France's being the pre-eminent representative of European Catholicism almost from the very earliest times of Christianity in the West of Europe." The French Revolution had proclaimed new principles and rent France's connection with Catholicism. Would this great nation return to its faith or would it become a hot-bed of atheism for all the world? "In this fatal question of the life and death of France," concludes the writer, "of the resurrection or suppression of its great genius, so sympathetic to mankind, is perhaps contained the question of the life and death of all European mankind, whatever the recent conquerors of France—the Germans—might have to say regarding this."

Apropos of Bismarck Germany's contention with the Catholic Church, Dostoevsky clearly defined the anti-Christian principle of the new

German empire. "Here we have not only the struggle of Roman Catholicism, of the Roman idea of universal world dominion, which does not want to die, cannot, and will die perhaps only with the end of the world,—*but we also have in germ the struggle of faith with atheism, the struggle of the Christian principle with the new coming principle of the new future society, which dreams of erecting its throne in place of the throne of God.*"

About seventy years have passed and Dostoevsky's prediction has been realized. Out of the "anti-Christian" germ grew the doctrine of the pagan totalitarian state.

The writer's political essays are illuminated by the fire of the Apocalypse. Here is a last mysterious prophecy of the Russian visionary: "The world will be saved only after its visitation by the evil spirit. . . . And the evil spirit is near: *our children, perhaps, will look upon him.*"

All of us, Dostoevsky's spiritual children, are passing through the terrible experience of this "visitation." He is the forerunner, we the spectators and witnesses.

On March 19, 1874, the writer retired from *The Citizen,* gave up the 3,000 ruble annual salary and was left without any means. In April he went to Moscow to try to sell the plan of his new novel to *The Russian Messenger.* But Katkov would not agree to pay him 250 rubles per sheet and gave an evasive answer. Dostoevsky returned to Petersburg upset and anxious. Then an unexpected event took place: his old ideational enemy, Nekrasov, came to the author of *The Devils,* the fierce exposer of nihilism and revolution, to buy the projected novel for *Fatherland Notes.* Anna Grigoryevna tells about this in her memoirs: "My husband was very glad to renew friendly relations with Nekrasov, whose talent he valued highly. . . . But in this matter there was also a side that was difficult for Fyodor Mikhailovich: *Fatherland Notes* was a journal of the opposite camp and not so very long before, when my husband was editing the journals *Time* and *Epoch,* he had carried on an embittered fight with them. On the editorial staff were several of Fyodor Mikhailovich's literary enemies: Mikhailovsky, Skabichevsky, Yeliseyev—at times Pleshcheyev —and they could demand that my husband modify his novel in the spirit of their tendency. But Fyodor Mikhailovich could not, under any circumstance, give up his fundamental convictions. *Fatherland Notes,* in its turn, could not want to print some of my husband's opinions, and then at the first somewhat serious disagreement, Fyodor Mikhailovich, without doubt, would have demanded his novel back, whatever sad consquences might have resulted for us from this."

However Anna Grigoryevna may underline her husband's loyalty to his "fundamental convictions," nonetheless his move from the conservative *Citizen* to the extreme-left *Fatherland Notes* could not fail to irritate his conservative friends. It is impossible to explain this rapprochement with Nekrasov's group simply as opportunism: a reversal took place in Dostoevsky's ideas; after his collaboration with Meshchersky, he realized that his path was not with the reactionaries. *A Raw Youth* testifies to the profound change in his view of the revolutionary youth of the seventies.

In the summer of 1874 the writer traveled to Ems to be treated for emphysema and worked on the plan for his novel. He made no progress. "When can I write a novel," he wrote his wife, "during the day, with such light and sunshine, when one is tempted to take a walk and the streets are filled with noise? Please God only that I can begin the novel and draw up at least some plan. Beginning is already half the affair." Instead of writing the novel he read Pushkin and "grew intoxicated with ecstasy." Once again he was struck by the brilliant concept of the *Covetous Knight*; and under the influence of Pushkin's tragic miser, he conceived his own hero—Arkady Dolgoruky with his "idea of Rothschild."

As always, Dostoevsky had difficulty sorting out the innumerable plans, ideas, plots which arose in his inexhaustible fantasy. "An abundance of schemes," he informed his wife, "here is the principal defect. When I have considered it as a whole, then I see that there are four novels combined in it." *A Raw Youth* is the most overloaded of all Dostoevsky's novels. It would be possible to extract not four, but seven or eight fully complete novels from it.

After having returned from Ems at the end of July, the writer settled with his family for the whole winter in Staraya Russa and plunged into writing *A Raw Youth*.

Dostoevsky's daughter Lyubov, in her memoirs, gives a detailed description of the family's life in the quiet little town. The Dostoevskys rented a villa from a certain Colonel Gribbe. It was

a small house built in the German taste of the Pre-Baltic Provinces, full of unexpected surprises, secret wall cupboards, sliding doors leading to dark, dusty, spiral staircases. The low and narrow rooms were arranged with old furniture in empire style; greenish mirrors reflected the distorted faces of those who had the courage to steal a glance into them. On sheets of paper pasted onto linen, which served as pictures, our astonished gaze, as children, beheld monstrous Chinese women, with nails two feet long and tiny feet squeezed in children's half-boots. A closed veranda with multicolored walls was our sole entertainment, and little Chinese billiards with their glass balls and bells diverted us on the long rainy days. Behind the house was a garden with funny little patches, planted with flowers. All possible kinds of fruit grew in this garden, which was cut through by a little canal. On the old colonel's death, my parents bought this house from his heirs for a ridiculously low price [in the spring of 1876].

Lyubov Dostoevskaya maintains that the topography of Skotoprigo-nyevsk, in which the action of the novel *Brothers Karamazov* takes place, reflects the features of Staraya Russa and old Karamazov's home recalls Colonel Gribbe's villa. Several of the local residents appear in the novel. So, for example, the merchant Plotnikov, from whom Mitya Karamazov buys the provisions to entertain the gypsies, really existed and was the writer's favorite purveyor. The coachmen Andrey and Timofey, who drove Mitya to Mokroye were good friends of the Dostoevsky family: every year they brought the children to the bank of the Ilmen, where in the autumn the boat docked. Lyubov Dostoevskaya even asserts that Grushenka was a "young provincial girl whom her parents knew in Staraya Russa."

In the lonely northern town the writer lived isolated and secluded. In his daughter's memoirs we find a curious description of his habits. Dostoevsky used to get up after eleven, did gymnastics, washed fastidiously; if he was in good humor, he would sing: "At dawn don't wake her." He never went about in a dressing gown, could not tolerate spots on his clothes; wore fine linen and starched collars. After praying, he drank two glasses of strong tea, and carried a third to his room.

In his study, over the divan, hung a copy of the Sistine Madonna. Things were laid out on his writing desk in the most pedantic order. After lunch he used to dictate the chapter which he had written during the night. "Mother would take it down in shorthand," writes Lyubov Dostoevskaya, "recopy it, he would make corrections, mother would once again transcribe it and send it to the printer. Mother did not criticize, would only sometimes change the heroine's dress from blue to rose; vary the cut of the hero's hat and remove his beard."

After the dictation, the writer used to distribute treats to the children; in the drawer of his desk always were stored confections, dried figs, dates, nuts, raisins.

At 4 o'clock he would go out for a walk: he walked with his head bowed in deep meditation; he used to hand out alms, without looking— once he gave a coin to his own wife. He loved to buy sweets, grapes, pears at the most expensive store. At 6 o'clock, they had dinner; at 9, supper. Dostoevsky sat down to work, having blessed the children and recited a prayer to the Mother of God with them. He worked with two candles, smoked a great deal. He used to read Pushkin's tales, the poems of Lermontov, Gogol's *Taras Bulba* and *The Robbers* of Schiller aloud to the children. He knew all the heroes of Dickens and Walter Scott by heart.

This quiet comfort and relative well-being Dostoevsky owed to his wife. Anna Grigoryevna showed great organizational and commercial talents. She knew how to come to an agreement and settle accounts with creditors, to protect her husband from his relatives' extortions and founded her own publishing house. In the year 1873 she became the publisher of her husband's works. *The Idiot* and *The Devils*, published in one volume, laid a foundation for the writer's material security.

Despite Nekrasov's courtesy and kindness, the writer continued to be troubled by his unexpected reconciliation with his recent enemies. In December 1874 he wrote to his wife: "Yesterday I read in *The Citizen* that Lev Tolstoy had sold his novel [*Anna Karenina*] to *The Russian Messenger*, in 40 sheets, and it will appear starting in January—at five hundred rubles a sheet, i.e., for 20,000. They couldn't decide right away to give me 250 r., but willingly paid L. Tolstoy 500! No, I'm valued too low, because of the fact that I live on my work. Now Nekrasov really can pressure me, if anything goes against their tendency: he knows that now (i.e., for the future year) I will not be taken in *The Russian Messenger*, since *The Russian Messenger* is overloaded with novels. But even if we should have to ask charity this year, I will not concede a line to their tendency!" Now he understood why Katkov could not immediately agree to give him 250 rubles a sheet for *A Raw Youth*: in his portfolio already lay Tolstoy's huge novel *Anna Karenina*. But his apprehensions regarding "pressures" on Nekrasov's side proved to be false.

In February 1874 the writer arrived for several days in Petersburg and brought the first two parts of the novel to the editors of *Fatherland Notes*. Nekrasov met him "with extraordinary friendship and kindness." On February 9 Dostoevsky informed his wife: ". . . Nekrasov came 'in order to express *his delight* on reading the end of the first part.' 'All night I sat, read, was so captivated, and yet at my age and with my health I shouldn't have allowed myself to do this. And what freshness you have, my dear fellow! . . . Such freshness does not appear in our day, and not one writer has it. In Lev Tolstoy's last novel there's only a repetition of what I have read before in him, only before it was better.'" Nekrasov particularly liked the first two chapters and the last scene with Liza; the story of the young girl's suicide he found the "crown of perfection." "In general, Nekrasov is terribly pleased." Dostoevsky quotes his words: "I came to talk over the remainder with you. For God's sake, don't hurry and don't spoil it, because it's begun too well." And the writer concludes: "In a word, the result is that I am utterly esteemed at *Fatherland Notes* and that Nekrasov wants to begin completely amicable relations."

Thirty years before Nekrasov had hailed Dostoevsky's literary birth and passed a sleepless night over his first novel *Poor People*. Then there was the quarrel, baiting the "knight of mournful figure," and the cruel journalistic polemics. And here, at the end of their lives the authors met once again—their friendship of years before came to life. On the other hand, recent friends, Maikov and Strakhov, could not forgive Dostoevsky his "apostasy." The writer informed his wife: "Maikov met me, to all appearances, pleasantly, but I saw at once that it was with strong reserve. Strakhov also turned up. Not a word about my novel, and, evidently, so as not to *irritate* me. They also talked a little about Tolstoy's novel, but what they said—they expressed with ludicrous enthusiasm. . . . In a word, I see that something is going on here. . . ." Several days later he again wrote to his wife:

Maikov, Anna Ivanovna, and all of them were very kind, but on the other hand Strakhov was for some reason reserved with me. And even Maikov, when he began to inquire after Nekrasov and when I relayed Nekrasov's compliments to him, assumed a distressed air, and Strakhov one that was altogether cold. . . . No, Anya, this is a nasty seminarian and nothing more: he already abandoned me once in my life, namely when *Epoch* failed and came running back only after the success of *Crime and Punishment*.

In fact, Strakhov did grow cold toward Dostoevsky: he felt an unbounded admiration for Tolstoy, whereas his attitude toward the author of *The Devils* was haughty and insincere. After Dostoevsky's death, he spread a hideous calumny about his late friend (a letter to Tolstoy).[3]

In the summer of 1875 the writer again took the cure at Ems and with difficulty wrote the third part of *A Raw Youth*. He felt melancholy and was brought to despair by the boring German resort. On June 10 he complained to his wife: "I think I will finally go out of my mind from boredom or commit some wild act. It is impossible to endure more than I'm going through. This is literally torture. This is worse than being shut up in prison. Most important, if only I could work, then I'd be distracted. However, I can't even do this, because my plan has not been settled and I see extraordinary difficulties. Without my thought having ripened, it's impossible to proceed, and there's no inspiration in such anguish, and it is primary." Three days later again he complained: "Most of all I'm tormented by the failure of my work; I'm still sitting, am tortured, and have doubts, and there is no strength to begin. . . . Everyone in literature, however, has decidedly turned

[3] Strakhov's much-quoted letter to Tolstoy (November 28, 1883) was first published in the October 1913 issue of *Contemporary World*. After Dostoevsky's death Strakhov wrote a biography of his former friend and then declared to Tolstoy that he had "struggled against his feeling of disgust" and tried to depict only a positive "façade of life" as was customary. He maintained that Dostoevsky was a "malicious, envious, immoral man," "ill-natured," without a "feeling of genuine goodness," but that "like Rousseau he regarded himself as one of the best and happiest of men." The characters which most resembled him were the "underground man," Svidrigailov and Stavrogin. Tolstoy, with good taste, answered this hypocritical letter by saying that Dostoevsky had a "physical nervous defect," and that as for his characters being self-portraits: "The deeper a writer penetrates into the human heart, the more universal he becomes and the more familiar and akin he is to us all. The result is that even in those exceptional characters not only we, but also foreigners, recognize ourselves and our own inner being." In the letter Strakhov resorted even to making the vicious and contemptible accusation that Dostoevsky had boasted to a certain Professor Viskovatov that he, with the complicity of a governess, had raped a little girl in a bathhouse. Anna Grigoryevna refutes this calumny by stating how "astonished" she was by Strakhov's reference to Viskovatov in that he had never been that familiar with Dostoevsky, had never been to their home, and Dostoevsky had not expressed a very good opinion of him. The episode about the bathhouse and the governess had been a real occurrence which someone had related to Dostoevsky and which he had intended as one possible "artistic characterization of Stavrogin." Lastly we need only recall how consistently and in what light Dostoevsky treats the theme of "cruelty to children." The rape of a young girl (Svidrigailov, Stavrogin) is an act of brutality for which there can be no forgiveness. It is only unfortunate that Strakhov's spite, limitations, and jealousy could have prompted him to spread such an infamous slander.

away from me. . . . I see that the novel is done for: it'll be buried with all honors under everyone's scorn."

On August 10 Dostoevsky's second son, Aleksey, was born. *A Raw Youth* was published in *Fatherland Notes* in the course of 1875. Between the printing of the second and third parts there was an interruption of three months.

X X

A Raw Youth

It is not fully possible for us to reconstruct the story of *A Raw Youth's* creation. The manuscript of the two final parts and the three notebooks with drafts of the novel have still not been published.[1] We are forced to content ourselves with the few fragments published by V. Komarovich and G. Chulkov.[A]

In the spring of 1874, Dostoevsky promised Nekrasov that he would deliver the novel by January 1, 1875. The copybooks show that the writer had not conceived even the most general plan of the new work. After his "bondage" on *The Citizen,* he felt spiritually depleted; inspiration did not come. Dejectedly, he understood that in fact he had no design, that he had only the *intention* of writing a novel. In this moment of creative breakdown, he returned to old plans he had used and remembered his earlier dream of writing a novel about children. While still working on *The Idiot* Dostoevsky had projected a picture of children's life: the idiot was portrayed at the head of a club of children; the children's community lived its own special life, perfected a new moral consciousness, passed judgment on adult society. And here, pondering over a new novel, Dostoevsky was captivated by an original concept: to describe the utopia of a "children's paradise." In the spring of 1874 he noted down in his copybook: "a novel about children, only about children, and about a child hero." The idea engaged him until July; during this month he wrote: "Try the children tomorrow, the children alone." After July this design disappeared

---

[1] These notebooks were finally edited by I. I. Anisimov and appeared in 1965. *F. M. Dostoevsky v rabote nad romanom "Podrostok"* (F. M. Dostoevsky in His Work on the Novel *A Raw Youth*). Literary Heritage, No. 77. Publ. by *Nauka* (Science), Moscow.

[A] W. Komarovitch. *Handschriftliche Aufzeichnung des Romans "Der Jüngling." Der unbekannte Dostoewski.* Piper Verlag. München, 1926. This scholar also published excerpts from the manuscript of *A Raw Youth* in the journal *Nachalo* (Beginning), No. 2. Georgy Chulkov. *Kak rabotal Dostoevsky* (How Dostoevsky Worked). *Sovetsky pisatel* (Soviet Writer). Moscow, 1939.

and was replaced by another. The writer returned to the abandoned plan of the novel-poem on which he was working in 1869: *The Life of a Great Sinner*. He recorded: "The novel's full title is *A Raw Youth*. The confession of a great sinner, written for himself." *A Raw Youth's* plot absorbed the unused material of the *Life*. In the new novel there was also to be a detailed biography of the hero; he too was an illegitimate son, spent his childhood in some other family, far from his parents, then returned to his father's home, took an involuntary part in the family drama; he also studied at Souchard's boarding school and Chermak's gymnasium; likewise became associated with his former school companion Albert (Lambert) and led a dissolute life. The father of the *Life's* hero bore the name Alfonsky: in *A Raw Youth*—the Frenchwoman, Lambert's mistress, is given the name Alfonsine. But *A Raw Youth* is not only dependent upon the *Life* for its subject matter: Arkady Dolgoruky inherits his "idea" from the "great sinner." The plan of the *Life* begins with the notation: "Accumulation of wealth." The hero is a proud individual, he yearns for power and might and "resolves on money"; "is terribly sure that everything will come of itself: money solves all questions." The author noted down: "Although money really establishes him on a certain firm point and solves all questions, however, sometimes the point wavers (poetry and much else) and he cannot find a way out. It is this state of vacillation that constitutes the novel." All these characteristics of the "great sinner" pass as a whole over to Arkady Dolgoruky. The *Life* transmits its ideational-psychological theme and a sketch of the subject to *A Raw Youth*.

The return to the "unwritten poem" took place without doubt under the influence of Pushkin. In Ems, Dostoevsky "grew intoxicated with ecstasy," rereading the great poet, and the idea of *The Covetous Knight*, which had absorbed him in his youth, was revived in his imagination. "Power through money" and "the power of money" is one of Dostoevsky's basic artistic ideas.

The outlines for the *Life* were again reworked in the rough notes for *A Raw Youth*. The writer cautioned himself against misuse of the device of enigma and endeavored to free himself from his main failing: excessively complicating the intrigue and overloading the action. From Pushkin he learned conciseness of exposition; in the novel there must be one hero and this hero—the raw youth.

Here is a curious note dated August 12, 1874: "Important solution to the problem. Write from one's self. Begin with the word: *I*. The confession of a great sinner. The confession is extraordinarily concise (learn from Pushkin). More concise, as concise as possible. . . . But as in Belkin's tales, Belkin himself is most important of all, so here— the raw youth is sketched first before everything."

Two months later another notation:

> In the course of the novel maintain two principles without fail: the first rule is to avoid the error in *The Idiot* and in *The Devils*, that secondary events (many) were depicted in a fragmentary, incomplete, romantic fashion, were extended over a long period in the action and scenes, but without the least explanation, in theories and allusions, instead of *explaining the truth directly*. As secondary episodes they were not worth the reader's attention and even, to the contrary, the principal design was obscured, and not clarified by this, precisely because the reader, who was led astray onto a bypath, lost the main road; his attention became confused. Endeavor to avoid this and to allot an insignificant, altogether shorter place to secondary matters, and concentrate the action around the hero.

> The 2nd rule is that the hero is the raw youth. And all the rest are secondary, even *He* [Versilov] is secondary. The poem is in the raw youth and in his idea, or better to say in the raw youth alone, as the exponent and discoverer of *his idea*.

And further on the schema of the action is presented as a function of the hero's fate. The novel was conceived in the form of a struggle between the raw youth's idea and reality. It could have been entitled *The Adventures of a Certain Idea*. Dostoevsky noted down the plan:

> The raw youth departs from Moscow, obsessed with the idea and faithful to it. He is armed by it and goes into the battle, and knows that he's already sacrificed something to it: namely the three years spent strengthening his character and denying himself higher education, specifically for the idea. In Petersburg *his idea* is subjected to reversal and upset for many reasons:

> 1) From encountering people and because he has not had patience and has disclosed his idea. *Shame* on account of it.

> 2) Socialism has caused his belief to waver: wants both the idea and to remain noble.

> 3) *His* [Versilov's] supercilious relation to the idea. *He* approves, but the raw youth has a presentiment that *His* idea is loftier, prouder,

and nobler than his. In what does *His* idea consist? The entire novel searches for a solution.

4) His clash with life, sensuality, ambition, not his own society, a young prince. Cynicism and other glittering paths appear. Everything is undermined because of insults which return him again to his idea, but now not theoretically, but in fact, angry and wanting to avenge himself. Cynicism and daring. Lambert and the prince. Conspiracy. Money. This period involves his regarding *Him* superciliously, loss of respect, of love for *Him*. A desire to avenge himself for *His* having so long constituted so much in his life. Here is a lack of respect for his own self. His meeting with Liza, the child, and so forth.

5) His relation to the princess [Akhmakova], ambition, passion, and conspiracy. Finally, the explanation what *He* is. But he has decided on the conspiracy not at all from an idea, but out of passion.

6) Makar Ivanov, etc. Jolting impression, but not nullifying his idea.

Dostoevsky rarely expressed himself about his artistic plans with such precision and clarity. This priceless document permits us to view the novel through the author's eyes and to compare the concept with its realization. All the points of the program were carried out in the final text, but yet it does not correspond to the original concept. It is true, the raw youth arrives with his idea and it undergoes modifications through conflict with people, through the revolt of his passions, his spiritual struggle with his father: and all the same the novel's significance does not lie in this, and the raw youth with his idea of Rothschild does not determine it. The schema of the action has been preserved intact, but its artistic stress has been shifted and its perspective sharply altered. This took place contrary to the author's designs: *a secondary personage arbitrarily assumed the central role, which was not destined for him.* The writer in vain prescribed the strict principle: "The hero is the raw youth. And all the rest are secondary, even *He* is secondary"; *He*—Versilov, having once entered the novel, could not remain "secondary": however the author might have tried to consign him to a second plane, to blanket him with obscurity and "vagueness," his image naturally thrust itself to the center and illumined the novel with the rays of its spiritual energy. In the struggle between the father and the son, the raw youth assumed a modest role: that of a timid disciple, an enamored listener, and conscientious narrator. Falling into the magnificent sphere of his father's thoughts and passions, he diffused himself like a pale shadow; instead of a hero he was transformed into a witness: his naiveté and moral irresolution chill the reader. From a fanatic and ascetic with an idea he quickly became a young fop and frivolous adventurer.

While Dostoevsky was working on *The Devils,* Stavrogin suddenly appeared and unceremoniously occupied the hero's place intended for Pyotr Verkhovensky. A similar mysterious occurrence took place when the writer was composing *A Raw Youth.* Versilov's ascendancy was as self-assumed as Stavrogin's domination.

The raw youth's fascinating and enigmatic father emerged, as did Stavrogin, out of *The Life of a Great Sinner.* The characteristics of the "poem's" hero apply in equal measure to both "strong personalities." The author wrote about his "sinner": "An extraordinary man— intelligent, gifted, having a strong will, broad, generous, capable of the loftiest feelings, self-denial. But the complete absence of a point of support. His faith wavers and disappears. Immense pride."

Versilov is a new embodiment of Stavrogin. The author condemned the hero of *The Devils* to a shameful death by hanging, but could not free himself from this seductive demon. Stavrogin continues to live in Versilov, experiences new falls and revolts, and his terrible vitality conquers.

In the notebooks we find a series of this enigmatic individual's characteristics. The writer made great efforts to take stock of the new character that had appeared before him, strove to grasp his features, which were still unclear, but the hero of *The Devils,* whom he had buried, burst into his work, and Versilov's outlines became as like Stavrogin's portrait as two drops of water. On reading the notes for *A Raw Youth* one is struck by the writer's obsession with the personality of his favorite hero. Sometimes it is difficult to believe that the remarks refer to Versilov, and not to Stavrogin. For example this note:

What's important here is that with all his force he preaches Christianity, freedom (Christ's in opposition to the social theory of crime) and the future life, openly holds that without Christ (Orthodox) and Christianity the life of man and of humanity is unthinkable, because it is not worth living otherwise. So that, when he smashes the icon, it shows that he himself did not believe in anything and was, in his soul, a profound atheist, always, from the very beginning of his life, was also tormented by that . . . "His suffering is now intelligible to me," says the raw youth.

But, he was not pretending, when he used *ardently* to preach Christ, on the contrary it was sincere to the highest degree. Convinced himself that he *believed*. Used to prove to himself that faith existed, struggled with the monster of his own doubts, choked it, but in the end it devoured him.

Stavrogin likewise preaches the Orthodox Christ to Shatov and endeavors to convince himself that he believes. He also yearns for an heroic feat, but does not know the feeling of penitence, and his humility reverts to diabolic pride.

About Versilov, Dostoevsky writes: "He has a lofty ideal of beauty, chains are an end for him, for the ideal is humility, but all his humility is based on pride. . . . The most shameful and terrible memories are nothing to him and do not elicit repentance, because he has 'his idea,' i.e., ideal. The ideal is impure. Self-adoration. For him people are mice."

Stavrogin plays cruelly and criminally with people and profoundly despises them: he marries the cripple for the sake of a drunken wager, senselessly destroys Liza, poisons Kirilov's soul with the bane of atheism, drives Shatov to destruction. Versilov's relationship to his son is just as haughty and pitiless. We read: "In order to possess the document and take advantage of the raw youth, he pitilessly lures him into debauchery and sin. He makes use of his love for the princess [Akhmakova], makes use of his thirst for excitement, his egoism, which he excites terribly by vices, pride. Scenting a loftier nature in him, at times, but offhandedly he tosses him bits of a higher thought (socialism, Christianity). But wheedling the document out of him does not take place systematically, jesuitically, because his goals themselves are not precise. . . . Either he flatters the youth's 'idea' of Rothschild and his proud isolation or suddenly refers skeptically, carelessly, and cynically to the raw youth's soul. Despite his self-worship, he is uneasy because he is frequently discontent with himself. He wants the heroic-feat of the higher man, wants chains and sacrifices, but his mouse opinion[B] and pride continually justify him in his own conscience. It is impossible to love people."

In *The Devils* Kirilov shoots himself; in *A Raw Youth* another monomaniac, Kraft, shoots himself. Stavrogin in the letter before his death writes: "Generous Kirilov could not withstand his idea and shot himself. . . . I have never been capable of losing my reason and could never believe an idea to the degree that he did."

B That is, that "for him, people are mice."

Analogous to this declaration is the notation concerning Versilov: " 'This is perhaps only the breadth of our Russian nature,' he says. 'Now, however, this breadth (i.e., passionate faith and at the same time cynicism) has somewhat narrowed; Krafts shoot themselves because of the idea that Russia is second-rate. But we have only grown handsomer from such ideas.' "

Stavrogin held the artist's imagination undividedly and dictated his will to him: instead of a new hero, Dostoevsky composed new variants on the old. Versilov was by degrees turned into Stavrogin's double. From several notations it is possible to conjecture the author's struggle with his hero-incubus. Preserving a family likeness to his older brother, Versilov began to be distinguished from him; the demonic features grew dim, the torpid pallor of doom disappeared; the new "strong individual" still had the possibility of salvation through Faustian "incessant striving." And mainly: he was provided with an ardent heart, capable of a dual love, earthly and heavenly (for Akhmakova and his wife). Versilov is not a corpse galvanized by devils, but a living man, doubting, tormented, loving and believing in an ideal. His emotional impetuosity is underlined in the notes. "N.B. Important. Everything with this Versilov proceeds in bursts: first there is no hope for the princes; now suddenly he himself returns the inheritance, then throws down a challenge, withdraws it; now keeps silent, then suddenly an impudent, abusive letter to Akhmakova beyond all propriety, beyond any measure. 'I can't understand how such a self-possessed, level-headed, calm, and solid gentleman as Versilov could make such leaps' (a remark of the raw youth)."

By his ardor, vitality, "viability," the hero of *A Raw Youth* overcame Stavrogin's frozen likeness to death. But this was not enough: in order for him to be cast as an independent personality, he must have his own idea. In Dostoevsky's world, an idea always forms the spiritual center of the personality: *the personality is always idea-bearing.* In the sketchbooks, Versilov's "idea" is marked unclearly: in one note an "idea of nobility" is spoken of; in another, a striving for good "at any price come what may."

Here is the first entry: "After shattering the image, he comes to the raw youth: 'All these last eight years I imagined myself a believer,' *He* says.

" 'How then have you suddenly lost your faith?'

" 'Dear friend! I've always suspected that I didn't believe anything.'

"'And so, you now begin to live . . . [illegible].'

"'No, my friend, in accord with the ideal of nobility that I've drawn up for myself.'

"'Who forces you?'

"'I am forcing myself.'"

Here is the second notation:

"1) Versilov is convinced of the loss and stupidity of every ideal and of the curse of stagnation on the whole moral world.

"2) For some time he compulsively believed in Christ.

"3) But all his faith was shattered. There remained only the moral sense of duty, self-perfection and good, at any price come what may (i.e., in spite of all loss of faith and all moral despair), as a result of his own conscious will, his desire at any price come what may."

The "conscious will," establishing a moral law for itself, the striving for good "at any price come what may" recalls Kant's moral imperative. The question of the autonomy of morality arose before Dostoevsky and he wanted to make Versilov the exponent of this idea. The misty ideal of "nobility" was to save the "dreamer" from the precipice of atheism. In the rough drafts the author calls Versilov an "idealist" and exclaims: "Blessed be the name of the last idealist." A utopia of good without God would be embodied in his dream of the golden age.

Thus the two heroes of the novel, Versilov and his son, are indicated and the two ideas that they embody: one is "generous," the other loves money; one embraces all humanity and inspires it to incessant striving for good "at any price come what may," the other locks himself up in haughty isolation, in wealth and power. The father's idea is the golden age, the son's idea—the underground. The clash of these ideas would determine the novel's action. The opposition of the light and dark element is underlined in Versilov's following aphorism: "In our society," he says, "on one side are despair and the pus of decomposition, while on the other is the yearning for restoration and ecstasies. They reject even God religiously." This dichotomy is the more tragic in that it is expressed not only in the confrontation of men, but also in the inner conflicts of consciousness. Versilov is no less divided than the raw youth; he is just as false to his ideal of nobility as his son is to the idea of Rothschild. Dostoevsky outlined a "preface" in which the novel's social meaning was explained: his heroes are the representatives of Russian society, "men of the Russian majority," "heroes of the tragedy of the underground." This exceptionally important self-assessment of the writer ends with a prophetic foreboding.

Here is what he writes about his novels: *"For the preface. Facts.* People pass by, they take no notice, there are no citizens, and no one wants to exert or force himself to think and take note. I could not remain indifferent, and all the critics' cries that I am not portraying real life, have not dissuaded me. Our society has no *foundations*, life has not produced principles, because there has not even been life. A colossal jolt and everything is broken off, collapses, is negated, as though it had not even existed. And this is not the external only, as in the West, but internally, morally. . . .

". . . Our writers have in a highly artistic way depicted the life of our upper middle circle (of the family). They've thought that they were depicting the life of the majority. In my opinion, they have depicted the life of the exceptions. . . . I pride myself that I've been the first to portray the real man of the Russian majority, and have for the first time revealed his distorted and tragic side. The tragedy lies in the consciousness of his deformity. . . . I alone have exhibited the hero of the tragedy of the underground, which is composed of suffering, of self-punishment, the consciousness of what is better, and the impossibility of attaining it, and, mainly, of the clear conviction of those unfortunate beings, that all [illegible], and, consequently, it isn't even worth reforming oneself. What can sustain those who reform? Reward, faith? A reward from no one, faith in no one?"

And in the margin, the postscript: "Future generations, who will be impartial, will be convinced of this; *truth will be behind me.* I believe in this."

Dostoevsky prided himself on having portrayed not the exception, but "the man of the majority." His was the discovery of this man's distorted and tragic countenance. He was the first to see that Russian society was uprooted and formless. The absence of "foundations" and "traditions" doomed Russians to the tragedy of the underground. Without religious convictions and moral supports, Russia was living *catastrophically.* "A colossal jolt and everything is broken off, collapses, is negated." The "jolt" of the war and revolution have confirmed these words with astonishing accuracy. The writer was not mistaken: future generations have become positively convinced that "truth was behind him."

So by degrees the idea of the novel arose: *"Our society has no foundations."* The author insisted on his realism: he was painting not fic-

tions, but authentic Russian reality. All his great novels were devoted
to one theme: a depiction of the tragic *Russian chaos*. But how paradoxical was his place in literature! He stood alone against everyone; he
saw "disorder" where all other writers found system, mores, stable
forms. Is it possible that Turgenev, Goncharov, Lev Tolstoy depicted
only "mirages"? Can all great Russian literature be "fantastic"?
Dostoevsky was constantly preoccupied by this question in the seventies. He wrote to Maikov: "But you know—why, this all is landowner's
literature. It has said everything that it had to say (magnificently
with Lev Tolstoy). But this word, aristocratic to the highest degree, was
the last. *A new word*, replacing the landowner's, still does not exist."
Dostoevsky asserted that the old "landowner" literature was finished
and that he was called upon to create a new one. Such a proud consciousness of his own innovational, almost revolutionary role, unavoidably led him into conflict with the old art's greatest representative—
Lev Tolstoy.[C]

With jealous attention the writer followed the work of his literary
antipode. In *The Humiliated and Wronged* he alluded to *Childhood*
and *Boyhood* and presented the type of Prince Volkovsky, "an aristocrat without any convictions" with clear reference to the heroes of Tolstoy. In the design of the grandiose novel *The Life of a Great Sinner*
one senses a concealed polemic with the author of *Childhood*. Dostoevsky informed his friends that his "poem" would be of the same dimension as *War and Peace*. Among the rough drafts to the *Life* we meet the
following words of Tikhon concerning children: "How they are stripped
of their childlike images while still in childhood. The study that has
been made of them, though exact (L. Tolstoy, Turgenev), reveals as
though a *different* life. Only Pushkin is a genuine Russian." Tolstoy's
growing fame intensified Dostoevsky's critical relationship to him: in
the year 1874 the *Russian Messenger* refused to pay him 250 rubles a
sheet for *A Raw Youth* and was not unwilling to pay Tolstoy 500 rubles
per sheet for *Anna Karenina*. Strakhov became Tolstoy's fanatic admirer
and broke off his old friendship with the author of *The Devils*. He and
Maikov spoke "with ludicrous enthusiasm" about their idol's new work,
Anna Karenina. The colossal figure of Tolstoy impeded Dostoevsky's
literary path, as once Turgenev's figure had.

The great writer's genius was incontestable; the author of *A Raw
Youth* had either to acknowledge that he himself was second-rate or
sharply to define his own special, independent domain from that of

[C] Cf. A. L. Bem. *Dostoevsky i Tolstoy* (Dostoevsky and Tolstoy).

his fortunate rival. Under the influence of his ideational struggle with Tolstoy, Dostoevsky realized his own *eccentric place* in Russian literature. *A Raw Youth* was conceived as an antithesis to the writer-nobleman's family chronicles; the idea of the novel becomes intelligible only on the plane of a polemic work against "landowner literature, which had outlived its time." Instead of families of the "middle aristocracy," which Tolstoy portrayed with such art, one encounters the "haphazard households" whose historiography Dostoevsky considered that he was writing. This social-philosophical opposition is clearly disclosed in the epilogue to *A Raw Youth*. There we read: "If I were a Russian novelist and had talent, then without fail I would have taken my heroes from the Russian ancestral nobility, for only in that type of cultivated Russian can one find *at least the appearance of beautiful order* and of beautiful impression which is so necessary in a novel to produce an aesthetic reaction on the reader." And further: "The position of our novelist in such a case would be perfectly defined: he could not write in any form, other than the historical. . . . Oh, in the historical form it is possible to depict a multitude of details still extraordinarily pleasant and comforting. . . . Such a work when one has great talent, would belong now not as much to Russian literature as to Russian history. It would be a picture, artistically complete, of the Russian mirage, but would exist in reality so long as no one guessed that it was a mirage." The thrust of these ironic encomia was directed against Tolstoy and his artistic picture of the "Russian world," *War and Peace*. Dostoevsky was the first to glean that the "beautiful order" of the nobles' forms was only a semblance, that under the "cosmos" of Russian culture chaos was raging. A cruel destiny committed him to dissipate the comforting mirage and to become the novelist of "haphazard households." "The work is thankless," he added, "and without beautiful forms."

A Raw Youth was Dostoevsky's reply to Tolstoy's *War and Peace*. In the author's manuscript we find an entire study on Tolstoy, definitively explaining the ideational genesis of this work. The "sightliness" of the Tolstoian heroes, which Versilov admires with such ironic rapture, had proved to be uncommonly fragile; one generation later it was transformed into the "unsightliness" of the heroes in *A Raw Youth*. "I have, my dear," says Versilov to his son,

> one favorite Russian writer, one novelist, but for me he is almost the historiographer of our nobility or, better to say, of our cultivated stratum, which crowns the "formative period" of our history. . . .

What I like most of all in him is that very "sightliness," which you looked for in the heroes that he has portrayed. He takes the nobleman from his childhood and youth, he sketches him in the family, his first steps in life, first joys, tears, and everything is so unshakable and incontestable. He is the psychologist of the nobleman's soul. But the main thing is that it is presented as incontestable and, of course, you agree. You agree and are envious. Oh, how one envies! . . . Oh, these are not heroes. They are dear children who have excellent dear fathers, who eat at the club, entertain in Moscow, their older children are in the hussars or are students at the university who have their own carriages. . . . However it may be, whether all this is good or bad in itself, here now there is a *tried and determined form,* here rules have been established, here is honor and duty of its sort.

Versilov's exaggerated ecstasy regarding the "sightliness" of the nobles' form unmasks its artificiality and frailty.

In his sketchbook the writer notes down: "According to a new plan from August 26. The name of the novel is *Disorder.* The characters' ideas and passions must illustrate this idea Versilov says to his son: 'Here you've chosen the idea of Rothschild. By this idea you only testify as well to a moral disorder, you want to withdraw into your hole, away from everyone, and take measures to that end. Liza is complete moral disorder: is unwilling to live without happiness. Dolgushin is moral disorder'—'Let them be wrong,' says the raw youth, 'but they do have convictions of honor and duty, consequently, there is no disorder.' 'Convictions of honor and duty to the point of universal destruction—a fine order, besides, I don't want to argue,' He says." Rejecting the "family forms" idealized by Tolstoy, Dostoevsky depicted the formlessness of the contemporary Russian family: Versilov has two families, two legitimate children and two illegitimate; he lives with a civil wife whom her legal husband, Makar Dolgoruky, continues to visit; means to marry the daughter of General Akhmakov, with whose wife he is passionately in love. This chaos is even more extreme in the rough drafts. The girl who commits suicide, Olya, is portrayed in them as Versilov's lover and bears the name Liza. "He was in fact living with Liza. Her mother found out in the end. Upon their meeting Liza first charms him, then torments him the rest of the time. Liza tried to seduce the young prince, but the latter spurned her. Offense. After the death of the step-mother, who had gone out of her mind, Liza hanged herself."

And another note: *"The essence of the novel:* His disorderly love for Liza and the suffering she causes. *His* love and adoration of his wife, and mutual torment. But the secret remains hidden: *His* love-hatred for the princess [Akhmakova]."

In this way, Versilov's original love life was to have been even more complicated and strained; his family relationships were also involved: Arkady was intended to have a brother, a sickly eight-year-old boy, in addition to a sister.Olya (in the novel Liza). The author projected a new dramatic situation: *"He* (Versilov), egoistically torturing himself, bore his wife's death and Liza's suicide [in the novel Olya]. He himself led the boy away and left him on the street. Or: *He* looked after him, used to amuse him by playing with him, [there was no aunt], but the child ran away, and this shattered his pride completely."

All these excess complications have disappeared in the final text. And nonetheless, after the reductions and "polishings," the novel strikes us as being entangled and cumbersome. The author set himself a paradoxical task—to portray formlessness in an artistic form, to contain a picture of chaos in the framework of art.

And so the novel's social-philosophical idea, its plot and heroes, are all antithetical to Tolstoy. The heroes of *War and Peace* have their strength in their fidelity to their birth; Versilov is an ideational traitor to his class; it is not without reason that in the rough drafts the name Brutilov (from Brutus) was first given to him; his family's history is set in opposition to the Rostov household. The author entered a reminder in his notebook: "N. B. Carefully go over the books on the Rostovs and so forth." The raw youth's severance from his ancestral tree is symbolized by his illegitimacy: he bears the celebrated noble name of the Dolgorukys; however, he is not a prince, but "simply Dolgoruky."[2]

The author proposed to show the "disorder" of Russian life not only in its family and social relations, but also in political movements. We have already cited Versilov's words: "Dolgushin is moral disorder." A letter of Dostoevsky's to V. F. Putsykovich testifies to his interest in the Dolgushin case, which was tried July 9-15, 1874: "Two weeks ago," he writes, "during my stay on my way through Petersburg, when

[2] The Princes Dolgoruky came from one of the most ancient and influential families in Russian history. They traced their descent from Yury Dolgoruky (the Long-Arm), son of Vladimir Monomakh and Grand Prince of Kiev intermittently from 1149 until his death in 1158. A Russian hearing the surname would naturally think of the noble family, and hence the misunderstanding that occurs in the novel.

you so obligingly promised to gather information from the newspapers for me about the trial of Dulgushin and comp., I did not succeed in calling on you for the papers. . . . *I absolutely* need those issues for the literary work in which I'm now engaged." Dostoevsky used the details of the trial to depict Dergachyov's circle in the novel. In the copybooks Dergachyov still bears the name Dolgushin. Dostoevsky says of him: "He was a technician and had a job in Petersburg." Dolgushin actually did manage a certain Vereshchagin's tinshop. The external appearance of Dergachyov, "medium height, broad-shouldered, a powerful dark-haired man with a big beard," corresponds exactly to Dolgushin's description. In the novel the circle consists of ten persons and meets on the Petersburg side. This was also true in reality. From Dergachyov's entourage the writer singles out "a tall, swarthy man, with black whiskers, who talked a lot, about twenty-seven years old," to whom he gives the name Tikhomirov, and "a young lad in a Russian jerkin, a peasant." They correspond to two Dolgushinists: Panin and the peasant Anany Vasilyev. The name Tikhomirov, which the novelist chose, was also mentioned at the time of the trial. At Dolgushin's on the wall there was an inscription: "*Quae medicamenta non sanant.* . . ." In the novel we read: "We had just entered the tiny anteroom, when voices were heard: it seems they were disputing heatedly and someone shouted: '*Quae medicamenta non sanant – ferrum sanat, quae ferrum non sanat – ignis sanat!*'"

At the trial it was stated that a crucifix hung in Dolgushin's apartment, and on it was the inscription: "Liberty, equality, fraternity." Dostoevsky changes the crucifix into "an icon without a silver covering, but with a lamp burning before it." Before the court Dolgushin's wife testified that she was often obliged to leave the sessions, since she was nursing a child. The writer did not let even this detail escape. In the novel, Dergachyov's wife "having nodded to the raw youth, immediately went out." And the latter adds: "It seems, apparently, she was also taking part in the dispute, and went out to feed her child."

With scrupulous precision the "realist" Dostoevsky reproduced the externals of the revolutionary circle's life. The internals are hardly noted in the novel. One small scene and several cursory references are devoted to Dergachyov's group. At the meeting "the teacher with black whiskers" (Tikhomirov) preaches "zeal for the cause that is universal to mankind." "Humanity is on the eve of its regeneration, and it has already begun," he cries to Kraft. "Leave Russia alone, if you've lost faith in her and work for the people of the future, those yet unknown, but who will be made up of all mankind, without distinction of race." The raw youth protests against this theoretical love of mankind, defending personality and its freedom. Dergachyov's wife, holding the child at her breast, says from behind the slightly opened door: "One must live according to the laws of nature and truth." These two ideals—"universal mankind" and "return to nature"—exhaust the characteristics of Dostoevsky's "revolutionaries." If one compares the scene *At Ours* in *The Devils* and the session of Dergachyov's circle in *A Raw Youth,* one is struck by the modification of the writer's view regarding the social movement in Russia. The nihilists in the first novel are criminals, murderers, destroyers: they are the devils and imps who have settled in the herd of swine; the revolutionaries in the second novel are utopians daydreaming in the spirit of Fourier, Christian socialists reminding one of the Petrashivists. The author treats the first with violent hatred, the second—with disdainful condescension. The raisonneur Vasin says of Dergachyov's circle: "All these young people are mostly talkers and nothing more." Another character in the novel, Kraft, remarks about them: "They're no more stupid than others and no smarter: they're crazy, like everyone."

Such unexpected indulgence toward the revolutionaries on the part of the writer is explained not simply by the fact that *A Raw Youth* was printed in the left-wing journal *Fatherland Notes.* Dostoevsky saw that the revolutionaries of the seventies were in many ways different from the nihilists of the sixties. The Dolgushinists were idealists, aspired to create a "religion of brotherhood" and based their communism on the Gospel ideal. Dolgushin's proclamation *To the Russian People* began with an epigraph from the Gospels. This new generation, seized by religious pathos, "went to the people."

The sketchbooks permit us to conjecture that the revolutionary populism of the seventies was originally allotted a much more important place in the novel. The author contemplated an encounter of the raw youth with Dergachyov's circle. He noted down: "At Dolgushin's they took him for a spy, but it proved to be someone else. Yet the youth was offended by their suspicion, and with his soul wronged on all sides, did not know to whom to go." In the novel, the self-satisfied theoretician Vasin visits the meetings at Dergachyov's, but ideationally is not connected with him. In the rough draft he is characterized as a nihilist and revolutionary: "Vasin (the ideal nihilist) is a model of reason and logic (and heart) with an abundance of folly. Vasin says: 'Though revolution will not be of any use to us now, nevertheless, since there is nothing else to occupy us, we must engage in revolution. There's no direct advantage, except that the idea is sustained, examples are pointed out and continual experience is gained for future revolutionaries. This alone is worthwhile so as not to give up the idea. Nothing is done in one stroke; unfortunately, it seems, I am the only one of us who admits this idea, whereas everyone else here, just as soon as he enters on a society, does so with the inevitable goal of suddenly attaining everything at once and believes in this. Believes to such an extent that if he did not believe, then he wouldn't have undertaken the affair. . . . I don't believe, but I begin. I believe in the future. And, besides, what activity is there, except revolution, when, except for it, there's nothing at all one can do.'" Dostoevsky recognized a new psychological type, the revolutionary-nationalist, logician, pragmatist. In the long run, he was destined to gain ascendency and overcome the old type, the enthusiast-dreamer. The utopian socialism of the French school was succeeded by "scientific" German marxism. The future bolshevism's passion for technology and industrialization is foreseen in the following remarkable notation: "The young generation has not forgotten the face of a young man, a rich landowner, who had studied with the Germans as a laborer in a factory, in a technical plant. He was at a gathering at Dolgushin's 'I advise you, gentlemen, to direct your attention to the technical side and study technology.' 'Serve a machine?' 'No, gentlemen, join with us through all Russia; if only the technical side goes well, then an upheaval (a revolution) will take place, incomparably more forceful and successful than all your appeals to the people.'"

These prophetic words were written in the year 1874!

The revolutionary-populist Dolgushin served Dostoevsky as the prototype of Dergachyov, the student Kramer—as Kraft's prototype. I. I. Lapshin has explicated the origin of this antipode of Shatov.[D] A. F. Koni, in his memoirs, tells about the student Kramer who constantly engaged Professor B. N. Chicherin in debate. He committed suicide because he had come to the conclusion that the Russian people had no historical future and were destined only to serve as manure

[D] I. I. Lapshin. *Obrazovaniye tipa Krafta v "Podrostke"* (The Development of the Character Kraft in *A Raw Youth*). *Sbornik statey o Dostoevskom* (A Collection of Articles about Dostoevsky), ed. A. L. Bem. Prague, 1929.

for younger peoples who, probably, would come from the East. Before his death, he wrote in his diary: "Soon it'll be 12 o'clock! Everything is ready. I have a slight chill and I'm yawning a little, but am completely calm. I wanted to drink some cognac, but wine, they say, increases the blood flow, and even without that I'll cause a mess here. What a bad book Donders' *Anatomy* is! Two big volumes of close print, and it's impossible to find how to determine where the heart is accurately. Now it's 12 o'clock. There's no one for me to send a last 'forgive me' to and no one to remember with thanks. There is one man for whom, dying, I feel deep respect. It's the former professor of Moscow University, Boris Nikolayevich Chicherin. If the person into whose hands this diary falls finds it possible to tell him of this, then I ask him to do so. It's time!!" And Koni adds: "Along this page of the diary there extended a dried trickle of spattered blood."

On the basis of these facts, the writer created the unforgettable image of the ideational suicide. The raw youth meets Kraft in Dergachyov's circle: "Kraft's face," he writes, "I shall never forget. There was no particular beauty in it, but something, which was perhaps too mild and delicate, although personal dignity was conspicuous in everything about him. He was twenty-six years old, rather thin, above medium height, fair-haired, with a serious, but tender face; there was something gentle about his whole personality." Dergachyov informs the circle of Kraft's idea. "He [i.e., Kraft], in consequence of a very ordinary fact, has come to a very extraordinary conclusion, that has surprised us all. He has deduced that the Russian people are a second-rate people, who are predestined to serve as the material for a nobler race, and not to have its independent role in the fate of mankind. In view of this deduction of his, which is perhaps even true, Mr. Kraft has arrived at the conclusion that all future activity on the part of every Russian must be paralysed by this idea, so to speak, everyone must sit with his hands folded." Kraft is Shatov's ideational antithesis; the latter passionately believes in Russia's calling, the former just as resolutely denies it. The first lives and breathes the idea of Russian messianism, the second has lost faith in it, and kills himself. It is said of Shatov that he shrinks under the stone of an idea that has gripped him. Kraft is also characterized this way. Vasin remarks about him: "Kraft doesn't have merely a logical conclusion, but so to speak, a *conclusion which has been transformed into feeling.* Not all natures are alike: with many people a logical conclusion is sometimes transformed into the most powerful feeling, which seizes the whole being. . . ."

But Kraft is not only related to Shatov ideationally: he also recalls him in his external appearance and character. Both of them are gentle, shy, pensive, and tender.

The student Kramer's suicide served the writer as material for his account of Kraft's suicide. Vasin informs the raw youth: "Kraft shot himself with a revolver yesterday, just at nightfall, as was evident from his diary. The last entry in the diary was made just before the fatal shot, and he remarks in it that he was writing almost in the dark, barely able to make out the letters: he didn't want to light a candle though, afraid that it might start a fire after him. 'And I don't want to light one so that I have to extinguish it again before the shot, as I will my life,' he added strangely almost in the final line...." The raw youth asks Vasin if he can recall any other notation from the suicide's diary and the latter cites several lines, approximately an hour before the shooting, about how "he had a chill and that he had thought of drinking a glass of wine to warm himself, but was stopped by the thought that this, perhaps, would increase the hemorrhaging."

Dostoevsky changed the hour of the suicide: instead of twelve o'clock—it is twilight; he added the detail of the candle—and with this underlined the symbolic meaning of the death: Kraft is extinguishing his own life, like a candle; the darkness of night and death follows.

Kraft is opposed to Shatov and parallel to another ideational suicide —Kirilov. The hero of *The Devils* has lost faith in God and cannot live without God. Kraft cannot live without faith in Russia. Both arrive at suicide through logic. But comparing the description of these two deaths, we are again persuaded of the difference of *artistic tonality* in *The Devils* and *A Raw Youth*. The scene of Kirilov's suicide is full of unbearable horror; Kraft's ruin is depicted in soft, lyric tones. The first is preceded by the "man-god's" unseemly, cynical argument with Pyotr Verkhovensky; the second, by the sad, poetic conversation of the "victim of an idea" with the raw youth.

In Dostoevsky's work *The Devils* is hell, *A Raw Youth*—purgatory.

The composition of *A Raw Youth* is based on those same laws of "expressive art," according to which all the "novel-tragedies" are built. In it we find the action concentrated around the main hero, dynamic development of the plot and the device of arousing the reader's interest. But the writer did not repeat himself: the compositional schema, worked out in *The Devils*, was rethought and acquired a new artistic import. The words of Hamlet: "The time is out of joint" could have served as an epigraph to the novel. Mankind has abandoned God and been left alone on earth. Together with the idea of God, the idea of the *unity of the world* is also out of joint. Mankind no longer forms a single family, all have been separated; fraternal communion has been replaced by hostility, harmony, by "disorder."

In his former novels the author depicted the fate of the man of this "troubled time" (Raskolnikov, Prince Myshkin, Stavrogin), he was occupied with the problem of the strong personality, who had lost God and fallen out of the old Christian world-order. In brilliant symbols he had shown its terrible freedom and tragic solitude. In *A Raw Youth* he posed a question not about the isolated individual, but about human society. *Can mankind establish itself on earth without God?* This religious-social idea predetermines the structure of the novel. The crisis of the communal is shown in that organic cell from which society grows—in the family. The novel is conceived in the form of a "family chronicle." As in *The Devils*, the action is concentrated around the hero, but Versilov's personality is revealed differently than Stavrogin's personality. The hero of *The Devils* is connected with the other dramatis personae ideationally; Versilov's personality embraces the entire history of his family; *it is organically collective.*[8] Stavrogin is the *idea center* of the novel; Versilov is the *center of life.* He is the progenitor, the father, and husband. His tragic fate determines the destiny of his double family, his dichotomy is transferred to the dichotomy of his children. The principle of constructing the action around the hero receives a new, deeper basis. The characters are joined to Versilov by natural blood bonds: they are his children or relatives. Shatov, Kirilov, Pyotr Verkhovensky are Stavrogin's embodied ideas; Arkady, Liza, Anna Andreyevna are parts of Versilov's soul, flesh of his flesh. The conflicts of *The Devils* are expressed in the disciples' struggle against their teacher; the conflicts of *A Raw Youth*, in the discord between father and children. The ideational drama passes over into a family tragedy.

[8] The term "organically collective" (*soborny*) is here not used in a purely technical sense. It is, however, associated with a central philosophical concept of the Slavophile theorist Aleksey Stepanovich Khomyakov (1804-1860). This remarkable and versatile thinker was an important philosopher, a founder of the Slavophile movement, one of the major 19th century Orthodox theologians, as well as poet, dramatist, and historian. In his ideational system "organic collectivity" is defined in reference to the Church as "the free unity of the members of the Church in their common understanding of truth and finding salvation together—a unity based upon their unanimous love for Christ and Divine righteousness." (See N. Lossky's *History of Russian Philosophy.*) Khomyakov's influence can readily be felt upon Dostoevsky's thought and the latter's ideas of personality, freedom, love for Christ and the "complete universality of mankind."

In the novel's complex counterpoint, it is possible to distinguish several themes, which are disposed according to the scales of their decreasing importance. The main subject, Versilov's love life, falls into two motifs: his love for his wife and passion for Akhmakova; the second theme, the raw youth's biography, is indissolubly interwoven with the first. The son's life depends functionally on the life of his father and is conditioned by love-hate, attraction and repulsion. Two secondary themes go further: the liaison of Versilov's daughter Liza with the young Prince Sokolsky and the intrigue of his other daughter, Anna Andreyevna, with old Prince Sokolsky. The duality of the father's feelings is reflected in the love life of his daughters: Liza's and Anna Andreyevna's affairs enter into Versilov's fate, revealing its organically collective nature. On a third plane are introduced episodic characters, caught in the centripetal force of the Versilov household. All of them help in the development of the action and by their participation bring it to the catastrophe. As such instruments of the plot we find Auntie Tatyana Pavlovna, Zverev, Kraft, Vasin, Lambert, and his entourage, Dergachyov and his circle, Olya with her mother. Thus, a family principle organizes the vast human world of the novel. The duality in Versilov's soul is the spark from which the flame bursts out in his family. It spreads onto society and engulfs it in its conflagration.

The novelist's art is manifest in the devices of combining and interweaving the four themes and several episodes. The novel is composed of three parts: the first is devoted to the exposition and the first stage of the contention between father and son. It ends with Versilov's complete triumph. The second shows us his spiritual features and leads up to the secret of his passion for Akhmakova. As a parallel, the love histories of his two daughters are developed. In the third, at the threshold of the catastrophe, the figure of the pilgrim Makar Dolgoruky is introduced. This image of spiritual beauty is set in opposition to the chaos of the crumbled world.

The principle of dramatic structure also attains a new style in the novel. The unity of time is observed with striking exactitude and underlined by chronological indications. All the varied events of the first part fall into three days, "the 19th, 20th, and 21st of September of last year." The events of the second part take place in the course of three days: "the 15th, 16th, and 17th of November." Finally, the catastrophe in the third part also occupies "three fateful days." Temporal boundaries are not marked out so precisely in any other novel of Dostoevsky's: the chaotic world of passions and events is set into a sharply delineated framework; not only are the days counted, but sometimes even the minutes. The reader has the hours before his eyes, and by comparison with mathematical time, can judge the precipitate rhythm of the action.

The unity of the novel is dynamic: the main plot, Versilov's passion for Akhmakova, creates the predominating tension: the other plots accompany it as smaller waves follow behind a big one. The writer knows that the force of the catastrophe is proportionate to the duration of tension and endeavors to delay as much as possible the interval between the complication and the denouement. Thus, the origin of the Versilov-Akhmakova motif is indicated only in enigmatic allusions in the second chapter of the first part, and its conclusion is presented in the very finale of the novel. This love-hate passes through the whole novel with a secret tension, now completely disappearing from the field of our vision, then manifesting itself in enigmatic hints, strange acts and ambiguous words. Akhmakova always stands at a distance, hidden, as it were, by a dense fog. The lovers meet only once before the catastrophe. But Versilov's passion constantly occupies and troubles our imagination: we feel it, like a terrible mysterious force which is felt in dull, subterranean bursts. The complication and denouement are the two ends of a bow between which a string is drawn: the farther they are removed from one another, the longer and more tense the string is and the farther the arrow will fly. With the other plots the string is shorter and the shot weaker: we begin to surmise that Liza is having an affair with young Prince Sokolsky at the end of the first part; it concludes long before the final catastrophe. Even weaker is the tension created by the intrigue between the old prince and Anna Andreyevna: it begins only in the second part and ends before the main theme's denouement. Dostoevsky's dynamic composition can be compared with a series of waves, racing toward the shore. The mightiest wave begins to swell earlier than the others, breaks later and with more force: coming in, the smaller waves anticipate the roar of its fall. So, the partial catastrophes prepare the main one and are joined with it in dynamic unity.

This unity subordinates to itself all the complex diversity of the exterior action. Versilov's passion for Akhmakova is suspended, like fate, not only over his beloved, but also over all the dramatis personae. A feeling of fear for the hero and for his entire world increases with each chapter of the novel. The more we learn about him, the deeper we penetrate his divided consciousness the more clearly we understand that he is capable of insanity and crime. The author is not content with our psychological certainty in the inevitability of the catastrophe: he has recourse to a commonplace device of the crime novel: the raw youth possesses a "document" which compromises Akhmakova. If Versilov succeeds in gaining possession of it, he can ruin her: the exterior interest of the intrigue sustains our concern for the heroes' destiny. The story of the fatal letter, its trials, the struggle for it, Lambert's theft of it, Versilov's participation in this plot and the catastrophe caused by the letter creates the novel's second plane—*adventure*. The spiritual discord between father and son is reduced to a base struggle for the document. Versilov's passion for Akhmakova is linked with an attempt at blackmail. Dostoevsky is not afraid sometimes to sacrifice artistry for the sake of sustaining "interest" and he attains his end. In the variety of its happenings, medley of characters, strained passions, and the effect of its conflicts, *A Raw Youth* is the most captivating of all Dostoevsky's novels.

The main hero is enigmatic and his past is plunged in semidarkness. In the beginning of his autobiography, the raw youth speaks about Versilov: "This man, who had so captivated me from my very childhood, who had such an immense influence on the formation of my whole soul and even, perhaps, has himself colored my whole future, this man remains even now in very many ways *completely an enigma* for me." The son knows that his father had been banished from society for a certain "scandalous behavior," that a year ago, in Germany, young Prince Sokolsky had slapped him in the face. The raw youth undertakes the unraveling of Versilov's enigma. "Without fail I must find out the whole truth just as quickly as possible," he says, "for I've come to *judge* this man." The exposition of *A Raw Youth* is parallel to the exposition of *The Devils*: in both cases the enigma of the hero is posited; but the difference that alters the whole ideational significance of the novel is that other people unriddle Stavrogin, whereas Versilov is studied and judged by his own son. The first are prompted by an interest in ideas, the second—by his blood ties and common fate.

The events in *A Raw Youth* strike us as being even more unexpected and strange than the events in *The Devils*. The whole catastrophe is built on a sudden and astonishing series of circumstances: Versilov shatters an icon, the raw youth decides to return the document and discovers its loss; Lambert blackmails Akhmakova, Versilov protects her and wants to kill Lambert; Anna Andreyevna kidnaps the prince and brings him to the raw youth's apartment, etc. In no novel of Dostoevsky's does the "whirlwind of events" rage so furiously as in *A Raw Youth*.

The novel is written in the form of the autobiography of twenty-year-old Arkady Dolgoruky, the landowner Versilov's illegitimate son. This is the "history of his first steps in the sphere of life." It is begun with brief remarks about his father. Versilov, a landowner, was married to a girl of higher society and had a son and daughter by her. He squandered away three fortunes and, having become a widower at the age of twenty-five, began to live with Sofya Andreyevna, the wife of his gardener Makar Dolgoruky; he bought her from her husband and took her abroad. A year later, a son Arkady was born to him and in another year, a daughter Yelizaveta. The boy was raised far away from his family. "I was an outcast," he recollects, "and lodged with strange people almost from my very birth. . . . Before my twentieth year I had scarcely seen my mother." On this, the raw youth's biography is broken off. A month before September 19, the date with which his tale begins, he decided in Moscow "to renounce everyone and now to enter into his idea decidedly." This idea originated with him while he was still in the sixth class of gymnasium, and for its sake he decided to sacrifice going to the university. His father proposes that he come to Petersburg and enter the service. Arkady is tempted by this proposal, although he also fears that this new life will divert him from his main object—from his idea. But a passionate desire to see his father vanquishes these doubts. The deciding reason for his leaving Moscow is a certain "most important document" that makes him "ruler and master of others' fates."

He comes to Petersburg, becomes acquainted with his family, serves as secretary to old Prince Sokolsky, a friend of his father's. Gradually he is drawn into a new life. His inner dichotomy intensifies; on the one side, there is his father's enigmatic world which disturbs and attracts him; on the other, his "idea," which presses him importunately. He wants to find out about his father in order to judge him, and simultaneously attempts to realize his idea: he buys some album at an auction and resells it at great profit. Versilov is carrying on a law suit with the Princes Sokolsky and wins it; a letter falls into Arkady's hands, from which it appears that Versilov's rights to the inheritance are doubtful. With each chapter the rupture between the father's idea and his son's idea is deepened. The proud boy worships Versilov and rebels against him. He says: "It's true that this man's appearance in my life, i.e., for an instant, when I was in my early childhood, produced that fatal shock which set my consciousness in motion. Had he not met me then, my mind, my way of thinking, my fate surely would have been different, despite even the character which fate destined for me, which nonetheless I would not have avoided." Thus the main theme of the novel is posed—*the problem of communality;* man is determined by his character, but his fate is defined in freedom, *in spite of his character;* the influence of one personality on another is limitless; the roots of human interrelationship extend into metaphysical depths; the violation of this organic collectivity of souls is reflected in social upheavals and political catastrophes.

In the raw youth's soul attraction for his father is as strong as repulsion. In opposition to the law of "unity" is set the law of "separation." The personality does not want to be only a part of the whole, it claims to be all. Arkady, cast out of his family, forgotten by his parents, bears in his heart an unhealed wound. He is a wronged and proud boy, who does not forgive injuries. He escapes from his humiliations and sufferings into his "idea." "My idea," he says, "is to be a Rothschild." If communality among people is violated, no communality is necessary. "The entire goal of my idea is isolation. . . . This is the same thing as in a monastery, the same thing as an anchorite's heroic feats." He has already tried his powers: lived half-starving, renounced everything, practiced asceticism. The young dreamer's loving heart is wounded by his adored father's indifference, and he begins to hate people. "Perhaps, from my very first fancies, i.e., almost from my very childhood, I was unable to imagine myself in any other way than in the first place, always and in all turns of life. . . . From twelve years old, I think, i.e., almost from the beginning of real consciousness, I began to dislike people. . . . Yes, I've yearned for might all my life, might and solitude. . . . Solitude and the calm consciousness of strength! Here is the most complete definition of freedom." The world, created by God, is directed by a centripetal force, by unity in love; the proud personality opposes to it a centrifugal force—might in solitude. Dostoevsky, the composer of the greatest contemporary tragedies, creates a dynamic image of world history: before him the tragic spectacle of the antagonism of two forces is revealed: the divine "gathering into one" and demonic separation and fragmenting. To unifying love he opposes not hate, but *might and power.* In this is the genius of his penetration. In God's world there is free accord; in the kingdom of the devil, scattered atoms are compulsorily consolidated by *power and despotism*. Power is by its very nature demonic: it creates not a spiritual community, but a materialistic collective, not the Kingdom of God, but a communistic anthill. The raw youth's idea prepares for the Grand Inquisitor's appearance in *Brothers Karamazov*.

The theme of "proud isolation" passes through all of Dostoevsky's creative work; there is in each soul an "underground." The writer boasted that he was the first to have fathomed the secret of the personality and depicted it as the tragedy of contemporary consciousness. He attributes his own greatest metaphysical discovery to the influence of Pushkin: "Solitude and the calm consciousness of strength!" exclaims the raw youth and quotes: *"For me, enough the consciousness of this. . . .* Even when I was a child," he continues, "I learned the Covetous Knight's monologue in Pushkin by heart; Pushkin produced nothing loftier in idea than this."

The raw youth's idea about "isolation and might" clashes with his dream of his father. In order decidedly to "close himself off and withdraw into his shell," he has to kill the dream. Gossip and vague rumors about Versilov incline him to think that he has been in love with a phantom. Versilov is a wretched, downcast individual, expelled from society, who has disgracefully borne a slap in his face. Arkady writes: "Why, it appears that this man has only been my dream, a dream from my childhood. . . . But what is absurd, is not that formerly I used to dream 'under my blanket,' but that I came for him, again for this *man that I had projected.* . . . And is it his fault that I came to love him and created a *fantastic ideal* out of him?" The first part of the novel—the son's struggle with his "projected father"—ends with the phantom's transformation into a living person. The real Versilov proves to be worthy of his son's love; reality is more beautiful than the dream. On the dramatic effect of "recognition" the finale of the first part is constructed.

Arkady conducts himself arrogantly and peevishly in his family; bitter quarrels take place with his father. After a month, a decisive explanation is given. Versilov guesses his idea and mockingly announces: "I know the essence of your idea: in any event, it is: 'I am withdrawing into a desert!' . . . My feeling is that he wants to become a Rothschild or something like that and withdraw into his own grandeur." The raw youth is amazed at his insight; he was proud of his isolation, and now his shell is broken; with his thoughts and sensations he is entirely contained in his father's consciousness. This real experience of spiritual unity deals a death blow to his idea. "I trembled inside," he notes down. "Of course, all this was chance; he didn't know anything and wasn't speaking about that at all, though he did mention Rothschild; but how could he define my feelings so exactly?"

Arkady is amazed, but not vanquished; he perseveres in his intention to break with his family and, before parting, takes revenge upon his father by telling about his childhood. In the excited, lyric confession are many of the author's personal memories. These pages are full of the most tender poetry. "I remember huge trees around the house, limes, I think, then sometimes the brilliant sunshine at the opened windows, the little front garden with the flowers, the path, and you, mama, I clearly remember, only at one moment, when I was once taken to communion in the church there and you held me up to receive the Gifts and kiss the Chalice: it was summer and a dove flew across through the cupola, in one window and out another. . . ."

He remembers how as a little boy he first saw his father: he was dressed in a pretty little blue frock-coat and driven to a grand house, where Versilov was staying. The latter was standing before a mirror with a notebook in his hand, rehearsing Chatsky's last monologue. His beauty and elegance struck the boy. Then Arkady's hair was pomaded and curled and he was taken in a carriage to an amateur performance at the home of a certain eminent lady. "When you came on, Andrey Petrovich," continues the raw youth, "I was ecstatic to the point of tears, why and for what reason, I myself don't know. . . . All night I was delirious, and by ten o'clock the next day, was already standing outside the study." But the boy was not allowed in, his father drove off from Moscow and he did not see him any more. "It ended by my being taken to boarding school at Touchard's, I who was in love with you and innocent, Andrey Petrovich." There begins the child's sad life at "the little Frenchman's, of Parisian origin, of course, from a family of cobblers." Touchard persecutes him, reproaches his illegitimate birth, beats him, and finally, turns him into a menial. The boy decides to run away to his father, but at the last minute despair seizes him and he stays. Arkady ends his confession with the words: "Here it was from that very moment, that I recognized that besides being a lackey, I was moreover a coward, and my real, genuine development began!"

In *Notes from Underground* Dostoevsky brilliantly analyzed the *disease of consciousness* and discovered the world of *underground psychology*, till then unknown. The "dreamer's" unappeased and wronged thirst for beauty is turned into the underground man's ineffectual malice and cynicism. The idea of Rothschild is the raw youth's underground; the image of beauty flashed before him for an instant in his father's face and after this shining vision the darkness of reality became even more obscure. The father deceived his son's love—he proved to be only an actor playing the role of Chatsky. But Touchard did not delude him: in his school the boy learned the truth about himself: he was a lackey and a coward. Versilov and Touchard are the symbols of Arkady's duality. From this duality, the disease of consciousness begins: a fetid underground is discovered in man's soul.

The confession ends in a sharp break with his father: the youth avenges himself for his statement of love, he throws cruel and unjust accusations into Versilov's face: "I don't love you, Versilov," he shouts at him and threatens: "Take care, Versilov, don't make me your enemy." On the following day he moves to other lodgings. This is the highest point of division: I love–I hate, a beloved father and the worst enemy; his consciousness, delirious with pain, is tossed about between these extremes.

Arkady suspects his father of shameful and base behavior; rumors circulate that he had had an affair with the late daughter of General Akhmakov, that he is concealing his illegitimate child, that Prince Sokolsky slapped him in the face on this account. Versilov helps a poor girl, Olya, and she accuses him of vile intentions; the son is inclined to believe this accusation. In order decisively to persuade himself of his father's moral fall, Arkady returns a letter to him relating to the lawsuit over the inheritance which he has won. And here the effectual disclosure of Versilov's secrets begins: it appears that it was not he who seduced the daughter of Akhmakov, but Prince Sokolsky. Versilov out of compassion for the wronged girl wanted to marry her and concerns himself with the upbringing of the prince's child; he answers Sokolsky's slap with a noble challenge to a duel; he wanted to help Olya disinterestedly and was punished for his good deed; upon learning from the letter that his rights to the inheritance are not fully incontestable, he renounces even his legal share. He unexpectedly grows up in our eyes: this is not an adventurer who has ruined himself and fallen, but a man of lofty soul and outright nobility. Arkady at once passes from hatred toward his father to enraptured adoration. He chokes with ecstasy, throws himself on Vasin's neck and exclaims: "I embrace and kiss you, Vasin!" "For joy?" the latter asks. "For great joy," answers Arkady. "For this man 'was dead and has returned to life, was lost and has been found!' " Thus the sense of the Gospel parable is reversed: it is not the prodigal son who is returning to his father, but a "prodigal" father, torn away from his native land and family roots, who returns to his son. The son's trial of his father is ended: the father is acquitted, his image is disclosed as the *ideal of human nobility*. The first part concludes with a hymn to life and love. Arkady meets his sister Liza on the street. "There was something terribly gay, and even a touch of cunning in her beaming eyes." With joyful exuberance he says to her: "I love you awfully, Liza! Ah, Liza! Let death come, when it must, but meanwhile let's live, live! Let us pity that unfortunate girl [the suicide Olya], but let us bless life all the same, don't you think so? Liza, you know, of course, that Versilov has refused the inheritance? You don't know my soul, Liza, you don't know what this man has meant to me." This astonishing scene on the street is flooded with light. Finding his father presages for the youth a return to life, to happiness, to faith. He breathes deeply, for the first time he has, as it were, come out onto God's earth. Ended is the "isolation and might," the idea of Rothschild is past, the musty underground is finished. Young life overcomes the malady of romantic dreaming. Arkady resurrects.

In the second part, the "revolt" of the raw youth's "passions" is depicted. Two months pass—he is not recognizable: he is dressed foppishly, tosses money around recklessly, dines at the best restaurants, rides in his own chaise. He resumes his tale with this preface: "I now begin the story of my shame and disgrace." His idea is abandoned. The young man is intoxicated with life and seduced by freedom. His mistakes and falls are from his inexperience, naiveté, and generosity. The experience of freedom is purchased at a dear cost. Arkady says to his sister, Anna Andreyevna: "We lived through the Tatar invasion, then two centuries of bondage and no doubt because the one and the other suited our taste. Now freedom has been given us and *we have to endure freedom:* will we know how? Will freedom appear equally according to our taste?—here's the question." The ingenuous dreamer believes that the tragedy of human communality is ended for him: his father loves him, he lives with his sisters in deep friendship, friends surround him with tender care. In a word, for him paradise has already come on earth. Reality deals this utopia a cruel blow. Arkady lives at Prince Sergey Sokolsky's and uses his money as his own. "Alas, all this was done in the name of love, generosity, honor," he writes, "but afterward it appeared unseemly, impudent, dishonorable." His friendship with the prince is broken off by a catastrophe: the raw youth sharply reproaches the friend who has wronged him and the latter hurls into his face: "Can you, having taken my money this whole month, dare say that you didn't know that your sister [Liza] is pregnant by me?" He likewise experiences a bitter disenchantment in love: Katerina Nikolayevna Akhmakova confesses that she encouraged him, counting on his "impulsiveness" and hoping to learn from him about the document compromising her. But for him most tormenting of all are relations with his father. Versilov frequently visits him, trustingly confides his thoughts, convictions to him, initiates him into his intimate life, and meanwhile a real closeness does not develop between father and son. The raw youth senses that his father has some kind of secret and he cannot penetrate it. Versilov sees his son's moral decline and does nothing to open his eyes and save him from disgrace. He does not wish to "intrude at another's expense into another's conscience." When his son reproaches him with indifference, he declares: "I repeat to you: Once I really did meddle with others' consciences—a most inconvenient maneuver!" No, this is not the apathy of a man who has lost faith in good, but profound regard for another's personality and preservation of its moral freedom.

The second part ends for Arkady with a double catastrophe: he suddenly surmises from a note of Versilov's to Akhmakova his father's tragic passion for the woman with whom he himself is in love: after winning at roulette, the money is stolen from him, he is accused of theft and is disgracefully thrown out of the gambling casino. He falls ill with a fever and for ten days lies unconscious.

In the third part, the youth is entirely caught up in the whirlwind of events taking place around him, is drawn into his father's tragedy; from a hero he is turned into a witness and chronicler. The bitter experience of his falls and passions teaches the impulsive adolescent a valuable lesson; from a raw youth he becomes an adult and perceives the dichotomy of his nature. Yes, in his soul coexist a yearning for beauty and a base longing for Akhmakova. "This was because," he writes, "I had the soul of a spider. . . . And this was the person who wanted to get away from them and from the whole world in the name of 'sightliness!' The longing for sightliness was still there, of course, and very intense, but in what way could it be joined with the other longings, really God knows what longings—this is a mystery to me. And it always has been a mystery and I have marveled a thousand times at this capacity in man (and, it seems, in the Russian man pre-eminently) to cherish in his soul the loftiest idea right alongside of the greatest villainy, and all quite sincerely. Whether this is breadth peculiar to the Russian, which takes him so far, or simple baseness—here is the question!"

The raw youth's self-knowledge culminates in a fatal question. Duality, antinomy of soul, is the final word about him and about Versilov. However, they are not the exception, but the rule. *Every human consciousness is inwardly contradictory.* All of Dostoevsky's creative work speaks about this "underground truth." It is summarized in the unforgettable words of Mitya Karamazov about God's struggle with the devil in the human soul.

The idea of the "family chronicle" and the meaning of the hero's drama is expressed by Versilov. "You see, my friend," he says to his son, "I have known for a long time already, that we have children who brood from childhood over their family, being offended by their fathers' unsightliness and their surroundings. . . . I always imagined you one of these little creatures, conscious of being gifted and doomed to isolation. Like you, I also never liked my school fellows. It is sad for those beings who are abandoned to their own resources and fancies alone and have a passionate, premature, and almost vindictive longing for sightliness."

So the idea of *A Raw Youth* is naturally connected with the idea of *The Devils.* The contemporary crisis is a crisis of aesthetic consciousness. The ideal of beauty has been muddled, but mankind cannot live without beauty. Dostoevsky resolutely affirmed that "it is possible to live without bread, but without beauty it is altogether impossible." The young generation is offended by the "unsightliness" of their fathers. At the core of social disturbance is the disintegration of the family. In its infirmity is reflected the world crisis, which mankind is experiencing. The idea of the "family tragedy" of *The Brothers Karamazov* evolves out of the family chronicle, *A Raw Youth.* Versilov's "haphazard household" in the process of its decomposition must generate the household of the Karamazovs.

But the raw youth's confession is only the "history of his first steps." The "revolt of the passions" and the investigation of freedom—this is his *éducation sentimentale.* At the conclusion of his notes he writes: "Having finished writing the last line, I suddenly felt that I had re-educated my own self. My old life has vanished altogether, and a new is scarcely begun." Arkady sends the autobiography to his old tutor Nikolay Semyonovich and the latter answers him: "Yes, Arkady Makarovich, you are a member of a haphazard household. . . . Oh, when the evil of the day has passed and the future has come, then some future artist will discover beautiful forms even for depicting past disorder and chaos!"

The Devils ends with universal destruction; Russia presented itself to the writer as sick, possessed by devils; the somber night was illuminated by a fire of sedition. *A Raw Youth* concludes with faith in a new life, in a new ideal of beauty. Dostoevsky dreamt of finding "beautiful forms" and creating an art with which to depict contemporary chaos. "Disorder" is only a stage in development; Arkady did not perish in chaos; the experience re-educated him and tempered him for a new life. After hell (*The Devils*) and purgatory (*A Raw Youth*) the writer intended a poem about paradise (*Brothers Karamazov*). Death cut short his ascent at the very beginning.

The theme of the raw youth brings us to the theme of the novel's main hero—Versilov. We cannot approach him by any other way: *the father is revealed to us through his son's consciousness.* Versilov does not exist for us objectively: we see him only through the eyes of Arkady, as a figure of his creative imagination. At first the son is hostile toward his father, and the father's character is presented to us as equivocal and depraved; to the degree they come together, the father's image clears up and grows in beauty. With brilliant perspicacity Dostoevsky depicts Versilov's communality with the raw youth as a spiritual unity, a mystical joining of "I" and "thou." In the father, the son unriddles his own personal enigma and together with that the *enigma of man:* he understands not only the unity, but also the universality of personality. The raw youth's dichotomy is reflected, as in a mirror, in Versilov's duality; his yearning for sightliness finds an ideal of beauty in him; his passions are answered by his father's "fatal" passion. This cognition of the father passes through stages corresponding to the son's perception of his vital experience and spiritual state. And only at the end of the novel does the father appear in all his stature before Arkady, now grown up and re-educated.

The child's first meeting with his unknown father is deeply symbolic. Versilov appears to him as a shining vision in a halo of beauty and nobility. "As now, I see you as you were then," Arkady recalls, "flourishing and handsome; what wonderful hair you had, almost completely black with polished lustre, without the least bit of grey: your face of a dull pallor—pale, your burning and dark eyes and gleaming teeth, especially when you laughed." How the ten-year-old boy committed all the details of his costume to memory: the dark-blue velvet jacket, the solferino-colored necktie, the shirt with Alençon lace! And the "image of beauty" pierced his heart forever. Versilov is as handsome a man as Stavrogin, but his beauty is not a dead mask, but passionate, exerted life. However this image may be divided and distorted afterward, the stamp of nobility on it will not be effaced. Stavrogin surrenders himself to the spirit of nonbeing, Versilov is saved by his "ardent heart." It is not without reason that the boy first see his father on the stage in the role of Chatsky. Versilov is the spiritual son of the fiery hero of *Woe from Wit*. He is just such a dreamer without family and race, an alien in his own land, an eternal wanderer. He also has a "mind not in harmony with his heart."

Versilov's two countenances are embodied in the two female figures, who stand on either side of him: the hero has a dual life, a dual love. His wife, Sofya Andreyevna, he loves with a deep, compassionate love; he is drawn to Katerina Nikolayevna Akhmakova by irresistible passion. The first love is depicted precisely, is illumined by a bright light, the second is plunged in obscurity and only at the denouement bursts out in dazzling and ruinous fire. The artistic device of the double illumination runs throughout the whole novel. His love for Sofya Andreyevna, "mama"—this is Versilov's day; his passion for Akhmakova is his night. The first is his free self-determination and joyful life; the second is "fate" and the enticement of ruin.

The young widower, a landowner, came to his village and took as his mistress an eighteen-year-old peasant girl, who had just been given in marriage to the old gardener Makar Ivanovich. She was not a beauty and Versilov's impulse is not explained by depravity and "a master's rights." In fact, there was not even an impulse. He himself did not understand how this happened. To his son's question, the father "on one occasion mumbled somewhat strangely that his mother was one of those *defenseless* individuals whom you do not fall in love with— quite the contrary; somehow, suddenly, for some reason *you pity* them for their meekness, though one cannot say what for. That no one ever knows, but you go on pitying them for a long time, pity them and grow attached." This love-pity is stronger than the most fiery passion, its source is mystical. It is an earthly reflection of a heavenly mystery. The semiliterate, silent, gentle, meek Sofya Andreyevna does not refrain from being unfaithful to her husband, takes the sin upon her soul, because *it must be so:* Versilov has from eternity been predestined as her companion, she is his heavenly friend. Her very name—Sofya— is mysteriously significant. In the poor orphaned peasant girl lives the image of the Eternal Feminine, Sophia, the Divine Wisdom. Makar Ivanovich gives up his wife to his owner and becomes a pilgrim. He visits her once in every three years; treats her with paternal tenderness and a certain enigmatic respect. Versilov's "strange liaison" with the "defenseless" orphan is in subject linked with Stavrogin's "strange" marriage to the cripple. Sofya Andreyevna is a mystical figure, as is Marya Timofeyevna. She too is the soul of the world, Psyche, oppressed in the bondage of evil and yearning for her savior. Marya Timofeyevna's guilt is indicated symbolically: she is a "halfwit" and lame; Sofya Andreyevna's guilt is defined psychologically: her sin against her "just" husband, Makar Ivanovich. Even in external appearance, the raw youth's mother is remarkably like Stavrogin's wife. "Her face had a look of simplicity, but by no means of stupidity; it was somewhat pale, anaemic. Her cheeks were very thin, even hollow, and her forehead was already strongly lined by wrinkles, but there were still none around her eyes and her eyes, rather large and open, shone always with a gentle and serene light. . . . In her face there was nothing at all particularly melancholy or drawn; on the contrary, her expression would have been even gay, if she had not been troubled so often." This is almost a portrait of Marya Timofeyevna. The cripple is connected with a monastery, a religious mode of life, prophetic pilgrim-women. Sofya Andreyevna is joined in her son's memoirs with the village church and the Chalice with the Holy Gifts. High above her head a dove flies past through the cupola. Thus her spirituality is symbolized. If Sofya Andreyevna is compared with Marya Timofeyevna, then Versilov is sharply set in opposition to Stavrogin. The divine light burning in his companion does not arouse diabolic malice in him; he senses her spiritual excellence and bows before it, in spite of all his skeptical derisions. He tells his son with affection and irony about his family life: "Your mother and I have spent all these twenty years together in silence. . . . The chief characteristic of all our twenty years' relationship has been its—reticence. . . . Humility, submissiveness, self-abasement, and at the same time firmness, strength, *real strength*, this is your mother's character. Keep in mind that she is the best of all the women whom I've met on earth." And Versilov adds that her strength comes from the common people. In his peasant wife, there is placed in opposition to him a Russian wanderer uprooted from the soil, the "Russian people's great viable strength." Sofya Andreyevna is not only the bearer of the religious principle, but also the embodiment of the people's soul. In her image Dostoevsky sees his own holy-of-holies, mystical Russia. The blessed image of the Russian mother is the writer's greatest creation. When he is shamefully thrown out of the gambling casino, Arkady, as he lies freezing on the street, recalls his mother. She had visited him at Touchard's boarding school, brought him a little parcel with treats. The boy felt ashamed of his poor guest. "I only looked sideways at her darkish, old dress, rather coarse, almost working-class hands, her quite coarse shoes and her terribly thin face." Leaving, the mother had asked Touchard and his wife "not to abandon the orphan, he is just an orphan now, but to show him your kindness" and with tears bowed down to the ground as "simple people" bow. Then saying goodbye to her son: " 'Well, Lord . . . well, the Lord be with you . . . well, the heavenly angels, Most Honorable Mother, Nikolay the Saint keep you. Lord, Lord!' she repeated, speaking rapidly, crossing me, and trying to make as many signs of the cross over me as she possibly could: 'You're my little dove, my darling. . . .' " And she gave him a little blue-checked handkerchief with a tightly fastened knot at the corner, in which there were four twenty-kopeck pieces. This image of the mother, sorrowing and humble, is almost an icon.

———————

Versilov's bright countenance is directed toward Sofya Andreyevna, his companion, not of this earth. . . . His dark one is turned toward his earthly love—Katerina Nikolayevna Akhmakova. Through the extent of the novel's first two parts, the truth of this love remains hidden from us by a dense veil of gossip, slander, hideous suspicions. The son has heard that something suspicious occurred abroad between his father and this woman and that an old enmity separates them. He is predisposed against Akhmakova, and, meeting her for the first time at Prince Sokolsky's, sees an enemy in her. "Her face seemed to contract, she threw a nasty glance at me and smiled impudently." And still he is struck by her beauty. The author repeats the device he used in *The Idiot* to depict Nastasya Filippovna: the hero first sees a portrait of the beauty, and then her herself.

"The side door opened," recalls the raw youth, "and *that woman appeared*. I already knew her face from the wonderful portrait that hung in the prince's study; I had been scrutinizing this portrait all that month. I spent about three minutes in the study in her presence and did not tear my eyes from her face for one second. . . . But if I had not known the portrait and had been asked, after those three minutes, what she was like—I wouldn't have answered anything because all was confused within me. . . . From those three minutes I only remember a certain *really beautiful woman*. . . ." This is how the "fatal" beauty, Akhmakova, is introduced. Beauty is a terrible force and its action on the human soul is inexplicable and powerful; we have already a presentiment of Versilov's tragedy. Arkady's hostility toward Akhmakova changes into devotion and ends in passionate love. Not suspecting that he is his father's rival, with the clear-sightedness of love, he divines Katerina Nikolayevna's character. She, whom he considered a fatal beauty, a dangerous and depraved aristocrat, proves to be an infinitely ingenuous and bashfully chaste woman. Her secret is that she has no secret; she is life itself, inconceivably simple and clear. The youth says to her, breathless with rapture and emotion:

"I can't bear your smile any longer. Why did I picture you even in Moscow as formidable, magnificent, and using spiteful drawing room phrases. . . . The expression of your face is childish mischief and boundless simplicity—there! . . . As soon as I saw you, I was blinded. Your portrait is not at all like you; your eyes are not dark, but light and only seem dark from your long lashes. You are plump, you're of medium height, but you have a buxom fullness, the light full figure of a healthy country girl. Yes, and your face too really is countrified, the face of a village beauty, a round, ruddy, clear, bold, laughing . . . and bashful face! That's right, bashful! Bashful! of Katerina Nikolayevna Akhmakova! Bashful and chaste, I swear it! More than chaste—childlike! . . . You have a cheerful mind, but without any embellishments. . . . Another thing I like is that your smile never leaves you: that's my paradise! I also like your calm, your quietness. Your bosom is high, your bearing light, you have extraordinary beauty, but you are not proud!"

The image of the mother is opposed by the image of the lover: the martyr-like humility of the one by the chaste and joyful beauty of the other. All of Dostoevsky's feminine world divides into these two categories: his heroines are either meek "sisters of mercy," knowing only how to love maternally (the clearest image of all is Sonya Marmeladova), or lovers dazzling in beauty and the enchantment of youth. The first come down into the world with sacrificial love; the second lacerate and destroy their victims in the fire of eros. Nastasya Filippovna, Akhmakova, Grushenka—psychologically distinct—are unified by the erotic element present in them. From his youthful years, Dostoevsky was filled with a vague yearning for the "living life." Its light used to flash before him for a second in the ecstasy before an epileptic fit. He *knew* it, but could not define it. Versilov expresses it "a vision inconceivable to the mind." Sergey Sokolsky asks him mockingly: "And what then is this *living life*, according to you?" "I don't know, prince," he answers. "I only know that it must be something terribly *simple*, quite ordinary, staring us in the face, every day and every minute and so *simple*, that we cannot in any way believe that it's so simple and have naturally been passing it by for many thousands of years, without noticing and without recognizing it."

After his meeting with Akhmakova, Arkady confides in his father and tells him of his love. Suddenly his voice trembles and he declares with emotion: "Listen, Andrey Petrovich, listen: that woman is what you were saying just before at the prince's about 'living life'—remember? Well, holding such a view, you have even met the ideal woman, and in perfection, in the ideal, you recognized 'all the vices.' "

The mystery of Versilov's dark countenance begins to unravel: the Russian European, the spiritual pilgrim, confusedly knows about "living life" and yearns for it. And here "living life" itself appears to him in Russian beauty, simple and ingenuous. But his soul is already poisoned by doubt, his heart is depraved by spiritual rambling and he does not see, does not understand, does not believe in the "perfection" offered to him. Akhmakova summons forth an evil passion in him and instead of salvation brings destruction to him. She is simplicity and integrity, he is complexity and dissipation. She lives, and in this is her grace-filled secret. He only longs for life, dreams and fantasizes. His heavenly companion, Sofya Andreyevna, is too lofty, his earthly love—Akhmakova—is so simple that he cannot come to believe in it. His consciousness is torn between unattainable ideals.

In the third part, the secret of his father's passion is suddenly revealed to the son. Upon recovering from his fever, Arkady is once again drawn into the "whirlwind of events." The catastrophe approaches; its effect is heightened by a false denouement. The pilgrim Makar Ivanovich dies; it seems to Versilov that his two years' obsession is ended, that he no longer loves Katerina Nikolayevna. He is free and can marry Sofya Andreyevna. In one of the most wonderful scenes in the novel, the father opens his soul to the son. He had met Katerina Nikolayevna abroad and from the first glance she "bewitched him." "It was fate," he says. The raw youth explains: *"He did not choose* this fate, did not want to love. I don't know if I'll be able to communicate this clearly, but only his whole soul was in turmoil precisely because this could have happened to him. Everything in him, he said, that was free was at one stroke destroyed by this meeting and the man was fettered for life to this woman who had really nothing to do with him. He did not desire this slavery of passion." So the tragedy of Versilov is finally formulized: the struggle of freedom with fate, the free personality's rebellion against the slavery of passion. Triumphantly, with a shining face, like one "resurrected from the dead," he speaks about his great and unique love for Sofya Andreyevna and tenderly kisses her portrait. But suddenly after this illumination, ominous gloom descends. The father does not come to Makar Ivanovich's funeral; "mama" waits for him in unbearable excitement; at last, he appears, speaks in a kind of delirium and laughs an insane laugh. "You know, I feel as though I were really split in two. Right beside you stands your double; you are sensible and rational yourself, and he wants without fail to do something absurd beside you and at times something very funny." "You know, Sonya," he remarks to his wife, pointing to the ancient icon left to him by Makar Ivanovich, "here I've taken up the icon again and you know, I have a terrible desire now, this second, to smash it against the stove, against this very corner. I am sure it would break into two halves at one stroke—neither more nor less." And he shatters the image.

Versilov's duality is underlined by the motif of a "double." The son does not believe that his father committed this terrible symbolic act in a fit of mental derangement, "but," he adds, "his double was unmistakably beside him, of that there was no doubt." Versilov stands on the border of insanity. Fate draws him into its abyss, he is threatened with the lot of Stavrogin and Ivan Karamazov, the struggle with God, demonic possession, a double-devil. A rendezvous of the lovers takes place; the whole movement of the plot has prepared us for this *sole* dialogue between the hero and the heroine. Akhmakova openly confesses to Versilov that she loves him with a "general love, with which you love everyone." He docilely asks her not to get married to anyone and suddenly fury breaks out in him: "I'll murder you!" he says with a distorted voice. But, having mastered himself, he lets her go with the words: "No, you and I are both possessed by the same madness! Be always as mad, don't change and we shall meet as friends." Dostoevsky believes that his wanderer will regain his native land, will believe in the "Russian idea"—and then he and Akhmakova will "meet as friends."

In the novel's melodramatic finale the scoundrel Lambert blackmails Katerina Nikolayevna with the letter. Versilov snatches his revolver away from him and strikes him on the head. Akhmakova falls into a faint. The youth relates: "He caught her as she fell unconscious, and with incredible strength lifted her up in his arms, like a feather and began carrying her aimlessly about the room, like a child." Then he laid her on the bed and, suddenly bending over, kissed her twice on the lips. . . . Then he waved the revolver over her. . . . He wanted to shoot both her and himself. The son draws his father's arm aside and the latter wounds himself in the shoulder.

Versilov does not perish: after a terrible crisis he spiritually rises from the dead. "He does not leave mother's side now and will never leave her again. He has even received the 'gift of tears.' . . . Everything that was ideal in him has grown still more." The hero of A Raw Youth drew near to Stavrogin's path, but did not enter upon it. He was saved by the mystical force of life—faith in it and love for it. In Dostoevsky's world-outlook this is the deciding moment. Porfiry Petrovich advises Raskolnikov to trust in life and promises him resurrection; Prince Myshkin preaches the grace of life; Stavrogin perishes because his heart is insensate to life. The elemental "Karamazov" vitality saves Ivan and Dmitry Karamazov. The writer forgives his sinful heroes everything, both crime and downfall; there is one thing he does not forgive: blasphemy against the Holy Spirit, who breathes in all living creatures. Versilov says about himself: "I indeed know that I'm infinitely strong . . . you will in no way destroy me, will not do away with me and will not astound me by anything. *I am as tenacious of life as a watchdog.*" The romantic Dostoevsky had a mystical religion of life.

A Raw Youth was conceived by Dostoevsky as an answer to Lev Tolstoy; in opposition to the households of the Irtenyevs, Rostovs, Bolkonskys are set the households of Versilov and the Sokolskys. The writer with bantering tone depicts the senile old Prince Sokolsky and weak, dishonorable Prince Sergey. But the novel is not merely a criticism of the nobility and exposure of the Tolstoyan "ennobling lie." Versilov is an inspired preacher of the idea of spiritual nobility, of a Russian aristocracy of the spirit.

Prince Sergey "values his title" and out of false pride gets involved in debts and ends with a serious crime and denunciations. Versilov attempts to inspire him to "a loftier thought." "Our nobility," he says, "even now that it has lost its privileges, could remain the leading class, as the custodians of honor, enlightenment, science, and the higher idea, and, what is most important, without closing themselves off into a separate caste, which would be the death of the idea. . . . Let every achievement of honor, science, and heroism here give a man the right to join the ranks of the upper class. In that way, the class itself is converted only into an assembly of the best people, in a literal and true sense." The prince is aroused: "And what sort of nobility would that be?" he objects. "This is a kind of masonic lodge you're proposing, but not a nobility." Versilov falls silent: his "utopia" is inaccessible to the representatives of the "noble caste." But at the end of the novel, in friendly conversation with his son, he returns to his beloved idea and discloses it in all its incomparable poetic brilliance. Versilov's confession to his son is one of the most perfect examples of Dostoevsky's "philosophical lyricism." "*Je suis gentilhomme avant tout et je mourrai gentilhomme!*" excitedly cries the Russian European. "There are perhaps, about a thousand of our sort in Russia: actually, perhaps, no more, but why, this is quite enough for the idea not to die. We're the bearers of the idea, my dear. . . . Yes, my boy, I repeat to you that I cannot help respecting my nobility. Among us there has been created by the ages a type of the highest culture, seen nowhere before, such as does not exist in the entire world—a type of worldwide compassion for all. This is a Russian type, but as it is taken from the most cultured stratum of the Russian people, I have the honor of belonging to it. It safeguards the future of Russia." Versilov is an aristocrat of the spirit, an exponent of the "loftiest Russian thought": the "complete *reconciliation of ideas*," "*worldwide citizenship*." After the emancipation of the serfs he was an arbitrator, and suddenly he was overcome by "the anguish of the Russian nobleman," and left for Europe. "In those days, especially, one seemed to hear the tolling of a funeral bell over Europe." Just after the Franco-Prussian War, the ruins of the Tuileries, burned down by the communards, were still smoking. The sun of European humanity was setting. Peoples were at enmity with one another, closed off in national pride: in Europe at that time there was not a single European. "I alone, as a Russian," declares Versilov, "was the *sole European* in Europe then."

The Russian incorporates a "complete union of ideas"; he becomes most Russian when he is most a European. "I am in France a Frenchman; with a German, a German; with an ancient Greek, a Greek; and by that very fact I am most typically Russian. By that very fact I am a true Russian and am most truly serving Russia, for I demonstrate her main idea. I am a pioneer of this idea." A thousand of the best men, created by the ages of Russia's history, bear the Russian *universal idea* to the world. It is the synthesis and culmination of all ideas. It is completely universal to mankind and worldwide. The assertion that the Russian cultured type is superior to all others, may seem too arrogant, and the universality of the Russian idea may cause doubt. One thing is indisputable: by his personality and creative work Dostoevsky demonstrated that the gift of "universality" does really lie in the depth of the Russian spirit. He justifies his teaching about the messianism of Russia by *his own genius*. Many vicious and unjust remarks about foreigners are met in his works; frequently he was blinded by hatred when he wrote about Europe. But not one Russian writer spoke with such devout love about the old, dying world. This hymn to Europe is for every Russian a patent of nobility. "I had lived in Europe before," relates Versilov, "but this was a special time and never had I gone there with such inconsolable grief and with such love, as then. . . . To the Russian, Europe is just as precious as Russia; every stone in her is beloved and dear. Europe has been as much our fatherland as Russia. Oh, more so! It's impossible to love Russia more than I love her, but I have never reproached myself that Venice, Rome, Paris, the treasures of their sciences and art, all their history—are dearer to me than Russia. Oh, these old alien stones are dear to Russians. These wonders of God's old world, these *fragments of holy wonders*: and this is dearer to us, than to those people themselves."

The Russian nobleman's completely universal love for mankind is embodied in *the dream of the golden age*. The writer simply excerpted the whole of Stavrogin's dream from the suppressed chapter, *At Tikhon's*, in *The Devils*, but without its tragic finale, the little red spider. The picture of the earthly paradise is inspired by Claude Lorrain's picture *Acis and Galatea:* the islands of the Archipelago, the azure waves, the setting sun, the beautiful and happy people. . . . All his life this dream pursued the writer: the utopia of the golden age illuminates all his novels by its distant radiance. Versilov exclaims: "Marvellous dream, sublime delusion of mankind! The golden age is the most improbable of all the dreams that have ever been, but for it men have given up their entire lives and all their forces; for the sake of it prophets have died and been killed; without it nations will not live and cannot even die!" Dostoevsky was himself such a prophet of this "improbable dream" and not only in the period of his enthusiasm for Fourier and Saint-Simon, but even after penal servitude—always.

Versilov wakes up, his eyes are wet with tears. Slanting rays of the setting sun break through the window of his room. "And here, my friend, and here," he says, "that setting sun of the first day of European humanity, which I had seen in my dream, was immediately transformed for me, as I woke up, in reality, into the setting sun of the last day of European humanity!" He understood that he had come to bury Europe; the great idea of Christian culture was dying, it was being escorted out with catcalls and the flinging of mud; atheism was celebrating its first victories. "I wept," confesses Versilov, "I wept for them, I wept for the old idea and, perhaps, I wept real tears, with no word of exaggeration."

The Russian European, presenting himself as a "philosophical deist," draws a shocking picture of mankind, left without God. . . . Dostoevsky turned many times to the apocalyptic theme; he prophesied a terrible destiny for atheistic humanity: the kingdom of Baal, the communist anthill, "the manners of tigers and crocodiles," troglodytism, transformation into a herd which is tended by the Grand Inquisitor.

In *A Raw Youth* instead of the Apocalypse we find an idyll. This "humanistic utopia" does not suggest horror; but it is full of such piercing, bitter grief, such heart-rending anguish, that the remembrance of it remains in the soul like an unclosed wound. Versilov imagines that the battle has already ended and the struggle ceased. A lull has come, and men have been left *alone*. "The great idea of old has forsaken them; the great source of strength that till then had nourished and warmed them was vanishing, like that majestic, inviting sun in Claude Lorrain's picture. And men suddenly understood that they were left quite alone and at once felt completely orphaned. And here then all the abundance of their former love for God would be turned by men upon nature, on the world, on people, on every little blade of grass. Having become conscious of their own finiteness, they would begin to press to another more closely and more lovingly. They would wake up and would hasten to kiss one another, eager to love, realizing that the days are short, that this is all that is left them. . . . Oh, they would hurry to love in order to extinguish the great sadness in their hearts. . . ." The idea of God's abandonment is turned into the most pure lyric theme: the final day of mankind, the setting sun, men having become orphans, their farewell kisses before eternal separation, the blinding outburst of love as it is extinguished on earth. . . .

Versilov completes his "fantasy" with an unexpected conclusion: "It is remarkable," he confesses, "that I have always ended my picture with a vision, as in Heine's *Christ on the Baltic Sea*. I could not get on without Him, could not help imagining Him finally, in the midst of His orphaned people. He comes to them, stretches out His hands to them and says: 'How could you forget Him!' And then the scales would, as it were, fall away from all their eyes and there resounds the great hymn of the new and last resurrection." In the manuscript the "vision's" religious finale is expressed even more strongly—Versilov says about Christ: "Never could I imagine men without Him. . . . Since once He was here, He cannot go away. And even if He did go away, they themselves would find Him." The picture of atheistic mankind's dying is completed by the "new and last resurrection." Logically this is contradictory and unaccountable, but mystically it is fully justified. If love will burst forth in abandoned mankind, Christ will return to it, for Christ is love. Atheistic humanity worships an unknown god: Dostoevsky believes that the history of the world will end with a new *divine revelation*. The prodigal son, after wandering in the desert, will return to his Father's house.

The father's philosophical conversation with his son occupies two whole chapters in the third part of the novel before the catastrophe. And these abstract deliberations are the apogee of the dramatic tension and artistic perfection. Versilov approaches the last act of his life's tragedy. He is not philosophizing, but deciding his fate; does not meditate, but lives ardently and with inspiration. The ideas-passions, ideas-energies, ideas-images are transformed in Dostoevsky into aesthetic values.

But Versilov, the philosopher-deist and bearer of the idea of "unity," and Versilov, shattered by two loves—is one and the same man. His ideological image is as divided in two, as is his psychological. He confesses that he can "in the most convenient way" feel two opposite feelings at one and the same time and this fills him with contempt for himself. The nobleman, the preacher of the ideal of honor and duty, with repugnance observes in himself the "dishonorable" breadth of his nature. Passionately loving life, he sometimes painfully feels the immorality of his Russian "viability" and "adaptability." "Of course, I love life," he says, "but for one such as me—to love life is vile."

Versilov weeps real tears over the grave of European humanity; in his soul burns a universal love for mankind. But a fatal dichotomy cleaves even this "great" idea in two. He speaks bitter and terrible words about love for mankind: "My dearest," he confesses to his son, "to love men such as they are is impossible. And yet one must. . . . To love one's neighbor and not to despise him is impossible. In my opinion, man is created physically incapable of loving his neighbor. Here there is a kind of mistake in the words from the very beginning, and one must understand 'love for mankind' only for that mankind which you yourself have created in your own soul and which consequently will never exist in actual fact."

In the manuscript, Versilov's paradox is even more pointed: "It is beyond all doubt that Christ could not love us such as we are. He tolerated us, forgave us, but, of course, despised us. At any rate, I could not otherwise understand His holy image, which therefore will never appear in reality."

And not only his "universal love for mankind," but also Versilov's "deism" is connected with tormenting doubts. "One must believe in God, my dear," he says to his son. The latter asks him: "Did you have such strong faith in God?" The father, joking, makes a tragic confession: "My friend, that is perhaps a superfluous question. Let's suppose that I didn't have very great faith. . . ." Old Prince Sokolsky ironically tells about Versilov's religious impulses abroad: "Well, what then?" he asks Arkady, "will your father preach God as before? . . . He particularly liked to frighten me with the day of judgment. . . . Out there, he became a Catholic. . . . Would you believe it, he used to behave as if he were a saint and his relics would be displayed. . . . He used to wear chains." All this is nonsensical gossip, but it faithfully reflects the impression that Versilov produced at that time. And this same man shatters the icon-shrine of the pilgrim Makar and Sofya Andreyevna; the symbolism of this is underlined by his words: "Don't take this for an allegory, Sonya, I broke it, not as Makar's legacy; I only did it to break something. But then, however, take it even as an allegory: *why, really, it must have been so!*"

Versilov is stricken with all the infirmities of contemporary civilization: everything shifts, wavers, and is doubled in his consciousness; ideas are ambiguous, truths—relative, faith—disbelief. But he has one point of support and it saves him from chaos: this point is the *moral imperative*. Versilov believes in the autonomy of the moral will, independent of personal volitions and religious convictions. He likes to repeat: *"One must* believe in God," *"one must* love people, *one must* do good, even if it's while holding one's nose and closing your eyes." To his son's question, what should he do and how is he to live, he advises him to be honorable, not to lie, to keep the ten commandments. "Fulfill them," he adds, "despite all your questionings and doubts and you will be a great man." Versilov's moral teaching is close to Kant's *Critique of Practical Reason;* he alone of all Dostoevsky's heroes presents the idea of *autonomous morality.* In the epilogue to the novel the raw youth's tutor Nikolay Semyonovich gives the definitive formula of Versilov's type: "He is a *nobleman* of the most ancient lineage and at the same time a Parisian *communard.* He is a true *poet* and loves Russia, but on the other hand also denies her completely. He is without any religion, but is ready almost to die for something indefinite, which he cannot even name, but in which he passionately believes, like a great number of Russian partisans of European civilization in the Petersburg period of Russian history."

It is not an idea and even not faith that save Versilov, but only his ability to die for some indefinite ideal. The Russian Faust is led onto the shore by his *incessant "dark striving"* (*der dunkle Drang*).

As the antithesis of the "European civilizer" Versilov, the author introduces the pilgrim Makar Ivanovich Dolgoruky. The novel's religious and artistic intention finds its culmination in him. He is the expression of that spiritual "sightliness" that has been lost by the upper class and about which the raw youth is so plagued. For his ideological portrait Dostoevsky employed the rough drafts for *The Life of a Great Sinner* and for *The Devils.* Makar Ivanovich inherits the spiritual riches of Bishop Tikhon. But the origin of this figure rises from the period of work on *The Idiot:* Dolgoruky embodies the writer's dream of a "positively beautiful individual." Psychologically, the just man from the people is linked not with the refinedly educated bishop, but with the hero of Nekrasov's poem *Vlas.* In the *Diary of a Writer* Dostoevsky recalls it with emotion, and the figure of the pilgrim, wandering through Russia and collecting alms for a church of God, did influence the conception of Makar Ivanovich's image. He also is a "vagabond," also is collecting for the building of a church. Describing his outer appearance, Versilov quotes a line from Nekrasov's poem. "This Makar," he says to his son, "bears himself with uncommon dignity and, I assure you, is uncommonly handsome. It's true, he's old, but he is 'dark-complexioned, tall, and erect.'" In actuality, Makar is just as much a heroic Russian type as Vlas. "He was tall in size," relates the raw youth, "broad-shouldered, of a very hale appearance, in spite of his illness." He has a rather long face, a "terribly" white beard, light blue, radiant eyes. His whole soul, kind-hearted and sinless, is expressed in his clear, joyful laugh. A "cheerful heart" is characteristic of all Dostoevsky's just men; it is the crowning of the spiritual way, the reflection of the Kingdom of God. The doctor asks Makar whether he considers him an atheist. The latter answers: "No, you're not an atheist, you're a *cheerful person*." Life in God is joy and tenderness. The writer underlines that the people's ideal of sanctity is foreign to Byzantine austerity and monastic asceticism. Makar goes on pilgrimages from monastery to monastery, extols the desert, but, the author adds, "will not go either into the desert, or into a monastery for anything, because he is essentially a 'vagabond.'" It is understandable that to the severe "Byzantine" Konstantin Leontyev,[4] Dostoevsky's religious mind could seem "rose-colored Christianity." The writer created his popular saints outside of the Church-monastic tradition. Their theology is limited by the mystery of this world and does not ascend to heavenly mysteries. They glorify God in His creation, devoutly revere the divine foundation—Sophia—but for them metaphysical heights are closed. The theme of mystical naturalism, begun by Prince Myshkin in *The Idiot* and Tikhon in *The Life*, is rapturously and touchingly developed by the pilgrim Makar. Paradise is revealed to the pure heart on earth. "What is a mystery?" asks Makar. "Everything is a mystery, my dearest; God's mystery is in all. In every tree, in every blade of grass, this same mystery lies hid. Whether the small bird sings, or the stars in all their host shine at night in the heaven— it's all this one mystery, ever the same. . . ." He recalls his pilgrimage to the Bogorodsky Monastery.

We spent the night in the field, and I woke up early in the morning; everybody there was still sleeping and even the dear sun had not yet

4 Konstantin Leontyev (1831-1891) was a philosophical and important critical thinker of the latter half of the 19th century. Even his earlier works reflect his deep religious sense, but at the period, one based upon the beauty, the aesthetics of liturgical experience and ritual. About 1870, while serving as a diplomat in the Near East, he underwent a "personal" conversion to the "authentic" Byzantine form of Christianity, and after a year spent at Mount Athos where he absorbed the ideals of monastic asceticism, he returned to Russia and began writing criticism in the spirit of his "absolute" Christian world-view. In the rigid dichotomy of his thought he now renounced any "humanistic" elements in the spiritual life and preached a "God of Fear." The end of his life was passed at Optina Pustyn.

peeped out from behind the forest. I lifted my head, dear, I gazed around me and sighed: *inexpressible beauty everywhere!* Everything was still, the air was light; the grass grows—grow, grass of God; a bird sings—sing, bird of God; a child yelled in a woman's arms—God be with you, little man; grow up and be happy, little babe! And here for the very first time in my very life then, I really took all this in.... It's good on earth, dear.... And that it's a mystery, why, so much the better: it is awesome to the heart and wondrous: and this fear makes the heart merry. All is in You, Lord, and I myself am in You, receive me.

For the sake of cosmic love the world is disclosed in its primeval beauty, as it was on the first day of Creation. The just individuals in Dostoevsky know neither sin nor evil. The radiance of the light of Mount Thabor hides Golgotha from them.[5]

Makar says solemnly about death: "An Elder should take leave with splendor. . . . An Elder ought to die in the full flower of his understanding, beautifully and blessedly, having fulfilled his days, sighing for his last hour and rejoicing when he is taken, as an ear of corn to the sheaf, and having accomplished his mystery. . . . It's no matter, even in death is love!" And not only in Makar's eloquent words, but also in his features, movements, and actions do we find underlined sightliness, beauty, lofty triumph. The religious ideal of the people is spiritual *beauty*. We know that according to Dostoevsky's conviction, society is governed by the aesthetic principle.

The figure of the pilgrim rises over the "disorder" of contemporary Russian society. They are all "searching," he alone has "found."

The great idea of God and immortality is withdrawn from people and simultaneously the human family disintegrates; communality is supplanted by separation. This is how Dostoevsky saw "the last day of European mankind." But in the Russian people, faith is strong and communality is not ruptured. In Makar there is a complete absence of self-love: he likes to visit the family of his wife who was unfaithful to him, tenderly loves Versilov's children, who bear his name. A feeling of personal wrong is incomprehensible to him: he lives in all and for all;

---

[5] St. Symeon the New Theologian (949-1022), one of the greatest Byzantine mystics, in his writings defends the *Hesychast* method of prayer, uniting all the faculties of man, spiritual, mental and physical, in the worship of God. In the final stage of mysticism the soul is united with God and experiences Divine, uncreated light. St. Symeon identifies this light with the Light the three disciples saw surrounding Jesus at His transfiguration on Mount Thabor. Hesychasm and the writings of St. Symeon and St. Gregory Palamas exercised a vast influence upon the development of Russian spirituality.

all are his own relatives. The author notes: "His yearning to communicate was painful." The Russian idea of "unity" is in the pilgrim Makar invested with living, artistic flesh.

The structure of *A Raw Youth* is analogous to the structure of *The Idiot*. Both here and there a just man is set in opposition to all the sinful world. But Prince Myshkin is a Russian nobleman with a dreamlike "religion of the heart," Makar Dolgoruky is a heroic Russian type, faithful to the people's holy-of-holies. In the first novel is a blind night, in the second—a dawn. New hopes had been born in the writer's soul.

X X I

The Diary of a Writer (1876-1877)

Upon completing his novel, *A Raw Youth*, Dostoevsky moved with his family from Staraya Russa to Petersburg, and ran an announcement in the newspapers that he intended to publish his *Diary of a Writer*. For a period of two years (1876-1877) he issued short installments; they appeared as a direct continuation of that section which he had printed in 1873 under the same name in *The Citizen*. The writer understood the vast difficulty of such an enterprise. "I'm undertaking a new project," he wrote to V. S. Solovyov, "but what'll result, I don't know." He proposed to write "about what I've heard and read, everything or a part of it, which has struck *me personally during the month*." "Undoubtedly," he continued, "the *Diary of a Writer* will be like a feuilleton, but with the difference that a monthly feuilleton, naturally can't be like a weekly feuilleton. Here the report of an event will not be as much concerned about novelty, as about what remains of it of more permanent interest, what is more connected with a common, entire idea. Lastly, I by no means want to confine myself to the rendering of an account. I'm not a chronicler: this is, to the contrary, a complete *diary* in the full sense of the word, i.e., an account of what has interested me personally most of all—*here there'll even be caprice*."

Dostoevsky was afraid that his monthly conversations with his reader could turn into banal feuilletons; he insisted on the word *diary* and sharply underlined the *personal* character of his publication ("which has struck *me personally*"; "*what has interested me personally*"). And in fact, the unprecedented originality of *The Diary of a Writer* lies in its revelation of the author's personality, in its singular tone of intimacy, the candidness and truthfulness of its communication. The literary work is not presented in its finished form; the writer was not partitioned off by the walls of his study; we penetrate the very laboratory of his creative activity, we see how his plans arose, grew and took form. Dostoevsky's work is inseparable from his life. And the closer we approach the man, the more intelligible the writer then becomes to us.

The Diary is an attempt at *an integral revelation of personality*, of full human communality. But the author did not succeed in realizing his plan; he soon perceived that a lyric confession in the form of monthly installments—unavoidably becomes conventional. "With great naiveté, I thought," he wrote in April 1876, "that this would be a real *Diary*. A real diary is almost impossible, and this is only a display, for the public." One could not offset the separation of human souls at one stroke and immediately create a spiritual "community"; one could not "confess" before strangers, as before close friends. But the writer's "naiveté" was his strength: it attracted a mass of sympathetic readers to the *Diary* and created for its author the reputation of a "teacher of life." Yet, in spite of the great success of the first January issue, Dostoevsky acknowledged bitterly that the *Diary* had not justified his hopes. He wrote to Ya. Polonsky: "I'm not very pleased with my Diary, I would have liked to say a hundred times more. I wanted very much to write about literature and precisely about what no one has written anything since the thirties: *about pure beauty*." This acknowledgment illuminates the connection of *A Raw Youth* with *The Brothers Karamazov*. Both novels narrate the crisis of the aesthetic consciousness, the tragic fate of "pure beauty."

But his purpose in publishing the *Diary of a Writer* was not confined to a desire to create a new form of personal communality: the monthly reports of current events helped the author prepare materials for his new novel. "I came to the irrefutable conclusion," he wrote to Kh. D. Alchevskaya, "that the creative writer, in addition to the poem, must know the reality he is portraying down to the finest particulars, historical and current. Here is why, in that *preparing to write a very big novel*, I also planned to immerse myself especially in the study not of reality proper, I'm acquainted with it even without that, but of the details of the current moment. One of the most important problems in this moment for me, for example, is the young generation and, along with that, the contemporary Russian family, which, I have a presentiment of this, is not in the least like it was even twenty years ago. I'm somehow drawn now to write some piece or other, having a full knowledge of the matter; here is why for a while I will both study and at the same time continue *The Diary of a Writer*, in order that this multitude of impressions might not be lost to no purpose."

A Raw Youth was devoted to the question of the young generation and the "haphazard Russian household." This same idea inspired the author to create a new "very big novel." We are again faced with the organic connection of Dostoevsky's two last novels. He speaks about this in even more detail in the January installment of the *Diary* for 1876.

> Long ago I had already set myself the ideal of writing a novel about present-day Russian children, well and, of course, about their present-day fathers, in their present-day mutual interrelation. The poem is ready and was created before everything else, as it must always be in the case of a novelist. I will take fathers and children, as far as possible, from all strata of society and will trace the children from their very earliest childhood. When a year and a half ago Nikolay Alekseyevich Nekrasov invited me to write a novel for *Fatherland Notes*, I very nearly began on my *Fathers and Children*, but I restrained myself and thank God: I was not ready. And in the meantime, I have written only *A Raw Youth*—this first sample of my thought.

Such is the origin of the concept of *Brothers Karamazov*. In 1876 the "poem was ready": at its center stood children "from all strata of society": the novel was planned in the form of an artistic answer to Turgenev's *Fathers and Children*, *A Raw Youth* was the "first sample of his thought." In the process of work the "story of early childhood" would withdraw onto the second plane and become an episode (Ilyusha and the schoolboys): the "sons" Karamazov would be introduced as adults while the "story of their fathers" would be reduced to the depiction of Fyodor Pavlovich alone. Versilov's "haphazard household" in *A Raw Youth* is a preparatory sketch for the picture of the Karamazovs' household.

The "poem is ready," declared Dostoevsky, but immediately added that he did not succumb to Nekrasov's proposal and did not begin to write his *Fathers and Children*, since he "was not ready." By the "poem" he understands the artistic thought of the novel: it was, in fact, "created before everything else"; *it is possible to ascribe* its origin to the year 1849, to the period when he was writing of his first "family tale"—*Netochka Nezvanova*. But to fully embody the "poem," enormous work was needed regarding the "facts": in order to study the "details of current reality," Dostoevsky set up a laboratory: he published *The Diary of a Writer*. The ideational riches of *Brothers Karamazov* was amassed in the thinnish issues of this publication. In all world literature there is no work whose history might be so accessible to our investigation.

In the May installment the writer tells about the midwife Pisareva's suicide and apropos of this article, develops in a letter to V. A. Alekseyev (June 7, 1876) the idea that will be at the basis of his brilliant *Legend of the Grand Inquisitor*. Comparing the original sketch with the completed form, we touch upon the mystery of artistic embodiment. Here is this remarkable letter: "In the temptation of the devil three colossal world ideas have become merged," writes Dostoevsky, "and here 18 centuries have passed, but there are no ideas more difficult, i.e., more trying, than these and even now no one can resolve them. 'The stones and bread' symbolize the present-day social question, the environment. This is not a prophecy, it always has been so. 'Rather than go to the ravaged poor, who from hunger and oppression look more like beasts than like men, rather than go and start preaching to the hungry abstention from sins, humility, chastity, is it not better first to feed them? That would be humane. Even before You, people came to preach, but why, You are the Son of God; the whole world has waited for You with impatience; then act as one who is superior to all in mind and justice, give them all food, make them secure, give them a social structure so that they might always have bread and order, and then ask them their sins. Then, if they sin, they will be ungrateful, but now they commit sin from hunger. It is sinful even to ask them.

" 'You are the Son of God—therefore You can do everything. Here are stones—you see how many. You have only to command and the stones will be turned into bread. Command then that from now on the earth bring forth without toil, teach men such a science or teach them such an order, so that their life might henceforth be provided for. Can you really not believe that the greatest vices and miseries of man have resulted from hunger, cold, poverty and from the impossible struggle for existence.'

"Here is the first idea which the evil spirit proposed to Christ. You must agree that it is difficult to deal with it. Contemporary socialism in Europe, and with us too, everywhere puts Christ aside and concerns itself above all else with *bread*, calls upon science and declares that the cause of all man's miseries is poverty alone, struggle for existence, 'the environment has gone bad.'

"To this Christ answered: 'Not by bread alone does man live,' i.e., He propounded the axiom of the spiritual origin of man. The devil's

· 538 ·

idea could only apply to man-brute; Christ, however, knew that by bread alone one could not keep man alive. If, moreover, there were no spiritual life, no ideal of beauty, then man would fall into anguish, would die, would go out of his mind, would kill himself, or would enter into pagan fantasies. But since Christ bore the ideal of Beauty in Himself and in His word, He decided: it is better to inspire man's soul with the ideal of beauty; possessing it in their souls, all will become brothers to one another and then, of course, working for one another, they will also be rich. Whereas, give them bread and out of boredom they will become, as it were, enemies of one another.

"But if one gave men both beauty and bread together? Then man would be deprived of labor, personality, the self-sacrifice of one's own goods for the sake of one's neighbor—in a word, he would be deprived of life, the ideal of life. And therefore it is better to proclaim only the spiritual ideal.

"By the way, just recall the contemporary theories of Darwin and others about the origin of man from a monkey. Not entering into any theories, Christ simply declares that in man in addition to the animal world there is also a spiritual one. Well and what then, let man have originated from where you like (it is not at all explained in the Bible how God formed him out of clay, took him from a stone), but on the other hand *God did breathe into him the breath of life.*"

Three years before the appearance of *The Brothers Karamazov* the idea of the Grand Inquisitor was already fully formed. Into the discussion about bread we find inserted a personal address to Christ ("Even before You, people came to preach . . ."), out of which afterward developed the Inquisitor's emotional, excited monologue. But in opposition to the arguments of the evil spirit was set Christ's teaching about the spiritual origin of man. In the final text it has disappeared. Christ does not argue and does not refute—He remains silent. The ideal of Beauty exists, and he does not have to prove its existence.

In another letter (to P. Pototsky, June 10, 1876), also in connection with the suicide of Pisareva, the writer once more returned to the "ideal of beauty." Pisareva could not endure the philosophy of utilitarianism and egoism. She wanted "to see the beauty of people and of the world, to display magnanimity herself," but she was answered: "Magnanimity does not exist, rather become a midwife, be useful there." Here she decided: "If magnanimity doesn't exist, there's no need even to be useful." Pisareva's suicide is proof of the spiritual nature of man; bread alone is not enough, it is impossible to live without beauty. "If one says to a man: magnanimity doesn't exist, but there is the elemental struggle for existence (egoism), then this means taking *personality and freedom* away from man." So, on the instance of the midwife who committed suicide, Dostoevsky founded his teaching about man. The most profound idea about personality and freedom grew out of a real fact. "Bread" became the symbol of every materialistic philosophy and every socialistic structure. "Bread" is the temptation of the evil spirit, of the prince of this world. He is opposed not by theories and doctrines, but by *personality*, the incarnated ideal of beauty, the living testament of man's spiritual nature—Christ.

Dostoevsky was delighted at the success of *The Diary*: he had 2,000 subscribers; in addition, 2,000 copies were sold by retail distribution. He received a mass of letters from the most diverse readers; two students from the Academy of Medicine came to him—"altogether new types." They struck him "by their most genuine seriousness and most genuine gaiety." One young girl confessed to him that she did not love her fiancé and wanted to continue her studies; another asked if she should marry a man whom she did not love. A third complained of her failure at her examination. The writer offered advice, comforted, took an ardent interest in the lives of his modest correspondents. He was taken back by an unexpected discovery: in all parts of Russia he had a multitude of supporters and friends! He would have liked to be in personal communality with them all, to realize his dream of unity. He wrote to Kh. D. Alchevskaya: "Moreover, here is the thought that occupies me most of all: what does our *community* consist in, where are those points about which we could all, of various tendencies, come to an agreement?" In this question is the first conception of his thought on the great synthesis of Russian culture, on the "complete reconciliation of ideas," on it would be constructed his speech on the Pushkin celebration.

The summer of 1876 Dostoevsky again spent at Ems and in the July-August issue of *The Diary* described his impressions of Russians abroad. He felt a great spiritual uplift in spite of the fact that his physical forces were growing perceptibly weaker. He wrote to his brother Andrey: "Our time has flown past like a dream. I know that my life will not continue for long, but meanwhile not only do I not want to die, but I feel, on the contrary, as if I am only beginning life. I'm not a bit tired, but meanwhile I am 55—ah!"

The Eastern war inspired him to write patriotic articles in which he "carried certain of his convictions to the end" and said his "very last word." It seemed to him that his prophecies about the destiny of Russia were already beginning to be realized. In the January issue of the year 1877, he ran an article about Foma Danilov, a noncommissioned officer of the Turkestan Rifle Battalion, who had been barbarously tortured to death by the Kipchaks for refusing to enter their service and accept Mohammedanism. The story of this unassuming martyr from the people would afterward serve the author in his creating of the scene *The Controversy* in *Brothers Karamazov*.

Pobedonostsev followed the *Diary* with sympathetic attention, supplied the editor with materials, and congratulated him on his success. On February 1, 1877, he wrote Dostoevsky: "Having just finished reading it through [the January issue], I hasten to thank you for your excellent articles—all are good, especially how you discuss Stundism, yes, and about Foma Danilov. Long life and happiness."

Toward the end of the spring of 1877, the writer felt greatly overfatigued and at the end of the April issue informed his subscribers that the May and June issues would come out in one installment at the beginning of July, since he would be forced, in the judgment of his doctors, to leave Petersburg. He apologizes touchingly: "In the face of such an unforeseen circumstance as the complication of an illness, it was difficult to anticipate all this."

Upon having learned of the Imperial Manifesto regarding the entry of Russian troops into Turkey, issued at Kishinev, April 12, 1877, Dostoevsky went to pray in the Kazan cathedral. Anna Grigoryevna writes in her memoirs: "Knowing that at certain solemn moments he liked to pray in silence, without witnesses, I did not go after him and only a half-hour later found him in a corner of the cathedral, so absorbed and in a prayerful, moved frame of mind, that at the first instant he did not recognize me."

In the summer of 1877 the writer took a rest at "Maly Prikol," the estate of his wife's brother, Ivan Grigoryevich Snitkin, in Kursk province. But at the beginning of July he was forced to return to Petersburg to publish the overdue May-June installment of the *Diary*. Much of his strength was wasted on difficulties with the printers and with the Censorship Committee on reading the proofs. On his journey back to Prikol, he stopped at his father's former estate Darovoye, walked in the Chermashnya grove and immersed himself in· the memories of his childhood. This landscape long familiar to him would afterward enter the novel *Brothers Karamazov*. Before his trip to Darovoye, Dostoevsky passed three "terrible" days in Petersburg. He did not receive any letters from his wife and in anticipation of a reply wrote Anna Grigoryevna a desperate letter. In the writer's love for his wife and children, there was morbid frenzy. He always experienced separation as a trying illness: he was continually haunted by the thought of threatening misfortunes. "Anya," he wrote his wife, "I've passed the last three days here in a terrible way. Especially the nights. I don't sleep. I think, weighing the chances, walk about the room, the children seem to appear to me, I think of you, my heart throbs in me (During these three days I have begun to have palpitations, which never occurred before). . . . Finally dawn begins to break, while I weep, walk about the room and cry with a kind of trembling (myself I don't understand it, this never happened before), and only take care so that the old woman won't hear. I throw myself into the bed at about five in the morning and sleep a total of about four hours and always there are terrible nightmares. . . .

". . . The accursed trip to Darovoye! How I would like not to go! But it's impossible: if one is to deny himself these impressions, then how afterward and what will a writer write about! But enough, we'll discuss all this. But all the same know, at this moment when you're reading this, that I cover all your whole dear body with a thousand most passionate kisses and pray to you, as to an icon."

Dostoevsky's letters to his wife surprise us in their unexpected manifestations of passion. Up to his very last days, he not only loved his "Anichka," but also was in love with her, as in the first year of their marriage. This feeling sometimes burst forth in fits of insane jealousy. Anna Grigoryevna describes a certain "family scene" (in 1876). Once unsuccessfully she "played a joke": she copied an anonymous letter out of S. Smirnov's *Strength of Character* and sent it to Fyodor Mikhailovich. In it was the sentence: "And if you don't believe me, so on your spouse's neck a medallion is hung, so you take a look, see whom she carries in this medallion on her heart." "I went into the room," continues Anna Grigoryevna, "sat down in my usual place by the writing desk and purposely started to talk about some sort of thing which required Fyodor Mikhailovich's reply. But he kept irritably silent and with heavy steps that must each have weighed forty pounds kept walking up and down the room. I saw that he was upset and I instantly began to feel sorry for him. In order to break the silence, I asked: 'Why are you so gloomy, Fedya?' Fyodor Mikhailovich angrily looked at me, paced twice more through the room and stopped almost in front of me. 'Are you wearing your medallion?' he asked in a constrained voice. 'Yes.' 'Show it to me.' 'Why? But you've seen it many times.' 'Show me the me-dal-lion!' F. M. shouted at the top of his voice; I realized that my joke had gone too far and in order to reassure him, began to unbutton the collar of my dress. But I could not get the medallion out myself. F. M. could not control the anger which had possessed him, rushed quickly up to me and with all his force tore off the little chain. . . ."

Anna Grigoryevna calmed her husband. He was taken back. " 'You're always laughing, Anichka,' began Dostoevsky in a guilty voice, 'but think what a misfortune could have taken place. *I could have strangled you in my anger.* . . . I implore you, don't joke with such things; when I'm enraged, I do not answer for myself.' "

In the October installment of the *Diary* the following notice was run: "To the reader." "For reasons of ill-health, which especially prevents me from publishing the *Diary* punctually on definite dates, I have decided to discontinue my publication for a year or two. With the December issue it will come to an end. It is hoped that neither I nor the readers will forget each other until the time."

In a letter to S. D. Yanovsky his decision is explained in more detail. "For a time (for a year)," he writes, "I have decided to discontinue it [*The Diary*]. There is a combination of many reasons: I'm tired, my epilepsy has grown worse (precisely because of the *Diary*), finally, I want to be freer next year, although scarcely do I pass even two months without working. I have a novel in my mind and heart and it asks to be expressed. . . ."

Not fatigue and not illness compelled the author to give up his publication whose success was increasing with each month (in 1877 the *Diary* had around 7,000 subscribers). He had a novel in his heart; the period of preparation was at an end: the mysterious time of birth was approaching. The novel "asked to be expressed"—and the creator complied with his still unborn creation's will to life. Taking leave of his readers in the December issue of the *Diary*, he spoke openly about his design: "In this year of rest from periodical publication, I will in fact be engaged in a certain artistic work, which imperceptibly and involuntarily has molded itself during these two years of publishing the *Diary*. . . . But I firmly hope to resume the *Diary* in a year. . . . With expectations of a happy meeting in the near future." Dostoevsky kept his promise: *The Diary of a Writer* was resumed in 1880: a single installment appeared in August. In 1881 one more issue—January's—came out. *The Diary's* continuation was cut short by his death.

Totaling the sums of the two years of exertion on *The Diary*, the writer recalled with gratitude the "happy moments" that he had experienced that year, society's interest in his activity, the hundreds of letters he had received from all the ends of Russia. He felt that he had learned many things.

"But the main thing I've discovered," he wrote to S. Yanovsky,

is that, contrary to what I used to think two years ago, it has proved that we in Russia have incomparably more truly Russian people— not with a distorted view, as of Petersburg intelligentsia, but with the true and just view of the Russian man. So many more, that even in my most ardent desires and fantasies, I could not have imagined this result. Believe me, my friend, that much in Russia is not at all as gloomy as formerly it seemed, and most important, there is much which testifies to a yearning for a new, just life, to a deep faith in the imminent change in the form of our intelligentsia's attitudes, those who have become detached from the people and do not even understand them at all.

The Diary of a Writer is an important stage in Dostoevsky's spiritual life. It kindled in him a new faith in Russia, excited him with a new joyful hope. It was in a brighter and encouraged frame of mind that he proceeded to the writing of his novel about the future resurrection of Russia, about the new *beautiful* Russian man. Alyosha Karamazov's image already shone in his heart.

In the writer's copybook we find the following remarkable notation for December 24, 1877.

"*Memento*, For the whole of my life.
1. Write the Russian *Candide*.
2. Write a book about Jesus Christ.
3. Write my memoirs.
4. Write a poem, *The Requiem Service on the Fortieth Day*.

"(All this, in addition to my last novel and the intended publication of the *Diary*, i.e., a *minimum* for 10 years' activity, and I'm now 56 years old)."

Dostoevsky was not destined to write these books; he was not destined to complete the "poem" of *The Brothers Karamazov*. His vast creative designs were a final blazing up of his fiery spirit: he had only three years left to live.

The contents of *The Diary of a Writer* for the years 1876 and 1877 are unusually varied: artistic works, literary criticism, lively responses to current events, accounts of court proceedings, journalistic essays, philosophico-moral reflections, political discussions, the preaching of mystical populism, and personal memoirs—all this complex material is organized by the idea of the author's direct communality with the reader. The personal tone of a friendly conversation is above all created by the abundance of autobiographical essays: the writer tells about his early childhood, about his meeting with the peasant Marey, about his nurse Alyona Frolovna's sacrificial love, about the journey with his brother Mikhail to Petersburg; then come stories about his youth, about working on *Poor People* and his enthusiasm for the novels of George Sand, about reading *The Double* at Belinsky's, about his acquaintance with Nekrasov. His life, "which has flown past, like a dream," is illumined by a soft poetic light. A grateful memory finds meaning in the sufferings that have been experienced. How regrettable it is that Dostoevsky did not succeed in writing the proposed book of his "memoirs"!

In the variegated context of the *Diary* several finished artistic works stand out prominently. Everyone knows the story *A Boy at Christ's Christmas Tree Party*. On a frosty evening before Christmas, the writer meets a boy about seven years old who is going along "with a little hand," i.e. is asking for alms. A description follows of the unhappy fate of little beggars who take shelter in cellars among drunken and dissolute "rag-pickers" and grow up tramps and petty thieves. This meeting evokes in the author the image of a boy freezing to death, whom Christ brings to see His Christmas tree. Everything is flooded with light; around "Christ's Christmas tree" radiant children revolve and fly; their mothers also stand there: "Each one recognizes her boy or little girl, and they fly up to their mothers and kiss them, wipe away their tears with their little hands and beg them not to cry, because they feel so happy here." The vision of Christ's Christmas tree party for the little children who have been tortured is a draft of Alyosha Karamazov's vision. In *Cana of Galilee* there is also a bright festival, also a victory over death and corruption. In the Christmas story we already find that unforgettable, tenderly moving tone that pierces us in *Cana of Galilee*. The boy who had died asks: "Who are you boys? Who are you little girls?" "This is Christ's Christmas tree party," they answer him. "Always on this day Christ has a Christmas party for the little children who have no Christmas tree of their own." "And *He Himself* is in their midst and holds out His hands to them and blesses them and their sinful mothers."

In this same way, Alyosha asks the elder Zosima, and in the same way, the latter joyfully points out to him "Our Sun"—Christ. In the story, the theme of the tormented children is still not separated from that of the mystical supper of the Lamb. The substitution of the Gospel account of the marriage in Cana for the Christmas subject (the party) carries us to a more lofty plane of religious symbolism. Thus, the dead boy's resurrection into the "children's paradise" anticipates the elder Zosima's resurrection at Christ's marriage feast.

The *Diary*'s November issue contains one of Dostoevsky's most accomplished artistic works—the tale *The Meek One*. The origin and development of this design can be followed in the "laboratory" of *The Diary of a Writer*. With absorbed and troubled attention the author studied the facts concerning suicides among the young generation. "It is true lately, suicides have so increased among us," he wrote, "that no one now even speaks of them. The Russian land seems to have lost the strength to hold people on it. . . . The so-called living force, the living feeling of being, without which no society can exist and the land is liable to fall, is decidedly vanishing—God knows where." A twenty-five-year-old girl—the midwife Pisareva—killed herself and left a note: she was very tired, so tired that she wanted to take a rest. Dostoevsky gives a profound analysis of the psychology of "tired souls." Several months later Pobedonostsev informed him of the details regarding the suicide of the daughter of the well-known writer —the emigré Herzen. This death struck him as being mysteriousness. "In this suicide," he writes in the *Diary*, "everything is a riddle both from the outside and within. Of course, following the instinct of human nature I sought somehow to unravel this enigma in order to arrive at something and reassure myself." Herzen's daughter was brought up in the most inconsolable positivism and her soul could not bear the "rectilinearness of phenomena." The author concludes: "This means she simply died of 'cold darkness and boredom,' with, so to speak, animal and unaccountable suffering, life simply became stifling for her, just as if there were not enough air. . . ."

Finally, a third case of a girl's suicide: "About a month ago," informs the author, "there appeared in all the Petersburg newspapers a few brief lines in small type about a Petersburg suicide: a certain poor young girl, a seamstress, threw herself out of a window, on the fourth floor—'because she was utterly unable to find work for her livelihood.' It was added that she jumped out and fell to the ground *holding in her hands an icon*. This icon in her hands is a strange and unheard-of trait in a suicide! This now was some kind of *meek*, humble suicide. Here, apparently, there was not even grumbling or reproach: simply it became impossible to live. 'God did not wish it'—and she died, having said her prayers. There are some things, *however simple* they may seem at first glance, about which one does not stop thinking for a long time, somehow they turn up in one's dreams and it is even as though you are to blame for them. This *meek soul that destroyed itself* involuntarily keeps tormenting one's mind. . . ."

The three young suicides haunted the writer's imagination. The "meek one," who threw herself out of the window with an icon in her hands is artistically embodied in the heroine's figure of a "fantastic story." The detail, reported in the papers in "small type," is turned into the tragic finale of a tale. The servant Lukerya describes the "meek one's" suicide: "She was standing by the wall close to the very window, had put her hand against the wall, and pressed her head to her hand, she stood like this and was thinking. And so deep in her thoughts she was that she didn't even notice how I was standing and looking at her from the other room. I saw, she seemed to be smiling, was standing, thinking and smiling. I looked at her, turned round very quietly, went away, and was thinking to myself; only suddenly I heard—the window has been opened. I at once went to say, 'It's cool, mistress, now don't catch a cold,' and suddenly I saw, she was standing on the window ledge and she was standing full height at the open window, her back to me, and in her hands she was holding a holy image. Then and there my heart sank, I cried: 'Mistress, mistress!' she heard me, made a move to turn toward me, but didn't turn, and took a step, pressed the image to her breast and—threw herself out of the window!"

The simplicity and sparseness of means which the writer needed to create this tragic scene are incredible. The "meek one's" humble death is sketched in a few pale strokes, but they are indelible. The miracle of transforming the material of life into a creation of art takes place here literally before our eyes.

The Meek One bears a subtitle: *A Fantastic Story*. In the foreword the author explains that the story itself seems "in the highest degree real" to him and that the "fantastic" is contained in its form. This is a husband's monologue before the body of his wife, who a few hours before had committed suicide. She is lying on the table, and he walks about the room and converses with himself, in an effort "to gather his thoughts into focus" and *explain* to himself what has happened. The author plays the role of a stenographer, writing down the unhappy hero's confused, broken speech. Dostoevsky justifies this new narrative form by reference to Victor Hugo's chef d'oeuvre *The Last Day of a Man Condemned to Death*. His hero's monologue is no more improbable than the notes of a man who has only a few minutes left to live.

The form of the tale is, in fact, unprecedented in literature: this is the first attempt at an exact notation of interior discourse (*monologue intérieur*). Many years before Proust, Joyce, the symbolists, and expressionists, Dostoevsky broke the convention of logical literary speech and attempted to reproduce the stream of thoughts and images in their immediate associationalist movement. In the seventies such a technical innovation was daring.

The recording of a confused and shaken man's *thinking aloud* raises the emotional pitch of the story almost to a physiological intensity: we actually hear his gasping voice, pauses, exclamations, and muffled sighs; even his heavy steps, now withdrawing, not returning to the same place, resound with a monotonous echo in our ears. His monologue begins: "Now as long as she's here, everything is still all right: I come near and look at her every minute; but, tomorrow she will be carried away—and how shall I remain alone then? Now she is on the table in the hall—I put two card-tables together—while the coffin will be here tomorrow, a white one, white gros-de-Naples, but then, this is not the point. . . . I keep walking and want to explain it to myself. It's six hours already that I've sought to explain it and I'm still not able to gather my thoughts into focus. The thing is that I keep walking, walking, walking. . . . This now is how it was, I will simply relate it in order (Order!)."

The story is arranged *retrospectively*. The catastrophe, the Meek One's suicide, is set at the beginning; slowly, thread by thread, the ball of causes that provoked her death is disentangled. The psychological analysis, incomparable in its penetration, uncovers the tragedy of the suicide.

The hero is a money-lender; once a girl of about sixteen years "thinnish, fair-haired, of medium-tall height" came to him with a pledge. "Her eyes were light blue, big, pensive." She was looking for a position as governess, was pawning her last possessions, some "remnants of an old hare mantelet." He was taken with her purity and pride, and he at once made a decision—she would belong to him. "I was looking at her then as if she were *mine* and didn't doubt my power. You know, this is an awfully sensuous thought when you no longer have doubts." And here he saves her from poverty and the attentions of some fat shopkeeper; he offers her his hand. It's true, he has a "pawnshop," but still he is a retired second-captain and a nobleman by birth. The "Meek One" becomes his wife; with the generosity of youth and the credulity of an inexperienced heart she surrenders her love to her husband. But he is not looking for love. He has his own idea: he wants *power*, limitless, despotic dominion over another soul. His life's failures, introverted ambition, and an exasperated self-love have infected him with a cadaverous poison. He has "gambled away" his life, been reduced to a pawnshop, and now "avenges himself" on society. He needs some human being, though it be only one to bow down before him as a hero and martyr. He wants to mold the Meek One, put her on her knees before his own greatness. The husband answers his wife's amorous impulse with sternness. "I at once threw cold water on all this ecstasy. Here is precisely what my idea consisted in. . . . First, sternness—so it was with sternness that I admitted her to my home. . . . I wanted complete respect, I wanted her to stand before me in prayer for my sufferings—and I deserved that. Oh, I was always proud, I always wanted either everything or nothing!" Having been wronged in her feeling, the Meek One begins to revolt: she closes herself off in silence, leaves the house for whole days and finally hurls a challenge at her husband: "And is it true that you were turned out of the regiment because you were afraid to accept a challenge?" He feels that contempt and hatred toward him are growing in his wife's soul, and performs a terrible experiment: lying down to sleep, he places a revolver on the table before her. In the morning he wakes up, feeling the cold contact of iron at his temple; the antagonists' eyes meet for a second. He continues to lie motionless, pretending to be asleep. "I knew, with all the force of my being, at that very instant a struggle was in process between us, a terrible duel for life or death, a duel here involving that very coward of yesterday, driven out by his comrades for cowardice." The minutes pass, the dead silence is prolonged. Finally, she lowers the revolver. "I got up from my bed; I had conquered—and she was forever vanquished!" The wife's revolt is checked; the rebellion of the free soul against the tyranny of an evil will is crushed. "In my eyes she was so vanquished, so humbled, so crushed, that I painfully pitied her sometimes, although in spite of all this I was sometimes decidedly pleased with the idea of her humiliation." He is above her love, above her hate, he pretends to the dignity of a divinity, inspiring a humble slave girl to trembling veneration. For six weeks the Meek One lies in a fever. Spring comes; she is grown thin and coughs. An uninterrupted silence separates them like a wall. And suddenly in the beginning of April—she begins to sing. She had never sung before in his presence. He is shaken: the scales fall from his eyes. "If she started singing in my presence," he thinks, "it means she forgot about me—that's what was clear and dreadful." His "dream of pride" is ended—ecstasy alone radiates in his soul. He understands that he loves her endlessly, that he cannot love otherwise. In repentance and pain he falls at her feet. "I fully understood my despair, oh, I understood! But do you believe, ecstasy was boiling in my heart so irresistibly that I thought that I would die. I kissed her feet in frenzy, in happiness." She looks at him with terror, astonishment, shame; she suffers a terrible fit of hysterics. When she comes to herself, the words somehow involuntarily slip out: *But I thought that you would leave me this way.* At the time he still did not understand the fatal meaning of this sentence. Ecstasy was flooding him. He believed that everything was still reparable, that tomorrow he would explain to her, she would again come to love him, they would go to Boulogne to bathe in the sea and they would begin a new, happy life. On the following day, he confesses to his wife all the falls and sins of his life. Her face grew ever more thoughtful and frightened. He loves her, her, who made an attempt on his life! He is magnanimous and noble, but she had thought so basely of him, had despised him so deeply! And most of all, she had believed that he would leave her *this way.* "And suddenly here I came forward, the husband, and a husband needs love!"

The Meek One's timid and humble soul does not sustain this shock. And now—her body is lying on the table. The husband looks attentively at her dead face and "the question hammers away in his brain" —why did she die? With torment he unpuzzles this enigma. The Meek One died because he had killed her love; she was too chaste, too pure, to pretend to be a loving wife. "She did not want to deceive him with half-love under the guise of love, or with quarter-love."

The story-monologue is entirely devoted to the story of the unfortunate suicide. It is only about her that the husband, insane with despair, can even talk. But alongside her figure there appears the silhouette of the narrator—he grows up, like a dark shadow, spurned by her shining image. Telling about his wife, the husband makes a confession and repents: we learn about him through contrast with her. His traits are long familiar to us: *this is Dostoevsky's eternal companion: the man from underground.* He has the same character and the same evil destiny, as the hero of the tale: *Apropos of the Wet Snow.* The Meek One's husband relates of himself: "My comrades didn't like me because of my difficult character and, perhaps, because of my ridiculous character. . . . Oh, I was never liked even in school. Always and everywhere I was disliked." He had been forced to leave his regiment after a certain cowardly act; then for three years he tramped about the streets of Petersburg, was reduced to complete disgrace and degradation. Upon receiving a small inheritance, he opened a pawnshop and closed himself off in proud solitude. But the memories of his tragic past did not leave him; he conceived a hatred for society and revenged himself on it for his ruined life. The hero of *The Meek One* is a disenchanted dreamer, as was the author of *"Notes From Underground";* and he has the psychology of a "harassed mouse," and he is poisoned by spite accumulated over years, and his love is perverted into tyranny and cruelty. The underground man saves Liza from disgrace, deceives her with his contrived love, and drives her to ruin; the hero of *The Meek One* also acts the same way. But in the character of the latter traits of despotism and the sensuality of power are reinforced. He absolutely must assert his own greatness, restore his own lost "nobility," and with this goal he "educates" his still very young wife. Like a demon, he demands that she "falling down, worship him."

In *The Meek One* Dostoevsky finds the final synthesis of his basic philosophical ideas. The themes of the "underground," "separation," "might," and "spiritual tyranny" are united here as leitmotifs in the pathetic finale.

The proud personality, shut off in desperate solitude, ruptures the tie of human communality. The law of God's world—love—is distorted into a diabolic grimace—despotism and force. The Meek One's "weak heart" is crushed by this dead weight. She escapes into death. The symbolic opposition of the divine principle and the demonic principle is expressed by the peculiarity of her suicide: she throws herself out of the window, *after having prayed* and holding an icon in her hands. This detail, which the writer found in an actual happening, was understood by him mystically and became the kernel out of which the story developed. The Meek One is dead. Her murderer understands his crime against love too late. Having begun to see clearly, he perceives the diabolic delusion, and a feeling of world loneliness seizes his soul. He has, with his own hands, violated the unity of God's creation. And the world is stretched out before him like a glacial waste. Dreadful is the cry of this living corpse:

"Inertia! Oh, nature! Men are alone—on earth this is the misery! 'Is there a living man in the field'? shouts the Russian warrior-knight. I am not a knight, I am shouting too, and no one answers. They say the sun gives life to the universe. The sun will rise, and look at it, isn't it really a corpse? Everything is dead, everywhere there are corpses. Men alone, and around them silence—here is the earth! 'Men, love one another,' Who said this? Whose testament is this? The pendulum is tapping, insensibly, disgustingly. Two o'clock at night. Her little shoes stand by the bed, as if they're waiting for her. . . . No, seriously, to-morrow when they carry her away, what will I be then?"

This is how fallen souls, plagued in the abyss of nonbeing dream and rave. And even there, at the bottom of the infernal crater, a vague echo carries to them the incomprehensible words: "Men, love one another." "Who said this?"

The third artistic work, printed in the *Diary of a Writer* (April 1877), *The Dream of a Ridiculous Man*, bears the same subtitle as *The Meek One—A Fantastic Story*. But its "fantastic element" lies not in its form, but in content. This work, wondrous and unique in its genre, brilliantly culminates Dostoevsky's utopian conceptions.

The "ridiculous man" is an image of the contemporary civilized European: in him is concretized a phase of the spiritual development of 20th century humanity. The personality in its assertion and separation absorbs the whole reality of the world. After Kant idealist philosophy is reduced to solipsism. Both God and the world are only phantoms of my consciousness. Life is a dream, everything only appears, and consequently "nothing matters." The ridiculous man's conviction is suddenly understood, that *nothing matters* in the world. . . . "I suddenly felt," he writes, "that it didn't matter to me whether the world existed, or whether there was nothing anywhere. . . . I began to hear and feel with all my being, that *around me there was nothing*. At first, it seemed to me that on the other hand there had at one time been much, but then I guessed that even before there had been nothing, and only that for some reason there had seemed to be."

Subjective idealism leads to pure nonbeing: the world of phenomena is only a semblance. But in the midst of phantoms personality itself becomes a phantom. On a gloomy, rainy evening the "ridiculous man" is returning to his home; in the sky, among the rent clouds, shines a little star and it "presented him with a thought"; he resolves to kill himself that very night. Suddenly a little girl about eight years old, in rags, wet, shivering, grabs him by the elbow. She is crying and shouts: "Dear Mommy! Mommy!" The hero stamps at her and chases her away. Having returned to his corner, he sits down at the table and places a revolver before him. He, of course, would have shot himself, had it not been for the little girl. . . . His meeting with the unfortunate little creature suddenly shattered the frozen wall of his isolation, of his murderous "nothing matters." Pity and an ache arose in his heart. Really, is not this feeling strange, incredible in a man who has sentenced himself to death? "I am turning into a zero, into an absolute zero," reflects the narrator. "And is it possible the consciousness of the fact, that in an instant I *shall completely cease* to exist, and that therefore, *nothing will exist,* could not have exercised the least influence upon a feeling of pity for the little girl?" The truth of the intellect: "I alone exist" clashes with the truth of the heart: another personality (the little girl) exists as really as I do. This *revelation of reality* saves the hero from suicide. He falls asleep, and he dreams a dream of paradise, about the *brotherhood of man.* Here he has shot himself in the temple, has been buried, he is lying in his grave—and heavy drops of water are falling slowly on his closed left eye. But suddenly the grave is opened and some mighty being carries him away into the cosmic expanses. He sees a sun and an earth, but knows that this is not our sun and not our earth. Love for his old native earth, which he quit willfully and with scorn, pierces him with an unbearable pain. "If this is an earth there," he asks, "then is it possibly the same kind of earth as ours . . . absolutely like it, unfortunate, poor, but dear and eternally beloved, and generating even in its most ungrateful children, a tormenting love of itself as ours does?" And he adds: "The image of the poor little girl whom I had offended, flashed past before me."

These last words clearly enlighten the symbolism of the story. The weeping girl is the eternal feminine principle of the world, the mystical soul of the earth; the rational idealist's sin is in his offense of the "Mother Earth." He has torn himself away from her living bosom and this estrangement is crime and suicide. Pity for the young girl was the beginning of his return to the maternal breast: from here, as from a spark, flashed the flame of his love for "*our* unfortunate, poor, but dear *earth*." Now he *knows the truth*: the scales have fallen from his eyes: he has seen the *real* earth in its primordial beauty, in its sophiac brilliance, has seen *real* mankind still not darkened by sin, has seen *paradise on earth*.

In order to depict paradise Dostoevsky employed those same picturesque strokes with which he sketched the painting of the "golden age" in Stavrogin's dream and in the dream of Versilov. Once again we have the islands of the Greek Archipelago, the sunlight, the "caressing emerald sea." Once again he was reminded of Claude Lorrain's painting, *Acis and Galatea*, which had captivated him forever. Amidst the beautiful trees, fragrant flowers, and flocks of birds live the "children of the sun"—a happy and joyful people. "Oh, at once," exclaims the narrator, "from my first glance at their faces, I understood everything, everything! This was an earth not defiled by the fall, upon it lived men who had not sinned; they lived in such a paradise as that in which, according to the tradition of all mankind, our fallen forefathers also lived."

The writer knows that "paradise on earth" is a dream, and a "most incredible" dream, but for this dream he was ready to surrender his life. This dream, with its magic lustre, illumined his romantic youth, brought him together with other dreamers—the Petrashevists; he paid for it with ten years of Siberia, struggled for it, and preached it in his novels; he endowed his favorite heroes with it (Prince Myshkin, Stavrogin, Versilov), and with it went down to the grave. The utopia of the "earthly paradise" is the mysterious source of his inspiration.

With tenderness and feeling the "ridiculous man" tells about the "beautiful people": they have a higher knowledge of life, they understand the language of the animals and trees; their souls are in contact with the stars, they love one another with an inexhaustible love. "Their children were children of all, because they all formed one family." They died as though falling asleep and sorrow did not accompany their dying, but "love grown as though to ecstasy." "They did not have temples, but in them was a kind of daily, living, and uninterrupted union with the entire world. . . . They glorified nature, the earth, the sea, forests, composed songs about one another. It was a sort of enamoredness of one another, complete, universal." The picture of the "earthly paradise," drawn by the ridiculous man, is an attempt to unfold in words the *mystical content of ecstasy*.

Dostoevsky's spiritual experience is ecstatic and at its center stands the cult of Mother Earth—the Mother of God. It is true, the writer calls the hero of his story a "ridiculous man"; but this precaution is futile: it is not the "ridiculous man" who tells us his fantastic dream, but the author himself, fifty-six-year-old Dostoevsky, permitted himself at last to fully disclose his "most incredible" idea, to remain, though for one instant, in the earthly paradise. He forgets for a moment the arguments of reason and casts himself into the ocean of "world harmony"—what a liberation, what bliss!

Prince Myshkin says that the sensation of harmony lasts not more than a second: more, a human being cannot endure. The "ridiculous man's" vision concludes with the "beautiful world's" destruction. After the intoxication of ecstasy comes the sobering; Dostoevsky remembers that his dream is "incredible": the doors of paradise have been closed forever to fallen mankind. There is no more paradise on earth; all creation groans and languishes.

The story of man's fall from grace follows the picture of paradisiacal bliss. It is depicted symbolically, as the sin of the "ridiculous man." "Here there occurred something so awful," he relates, "something so horribly real that it could not have been conceived in a dream. . . . Oh, judge for yourselves: up till now I have been concealing the full truth, but now I will complete my story. The thing is that I—*debauched them all!*"

The outbreak of evil and its spread is depicted with jolting force. "I know only," confesses the hero, "that I was the cause of their fall into sin. Like a *filthy trichina*, like an *atom of pestilence*, infecting whole nations, so I myself infected all this happy earth which was sinless before my coming." This theme is disclosed in images, that recall Raskolnikov's dream in *Crime and Punishment* to us. In penal servitude the murderer dreamt: "The whole world was condemned to fall a victim of some strange *plague*, unheard-of and as yet unseen, coming out of the depths of Asia onto Europe. There appeared certain new *trichinae*, microscopic creatures, which settled into men's bodies. The people, who were infected with them, became at once like men who were possessed and out of their minds." Both in *The Dream of a Ridiculous Man* and in *Crime and Punishment* there is described the origin of hostility, discord, bloody wars. "Unity" in love is replaced by dividedness in hatred. . . .

In Stavrogin's dream the fall is indicated symbolically. It is only pointed out by one *mystical token—a little red spider*. In Dostoevsky's work the spider is an image of the evil principle. Stavrogin writes in his *Confession*: "But suddenly, as though in the bright, bright light, I saw a kind of tiny dot. . . . This dot began suddenly to assume a certain form and suddenly there clearly appeared before me a *tiny, little red spider*." The spider causes him to remember the young girl Matryosha whom he had wronged. Evil enters the earthly paradise in the form of murderous sensuality. Stavrogin, like the "ridiculous man," offending the young girl, commits a sin against Mother Earth. But their fates are different: Stavrogin does not repent and perishes in his own deathlike indifference; the "ridiculous man" is saved by his pity for the injured being: after the dream about the golden age, he recognizes the truth and becomes a different man. He concludes his story with the words: "*And I have found that little girl.*"

The "ridiculous man" has awakened. The earthly paradise was only a dream. It would seem the hero should forget about it and return to reality. The reverse takes place: the dream becomes the sole reality for him, in comparison with which all the rest is delirium. In the dream truth was disclosed and he goes forth to preach it. Let reason prove to him that this truth is utopia, a dream; he will not believe reason: "I saw truth, not that which my *mind* invented, but *I saw, saw it*, and its *living image* filled my soul forever. I *saw* it in such complete integrity that I cannot believe that this cannot exist among men." Here there is opposed to rational consciousness the *super-rational*, overwhelming authenticity of the "vision." He *saw a living image*, and he is convinced that this image does not exist. And he himself *understands* that paradise on earth is impossible, but really is *understanding* the point here? He *knows* that there will be a paradise. "This is so simple," assures the "ridiculous man": "in one day, in one hour—everything would be at once established! The main thing is—love others as yourself—here is the main point and that's all, and nothing more is needed: you will immediately find how things should be arranged. . . . If only everyone would begin to desire it, then everything could at once be arranged."

This is said with passionate faith and without any irony. Dostoevsky had already written about brotherhood in love in *The Winter Notes on Summer Impressions*. Such a brotherhood is paradise on earth. "Because I saw the truth, I saw and know that men can be beautiful and happy, *without losing the ability to live on earth*."

The Dream of a Ridiculous Man is the key to Dostoevsky's complex religious philosophy; here is the synthesis and culmination of his entire world-outlook. He believed not in the other-worldly bliss of bodiless souls, but in the coming of the Kingdom of God on earth, in the realization of man's unity in love according to Christ's testament. He believed in the *resurrection and transfiguration of the flesh*.

". . . People can be beautiful and happy, without losing their ability to live on earth! . . ." The "earthly paradise" is not the socialist anthill, not a humanitarian utopia, but the Second Advent of Christ. It is true, the "ridiculous man" does not mention the name of Him Who will gather around Him the family of man. But for him this "final truth" was already said by the "deist" Versilov, who dreamed that same dream of paradise. "I have always ended my picture," he confesses, "with a vision, as in Heine's—*Christ on the Baltic Sea*. I could not get on without Him. . . . And then the scales would, as it were, fall away from all their eyes and there resounds the great hymn of the new and last resurrection. . . ."

The three dreams—Stavrogin's, Versilov's, and the "ridiculous man's" —are united by the vision of Claude Lorrain's "golden age." This is a triptych, forming one whole: the most fantastic utopia, "the most incredible dream," is completed by the image of Christ and the "hymn of the last resurrection."

In the vast philosophico-journalistic material of *The Diary of a Writer* of 1876 and 1877 we should single out, above all, those elements of the "prehistory" of *The Brothers Karamazov*. The writer amassed facts, observations, reflections, and notes for his "ideological novel." The most insignificant events, the most trite facts were precious to him, as concrete images of his "*idea*." The artist declares: "Not only to create and write an artistic work, but even to *notice* a fact, an artist is needed in his own way."

Dostoevsky too was an artist who, in the pages of *The Diary* was preparing his last, greatest work. *The Diary* is the laboratory of *The Brothers Karamazov*. Observations on children occupy an important place in it. At the Christmas tree party at the Artists' Club, the writer carefully observed the well-dressed children who were dancing. "Of the children, I liked most the smallest ones; they were very charming and unconstrained. Those a little older are also unconstrained, but with a certain boldness. . . . More gifted and segregated children are always more reserved, or if they are joyous, then it is invariably with a streak of leadership and command." In the tenth book of *The Brothers Karamazov*, entitled *The Boys*, this difference is maintained: we meet in it the "commanding" Kolya Krasotkin, the reserved and segregated Ilyushechka and the group of cheerful schoolboys, who are "all charming and unconstrained."

The trial of Kroneburg, who had tortured his seven-year-old daughter with *spitzruten* ("with sticks"), ended in the sadistic father's acquittal. The talented lawyer Spasovich defended the accused in a brilliant speech. Dostoevsky came down upon the cleverness of the defense's eloquent resourcefulness and with emotion speaks about the sanctity of the child. "Listen," he addresses the lawyer, "we ought not extol ourselves over children, we are worse than they. And if we teach them anything, in order to make them better, then they too teach us many a thing and also make us better, merely by our contact with them. . . . And therefore we should respect them and approach them with respect for their angelic countenances, for their innocence, for their irresponsibility and their touching defenselessness." The "angelic countenance" of a child would be revealed in the elder Zosima's instructions; the torturing of children would become the main argument against "God's world" on Ivan Karamazov's lips; the lawyer Spasovich would appear at Mitya Karamazov's trial under the name of Fetyukovich.

The author visited a colony of juvenile delinquents and described the life of these little rejected creatures. "Yes," he exclaims, "these children's souls have seen somber pictures and have grown accustomed to strong impressions, which will remain with them, of course, forever, and which they will dream about all their life in terrible dreams." Then he chances upon a Foundling Home and he became interested in the psychology of the "castoffs" of society. . . . "I kept asking myself and wanted terribly to fathom; when precisely do these children begin to learn that they are inferior to all the rest, i.e., they are not children such as 'those others,' but much inferior and are not living at all by right, but only, so to speak, out of humaneness!" And once again "facts" of children's sufferings: the case of Kornilova, a stepmother, who threw her six-year-old stepdaughter out of the fourth story; the case of Djunkovskys who savagely tortured their children. Dostoevsky ends his account of the trial with an inspired appeal to love; the religious pathos of this "sermon" anticipates the elder Zosima's instruction, "Seek love and store love in your hearts," he exclaims. "Love is so omnipotent that it even regenerates ourselves. It is only with love that we will buy our children's hearts. . . . And how can one not love them! If we cease to love children, whom then would we be able to love and what will happen to us? Remember that it was only for the sake of children and for their little golden heads that our Savior promised us to 'shorten the times and the seasons.' It is for their sake that the pain of the regeneration of human society into a more perfect one shall be shortened. Let this perfection come to pass and let the sufferings and doubt of our civilization at last come to an end!"

"The regeneration of society into a more perfect one" is his same eternal dream of an "earthly paradise," of the transfiguration of the world. From this mystical kernel grows *The Brothers Karamazov*. It is the children who first enter into the Kingdom of God; here is why the "children's theme" occupies such an important place in the novel's composition. The promise of future perfection is already shown in the angelic countenance of a child. The beginning of the transfiguration of the world is put in Alyosha's speech *At the Stone*, over the grave of the boy Ilyusha.

Dostoevsky's "earthly paradise" opens like a mystical flower on the "holy" land, in the bosom of Mother Earth–the Mother of God. Therefore, the theme of children is united in his work with the theme of land, forms a consecrated Trinity: *paradise–children–the earth*. In the July-August installment of the *Diary*, for 1876, in the article *The Land and the Children*, we read: "Land is everything, I am not differentiating between the land and the children and somehow with me this comes out of its own accord. . . . Children must be born on the soil, and not on the pavement. . . . *Que diable*, every decent and healthy urchin is born together with a little horse; every decent father must know this if he wishes to be happy. . . . Later on they can live on the pavement, but a nation in its vast majority should be born and *sprout* on the earth, on the soil, upon which corn and trees grow. . . . There is something sacramental in the earth, in the soil. If you want to regenerate mankind into something better, to make men virtually out of beasts, then give them land and you will achieve your goal."

The writer's political doctrine about being rooted in the soil and his religious teaching about the earth are united with faith in the regeneration of mankind. Children are the symbol of this union. Dostoevsky for the first time expressed himself to the end. "There is something *sacramental* in the earth, in the soil."

Other notes prepare characteristics of the novel's dramatis personae. Here is the first "social" drawing of Fyodor Pavlovich Karamazov. Talking about "liberal fathers," the writer remarks: "On the contrary, the majority was made up only of a coarse mass of petty atheists and gross scoundrels, in substance, mere bleeders and petty tyrants, but braggarts of liberalism, in which they contrived to see only the *right to dishonor*. . . . And just then the emancipation of the peasants had come, and along with it the decomposition of our educated society." Fyodor Karamazov is a "liberal father," who has understood liberalism as the "right to dishonor." Such is the "idea" of the head of the Karamazov household.

Intending to write the history of a Russian family, the writer by no means defined it as a biological cell, the development of which is determined by the laws of race, blood, and heredity. The family for him was a *spiritual whole*, unified by an ideational succession. Dostoevsky the idealist is the antipode of the naturalist Zola: the Karamazovs are the direct antithesis of the Rougon-Macquarts. In the *Diary* he talks about the "life of ideas" and has in mind the theme of Smerdyakov. "Ideas go flying about the air," he writes, "but certainly in accord with laws: ideas are alive and spread according to laws that are too difficult for us to perceive; ideas are infectious, and do you know that in the general temper of life some idea, some anxiety, or grief accessible only to the highly educated and developed mind, can suddenly be communicated to an almost semiliterate being, one that is crude and has never been concerned about anything, and *suddenly will infect his soul with its influence*." In this way the "idea" of Ivan Karamazov's philosophy infects the "semiliterate" lackey Smerdyakov.

Finally, there grows out of observations on a new "contemporary type," the author of anonymous abusive letters, the ideational image of the "exposer" Rakitin in *Brothers Karamazov*. "Discontented, skeptical, fathers" have bequeathed to their sons their own "impotent laughter" and a "heritage of baseness." "The son is smart, egotistic, considers himself a genius, begins to send manuscripts to an editor, and ends with denunciations and anonymous slander." The author concludes: ". . . In a word, it seems to me that the type of an anonymous libeler would be an extremely good theme for a tale. And a serious one. Here, of course, Gogol would be needed, but I am glad at least that by chance I struck upon the idea. Perhaps, in fact *I will even try to put it into a novel*."

Thus a chance and insignificant fact suddenly disclosed its ideational depth to the artist. He had "struck upon the idea": the idea would be embodied in a personality; there would be born the unforgettable figure of the "seminarian-careerist" Rakitin.

In the journalistics of *The Diary of a Writer* Dostoevsky's basic philosophical themes are clearly presented: catholicism and socialism, Europe and Russia, the intelligentsia and the people, the idea of immortality and Western atheism. The ideological constructions, already known to us through the author's journal essays and great novels, in the *Diary* are developed with the tone of a sermon and prophecy. The writer predicts the "colossal" revolution approaching Europe. "It seems to me," he wrote in June 1877, "that even the *present age will end in old Europe with something colossal, i.e.*, perhaps, with something, although not literally identical with the events that ended the 18th century, but nevertheless equally colossal, elemental, and dreadful and also involving a change of the face of this world. . . . For precisely now everything has risen up in Europe simultaneously, all world questions at once, and at the same time all world controversies."

In November 1877 Dostoevsky again returned to the theme of Europe: "Yes," he wrote, "vast cataclysms are awaiting Europe, such that men's minds refuse to believe in them, considering their realization as though something fantastic. . . . *Social revolution and a new social period are indubitable in Europe.*" In our time Dostoevsky's prophetic insights have been realized. The "colossal and elemental" have already seized all the old world. . . .

As ever, at the center of the writer's historiosophic reflections stand Russia, the faith of her people and her religious mission. With new forces he preaches his *mystical populism.* Christ's image is mysteriously impressed onto the people's hearts: "The people know Christ, their God, perhaps, even better than we," wrote Dostoevsky; "though they did not study in school. They know Him because for many centuries they have borne many sufferings and in their grief have always, from the beginning and till now, heard about this God—their Christ— from their saints." The people's Christianity is not dogmatic and not even mystical: this is a *living feeling, a living force,* which stirs the nation. The writer declares that the whole of Orthodoxy is reduced to *love of mankind in Christ* alone. "The Russian man," he states, "knows nothing more lofty than Christianity, and cannot even imagine anything. He has called his whole land, his whole community, all Russia, 'Christianity' [*Khristianstvo*]—the 'peasantry' [*krestyanstvo*]. Consider Orthodoxy: this is by no means the church and ritual, this is a *living feeling* which among our people has been turned into one of those basic *living forces* without which nations do not live. In Russian Christianity, strictly speaking, there *is no mysticism* at all, in it there is only *love of mankind, only the image of Christ.*" Later, Dostoevsky was to transmit his own *very personal* religious consciousness to the "people's saint"—the Elder Zosima.

This chain of syllogisms brings the author of the *Diary* to the idea of *Russian messianism*. The soul of the people is Orthodoxy, the idea of Orthodoxy is completely universal to mankind and ecumenical, Russia's vocation is the unification of all nations at the foot of the Cross. He writes about the Russian idea: "This is, actually and in fact, almost our brotherly love for other peoples, this is our need *to serve all mankind*, this is our reconciliation with their civilizations." The Eastern question aroused the writer with a presentiment of great accomplishments: he believed that Russia would enter upon its authentic historical path; it would become the protectress of its brother Slavs, the leader of Orthodoxy. But in the tragic dialectic of his ideas, Dostoevsky lapsed from the theme of religious service to the theme of national might; Russian messianism was converted into warlike imperialism: the last became the first. In the article *The Utopian Conception of History* this transition strikes us in its sharpness. "We will begin now that the hour has come," he writes, "precisely by becoming servants to all, for the sake of universal reconciliation. He who wishes to be first in the Kingdom of God—let him become a servant to all. . . . Here is how I understand Russia's predestination in its ideal." And a few lines later he declares: "*Of course and for this very purpose, sooner or later, Constantinople must be ours . . .*" (June 1876).

The beginning of the war to liberate the Slavs seemed to the writer the approach of a new era in Russia's history. In the November installment of the *Diary* for 1877 he spoke still more resolutely about Constantinople: "Constantinople must be ours, conquered by us, Russians, from the Turks and remain ours forever. . . . Constantinople is the center of the Eastern world, while the spiritual center of the Eastern world and its head is Russia. . . . She will stand on guard over all the East and its future order. . . . For, what is the Eastern question? The Eastern question is in its essence the solution of the destinies of Orthodoxy. . . . During the ages the lost image of Christ has been preserved in all the light of its purity in Orthodoxy. . . ."

Shigalyov in *The Devils* announces: "I have confused my own givens and my conclusion is in direct contradiction to the original idea, from which I set out. Starting out from limitless freedom, I end with limitless despotism."

The same tragic contradiction lies in Dostoevsky's *Christian imperialism*. Setting out from the idea of "serving all," he concluded with an apology of war. Russia's religious mission required the capture of Constantinople.

But the writer's presentiments were not realized: the Lord prepared for Russia not a coronation in the ancient capital of the Byzantine emperors, but a way of the cross and a martyr's crown.

The two years spent working on the *Diary* were culminated by that religious-philosophical idea, from which issued the concept of the novel *The Brothers Karamazov*. The Russian writer's historical mission consisted in asserting the *failure of humanism* and exposing its religious lie. All his great novels are devoted to struggling against the seductions of *atheistic love for mankind*. Love for men can be only in Christ and man's brotherhood is possible only on a Christian foundation. In *The Diary of a Writer* Dostoevsky's many years of reflections on the ultimate destinies of mankind are concentrated in a few aphorisms which are astounding in their force: all the rays are brought into focus and the greatest of the writer's thoughts are illuminated with a blinding lustre.

Humanists profess that love for others is *naturally* innate to man. Dostoevsky retorts: love for others is *not natural*, but supernatural. Without faith in immortality, this idea is incomprehensible to human reason. He goes even further, and daringly asserts that without belief in God and in the immortality of the soul, love for mankind can be transformed into hate. Here is what he writes in the *Diary* (November 1876).

"Without a higher idea, neither a man, nor a nation can exist. But on earth there is *only one* higher idea, and namely—the idea of the immortality of the human soul, for all the other 'higher' ideas of life, by which man can live, flow from it alone. . . .

"I assert that the consciousness of our own utter inability to help or to bring, if only some, benefit or relief to suffering mankind, while at the same time remaining completely convinced of this suffering, can even *transform the love of mankind in your heart into hatred for it*. . . . I declare (again still *for the time being* without offering proofs for it) that love for mankind is even altogether *unthinkable, unintelligible,* and *altogether impossible* without concomitant faith in the immortality of the human soul. . . . I even maintain and make bold to say that love for mankind is, as an idea, *one of the most incomprehensible ideas* to the human mind. . . . Without being convinced of his own immortality, man's ties with the earth are severed. . . . In a word, the idea of immortality—this is life itself, *living life*."

In these assertions for which "proofs were not offered"—is the synthesis of all Dostoevsky's thoughts on faith and atheism, on socialistic utopias, on the fate of Christianity and Russia's mission. The humanism of the 19th century, torn away from its Christian roots, was transformed into hatred and universal war. The mankind-loving disciples of Rousseau became Parisian Communards; love for humanity led to the destruction of nine-tenths of it by fire and the sword.

Out of these reflections grew the idea of Ivan Karamazov. He is a representative of atheistic humanity, of "distant and remote love"; he is opposed by Alyosha, the "Christian humanist," the bearer of "immediate love for one's neighbor." A quarrel develops between them. If there is no God and immortality, Ivan is right; if God exists, Alyosha wins.

Behind Ivan's shoulders stands the spirit of nonbeing—the devil; behind Alyosha, the elder Zosima, feasting after death at the marriage in Cana of Galilee. Thus, the idea of immortality is embodied in the artistic design of *The Brothers Karamazov*.

X X I I

The Final Years. The History
of the Creation of *The Brothers Karamazov*

In November 1880, sending the epilogue of *The Brothers Karamazov* off to *The Russian Messenger*, Dostoevsky wrote to Lyubimov: "Well here, the novel is finished! I've worked it for *three years*, I have been printing it for two—a significant moment for me." And so, according to the author's testimony, the beginning of his work on the novel goes back to the year 1877. Here is why in the October issue of *The Diary of a Writer* for 1877 he informed his readers of his decision to discontinue the publication for a year or two, and in the final December installment he confessed that he wanted to occupy himself with a certain "artistic work." The conception of *Brothers Karamazov* already completely possessed his imagination.

In the spring of 1878 he began to arrange the material he had collected in *The Diary of a Writer* in order and to work out the plan of the novel. Dostoevsky had been engrossed by his "children theme" and with the conscientiousness of a scholarly researcher he studied the facts. He wrote to the pedagogue V. V. Mikhailov: "In your letter, I was very interested in the fact that you love children, have lived a great deal with children, and even now spend time with them. Well, here is my request, dear Vladimir Vasilyevich: *I have planned, and soon will begin a big novel* in which, among other things, children will play a large part, especially young ones from 7 to 15 years, approximately. Many children will be introduced. *I am studying* and have studied them all my life, love them very much, and have some of my own. But the observations of a man such as yourself (I understand this) will be invaluable to me. And so write me what you yourself know about the children in Petersburg who have called you dear uncle and about the Yelisavetgrad children and *about what you know*. Things that happen, their habits, answers, words and little sayings, traits of character, their relations to their families, faith, misdeeds, and innocence; nature and the teacher, the Latin language and so forth, and so forth—in a word, what you yourself know."

The letter is dated March 16; the project had already matured to the point that the writer could "soon begin" the novel. In fact, the first entries in the notebooks are from April 1878. The novel's ideology is built, however, not on facts and observations alone. Two great thinkers entered Dostoevsky's life at this period, whose influence determined his religio-philosophical conception. These were Vladimir Sergeyevich Solovyov and Nikolai Fyodorovich Fyodorov.

The young docent at Moscow University, the author of a brilliant Master's dissertation, *The Crisis of Western Philosophy*, and of the extraordinary study, *The Philosophic Principles of Integral Knowledge*, V. S. Solovyov, captivated Dostoevsky by the boldness of his constructions and by his inspired teaching regarding the mystical transfiguration of the world. He preached the theory of Sophia, the Divine Wisdom, and explained the meaning of history in terms of a divine-human process. The twenty-five-year-old philosopher, mystic, and poet, sought to express his personal religious experiences in logical concepts and abstract schema. In his poem *Three Encounters*, he wrote:

> Though still enslaved to the idle world,
> Beneath the crude outer husk of matter
> Thus I perceived the incorruptible purple
> And felt the radiance of the Divinity.

Dostoevsky also knew the mystical experience of the divine foundation of the world (Mother Earth, the Mother of God); he was also a visionary and in his ecstasies had experienced the moment of "world harmony." Solovyov became his closest friend and companion. Anna Grigoryevna informs us that Fyodor Mikhailovich was fervently attached to the young philosopher; his relation to him resembled the relation of the Elder Zosima to Alyosha Karamazov; he used to say that Solovyov's spiritual appearance reminded him of the friend of his youth, I. N. Shidlovsky, and he compared the young philosopher's beautiful face to the face of Christ in Carracci's painting. In 1877 Solovyov delivered to the Society of the Friends of Russian Literature an inspired speech *Three Forces*. His ideas were very close to the ideas of Dostoevsky; the lecturer violently attacked Western civilization, which had culminated its development by affirming the "atheistic individual," and he believed that Russia "would bring life to those elements that were dead in their hatred through a loftier principle of reconciliation. . . ." "The great historic mission of Russia," he concluded, "is a religious mission." We are familiar with these ideas from *The Diary of a Writer*. The concept of the universality of the Russian spirit, which lies at the base of Dostoevsky's Pushkin speech, was formulated by Solovyov before him. In the beginning of 1878 the young philosopher gave a series of lectures *On God-manhood* at Solyanoy Gorodok in Petersburg; these lectures became a great event in the spiritual life of the capital. They were frequented by prominent officials, ladies of the aristocracy, men in public life, writers, the university youth. Dostoevsky enthusiastically attended Solovyov's talks, and his system is reflected in the ideational structure of *Brothers Karamazov*. In the philosopher the writer found a clear and pointed formulation of his own cherished thoughts. This is how Solovyov defined the problem of "Christian philosophy":

"The old traditional form of religion arises from faith in God, but does not pursue this faith to its limit. Contemporary civilization outside of religion arises from faith in man, but even it does not pursue its faith to the limit; consistently pursued and brought to their ultimate realization, both these faiths—faith in God and faith in man—are united in the sole, complete, and integral *truth of God-manhood.*"

The Brothers Karamazov was inspired by this truth. Anna Grigoryevna holds that several characteristics of the author of *Lectures on God-manhood* passed over to Ivan Karamazov. In fact, the brilliant dialectician Ivan, with the power of his formal logic and rational ethics, with the range of his social utopia and religious philosophy, does recall Solovyov. It is not without reason that in the novel it is Ivan who expounds the "idea" of theocracy, on which the young philosopher was working at that very time.

Another remarkable individual who exercised influence on Dostoevsky, was N. F. Fyodorov, the brilliant author of *The Philosophy of the Common Task,* also as much a solitary and misunderstood thinker as was Solovyov. A follower and disciple of Fyodorov, N. P. Peterson, who taught in a peasant school, sent the writer an account and précis of his book. It deeply excited Dostoevsky and on March 24, 1878, he answered his correspondent: "I will say that in essence I am completely in accord with these thoughts. I read them as though I might have written them myself: I read them today (anonymously) to Vladimir Sergeyevich Solovyov. I waited for him on purpose in order to read your account of your thinker's ideas, inasmuch as

I found a great deal that is analogous in his outlook. This provided us with two beautiful hours. He is in profound sympathy with your thinker." And in conclusion the writer solemnly declared: "We here, i.e., Solovyov and myself, at least, believe *in a real, literal, personal resurrection and that it will take place on the earth.*"

Having studied Fyodorov's system, Solovyov wrote to its author: "I have read your manuscript greedily and with spiritual delight. . . . Your 'project' I accept categorically and without any discussion. . . . For the present I will only say that, since the coming of Christianity, your 'project' is the human spirit's *first move* along the way of Christ, I, from my side, can only acknowledge you my teacher and spiritual father." What precisely was the nature of this teaching which captivated two such people as Dostoevsky and Solovyov?

Fyodorov's *Philosophy of the Common Task* reduces to a paradoxical proposition: the joining together of sons for the resurrection of their fathers. Men live divided and their spiritual forces are paralyzed by enmity and conflict. One must do away with the struggles between governments, peoples, classes; a classless society, a single family, a brotherhood must be created. And then united mankind will be able to realize its great vocation. All living sons will direct their forces to a single problem—the resurrection of their dead fathers. "For the present age," writes Fyodorov, "father is the most hateful word, and son is the most degrading." When humanity is converted into one family, it will accomplish Christ's work on earth. "Religion also is the task of resurrection," the philosopher maintains. Christ by his own resurrection showed us the way; all things will be possible to the human brotherhood; it will, in fact, begin to master the earth and control the elements. Science and technology will transfigure the world. Then the destructive force of nature will itself become life-bearing; life will be replaced by resurrection, sexual love by filial love. "The regulation, the direction of the forces of nature," writes the author, "are also encompassed by that great task which can and must become common." If mankind unites in love, the world will not end in a catastrophe nor will there be a Final Judgment. Without a disaster, our earthly world will, through evolution, be transformed into the Kingdom of God. Fyodorov's "project" is astonishing in its fiery heroic spirit. Throughout all world philosophy there is no construction more mysterious and audacious. Fyodorov talks about religion as a genuine cosmic force which is transfiguring the world; sets before Christianity a vast *practical* problem—of universal resurrection; requires the full actualization of man's creative power, religious, social, scientific, and technical, and ardently believes that the Kingdom of God will appear as the culmination of the *God-manhood* process.

In Fyodorov's strange project, Dostoevsky encountered a bold expression of many of his own confused expectations and dim hopes. His ideas of "unity," "the family" and "brotherhood," his faith in the religious meaning of history and in the transfiguration of the world by love found in the teaching of the Moscow philosopher a brilliant corroboration. The practical, concrete character of the "project" captivated him; he kept in mind the phrase that "for the present age the word father is the most hateful." Fyodorov called sons to the resurrection of their fathers; at the center of *The Brothers Karamazov* stands a *parricide:* these sons mortally hate their father. The crime whose responsibility falls on Smerdyakov, Ivan, and Dmitry, becomes the symbol of mankind's denial of unity. Through a "proof by the contrary" the author leads us to an affirmation of the religious significance of life. Sonship of blood is opposed by sonship in the spirit (Alyosha—the Elder Zosima); murderous hate, by resurrecting love. Fyodorov's "project" affected the "practical" character of Alyosha's Christian ministry. He leaves the monastery for the world and lays the first foundation for future human brotherhood (his speech at Ilyusha's grave). Like Fyodorov, he also believes in "a real, literal, personal resurrection" here on earth.

Here is why among the rough drafts to the novel we find such entries: "The resurrection of our forefathers." . . . "The resurrection of our forefathers depends on us." Under Fyodorov's influence, Dostoevsky developed the theme of parricide as the ultimate expression of world tragedy.

———————

In April 1878 the first notes for the novel were entered in his sketchbook.

Memento (concerning the novel).

—Find out whether it's possible to lie between the rails with a train passing over you at full speed.

—Inquire: the wife of a man condemned to penal servitude—can she marry again right away.

—Does an idiot have the right to keep such a crowd of adopted children, to have a school, etc.

—Inquire about child labor in factories.

—About gymnasiums, life in a gymnasium.

—Inquire about whether a young man, a nobleman and land-owner, can shut himself off for many years in a monastery (although it's at his uncle's) as a novice? (N.B. In connection with Filaret, who stank.)

—In an orphan asylum.

—At Mikhail Nikolayevich's (Foundl. Home).

—About Pestalozzi, about Froebel. Lev Tolstoy's article on contemporary school instruction in *Fath. Notes*.

—To take part in a Froebel walk.

———

The first rough drafts are devoted to the "children's theme." The author visited schools and asylums, read pedagogical works. Amidst "the great crowd of children" there rose up the image of Alyosha Karamazov. It is very curious that he was still called the "idiot." Alyosha genealogically is connected with Prince Myshkin. He inherits from him the idea of founding a brotherhood of children. The author was still unclear regarding the character of his activity ("adopted children," a school), but had already conceived the idea of "shutting him off" for many years as a novice in a monastery. The note about "Filaret, who stank" refers to the plan of the chapter *The Smell of Decay*. The writer even has Kolya Krasotkin in view and the story of how he lay between the rails under a train: the author wanted to inquire whether this fact was possible. On the secondary plane appears the image of Mitya Karamazov, sentenced to penal servitude. The novel's plan was clear to the author in its most general features; individual details were concretized; "inquiries" were made; "factual" material was collected.

———

On April 18 Dostoevsky wrote a long letter "To the Students of Moscow." For the first time he came forward as an instructor of Russian youth and as a teacher of life. Working on the theme of "fathers and children," the author tried to determine his position exactly. Children were in no way guilty, the entire responsibility fell on their fathers. "Never," he wrote, "has our youth been more sincere and honest (which is not an insignificant fact, but something extraordinary, great, historic). However, the trouble is that youth have inherited the lie of two whole centuries of our history. . . . In my opinion, you are in no way guilty. You are only children of that 'society' which you now are forsaking and which is a 'lie from all sides. . . .'" What possibilities then are open for the young Russian generation? Dostoevsky clearly saw two paths—one false, the other true. The false path led to "Europeanism," the true to the people. "But," he continued, "tearing himself away from society and forsaking it, our student goes not to the people, but away somewhere abroad, to 'Europeanism,' to the abstract kingdom of a universal man who has never existed and in this way breaks with the people, holding them in contempt without knowing them. . . . And yet our whole salvation lies in the people (but this is an extended theme). . . ." The true path leads to the people: it was hard for the contemporary generation. "In order to go to the people and to remain with them, one must above all learn not to despise them. Secondly, *one must, for example, also believe in God.*"

Under the guise of a moral admonition to the students, Dostoevsky set forth the ideological plan of his future novel. In the children's tragedy, the fathers, who are "a lie from all sides," were guilty. Fyodor Pavlovich Karamazov would be presented as this type of corrupted father. The two paths which were open to the children determine the fate of two of his sons: Ivan would turn to "Europeanism," to the "abstract kingdom of a universal man"; he would tear himself away from the soil and lose his faith; Alyosha would go to the people and believe in that which is holy and sacred to the people—Christ. The ideological schema of "fathers and children" was ready; the antithesis between the "universal man" Ivan and the Russian novice Alyosha was finally determined.

Work on the novel was interrupted by a tragic occurrence in the writer's family life: on May 16 his favorite—his three-year-old son Alyosha died. Lyubov Dostoevskaya tells us in her memoirs: "Aleksey had a strange, oval, almost angular forehead, a little head egg-shaped in form. . . . He had a seizure of convulsions; in the morning he woke up healthy, and asked for his toys in his bed, played for a moment and suddenly once again fell down in convulsions." The poor child had inherited his father's epilepsy. Anna Grigoryevna describes the writer's grief.

F. M. went to accompany the doctor, returned terribly pale, and knelt by the sofa to which we had moved the tot so it would be more convenient for the doctor to examine him. I also knelt down next to my husband; I wanted to ask him what precisely the doctor had said (as I found out later, he had told F. M. that the final agony had already begun); however, he motioned me with a sign not to speak. . . . And what was my despair when suddenly the baby's breathing stopped and death came. F. M. kissed the child, blessed him three times, and began to sob. I also wept.

Lyubov completes her mother's story. "His little coffin was taken in a carriage to Okhtensky cemetery. On the way we cried a great deal; petted the little white coffin covered with flowers." "F.M.," continues Anna Grigoryevna,

> was terribly affected by this death. Somehow he especially loved Lyosha, with an almost morbid love, as though sensing that he would soon lose him. It particularly distressed F. M. that the child perished from epilepsy—a sickness which had been inherited from him. Judging from his appearance, F. M. was calm and courageously bore the blow of fate which had befallen us, but I strongly feared that this suppression of his deep affliction would fatally reflect upon his health, which even without that was faltering. In order somewhat to comfort F. M. and to distract him from melancholy thoughts, I begged Vl. S. Solovyov, who was visiting us in those days of our sorrow, to persuade F. M. to go with him to Optina Pustyn, where Solovyov was preparing to go that summer.

Dostoevsky sent his family to Staraya Russa, and on June 20, went to Moscow; after making arrangements regarding the novel with the editors of *The Russian Messenger*, he left with V. Solovyov for Optina Pustyn.

The dead boy's name Alyosha was given to the youngest of the Karamazov brothers who earlier in the rough drafts had been called the "idiot." And together with the name, all the father's tenderness, all the unrealized hopes for his son's brilliant future, were transmitted to the novel's young hero. Dostoevsky was destined to undergo this onerous trial, so that the greatest of his creations might immortalize his love and torment. Anna Grigoryevna informs us that in the chapter *Peasant Women Who Have Faith*, Fyodor Mikhailovich included "many of her doubts, thoughts, and even words."

The writer's personal grief was poured out in the plaints and lamentations of the cab man's wife who seeks consolation from the Elder Zosima. "What are you weeping about?" the Elder asks her. "It's my little son, I'm grieving for, Father," answers the peasant woman.

He was three years old, just two more months and he would have
been three years. For my little son I'm tormented, Father, for my
little son. He was the last son left; we had four, Nikitushka and me,
and they're all gone from us; the little children, they're all gone;
what was longed for, they're all gone. . . . I've buried the last, and
I can't forget him. Look, just as if he stands here before me, he
never leaves me. He's dried up my soul. I'll look at his poor little
clothes, at his little shirt, or at his shoes and I'll start wailing. . . . I'll
lay out what was left after him, every thing of his, I look and wail.
. . . If only I could look at him one little time, if only one time I'd
have the chance again to peep at him and I wouldn't go up to him,
wouldn't speak, I could hide myself in a corner, only to see, to hear
him for a single moment, playing in the yard; he used to come, he
would cry in his little voice: "Mommy, where are you?" If only I
could hear how he passes through the room with his tiny feet just
once, just one time, with his tiny feet tap-tap, and so often, often,
I remember, how he used to run to me, shout, and laugh; if only I
might hear, might hear his tiny feet, I would know him! . . .

Dostoevsky's artistic realism here attains genuine clairvoyance. Maternal love *resurrects* the image of the dead child; the concreteness of
its vision verges on a miracle.

The father's anguish caused by the death of his favorite son intensifies the emotional tone of the story regarding the children; the description of Ilyushechka's death and Captain Snegiryov's grief will forever
pierce the heart with an unforgettable pain. In this "torment," it is impossible not to feel the author's personal anguish.

In his letters from abroad, Dostoevsky frequently spoke of his desire
to visit a Russian monastery. Long before (in the rough drafts for
Atheism and for *The Life of a Great Sinner*) he had already decided
to depict a monastery. Optina Pustyn to which he traveled with V.
Solovyov, was located in Kaluga Province, near Kozelsk, and in the
19th century was celebrated for its Elders. Gogol appealed to their
wise direction. The well-known Slavophile Iv. Kireyevsky worked
with them in a venture to publish ascetic treatises. Konstantin Leontyev, lived for a long time at the hospice. Even Lev Tolstoy used to
come there. The holiness of the monastery shone over all Russia. Legends about the Elder Amvrosy—the ascetic, healer, and miracle worker
—circulated among the people.

Dostoevsky passed two days and nights at Optina Pustyn. "The then renowned Elder Fath. Amvrosy," writes Anna Grigoryevna, "F. M. saw three times: once in a crowd surrounded by the people, and two times privately." In the novel, the Elder Zosima offers touching consolation to the unfortunate mother. Anna Grigoryevna thinks that Dostoevsky placed on his lips words that had been said to him personally by Father Amvrosy: "And don't be consoled, consolation is not what you need," says Zosima, "Don't be consoled, and weep. . . . And for a long time yet you will have this great mother's lamentation, but in the end it will turn into quiet joy for you, and your bitter tears will be only tears of quiet tenderness and heartfelt purification, which delivers one from sins. And I shall remember your little child's repose; what was his name?" "Aleksey, Father." Dostoevsky returned from the monastery comforted and set about the writing of the novel with inspiration.

The first two books of *The Brothers Karamazov*—*The History of a Certain Family* and *An Unfortunate Gathering*—were prepared in their final form at the end of October 1878; the rough drafts for them are devoted primarily to the characteristics of Alyosha Karamazov.[A] The author provided motivation for his hero's entering the monastery: "The straightforwardness of youth. Perhaps this force acted on his youthful imagination—he saw how particularly the garrulous and peasant women flocked together. And perhaps the good Elder struck him at that time by some special attributes of his soul, only he became attached to him entirely without reserve." "The hermitage's beauty, the singing, then most of all, the Elder." "The honesty of the generation. A hero from the new generation. Conceived the desire and acted." "Chapter—why the monastery? Is he a mystic? never, a fanatic—by no means." "He had faith as a realist. Such a person, once he believes completely, then he will believe irrevocably. The dreamer and poet will have faith on condition, as a Lutheran. . . . He understood that knowledge and faith are different and opposite, that if there are other worlds and if it's true that man is immortal, i.e., he himself is from other worlds, then, it means everything is connected with other worlds. There is also miracle. And he longed for a miracle. But here the Elder in sanctity, in the holy of holies." These reflections on other worlds were transferred to the novel in the Elder Zosima's exhortations and turned into Alyosha's ecstatic experience.

[A] *Literaturny Arkiv. F. M. Dostoevsky. Materialy i issledovaniya* (Literary Archives. F. M. Dostoevsky. Materials and Studies). Ed. A. S. Dolinin. Leningrad, 1935.

Alyosha's conversation with the children was conceived on a broad scale. "He explains to the children the situation of mankind in the tenth century (Taine). Explains *The Funeral Dinner* to the children: evil leads to an evil end. Explains the devil (Job, the prologue). Explains the Temptation in the Wilderness. Explains the future socialism, new men. Maxime du Camp, negative, there is no *positive*, Russia is positive—Christians." *The Funeral Dinner*, is Schiller's poem *Das Siegesfest* from which Dostoevsky quotes one verse in Tyutchev's translation;[2] an "explanation" of it did not enter the text of the novel. In the final edition, it is not Alyosha, but the Elder Zosima who talks about the Book of Job. The "Temptation in the Wilderness" becomes the main theme of the *Legend of the Grand Inquisitor;* Maxime du Camp's book *Convulsions de Paris* which is devoted to the Paris Commune, was employed by the writer in his condemnation of socialism. Originally, Alyosha was also conceived as a philosopher like Ivan.

Notes were assembled for the description of the monastery and its life; the monk Parfeny's book and the author's personal impressions from Optina Pustyn served as material for it. He wrote down: "The institution of Elders, the monk Parfeny."

"The Elders of Optina: peasant women used to approach them on their knees." At this point, Zosima still bore the name Makary; his image had not been completely diassociated from the figure of the pilgrim Makar Dolgoruky (*A Raw Youth*). "They used to say, Makary could read in their eyes."

"There were monks in the monastery who were hostile to the Elder, but there were not many of them. They kept silent, concealing their malice, although they were important personages. One used to fast, the other was a half-fool for Christ. In the novel these two enemies of Zosima are merged into one person—Ferapont.

Ivan Karamazov appears in the rough drafts under the names "the learned one," "the learned brother," "the murderer." We find the novel's ideational construct already developed; the real parricide is not Smerdyakov, but the atheist Ivan. The author noted down: "The learned brother, it turns out, had been at the Elder's before." In the

[2] Fyodor Ivanovich Tyutchev (1803-1873), perhaps, after Pushkin Russia's greatest poet. His style employs archaic effects, is lofty in tone, with an absolute mastery of rhythm and the arrangement of sound. The main vision of his work is metaphysical and based upon a dualistic conception of the universe: there exist two worlds—Chaos and Cosmos, Night and Day—and the latter is illusory, unreal. His influence upon the Symbolists, of course, was great. No less beautiful, though quite different in texture, are his love poems. His translations from German, French, Italian, and English are extraordinary and in some instances overshadow the originals.

novel there are no traces of this original design. It is possible that the author wanted to set the ideational opponents Zosima and Ivan in a more intimate connection, as he had done in *The Devils* (Bishop Tikhon's meeting with Stavrogin). The dispute in the Elder's cell was planned differently than it appears in the final text. Ivan was to defend his thesis: "Is there such a law of nature—to love mankind? This is a divine law. There is no such law of nature." Miusov—the advocate of the theory of rational egoism—offered objections. Here is the entry of this dialogue:

He (the murderer) maintains that there is no law and that love exists only out of faith in immortality.

Miusov. I most strenuously disagree. Love toward mankind lies in man himself as a law of nature.

All are silent: "There is no reason to submit to suffering," somebody mumbles.

(*Ivan*). How does one determine where the limit is?

(*Miusov*). The limit is when I injure mankind.

(*Ivan*). And why restrain oneself?

(*Miusov*). If for no other reason, to live one's life more conveniently. If there is no love, then it will be founded on reason.

(*Ivan*). If everything were based on reason, we'd have nothing.

(*Miusov*). In this case can one do what one likes?

(*Ivan*). Yes, if there's no God or immortality of the soul, then there can be no love for mankind.

This curious dialogue did not enter into the novel.

In the rough drafts Dmitry Karamazov bears the name of Ilyinsky. According to Anna Grigoryevna's testimony, this was the name of the parricide whose story is related in the first chapter of *Notes from the House of Death.* "I especially cannot forget a certain parricide," wrote the author. "He was of the nobility, had been in service and for his sixty-year-old father was something like a prodigal son. He was completely immoral in his behavior, had become involved in debts. His father tried to confine him; but the father had a house, had a farm; it was suspected that he had money and that the son killed him, through greed for his inheritance. The crime was only discovered a month later. This entire month he spent in the most dissolute manner. Finally, in his absence, the police found the body. . . . He did not confess, was deprived of his nobility, rank, and exiled to hard labor for twenty years.

All the time that I lived with him, he was in the most excellent, in the most cheerful frame of mind. This was a flighty, light-headed individual, irresponsible in the highest degree, although by no means a fool. I never noticed any particular cruelty in him. . . . It goes without saying, I did not believe in this crime. But people from his town, who must have known all the details of his history, related the whole affair to me. The facts were so clear that it was impossible not to believe them." However, intuition did not deceive the writer. In the seventh chapter of *House of Death*, which was printed in the journal *Time* a year and a half after the first chapter, the author tells how he had received information from Siberia. "The criminal was, in fact, innocent and for ten years had suffered in penal servitude—for no reason; his innocence has been established by the court officially: the real criminals was found and has confessed; the unfortunate man has already been released from prison." And Dostoevsky concludes: "There is nothing to say or add regarding all the tragic depths in this fact, regarding the life that was already ruined in the time of its youth, under such a terrible charge."

The writer was shaken by the *tragic* fate of this innocent convict who had borne the accusation of parricide. For sixteen years this terrible recollection lived in his memory, and determined the plot of his last novel. Flighty and light-headed Mitya Karamazov is placed in the same relation toward his father "of whom it is suspected that he has money," as Ilyinsky. Like the hero of the novel, the alleged murderer was a healthy and strong individual, lived in a small provincial city (Tobolsk), came from a noble family, and had the rank of sublieutenant in a line battalion. Ilyinsky's father was sixty years old, Fyodor Pavlovich Karamazov fifty-five. Ilyinsky was exiled to penal servitude by Imperial decision. Mitya "will smell the mines for twenty years."

The clash between Dmitry Karamazov and his father in the Elder Zosima's cell was conceived by the author in direct connection with Fyodorov's idea about the resurrection of our forefathers. He noted down: "The resurrection of our forefathers. The landowner [i.e., Fyodor Pavlovich] about Ilyinsky: 'He not only will not raise anyone from the dead, but he'll even bake them till they're done.' Ilyinsky gets up: 'A disgraceful comedy.' " Apparently, Fyodorov's "project" was originally one of the themes of conversation among the Elder's guests. When Dmitry appeared, Fyodor Pavlovich, pointing to his son-rival, made a buffoonish exit out of the conversation. In the printed text, allusion to the philosopher who was unknown to the general public was omitted. However, this important entry shows that the theme of parricide was consciously chosen by Dostoevsky as the antithesis to Fyodorov's teaching. In the transfigured universe carnal love will be turned into family love, and sons will restore life to their fathers; in our fallen world, carnal passions lead to parricide.

On the following page we read: "A bludgeon. A compromising word —onward (about the father's murder). . . . 'Karl Moor and Franz Moor. *Regierende Graf von Moor.*'" In the novel, this entry is developed in the words of Karamazov senior. " 'Heavenly and most holy Elder!' he exclaimed, pointing to Ivan Fyodorovich. 'This is my son, flesh of my flesh, the most beloved of my flesh! This is my most respectful, so to speak, Karl Moor, and there—that one, my son who has just come in, Dmitry Fyodorovich, and against whom I am seeking justice from you, he is now the most disrespectful Franz Moor—both out of Schiller's *The Robbers*, and I, I myself, in such case, am the *Regierende Graf von Moor*!'"

In fact, the plot of *Brothers Karamazov* remotely recalls the subject of Schiller's drama. Ivan, who under a mask of respect, conceals hatred for his father and is morally responsible for his death, and Dmitry whom his father suspects of wanting to make an attempt on his life and who is crushed by a false accusation occupy places in the composition of the novel analogous to the places of the brothers-enemies in *The Robbers*. Dostoevsky had seen Schiller's drama while still a child and throughout his entire life remembered the celebrated actor Mochalov's performance. The figure of the noble but dissolute son, Karl Moor, was joined in his imagination with passionate and generous Dmitry. In Schiller's romanticism of the pathetic, he found a tone for the image of the "most disrespectful son." Not without reason does Dmitry declaim the German poet's hymn *To Joy* and is inspired by his cosmic sense of life.

Fyodor Pavlovich's figure is clearly sketched in the rough drafts. The writer perceived it not visually, but, as it were, by ear. He amassed a great number of words and expressions with which to characterize this cynic buffoon. We again have before us the fact of a character's springing up from the element of speech. For the old Karamazov's "buffoonery" sayings, puns, and anecdotes were collected. "I'm a knight.

I'm a knight of honor. . . ." "The money's in the envelope for my little chick." "In love like a pugdog!" "I'm a passionate individual . . ." "*La Russie se recueille.*" "A certain most high Government personage. I say to him:, *mon cher.* But here comes that most high Government personage now." "Diderot and Platon. The fool says in his heart: there is no God. He bowed down." "With a walling in." "He genteelly kissed his head." "Dmitry Fyodorovich, from now on, do not know me! Yes; I'm ready to challenge you to a duel." *Ilyinsky* to him: "Comedian, I curse you." Out of this chaotic verbal material, grew up the personality of Karamazov senior. The expressions, devised and noted beforehand, were colors on the artist's palette: distributing and combining them on his canvas, he painted the portrait of his hero.

Like Fyodor Pavlovich, the murderer Smerdyakov also arose from *speech.* The author heard his voice, penetrated his intonations. He noted down: "*Smerdyakov*—he struck with a knife, she cried out and began to catch at the knife. *Smerdyakov.* No, sir, I would hold a woman in obedience." In the novel, these expressions remained unused: the sense was not important to the writer, but the intonation and sound of these expressions: he was practicing his hero's "articulation." Smerdyakov's psychological image was fixed with the help of quotations from Victor Hugo. Dostoevsky notes: "Humble et hautain comme tous les fanatiques (V. Hugo)" and "L'âme d'un conspirateur et l'âme d'un laquais."

The first quotation is taken from Hugo's novel *Les Misérables,* the second from his play *Ruy Blas.* Komarovich points out the illegitimate son Smerdyakov's resemblance to the detective Javert in *Les Misérables.* Javert was born in some dark corner to a woman of the streets, and began to avenge himself for his illegitimate origin—on whom, on what "this he could never decide or understand." Dostoevsky cites Javert in an unpublished article that had been intended for *The Diary of a Writer* for 1876. The purposeless vindictiveness and spite of Hugo's hero the author transferred to his own "illegitimate"—Smerdyakov.

In November 1878 the two books of the novel's first part were completed and the writer brought them to the editor of *The Russian Messenger* in Moscow. Katkov "looked over" the manuscript and was satisfied: his coeditor Lyubimov "read through the first third and found everything very original." On January 31, 1879, Dostoevsky sent off the third book of the novel *The Sensualists.* "This third book which I am now sending off to you," he wrote to Lyubimov, "I by no means consider bad, to the contrary, it has turned out well."

The writer's friendship with Pobedonostsev became each year more and more intimate. The prominent dignitary introduced the author of *Karamazov* into government circles and the Sovereign entrusted him with the spiritual guidance of the younger Grand Dukes Sergey and Pavel. Dostoevsky made the acquaintance of the heir to the throne and his Imperial spouse, became friends with the Grand Duke Konstantin Nikolayevich and carried on conversations with his sons: the future poet K. R. and Dmitry. The writer most respectfully presented the heir Aleksandr Aleksandrovich with copies of *The Devils* and *The Diary of a Writer*. At the end of the seventies he served as vice-president of the Slavic Philanthropic Society, whose membership included Slavophiles, representatives of the military world, and of rightist journalism. The celebrated writer became a constant guest at the aristocratic salons: he frequented the homes of Countess S. A. Tolstaya, Ye. Naryshkina, Countess A. Komarovskaya, Abaza, Princess Volkonskaya, S. P. Khitrovo, Geiden, A. Filosofova. In 1906 Pobedonostsev wrote to Anna Grigoryevna: "And during his last years he often came to my house on Saturday evenings for a chat—and I remember as though now, how, animated and running about the room, he used to relate chapters of *Karamazov*, which he was writing at that time." After Dostoevsky's death, his high-ranking friend assumed the guardianship of the dead man's children.[B]

The ideology of the author of *Diary of a Writer* in significant measure determined the direction of the politics of Aleksandr III's reign.

In 1878 a jury acquitted the terrorist, Vera Zasulich. In the rightist press a bitter campaign was begun against the court systems. The editor of *The Russian Messenger*, a militant nationalist, M. Katkov wrote some indignant articles. Dostoevsky was at the trial and shared Katkov's indignation. He made up his mind to depict the new courts satirically in *The Brothers Karamazov*. Many details of Dmitry's trial were borrowed from the legal investigation of Vera Zasulich's case.

In February 1879 Dostoevsky worked on the novel's fourth book, *Lacerations*. Here was created the picturesque figure of the Elder Zosima's ideational adversary—Father Ferapont—the champion of fasting and religious silence.

[B] See L. Grossman, *Dostoevsky i Pravitelstvennye Krugi 1870 Godov* (Dostoevsky and the Governmental Circles of the 1870 years). Literary Heritage, No. 15. Moscow 1934.

V. Komarovich[c] has established the genealogy of this representative of the old monasticism. In the eleventh chapter of *The History of Optina Pustyn* the writer found an account of a Father Pallady who lived in a hut in the forest and had been subjected to many temptations by the devil. A rigid legalist, he knew all the canons of the code thoroughly; abstained from conversations and contact with women; used to say: "Do not believe their tears, brother; hostility exists between us and them until the grave. . . . Devils come in throngs to monks who remain in idleness, but to those who are occupied with manual labor, they appear only one at a time." When visitors once asked Father Pallady if he had any antiquities, he showed them a picture of the Final Judgment, and pointing to Satan, said: "Here is the most ancient antiquity that we have, there is nothing more ancient than it. Even our old fathers used to call him the ancient enemy."

Luminous Christianity, according to Dostoevsky's thought, is a gift of the Holy Spirit. That is why in censuring it, Father Ferapont substitutes "the heresy of the holy spirit" for the Holy Spirit. The anchorite's conversation with the monk from Obdorsk about the Holy Spirit Who flies down like a bird and talks in human language, was taken by the author from the life of the Optina Elder Leonid. During his time there lived in a solitary cell a priest-monk, Feodosy, who knew how to predict the future. Father Leonid asked him how he did this; Feodosy answered that the Holy Spirit flew down to him in the form of a dove and spoke with him in a human tongue. Out of these scanty details, Dostoevsky created the fanatic Ferapont, overcome by devils, a figure remarkable in its expressiveness. . . . "An old man, strong, tall, who held himself erect, without stooping, with a fresh face, although it was also thin, but healthy. He was of athletic build. His eyes were gray, large, shining, but so extraordinarily prominent that it was even striking. He used to speak with a broad stress on the letter 'o.' He was dressed in a long, reddish, peasant's coat made of coarse, convict's cloth, as it used to be called, with a thick rope around his waist. His neck and chest were bare. From beneath his coat, a shirt of the most heavy cloth looked out, which had turned almost completely black and had not been taken off for months. His bare feet were thrust in old shoes almost falling to pieces." This "realistic" portrait was without doubt copied from nature; one can conjecture that

---

[c] W. Komarovitch, *F. M. Dostoyewski. Die Urgestalt der Brüder Karamazoff.* Piper Verlag. München.

the author sketched in it one of the monks of Optina Pustyn who had struck him by his peasant-like appearance.

In 1879 Turgenev arrived in Russia; the young students arranged a triumph for him. Dostoevsky met with his old enemy and outwardly a reconciliation took place between them. In March both writers appeared together at a literary soirée. Dostoevsky read excerpts from *Brothers Karamazov.* His masterful reading enjoyed vast success; he was swamped with invitations and surrounded by female and male admirers. One reading followed another: on April 3 he appeared at Solyanoy Gorodok; on Easter he read chapters from *Crime and Punishment;* in December—the story *A Little Boy at Christ's Christmas Tree Party,* and *The Legend of the Grand Inquisitor.* These public appearances caused him great strain; he was suffering from emphysema, easily lost his breath, controlled his muted and hoarse voice with difficulty. But Dostoevsky loved communion with his public, the ecstasies of the young, and bursts of applause.

In April 1879 the writer worked on the fifth book of the novel—*Pro and Contra.* For the chapter *Smerdyakov with a Guitar* he outlined the story of Smerdyakov's romance with a neighbor's daughter. Traces of it have remained in the following passage of the novel. By chance, Alyosha is present at the lackey's rendezvous with the chambermaid. " 'The man, I believe, is Smerdyakov,' he thought, 'at least, from the sound of his voice, and the lady, certainly is the daughter of the owner of the little house here, who has come from Moscow, the one who wears the dress with a train and goes to Marfa Ignatyevna for soup.' . . ." In the rough notes to Alyosha's conjecture, there corresponds a detailed description of the old Karamazov neighbors.

Fyodor Pavlovich's garden was separated from the other neighboring garden by a fence. . . . The owners of the little cottage were an invalid old woman, a widow of lower middle class, and her daughter. . . . The old woman was able to walk two years ago, engaged in some work, acted as an agent for people, used to sell things and took a percentage, but was earning less and less. When she completely lost the use of her legs, her twenty-two-year-old daughter, Marya Nikolayevna, came home. She had been "living in" with a certain rich family in the capital of the province. Although she had really only been a chambermaid, nonetheless she carried herself like a young lady, and had two or three dresses that weren't bad. She didn't know how to do anything, even sew. . . .

She made one mistake at the very beginning, namely, she seemed to take no notice of Smerdyakov because of some prejudice, a distant tradition or generally, for some reason or other, not deeming him worthy of attention. . . . And so what? Something happened which was even impossible to expect. Marya Nikolayevna who had been fascinated by gentlemen and higher society, was favorably taken precisely by Smerdyakov's stubbornness, precisely by his cold tone and the fact that he was thoroughly unlike any "person" in the class to which Smerdyakov belonged. And Smerdyakov was struck by her two dresses—one with the tail and the fact that she knew how to maneuver this tail. At first he turned from the tail with indignation, but then it greatly pleased him. Both discerned higher people in one another. In spite of all this, Marya Nikolayevna was not distinguished by any great beauty; she was tall and very lean and on her face there were even a few little pock marks—it's true only a few, but which spoiled her all the same. Good Marfa Ignatyevna found her even a pretty little thing.

For a long time, Marya Nikolayevna invited Smerdyakov to pay them a visit and become acquainted, in doing which she expressed herself pleasantly: to visit their refuge (i.e., shelter), to visit their little nook or cozy nest. Smerdyakov always bellowed something in reply, at least, he was not abusive. Nonetheless, she invited him with a certain smile and even jauntiness. Smerdyakov did not go. But now, finally, she started inviting him without any trace of jauntiness, and directly with a beseeching face.

"And why is it you don't want to come, is it you haven't time," at last Marfa Ignatyevna once remarked, who found it very pleasant to see the two young people acquainted. If in that regard Marfa Ignatyevna had made some kind of blunder, if she had hinted at that—"Look," she might have said, "you're young people and our fate is completely in the hands of God'—she would have spoiled everything. Smerdyakov would never have gone to his neighbors for whatever reason and he would even have given up talking to them. But God drove away the storm-cloud and Smerdyakov went to visit them; not on the next day, nor on the third, but only on the fourth. Of course, he considered this more elegant.

This episode, which contains priceless little traits that fill out the picture of Smerdyakov's personality, is artistically complete. But the author feared that it would introduce a slowing down in the precipitous action of the novel, and sacrificed it.

On May 10 Dostoevsky sent off to Moscow the first four chapters of the book *Pro and Contra* (*The Engagement, Smerdyakov with a Guitar, The Brothers Become Acquainted*, and *Revolt*). In the accompanying letter to Lyubimov he wrote:

This fifth book is, in my opinion, the culminating point of the novel and must be completed with special care. The thought, as you see from the text which has been sent to you, is to represent utter blasphemy and the core of the destructive idea of our times, in Russia, among young people who have been torn away from reality—and along with the blasphemy and anarchism, the refutation of them which I am preparing now in the words of the dying Elder Zosima, one of the characters in the novel. . . . On the whole, the chapter will be full of action. In the manuscript which I have now sent, though, I have simply depicted the character of one of the central personages in the novel who is expressing his fundamental convictions. These convictions are just what I recognize as a synthesis of contemporary Russian anarchism. A denial not of God, but of the meaning of His creation. All socialism has arisen and begun with the denial of the significance of historical reality and has proceeded to a program of destruction and anarchism. The original anarchists were, in many instances, men who were sincerely convinced. My hero takes a theme which is, in my opinion, irresistible, the senselessness of children's suffering and deduces from it the absurdity of all historical reality. I don't know whether I have executed this well, but I do know that the person of my hero is in the highest degree real. . . . All that my hero says, is based on fact. All the accounts about children really took place, were printed in the papers, and I can point out where; I have invented nothing. The general who hunted down a child with dogs, and all the circumstances, was a real incident, was reported this winter, I think, in *The Archives* and reprinted in many newspapers. My hero's blasphemy will be triumphally refuted in the next (June) number for which I am even working now with fear, trembling, and reverence; I consider my task (the overthrowal of anarchism) a civil heroic feat.

Dostoevsky's letters of this period, especially those to Lyubimov and Pobedonostsev, are exceptionally valuable for the author's commentary upon his novel. The writer expounded in detail the ideology of the work that he was in the process of creating. He recognized the ingenious fifth book, which contains *The Legend of the Grand Inquisitor*, as the *culminating point*. One is struck by the author's statement that his hero's *theme* is *irresistible*: the suffering of children is senseless, and consequently, all historical reality is absurd. Destruction and anarchism are the completely logical conclusion of this terrible syllogism. The author "with fear and trembling" presented a refutation of this "blasphemy." The Elder Zosima was conceived as the antagonist of the "learned brother" Ivan.

Ten days later the writer returned to the same theme in a letter to Pobedonostsev. Why does Ivan deny not God, but His creation? He explains:

I chose this blasphemy [i.e., Ivan's] as I myself have understood and felt it more strongly, i.e., just as it now appears among us, in our Russia, among almost *all* of the upper stratum and chiefly among the young people, i.e., the scientific and philosophical denial of the existence of God has now been abandoned, present-day *practical socialists* simply do not occupy themselves with it (as they used to throughout the entire past century and in the first half of the present), but on the other hand, God's creation, God's world, and its meaning is with full force denied. Here in this alone does contemporary civilization find nonsense. And so, I flatter myself with the hope that even in such an abstract theme I have not betrayed realism.

In May 1879 Dostoevsky finished the most sublime of all his creations—*The Legend of the Grand Inquisitor*. In the notebook, the rough drafts to the chapter *Revolt* are at first interwoven with entries regarding the *Grand Inquisitor*, then gradually they are joined in a coherent text, very close to the printed edition:

"*Ivan:* 'And, why, we know that He found nothing there. A foolish attempt, so now even I feel cheated, and that's how it is.'

"*Inquisitor:* 'You are truth itself, you cannot lie.'

" 'Don't curse. . . .'

" 'You think I'm talking about the poor, about the peasant, about the workers? They're so stinking, coarse, drunk, I wish them all the best, but I don't understand how Christ consented to love them, I don't understand Christ's love. . . .'

"*Inquisitor:* 'What business do we have "there"? We are more human than you. We love the earth. Schiller sings about joy, John Damascene. What is this joy purchased with? With what a torrent of blood, tortures, baseness, and brutalities which are impossible to endure? They don't talk about this. Oh Crucifixion, this is a terrible argument.'

"*Inquisitor:* 'God is like a merchant. I love mankind more than you.'

"'Oh yes, He gave His own Son, He Himself sent Him to a curse—He threw him into confusion. Oh, this is an argument of terrible force, an eternal argument.'

"'Euclid's geometry. And therefore I'll accept God all the more that this is the eternal, old, dear God and you'll not resolve Him. And so, let there be a dear God. It's more shameful. . . .'

"'This was an act of love: though I'll look at them, though I'll pass among them, though I will touch them. . . . From His garments power comes forth.'

"'How did they know Him? And is it possible that He was like us, why He is a miracle, a heavenly mystery?'"

In the rough draft Ivan's "blasphemy" is shown with great incisiveness. Christ has not risen; this was a foolish attempt; Ivan accepts God, but with what murderous derision: "The eternal, old, dear God, you'll not resolve Him." The idea that it is impossible to love men is expressed in the words about the poor who are "stinking, coarse, and drunk." On another page of the sketchbook, an entry is noted which beyond all doubt belongs to Ivan: "*I would like to absolutely do away with the idea of God.*" In this lies the whole meaning of his "revolt": The atheist's denial is immediately concretized in an historical-philosophical picture; the senselessness of the world is related in the myth of the Grand Inquisitor. Ivan wants to do away with the idea of God; the Inquisitor has already destroyed it in his heart and acts just as if God did not exist. He struggles against the "terrible argument of the Crucifixion," inasmuch as he does not believe in this "attempt," he denies life beyond the grave and contrasts it with the "earth." So Ivan's atheistic argumentation logically gives birth to *The Legend.* The rough drafts clearly reveal Ivan's spiritual tie with the atheist Kirilov in *The Devils.* The "learned brother" wants to do away with the idea of God and crosses over to the side of the *Grand Inquisitor*—the Antichrist. Kirilov is convinced that this idea will be extinguished in the consciousness of mankind; therefore he renounces God-manhood for the sake of man-Godhood and, in order to kill God—kills himself. The final entries about Christ ("This was an act of love," "From His garments power comes forth," "How did they know Him") presumably relate to a refutation of the blasphemy and must be ascribed to the Elder Zosima. On the following page we find this note: "The Elder's confession. I do not want to leave you in ignorance as I myself understand this."

In the rough draft the Inquisitor's disbelief is expressed most openly. The hero of *The Legend* repeats Ivan's thought that after death there is no resurrection. The banner of "earthly bread" would have united all men in indisputable harmony, whereas the ideal of "heavenly bread" has condemned the Christian world to eternal war. Here is this extraordinary passage: "Then where will there be community of worship, when the majority of people don't even understand what such a thing is. In place of harmonious worship the banner of discord and war without end has been raised up; this would not have occurred under the banner of earthly bread. But remember that religion is not suited to the vast majority of people; and it cannot be called a religion of love, in that He came only for the elect, for the strong and powerful, and that even those who have undergone His cross, will not find anything that was promised, just as *He Himself did not find anything* after His cross. Behold your One Without Sin, Whom you have set to the fore. And consequently, the idea of slavery, subjugation, and mystery—the idea of the Roman Church and perhaps also of the Masons, is much more suited to the happiness of people, although it has been based on universal deceit. Here is what your One Without Sin means."

The representation of the history of Christianity as eternal hostility and the thought that *religion is impossible* for the majority of men do not correspond to the image of the Inquisitor who is "correcting" the work of Christ while covering himself with His name. These terrible words were omitted from *The Legend*

In June and July Dostoevsky prepared the novel's sixth book, *The Russian Monk,* for printing. It cost him tormenting effort. In a letter from Staraya Russa to A. P. Filosofova (July 11), the writer complained, "For the whole time I've been here in Russa in an unbearable, oppressive state of spirit. Mainly—my health has become worse, everybody's been sick, first my son—with typhus, and then the two of us now with whooping cough. In this state of mind and under such circumstances, I've been writing all the time, have been working at night, listening to how the storm howls and breaks down century-old trees. . . ."

The notes to the sixth book consist of short remarks on the Elder Zosima's life and conversations. The author marked the basic themes of his exhortations. The motif of "paradise on earth" is repeated many times as the core of the Elder's religious world-outlook. "Everything is paradise. It has been given to a few, but it's so easy to see." "Life is a great joy." "You can save the entire earth." "All are happy, all are beautiful, all *could establish* paradise right now." "In truth, life is paradise! It is given once in the myriads of ages." "Life is paradise, well, what a paradise, my dearest one! Therefore I say that I have paradise in my soul."

The writer prepared a "triumphant refutation of Ivan's blasphemy." The atheist scornfully does not accept God's world. Zosima affirms that life is joy and the world is paradise. Ivan does not want universal harmony that has been purchased with the sufferings of children: Zosima affirms that "all men are guilty for everyone," and consequently it is possible also to forgive all. This idea is developed in detail: "All men are guilty for all and everyone." "And if a baby is killed? Go and accept suffering for some one—it will be easier." "Above all. They are guilty for everyone, they have covered the earth with filth. You can shine like the One without Sin. *For each man can take up His burden,* each, if he wants such happiness. He was the image of man." "Forgive the evil-doer—the land forgives and tolerates him. And if you are very dejected—seek suffering *for yourself*." "You are guilty for all and everyone, without this you cannot be saved. You cannot be saved, you will not be able to save. In saving others, you will save yourself." Zosima's answer to Ivan finally acquires, its definitive formula. "But if everyone forgave everything done to himself, really, is not *everyone* strong enough to forgive also everything done to others? Each man is guilty for all and everyone; each therefore has the strength to forgive all men everything, and all will become then a work of Christ's, and He Himself will appear among them, and they will know Him and will be merged with Him; He will forgive even the High Priest Caiphus, for he loved his people in his own way, yes, he loved them; He will also forgive Pilate, who was high-minded, who was pondering about truth, for he knew not what he was doing." Several of the Elder's sayings could appear as too daring and were eliminated from the final text, for example: "*Love men in their sins, love even their sins."* "Children, love one another and do not fear men's sin; love in sin, for this is now Divine love," and finally, the seductive entry: "Love sins!"

At the end of July Dostoevsky left for Ems to be treated and on August 7 sent off the sixth book from there. He commented upon it, as was his habit, in the accompanying letter to Lyubimov:

> I called this sixth book *The Russian Monk*—a bold and provocative title, for all the critics who are hostile to us, will cry out: "Is this the type of the Russian monk; how do you dare to place him on such a pedestal!" But, so much the better, if they shout, isn't that so? (And, really, I know that they won't be able to restrain themselves.) I feel that I have not transgressed against reality; not only is it justified as an ideal but it is also justified as a reality. I only do not know whether I've succeeded. I myself feel that I have not succeeded in expressing even one-tenth part of what I wanted. I look, however, upon this sixth book as the culminating point of my novel. It goes without saying that many of the Elder Zosima's exhortations (or better to say, the manner of their expression) refer to his person, i.e., to the artistic representation of it. Though I too am fully in accord with these same ideas which he expresses, however, if I personally expressed them *myself*, then I would have expressed them in a different form and different language; but he could not express himself in different language, or in a different form than that which I have given him. Otherwise I would not have created an artistic character. I took this character and figure from the old Russian monks and prelates. Along with deep humility, there are infinite naive hopes in the future of Russia, in her moral and even political destiny. St. Sergius, the Metropolitans Pyotr and Aleksey—really did they not always have Russia in view in this sense?

However, not only liberal criticism, but also those who venerated the "old monks and prelates," such as Konstantin Leontyev, did not acknowledge the Elder Zosima as the ideal of the "Russian monk." The image that Dostoevsky created was likewise rejected by the Elders of Optina.

The writer was depressed at Ems and complained to Pobedonostsev (August 9, 1879):

> I lie here and constantly think about what I already realize: I will die soon, will after a year or after two, and what will happen to those

three little heads which are golden for me—after I'm gone? But then I'm here and in general in the most gloomy frame of mind. There's the narrow gorge, though it's true it's picturesque, as a landscape, but which I'm visiting for the fourth summer and in which I hate every stone because it's difficult even to imagine how much anguish I've borne here these four trips. The present trip has been the most awful: an immense crowd of every riff-raff from all over Europe (there are few Russians, and all of them nobodies from the border-lands of Russia) on the most narrow tract of land (the gorge); there is no one with whom to speak a single word, and mainly, ev-erything is alien, everything is completely alien. It's unbearable. . . .

Pobedonostsev read through the *Grand Inquisitor* and was trou-bled. "Your Grand Inquisitor," he wrote to Dostoevsky, "produced a strong impression on me. Little that I have read is so strong. Only I was waiting to see where the rebuff, rejoinder, and explanation would come from, but I still have not found any."

Pobedonostsev's remark greatly disturbed the writer, and he an-swered him from Ems (August 24, 1879). This is one of the most im-portant of the author's commentaries to *Brothers Karamazov*. He wrote:

Your opinion of what you have read of *Karamazov* was very flatter-ing to me (as regards the strength and energy of what was written), but at that point, you pose a most necessary question: that I have not as yet shown an answer to all these atheistic theses, and one is needed. Exactly so, and it is in this precisely that now my anxiety and all my concern lie. For this 6th book, *The Russian Monk*, which will appear on August 31, was intended as an answer to this whole negative side. And therefore I also tremble for it in this sense—will it be a *sufficient* answer? The more so that this answer now is not direct, not point by point to the theses that were expressed earlier (in the *G. Inquisitor* and before), but is only implied. Here something is presented directly opposed to the world-outlook expressed above, but again it is presented not point by point, but, so to speak, in an artistic picture. This is what disturbs me, that is, will I be understood and will I attain even a particle of my aim? And here there was a further obligation of art: I had to present a modest and majestic figure, whereas life is full of the comic and is only majestic in its inner sense, so that in the biography of my monk, I was forced, will or nill, by artistic demands to touch upon even the most trivial aspects so as not to spoil artistic realism. Then there are several things in the monk's teaching against which they will simply cry out, that they are absurd, for they are too exalted; of course, they are absurd in the everyday sense, but in another, inward, sense, it seems they are justified.

And so, *The Russian Monk* was conceived as a *theodicy*. The writer discarded scholastic "proofs of God's existence" point by point, following articles. Ivan Karamazov's logical *argumentation* is opposed by the Elder Zosima's religious world outlook. Euclid's *reason* negates; mystical *experience* affirms. The answer is given not on the plane of the question. Dostoevsky feared that his answer would appear "insufficient"; he himself was not conscious of all the depth of genius of his religious dialectic.

The writer wrote love letters to his wife from Ems. He was fifty-eight years old, was convinced that he would die in a year or two; he was suffering with an incurable illness, but his heart flamed with love. "There are a terrible lot of flowers here and they're sold in bunches. But I don't buy any, there's no one to give them to as a gift; my tsaritsa is not here. And who is my tsaritsa—you are my tsaritsa, I have decided so here, for sitting here, I am so in love with you that you cannot even imagine. . . ."

"And now I am convinced, Anya, that I not only love you, but also am in love with you and that you are my only Lady, and this after 12 years! And even speaking in the most mundane sense, it is also so, in spite of the fact that why, of course, you have changed and grown older since the days when I came to know you, at nineteen. . . . But now, do you believe me, you please me in this sense incomparably more than then. This may be unbelievable, but it is so. . . ."

Having returned from Ems, Dostoevsky worked intensely on the seventh, eighth, and ninth books of the novel and completed them in the beginning of January 1880. The rough notes are very close to the printed text. In the draft to the chapter *Such a Moment* in the seventh book we encounter a plan of the ideological dispute between Alyosha and Rakitin. In the novel, Rakitin is portrayed as an unprincipled careerist without ideas of his own. He is seminarian, the author of a brochure of spiritual tenor *The Life in God of the Deceased Elder Zosima*, but he does not believe in God and scoffs at everything. Ivan predicts a brilliant future for him: "He wanted to express the thought," says Rakitin, "that if I, he said, did not decide upon the career of archimandrite in the very near future, and I didn't agree to be tonsured, then undoubtedly I would go away to Petersburg and join the staff of some literary-political monthly, undoubtedly in the criticism section, I would write for about ten years, and, ultimately, would take over the journal. Then I would again publish it and undoubtedly in a liberal and atheistic tenor, with a socialist overtone." Dostoevsky had in mind his own journalistic enemy of the sixties, a contributor to *The Spark* and *The Contemporary*, G. Yeliseyev, and sketched a malicious caricature of him. Yeliseyev had received a bachelor's degree from the Spiritual Academy of Kazan, had written *A History of the Lives of the First Founders and Propagators of the Church of Kazan, the Prelates Gury, Varsonofy, and German,* but later on became himself a contributor to the *Contemporary*, wrote an "inner review" with a "socialist overtone" and, after his death, left a fortune of 50,000. In the notebook the seminarian-atheist Rakitin argues with Alyosha about religion and the people. Here is this rough draft:

"*Alyosha*: 'And this the people will not allow.'

"*Rakitin*: 'Well then, eliminate the people, curtail them, force them to be silent. Because the European enlightenment is more important than the people. . . .'

"—Rakitin left Grushenka's in anger. Alyosha was silent, but Rakitin started to talk: 'Do everything without religion, enlightenment. . . . People are becoming more and more humane. Religion costs a lot. *You ought to read Buckle.* But we will do away with it.'"

The rough notes complete the portrayal of Rakitin's personality. This is a man of the sixties, a future socialist and exposer, an adherent of European "enlightenment," and admirer of Buckle.

Sending the eighth book, *Mitya*, to his editors, Dostoevsky informed Lyubimov that the ninth book, *The Preliminary Investigation,* came to him "suddenly and unexpectedly." "Originally," he wrote, "I wanted to limit myself only to one *judicial investigation* at the trial itself. But being advised by a certain procurator, with a great practice [undoubtedly A. F. Koni], I decided to elucidate also that part of the judicial process which is called 'the preliminary investigation' with its old routine and with its latest abstractions in the persons of the young jurists, examining magistrates, etc." The rough draft shows that the author conceived his criticism of the state court system on a broad scale, in the spirit of those accusations that we find in Tolstoy's *Resurrection*. In the final text the satire has been very much subdued. Moreover, in the ninth book the writer wanted "to emphasize more strongly the character of Mitya Karamazov: he is purified in his heart and conscience by the storm of unhappiness and false accusation. His soul accepts punishment, not because he has committed the crime, but because he was *so unseemly* that he could have, and wanted to commit it." This theme became predominant in the printed text and overshadowed the criticism of the legal processes. On December 8 Dostoevsky wrote to Lyubimov:

Again I emerge as guilty to the extreme before you and before *The Russian Messenger*. The ninth book of Karamazov which was so categorically promised you for December—I cannot send in December. The reason is that I have worked myself to the point of sickness, that the theme of the book (the preliminary investigation), has grown and become complicated, and chiefly, that this book is turning out one of the most important in the novel, and demands (I see this) such careful refining, that if I should bend every effort and made a hash of it, then I would hurt myself as a writer both now and forever. And even the idea of my novel would be extremely impaired, and it is dear to me.

He worked on this book for two whole months and sent it to the editors only in the beginning of January 1880. The most pathetic passage in the ninth book is Mitya's dream in Mokroye: he sees a village that has been burned down, hears how a "babe," shivering with cold and hungry, is crying. And suddenly in his heart "there rose up a certain tenderness that he had never known before, so that he wanted to cry, so that he wanted to do something for them all, so that the 'babe' would not cry any more, that the baby's dark-colored, dried-up mother also would not cry, so that no one at all would have tears from that very moment." This is "Mitya's ecstasy," corresponding to Alyosha's ecstasy (Cana of Galilee). Both brothers after a spiritual blow and suffering—(with Alyosha, the Elder's death; with Mitya, the accusation of parricide)—are cleansed in their heart and experience a luminous emotion. The rough drafts show that the juxtaposition of two brothers' "visions" was a conscious artistic device on the author's part. In the manuscript we find the following note. "The district police officer conducts Mitya away. He remembers Grushenka and her cry. The beginning of spiritual purification (*pathetically, as with the chapter Cana of Galilee*)."

Dostoevsky did not succeed in finishing the novel at the beginning of 1880. The tenth book, *The Boys,* was only forwarded to the editors in April 1880. Then came a long interruption in the work: the author was engaged in preparing his speech on Pushkin; he made the journey to Moscow for the Pushkin celebrations and returned only on June 12. The eleventh book was ready in the beginning of August, the twelfth in October. The author's striving for absolute precision in his representation of his heroes' psychological states is attested in a letter to Lyubimov regarding Ivan Karamazov's nightmare:

> I consider it my duty, nevertheless, to inform you that I have for a long time consulted the opinion of doctors (and not of only one). They maintain that before "a cerebral fever" not only are such nightmares possible, but also hallucinations. My hero, of course, does see hallucinations too, but he confuses them with his nightmares. Here we find not only a physical (sick) trait when an individual at times begins to lose the distinction between the real and the illusory (which has happened to almost everybody at least once in his life), but also a moral trait which concurs with the hero's character: denying the reality of the illusion, when the illusion has disappeared, he stands up for its reality. *Tormented by unbelief, he unconsciously desires at the same time that the illusion might not be a fantasy, but something in actual fact.*

The devil is the product of Ivan's unbelief: but before the terror of nonbeing which is drawing upon him, the atheist clutches at the *illusion of reality*: he wants the devil to be "something in actual fact." The author polished each sentence in this chapter with great care; he was afraid that the censor would not allow "two words" to pass. "I also don't think," he wrote at the end of the letter, "that the censorship will find anything objectionable, except perhaps two little expressions: 'the hysterical squeaks of the cherubim.' I implore you, get these passed in that here it is the devil who is talking; he cannot speak otherwise. And if it is absolutely impossible then in place of *hysterical squeaks*, insert: *joyful cries*. But would *squeaks* be impossible? And then it would be very prosaic and not in the tone."

Dostoevsky was right: the substitution of *one single word* by another destroys the stylistic unity of this extraordinary chapter.

At the beginning of November 1880 *The Brothers Karamazov* was completed.

XXIII

The Brothers Karamazov

Dostoevsky worked for three years on his last novel. For three years the concluding stage of the labor—its artistic embodiment—continued. But spiritually he had worked on it his entire life. *The Brothers Karamazov* is the summit, from which we see the organic unity of the writer's whole creative work disclosed. Everything that he experienced, thought, and created finds its place in this vast synthesis. The complex human world of *Karamazov* grew up naturally, over the course of a decade, absorbing the philosophical and artistic elements of the preceding works: the *Diary of a Writer* is the laboratory in which the ideology of the final novel is given its definitive form; in *A Raw Youth* there is established the structure of the family chronicle and the tragedy of "fathers and children" is delineated; in *The Devils*, the atheist Stavrogin's clash with the prelate Tikhon anticipates the tragic conflict of faith and disbelief (the Elder Zosima—Ivan Karamazov); in *The Idiot* the subject schema, similar to *Karamazov*, is worked out: at the center of the action stands a major crime; the wronged beauty Nastasya Filippovna calls Grushenka to mind, the proud Aglaya—Katrina Ivanovna; the motif of a dramatic meeting between the rivals is repeated in both novels.

The "passionate" Rogozhin is just as engulfed by eros as is Mitya Karamazov; the "positively beautiful individual"—Prince Myshkin—is Alyosha's spiritual brother. In *Crime and Punishment* Raskolnikov steps beyond the moral law, declaring that "everything is permitted" and becomes a theoretician-murderer: his fate determines the fate of Ivan; the struggle between the prosecutor Porfiry Petrovich and the criminal develops in *Karamazov* into the "preliminary investigation" of Dmitry's case. But Dostoevsky's last and greatest creation is genetically linked not only with the "great novels." Mitya's erotic possession had already been delineated in the portrayal of the hero's passion for the fatal woman Polina in *The Gambler*; Ivan's "disease of consciousness" and Fyodor Pavlovich's "underground philosophy" had been outlined in *Notes from Underground*. Prince Volkovsky in *The Humiliated and Wronged* already possesses the Karamazov element—sensuality; in *The Village of Stepanchikovo* appears the first draft of the figure of Smerdyakov (the lackey Vidoplyasov). Even the tales of the period before penal servitude are related by countless threads with the last novel: the theme of "romantic dreaming" and the "solitary consciousness" is culminated in Ivan's "abstractness" and uprootedness; Schiller's romanticism finds its poetic expression in Dmitry's "hymn"; the idea of the *Grand Inquisitor* grows out of the tragedy of the "faint heart" (*The Landlady*). Finally, the motif of the personality's duality (Ivan Karamazov's devil) rises from his youthful work, *The Double*.

The *Brothers Karamazov* is not only a synthesis of Dostoevsky's creative work, but also the culmination of his life. In the very topography of the novel his memories of childhood are united with the impressions of his final years: the city in which the novel's action is placed reflects the features of Staraya Russa, but the villages surrounding it (Darovoye, Chermashnya, Mokroye) are related to his father's estate in Tula province. Fyodor Pavlovich inherits several traits of the writer's father, and his violent death corresponds to Mikhail Andreyevich's tragic end. Dmitry, Ivan, and Alyosha are three aspects of Dostoevsky's personality, three stages of his spiritual way. Fiery and noble Dmitry, declaiming the *Hymn to Joy*, embodies the *romantic period* of the author's life; his tragic fate, the charge of parricide and exile to Siberia, was inspired by the story of the innocent criminal Ilyinsky and by this is connected with memories of the years of penal servitude. Ivan, the atheist and creator of a social utopia, reflects the *epoch of his friendship with* Belinsky and captivation by atheistic socialism; Alyosha is a symbol of the writer after the period of his penal servitude, when a "regeneration of his convictions" took place within him, when he discovered the Russian people and the Russian Christ.

The novel *Brothers Karamazov* opens before us as its author's *spiritual biography* and his *artistic confession*. But, having once been transformed into a work of art, the story of Dostoevsky's personality becomes the history of man's personality in general. The accidental and individual disappears, what is ecumenical and universal to mankind grows up. In the fate of the brothers Karamazov each of us recognizes his own fate. The writer portrays the three brothers as a *spiritual unity*. This is an organically collective personality in its triple structure: the principle of reason is embodied in Ivan: he is a logician and rationalist, an innate skeptic and negator; the principle of feeling is represented by Dmitry: in him is the "sensuality of insects" and the inspiration of eros; the principle of will, realizing itself in active love as an ideal, is presented in Alyosha. The brothers are joined to one another by ties of blood, grow up from one familial root: the biological given—the Karamazov element—is shown in the father Fyodor Pavlovich. Every human personality bears in itself a fatal dichotomy: the legitimate Karamazov brothers have an illegitimate brother Smerdyakov: he is their embodied temptation and personified sin.

Thus in the novel's artistic symbols the author expounded his own *teaching about personality*. The conflicts of consciousness are converted into a struggle of the passions and into "whirlwinds of events."

The conception of the *organically collective personality* determines the novel's structure. All of Dostoevsky's works are personalistic: their action is always concentrated around the personality of the main hero (Raskolnikov, Prince Myshkin, Stavrogin, Versilov). The main hero of *Karamazov* is the three brothers in their spiritual unity. Three personal themes are developed parallel, but on the spiritual plane the three parallel lines converge: the brothers, each in his own way, experience a single tragedy, they share a common guilt and a common redemption. Not only Ivan with his idea "everything is permitted," not only Dmitry in the impetuosity of his passions, but also the "quiet boy" Alyosha—all are responsible for their father's murder. All of them consciously or semiconsciously desired his death; and their desire impelled Smerdyakov to the crime: he was their docile instrument. Ivan's *murderous thought* was transformed into Dmitry's *destructive passion* and into Smerdyakov's *criminal act*. They are guilty actively, Alyosha passively. He knew and permitted it, *could have* saved his father and did not. The brothers' common crime also involves a common punishment: Dmitry atones for his guilt by exile to penal servitude, Ivan—by the dissolution of his personality and the appearance of the devil, Alyosha by his terrible spiritual crisis. All of them are purified in suffering and attain a new life.

The architectonics of *Karamazov* are distinguished by their unusual rigidity: the law of balance, of symmetry, of proportionality is observed by the author systematically. It is possible to conjecture that Vladimir Solovyov's harmonious philosophical schema influenced the

technique of the novel's structure. This is the most "constructed" and
ideologically complete of all Dostoevsky's works. The human world
of the novel is disposed in a symbolic order: at the center of the plot
appears Dmitry—he is the promoter of the action and the source of
dramatic energy. His passion for Grushenka, rivalry with his father,
his romance with Katerina Ivanovna, the apparent crime, the trial and
exile constitute the external content of the novel. On both sides of him
stand Ivan and Alyosha; the first prepares the parricide by his ideas
and by this influences Dmitry's fate: he is his ideational adversary and
spiritual antipode, but is joined to him by blood, by their common
hatred for their father and their common guilt. Alyosha sets his "quietness" in opposition to Dmitry's violence, his purity—to his sensuousness; but even in his modest chastity lives the "Karamazov element,"
he also knows the gnawing of sensuality. They are different and alike:
The ecstatic sense of life mysteriously unites them. Therefore, Dmitry's
sin is Alyosha's sin.

Behind the group of legitimate sons, set on the first plane, in the
distance, in half-illumination, stands the figure of the illegitimate
brother, the lackey Smerdyakov. He is separated from them by origin,
descent, social position, character; the spiritual unity of the family is
rent by his wanton isolation. But nonetheless how mysteriously profound is his tie with his brothers: as a medium, he executes their subconscious suggestion; Ivan determines Smerdyakov's destiny by his
ideas, Dmitry by his passions, Alyosha by his squeamish indifference.
The theme of "children" in its four ideational aspects is developed by
the four brothers; the theme of "fathers" is represented only by Fyodor Pavlovich. It is unique and simple: the impersonal, innate element
of life, the terrible force of the earth and sex.

A tragic struggle takes place between the father and his children.
Only the men contend, masculine ideas clash together. Dostoevsky's
women do not have their own personal history—they enter the heroes'
biography, constitute part of their fate. Each of the brothers Karamazov has his own complement in a female image: beside Ivan stands
Katerina Ivanovna, beside Dmitry—Grushenka, by Alyosha—Liza
Khokhlakova; even Smerdyakov has his own "lady of his heart"—the
maidservant Marya Kondratyevna. The brothers' indivisible unity
comes forward on the "amorous" plane with special precision. The
threads, uniting them with their loves, cross and intertwine. Ivan loves
Katerina Ivanovna, Dmitry's fiancée; Alyosha for an instant becomes his
rival, feeling himself stung with passion for Grushenka; Katerina Ivan-

ovna is a fatal woman both for Ivan and for Dmitry; Grushenka unites in her love Dmitry and Alyosha. Finally, the unity of the Karamazov family is symbolically shown in Fyodor Pavlovich's and Dmitry's passion for one woman—Grushenka. The remaining dramatis personae are disposed around this central group. Fyodor Pavlovich is surrounded by his own "world" of boon-companions and dissolute women; Grushenka brings with her her admirers and a company of Poles; Mitya bursts in with gypsies, chance friends and creditors. Richest of all is Alyosha's world: the "young lover of mankind" introduces two aspects of human communality into the novel: the monastic communal life and the "brotherhood of children." He connects the dark Karamazov kingdom with the world of the Elder Zosima and Ilyusha Snegiryov. Only Ivan does not have his own world: he does not accept God's creation, that which is human is alien to him, he is disembodied. His sole companion is a phantom, the spirit of nonbeing, the devil.

The story of the Karamazov brothers' collective personality is depicted in a *novel-tragedy*. Everything is tragic in this artistic myth about man, both the enmity of the children toward the father, and the brothers' struggle among themselves, and the inner strife of each brother individually. The disclosure of the metaphysical significance of human fate belongs to Dmitry. In his experience of the passions he came to understand that "the devil struggles with God, and the field of battle is the human heart." Before him are revealed two abysses— above and below. But he is powerless to make a choice and in this lies his personal tragedy. Among the brothers he occupies a middle, neutral position. Ivan and Alyosha, standing on his left and on his right side, already have made this choice. Ivan is irresistibly drawn to the lower abyss, Alyosha reaches for the higher. The one says "no," the other "yes." Fyodor Pavlovich, sitting over his "little cognac," asks Ivan: "Is there a God or not?" The latter answers: "No, there is no God." He appeals to Alyosha: "Alyosha, does God exist?" Alyosha answers: "God does exist." Ivan's personal tragedy is in that "his mind is not in harmony with his heart": with his feelings he loves God's world, although with his reason he cannot accept it.

Of the three brothers the most in harmony is Alyosha, but even in his integral nature there is a split: he knows the temptations of Karamazov sensuality and his faith passes through a "furnace of doubt." The religious idea of the novel—the struggle of faith with disbelief— emerges beyond the limits of the Karamazov household. Ivan's negation begets the ominous figure of the inquisitor; Alyosha's affirmation is mystically deepened in the Elder Zosima's image. Human hearts are only the field of battle, and God and the devil struggle. Under the psychological exterior of the personality, Dostoevsky unveils its ontology and metaphysics. The history of the Karamazov family is an artistic myth which encompasses a *religious mystery*: here is why the *Legend of the Grand Inquisitor* stands at its center.

Dostoevsky was writing not a philosophical treatise or a theological system, he was composing a novel. Religious-philosophical material was introduced into the framework of the novel genre and treated according to its laws. A tense dramatic plot is constructed, at the center of which stands an enigmatic crime; the ideological masses are drawn into the whirlwind of the action, and clashing together, produce effective outbursts. In *The Brothers Karamazov*, the religious mystery-play is paradoxically joined with a crime novel. Notwithstanding all its depth, this is one of the most captivating and popular works of Russian literature.

To the harmony of its architectonics corresponds the masterful technique of its construction. The novel begins with a short prehistory. In the first book (*The History of a Certain Family*) necessary information is given about the landowner Karamazov and his three sons. The second book, *An Unfortunate Gathering* is an exposition of the characters and complication of the plot. The main protagonists are all presented together in a dramatic scene. Without preliminary explanations and descriptions we are at once led into the action. The first clash between old Karamazov and Dmitry takes place in the Elder Zosima's cell; Fyodor Pavlovich is characterized by his cynical anecdotes, blasphemous sallies and the "scandal"; Ivan—by his essay about the Church and his idea of the impossibility of loving mankind; the Elder Zosima —by his instruction and perspicacity (his prostration before Dmitry); the "scandal" anticipates the novel's tragic denouement.

" 'Dmitry Fyodorovich!' yelled Fyodor Pavlovich suddenly in a kind of unnatural voice, 'if only you were not my son, then I this very minute would challenge you to a duel . . . with pistols, at a distance of three paces . . . across a handkerchief!' " And Dmitry in anger pronounces the fatal words: "Why does such a man go on living?" The enmity between father and son is at once shown at its highest tension. The catastrophe is not only foreboded, but is foretold: Fyodor Pavlovich replies to Dmitry's words: "Do you hear, do you hear, you monks, the parricide?"

In this scene, three lines of intrigue are dramatically introduced.

The father Karamozov maliciously calumniates his son, depicting in a distorted form his romance with Katerina Ivanovna, his passion for Grushenka, and his insult to Captain Snegiryov. Here in what passionate and raging tones this exposition is expounded. "Holiest Father," cries Fyodor Pavlovich, "do you believe, he has captured the heart of the noblest of young girls, of a good family, with means, the daughter of his former commander, a valiant colonel, who was very distinguished, who wore the Anna Cross with swords on his neck,[1] he compromised the girl by the promise of his hand, now she is here, now she is an orphan, his fiancée, and before her very eyes he is running after a certain local enchantress. But though this enchantress has lived, so to speak, in civil marriage with a certain respectable man, yet she is of an independent character, an impregnable fortress for everyone. . . . And Dmitry Fyodorovich wants to open this fortress with a golden key, and that's why he is bullying me about now, hopes to get money from me. . . ."

And further on regarding Snegiryov:

Gentlemen, just imagine: there is a poor but respectable man here, a discharged captain; he got into trouble, was discharged from the service—but secretly, not by court-martial; who has preserved his honor intact—and this man is burdened with a numerous household. And three weeks ago, Dmitry Fyodorovich seized him by the beard in a tavern, dragged him by this very beard out onto the street and in the street publicly thrashed him.

The tragedy of Dmitry, filling the novel with its stormy peripeteias, is shown to us in his father's perception, distorted by hatred. Around it at once is created an enigma which raises the emotional tension of the novel. The theme of Captain Snegiryov prepares for the theme of the schoolboys and Ilyusha: Dmitry's sin will be redeemed by Alyosha.

The presentiment of the inevitability of a clash between old Karamazov and Dmitry is strengthened in the scene between Alyosha and Rakitin (*The Seminarian-Careerist*). Alyosha's friend talks about the elder's prostration before Dmitry: "In my opinion the old man is, really, keen-sighted: he smelled out a crime. Your house stinks of it. . . .

[1] In Imperial Russia orders or decorations were awarded in various categories. The first class wore a star and sash over one's breast, the second a cross under one's collar, the third and fourth were worn in the buttonhole. The order that Katerina Ivanovna's father received was that of St. Anne, and the crossed swords indicate that it was a military honor.

It'll be in your family circle, this crime. It'll take place between your dear brothers and your rich old dad." And Rakitin forces Alyosha to confess that even he himself had been thinking about a "crime." "You see, you see?" he says in triumph, "Today, looking at your papa and your brother Mitenka, you thought about a crime? So, I'm not mistaken then?"

Dmitry's image is distorted by his father-rival Fyodor Pavlovich; Ivan's image also by a rival—Rakitin. The jealous and egotistical seminarian depicts Ivan as a vile intriguer, "sitting in clover" and carrying his rich fiancée off from his brother. A riddle is once again posed to the reader; the figure of Ivan acquires traits of craftiness and duplicity.

In the third book (*The Sensualists*), the conflict between Fyodor Pavlovich and Dmitry is disclosed in all its depth. The calculations regarding money are only a pretext, the rivalry for Grushenka is only the exterior reason for their struggle: two sensualists have clashed; the "earthly Karamazov force" has risen up against its own self. Immeasurable, irresistible, mad, it sweeps away all obstacles and "steps beyond" all boundaries. Dmitry opens his soul to Alyosha (*The Confession of an Ardent Heart*); Fyodor Pavlovich, over his cognac, makes intimate avowals to his "dear children—piglets." One confession is parallel to the other: these are two raging forces, rushing toward one another. The collision seems inevitable. Dmitry sits in ambush and watches for Grushenka: if she comes to the old man, he will break in and confront them. "And if . . ." asks Alyosha; the other interrupts: "if there's an if, then I will commit a murder. I couldn't survive it." "Whom will you murder?" "The old man. I won't kill her." "Brother, what are you saying!" "Why, I don't know, I don't know. . . . Perhaps I won't kill him, and perhaps I will. I'm afraid that I will suddenly find his face loathsome at that very moment. . . . I feel a personal disgust. Here's what I'm afraid of. Here, maybe, I won't restrain myself."

And so we become convinced of the *possibility* of the murder. It is possible both practically and psychologically. But this is not fate; Mitya does not *of necessity* have *to kill.* He feels his own freedom; *he can also not commit the murder.* The mystery of his personality is impenetrable even to himself. At the last moment who will conquer in his heart—God or the devil? This he does not know: "Perhaps I won't kill him, and perhaps I will."

The tension mounts with each scene. The father's second clash with his son ends in a fight. Suspecting that his father is concealing Grushenka, Dmitry breaks his way into Fyodor Pavlovich's house. "He threw up both hands and suddenly seized the old man by the two last tufts of hair that remained on his temples, tugged at him, and threw him with a crash onto the floor. He even managed to kick the fallen man in the face two or three times. The old man groaned shrilly. . . ." Dmitry beats his father, but does not kill him. This *false denouement* with its base character by contrast prepares the tragic tone of the catastrophe. The figure of the alleged future murderer is clearly illumined: we already know his impetuous nature, his passion for Grushenka, his debt of honor in relation to his fiancée. The real future murderer is still surrounded by impermeable darkness. The author concisely describes three of Fyodor Pavlovich's servants: the old man Grigory, his wife Marfa Ignatyevna, and the lackey Smerdyakov. Having told about Smerdyakov's birth by the idiot-girl, Stinking Lizaveta,[2] he concludes:

> I really ought to say something about him specially, but I am ashamed of diverting my reader's attention so long with such common lackeys, and therefore I am going back to my story, trusting that somehow I will come back myself in the future course of the tale to Smerdyakov.

By a skillful device the author directs the reader's suspicions onto Dmitry, diverting them from Smerdyakov: he is "such a common lackey," that it is not worthwhile saying much about him. The importance of this character and his role in the crime will by degrees be explained in the course of the novel; slowly the reflector is shifted: proportionally as the apparent murderer withdraws into the shadows, the real murderer steps out in full illumination. No less skillfully is the false murderer Dmitry placed in opposition to the moral murderer Ivan. Dmitry thrashes his father, Ivan restrains him and protects the old man. But the frenzy of the first is not so terrible as the latter's cold hatred. Ivan maliciously whispers to Alyosha: "One reptile will devour the other reptilian, and it serves them both right." He reserves for himself the right to desire. . . . "Not for another's death?" asks Alyosha. "And what if it is for another's death," he answers. "Why lie to oneself, when all men live this way, and, I daresay, cannot live otherwise." In the chapter *The Sensualists*, the three accomplices to the murder are contrasted: Dmitry, Smerdyakov and Ivan. The heroines are also "shown" in equally dramatic fashion; we are introduced to Katerina Ivanovna and Grushenka in the effective scene of the "rival's meeting." The

---

[2] Lizaveta Smerdyashchaya; from which Fyodor Pavlovich contrived the name Smerdyakov.

exultant dreamer Katerina Ivanovna invites the "enchantress" Grushenka to her home, overwhelms her with enraptured praises and kisses her hand. Grushenka with "reverence" takes Katerina Ivanovna's "little hand," brings it up to her lips and does not kiss it. " 'And do you know what, angel mistress,' she suddenly drawled in now the most tender and sugary voice, '—you know that I will take your little hand and shan't kiss it.' " Katerina Ivanovna in an hysterical fit cries: "This is a tiger. She needs a whipping, on the scaffold, by an executioner, before the public."

Mitya says of Grushenka: "I understand the queen of insolence, that's her all over, that's her all over, expressed in this little hand, *the infernal woman*! She's the queen of all infernal women, that one can even imagine in the world! It's ecstasy in its own way." Katerina Ivanovna's fit characterizes her completely. "That is precisely the same Katenka, the institute student," continues Mitya, "who, out of a generous impulse to save her father, was not afraid to come running to an absurd, rude officer and run the terrible risk of being wronged! But our pride, but the need of risk, but the challenge to fate, the infinite challenge! . . . She really was taken with Grushenka, i.e., not with Grushenka, but with her own dream, with her own delirium—because, she said, this is *my* dream, my delirium."

The fourth book (*Lacerations*) is devoted to the story of the wronged Captain Snegiryov and prepares the development of the "children's theme" (Ilyusha and the schoolboys). There is introduced, parallel, a third heroine—Liza Khokhlakova and the romance between her and Alyosha is indicated. In the fifth book (*Pro and Contra*), which is ideologically central, we have Ivan's confession and his *Legend of the Grand Inquisitor*. On the second plane there slowly grows the shadow of his double, Smerdyakov. In the chapter, which the author calls *For the Present, One Still Very Obscure*, the lackey persuades his "learned brother" to go to Chermashnya: he is convinced that on this night Dmitry will kill their father, and therefore it is not worthwhile for Ivan "to stay on for such an affair." The latter vaguely surmises Smerdyakov's dark calculations. "You are, it seems, a perfect idiot and, of course, . . . a dreadful, loathsome—scoundrel," he says to him. And nonetheless, he decides to go away. Getting into the carriage, he hurls at the lackey, "You see . . . I'm going to Chermashnya." . . . " 'It means that it's true what people say that it's interesting even to speak with a clever man,' firmly answered Smerdyakov, having looked penetratingly at Ivan Fyodorovich." Ivan knows that there will be a murder—and washes his hands. He is not his brother's keeper; he is not accountable for another's acts. But his tolerance is fatally turned into complicity. Smerdyakov was hinting at that. He would kill the old man and was sure that Ivan understood him and gave his consent. He decided to commit the murder since he knew that the other wished his father's death. Ivan was the inspirer, Smerdyakov only the tool.

The sixth book (*The Russian Monk*) follows immediately after Ivan's confession. The Grand Inquisitor is answered by the Elder Zosima. In the seventh book (*Alyosha*) there is disclosed Alyosha's spiritual drama, his fall and rebirth. His theme is interwoven with the theme of Grushenka. The heroine goes away to Mokroye to her "seducer," for whom she has waited five years and who, at last, has called her. Her departure is the deciding moment in Dmitry's fate. The fear of losing Grushenka brings his inner dismay to half-mad frenzy. We are drawing near to the catastrophe. In the eighth book (*Mitya*) the author relates "only what is most indispensable from the story of these two terrible days in Mitya's life, which preceded the dreadful catastrophe that so unexpectedly burst over him." Mitya has to get three thousand in order to repay his debt of honor to Katerina Ivanovna. Then he will be clean and then another "renewed" life will begin. The hero's trials in his quest for money begin with his visit to Grushenka's protector, the merchant Samsonov: the latter sends him to the peasant Lyagavy in the village of Ilyinskoye; from there he falls in with Mrs. Khokhlakova who advises him to set out for the goldmines. Having learned that Grushenka has gone away, Mitya seizes a small brass pestle from the table and runs to his father's house. The plot's culmination point is the scene of the mysterious murder. The dark garden, concealing the "apparent murderer"; amidst the bushes of elder and snowballs, the brightly illumined window; in it Fyodor Pavlovich, "decked-out" in his striped silk dressing gown and "foppish linen"; Dmitry's giving the signal raps in answer to which the window is opened and we hear the old man's trembling half-whisper: "Grushenka, is it you? Is it you then? Where are you, mommy, my little angel, where are you?" These images are unforgettable. Fyodor Pavlovich leans out of the window. "Mitya looked sideways and did not stir. The old man's whole profile, that he found so loathsome, his whole Adam's apple hanging down, the hooked nose, his lips smiling in sweet expectation, *all this was brightly illumined by the slanting lamplight falling on the left from the room.* A terrible, furious malice suddenly began to boil up in Mitya's heart. . . . This personal disgust was growing unbearable. Mitya was now beside himself and suddenly snatched the brass pestle out of his pocket. . . ."

But "God was watching over him": Mitya did not kill his father. The servant Grigory chases after him, shouting "parricide." Climbing over the fence, Mitya strikes him on the head with the pestle. On this overwhelming scene the first part of the novel ends. The tension, having increased from the very beginning of the action, has been resolved. The dynamic charge of this device is exhausted.

The second half is built on another dominant: the enigma of the murder. It is prepared with extraordinary dramatic art: having learned that Grushenka has gone away to Mokroye to her fiancé, Mitya rushes after in pursuit. The Pole fiancé is won over by money and renounces his rights to Grushenka. There begins a dissipated, raging spree. The drunken madness of pleasure is interrupted by the appearance of the police. The examining magistrate "firmly, loudly, and solemnly" pronounces: "Ex-lieutenant Karamazov, I must inform you that you are charged with the murder of your father Fyodor Pavlovich Karamazov, perpetrated this night." Dostoevsky never created a more pathetic situation.

The following book (*The Preliminary Investigation*) is devoted to the interrogation of the apparent criminal. The "soul's way through suffering" is depicted in the form of dramatic duels between the accused and the representatives of justice—the district police inspector Makarov, the examining magistrate Nelyodov and the public prosecutor Ippolit Kirillovich; the noble trustfulness, sincerity and lofty humanity of Mitya are smashed against the stone of "old routine and the latest abstraction." On this contrast between the "letter of the law" and a living human heart is founded the vast psychological expressiveness of this scene. We know that Mitya did not commit murder, that, defending himself from the charges, he is speaking the purest truth, but at the same time we feel that he cannot clear himself; the secret of the crime is still hidden from us, but with each minute we grow more certain that the hero will be crushed by fate—by a force blind and merciless.

The tenth book (*The Boys*) develops the "children's theme." In it the dying boy Ilyusha steps forward onto the first plane.

The eleventh book (*The Brother Ivan Fyodorovich*) is parallel to the ninth (*The Preliminary Investigation*). There we saw depicted the investigation made of the apparent murderer's affair; here, the moral murderer himself comes forward in the role of prosecutor (the three meetings with Smerdyakov). The enigma of the murder, at last, is disclosed. The lackey says to Ivan: "The main murderer in this all is only you, sir, and I'm not really the main murderer, though I did kill him. But you are the rightful murderer." Ivan judges and condemns himself (the celebrated scene of the nightmare).

The twelfth and last book (*A Judicial Error*) is devoted to a detailed description of Dmitry's trial. Much satiric material and parody is introduced. The witnesses' examinations in their dramatic effect border on "sensationalism." *The Muzhiks Stood Firm*: innocent Mitya is condemned to penal servitude. He "will smell the mines for twenty years."

In the epilogue the theme of Ilyusha is finally merged together with the theme of Alyosha. At the poor boy's grave the "young lover of mankind" confesses his faith in universal resurrection.

Having examined the novel's ideational architectonics and its dramatic composition, we turn now to the third side of Dostoevsky's art—to the artistic embodiment. His heroes are not allegorical figures, but men endowed with the powerful force of life. It seems that they breathe not air, but pure oxygen, do not live, but burn themselves up. The whole Karamazov family possesses an intense vitality.

Fyodor Pavlovich is a fifty-five-year-old man who has grown flabby. He has long, fleshy bags under his eyes, little, impudent, suspicious, and mocking eyes, a great number of wrinkles on his little fat face, a sharp chin with a great and fleshy Adam's apple, a long mouth with thick-set lips. He spatters himself with saliva when he speaks; he has a "repulsive-sensual appearance." The old man prides himself on his large, thin, aquiline nose. "A real Roman one," he used to say, "together with my Adam's apple the genuine physiognomy of an ancient Roman patrician of the times of the fall." Fyodor Pavlovich indistinctly senses his relationship: in him, in fact, lives the soul of the ancient pagan world, a cosmic force, the irresistible element of sex.

There is in his nature something of the faun and the satyr. His lust is insatiable, since it passes into infinity. This is by no means physical sensuousness, seeking and finding satisfaction, this is a spiritual passion, thirst, an eternal excitement, sensuality. The "earthly Karamazov force" in Fyodor Pavlovich is elementary and impersonal. He loves not women, but *woman*, his lasciviousness still does not rise to eros. *Over a little Cognac* the father talks intimately with his sons. Something ancient and painful breathes from his confessions. "To my thinking in my whole life I have never found an unseemly woman, here has been my rule! Can you understand me? . . . According to my rule one can find in every woman something, damn it, extraordinarily interesting, which you won't find in any other; only one must know how to find it, here's where the trick is! This is a talent! For me ugly women have not existed: the very fact that she is a woman already is half everything. Even in *vieilles filles*, even in them, you sometimes will discover a thing that makes you simply wonder at the rest of fools, how they allowed her to grow old and up till now did not notice her! With a bare-footed girl or an ugly one you must take her by surprise right from the start; here's how one should go after them."

But ancient paganism has ended. Great Pan is dead and the fauns have turned into demons. Fyodor Pavlovich is not only a sensualist, but also a wicked buffoon, cynic, and blasphemer. The innocent shamelessness of the natural demigod passes into delight in one's personal ignominy and fall. The faun is no longer innocent; he knows that his lust is sinful and protects himself by buffoonery and cynicism. His shamelessness is a perversion of the feeling of shame. After the "sensualist's" indecent sallies in the monastery, the Elder Zosima says to him: "*Don't be so ashamed* of your self, for this alone is the cause of everything." And Fyodor Pavlovich exclaims that by this remark the elder's perspicacity "pierced right through him." "Precisely, I always feel just like that," he adds, "when I meet people, that I'm lower than everyone and that they take me for a buffoon. . . . Here's why I am a buffoon, *a buffoon from shame*. . . . It's simply from over-anxiety that I am rowdy." Shame, over-anxiety, wounded dignity, vindictiveness, and rapture in his personal shame—such is the complex composition of old Karamazov's buffoonery. Absorption in the sexual element makes a man weak and timid. Fyodor Pavlovich does not believe in God, but is afraid of hell. He "intends to remain on the earth as long as possible," wants "to belong to the line of man for about twenty years yet," and therefore he amasses money; the sensualist is naturally greedy. Money allows him to devote himself without concern to his "filth," but does not save him from the fear of death. He knows his sin and for his tranquility he must be convinced that there is no God, no life beyond the grave. . . . "Do you see," he confesses to Alyosha, "however stupid I am about this, yet I keep thinking, keep thinking, now and then, of course, not all the time. Why, it's impossible, I think, for the devils to forget to drag me down by them with their hooks, when I die. . . . And if there are no hooks, everything just falls apart, which again is not very likely: for then who will drag me down with hooks, because, if they don't drag me down, what will there be then, where will justice be in the world?" This unexpected confession sheds a new light on the cynic and blasphemer. The enormous "Karamazov" force of life has in Fyodor Pavlovich passed into lust and debauchery; but, however stifled it is by this base element, its nature remains spiritual and creative. The sensualist condemns himself and *thirsts for justice*. More than that: sitting up to his neck in "filth," he is, at moments, capable of perceiving beauty and loving good: his second wife, the "orphan" Sofya Ivanovna he married without any calculation, for her beauty alone. " 'Those innocent little eyes slashed my soul then, like a razor,' he used to say afterward."

He loves Alyosha sincerely and tenderly and trusts in him "as in the last thing": he does not offend his religious feelings and even asks him to say a prayer for him. Alyosha sadly reflects upon his family: "Here there is the 'earthly Karamazov force,' earthly and raging, unfashioned. . . . I don't even know if the Spirit of God hovers over this force." . . . But Dostoevsky believed in the great and saving force of Mother Earth: the father Karamazov's "impetuosity" is the chaotic ebullition of creative powers, which are predestined to transfigure the world.

This transfiguration already begins in Karamazov's oldest son, Dmitry. His youth was spent in wild passions: "He did not finish his studies in the gymnasium, got then into a certain military school, then turned up in the Caucasus, rose in the service, fought a duel, was demoted to the ranks, again was promoted, caroused a lot and, comparatively, squandered a sufficient amount of money." Mitya is twenty-eight years old; he is of medium height and a pleasant face, is muscular and strong. . . . "His face was thin, his cheeks were sunken in; their color was distinguished by an unhealthy sallowness. His rather large, prominent dark eyes, had apparently an expression of firm determination, yet somehow there was a vague look in them." Fyodor Pavlovich's sensuality is expressed by two "exterior marks": his Roman nose and great Adam's apple. Dmitry's all-engulfing passion is indicated by his sunken cheeks and the vague expression of his dark eyes. Of the three sons the oldest most resembles the father. He is also a sensualist, also knows the shameful sweetness of debauchery. "I have always loved little side-streets," he confesses to Alyosha, "deserted and dark blind alleys, behind the public square; there one finds adventures and surprises, virgin nuggets in the dirt. . . . I loved debauch, loved even the ignominy of debauch. I loved cruelty. Really am I not a bug, not an evil insect? In fact, it is said—a Karamazov!" Rakitin characterizes Dmitry: "He may even be an honest man, your Mitenka, but he's a sensualist. Here is his definition and whole inner essence. It's your father who transmitted his own base sensuality to him. . . . Why, in your family sensuality is carried to an infection." But the materialist Rakitin knows only half the truth about Mitya: sensuality is by no means "his whole inner essence." The dark earthly element is in Mitya's "ardent heart" transfigured into the blinding flame of Eros. He perceives it as a great birth-giving and creative force. Nature reveals itself to him as the "ancient Mother Earth," as the divine fire, which gives life and joy to all God's creation. Mitya's cosmic sense finds its expression in Schiller's *Hymn to Joy*. Trembling with ecstasy, he declaims:

> Joy eternal offers drink
> To the Soul of God's creation,
> By her secret force of ferment
> The cup of life inflames.
>
> At the breast of kindly nature
> All that breathes, drinks joy,
> All creatures, and all peoples
> She compels to follow her;
>
> Her gifts to us are friends in sorrow,
> The juice of grapes, garlands of the Graces,
> To the insects—sensuality—
> The angel stands before God.

Mitya declaims these verses and weeps: to him, a rough and uneducated officer, is sent this revelation of the Mother Earth, he, a sensuous insect, is accorded a knowledge of cosmic rapture! Where does his mystical ecstasy come from? In his life there took place an event, which decided his fate forever. Mitya saw Grushenka. "The storm thundered," he says, "The plague struck, I was infected and am infected till now and I know that everything is now over, there'll never be anything else. The cycle of the times is fulfilled." Dmitry has become the victim of the terrible and merciless god—Eros. In his passion the fiery heart of the world was disclosed to him; his cosmic inspiration is a gift of Eros. But Mitya knows also another, dark countenance of the god "the sensuality of the insects." This enigmatic ambiguity, this contradiction between the chaotic element of sex and Eros' "creation in beauty" strikes him with superstitious horror. "I go on and don't know whether I've fallen into a mire and shame, or into light and joy? Here's just the trouble, for everything in the world is a riddle! And whenever I've happened to sink into the most, into the most profound shame of debauchery (and it's always been happening), then I always read that poem about Ceres and about man. Has it reformed me? Never! Because I am a Karamazov. . . . And here in this very shame I would suddenly begin a hymn. Let me be damned, let me be base and vile, but let me too kiss the hem of that garment in which my God is clothed; let me go at the same time right after the devil, yet all the same I am Your son, O Lord, and I love You and feel the joy without which the world cannot stand or be."

The fatal discord between sex and Eros is the first enigma which Mitya encounters. The second and even more terrible is ahead of him. Sex is motion about a circle, continual and without any issue; Eros is an ascension, a ladder, leading to a height. Eros has an *aim* and an ideal—Beauty. It creates Beauty and worships it. And here is the second enigma. "Beauty—this is a terrible and awful thing," says Mitya, "terrible because it is indefinite, and to define it is impossible, for God has posed only enigmas. Here the shores meet, here all contradictions live side by side. . . . Beauty! I cannot, besides, endure the thought that a man with a lofty heart and with a lofty mind begins from the ideal of the Madonna, and ends with the ideal of Sodom. . . . What is presented to the mind as shameful, to the heart is uninterrupted beauty. . . . What's awful is that beauty is not only a terrible, but also a mysterious thing. *Here the devil struggles with God, and the field of battle is the human heart. . . .*"

This is one of the most brilliant pages in Dostoevsky. The mystery of beauty, the tragic duality of the aesthetic consciousness is expressed with astounding force. Dmitry knows only one way to God—through Eros. In his amorous inspiration he longs to press himself "to the garment of the Divinity" and recoils with horror: his divinity is two-faced, Beauty comprises the ideal of the Madonna and the ideal of Sodom. "Is there beauty in Sodom?" asks Mitya and answers: "Believe me that for the vast multitude of people it is found in Sodom; did you know this secret, or not?" Beauty is from God; Beauty is the breath of the Holy Spirit. But in this fallen world its face has been darkened and distorted. It is not Beauty which will save, but it itself must be saved. In the aesthetic consciousness there are most subtle temptations: Beauty can be an evil demonic attraction. Mitya does not see the way out of these tragic contradictions. He has to pass through the purification of suffering, through the torment of conscience and the spiritual death of penal servitude in order that the flame of Eros, which has caught fire in him might become a spiritual force that transfigures the world. As an epigraph to his novel Dostoevsky took the words from the Gospel of John: "If a kernel of wheat, which has fallen onto the earth, will not die, then it will remain alone, but if it will die, then it shall bring forth much fruit."

Fyodor Pavlovich's second son, Ivan, is four years younger than Dmitry. He grew up in a family of strangers as a sullen boy and early manifested brilliant talents. He studied natural sciences at the University, supported himself by giving penny lessons and journal work, wrote an article about the ecclesiastical courts, which attracted universal attention. His arrival at his father's is surrounded by mystery. Alyosha does not understand how his brother, so proud and isolated, can get on with the unseemly Fyodor Pavlovich. In the scene in the tavern he confesses to Ivan: "Brother Dmitry says about you: Ivan is a tomb. I say about you: Ivan is an enigma. Even now you are an enigma to me." Alyosha feels that Ivan is occupied with something interior and important, is striving for some goal, perhaps, a very difficult one. "He knew perfectly well that his brother was an atheist." In this enigmatic fashion the author introduces the figure of the "learned brother." His behavior is incomprehensible and ambiguous: why, being an atheist, does he write about a theocratic organization of society? Why does he suggest to his father that he appeal to Zosima's mediation and arrange a family council at the monastery? Why does he "firmly and seriously" receive the Elder's blessing and kiss his hand?

The clear-sighted Zosima at once guesses the young philosopher's secret. "God frets" Ivan; his consciousness is torn between faith and disbelief. The Elder says to him: "This idea is still not resolved in your heart and frets you. . . . In this lies your great grief, for it urgently demands a solution. . . . But thank the Creator that He gave you a loftier heart, capable of suffering such torture, of 'thinking exalted thoughts and seeking exalted things, for.our dwelling is in the heavens.'"

Ivan is not a self-satisfied atheist, but a lofty mind, a "loftier heart," the martyr of an idea, who experiences lack of faith as a personal tragedy. Zosima concludes with the wish: "God grant you that your heart may attain the answer while you are still on earth, and may God bless your path." The just man blesses the sinner's "incessant striving" and predicts that he will fall and rise up. The author of *The Legend of the Grand Inquisitor* will not perish like Stavrogin, whose heart was frozen. In the epilogue, Mitya prophesies: "Listen, our brother Ivan will surpass everyone. He ought to live and not us. He will recover."

Ivan will be saved by the "earthly Karamazov force" which he inherits from his father. His blood also overflows with the poison of sensuality; as Dmitry, he too knows the inspirations of Eros and cosmic raptures. In him there is "such strength, that it will endure everything."

Alyosha asks: "What strength?" Ivan answers: "The Karamazov . . . strength of baseness." "That is to sink in debauchery, to stifle your soul with corruption, yes, yes?" "I daresay even that. . . ."

But the "sensuality of insects" is for Ivan only a *possibility*, a remote threat in old age. He is still young and pure, human passionate love is accessible to him. Upon becoming acquainted with Katerina Ivanovna, "wholly and irrevocably" he surrendered to his flaming and mad passion for her. His love for the world is just as ecstatic as Dmitry's. Ivan confesses to Alyosha: "But I still would want to live and now that I've touched upon this cup, so I would not tear myself away from it until I have drained it. . . . I've asked myself many times: is there in the world such despair that might overcome *this enraptured and, perhaps indecent, thirst for life* in me and have decided that, apparently there is not. . . . I have a longing for life and I go on living even contrary to logic. I may not believe in the order of things, but the sticky, little leaves, as they open in spring, are dear to me; the blue sky is dear, another man is dear. . . ." Ivan inwardly is linked to the hero of *A Raw Youth*, Versilov: he also would like to travel to Europe, to bow down before the holy graves. He, a logician and rationalist, makes a surprising confession: "I know beforehand," he says, "that I shall fall on the ground and kiss the stones and weep over them. . . . *I shall get drunk on my own emotion.*" Tears of rapture and emotion are accessible to the atheist Ivan! And he, like Alyosha, is capable of falling onto the ground and watering it with his tears. But the Karamazov force—the love for life—conflicts in his soul with another force—atheistic reason, which breaks it down and kills it. With his mind he rejects that which he loves with his heart, considers his love senseless and indecent. Really is it worthy of man to love "with his inners, and his bowels" that which presents itself to his reasonable consciousness as "a disorderly, accursed and, perhaps, diabolic chaos?"

In Ivan we find completed the age-old development of the *philosophy of reason* from Plato to Kant. . . . "Man is a rational being"— this axiom has entered his flesh and blood. Ivan is proud of his reason and for him it is easier to renounce God's world than reason. If the world is not justified by reason, it is impossible to accept it. The rationalist does not want to be reconciled with a kind of "nonsense." Here begins the tragedy: rational consciousness finds no meaning in the world-order. In the world there is an irrational principle, evil and suffering, which is impervious to reason. Ivan builds his own ingenious argumentation on the most pure form of evil—the suffering of children. It is in no way possible either to explain or to justify the tears of a five-year-old girl, tortured by her sadist-parents, the torments of a boy, hunted down by wolf-hounds, the whines of infants, massacred by the Turks in Bulgaria. If world harmony is *necessarily* founded on tears and blood, then away with such harmony! "It isn't worth the little tear, though it be only of that one tormented child who beat itself on the breast with its little fists and prayed in its stinking hole, with its unexpiated tears, to 'dear, kind God,'" declares Ivan and derisively concludes: "Too high a price has been set on harmony, and it's not at all within our means to pay so much to enter it. And therefore I hasten to return my admission ticket. . . . It's not God that I don't accept, Alyosha, only I most respectfully return my ticket to Him."

The "learned brother" disdains mockery à la Voltaire and banal refutations of God's existence. His tactics are more cunning and dangerous. Disputing with an imaginary opponent, he begins by conceding to him the main and, it would seem, most important thing: *he admits the existence of God.* By this crafty device he only reinforces the import of his basic argument. "It's not God I don't accept, understand this, I do not accept the world, that He created, this world of God's, and cannot agree to accept it." God he does accept, but only so as to lay upon Him the responsibility for the "accursed chaos," created by Him, so as to blaspheme His holy Name and with murderous "respect" return his ticket to Him. Ivan's "revolt" is more terrible than the naive farces of the atheists of the 18th century. Ivan is not an atheist, but struggles with God. His argumentation seems completely irrefutable. He appeals to the Christian Alyosha and *forces* him to accept his atheistic way out. "Tell me yourself frankly," he says, "I challenge you—

answer me: imagine that you yourself are raising up the structure of man's destiny with the aim of making men happy in the end, of giving them, at last, peace and rest; but it was necessary and unavoidable for this to torture only one tiny creature to death, that child who was beating itself on the breast with its fist—and to found this edifice on its unrevenged tears, would you consent to be the architect on these conditions, tell me and don't lie!"

And Alyosha, believing and ardently loving God, is forced to answer this question: "No, I would not consent." This means: I do not accept the architect, Who has created the world on the tears of children; I cannot believe in such a God. Ivan triumphs: he has caught the "monk" in the snare of his logical syllogisms and drawn him into his "revolt." In fact, Alyosha could not have answered differently: if he had agreed to purchase the happiness of mankind at the price of "a child's little tear," at that very moment he would have lost his image of God and ceased to be a man. The keenness of Ivan's reasoning lies in that he renounces God *out of love for mankind,* comes forward against the Creator in the role of the advocate of all suffering creation. In this imposture is hidden a diabolic deceit. The atheist appeals to the noble human sentiments of compassion, magnanimity, love, but on his lips this is pure rhetoric. Alyosha could have reminded his brother of his favorite idea: "There is decidedly nothing on the whole earth which could force men to love others as themselves . . . if there is love on the earth and has been till now, then it's not from any natural law, but solely because men have believed in their immortality. . . ." Ivan does not believe in immortality and cannot love others. He himself dons the mask of love for mankind in order to raise himself to the place of the lover of mankind—God. He is, he says, more kind and more compassionate than God; he would have created a more just order. Lucifer's arrogant pretension is ancient as the world. If one were to remove its deceitful humane veil from the God-struggler's "revolt," it would emerge as a sole thesis: the existence of evil in the world shows that there is no God. Christianity acknowledges the Fall from grace and believes in the coming of the Final Judgment; Ivan denies the first and contemptuously rejects the second: he does not want any reward for innocent sufferings. To the Christian all mankind is only Adam; in him all have sinned, all are "conceived in iniquity and born in sins." Ivan declares that there is no original sin, that man is born without guilt. Consequently, the sufferings of children are *unjust* and the Final Judgment is *senseless.* Denying original sin, he absolves man of any responsibility for evil and fixes it upon God. *But an evil God is not God*—which is the proof he required. All the force of Christianity is in the personality of Christ, who overcame sin and death. But if there is no sin, then redemption is not needed. The dialectics of his ideas unavoidably lead the atheist to an encounter with the most shining Face of the God-man. Alyosha, crushed by Ivan's arguments and forced to share his "revolt," suddenly becomes aware: he remembers that "in the world there is a Being, Who can forgive everything, everyone, and all, and *for everything*, because He Himself gave His innocent blood for everyone and for everything. . . ." Alyosha, naively thinks that Ivan "has forgotten about Him." But the latter has for a long time been waiting for this objection; he knows that all his proofs will appear impotent, if he does not succeed in subverting the *work of Christ*.

Having destroyed the idea of the *fall* and *reward*, the atheist must do away with the idea of *redemption*. His task involves titanic daring. How is one to struggle with the Living God? Of what can one accuse the "One Without Sin"? How can one raise up one's hand against the "everlasting ideal of Beauty"? The God-struggler understands the infinite difficulty of the conflict. He sharply changes his tactics. In place of logical proofs there is set a religious myth, in place of facts from contemporary reality—a legend whose action takes place in Spain in the 16th century. *The Legend of the Grand Inquisitor* is Dostoevsky's greatest creation. Here is the culmination of his work, the crowning of his religious philosophy.[A]

Once again the Savior comes upon the earth. In Seville, at the most terrible period of the Inquisition, He appears among the crowd, and the people recognize Him. Rays of light and power shine from His eyes, He stretches forth His hand, blesses them, performs miracles. The Grand Inquisitor, "a ninety-year-old man, tall and erect, with a withered face and sunken eyes" orders the guard to shut Him in the jail. At night he comes to his prisoner, "stops at the entry and for a long time, a minute or two, looks attentively at His face." Then he begins to speak. The *Legend* is the Grand Inquisitor's monologue. Christ remains silent. The aroused, fiery, and pathetic speech of the old man is directed against the God-man's work and teaching. Accus-

[A] V. Rozanov. *Legenda o Velikom Inkvizitore F. M. Dostoevskogo* (*F. M. Dostoevsky's Legend of the Grand Inquisitor*). Berlin, 1924.

ing Him, he justifies himself, his own spiritual betrayal. The "terrible and wise spirit, the spirit of self-destruction and nonbeing" tempted Christ in the wilderness—and He rejected him. The Inquisitor maintains that *the tempter was right.* "You want to go into the world," he said to Christ, "and you are going with empty hands, with some promise of freedom, which they, in their simplicity and their natural unruliness, cannot even comprehend, which they fear and dread, for nothing has ever been more unbearable for man and for human society than freedom! But do you see these stones in this barren and scorched wilderness? Turn them into bread and mankind will run after You, like a herd, grateful and obedient. . . ."

The Savior rejected this counsel of the evil spirit, for He did not wish to buy obedience with bread, did not want to deprive men of freedom. The Inquisitor prophesies: in the name of earthly bread the spirit of the earth will rise up against Christ and mankind will follow Him; on the place of the temple a tower of Babel will be erected; but after they have suffered for a thousand years, men will return to the Roman Church, which has "corrected" Christ's work, will bring to it their freedom and will say: "Better make us slaves, but feed us." The first temptation in the wilderness is a prophetic image of the history of mankind; the "bread" is a symbol of atheistic socialism; not only contemporary socialism, but also the Roman Church has succumbed to the temptation of the "terrible and wise spirit." Dostoevsky was convinced that Catholicism, sooner or later, would unite with socialism and form with it a single tower of Babel, the kingdom of the Antichrist. The Inquisitor justifies his betrayal of Christ by the same motive to which Ivan resorted in justifying his own struggle with God: *love of mankind.* The Savior was mistaken about men: He had too high an opinion of them, demanded too much from them. The Inquisitor says: "Men are feeble, vicious, insignificant, and rebels. . . . The weak, eternally vicious and eternally ungrateful race of men. . . . You thought too highly of men, for, of course, they are slaves, though rebellious by nature. . . . I swear, man is much weaker and baser by nature, than you believed him. . . . He is weak and vile." Thus in opposition to Christ's teaching concerning man is set the teaching of the Antichrist. Christ believed in the image of God in man and respected his freedom; the Inquisitor considers freedom the curse of these pitiful and weak rebels and, in order to make them happy, proclaims slavery. "I tell You that man does not have an anxiety more tormenting than finding someone to whom he may most quickly surrender this gift of freedom with which the unfortunate creature is born." Only a few elect are capable of assimilating Christ's testament. Is it possible then that He did not think about the millions and tens of thousands of millions of the weak who do not have the strength to prefer the bread of heaven to earthly bread?

In the name of this same freedom of man Christ also rejected the two other temptations—*miracle and the earthly kingdom;* He "did not want to enslave man by a miracle and craved faith given freely, and not based on miracles." The Inquisitor has accepted all three proposals of the "wise spirit." "We have corrected Your feat and have founded it on *miracle, mystery, and authority.* . . . We have taken Caesar's sword and, having taken it, of course, have rejected You and followed *him.*" Freedom will bring men to mutual destruction and anthropophagy. . . . But there will come a time and the feeble rebels will crawl to him who will give them bread and harness their rowdy freedom. The Inquisitor draws a picture of the "childlike happiness" of enslaved mankind: "They will tremble impotently before our wrath, their minds will grow timid, their eyes will become quick to shed tears, like children and women. . . . Yes, we will make them work, but in their hours free from toil, we shall organize life for them, like a child's game with children's songs, a chorus, with innocent dances. Oh, we will allow them even sin. . . . And all will be happy, all the millions of creatures, except the hundred thousand ruling over them. . . . Peacefully they will die, peacefully they will expire in Your name, and beyond the grave they will find only death. . . ." The Inquisitor falls silent, the prisoner says nothing. "The old man longed for Him to say something, even if it be bitter, terrible. But suddenly in silence, He approaches the old man and gently kisses him on his bloodless, ninety-year-old lips. Here is His whole answer. The old man shudders. Something stirred at the corners of his mouth; he goes to the door, opens it, and says to Him: 'Be off, and come no more. Come never again. . . . Never, never!' And he lets Him out onto the 'dark squares of the town.'"

What then is the Grand Inquisitor's secret? Alyosha guesses: "Your Inquisitor doesn't believe in God, here is his whole secret." Ivan readily agrees: "What if it's so!" he answers. "At last, you have guessed it. And in fact, it is so, in fact, the whole secret is in this alone. . . ."

The "legend's" symbolism consists of many levels: on the surface lies an exposure of the "Antichrist" principle of the Roman Church and contemporary socialism. Dostoevsky was tempted by the fantastic idea that the tower of Babylon, erected through atheistic socialism, would be crowned by Rome. But this unjust and un-Christian condemnation of Catholicism is only the exterior veil of the religious myth. Beneath it lies concealed a most profound investigation of the metaphysical meaning of *freedom* and *power*.

The hero of the legend, the Grand Inquisitor, is portrayed with colossal art. This is not a vulgar atheist, not a "petty devil," like Pyotr Verkhovensky. The old cardinal is a majestic and tragic figure. He had given up his life to self-abnegation and the service of Christ, to an heroic feat of sanctity in the wilderness—and suddenly in the decline of his years, has lost his faith. "Really would not one such be enough to make a tragedy?" asks Ivan. In actual fact, the loss of his faith is the Inquisitor's most profound tragedy: not believing in God, he takes on himself a lie and deceit and accepts *this suffering* out of "love for men." The author scorns those weapons generally accessible in the struggle with atheism: he does not depict his hero as a villain and monster. The Inquisitor is an ascetic, a wise man and philanthropist. In this conception lies the insight of Dostoevsky's genius. The Antichrist steps forward against Christ in the name of Christ's testament of love for one's neighbor. He presents himself as His disciple, as continuing His work. The Antichrist is a false-Christ, and not an anti-Christ. In the same way Vladimir Solovyov too understood the idea of the Antichrist. In his remarkable tale *Three Conversations*, like Dostoevsky, he depicted the Antichrist as a lover of mankind and social reformer.

The author of *Karamazov* represents the struggle with God in all its demonic grandeur: the Inquisitor rejects the commandment of love for God, but becomes a fanatic of the precept of love for one's neighbor. His powerful spiritual forces, which earlier were spent in worshiping Christ, are directed now to the service of mankind. But atheistic love is inevitably turned into hatred. Having lost faith in God, the Inquisitor must also lose *faith in man*, for these two faiths are indivisible. Denying the immortality of the soul, he rejects *man's spiritual nature*. And at once man is transformed for him into a pitiable, weak, and vile creature; the history of mankind—into a senseless accumulation of miseries, crimes, and sufferings. If man is only an earthly creature, then his lot is, in fact, a "devils' vaudeville"; if "beyond the grave, men will find only death," then they are indeed "incomplete, experimental creatures, fashioned in mockery." Then there remains for the lover of mankind one goal: to alleviate these unfortunate creatures' brief life, to "organize" this disobedient herd on the earth. Man has been given only an instant of earthly life; let him then spend it in contentment and calm. And the Inquisitor establishes "universal happiness:" He will feed men "bread," will harness their rowdy freedom with "miracle, mystery, and authority," will take up the sword of Caesar and will collect the feeble rebels into a single herd. Then the great tower of Babylon will be erected and the whore will mount the beast —and now forever. Ivan declared that without faith in God and in immortality it is impossible to love mankind. The Grand Inquisitor proves this. He began with loving mankind and ended by transforming men into domestic animals. In order *to make* mankind *happy,* he took away everything human from it. Like Shigalyov in *The Devils,* the hero of the *Legend* ended with the idea of "limitless despotism."

The Inquisitor's monologue is a chef d'oeuvre of oratorical art: his deductions follow logically from the premises, his conclusions strike one as irrefutable; but his negative argumentation suddenly is transformed into a positive one; the accusator's speech becomes the greatest theodicy in world literature. The *Legend* culminates the work of Dostoevsky's whole life: his struggle for man. In it he discloses the religious foundation of the personality and the inseparability of faith in man from faith in God. With unheard-of force he affirms *freedom* as the image of God in man and shows the Antichrist principle of power and despotism. Without freedom, man is a beast, mankind—a herd; but freedom is supernatural and superrational; in the order of the natural world there is no freedom, there is only necessity. Freedom is a divine gift, the most precious property of man. Not by reason, nor by science, nor by the natural law can one prove it—it is rooted in God, is revealed in Christ. *Freedom is an act of faith.* Atheistic lovers of mankind reject God, in that evil exists in the world. But evil exists only because there is freedom. Under this false compassion for the sufferings of mankind is hidden a diabolic hatred of human freedom and the "image of God" in man. Here is why, beginning with love of mankind, it ends in despotism.

The *Legend of the Grand Inquisitor* contains a "proof by the contrary." While accusing Christ, the Inquisitor pronounces a mortal judgment upon his own Antichrist work. He ends with a "herd" and the Babylonian whore. Christ's silence conceals in itself a justification of man and the affirmation of his divine-human dignity. The anthropodicy is crowned by a theodicy. The censure of Christ is turned into His glorification. The Inquisitor reproaches the Savior for having imposed an intolerable burden of freedom upon mankind, having demanded an impossible perfection from it and, consequently, having acted *as if He did not love it at all*. And, here he, the Inquisitor, in fact, "has loved" men: he has fed, enslaved, and turned them into a herd. Dostoevsky makes the greatest spiritual disclosure: *the free personality of man is revealed only in Christ*. Love for one's neighbor is characteristic not of fallen human nature, but of the divine nature. *The lover of mankind is not a man, but God*, who has given His Son for the salvation of the world.

Dostoevsky thought that in *The Legend* he was unmasking Catholicism's deception and the lie of socialism; but his exposure went further and deeper. The Inquisitor's kingdom of the Antichrist is built on miracle, mystery, and authority. In the spiritual life the principle of domination always stems from the evil one. Never in all world literature has Christianity been advanced with such striking force as *the religion of spiritual freedom*. The Christ of Dostoevsky is not only the Savior and the Redeemer, but also the Sole Emancipator of man.

The Inquisitor with dark inspiration and burning passion unmasks his Prisoner; the latter remains silent and answers the exposure with a kiss. He does not have to justify Himself: His enemy's arguments are refuted by the presence alone of Him Who is "the Way, the Truth, and the Life."

Ivan has finished. Alyosha asks about the Inquisitor's subsequent fate. "The kiss burns in his heart," answers Ivan, "but the old man adheres to his former idea." " 'And you along with him, you too?' exclaimed Alyosha sadly. *Ivan burst out laughing*."

Yes, Ivan is with the Inquisitor, with the "terrible and wise spirit" against Christ. He must follow the road of apostasy and struggle with God to the end. His idea "everything is permitted" is realized in Smerdyakov's parricide, the "spirit of self-destruction and nonbeing" is embodied in his "devil." The celebrated scene of Ivan's nightmare is a brilliant creation of the artist and philosopher. In the beginning of the novel the Elder Zosima says to the "learned brother" that the question of God is "still not resolved in his heart and frets him." The dichotomy of his consciousness between faith and disbelief is shown in the hero's dialogue with the devil. The derisive guest does everything in his power to compel the atheist to accept his reality: he has only to believe in the supernatural, and his positive concept of the world is destroyed, his "Euclidean mind" is demolished. Ivan struggles desperately with the "nightmare"; in rage he shouts at the devil: "Not for one minute have I taken you for real truth. You are a lie, you are my illness, you're a phantom. You are the incarnation of myself, only, however, of one side of me . . . of my thoughts and feelings, only the most nasty and stupid of them." Nonetheless, he jumps up so as to thrash his "hanger-on," to shower him with blows; he hurls a glass at him, and after his disappearance says to Alyosha: "No, no, no, this wasn't a dream! He was here, he was sitting here, right on that divan. . . ." So the question of the enigmatic visit will remain unresolved in Ivan's heart. He believes, when he does not believe, denying, he affirms. Reality escapes the man who has lost the highest reality—God; fact merges with delirium, nothing exists, everything only seems. With extraordinary art the author reproduces this confusion of the fantastic and real. The devil is an hallucination; Ivan is on the eve of falling ill with cerebral fever, but the devil is also a reality: he says that which Ivan could not have said, relates facts which the latter did not know.

In the scene of the "nightmare" Dostoevsky treats the theme of apparitions, which was noted in the novel *The Devils*. To Stavrogin appears a "nasty little scrofulous imp with a cold in his head, one of those who have miscarried"; he has the "self-contentment of the sixties, is a lackey in thought and a lackey in soul." Ivan Karamazov's visitor, a Russian gentleman-parasite is also "simply a devil, a wretched petty devil." With hatred the hero says of him: "Undress him and, be sure, you'll find a tail, long, smooth, like a Danish dog's, it'll be two feet long. . . ." What concreteness there is in this description of the fantastic, with what mean triviality the supernatural is arrayed! Stavrogin in his fate is linked with Karamazov: he prided himself on his demonic grandeur and was humiliated by the appearance of the nasty imp "with a cold." The same humiliation also befalls Ivan. The devil provokes him: "You're angry at me because I didn't appear to you somehow in a red light, 'thundering and flashing' with singed wings, but have appeared in such an unassuming form. You're offended, in the first place, in your aesthetic feelings, and, secondly, in your pride: how, you say, could such a banal devil have come to such a great man?" Stavrogin's demon and Karamazov's devil are two variations of one theme: both in the one and the other the falsehood of satanic beauty is unmasked. In his *Legend* Ivan represented the devil in the majestic image of a terrible and wise spirit, and here he has proved to be a vulgar hanger-on with a dark chestnut tail, like a Danish dog's. . . . The spirit of nonbeing is an impostor: this is not Lucifer with singed wings, but an imp "one of those who have miscarried," the incarnation of world boredom and world vulgarity.

However, Ivan Karamazov has not one double, but two: alongside the "hanger-on" stands the lackey, next to the devil—Smerdyakov. The face of the "learned brother" is distorted in the reflection of two mirrors. The devil repeats his thoughts, but only "the most nasty and stupid." Smerdyakov reduces his "idea" to a hideous capital crime. In the lackey's base soul Ivan's theory, "everything is permitted," is turned into his design of murder in order to commit theft. Ivan thinks abstractly, Smerdyakov accomplishes the practical conclusion. "You killed him," he declares to his "teacher," "it's you who are the main murderer, and I was only your helper, your faithful servant Licharda[8] and even committed this deed with your words in mind." Smerdyakov follows Ivan as the "executor": this same way Pyotr Verkhovensky follows Stavrogin. Son of the libertine Fyodor Pavlovich and the idiot-girl Stinking Lizaveta, Smerdyakov, the lackey-murderer is a sickly and strange man. He suffers from epilepsy, talks self-contentedly, in a doctrinaire tone and profoundly despises everyone. "In his childhood he was very fond of hanging cats and then burying them with ceremony." This little trait alone sketches the character of the malicious and pompous degenerate. Smerdyakov is an egoistic, arrogant, and suspicious nonentity. He is an innate skeptic and atheist. The servant Grigory was teaching the twelve-year-old boy sacred history. The latter mockingly and haughtily asked him: "The Lord God created light on the first day, and the sun, the moon and stars on the fourth day. Where then did the light shine from on the first day?"

For a few years he lived in Moscow and there studied the art of cooking. He returned, aged, "had grown wrinkled, yellow, had begun

[8] Smerdyakov is here alluding to the *Tale of Bova, the King's Son,* a Russian adaptation of the Italian romance *Buova d'Antona,* dating back to the late 16th century. In the story Licharda, servant of King Gvidon, is sent by Queen Militrisa to King Dodon with a message that she has decided to kill her husband. In this way, the faithful Licharda becomes a tool in the murder of his master. King Dodon is the real murderer (as is Ivan Karamazov in the novel). By the late 19th century this tale had become a favorite of uncultured readers of the Russian lower middle class. Thus Smerdyakov's words (his identification with Licharda) acquire a deeper meaning in the novel. Smerdyakov is not only an instrument in the murder of his master and father; the books which he reads also disclose his aesthetic interests, divulge his banality and vulgarity.

to resemble a eunuch." He adopted culture in the manner of a lackey, as foppishness; twice a day he carefully brushed his clothes and liked terribly to shine his boots with a special English polish. But as before he was sullen, unsociable, and haughty. Ironically the author calls him a "contemplator." Smerdyakov is by no means a fool; he has a base mind, but clever and resourceful. Fyodor Pavlovich calls him a "Jesuit" and "casuist."

And into this deformed soul falls the kernel of Ivan's teaching. The lackey accepts it with rapture; "God frets Ivan"—for him, the question of immortality is not resolved. In Smerdyakov's heart, God never existed; he is an atheist by nature, a *natural atheist;* and the principle, "everything is permitted," fully corresponds to his inner law. Ivan only desires the death of his father; Smerdyakov kills him.

In the accomplices' three meetings there is unfolded the tragic struggle between the moral murderer and the actual murderer. Smerdyakov simply cannot understand Ivan's horror and torment; he feels that the other is pretending, is "playing a farce." In order to prove that Dmitry did not kill their father, but that it was he, the lackey shows him the bundle of money that he stole after the murder. Dostoevsky finds details that give this scene a character of unutterable horror. " 'Just wait, sir,' said Smerdyakov in a weak voice and suddenly, drawing his left leg out from under the table, began to turn up his trouser leg. He had on *a long white stocking* and a slipper. Without hurrying, he took off the garter and reached his fingers deeply into the stocking. Ivan Fyodorovich looked at him and suddenly trembled in convulsive alarm. . . . Smerdyakov drew out the packet and laid it on the table." One further detail. The murderer wants to call the landlady and have her bring some lemonade and searches for something with which to cover the money; finally, he covers it with a thick yellow book: *The Sayings of Our Holy Father Isaac The Syrian.*

The "long white stocking," which conceals the packet of rainbow-colored notes, and the *Sayings of Isaac The Syrian*—the expressiveness of these artistic symbols can be only shown, but not explained.

Smerdyakov gives the money to Ivan: "I have really no need for it," he says. He thought that he had committed the murder for the money, but now has understood that this was a "dream." He has proven to himself that "everything is permitted"; for him this is enough. Ivan asks: "And now, therefore, you have come to believe in God, since you are giving back the money?" " 'No, I do not believe, sir,' whispered Smerdyakov."

Like Raskolnikov, he had only to assure himself that he could "step beyond." Also like the student-murderer, the stolen goods do not interest him. "Everything is permitted" means "it's all, all the same." Once having transgressed God's law, the parricide surrenders to the "spirit of nonbeing." Smerdyakov ends with suicide and leaves the note: "I am doing away with my own life *by my own personal will* and inclination so as not to throw blame on anyone." Thus he performs his final act of demonic *self-will*.

The youngest of the Karamazov brothers, Alyosha, is drawn more palely than the others. His personal theme is suppressed by Dmitry's passionate pathos and Ivan's ideational dialectics. Like his spiritual predecessor Prince Myshkin, Alyosha shares in the feelings and experiences of the others, but the action of the novel is not determined by him and his "idea" is only noted. But meanwhile *Karamazov* was conceived by its author as Alyosha's biography and in the preface he is directly named the *hero* of the novel. Dostoevsky attempted to explain this discrepancy between the design and its execution: Alyosha does not resemble a hero because "his acts are vague, unexplained." His image was to be disclosed in the future. "The main novel is the second," wrote the author; "this is my hero's activity now in our time, namely in our present current moment. The first novel took place thirteen years ago and is almost not even a novel, but only one moment out of my hero's early youth." But the second novel was not written and Alyosha has been left just as "incomplete" as Prince Myshkin. Working on *The Idiot*, the author confessed: "depicting the *positively beautiful* is an immeasurable task." In *Karamazov* the ideal image of man is only a presentiment and prevision.

Alyosha was born to the same mother as Ivan. His mother, the humble, "meek" Sofya Ivanovna, was epileptic. From her he inherited the religious formation of his soul. One memory of early childhood has determined his fate. "Alyosha recalled one evening, summer, peaceful, an open window, the slanting rays of the setting sun, in the room, in the corner, a holy icon, before it a lighted lamp and on her knees before the icon, sobbing hysterically, with moans and shrieks, his mother, who grasped him in both arms, clasped him violently, till it hurt, and praying for him to the Mother of God, held him out in both arms toward the image, as though to put him under the Mother's protection." Sofya Ivanovna, the martyr-mother, is as mystically joined with the most Holy Mother of God, as the Raw Youth's Mother—Sofya Andreyevna. Alyosha was placed by her under the Mother's veil; he was consecrated, and from his childhood years grace would rest on him. He was brought up in another family, did not finish his course in the gymnasium and suddenly returned to his father. The old Karamazov was astonished by the reason for his return: Alyosha had come to seek out his mother's grave. Shortly after he entered the monastery as a novice to the famous Elder and healer Zosima. The author is afraid that his young hero will seem an exultant eccentric and fanatic to the reader. He insists on his hero's physical and moral health. . . . "Alyosha was at that time a well-built, clear-eyed, *red-cheeked*, nineteen-year-old lad, *radiant with health*. He was at that time even very handsome, slender, moderately tall in height, dark-haired, with a regular, although somewhat long oval-shaped face, with brilliant wide-set dark grey eyes; he was very pensive and, apparently, very serene." He has the special gift of inspiring universal love; he loves everyone, does not remember injuries, never is troubled on whose resources he is living; is steady and clear; he has an extravagant, enraptured modesty and chastity.

The first attempt to portray a "positively beautiful individual"—Prince Myshkin—did not satisfy the writer; in *Karamazov* once again he reworks his draft. Prince Myshkin is a holy fool, epileptic, is "not fully embodied"; Alyosha "radiates with health," is red-cheeked, stands firmly on the ground and is full of Karamazov elemental vitality. But why did this youth, so full of life, become a novice? The writer explains: his hero is "not even a mystic at all"—he is a realist. "In the realist faith does not arise from a miracle, but the miracle from faith."

In Alyosha's image a new type of Christian spirituality is projected —*a monk serving in the world*: he passes through the monastic ascesis, but does not remain in the monastery; before his death the Elder Zosima says to his favorite: "I think of you in this way—you will go forth from these walls, but you will live like a monk in the world. . . . Life will bring you many misfortunes, but it is in them that you will attain happiness and will bless life and will cause others to bless it— which is most important of all. . . ." Such was Dostoevsky's plan regarding Alyosha; the Elder's predictions were to have been realized in the second novel.

The "youthful lover of mankind" clashes with his brother, the atheist; Alyosha believes in God and lovingly admits God's world; he says to Ivan: "I think that everyone should come to love life above all else in

the world. . . . Love it before logic—and only then will I understand its meaning." Ivan does not believe in God and before loving
the world, wants to understand its meaning. Christian love is opposed
by atheistic reason. *Pro and Contra* enters into Alyosha's very soul, becomes his inner struggle, temptation, and victory over temptation. The
Elder dies; his disciple expected that his teacher would be glorified,
but instead of this, he is present at his disgrace: from the esteemed
just-man's coffin a "decaying smell" emanates prematurely; the "temptation" seizes both the monks and the pilgrims; even the "realist" Alyosha, "firm in his faith," is scandalized. Where now is the spiritual transfiguration of nature, about which the Elder used to preach? And if it
does not exist, then Ivan is right. Alyosha's "revolt" is an echo of Ivan's
revolt. He also rises up against Providence and demands "justice" of
it. "It was not miracles he needed," explains the author, "but only
the 'higher justice,' which had, in his belief, been violated by the blow
that had wounded his heart so cruelly and unexpectedly. . . . And
what if there had been no miracles at all, if nothing marvelous had
been proclaimed and what was expected had not been realized at
once—but then why has the disgrace been proclaimed, why had this
humiliation been permitted, why this sudden decay, which even anticipated nature? . . . Where is Providence and its Finger? Why did it
hide its Finger at the most critical moment (so Alyosha thought), and
as though voluntarily submit to the blind, dumb, pitiless laws of nature." These questions about "justice," about Providence, about world
evil, which Alyosha experiences so tragically, are Ivan's questions. At
this fatal moment the novice suddenly feels his spiritual proximity to
his brother, the atheist. Incessantly he calls to mind his conversation
with Ivan. "A certain vague, but tormenting and evil impression from the
memory of yesterday's conversation with his brother Ivan now suddenly began to stir in his soul and more and more urged to break onto
its surface." But Ivan's "revolt" ends in his struggle with God and
negation of God's world; Alyosha's "revolt" is completed by his mystical vision of the resurrection; he is saved by a feat of personal love.
Alyosha goes out of the monastery, falls into the power of his Mephistopheles—Rakitin—and the latter takes him to Grushenka. In the chaste
youth awakens the Karamazov sensuality. The "infernal woman" sits
on his lap, entertains him with champagne. But, upon learning about
the death of the Elder Zosima, she piously blesses herself and "as in
alarm" springs from his knees. "Loudly and firmly" Alyosha says to
Rakitin: "Did you see how she has had pity on me? I came here to find

a wicked soul—I felt myself drawn to it because I was base and evil, but I've found a true sister, have found a treasure—a loving soul. Agrafena Aleksandrovna, I'm speaking of you, you have just now restored my soul."

Grushenka relates a fable about an onion. A wicked, very wicked old woman has during her whole life done nothing good; only once she had given a beggar woman an onion and after her death this onion helped her to get out of the fiery lake. For Alyosha, Grushenka's pity was the "onion," Alyosha's compassion proved also to be an "onion" for her wronged heart. "He has turned my heart upside down. . . . He's the first, the only one who's shown me pity, that's what! Why didn't you come before, you cherub'—she suddenly fell before him on her knees, as though in a frenzy. 'I've been waiting my whole life for someone like you, knew that such a one would come and forgive me. I believed that someone would love even me, nasty as I am, not only with a shameful love.'"

Alyosha's meeting with Grushenka is the bridegroom's mystical betrothal with his fiancée—earth; in *The Devils* we find the same nuptial symbolism (Stavrogin—the cripple). The law of death (sensuality) is overcome by resurrecting love. The souls understand their relationship and mystical unity. Alyosha bears Grushenka's guilt, Grushenka, Alyosha's guilt. "All men are guilty for everyone." In their common guilt they are loving brother and sister. The spiritual regeneration has been accomplished: Grushenka is ready to sacrificially share "Mitya's redemptive feat." Alyosha is open for the mystical vision of "Cana of Galilee."

The novice returns to the monastery and prays at the Elder's coffin. In a state of drowsiness he hears Father Paisy read the Gospel story about the wedding in Cana of Galilee. And now the walls spread apart—the coffin is no longer there; he sees guests, a wedding chamber. The Elder Zosima "joyful and gently laughing" says to him: "We are rejoicing, we are drinking the new wine, the wine of the new, great joy; you see how many guests? Here are both the bridegroom and bride, here is the all-wise Governor of the Feast; he is tasting the new wine. . . . And do you see our Sun, do you see Him? Do not fear Him. He is dreadful in His majesty before us, terrible in His sublimity, but infinitely merciful. . . ." Alyosha's vision is a symbol of the resurrection, the joy of the Kingdom of God.

He leaves the cell; like one mown down, falls onto the earth, embraces and kisses it. "He was weeping in his rapture even over those stars that were shining to him from the abyss, and 'was not ashamed of this ecstasy.' As it were, threads from all these innumerable worlds of God had joined together at once in his soul and it was trembling all over, 'touching other worlds.' He longed to forgive everyone and for everything and to beg forgiveness, oh! not for himself, but for all men, for all and for everything. . . ."

After the light of the resurrection comes cosmic rapture and a vision of the transfigured world. This is that second of "world harmony" of which Dostoevsky's heroes have a presentiment and for which they are oppressed. Man's heart is the mystical center of the universe, threads from all the worlds join together in it and the new Adam, re-established in his original glory, "weeping, sobbing, and shedding tears," kisses the earth, the holy Mother, whom once before he had profaned by his fall from grace.

The Karamazov "earthly" force is turned into a transfiguring force. Alyosha's ecstasy answers Ivan's confession. Ivan does not understand how the mother of a child tormented to death can forgive. Alyosha has understood: in the new world one forgives "for all men, for everything and for all."

The novice's mystical experience becomes the source of his spiritual energy. It empties onto the world, enlightening it from within. In the novel only the beginning of this service is shown. Inheriting from Prince Myshkin his children's theme, Alyosha enters into the life of the schoolboys, makes friends with them, reconciles them with Ilyusha, who is dying of consumption, and on his grave lays the foundation of a "completely universal brotherhood of mankind." The new community, in opposition to the socialistic anthill, is built on *personality and love.* This is a free society of friends of the late Ilyusha: the personal love for one becomes the common love of all. "All you, lads, are dear to me from this day on," Alyosha says to the boys, "I will gather you all into my heart, and beg you to gather me also in your hearts! Well, and who has united us in this kind, good feeling. . . . Who, if not Ilyushechka, the good boy, the dear boy, the boy precious to us for ever and ever."

Ilyusha is not dead: he will live in the love of friends whom he has united "for ever and ever."

Kolya Krasotkin makes the "youthful lover of mankind" explain his thought completely.

" 'Karamazov!' cried Kolya, 'Is it really true now what religion says that we all will rise from the dead and come to life and see each other and everyone again, even Ilyushechka?"

" 'Certainly we will rise, certainly we will see and gladly, joyfully tell each other all that has passed,' answered Alyosha, half-laughing, half in ecstasy."

The novel concludes with a triumphal confession of faith in the resurrection.

The spirit of nonbeing—the devil—stands beside the atheist Ivan; the holy Elder Zosima with his light illuminates Alyosha's path. For his depiction of the just-man, Dostoevsky made use of the rough drafts to *The Life of a Great Sinner*, in which he had already delineated the "majestic figure" of St. Tikhon Zadonsky. Bishop Tikhon in *The Devils* and the pilgrim Makar Dolgoruky in *A Raw Youth* are directly related to the image of Alyosha's spiritual father. The journey to Optina Pustyn and his study of the history of Russian "Elders" helped the author to give artistic form to the "monastic" episodes in the novel. The picture of the monastery in *Brothers Karamazov* reproduces the external aspect of Optina Pustyn with extraordinary accuracy. Here is how the Archpriest S. Chetverikov describes it.[B] "The cloister stands above a river. The white monastery buildings and blue cupolas of the churches with their golden crosses are visible from a distance against the green background of pines and fir-trees. Near the road itself is a post with an icon of the Mother of God. There is an apple orchard, a guest-house; between the four churches, the cemetery. Not far off from the monastery, beyond a small copse is the hermitage in which the Elder Amvrosy lives. His cell is a small little house whose windows look out onto a flower bed. A wooden flight of steps, a narrow entrance-way hung with popular engravings. From the entrance-way is a little corridor which divides the house into two halves. The first door on the right leads to a small chamber, the Elder's formal reception room. In this room the whole front corner is filled with icons, before which there are lamps burning. The wall is hung with portraits of famous ascetics, views of monasteries and other pictures of spiritual content. The furniture consists of an oldish sofa, a few tables and chairs. On the other side of the corridor is the Elder's own cell. Not far off is a pond and an apiary."

[B] Archpriest S. Chetverikov. *Optina Pustyn. Istoricheskiye ocherki i lichnye vospominaniya* (*Optina Pustyn. Historical Sketches and Personal Memories*). Imka-Press, Paris.

In Dostoevsky's novel the visitors enter the monastery gates. . . . Miusov absent-mindedly looks at the tombstones around the church. The hermitage, where the Elder Zosima lives, lies about four hundred paces from the monastery through a little grove. . . . It is all planted with flowers. "There were numbers of rare and beautiful autumn flowers," writes the author, "everywhere, wherever it had been possible to set them. They were tended, evidently, by an experienced hand. . . . The little wooden, one-storied house, with a gallery before its entrance, in which the Elder lived, was also surrounded by flowers."

The Elder Zosima's reception room reproduces Father Amvrosy's "chamber" with almost photographic exactness. Dostoevsky noted everything, remembered everything: "A very old-fashioned leather mahogany sofa," "along the opposite wall, four mahogany chairs covered with black, badly worn leather," "pots of flowers on the window," "in the corner a number of icons, one of them of the Mother of God was huge in size and painted, probably, long before the schism. Before it was burning a lamp. Near it were two other icons in shining settings." On the walls there were "several foreign engravings," and beside them "reproductions of the cheapest Russian prints of saints, martyrs, prelates, and so forth, such as are sold for a few kopecks at all the fairs. There were also several lithographic portraits of Russian bishops, contemporary and past."

The Elder Zosima's "bedroom" is just as poor, as Father Amvrosy's "own cell." "This was a little room," writes the author, "furnished with the barest necessities: the bedstead was of iron, narrow, and on it in place of a mattress, was only a strip of felt. In the corner by the icons stood a lectern, and on it lay a cross and the Gospels."

With the same painstaking exactness we find described in the novel the apartments of the Father Superior and Father Ferapont's dilapidated cell. Dostoevsky attached enormous spiritual significance to the most unimportant "factual" detail. His realism transfigures but never distorts reality. Zosima, in his external appearance very closely resembles Father Amvrosy. During the last years of his life, visitors were struck by the celebrated Optina Elder's frailty and sickliness. Thin, pale, somewhat stooped, he was distinguished, however, by his inexhaustible joy of life. He had a rather sparse beard and small, lively, kind, and penetrating eyes. The writer employed these features to create the image of Zosima. "He was a short, stooped man, with very weak legs," he writes, "and though he was only sixty-five, he seemed, from illness, much older, at least ten years. His whole face, besides,

was very shriveled, was sown with fine wrinkles and they were especially numerous around his eyes. His eyes were small, light-colored,
quick, and shining, like, as it were, two brilliant points. His fine greyish hair still remained on his temples, his beard was very small and
rather sparse, wedge-shaped, and his lips, which smiled frequently,
were thin as two threads. . . . His nose, not that it was long, but sharp,
was like a bird's beak."

Exteriorly the Elder Zosima resembles Father Amvrosy, interiorly
he is related to St. Tikhon Zadonsky, whom Dostoevsky even in the
sixties "had taken to his heart with enthusiasm."

The Voronezh Prelate's life served the writer as material for the Elder's biography. Zosima's love of the young novice reflects St. Tikhon's
regard for the son of the landowner Bekhteyev—Nikandr. The latter
fled from his home to the monastery and that same night the prelate,
having been inspired, went out to meet him on the bank of the Don. At
eighteen, Nikandr became a novice and for three years lived in Tikhon's cell.

Zosima sends Alyosha out into the world; in Tikhon's life we read:
"When Bishop Tikhon moved to Zadonsk, Vasily Ivanovich Chebotaryov became his lay-brother, but died a layman at Yelets, since the
bishop for some reason did not bless his remaining in the monastery."
Metropolitan Yevgeny informs us that St. Tikhon "often went to his
friends uninvited, and usually came on such occasions when they very
much needed his presence because of the circumstances. . . . This
used to happen at times of quarrels in the family, *at times when inher-
itances were divided, at times of disorder involving the children and
similar to that.*" It is possible that these biographical data inspired
Dostoevsky with the idea of the family gathering of the Karamazovs
in the Elder Zosima's cell. Tikhon had enemies in the monastery
(Zosima has Ferapont); he was condemned by the idle curious (like
Mrs. Khokhlakova); he loved to converse with the simple people.
"He often used to go out, onto the stoop or the vestibule of his cell,
would seat them around him and converse then about their condition
of life, and with the very old muzhiks about former times." In the same
way the Elder Zosima goes out onto the gallery and converses with the
"peasant women who have faith."

The writer fervently read St. Tikhon's religious-moral work, entitled:
A Spiritual Treasure Collected from the World and imitated his style
in his *Life in God of the Deceased Priest-monk, the Elder Zosima.*
The *Conversations and Exhortations* of Alyosha's spiritual father are

written in the sentimental religious style of the 18th century; in them archaisms and Church Slavonicism are combined with endearing diminutive nouns. The author reproduces artistically the didactic narrative style of the period, with its cult of "heartfelt emotion," tears of joy and tenderness, of friendship and virtuous nature.[C] Here is how St. Tikhon writes "about love for one's neighbor."

Without love nowhere is there joy and consolation; where there is love, there we find an everlasting spiritual feast and rejoicing. Souls united in love are pleased even to sit in a dungeon; it is sweet to shed tears for one another; without love even beautiful palaces are no different than a dungeon. Houses, cities, empires stand with love; without love they fall. . . . Oh, blessed is that society, that city, that house, in which mutual love flourishes! Like to an earthly paradise, filled with joy and sweetness, is the place, in which love, like a tree, abounding in sweet fruits, resides. Oh, love, love, the priceless treasure, love! Mother of all goods, love!

Dostoevsky was struck by St. Tikhon's inspired teaching about Christian love and his joyful acceptance of God's world. The prelate perceived the presence of the Creator in His creations and often immersed himself in the loving contemplation of nature. Every day in summer, he took a walk, rode in a cart through the forest, cut grass for his horse. The Elder Zosima also teaches that love transforms the world into paradise, that the beauty of nature proclaims the glory of the Creator.

St. Tikhon respected the image of God in man and believed in its restoration in the very worst sinner. He used to say that the universe is gradually drawing near to God, that Christ has already gained victory over death. The *Spiritual Treasure* is full of the joyful expectation of the universal resurrection.

Dostoevsky the anthropologist remembered the prelate's teaching about the dignity of the human personality. "Recognize, Christian," wrote St. Tikhon, "the nobility, honor, dignity, and pre-eminence of the human soul. He honored us in our creation, when He made us in His image and in His likeness; but He honored us more when He Himself came to us, fallen and lost, in our image and suffered and died for us. So dearly did the Lord establish the human soul."

Alyosha sees the risen Zosima, feasting at the marriage in Cana of

[C] R. Pletnyov. *Serdtsem mudrye* (*O "startsakh" u Dostoevskogo*). (*Wise in Heart* [*About "Elders" in Dostoevsky*]). The Second Collection on Dostoevsky, ed. A. Bem. Prague, 1938.

Galilee; after this vision he throws himself down onto the earth and experiences *cosmic ecstasy*. It is possible to suppose that Dostoevsky conceived the idea of this scene after reading the memoirs about St. Tikhon written by his lay-brothers, V. Chebotaryov and I. Yefimov. The first of them tells the following story of the prelate: "In the month of May the night was exceedingly pleasant, peaceful, and bright; I went out of my cell onto the stoop, which was on the north side, and standing there was meditating on eternal bliss. Suddenly the heavens opened and there was such light and radiance that my corruptible tongue can in no way relate it or my intellect understand it; but only this was brief and the heavens returned to their ordinary form, and I, from such a wondrous appearance, conceived a more ardent desire for the solitary life." I. Yefimov completes: "And again another vision our friend saw: he was led to crystal chambers, ones of most astonishing beauty and saw in them tables adorned, men feasting and singing and choirs, though he did not comprehend the verses. 'Do you find it good?' they asked him. And he answered: 'Exceedingly good.' 'Go and merit it,' was the answer to him."

From the artless and simple memoirs of the lay-brothers, Dostoevsky created his *Cana of Galilee*.

But the Elder Zosima is not a portrait of Tikhon Zadonsky. The writer freely reworked the hagiographical material and created a new type of holiness, different both from 18th century "religion of the heart" and from the Elders of Optina Pustyn. Zosima is not a representative of historical Russian monasticism; he is directed toward the future as a herald of the new spiritual consciousness of the Russian people. In his religiosity there is an enraptured sense of the divinity of the world and the Godlikeness of man; he sees the mystical unity of the cosmos and its illumination by the Holy Spirit (Beauty); this is the source of his teaching that "all men are guilty for everyone." The Elder lives in the light of the coming resurrection, believes that creation will freely return to its Creator and God will be "of everything and in all." His faith is alien to dogmatism; his teaching about man and about the world predominates over doctrines about God; he says little about the Church and nothing about its mystical heart—the Eucharist.

The treasure store of Orthodoxy is inexhaustible: Zosima with his spiritual outlook does not embrace all its riches; he takes from it only a few pearls, but in his hands they flare up with a new luster.

On the lips of his Elder, Dostoevsky puts the definition of the essence of his religious sense: these words belong to the greatest words of man.

"God took seeds from different worlds and sowed them on this earth and His garden grew up, and everything came up, that could come up, but what has grown, lives and is alive only by the feeling of its contact with other mysterious worlds; if this feeling grows weak or is destroyed in you, then that which has grown in you also dies."

Zosima teaches about the soul's ascent to God. The steps of this spiritual "ladder" are: suffering, humility, responsibility for all, love, tenderness, joy; its summit is ecstasy. "Kiss the earth and love unceasingly, insatiably, love everyone, love everything, seek after rapture and this *ecstasy*. Water the earth with the tears of your joy and love these tears of yours.

"Do not be ashamed of this *ecstasy*, value it, for it is a great gift of God, and is given not to many, but to the elect."

Dostoevsky in the touching image of the Elder Zosima embodies his own *ecstatic world-sensation*.

X X I V

The Pushkin Speech · Death

The solemn unveiling of the monument to Pushkin in Moscow was set for May 26, 1880. Dostoevsky and Turgenev received invitations from the Society of Lovers of Russian Literature to speak about the great poet at the celebration.

The author of *Karamazov* interrupted his arduous work on the novel and in a state of inspiration prepared a speech about Pushkin, whom he had admired all his life, whom he considered the greatest Russian genius and his own spiritual teacher. In a letter to Pobedonostsev, Dostoevsky wrote: "I've prepared my speech about Pushkin and precisely in the most extreme spirit of my (our, that is, I'll venture to express myself this way) convictions, and consequently expect, perhaps, some abuse. The professors there court Turgenev, who has decidedly turned into a kind of personal enemy toward me. . . . But I cannot extol Pushkin and preach Verochka. . . ."

Once more he was struggling for the convictions of his entire life, once more he was engaged in combat with European evil, embodied in his personal enemy—Turgenev. The last words allude to Turgenev's passion for the actress Savina, who with enormous success performed the role of Verochka in his play, *A Month in the Country.*

In spite of an aggravated lung condition and monetary difficulties, on May 22 Dostoevsky left Staraya Russa. On the next day in Tver he learned of the death of the Empress Mariya Aleksandrovna (Aleksandr II's wife) and of the Imperial decree to postpone the unveiling of the monument. Nonetheless out of civil courage he decided to continue the journey. Moscow received him warmly: his Slavophile friends honored him. Dinners and suppers followed one after the other; the writer was sincerely astonished at the lavish Moscow hospitality. . . . The Pushkin festivities began June 5 with a solemn prayer service; on the following day the unveiling of the monument took place; Dostoevsky delivered his famous speech on June 8 at a session of the Society of

Lovers of Russian Literature in the hall of the Noblemen's Assembly. He describes in detail these joyful days in letters to his wife.

"Moscow. Hotel Loskutnaya No. 33. May 28-29, 2 o'clock in the morning. . . . The main thing is that not only the Lovers of Russian Literature, but all our party are in need of me, our whole idea, for which we have struggled now 30 years, because the hostile party (Turgenev, Kovalevsky, and almost the entire University) want decidedly to diminish the significance of Pushkin as the spokesman of the Russian national spirit, denying that national spirit itself."

The first triumph awaited him June 6 at a literary soirée in the Noblemen's Assembly, where he read Pimen's monologue from *Boris Godunov*. He wrote to his wife:

"Moscow, June 7 . . . The unveiling of the monument took place yesterday, but how to describe it, where to begin. . . . Next followed a dinner with speeches. Then a reading during the evening literary festival at the Noblemen's Assembly with music. I read Pimen's scene. In spite of the impossibility of this choice (for Pimen cannot shout through an entire hall) and reading in what was acoustically the worst possible hall, I, I'm told, read superbly, but they tell me that little of it was heard. I was received excellently, for a long time was not permitted to read, there was such applause, and after the reading I had to answer three calls. But Turgenev, who read wretchedly, received more applause than I. Behind the wings (a huge place in the dark) I noticed about a hundred young people, who bawled in ecstasy, when Turgenev came out. At once I had the feeling that these were claqueurs, a *claque*, seated by Kovalevsky. So it turned out: today in view of this claque Ivan Aksakov refused at the morning sessions of speeches to read his speech after Turgenev's (in which the latter slighted Pushkin, having deprived him of the title national poet), having explained to me that the claqueurs had been engaged long ago and were seated expressly by Kovalevsky (they were all his students and all Westernizers), so as to indicate that Turgenev was the leader of their tendency, and to slight us if we should go against them. Nonetheless, the reception accorded me yesterday was quite astonishing, although only one part of the public who were seated in the stalls, clapped. Moreover—men and women came to me in crowds behind the wings to shake my hand. In the intermission I was passing through the hall and a swarm of people, young and old and ladies rushed up to me, saying: 'You are our prophet, you have made us better, since we have read *Karamazov*.' In a word, I am convinced that *Karamazov* has a colossal significance. Today, leaving the morning session, at which I did not speak, the same thing happened. On the stairs and at the cloakroom I was stopped by men, ladies, and others. At yesterday's dinner two ladies brought me flowers. . . . Today there was a second dinner, a literary one—about two hundred people. The young people met me on my arrival, regaled, attended me, made me enraptured speeches—and this even before the dinner. At the dinner many people spoke and made toasts. I didn't want to speak, but toward the end of the dinner they jumped up from behind the table and forced me to speak. I said only a few words—a roar of enthusiasm, literally a roar. Then in another hall where I sat I was surrounded by a dense crowd —they spoke a great deal and heatedly (over coffee and cigars). And when at half-past nine I got up to go home (two thirds of the guests were still left), then they shouted out hurrah, in which even those not sharing my sentiments, will or nill, had to take part. Then the whole crowd rushed down the stairs with me and without their coats, without hats, went out with me onto the street and helped me into a cab. And suddenly they rushed to kiss my hand—and not one, but tens of people, and not only the youth, but grey-haired old men. No, Turgenev has only claqueurs, but mine have sincere enthusiasm."

But all these ovations were nothing compared to the triumph that awaited the writer on the historic day of June 8. After his speech about Pushkin an enraptured ecstasy, inspiration seized his audience. This amazing day does not have a parallel in the whole history of Russian spiritual culture. Upon having returned from the festival, Dostoevsky wrote his wife: "This morning was the reading of my speech to the Society; the hall was crammed full. No, Anya, no, you can never imagine or conceive the effect which it produced. . . . I read loudly, with fire. All that I had written about Tatyana was received with enthusiasm (this is a great victory for our idea after 25 years of error!). Then when at the end I proclaimed the *world-wide union* of men, the hall was almost in hysterics; when I finished—I won't tell you about the roar, about the cry of ecstasy: strangers in the audience were weeping, sobbing, embracing one another, and *swearing to one another to be better, not to hate each other in the future, but to love.*"

Cries resounded: "You are our saint, you are our prophet," "You're a genius, you are more than a genius." For a half-hour the applause continued; the public was in a frenzy. Some student in tears ran up to the orator and fell senseless at his feet. Turgenev, deeply moved, embraced his old enemy. The session adjourned for an hour. Then Ivan

Aksakov announced to the public that he could not speak following Dostoevsky's brilliant speech, that he considered his talk an event in Russian literature. Once again a storm of applause. Aksakov was forced to deliver his speech, then Dostoevsky was called out; he was presented a laurel wreath in the name of Russian women.

In the evening at a literary festival the author of *Karamazov* read Pushkin's poem *The Prophet*. Utterly exhausted, he strained his weak and hollow voice to a shout. Once more the hall was "in hysterics," once more a "howl of ecstasy." All literate Russia crowned its "prophet." One image, which he loved, passes throughout Dostoevsky's works—the slanting rays of the setting sun. His glory was also such a final ray: he had less than eight months remaining to live.

The writer's speech about Pushkin was the fruit of twenty years' reflections on the great Russian poet. We find its rough draft already in the articles of 1861 in the journal *Time*. Pushkin always stood at the center of his historiosophical structures: in his image he sought the solution of the fate and mission of Russia. In the speech at the Pushkin celebration Dostoevsky invested his own inviolable thoughts and hopes with a brilliant artistic form. The orator's eloquence was united in it with the fiery pathos of a prophet.

In the appearance of Pushkin, said Dostoevsky, there was something indisputably prophetic for all Russians. He was the first—in Aleko and in Onegin—to depict the "historical Russian wanderer," torn away from his native soil, oppressed and suffering; he also proposed the Russian solution to this accursed question: "Humble yourself, proud man, and above all dissolve your pride. Humble yourself, idle man, and first of all, exert yourself on your native field." Next to the "wanderer" Onegin, Pushkin set Tatyana, the Russian woman, a "type of positive and indisputable beauty." Having defined our sickness, he also gave us great comfort. "Everywhere in Pushkin is heard faith in the Russian character, faith in its spiritual power, and if there is faith, consequently there is also hope, great hope for the Russian man." Not one world genius possessed Pushkin's capacity for universal sympathy. "How he was able to reincarnate in himself an alien nationality!" In *Don Juan* he is a Spaniard; in *A Feast During the Plague*—an Englishman; in *Imitations of the Koran*, he is an Arab; in *Egyptian Nights*—a Roman. This sympathy was a prophetic appearance, for in it has been expressed the national Russian force. Peter's work responded to the deepest aspiration of the popular spirit, which yearned for the completely universal union of mankind. "Yes, the Russian's destiny is incontestably all-European and world-wide. To become a real Russian, to become fully a Russian, perhaps, means only to become brother of all men, *a completely universal man,* if you want." Therefore, the hostility between the Westernizers and the Slavophiles was a sad misunderstanding. Russia was called to "utter the ultimate word of great common harmony, of the brotherly definitive accord of all races following Christ's evangelical law! . . . Let our land be poor, but through this poor land 'in the likeness of a slave, Christ has gone forth, bestowing His blessing.'[1] Why then should we not contain His ultimate word? And was not He Himself born in a manger?"

After this inspired messianic prophecy, the orator concluded with pathos: "Pushkin died in the full growth of his powers and without doubt carried with him into the grave some great secret. And now we, without him, are trying to solve this secret."

Dostoevsky passionately believed in the "great common harmony," in the "complete reconciliation of ideas." In his Pushkin speech he attempted to reconcile the Slavophiles with the Westernizers, the intelligentsia with the people, Russia with Europe. For an instant it seemed that the miracle had been accomplished: yesterday's enemies embraced one another. In tears Turgenev shook the hand of the author of *The Devils.* But this reconciliation was not lasting; when the intoxication of ecstasy had passed, the malicious criticism began, factional differences and polemics in the journals were resumed. Russia of the eighties was not ready for "the completely universal brotherhood of mankind."

———————

On June 10 Dostoevsky left Moscow; in Staraya Russa he set about the conclusion of *Karamazov.* Pobedonostsev congratulated him on the success of his Pushkin speech. "I was delighted with all my heart," he wrote, "that you fulfilled your wish, about which you wrote me, and achieved it with such success—to thrust back the insane wave which was preparing to besmirch the monument of Pushkin. I am delighted for you and particularly for the just cause which you have rescued."

In his letters to Pobedonostsev the writer complained of having to work beyond his strength. "I definitely decided not to go to Ems: I've too much to do. Owing to the spring confusion I neglected *Karamazov* and now propose to finish it before leaving Staraya Russa, and there-

[1] The lines from Tyutchev's poem: *Eti bedrye selenya* (*These poor villages*).

fore am sitting at it day and night." In another letter he informed him: "Besides *Karamazov,* in the near future I'm publishing in Petersburg an issue of *The Diary of a Writer.* . . . However, this is not an answer to the critics, but my *profession de foi* for the entire future. Here now, I'm declaring myself definitely and openly, I call things by their own names. . . . What is written there—*is for me fatal.* Starting next year I intend to resume *The Diary of a Writer!*

In August the sole installment of *The Diary of a Writer* for 1880 appeared. In it was included the speech on Pushkin and his reply to Professor A. Gradovsky's critical essay, which had been printed in the *Voice* under the title *Dream and Reality.* His ideational opponent acknowledged "a powerful sermon of personality in Dostoevsky's speech," but did not see "even a hint of social ideals" in it. The author of *The Diary* attributed vast significance to his reply: this was "his *profession de foi* for the entire future." In fact, in refuting Gradovsky, he found the definitive expression of his own religious-moral world-view. This *answer was Dostoevsky's spiritual testament.*

At the basis of social life, citizenship, nationalism lies the idea of personal self-perfection: it "comprises everything, all aspirations, all yearnings," and from it issue all civil ideals.

"In the origin of every people, every nationality, the moral issue always preceded the genesis of the nationality itself, for *it is the former which created the latter.*"

But the moral idea is always of religious origin: it emanates "from mystical ideas, from the conviction that man is eternal, that he is not a mere earthly animal, but is joined with other worlds. These convictions always and everywhere were formulated in religion, in a confession of the new idea and always, as soon as a new religion came into being, immediately a new civil nationality was also created. . . . Consequently 'self-perfection in the religious spirit' in the life of the peoples is the foundation of everything, whereas 'civil ideals' themselves, without this striving for self-perfection, never do appear, and never can be engendered. . . ."

Dostoevsky demonstrated his idea by the history of Christianity. "By the way, remember," he addressed the critic, "what was the ancient Christian Church and what did it strive to be. It came into being immediately after Christ; it comprised in all just a few men and at once, almost in the first days after Christ, it sought to find its 'civic formula,' wholly based on the moral hope of quenching its spirit in accordance with the principles of personal self-perfection. Christian communes-churches were begun, then quickly a new, till then un-heard-of nationality began to be formed—completely *fraternal, completely universal to mankind, in the form of a common Ecumenical Church.*" At the same time, over the Church, another enormous edifice was being erected—the anthill of the Roman Empire. "But the anthill did not come to pass, it was undermined by the Church. There occurred a collision of the two most opposed ideas, which could have existed on earth: *the man-god encountered the God-man, Apollo of Belvedere—the Christ. . . .*"

This celebrated formula culminates Dostoevsky's philosophy of history. At the center of the world-process stands man, his personal mystical experience, his moral idea of self-perfection. Society is organized through religion; the nation grows out of a common faith; opposed to the commune—the Church there created is the anthill of the state; the Antichrist rises up against Christ.

The author of the *Grand Inquisitor* did in fact "declare himself definitely and openly." A monarchist and imperialist, he came to acknowledge the pagan, *Antichrist principle of the State.* "What is written there," he declared to Pobedonostsev, "is *for me* fatal." We have understood this "fatal" only in our epoch, when the totalitarian state in struggle with God has revealed to us its demonic face.

The installment of *The Diary of a Writer* was sold in a quantity unprecedented for that time: 6,000 issues were bought up in several days. A second edition was exhausted in autumn. The writer exerted his last forces and succumbed from the "penal labor." On August 28 he wrote to Ivan Aksakov: "You won't believe how busy I am day and night, like a man sentenced to penal labor: namely, *I'm finishing Karamazov*; hence, am reckoning up a total of the work which I, at minimum, value, for it contains much of me and mine. Generally, I work in a nervous state, with torment and anxiety. When I work intensely, then I'm even sick physically. And now a total is being summed up of what for three years I have pondered, composed, written. . . . Besides, despite the fact that for three years now I've been making notes, I will write many a chapter and then reject it, will write it again and reject it again. Only the inspired places flow all at once, at a toss, but all the rest is arduous work."

In a letter to P. Ye. Guseva (October 15) the complaints of the utterly tired and sick writer, worn out by "penal labor," sound pathetic.

"I didn't answer you," he writes; "you won't believe why. Because if there's a man condemned to penal servitude, then it's me. I was in Siberia 4 years, but there my work and life were more endurable than at present. From June 15 up to October 1, I wrote 20 printed sheets of the novel and published *The Diary of a Writer* in 3 printed sheets. And, still, I can't write off the top of my head; I must write artistically. I'm bound in this to God, to poetry, to the success of what's been written and literally to all the readers of Russia, who are waiting for the conclusion of my work. And therefore I've sat and written literally day and night. . . . Do you believe that I can't and do not have the time to read a single book or even a newspaper. It's even impossible for me to speak with the children, and I don't. Then my health is so poor that you can't even imagine. The catarrh of my respiratory passages has formed emphysema, an incurable thing (choking, lack of air), and my days are numbered. As a result of my strenuous activity, my falling sickness has also become exasperated. I have neglected everything, given up everything, do not talk about myself. It's night now, 6 o'clock in the morning. The city is waking up and I still haven't lain down. And the doctors tell me that I ought not risk tormenting myself with work, ought to sleep at night and not sit up 10-12 hours, bent over my writing. Why do I write at night? But here I'll wake up now at one in the afternoon; then visitor after visitor will arrive. One will come in, ask for something, another for something else; a third demands; a fourth urgently demands that I resolve some insoluble, accursed question for him. Otherwise, he says, I am driven to the point of shooting myself (and I've just met him for the first time). Finally, a deputation of students, of women students, of gymnasiums, of a charitable society—they want me to read for them at a public soirée. But when can one think, when can one work, when is one to read? When to live? Don't be surprised at me for letting myself enter upon such conversations. I am so tired and I have a tormenting, nervous disorder. Literally, all literature is hostile to me, I am loved to enthusiasm *only* by all reading Russia."

But he did not give in: he completed the novel, carried on a passionate polemic, took part in literary soirées and intended the following year to resume publication of *The Diary*. "I confess to you as a friend," he wrote to Iv. Aksakov, "that, undertaking *The Diary* for the next year (in a few days I'm sending out the announcement), I've often and repeatedly now prayed on my knees to God, that He give me a pure heart, a word that is pure, sinless, not irritable, not envious."

Sending off the epilogue of the novel *Brothers Karamazov* to Lyubimov and saying good-bye to the editors of the *Russian Messenger*, the writer jokingly declared that he intended to live and write for another twenty years. . . .

In December 1880 he personally presented his last novel to the Heir Apparent—the future Emperor Aleksandr III. The Grand Duchess Mariya Fyodorovna was present at his reading in the home of Countess Mengden and shortly after this Their Highnesses received the author of *Karamazov* in the Anichkov Palace. Dostoevsky did not follow court etiquette: "He spoke first, stood when he found that the conversation had continued long enough and, having taken his leave of the Tsesarevna and her spouse, left the palace hall, as if it were the drawing-room of one of his friends. The Grand Duke was not offended by this."

During the last months of his life, Dostoevsky prepared the January issue of *The Diary of a Writer* for 1881. In it he boldly talked about the Russian people as the Church and paradoxically called the populist idea "Russian socialism." "The whole profound error of our intellectuals lies," he wrote, "in the fact that they do not acknowledge the Church in the Russian people. I am now not speaking of church buildings and not of the clergy; *I am now speaking of our Russian socialism* (and I use this term, diametrically opposed to the Church, precisely in order to elucidate my thought, however strange this may seem), the aim and end of which is the Church of all peoples and of all the world, realized on the earth, insofar as the earth is capable of embracing it. . . . Not in communism, not in mechanical forms is the socialism of the Russian people expressed: they believe that they shall be saved only, ultimately, *through universal union in the name of Christ*. Here is our Russian socialism!"

The people must be allowed to say their own word; attention must be paid to their truth. The writer dreamed of drawing the people into collaboration with the Tsar, of some new form of an all-Russian national assembly. "Yes," he writes, "we can show confidence in our people, for they are worthy of it. Summon the grey peasants' coats and ask them about their needs, about what is necessary for them, and they will tell you the truth, and perhaps for the first time we all will hear the real truth."

Dostoevsky's last days were poisoned with anxiety regarding the fate of this article: he feared that the censors would not let it pass. But *The Diary* appeared after the author's death. At the moment of his posthumous apotheosis, the authorities did not dare to touch the political testament of the author who had just passed away.

The concluding article of *The Diary* is dedicated to Skobelev's victory over the Turkomans and the Russian army's capture of Geok-Tepe. The author saw in this event a turning point in Russia's history and with inspiration spoke of the Russian mission in Asia. This is Dostoevsky's last and, maybe, most astonishing prophecy: contemporary Eurasian theories, the Asiatic politics of post-revolutionary Russia were already outlined in this article written before his death. "Russia," he declared, "is not only in Europe, but also in Asia: the Russian is not only a European, but also an Asiatic. Moreover, in Asia, perhaps, we have even greater expectations than in Europe. Moreover, *in our future destinies, perhaps Asia is our main outlet!* . . . In Europe we were hangers-on and slaves, but in Asia we shall appear as masters. In Europe we have been Tatars, but in Asia we are Europeans. Our *mission,* our civilizing mission in Asia will bribe our spirit and carry us there. . . . *A new Russia would be created,* which would in time regenerate and resurrect the old one. . . ."

In the eighties this "asiaticism" seemed pure fantasy; in our time we see in it a mysterious presentiment of the coming destinies of Russia.

There came the year 1881. Dostoevsky was full of far-reaching plans: he intended to publish *The Diary* over the course of two years, and then to begin writing the second part of *Karamazov;* all the former characters would appear in it, but now twenty years later, almost in the contemporary period. The main hero of the novel would be Alyosha Karamazov. Anna Grigoryevna writes: "The first half of January F. M. was in excellent spirits, visited acquaintances, and even agreed to take part in an amateur play which was intended for performance at Countess S. A. Tolstaya's the beginning of the following month. They talked about staging two or three scenes from Count A. K. Tolstoy's trilogy, and F. M. took the role of the hermit in *The Death of Ivan the Terrible.*"

On the night of January 25th to the 26th, while working in his study, he began to cough blood. The extravasation was so insignificant that he paid no attention: on January 26 there were two new hemorrhages. The doctor was summoned; the patient lost consciousness. Coming to himself, he said to his wife: "Anya, I beg you, call a priest at once, I want to confess and receive Communion." After his Communion, his condition improved and the night passed quietly. On the 27th he again set about business: talked with his compositor, was troubled regarding *The Diary*. Early in the morning of the 28th the sick man woke up his wife: "You know, Anya," he said, "it's three hours now that I haven't slept and all the while I've been thinking and only now I've realized clearly that today I'm going to die." Anna Grigoryevna assured her husband that he would not: he interrupted her: "No, I know, I must die today. Light a candle, Anya, and give me the Gospel."

He opened it at random, to the third Chapter of Matthew: "But John restrained Him and said: 'I need to be baptized by You and do You come to me.' But Jesus said to him in reply: 'Do not restrain me, for so it is fitting that we fulfill all righteousness.' "[2]

Dostoevsky said to his wife: "You hear—do not restrain me, this means I am going to die" and added: "Remember, Anya, I have always loved you ardently and have never been unfaithful to you, even in thought." Lyubov Fyodorovna recounts that before his death her father gave the following instruction to the children. The dying writer called his son and daughter to his side, asked that the parable of the prodigal son be read to them, and said "Children, never forget what you have just heard here. Preserve an unbounded faith in the Lord and never despair of His forgiveness. I love you very much, but my love is nothing in comparison with the Lord's infinite love for all men, whom He has created. If ever it should happen that in the course of your life you commit an offense, still you must not lose hope in the Lord. You are His children—humble yourselves before Him, as your father; beg Him for forgiveness and He will rejoice at your repentance, as He rejoiced at the return of the prodigal son."

The whole day Anna Grigoryevna did not leave the dying man for a minute: he held her hand in his and in a whisper said: "My poor, dear one, what do I leave you with. . . . My poor love, how difficult life will be for you." The hemorrhaging did not stop; they called the doctor, he found the patient already in agony. At thirty-eight minutes past eight on the evening of January 28 Dostoevsky passed away.

During his last months the writer often talked about his death and

---

[2] The New Testament, from which Dostoevsky read, had been presented to him thirty years earlier by the wives of the Decembrists in Tobolsk. Anna Grigoryevna in her memoirs notes that subsequent Russian translations render the words: "Do not restrain me" as "Suffer it to be so," and that because of the profound significance the Gospels assumed in their lives, had Dostoevsky read the more recent translation, he would have recovered, although, she goes on, he would not have survived the assassination of Aleksandr II on March 1.

asked to be buried in the cemetery of the Novodevichy Monastery. Once Anna Grigoryevna said jokingly that they would bury him in the Aleksandr-Nevsky Laura. "What a wonderful funeral I'll arrange for you!" she added. "Archbishops will serve your funeral liturgy, the metropolitan choir will sing. An immense crowd will escort your coffin and when the procession approaches the Laura, the monks will come out to meet you." "They do that only for the Tsar," answered Dostoevsky. But Anna Grigoryevna's words proved prophetic. The writer was interred at the cemetery of Aleksandr-Nevsky Laura.

His funeral turned into an historical event—thirty thousand people accompanied his coffin, seventy-two delegations carried wreaths, fifteen choirs took part in the procession. February 1 the writer's body was laid into the earth: Palm, Miller, Gaideburov, and Vl. Solovyov delivered speeches at his grave.

Dostoevsky's death was experienced by every Russian as a national mourning and personal grief.

Conclusion

In 1839 the eighteen-year-old youth Dostoevsky wrote to his brother: "Man is a mystery: if you spend your entire life trying to puzzle it out, then do not say that you have wasted your time. I occupy myself with this mystery, because I want to be a man."

The great psychologist had a presentiment of his vocation: all his creative work is devoted to the mystery of man. In Dostoevsky's novels there are no landscapes and pictures of nature. He portrays only man and man's world; his heroes are people from contemporary urban civilization, fallen out of the natural world-order and torn away from "living life." The writer prided himself on his *realism;* he was describing not the abstract "universal man," contrived by J. J. Rousseau, but the real European of the 19th century with all the endless contradictions of his "sick consciousness." The Russian novelist first discovered the real face of the hero of our "troubled time"—the "man from underground": this new Hamlet is struck by the infirmity of doubt, poisoned by reflection, doomed to a lack of will and inertia. He is tragically alone and divided in two; he has the consciousness of an "harassed mouse."

Dostoevsky's psychological art is famous throughout the world. Long before Freud and before the school of psychoanalysts he plunged into the depths of the subconscious and investigated the inner life of children and adolescents; he studied the psychics of insane, maniacs, fanatics, criminals, suicides. Special commentaries exist on Dostoevsky, the psychopathologist and criminalist. But his analysis was not limited to individual psychology; he penetrated the collective psychology of the family, of society, of the people. His greatest insights concern the soul of the people, the metapsychic "unity" of mankind.

Psychology is only the surface of Dostoevsky's art. It was for him not an end, but a means. The province of the inner life is only the vestibule of the kingdom of the spirit. Behind the psychologist stands the *pneumatologist*—the brilliant investigator of the human spirit. In one of his notebooks we find the following remark: "I am called a psychologist, it's not true, I am only a realist in the highest sense, i.e., I depict all the depths of the human soul." Dostoevsky had his own doctrine of man—and in this is his great historical importance. He devoted all his creative forces to struggling for the spiritual nature of man, to defending his dignity, personality, and freedom.

In his own personal experience, the author of *Crime and Punishment* lived through the tragic epoch of the *shattering of humanism.* Before his eyes humanism tore itself away from its Christian roots and was transformed into a struggle with God. Having begun with the emancipation of man from "theology" and "metaphysics," it ended by enslaving him to the "laws of nature" and "necessity." Man was conceived as a natural being, subject to the principles of profit and rational egoism: his metaphysical depth was taken away from him, his third dimension—the image of God. Humanism wanted to exalt man and shamefully degraded him. Dostoevsky himself was a humanist, passed through its seductions and was infected by its poison. The romantic idealist of the years of *Poor People* was captivated by utopian socialism and passed through the whole dialectical course of its development: he "passionately accepted" Belinsky's atheistic faith and entered Durov's secret revolutionary society. Starting out from Christian humanism, he came to atheistic communism. In the year 1849, sentenced to capital punishment, the writer stood on the scaffold. During these terrible minutes the "old man" in him died. In penal servitude a "new man" was born; there began a cruel judgment of himself and the "regeneration of his convictions." In Siberia, two events took place in the life of the exiled writer which decided his whole subsequent fate: his meeting with Christ and his acquaintance with the Russian people. Amidst inhuman sufferings, in a struggle with doubt and negation, faith in God was won. Apropos of the *Legend of the Grand Inquisitor* Dostoevsky wrote in his notebook: "Even in Europe there are not and have not been atheistic expressions of such force; consequently, it is not as a boy that I believe in Christ and confess Him, but *my hosanna has passed through a great furnace of doubts. . . .*"

After penal servitude, the religious theme formed the spiritual center of his work. The question of faith and disbelief was posed in all the great novels. In 1870 he wrote to Maikov: "The main question, which has tormented me consciously or unconsciously throughout my entire life—the existence of God."

"God torments" all of Dostoevsky's heroes; all of them decide the question of God's existence; their fate is wholly determined by the religious consciousness.

Dostoevsky lived through a period of crisis in Christian culture and experienced it as his personal tragedy. Shortly after the Franco-Prussian War and the Parisian Commune, the hero of the novel *A Raw Youth* went abroad. Never had he traveled to Europe with such sadness and with such love. "In those days especially, one seemed to hear the tolling of a funeral bell over Europe." The great idea of Christian culture was dying; it was being escorted out with catcalls and the flinging of mud; atheism was celebrating its first victories. "I wept," confesses Versilov, "wept for them, I wept for the old idea and, perhaps, I wept real tears."

The Russian Dostoevsky, at the end of the 19th century, felt himself the only European who understood the significance of the world tragedy, which was being experienced by mankind. He alone "wept real tears." And now the "old idea" was gone and mankind was left on earth without God. The writer's "novel-tragedies" are devoted to depicting the fate of *mankind abandoned by God*. He prophetically indicated two paths: man-godhood and the herd.

Kirilov in *The Devils* declares: "If God doesn't exist, then I am God." In place of the God-man appears the man-god, the "strong personality," who stands beyond morality, "beyond the confines of good and evil," to whom "everything is permitted" and who can "transgress" all laws (Raskolnikov, Rogozhin, Kirilov, Stavrogin, Ivan Karamazov). Dostoevsky made one of his greatest discoveries: *the nature of man is correlative to the nature of God;* if there is no God, there is also no man. In the man-god, the new demonic being, everything human must disappear. The Russian writer predicts the appearance of Nietzsche: the superman of the author of *Zarathustra* also signifies in his presence the destruction of man: "the human, the too human" is eradicated in him as shame and disgrace.

The other path of atheistic mankind leads to the herd. The culmination of Dostoevsky's work is the *Legend of the Grand Inquisitor*. If men are only natural beings, if their souls are not immortal, then it is fitting that they be established on earth with the greatest possible well-being. And since by their nature they are "impotent rebels," then one must enslave and transform them into a submissive herd. The Grand Inquisitor will tend them with an iron rod. Then at last, an enormous anthill will be built up, the Babylonian tower will be erected, and now forever. Both ways—man-godhood and the herd— lead to one and the same result: the suppression of man.

Dostoevsky saw history in the light of the Apocalypse; he predicted unheard-of world catastrophes. "The end of the world is coming," he wrote. "The end of the century will be marked by a calamity, the likes of which has never yet occurred." The tragic world-outlook of the author of *The Devils* was inaccessible to the positivists of the 19th century: he was a man of our catastrophic epoch. But God's abandonment is not the last word of Dostoevsky's work; he depicted the "dark night," but had presentiments of the dawn. He believed that the tragedy of history would be culminated in the transfiguration of the world, that after the Golgotha of mankind would follow the Second Advent of Christ and "there would resound the hymn of the new and last resurrection."

To Dostoevsky belongs a place beside the great Christian writers of world literature: Dante, Cervantes, Milton, Pascal. Like Dante, he passed through all the circles of human hell, one more terrible than the mediaeval hell of the *Divine Comedy,* and was not consumed in hell's flame: his *duca e maestro* was not Virgil, but the "radiant image" of the Christ, love for whom was the greatest love of his whole life.

Appendix

Dostoevsky's Plans and Rough Drafts
1. *The Emperor*
2. *The Holy-Fool*
3. *The Tale of Captain Kartuzov*
4. *The Death of a Poet*
5. *The Novelist*
6. *A Thought on Summer*

1. The Emperor[A]

The plan for the novel *The Emperor* is related to Mirovich's attempt to free Ivan VI Antonovich[1] from prison.

"The prison, darkness, the youth: he doesn't know how to speak, Ivan Antonovich, almost twenty years old. Description of character. His development. He grows up alone, fantastic image and figure, snow, sees a girl in a dream. Represent all objects. Terrible fantasy, mice, a cat, dog.

"A young officer, the commandant's adjutant plans a coup d'état, to proclaim him tsar. Becomes acquainted with him, bribes the old soldier who attends him, and goes to him. Their meeting. His astonishment, joy and fear; friendship. He opens the prisoner's soul, teaches him, talks with him, shows him a girl (his fiancée). The commandant's daughter, through whom all this takes place, is tempted by the idea of becoming tsaritsa. Finally, he discloses to him: 'You are tsar, you can do everything.' Image of power ('Therefore, I treat you with such respect, I am not your equal'). The prisoner has come to love him so, that he at once says: 'If you are not my equal, then I don't want to be tsar.' This means that he doesn't want to lose his friendship.

"From the window of the garret he shows him the world (the girl and the rest). Finally, an uprising. The commandant kills the tsar with his sword. The latter dies nobly and sorrowfully.

[A] Notebook No. 1/3, 1867.

[1] Peter the Great enacted a law whereby the reigning Emperor would choose his heir, rather than adhering to an ordinary hereditary succession. The years following his death were marked by continuous court struggles, turmoil and coups d'état. After the death of Empress Anna, the grandson of her sister, the Duchess of Mecklenburg, was named Emperor—Ivan VI—under a regency. The officers of the Guards summoned Peter's daughter Yelizaveta to the throne and the young Ivan was arrested and imprisoned on January 5, 1742.

"N.B. He shows him God's world. 'Everything is yours, you have only to wish it! Forward!' 'This is not possible! If this doesn't succeed, then there will be death.' 'What is death?' He kills a cat in order to show him blood. 'The impression is so horrible, I don't want to live, if this happens, if on my account anyone dies, if you will die, if she will die.' Mirovich, inspired, explains the opposite view to him and talks a great deal about how he, once he is tsar, can do so much good. This excites him.

"Mirovich is an enthusiast, he explains an understanding of God and Christ to him. (He shows him his fiancée, the commandant's daughter, with whom he is in agreement.) She does not attempt to involve her father: the austere old man, a zealous soldier, would not agree to the insane venture.

"The fiancée is willing. She comes to show herself, dressed sumptuously in a ball gown, with flowers. The tsar's rapture. The fiancée is astounded by the impression that she has produced upon him, she begins to dream about becoming tsaritsa. Mirovich observes this, is jealous, the tsar sees his hatred, his jealousy, his evil glances, does not understand, but senses what the matter is. Mirovich sets out for Petersburg. At the sight of the commandant, Ivan Antonovich is disturbed: 'I saw him in childhood!' "

The proposed draft of *The Emperor* stems from the period of Dostoevsky's work on *The Idiot*. Ivan Antonovich resembles Prince Myshkin. A man "not of this world," a "strange man," pure in heart, who lives his fantastic life outside of history and culture. The prince is an "idiot," sickly, has the sanatorium; the "tsar" has been imprisoned for life, is retarded, also an idiot in his way. Mirovich simultaneously plays the roles of Professor Schneider, by making the idiot a man, and Rogozhin, in his jealousy of his fiancée; the commandant's daughter—an ambitious beauty—calls Nastasya Filippovna to mind. The tsar is shaken by his first encounter with death (the killing of the cat) and astounded by the revelation of feminine beauty (his meeting with the commandant's daughter). This is the same in the case of Prince Myshkin (the impression of Legros' execution and of the portrait of Nastasya Filippovna). The tsar is just as trusting, naive, and full of love, as the hero of *The Idiot;* both perish tragically. A motif out of *Crime and Punishment* passed into the plan of the new novel: acquiring power by way of bloodshed and a justification of "revolt" by the possibility of doing much good.

2. *The Holy-Fool* (*The Sworn Attorney*)[B]

"A lover of old clothing. A good and noble man. Takes in his home orphans (a little girl with a dog). The benefactor of many. Those to whom he has been kind accuse him: he goes to ask their forgiveness and conciliates them. An apartment full of children, he is foster-father and nursemaid. Pacifies the children. (Marries. His wife is unfaithful and leaves him. The reason on account of the children. Afterward again comes to him: forces him to fight for her in a duel. Chivalrous acts. The wife dies.) Old clothing. The tailors, domestics laugh because they are old. He assures them that they are quite new. Duel over the clothes. He did not shoot and thought better at a distance (came in contact with a criminal-murderer). Defended him at the trial: his speech. After the duel, reconciliation. A great quarrel, why didn't he shoot at a distance? After several bottles! But is it possible, is it possible my cloth doesn't turn blue (already after the duel? He was told, at last, that it does)."

While working on his plan for *The Idiot* Dostoevsky outlined this variant of the "positively beautiful" individual. The children's presence relates this notation to the rough drafts for *The Idiot*.

The Tale of Captain Kartuzov[C]

In the notebooks, filled with rough drafts for *The Idiot* we find the plan of *The Tale of Captain Kartuzov* worked out in detail. Dostoevsky composed it in 1868 at the same time that he was working on *The Idiot*. It is not easy to sort out the disconnected remarks, the disorderly notations written out of all chronological sequence, the variants contradicting each other, the enigmatic allusions to one or another situation, the fragments of dialogues, the verbal formulas jotted down in the books as reminders; and yet from the chaos of accumulated materials it is possible to distinguish the fundamental line of the plot and to reconstruct the hero's image.

Captain Kartuzov is Prince Myshkin's spiritual brother. In the course of the novel's construction, he emerged out of that same psychological "haze" from which Myshkin was formed. He embodies one of the possibilities that was not realized in the Prince: the "beautiful individual" in a comic aspect, a foolish knight, a ridiculous provincial Don Quixote.

[B] Notebook, No. 1/5, 1868.
[C] Notebook No. 1/5 and No. 1/4, 1868.

It is possible to conjecture that at those moments when *The Idiot* seemed a "positive failure" to Dostoevsky, he grasped in despair at the other possibility of depicting the "beautiful individual," a humorous conception. This way presented itself as easier, more traditional; here he had great predecessors: Cervantes and Dickens. And yet, the tale was left unwritten. Dostoevsky quickly understood the delusion: to his tragic and cruel genius the geniality of humor was thoroughly uncharacteristic.

The Tale of Captain Kartuzov is the story of the love of a knight pure at heart, the ridiculous story of an "awkward man," a Platonic lover and absurd poet, and at the same time a sad tale concerning the ruin of a beautiful individual, scoffed at, and ignorant of his own value. The Russian Don Quixote is also a soldier; he is a captain who has recently been transferred to Reval from some fortress or other. His past lies in obscurity; he used to live in some remote place, in a fantastic world; he does not understand life at all, to the point of its being strange: he has "as though tumbled down from the moon." This fortress, half-real, far away, out of which suddenly Kartuzov appears, corresponds to the no less hazy Swiss sanatorium of Prince Myshkin. Both of them are strange men, eccentrics, holy-fools, wandering about in this world as in the dark, bewitched by their dream, grown-up children with unlimited naiveté and trust. Kartuzov is in love with a beautiful Amazon and worships her, as Don Quixote does Dulcinea. Dostoevsky concentrates his regard for the lady in a gesture-symbol: in order to "show esteem" for his chosen one, upon meeting her, he invariably puts his hand to his cap—whence his ideological name: Kartuzov.[2]

The Tale of Captain Kartuzov is divided into two parts; in the first of them the action takes place in Reval, in the second in Petersburg. The narrator is a man "off to the side"; he is in no way connected with the milieu in which he is living, or with the society which surrounds him; his narration can be completely objective. This is a "chronicle."

Here is the beginning of the tale:

Reval is a maritime city, on a gulf; people come there to bathe. . . . It's a German city and has a pretension of being chivalric, which for some reason or other is very ridiculous (though it was in fact once settled by knights). . . . By chance I belonged or, more precisely, did not

[2] *Kartuza*=peaked cap.

belong to but was peculiarly associated with a small cluster of officers from the buildings along the shore. Among the youth there were several amusing people, but at that time our attention was most of all provoked by a Captain Kartuzov. He had once again enlisted, had been transferred from some fortress. . . . Kartuzov was new in Reval. He paid everyone visits. . . . Little by little I noticed that he confided in me more than the others and even noticed his attempts to become friends with me.

For the "ridiculous knight" Kartuzov is found a worthy place of action, the "ridiculous" chivalric town Reval. The beginning of the tale sounds really "à la Pushkin." Involuntarily one recalls the first lines of *The Shot*: the officers' milieu, in the center of which is an enigmatic romantic hero (Silvio-Kartuzov).

The hero's detailed characteristics go on: "Nota bene: from the first moment set up Kartuzov's figure before the reader more comically, more enigmatically, and interestingly. All the rapacious and romantic moments in all their truth and reality must be *caught from nature* with a comic overtone."

And so, Kartuzov is a romantic hero, he is genetically connected with Pushkin's Silvio, although in the development of the tale the motif of "rapaciousness" was not elaborated. His romantic enigma is undercut by a "comic overtone." His exploits in the first part of the tale recall not so much Silvio, as Grushnitsky.[3] "Is taciturn, dry, well-mannered, naive, trusting. Suddenly utters thoughts. More frequently keeps silent and blushes, does not know how to talk. Is chaste. Comes, is silent, sits, will go away, smokes. Han the Icelander. . . . Kartuzov is a mad (unsociable) and taciturn person. The most awkward man I've ever known. In general, the whole tale could have been called *The Story of an Awkward Individual.* . . . Kartuzov speaks poorly, does not come to the point. He's never nonplused, apparently, not suspecting that he is ridiculous. Businesslike enough, if necessary, holds himself well, strictly according to form. But well only up to a certain extent, so long as it's possible to keep silent and doesn't require doing anything. But when it's necessary to move or begin speaking, he often at the first gesture compromises himself, and sometimes commits such a faux-pas that all find it unexpectedly strange and in the end it becomes ridiculous. . . . He was dreadfully ignorant. It was terribly difficult for me to find out what he knew and what he didn't. About Pushkin, verse–he would blush and was silent, but answered politely if he was asked. . . .

[3] A character in Lermontov's tale *Princess Mary* in *A Hero of Our Time.*

I used to ask in terrible amazement: 'Where have you been up till now, Captain (that is, where have you served, with whom have you lived, and how could you have attained such an age without a catastrophe)? For you should,' I said, 'have a nursemaid. It's impossible to leave you alone.' Kartuzov does not understand the question. Besides, he relates indifferently and without connection two or three features from his former life of which much is terribly strange. The conversation is interrupted and then he does not resume it."

Kartuzov's figure is advanced by the author as being really enigmatic. What kind of man is he, what is his past? What is the significance of his peculiarities? True to his habit, Dostoevsky hints at the tragic denouement of the tale—Kartuzov's ruin: "How could you have attained such an age *without a catastrophe?*" And a catastrophe is already approaching.

A rich and well-known beauty, Yelizaveta Karmazina comes to Reval for the waters with her·fiancé, a count. Kartuzov sees her riding on horseback and at first censures her, finds that for a girl it is indecent to ride about like an Amazon; however, at the very first glance she strikes his imagination. He feels sudden hatred toward the count. In the circle of officers Karmazina's arrival with her fiancé is discussed.

"Kartuzov expresses himself sharply about being a lackey, blushes, is silent; says that if I dropped my cap . . . (became terribly confused, and did not finish and grew silent). Got up: to spurn him. Whom? The count. I'm convinced that he is a scoundrel. Kartuzov's first opinion about the fact that the count must be a scoundrel is completely without foundation, not corroborated by any proofs, but is expressed with incredible violence."

Thus the author notes the complication of the tale: the sudden origin of Kartuzov's love for Karmazina and hatred for her fiancé. He behaves in a provoking manner toward the count, "clamors for a fight." Upon meeting him, he does not yield him the road and they collide "shoulder to shoulder." Dostoevsky here repeats the famous episode out of *Notes from Underground*. The count is indignant, Kartuzov triumphs. "A little scandal."

Finally, the distracted dreamer chances to fall under the "Amazon's" horse. He gets up unharmed, but this occurrence decides his fate: he is in love. "Flame and rapture." Karmazina sends to inquire about his health. On the next day he goes to thank her for her attention and says to her: "For the sake of such beauty I am glad to die thirty times." . . . The Count, who is present during this meeting, laughs at him.

"This is too much." Kartuzov flies into a rage. "And here you are not being asked." In confusion he breaks a cup.

After the visit to Karmazina, Kartuzov returns to the narrator and shares his impressions with him.

" 'I broke a cup there, but they surely will forgive me everything . . . and I . . . in a word—I'm a clever lad!'

" 'Oho, captain!'

" 'It's all this damned count, all the more that I expressed myself so delicately. In appearance it was rude: I'm ready to fall under your horse thirty times. To fall means to tumble head over, nastily, coarsely, and impudently; the thought alone that a decent man, i.e., a captain, and then what sort of captain, is flying flying in his trousers and his epaulets and all this head over and more, thirty times along the road. A rude and absurd idea, which can in the last extremity be allowed, but at the same time is also in the highest degree a delicate idea. A subtle idea! Therefore, why does he go flying, why, it is asked, does he agree to fly a subtle somersault, be it even head over heels? Here is understood such a subtle, such a lofty thought, that everything together forms an uncommon delicacy. Such a delicacy that, although it be the very highest society, here's what! Such is my opinion! But then, this count spoiled everything. In fact, I didn't go to see him at all. Why did he interrupt me and mock my every word?"

There comes a time of complete bliss for Kartuzov. "Kartuzov's first love was the time of his loftiest happiness." He calls on the Karmazins many times, but they do not receive him. He would like to "prove his love" in some way. In the taciturn and bashful man there suddenly are aroused romantic and even "rapacious" feelings. The author notes various exploits of Kartuzov: he fires a gun, buys a bear, and leads him about everywhere, intends to take a flight in a balloon. The captain begins to be concerned regarding his appearance, plays the dandy, pomades himself. The officers make fun of him and in his presence publicly discuss his love for the "Amazon." Once, in order to badger him, they force him to jump into the water in full uniform, claiming that a certain one of the women bathers is drowning. Kartuzov, "saving beauty," triumphantly carries a naked woman out of the water. They asked him whether he would have dared to touch the bather, if it had been Karmazina. He answers: "She won't bathe this way, like everyone else, not out of the baths, but somehow specially. . . . Surely they have their own bath covered with velvet." "But of course, velvet will subdue noise," they reply. He sends his lady love letters and verses and tells everyone about this. Dostoevsky noted down for himself a detailed and fine analysis of Kartuzov's feeling.

"Kartuzov falls in love immediately and suddenly by such a process that, as it were, this is inevitable, à la Orientale and it could not be otherwise. This is strictly not even being in love and not love, but only a *necessary* and *inevitable adoration*. It began with the lady's saddle, literally, and through the saddle (i.e., through the beautiful) Kartuzov directly ascribed all perfections to her, moral and physical, up to the highest ideal, but once having ascribed them to her, Kartuzov not only does not doubt these perfections of the ideal but is unable even to consider and to allow specks of thoughts and doubts. . . . The main thing struck him: an *Amazon*. It must be he had seen few Amazons and maybe none at all. . . . In him this is not a sort of opinion, not a conclusion, not a conviction, but something like faith, like a positive fact which is so tangible and positive that not only is the possibility of forming a question lost, but it even becomes imperceptible; thus, for example, one can live in a house before which there are four trees on the lawn, and, after having spent a year, not know precisely how many trees there are—four or three; or live in Vevey, delight in the mountains on the other shore of the lake and not know and not even once ask oneself what are the contours of these mountains. His conviction is thoroughly Don Quixotic, with the difference that Don Quixote nevertheless drew a *question* for himself from his conviction, or else he would not have found it necessary to ride out onto the road and defend this conviction with the lance, while Kartuzov does not presume and did not once have the thought that it was possible that not everyone agreed with her perfection. . . .

"Kartuzov, being in the highest degree of adoration, does not find the slightest indecency either in his adoration or in his behavior, i.e., the verses, and precisely because he does not even presume the possibility of marrying her, does not allow even the speck of a thought as to his equality with her (but it is possible to accept verses from him because he is a captain). So that, when a question by chance comes up about this, he calmly, without emotion and without any pain even judges that he is not worthy.

"I was shocked at first, that Kartuzov was so unchaste, that he let everyone discuss his love and passion, but I came to understand that here there was a great deal of naiveté, respect for others, respect for the loftiness of his passion, and the principal thing was the impossibility of comparing himself, as an equal, in his categorical opinion of himself as an inferior. Perhaps there was also a certain annoyance and vengeance against the Karmazins who did not acknowledge his passion."

Thus the lofty love of Don Quixote is indicated: more faith than feeling, infantilely pure and innocent. In a sinful world the shrine of this love invites derision, is disfigured in the comic. The "beautiful, not knowing its own value," is condemned to ruin. After his visit to the Karmazins, the captain lives in the world of his dream; in their drawing room he cursorily saw vases and statues, and they especially struck his imagination. He dreams that he will have an apartment with vases and statues.

"'I'm terribly fanciful. I am absorbed for a time, about two days in a row, by dreams: an apartment, vases, carpets, several expensive pictures, and one statue: a bacchante is looking for a strawberry. And besides, I do good deeds. . . .' Suddenly the question: 'why are statues naked? . . . Tell me, if a bacchante is looking for a strawberry, why a bare behind? . . . You think? . . . I think that this is only the declaration of a poetic dream and nothing more. . . .' He came, sat down, was silent, asked a question, got up and left. Smoked continually. . . . Kartuzov, to whom one thing is just like a million others, is in ecstasy over the vases, paintings at *her* place."

And the author adds that the captain perhaps did see vases at the Karmazins, but is exaggerating, while perhaps there weren't any vases; "he invented everything." Finally, Kartuzov brings his verses to the narrator:

> Oh, how dear she is
> Yelizaveta Karmazina,
> When on her saddle she flies with her friend,
> While her curl plays with the winds,
> Or when with her mother in church she bows down,
> And only the flush of devout faces is seen.
> Then I pray and tremble and desire pleasures.
> And after her, with her mother, send my tear.

And here is an excerpt from another poem:

> The father with rank in the Tsar's service,
> A domestic angel lived in the family. . . .
> (The father important in the service)
> Had children. But I could not see
> A rhyme on E, that does not disturb our amity.

In his letter to Karmazina Kartuzov writes: "You bear a name of Russian glory. Bearing a name of Russian glory, you naturally have not noted Captain Pyotr Kartuzov, who adores you." And further he naively informs her of his hopes and successes in the service.

Kartuzov confesses to the narrator that he has already sent off the letter with the poems. The following dialogue takes place between them:

"I ask: does he really have hopes?

" 'No, no, I know that it's impossible for me. Impossible!'

" 'Why do you write in the letters there then about your salary, service, hopes, and even paint a picture of an apartment in a little cottage?'

" 'Just so. For the sake of a game and for naiveté. I know myself that it's imagination. Just so. But imagining amuses me. I am dreaming by the minute: and what if it's possible?'

" 'But how could you send that?'

" 'But what?' (Surprise) . . . 'And why, this is all true; why, I myself keep dreaming each moment and she has to accept that this is only my imagining.'

" 'But suppose this is disagreeable to her?'

" 'I don't think so.'

" 'But it's a scandal. You're disgracing her.'

" 'Why? I declare to everyone that I'm in love, but I don't express any pretension.'

" 'It's indecent. You're placing yourself in a false position.'

" 'How?'

" 'Why, they consider you a buffoon.'

" 'Buffoons are also the ones who are considering. But Yelizaveta Nikolayevna cannot laugh in derision. If she begins to laugh, then it's some kind of divine laughter. And, besides, let her, even if it be in derision: why, I'm writing sincerely. Besides, what's it to me to spit on everyone? Except, of course, Yelizaveta Nikolayevna. Besides, I'm sure that here that scoundrel has besmirched me, and therefore, the laughter.'

" 'You yourself, then, why do you say that it's "flame and rapture?" '

" 'Indeed this is a strong expression.'

" 'Let it be. Be engulfed by flame and rapture, but one doesn't talk about it, as though even you did not know it. This is stronger.'

" 'Why?'

" 'You're just a child. To you everything is why. Well, because if you become aware of it, it means that natural flame has already somewhat died down in you.'

" 'Somewhat died down. Hm. When we meet, I shall express my esteem, i.e., that I esteem you alone.'

" 'Please, don't add that you will not address yourself to a certain count. And in general I would advise you not to address anyone at all and simply to pass by.'

" 'No, no, no, no! . . . This means, whatever calculations regarding the service might have filled my head, in spite of that—only a challenge will be heard—and Kartuzov is ready: esteem!' "

The narrator does not approve of his verses.

"One thing offends me: this 'with the winds.' " Kartuzov bursts out: "Only a scoundrel can give this another meaning."

About the second poem he says: "The father—this is me, a husband, and concerning the rhyme: this is a droll tone." And he adds: "I must make the acquaintance of some poet or other."

"Went calling on Polonsky, left his card. Although he insists that he is insignificant and unworthy, nonetheless in the letter he makes a proposal. . . . When he reads to me: 'the father in the service,' then after my admonition says: 'I am dreaming!' But at the same time he's thinking about marriage. 'And why couldn't she marry me? Simply because there is the count, but really does she love this count? But he is a scoundrel.' "

"You want to inform her that he is a scoundrel?" asks the narrator. "He grew pensive, wanted to write a letter, but then said: 'This is impossible.' "

"If one explains something to Kartuzov, he listens with amazement and then suddenly will plunge into thought, and he'll lose himself. . . . He has sometimes suddenly unrelated judgments after a melancholy reflection: 'How is it people are not able to organize themselves? They might live, loving one another, and might find in this true happiness.' "

Suddenly he poses the question: "Is it possible to die from nobility of soul?"

Kartuzov's letters and verses pass from hand to hand. The officers set up a mock tribunal to consider his affairs of the heart. The "commission" decides that Kartuzov must abduct his beautiful lady. The latter listens attentively, but does not approve. The narrator, angered by this scene, leads the captain away from the meeting.

" 'But, they are laughing at you!'

" 'Really?'

" 'Ah you! Why does one have to spell everything out to you? You're

like Don Quixote, you don't care that the maiden is practically married
—you always love so faithfully.'

" 'Can they have loved *this way?'* " answers Kartuzov.

And suddenly the captain resolves to make peace with the count.
He goes to him in order to find out whether he is worthy of his fiancée. He poses the question to him: "Do you love sincerely, or is it for
money? Is it true that you are marrying for calculated reasons? How
can I not know the truth, if I'm ready to give up my body for her slightest advantage?"

Dostoevsky notes the psychological motivation of his hero's strange
behavior. "Of course, everything since this time that touched upon
the Karmazins has constituted for Kartuzov a question of life and
death and therefore the idea appears: to *protect* Karmazina. There is
no experience of jealousy and he is not in the least tormented by
jealousy. He is not in the least jealous of the count, but a *higher
human ordination*, anxiety, role are awakened in him in the question: is the count completely worthy? . . . So that his main concern is
not that the count does not love (and is rival), but that the count is
not really worthy of her, and almost that he doesn't love her enough.
Kartuzov is precisely anxious that the count might love her not *somewhat*, but *deeply*. Having made peace with the count, he becomes his
trumpet, trumpets forth his merits, virtues, future successes, wealth,
looks, writes them both verses. Finally, he becomes friends with the
count, does not leave him, enters into his interests and his favorite conversation with the count is about the count's future and with the enraptured frenzy of a dreamer how to establish this future. However,
Kartuzov, although the count also finds him ridiculous because of his
unexpected friendship toward him, behaves so simply and with such
dignity that the count can in no way turn him into buffoon (what he
would like). He is very clever, so as not to understand Kartuzov,
though he's also nasty at heart. When, in the end, the count turns him
out, rudely and with spite, Kartuzov leaves, quietly forgiving him."

There comes the denouement of the first part of the tale. In the
evening a certain rogue appears at the officers' club and relates nasty
stories about the count: he had had an affair with a governess, a
Frenchwoman, who suddenly is coming to Reval, is slandering the
count, and insists that he owes her 60,000. Defending the honor of
Karmazina, Kartuzov sets out to see *mam'selle*. "Hers is a laughable,
serious, and insolently naive story." "Kartuzov politely takes leave of

her without saying anything, but then in conversation drily and briefly: a carrion." At once he sends the count a letter:

"There are various tones, among which the tone of a scoundrel sometimes rises to the surface. I have heard this tone of a scoundrel and unless I will confide the secret to paper, this tone will resound in my ears. I am sparing my ears and if a scoundrel looks into my private life, I seek a scoundrel's ears. Man's inner tranquility, observing the lot given to it, sleeps without being perturbed by extraneous circumstances. But when it awakes, it alters with the circumstances. I am unburdening everything in complete candidness. As to the name "scoundrel," I will see what you will do. . . .

> Without respect and binding upon everyone
> who signs a letter,
> Your servant P. Kartuzov.

In a rage the count beats Kartuzov with a whip; the latter challenges him to a duel. The count agrees, but the captain "lays down a condition" that the count should fire first, and that he will not shoot. The count laughs at this, is surprised and angry. Kartuzov explains:

"It is for the sake of Katerina Grigoryevna.ᴰ He is the chosen one. Let him know that I fully give to him Katerina Grigoryevna." "But this is stupid!" exclaims the count. "He's a fool!"

Three hours later rumors about the imminent duel reach the commandant, he arrests Kartuzov but, at the request of the Karmazins and the count, promptly releases him.

So, the duel did not take place: on the same day the "Amazon" fell from her horse and broke her leg. "Kartuzov was struck. grew silent, fell ill with a fever."

The first part ends on this.

In the second part the action is transferred to Petersburg. Karmazina was bedridden for six weeks, and her leg was amputated. Kartuzov, upon recovering from the fever, "without hair, with eyes still distended and sunken," arrives in Petersburg. He has found out that the count has refused to marry the crippled Karmazina and in notes demands an explanation from him. After long efforts, he finally gains an interview with the count and asks him:

"Where is your love?"

The count answers: " 'You're such a Don Quixote. You'll admit yourself that I could very easily have spared myself an explanation with you. I'm not bound.'

ᴰ In the rough draft to *The Tale* Karmazina is called first Yelizaveta Nikolayevna, then Katerina Grigoryevna.

" 'Nevertheless, explain yourself.'

" 'Yekaterina Grigoryevna has herself refused me. She wants to enter a monastery—poetry, the ringing of the evening bell and tears.'

" 'If she has herself, then you, of course, could not oppose her intentions, but you ought to have pressed.'

" 'But, allow me, you're acting against your own interests if you force me to get married, you ought to be delighted that a place is free. Indeed, you're also in love with Katerina Grigoryevna; why don't you marry her yourself?'

" 'I'm a monster, etc.'

" 'Not at all, you're a fine fellow.'

"Kartuzov blushed.

" 'You're a scoundrel.'

" 'Well, and you're a fool. You're looking for the whip again. Only this time I'll act not with the whip, but you should be locked up in a madhouse.'

" 'Wait now, I will inquire whether you are bound or not, and then we will meet.'

"The count throws him out."

Kartuzov goes to seek the narrator and "discloses the thought that it would be vile and vulgar for him to turn up under these circumstances as a suitor and the count, consequently, is a scoundrel. But the thought ripens; three days later: 'But why not? (real life takes its own). She broke her leg, so she'll be glad even to have me.' Dreams and ecstasy. Kartuzov arouses and makes a proposal; in a letter he expounds his general hopes and encloses verses concerning future happiness."

He writes: "From the time that I was knocked down by your horse, from that time my happiness (the duel was only a game), was established and suddenly everything has collapsed. . . . Derzhavin and Sumarokov[4] wrote Catherine, and what's more, how: the intimate form thou in the grand style:

" 'In thy joyful destiny, exult, O Russia, now.' "

He adds to the letter the verses:

> The ornament of beauty broke a limb
> And became three times more fascinating.
> And he three times over has grown enamored
> Who before was not untouched by love.

[4] Eminent poets during the reign of Catherine the Great.

Everything has disappeared! Buried is
One of the young limbs,
But I am captivated by what remains
And even as though they had been not at all.

Allow me then to pour out my love,
Deign to accept my proposal,
So as together in marriage to forget the lost limb,
And with that remaining to experience legitimate
    pleasure.

Having made the proposal, the captain "for the sake of tone" moves
to the Hotel London. In conversation he remarks: " 'The Hotel London; the most important persons stay there. . . . But in Petersburg
there is the Red Public House, so all the generals and the most important of the chamberlains ·gather there.'

" 'D-don't know. . . .'

" 'I do. This is so. Therefore, I now want to gather there too, so
that at Lizaveta Nikolayevna's they might know that I am most
sophisticated, so to speak, with a certain rich and noble tossing of gold
on the green cloth.' "

"He changed his gold before his departure for the Red Public
House. Didn't find anything. Fight with the waiters."

Finally, Karmazina receives him and politely refuses. Kartuzov hears
her out, becomes pensive and says: " 'Yes, I am a scoundrel!'

" 'Why?'

" 'The sense that I took advantage of an invalid's condition and dared
to think that I myself was equal to you to such an extent that I could
make a proposal.'

" 'But why? But why?'

"Interrupts: 'I am a monster. Without birth and family. My auntie,
the Finn, used to live at their pastor's, in a country house. She didn't
know how to speak human language all her life.'

" 'This, of course, could have served as an obstacle, but . . . but, in
the first place, captain, there has not even been talk of this and I
very, very much entreat you not to return to this subject. I am refusing not because, etc.'

" 'It's he, the scoundrel, that taught me!'

" 'Who?'

" 'The count! He'll be at your feet.'

· 667 ·

"'Don't dare. What do you want to do with him?'

"'A duel.'"

"She takes his word that he will not start a scene.

In the notebooks, the beginning of the second part has been preserved in two variants. According to the second variant, Kartuzov calls on the Karmazins several times, he is not received; finally, a superintendent comes out to him and asks him to stop his visits. The captain declares that "having a noble rivalry and honorable intention," he cannot discontinue them. "I will not leave off." The superintendent answers:

"'But, my dear sir, we shall find a restraint against you, we shall employ all severities.' (To Kartuzov they talk of measures of severity! Horror!)

"'But who are you?'

"'But who then are you? I wish to hear an answer from Yekaterina Grigoryevna's own lips.'

"'This you will not hear, and as to who I am, I already have announced to you that I am a person authorized to act in this matter and, moreover, I am going right now to the chief of police with the factual explanation of the affair, in order to find restraint against you.'"

Kartuzov decides to inform the chief of police that a complaint will be lodged with him. They admit him; he relates the story of his courtship. The chief of police:

"'This is very funny what you're saying.'

"The chief of police thought.

"'But they have refused you.'

"'But I haven't heard a reply from Yekaterina Grigoryevna.'

"'To be sure, and you'll not hear one. And what right do you have to expect an answer from her lips, as you put it, when you're not even acquainted. Why, you've already received an answer.'

"'Not a delicate answer, Your Excellency.'

"'But indeed you yourself have acted not delicately. You don't deserve any other.'

"'But I'm in love, Your Excellency.'

"'Hm. In love! This is stupid, my dear sir, what you're saying.'

"'For the first time I'm told, Excellency!'

"'You have been refused.'

"'I don't believe it, Excellency! I cannot believe it. I'm convinced that there is a mistake and malice here. They took me for someone else.'

"'It's really strange that you are so self-confident.'

" 'It's very hard for me to believe it, Excellency! If one makes a noble proposition, then there follows a noble refusal, and not an ignoble refusal, Excellency!'

" 'Who then is the source of the malice?'

" 'My enemies, Excellency.'

" 'Enemies! How is it you can even have enemies!'

" 'Why shouldn't I have enemies, Excellency?'

" 'Enemies, my dear sir, are had by people a little better than you, and you're what? But allow me, for all that I can in no way understand the reason for which you've been pleased to disturb me.'

" 'To inform you, Excellency. They wanted to slander me, Excellency, and the superintendent threatened to complain to your Excellency.'

" 'Maybe you have done something more than that? Have you misbehaved there, carried on?'

" 'Misbehaved! Excellency, such an expression! I've in no way misbehaved.'

" 'Perhaps they take you simply for a scamp? Yes, and of course so.'

" 'For a scamp, Excellency. I blush at the thought alone; I don't believe it and don't want to.'

" 'It's no matter what you want! What else did you write there in the letter?'

" 'There were also some verses, Excellency.'

" 'But here, now it comes out. What sort of verses?'

" 'The acme of respect, Excellency. I have a copy with me.'

" 'Give it here. . . . How is this possible to fly on a lady's saddle? With the winds? A strange expression.'

" 'A curl with the winds, Excellency. When the winds blow, then the curl flutters. This is a poetic thought, Excellency.'

" '. . . and desire pleasure. Pleasure . . .' (the general twisted his mouth). 'Now this is too outspoken.'

" 'But this is poetry, Excellency. In poetry it is permitted, Excellency!'

" 'In the service, my dear fellow, there is no poetry. In the service one has to serve, and not to poetize. Well, my good fellow, you're such . . .' (laughs. Suddenly Kartuzov also began to laugh).

The general frowned.

" 'Why are you laughing, my dear sir? Why are you grinning? It suits you not to laugh, but to blush, dear sir, to blush! What were the pleasures you suddenly begin to desire?'

" 'A poetic thought, Excellency, in poetry it is permitted.'

" 'Nonsense, dear sir, nonsense! Even in poetry indecencies are not permitted.'

" 'Indecencies! Your Excellency!'—burst out Kartuzov.

" 'And you express your thought so shamelessly—I can even say unscrupulously. Did you have any such right *before marriage?*' "

On this the second variant breaks off. Let us return to the first. After his meeting with Karmazina the captain goes to the count and declares to him: "I am convinced that she loves you and you must get married." The count chases him, Kartuzov slaps him in the face. He is arrested and at the count's insistence is placed under observation in a hospital. The author adds: "Insanity resulting from the count's intrigue, but also in fact."

"Kartuzov tried to call the chief of police to the hospital, wanted to expose the plot. A simpleton and with not the slightest disturbance, but to the contrary, an appearance of a certain kind of triumph. A peaceful and Socratic tone, steady glance. Drinks tea."

The narrator visits Kartuzov in the madhouse and converses with him. Kartuzov says:

" 'I find that a great deal is very strange.' He grew pensive and began to talk about engineering transactions, timber, the manufacture of brick."

The narrator asks him:

" 'So really you would have given way to the count?'

" 'Hm. The count is a scoundrel, but the count has imposing presence. At the nuptial the two of them together would have composed a charming picture. Just what is to be done, if there were no one except for the count. Well, but I . . . I . . . I would have thrown confetti at the wedding and, believe me, I wanted nothing more. I would have driven in a sledge with a bear.' "

And the author notes down:

"*The main thing.* Kartuzov goes out of his mind simply from the thought that he dared give in to the count and make her a proposal in her misfortune. Considers himself a scoundrel. The thought *literally* kills him that he wronged her by the fact that, taking advantage of her situation, he compared himself to her as *an equal.* He insists that she is an *ideal.*

"He apparently was struck by a stump of wood. He could not digest the compassion. One time he cried out: 'Why she almost married me, why I saw this! What a humiliation, what a fall! My God! My God! Why, she came out to me, maybe, with herself in mind! But is it not impossible, they say, to marry even this one. What's this. And finally, this stump of wood: rat-a-ta-ta! I can't forget. Such a stream, such a lily. . . . And on a lady's saddle. . . .' "

One can suppose that it is in the hospital that Kartuzov writes his last poem *The Cockroach.*

> There lived on earth a cockroach,
> A cockroach from his childhood,
> But then he fell into a glass
> (Upon receiving his inheritance),
> Which was full of fly-cannibalism.
> The cockroach took up space,
> The flies raised up a grumble,
> The glass now became crowded,
> At once they began to cry.
> But while their cry resounded
> Nikifor came up near,
> Truly, he was a wise old man. . . .

Kartuzov offers a commentary:

"Here I stopped; in a word, he took them all and rinsed them out in a tub; this was right and with that the matter ended." "Here he grew thoughtful, but not terribly, but as he used to; he put his hand to his eyes and then looked at me calmly but rather importantly, thinking wholly about something else altogether and perhaps even completely forgetting the poem. In general he looked as if he was gazing.

" 'Then, what is the meaning of the verses?' I was at the point of asking.

" 'Hm. And? What? What meaning? A satire, a fable, an *unimportant link*,' he pronounced listlessly but indulgently and as though in fact he now barely remembered the poem. He even tossed the paper aside.

" '. . . I intended to say here: upon receiving his inheritance, just that way as a witty remark, but since cockroaches do not receive an inheritance, then I chose to write: full of fly-cannibalism.'

" 'Well, and what does fly-cannibalism mean?'

" 'When a table is dirty, then the flies stick to it and fall; fly-cannibalism takes place.'

" 'I didn't understand just how he is a cockroach from childhood?'

" 'From his childhood, i.e., from his very swaddling clothes, or better to say, from birth. . . .'

" 'Who can Nikifor represent? The government?'

" 'Here it is not the government, but misunderstanding.'

" 'Misunderstanding?'

" 'Misunderstanding, misunderstanding in everything. So God is necessary. And we must create God. Russia is misunderstanding, or better to say—a play of nature. All Russia is the play of nature. Nikifor is also the play of nature. In Nikifor I portrayed nature. . . . I note one more thing: a cockroach does not grumble. . . .'

" 'Does it stand firm in its character?'

"Kartuzov looked at me severely.

" 'In a washtub, one doesn't stand firm. But then, perhaps you would like some more tea?'

" 'No, thank you.'

" 'And I thank you.' "

On the fourth day Kartuzov died.

"Having yearned for success in love and, so to speak, for marital pleasures (if it is even necessary to mention this word) but here, he's lying before me with his stretched-out bare, calloused feet. . . . So that for a long time afterward I recalled this. I am by no means a litterateur and a poet, above all not a poet, but there is much for me in Petersburg that is terrible. Of course, all this was more in my youth, at an age of inexperience and impressions, but, in spite of my years, nonetheless sometimes. . . ."

And the author composes a "funeral speech for Kartuzov."

"Had he been educated—he would have become a revolutionary. He was in conscience a pure fanatic."

Out of all Dostoevsky's unrealized projects the plan of the tale of Captain Kartuzov is the most elaborately developed. Substantial segments of text, long dialogues, detailed characteristics are noted down. Undoubtedly the author attached great significance to this work and labored over it with effort. Work on *The Idiot* turned his attention from Kartuzov; then new concepts arose and he no longer returned to the tale. It is also possible, that Kartuzov's image did not altogether satisfy him. The verses that the author ascribed to the noble knight were not only absurd, but also grossly cynical. Instead of good-natured humor in the style of Dickens a dark and heavy irony resulted. But nonetheless this unfinished tale appears to us as artistically very significant. It is skillfully constructed and presents a new revelation of the type of "romantic dreamer" so dear to Dostoevsky. Love—the faith of the Russian Don Quixote, his humble and ardent service to the "ideal of beauty," his ruin from the consciousness of his crime against his "holy-of-holies," his understanding of the "higher ordination of man" as complete self-sacrifice—all this adds features of profound spirituality and humanity to the figure of the enamored captain. Kartuzov remained in the limbo of unborn souls, having ceded his right to life to his brother in the spirit—Prince Myshkin. But Myshkin "having replaced him, did not take his place."

Two years after formulating the outline of the *Tale*, Dostoevsky began to write *The Devils*. His unused notes were not forgotten; part of them in a reworked mode entered the new novel. Above all is the "tone": *The Devils* is written in the form of a "chronicle" such as *The Tale*; the story is reported by a "disinterested personage." In the *Tale* the narrator does not belong to the officers' milieu and is related only through personal friendship to Kartuzov; in *The Devils* he is an extraneous personage in the town, and is friends only with Stepan Trofimovich Verkhovensky. In the "beautiful Amazon" Yelizaveta Nikolayevna (or Yekaterina Grigoryevna) Karmazina and her companion-fiancé it is not difficult to divine Yelizaveta Nikolayevna Tushina, riding about on horseback in the company of her fiancé, Mavriky Nikolayevich. Kartuzov's letter to the count, in which he calls the latter a scoundrel, the blow in the face, the challenge to a duel, and his declaration that he will not fire, correspond in *The Devils* to Gaganov's letter challenging Stavrogin ("Your beaten mug"), Stavrogin's challenge to the duel, his three shots into the air, and the slap that Shatov gives Stavrogin. The lame Karmazina calls the cripple Marya Timofeyevna to mind. Both in *The Tale* and in *The Devils* one encounters the motif of a marriage out of compassion. Kartuzov appears before the count and declares to him: "I am convinced that she loves you and you must marry her." In *The Devils* Mavriky Nikolayevich, in love with Liza, comes to Stavrogin with the same proposal. Finally, Kartuzov's image is genetically connected with two characters in *The Devils*. The blushing, taciturn, unassuming, and faithful knight Mavriky Nikolayevich, who unselfishly loves Liza, has inherited from the captain his romantic Don Quixotism. His figure is sketched in a few simple strokes on the novel's second plane. He is as though a pale shadow cast by Kartuzov onto the pages of *The Devils*. But the Reval captain's main heir is to be found in another captain—Ignat Lebyadkin. At first glance this transformation of the knight "pure at heart" into a drunken buffoon and extortionist seems incredible. And yet it is so; through the enigmatic dialectics of the idea, the character that the author originally conceived as an embodiment of the "beautiful individual" is reduced to a repulsive caricature, to the mask of a vile hanger-on, the brother of the cripple Marya Timofeyevna. This character is traced maliciously and sarcastically, and included in the legion of devils who are led by Pyotr Verkhovensky.

What induced Dostoevsky to ascribe two traits of Kartuzov's character—being in love with the "Amazon" and the composition of absurd verses—to one of the devils in his new novel? It seems to us that the reversal from the noble to the base took place precisely on the ground of poetic material. It was impossible to justify Kartuzov's poetry by any ignorance or naiveté: his verses are not only absurd, but cynical and vulgar. Really, could the chaste knight Kartuzov, who used to worship his lady as an unattainable ideal, have been the author of such doggerel?

And from the other side, really, did not this drunken and crude volubility already contain Captain Lebyadkin's *verbal image*? In *The Tale* the narrator persuades Kartuzov not to tell all and everyone about his affairs of his heart: "They consider you a buffoon," he adds. Out of the knight *who seemed* to be *a buffoon* develops the *real buffoon—Lebyadkin*.

Kartuzov in the beginning criticizes the "Amazon" Yelizaveta Nikolayevna and then unexpectedly falls in love with her; this is also true of Lebyadkin. Liputin says of him: "He's in love, in love, like a cat, and do you know that it began with hatred. At first he so hated Lizaveta Nikolayevna because she used to go riding on horseback, that he nearly reviled her out loud on the street, and in fact did revile her! . . . And suddenly today verses! Do you know that he wants to risk proposing to her? Seriously, seriously!" Lebyadkin sends verses *To the Star Amazon* and a letter to "The Perfection of the Maiden Tushina," into which Kartuzov's poem, which we already know, is transposed as a whole.

> Oh, how dear she is
> Yelizaveta Karmazina

with the substitute *Karmazina—Tushina*.

From another work of Kartuzov's *The Embellishment of Beauty Broke a Limb*, only the first strophe has been preserved in *The Devils*.

In conversation with Stavrogin Lebyadkin explains the origin of these verses. In his story we find not only a brief interpretation of the idea of *The Tale of Captain Kartuzov*, but also the most characteristic expressions of the Reval hero. Dostoevsky parodies himself. Lebyadkin says: " 'In the event she should break her leg,' that is, in the event of riding on horseback. . . . I was once struck, passing by, upon meeting a lady rider, and set myself the pertinent question: 'What would happen then?—that is, in such event?' It's obvious: all her suitors would take back their· word, all her fiancés are off. *Morgen früh*, what's to be; only the poet would remain faithful with his heart crushed inside his breast. Nikolay Vsevolodovich, even a louse may be in love and it is not prohibited by the laws. And yet the person was offended both by my letter and the verses. And you, they say, became angry; were you, sir? It's a pity: I didn't even want to believe it. Well, who could I harm by my imagination?"

Finally, Kartuzov's third poem *The Cockroach* also passes to Lebyadkin. His commentaries upon his verses reproduce rather exactly the Reval Captain's remarks as author. After reading the first line, Lebyadkin interprets, "That is, when flies in the summer time will fall into a glass, fly-cannibalism takes place; any fool will understand." Having finished his recitation, he adds: "Here, I still haven't completed it, but no matter I'll explain in a few words: Nikifor takes the glass and, despite their cries, pours the whole comedy out in a washtub, both the flies and the cockroach, which he should have done long ago. But mind you, take note, madame, the cockroach does not grumble! . . . As for Nikifor, he represents nature."

Kartuzov, having fallen in love, begins to play the dandy and dreams about "worldliness." Lebyadkin cries: "Do you understand, you ass, that I am in love: I've bought a frock coat; look: a frock coat of love, fifteen silver rubles; a captain's love requires worldly proprieties."

Faint reflections of Kartuzov's chivalry fall on Lebyadkin; some of the former's aphorisms are transferred to the latter. Lebyadkin says: "Report that *I am a knight of honor*." "There are moments of a *no-o-ble* character." "Is it possible to die solely from the *nobility* of one's soul?" "In my opinion Russia is a play of nature, no more!" "Your truly magnificent chambers could belong to the *noblest* of persons." "Temperance, solitude, and poverty—this is the vow of the ancient *knights*."

The artistic significance of Dostoevsky's ideological structures and stylistic devices is always dual: behind the "knight's" back stands the buffoon parodying him; behind the shoulders of the God-seeker grimaces his "scrofulous imp with a cold." In the figure of Lebyadkin, Dostoevsky, as it were, revenges himself on his unrealized dream of the "beautiful individual."

---

4. The Death of a Poet[E]
Very briefly

The Corners. A poet aged 26, poverty, is overworked, inflammation of the blood and nerves, pure at heart, does not grumble, is dying, a pregnant wife and two children. Runs about and feeds them, loves. The father is an aesthete (the leather case that has been found). A priestling, an atheist and a nihilist doctor. The priest is a pure Avvakum *en herbe* for Orthodoxy. The poet took his part against the atheist—the priest feels that he is a friend. The priest is poor, having been left only recently without even a place; from the Baltic land; through collecting with another; the mother—the priest's wife—an Old Believer; once interceded and engages with the atheist about freedom and the free individual (N.B. according to the Apostle Paul); meddles when now the priest has passed and proves that he understands freedom better. The poet regarding the deification of nature, a pagan. The poet's confession aloud—instead of that proposed by the priest at his wife's request; the kind, elegant, and enraptured woman; it ended with champagne for all. . . . even the Schismatic drank. For everything, for Christ, for a tiny flower, for his wife. Enraptured words about his wife. The Schismatic to the priest: and you, don't drink wine, or are you giddy and unsteady; you're young yet—and pure in heart—God will make demands upon you—Raving, the last instants of *Götter Griechenlands*. Death, the Schismatic praises and encourages the wife, praises also the priest.

Do not overwrite the tale (it will be like *Poor People*, only more enthusiasm)—in the corners a theft or a crime or something has been committed, but maybe not.

The wife to be a relative of the Schismatic—etc.

(in all 12 sheets maximum).

A gentleman who has come back from abroad. 6 years (is guilty that he did not hold out and returned). A nephew introduces him at the Corners. A stranger from abroad has business with the proprietor of

E Notebook No. 1/4, 1869.

the Corners and the house—Nechayev. Kulishov informs against Nechayev (but maybe even the landlord himself)—the landlord has supported the priest and then—I don't believe anything. The poet's wife is on good terms with the landlord, but not having an affair, the landlord tries; but she loves the stranger's nephew, and waits. He (i.e., the nephew) is jealous of the landlord, spies on him, and is surprised when his uncle informs him that he, it seems, saw her at the landlord's. The strained poet's last confession aloud (shot himself); touching humor and high art—

> The Doctor is a nihilist.
> Pan Pszepjardowski.
> and B-nov.
> The police enter and seize

N.B. In part the poet has (*chiefly*) shame that his wife knows about his indulgences toward the landlord, on account of weakness, for money. The poet is in debt to the landlord.

Dyrochkin.

In the first note, the poet's death is joined to an effective confession before death—an enraptured benediction of everything, in the spirit of Schiller's *Gods of Greece*. Around him are placed the little priest (the representative of Orthodoxy), the Schismatic, deliberating on freedom according to the Apostle Paul, an atheist, and the nihilist doctor. A dispute over faith takes place among them. The author wanted to write a sentimental tale like *Poor People*, but with great enthusiasm. Later (the end of November) he complicated the plot: the poet's wife loves the "nephew" who has returned from abroad; the landlord of the Corners seeks her affection. There appear the names of Nechayev and Kulishov, relating this notation to the rough drafts of *The Devils*. The poet has traits in common with Shatov. The "priestling" is often met in the notes to the *Devils*.

The ideological theme of *The Devils* is already marked: we find set in opposition to Orthodoxy (the future Shatov), paganism (the future Stepan Trofimovich), atheism (the future Stavrogin), and nihilism (the future Pyotr Verkhovensky).

---

5. The Novelist[F]

A *novelist* (writer). In old age, but primarily because of attacks,

[F] Notebook No. 1/10, 1870.

fell into a decline of his talents and thereupon into poverty. Recognizing his weaknesses, he prefers to stop writing, and submits to poverty. A wife and daughter. All his life he wrote on demand. Now he no longer considers himself equal to his former society, but is obligated before it. The critics, to whom he talks about himself, are *scoundrels* (lower than everyone, as it were: and as a result, superior to all); episodes out of his past life, as though in edification to the children, and so forth. Public lectures. About how many ideas he has conceived, both literary and all kinds. A tone, as it were, in mockery of himself, for himself: "But indeed this is so." How even the children and his wife and M-v[G] consider him nothing. How T-v,[H] Goncharov, Pleshcheyev, Aksakov give to him, quarreled with S.[I] How suddenly he wrote an excellent work about himself, fame and money, and so forth, and so forth. *N.B. the theme is rich.* Well, supposing I don't compare with Count L. Tolstoy or with Mr. Turgenev (N. B. never simply Turgenev, without Mr.): I don't compare even with the other Count Tolstoy, but the realist Pisemsky this is another matter. For this is French vaudeville which they offer us as Russian realism.

N. B. about the transiency of life and the story—a poetic work like Oblomov's dream about Christ—(and about oneself then). This is worth 200 rub. a sheet, and I'm giving this to them for nothing, and they think they're doing me a favor.

About currents and ideas that have existed.

The novel about the writer is purely autobiographical. Into it were to have gone literary polemics, memoirs, and reflections on literary tendencies. The tone was intended as sarcastic.

---

6. *A Thought on Summer*[J]

A field marshal arrives with his pregnant mistress in the provincial capital. (To entice the husband again.) The husband with principles, self-perfection, abandoned children. He is not captivated, but stable and loves. Entering into the desire to seduce her husband, she is seduced herself. The prince is a lost man. She wants to run away, at the end, from the seduction, for she has yielded; she exhausts the prince's patience; the latter is jealous of the husband, strikes him in the face, tries to kill him (but does not succeed). (N. B. she provoked him

[G] Milyukov.   [H] Turgenev.   [I] Saltykov-Schedrin.   [J] Notebooks 1/10, 1870.

to do it, yet did not put it into words, but aroused his jealousy.) Then when he fired at her husband, she abandoned the prince and gave herself unconditionally to her husband—did the prince kill himself? (N. B. the husband accepted, but just as he accepted, so she felt bored.) With a gymnasium student, with the governor—a hermit—Mary of Egypt. Forces the prince to insult his own mother. (Experiments on the prince every minute.)

N. B. seduces the husband to the point that she surrenders to him. N. B. She is from abroad and would like to look at a nihilist. There arrives—a certain teacher—a nihilist. (The husband's murder; the prince becomes friends and decides[?] to kill nihilists.)

Tropmana was at an execution. Description of the execution. About how he was charming.

N. B. Or the teacher spurns her, i.e. does not spurn her, but she does not captivate him (though perhaps he had). Then she revenges herself on him and when she takes revenge—(kills) then weeps; the prince is a tragic figure (the kernel of the novel's events and occurrence lies in him). The wife, who had been in the field marshal's keep, surrenders to them with recompense for the husband—to the teacher; sets his head spinning, forces him to insult his mother, kills the field marshal, forces her husband to fight a duel with someone who has wronged her (a certain young prince, her lover for the moment), overturns the whole province, dies finally in the presence of her weeping husband.

In June 1870 Dostoevsky was working out the ideological relations between Stavrogin and Shatov. In the teacher, to whom the pregnant wife returns, it is possible to see an outline of Shatov's figure. The prince's "tragic figure" displays features of Stavrogin. In *The Devils* the personality of Shatov's wife withdraws onto a secondary plane and is divested of its "demonic" properties.

Index

Acis and Galatea (*see also* Lorrain), 324, 527-28, 554, 557
Akhsharumov, D., 116
Aksakov, Ivan Sergeyevich, 225, 235, 331, 640, 643-44
Aksakov, Konstantin Sergeyevich, 46, 223, 235
Alchevskaya, Kh. D., 536
Aleksandr II, Emperor, 166
Aleksandra Fyodorovna, Empress, 165
Aleksey Svobodin, 126
Alekseyev, N., 173
Alekseyev, V. A., 538
Alyona Frolovna, 8
Antonelli, P. D., 52, 122-23, 133
Anna Karenina, 484, 494
Annenkov, Pavel, 45-46, 60, 79, 103
Averkiyev, Dmitry, 129

Bakhtin, M. M., 246
Bakunin, Mikhail, 117, 130, 329-30, 418
Balasoglo, 123
Balzac, Honoré de, 16, 22-25, 30, 45, 54, 101, 114, 280
Barber of Seville, 96-97
Belinsky, Visarion, 33, 36-38, 41, 43, 45-46, 53, 59, 60-61, 69, 78-79, 82, 103, 117-19, 122-23, 152-53, 227, 397, 474, 545, 597, 650
Beketin, 61, 114
Belkin Tales, 31, 230, 490
Bell, The, 231
Bergson, Henri, 296
Berezhetsky, Ivan, 13-15
Bestuzhev, Aleksandr, 73
Bible, the, 136, 333, 353, 372, 431
Boborykin, 240
Botkin, Nikolai, 117
Bryanchaninov, Ignaty, 11
Buckle, 592
Byron, Lord, 12, 16, 170, 222

Candide, 383
Carracci, A., 566
Casanova, Giovanni, 220
Catechism of a Revolutionary, The, 121, 126, 418
Cervantes, Miguel, 60, 346, 652
Chaadayev, Pyotr Yakovlevich, 397
Chebotaryov, V., 635
Chelverikov, S. Archpriest, 631

Chermak, Leonty Ivanovich, 10, 399, 400, 489
Chernyshevsky, Nikolai, 224, 243, 250-51, 265-66, 274, 326-27, 398n, 474
Chikhachyov, 11
Christ on the Baltic Sea, 529, 557
Chulkov, G., 488
Cid, Le, 16
Citizen, The, 470-74, 480-82, 488, 535
Communist Manifesto, 131
Constant, V. D., 168
Contemporary, The, 58, 61, 64, 69, 79, 99, 104, 173, 223-24, 231, 250, 261-63, 270, 326, 592
Corneille, Pierre, 16
Correspondence With Friends, 122, 167, 173-77
Covetous Knight, The, 64-65, 288, 314, 354, 395, 482, 489, 512
Crisis of Western Philosophy, The, 566
Critique of Pure Reason, 155, 531

Dahl, Vladimir Ivanovich, 136
Danilevsky, 331
Dante, 185, 188, 652
Dawn, 383, 386
Dead Souls, 46-47, 52, 397n, 398n
Death of Ivan the Terrible, 646
Derzhavin, 9
Dickens, Charles, 108, 199, 345-46, 484
Dobrolyubov, Nikolai, 131, 190, 198, 224, 227
Dombey and Son, 108
Don Carlos, 14-15, 22, 28
Don Juan, 640
Don Quixote, 60n, 345-46, 349, 374
Dorovatovskaya-Lyubimova, V. S., 263n, 359n
Dostoevsky, Aleksey Fyodorovich, 487, 571, 574
Dostoevsky, Andrey Mikhailovich, 4-6, 18-19, 21, 134, 147
Dostoevskaya, Anna Grigoryevna, *née* Snitkina, 4, 12-13, 162-63, 240, 267, 277, 321-25, 332-33, 383, 386, 405, 470, 472, 481-84, 486, 542-43, 571-72, 576, 591, 646-47
Dostoevskaya, Emiliya Fyodorovna, 19, 146
Dostoevsky, Fyodor Fyodorovich, 386, 470

Dostoevsky, Fyodor Mikhailovich
  acceptance by critics, 36-37, 41, 43, 45, 53, 638-39
  ancestry, 3
  arrest, 69
  birth, 4
  childhood and youth, 3-12
  death, 645-48
  epilepsy, 6, 162, 221, 323-25, 373, 385, 408
  exile, 155-62
  feuilletonist, 71
  first marriage, 157-62
  health, 26, 54-57, 62, 99, 132, 135-36, 159, 332, 582, 587, 637, 645
  literary images, 8, 77, 94, 105, 135, 145, 175, 191, 194, 217, 233-34, 253-56, 294-96, 353, 364, 389, 448-49, 521, 555-56, 640
  parodies of, 60-61, 140, 243, 485
  penal servitude, 133-47; 184-86
  rejection by critics, 69, 82, 198, 262, 485-86
  revolutionary activity, 114-32
  romanticism, 70, 73, 84
  second marriage, 321-28; 541-43
  self-deprecation, 82, 103
  spirituality, 103, 217
  travels, 229, 271
  use of folklore, 77-78
  VIEWS ON
    anarchism, 422, 584
    beauty, 374, 380-81, 412, 452, 454, 467, 507, 519
    Christ, 81, 118-19, 144, 152-53, 157, 165, 256-57, 260-61, 281-83, 285, 288, 294, 313, 327, 329, 345, 349-50, 352, 362-63, 368-69, 404, 411, 413, 415-16, 424, 429-31, 460-62, 467, 476, 492, 529, 538-40, 557, 561-63, 575, 586-87, 617-22, 642, 652.
    Christian humanism, 157, 195, 211, 214, 256, 306-7, 563, 620, 650
    crime, 68, 113, 193, 271-313, 356, 553, 598, 603, 606
    criminal, 189-93
    disbelief, 117, 122, 340, 625
    ecstasy, 554, 636
    eros, 182-83, 236-40, 267, 322, 324, 591
    evil, 193-95, 257, 307, 364
    Europe, 225-26, 229-33, 526, 530
    free will, 251-53, 329, 450
    guilt, 66-67, 113, 277
    "haphazard households," 106, 498-99, 517
    human nobility, 17, 191, 196, 515

idealism, 210, 339, 447, 495, 553
immortality, 144, 306, 363-64, 376, 449, 477-78, 533, 564, 574, 576
justice, 196, 616, 628
loneliness, 66, 303, 512, 552
love, 112, 153, 208, 221, 234, 259-60, 275, 281, 285, 379, 443, 511, 552, 554, 586-88, 616, 622, 627-28, 634
madness, 47, 308, 524
nature of reality, 27, 29, 58, 358, 382, 553, 594
Nationalism, 165, 219-22, 230, 330, 368-69, 430, 443, 526-27
"natural school," 31, 69, 73, 101, 222
Orthodox faith, 220, 234, 286, 368, 380, 398, 411, 414, 429-30, 445, 562
"positively beautiful individual," 343-46, 352, 380, 404, 424, 465, 596, 627
poverty, 33-35, 105
personality, 48-50, 66
pride, 284-85, 304, 309, 311, 337-38, 370
problem of communality, 234, 259, 521, 533, 536, 553
problem of consciousness, 245-49, 257-58, 356, 363, 392, 394, 399, 429, 443, 513-14, 517-18, 615
problem of freedom, 151, 189-91, 197, 234, 288, 301-2, 313, 377, 451, 453, 460, 474, 511, 540, 618, 621
psychology of children, 92, 105-6, 108, 350, 584
purpose of literature, 17, 58, 103, 167, 224
repentance, 193, 282, 303, 428, 444
resurrection, 151, 332, 338, 385, 557, 568-69, 573, 577, 630-31
romantic dreaming, 70, 76, 78, 80, 86, 93-94, 105, 172, 189, 205, 212, 244, 393, 399, 403, 434
romanticism, 16, 103, 114, 172, 213, 259, 393
romanticism, Russian, 13, 39, 101, 259-60
Russian People, 11, 166, 193, 196, 368, 405, 495-96, 501, 521, 544, 646
sensuality, 92, 108, 307, 317-18, 340, 598, 610-11, 614, 624
Slavophiles, 219-20, 223, 240, 430, 473, 641
Socialism, 114-16, 262-63, 444,

473, 538, 575, 584-85, 618, 620, 645

suffering, 217, 261, 289, 298, 476, 607, 613, 620

utopianism, 87, 114-17, 195, 211-12, 216, 227, 253, 375, 385, 528

weak individual, the, 80-82, 87, 195, 207, 213, 519

Western Christianity, 16, 115, 118-19, 167, 196, 234, 376, 386

Westernizers, 219-20, 223, 240, 430, 473, 641

WORKS

Another Man's Wife and the Husband Under the Bed, 82-83, 170

Apropos of the Wet Snow, see Notes From Underground

Brothers Karamazov, The, 565-95; 596-636; 7-8, 13, 36, 50, 58, 67, 87, 106, 108-9, 132, 135, 178, 179n, 207-8, 234, 254, 263, 299, 320, 326, 333, 338, 342, 365, 379, 381, 383, 392, 394, 398, 402-3, 480, 483, 512, 517-18, 524-25, 536-39, 541, 544, 557, 559-60, 563-64, 637, 640, 641-42, 645-46

Christmas Tree Party and a Wedding, 21, 71, 91-92, 112, 139, 215

Crime and Punishment, 270-313; 11, 21, 23, 33, 35, 62, 68, 105, 109, 134, 147, 153-54, 164, 179, 193, 207-8, 254, 318, 322, 326, 336, 351-52, 355, 358, 361, 376, 382, 387, 479, 485, 506, 555, 582, 596, 598, 626, 650-51

Devils, The, 433-69; 52, 62, 82, 109, 121, 129, 132, 162, 171, 179n, 181-82, 207-9, 254, 262, 299, 324, 331, 340-41, 366, 379, 381, 385-86, 388, 394-95, 398, 402-3, 479, 481, 492-93, 502, 505-6, 509, 517-18, 527, 531, 563, 576, 580, 586, 596, 598, 621, 623, 631, 641, 651-52

Diary of a Writer, 535-65; 10, 36-37, 45, 50, 71, 109, 115, 118-21, 129, 146, 150, 166, 260, 331, 337, 473-74, 477-79, 531, 546-52, 567, 579-80, 596, 642-46

Double, The, 40-68; 69, 95, 99, 103, 181-82, 545, 597

Eternal Husband, The, 382-403; 163, 277

Faint Heart, The, 71, 84-89

Gambler, The, 314-33; 109, 207, 236-37, 278, 354, 376, 597

Grand Inquisitor, The, 81, 191, 235, 538-39, 582-87, 590, 597, 614, 617-23, 650-51

Humiliated and Wronged, The, 198-218; 38-39, 56, 58, 161, 169, 182-84, 220-21, 227, 237, 258, 366, 479, 497, 597

Idiot, The, 334-81; 8, 62, 82, 108, 142-44, 179, 182, 207-8, 382, 386, 402, 479, 488, 521, 531-34, 596, 626, 630

Landlady, The, 13, 71, 73-81, 99, 120-21, 172, 208, 366, 597

Little Hero, The, 134, 136, 138-44

Mister Prokharchin, 40-68, 85, 336, 354

Nasty Predicament, A, 183, 226-27

Netochka Nezvanova, 99-113; 92, 121, 138-39, 164, 171, 203, 208, 376, 537

Notes From the House of Death, 182-97; 147-54, 172, 198, 215, 221, 274, 314-15, 576-77

Notes From the Underground, 242-69; 48n, 191, 217, 234, 274, 317, 362, 386, 394, 475, 513, 551

Novel in Nine Letters, A, 43

Poor People, 24-39, 20-22, 40, 50, 53, 56, 59, 63, 68, 73, 85, 96-97, 156, 198, 205, 208, 227, 289, 376, 485, 545, 650

Pushkin Speech, 222, 567, 637

Raw Youth, A, 488-534, 7, 10, 106, 108-9, 207-8, 254, 290, 324, 354, 366, 381, 394, 402, 482, 486-87, 536-37, 575, 596, 598, 614, 631, 651

Uncle's Dream, 155-81; 83-84, 184, 366

Village of Stepanchikovo, 155-76; 83, 184, 199, 209, 597

White Nights, 71, 92-98, 172, 205, 208

Winter Notes on Summer Impressions, 219-25; 191, 261, 556

FEUILLETONS

Petersburg Chronicle, 71-73

Petersburg Dreams in Verse and Prose, 27-28, 64, 67, 72, 84

JOURNALS

Citizen, The, 470-88; 535

Epoch, 242-69; 481, 485

Time, 219-42; 185, 198, 267, 481, 640

NOTEBOOKS, 207, 260, 278-80, 334-43, 346, 348, 380, 398-99, 402, 404-32, 433, 440, 488-99, 501-2, 544-46, 565-95

PROJECTS
Apathy and Impressions, 182
Life of a Great Sinner, The, 382-414; 631
Shaved Whiskers, The, 62-63, 73
Story of the Suppressed Chancery Offices, 62, 66
Dostoevskaya, Lyubov Fyodorovna, 6-7, 134, 149, 163, 171, 383, 470, 482-83, 571-72
Dostoevskaya, Mariya Dmitriyevna, *née* Constant, 157-64, 235-37, 242, 260-61
Dostoevskaya, Mariya Fyodoroyevna, *née* Nechayeva, 3-4, 10
Dostoevskaya, Varvara Mikhailovna, 4, 22, 277
Dostoevsky, Mikhail Andreyevich, 3-8, 10
Dostoevsky, Mikhail Mikhailovich, 4, 9-10, 11-14, 18-20, 22, 24-27, 41-45, 51, 55-57, 99, 114, 134-36, 140-41, 145-47, 155, 162, 164-68, 178, 181, 183, 198, 238-39, 243, 263, 268, 319, 323, 649
Durov, Sergey, 123-27, 130-31, 141, 145-46, 650
Dumas, Alexandre, 367

Egyptian Nights, 640
Engels, Frederich, 131
Epoch, 264-67, 481, 485
Eugene Onegin, 222, 640
Eugénie Grandet, 16, 22-25

Fatherland Notes, 24, 41, 46, 53, 58, 63, 69, 73, 82, 84, 89, 91, 100, 136, 155, 173, 270, 481-82, 485, 487, 502, 537
Fathers And Children, 224, 231, 329, 537
Feast During the Plague, 640
Fet, A. A., 266
Feuerbach, Ludwig, 117, 212
Filippov, P. N., 123, 126, 129, 471
Filosofova, A. P., 587
Fonvizina, N. D., 119, 146, 151, 158
Fourier, Charles, 51, 114-16, 253, 266, 453, 502, 528
Freud, Sigmund, 6, 108, 649
Fyodorov, M. P., 169
Fyodorov, N. F., 566-69

Geilovich, A., 180
Glinka, Mikhail Ivanovich, 18, 268
Goethe, Johann Wolfgang von, 17, 182, 204, 335
Gogol, Nikolai, 25, 27, 29, 30-32, 41, 43, 46-47, 63-66, 77-79, 101, 122-23,

167, 170, 176-77, 180, 222, 263, 265, 346, 368, 397n, 398n, 422-23, 469, 484
Golovinsky, 125
Goncharov, Ivan Aleksandrovich, 397, 433, 497
Gorsky, 357-59
Gospels, the, 9, 13, 146, 151, 233, 276-77, 308, 345, 411, 443, 502
Gradovsky, A., 642
Granovsky, Timofey, 397-98, 417
Greatcoat, The, 29-32, 63-66, 263
Griboyedov, Aleksandr, 212, 231, 320, 513-14, 519
Grigorovich, D. V., 24, 37, 45, 59-60
Grigoryev, Apollon, 198, 220, 263, 386
Grigoryev, Nikolai Petrovich, 126-27, 133
Guseva, P. Ye, 643

Hamlet, 17, 248, 277, 505
Hegel, Georg Wilhelm Friedrich, 117, 155, 157, 362
Heine, Heinrich, 277, 529, 557
Hero of Our Time, 9, 340
Herzen, Alexandr, 60, 117-18, 226, 231-33, 236, 327, 397, 417, 474, 546
Hoffman, E.T.A., 17, 27, 57, 79, 94, 101-2, 202, 469
"Holy Fools," 339, 370
Homer, 12, 16, 120
Hubert, E. I., 71
Hugo, Victor, 16, 114, 120, 142, 156, 199, 226, 346, 471, 548, 579
Hymn To Joy, 578, 597, 611

Illusions Perdues, 45
Imitation of the Koran, 640
Inspector General, 41, 212, 422-23
Isayev, Pavel, 470
Ivanov, A. P., 277
Ivanova, Sofiya Aleksandrovna, 345, 347-48, 358n, 382-84, 386, 395-96, 407-8, 458

Jaclard, Charles Victor, 268
Job, Book of, 333, 575
Joyce, James, 548

Kant, Emmanuel, 155, 214, 495, 531, 552, 615
Karamzin, Nikolai, 9, 32, 229
Karepin, Pyotr Andreyevich, 20-21
Kaspirov, V., 408
Katkov, Mikhail, 168-69, 223, 235, 272-74, 277, 279, 325, 332, 481, 484, 579
Khlebnikov, K. D., 14
Khomyakov, A. S., 506n

Kierkegaard, Søren, 197, 244, 250, 255
Kock, Paul de, 83
Komarovich, V., 77, 251n, 488, 579, 581
Koni, A. F., 503, 592
Koran, The, 155
Korvin-Krukovskaya, A. V., 277
Kostomarov, Koronad, 10-11
Kostomarov, Nikolai, 224, 243
Kovalevskaya, Sofya, 268
Kovalevsky, Ye P., 268, 638
Kramer, 503-5
Krayevsky, Andrey Aleksandr, 58, 69, 82, 99-100, 146, 173, 265, 271

Lamennais, 115
Lapshin, I. I., 503
Lawsuit, The, 43
Lectures on Godmanhood, 567
Leontyev, Konstantin, 60, 532, 573, 589
Lermontov, Mikhail, 9, 222, 340, 377n, 484
Les Misérables, 226, 346, 471, 579
Letters of a Russian Traveller, 229
Library for Reading, 22, 270
Liprandi, 117, 124-25, 127, 133
Liszt, Franz, 18
Lomonosov, Mikhailo, 368
Lorrain, Claude, 324, 527-28, 554, 557
Lossky, Nikolai, 506n
Lukerya, 8, 78
Lvov, Fyodor Nikolayevich, 126
Lyubimov, Nikolai, 322, 565, 579, 584, 589, 592-93

Magnetizer, The, 57
Maikov, Apollon, 62, 128-29, 164-66, 184, 324, 326-27, 330-31, 333-35, 343, 346-47, 383-84, 394, 396, 471, 485, 497, 650
Maikov, N., 54, 62
Makarov, 6
Marlinsky, 73n
Marx, Karl, 117-18, 131
Mathilde, 22
Meshschersky, Prince Vladimir, 470-71, 482
Mikhailov, V. V., 565
Mikhailovsky, Nikolai, 481
Miller, Orest, 648
Milton, John, 652
Milyukov, Alexsandr, 115, 125-27, 133, 145, 270, 276, 278
Mochalov, P., 9
Molière, 139, 173-75
Mombelli, Nikolai Aleksovich, 126, 131
Month in the Country, 637
Mysteries of Paris, 202

Napoleon, 66-68, 278, 306, 309, 282-84, 288
"Naturphilosophie," 17
Nechayev, 120-32; 406, 409, 410, 411, 412-13, 417-18, 420-23, 440, 474
Nekrasov, Nikolai, 36-37, 42-43, 58, 60-61, 87, 99, 173, 177, 260, 481, 484-85, 488, 531, 537, 545
Nest of Gentlefolk, 173, 328, 379n
Nevsky Prospect, 25, 29
Nietzsche, Friedrich, Wilhelm, 195, 244, 250, 255, 464, 651
Nikolai I, Emperor, 140
Nikolsky, Yu, 327n
Nikolayevich, Grand Prince Konstantin, 580
Nose, The, 46-47
Notes of a Madman, 46, 101, 266
Notes of a Demon, 25
Novalis, 12

Oblomov, 397n, 398
Ogaryov, Nikolai, 60
"Old Believers," 80n, 192n, 427-28
Odoyevsky, Prince Vladimir, 41, 101
Orlov, Count, 133
Ostrovsky, Alexander, 220
Othello, 338

Pallady, Father, 581
Pahn, Ivan Ivanovich, 123, 126, 648
Panayev, I., 43, 60-61, 87
Panayeva, Avdotya, 43-45, 59, 61, 163
Parfeny, Monk, 398, 576
Pascal, 652
Pavlovsky, I., 60-61
Père Goriot, Le, 22-23, 42-43, 280
Petersburg Collection, 46
Peterson, N. P., 567
Petrashevsky, Mikhail, 87, 116-17, 121-23, 131, 133-34
Phantoms, 236, 239, 242, 468-69
Philosophic Principles, 566
Philosophy of the Common Task, 567-63
Pickwick Papers, 345-46, 349
Pisarev, Dmitri, 155, 261
Pisemsky, Alexey, 243, 268
Plato, 615
Pleshcheyev, A. N., 115-16, 122, 131, 138, 481
Pletnyov, R., 634
Pogodin, M. P., 224, 471
Polonsky, Yakov, 225, 536
Polevoy, N. A., 101
Proust, Marcel, 548
Prokhorov, G., 266n
Prolinsky, I. I., 227-28

Proudhon, Pierre Joseph, 114-15, 236
Pugachov, 230
Pushkin, Aleksandr, 9, 16, 25, 31, 37,
    64-65, 127, 156, 165, 220, 222, 230,
    288n, 290, 314, 354, 368, 395, 397,
    442, 482, 484, 489-90, 497, 512, 567,
    637-46

Queen of Spades, The, 290

Racine, Jean, 16
Radcliffe, Ann, 27
Raphael, Sanzio, 25, 333, 442
Riesenkampf, Aleksandr, 19, 45
Robbers, The, 22, 484, 578
Rossini, Giocchino, 96-97
Rousseau, Jean-Jacques, 210, 257-58,
    385, 649
Rozanov, V. V., 241
Repertoire and Pantheon, 22
Resurrection, 593
Russian Messenger, The, 168-69, 173,
    223, 275-76, 346-48, 396, 481, 484,
    497, 565, 579, 593
Russian Word, 168-69, 172, 250
Russian World, The, 185
Ruy Blas, 579

Saint-Simon, 114-15, 377, 528
Sand, Georges 30, 114, 222, 367, 377,
    545
Schelling, Friedrich Wilhelm, 12
Schiller, J. C. Friedrich von, 9, 12-17,
    22, 27, 114, 137, 140, 172, 212-13,
    216-18, 253, 311, 393, 484, 575, 578,
    597, 611
Scott, Walter, 9, 27, 105-6, 111, 484
Schubert, Aleksandra Ivanovna, 183-84,
    198
Semevsky, 130
Semyonov-Tyan-Schansky, 127
Shakespeare, 12, 16-17, 136-37, 225,
    338, 442, 505, 649
Shchedrin, 223, 228, 261, 326
Shestov, Lev, 197
Shevyryov, S., 46
Shidlovsky, I. N., 11-13, 27, 566
Sluchevsky, K. K., 224
Smirnov, 542
Smoke, 327-29
Snitkin, Ivan Grigoryevich, 405
Socrates, 129
Sologub, Count Vladimir, 41, 44
Solovyov, Vladimir, 13, 566-68, 572,
    620, 648
Solovyov, Vsevolod, 134, 535

Souchard, Nikolai, 10, 489
Soulie, Frederick, 25, 27, 199, 210
Spark, 228n, 592
Speshnyov, Nikolai, 128, 130-32
Sportsman's Notebook, 328
Strakhov, N. N., 29, 220-21, 223-24,
    231, 235, 323, 382, 385, 394, 471,
    485-86, 497
St. Ronan's Wall, 111
Stellovsky, F. T., 51, 268, 277, 322
Sue, Eugene, 22, 199, 202, 210
Suslova, Apollinariya, 236-41, 270, 315-
    16, 317, 321, 369
Suvorin, S., 6-7
Symeon, St., the New Theologian, 533n

Tale of Bova, 624
Taras Bulba, 484
Tartuffe, 173, 175, 177, 139
Terrible Vengeance, The, 78
Thomas à Kempis, 267
Three Conversations, 620
Tikhon Zadonsky, St., 396n, 398, 497,
    631, 633-35
Timkovsky, K. I., 115
Time, 185, 198, 267, 481, 640
Timashev, 181
Tolstoy, Aleksey Konstantinovich, 646
Tolstoy, Lev, 320, 383, 402, 498-99,
    500, 525, 573, 593
Troubled Sea, The, 243
Trutovsky, K., 15
Turgenev, Ivan, 42-43, 45, 59, 60-61,
    103, 139, 140, 188, 220, 224, 231,
    235, 239, 242-43, 326-29, 383, 397n,
    433-34, 468-69, 497, 537, 582, 637,
    638
Tynyanov, Yury, 77
Tyutchev, Fydor Ivanovich, 575, 641n

Utin, 327

Vergunov, 161-63, 237
Vergil, 652
Vernet, Horace, 25
Viskovatov, 128
Voice, The, 265, 359, 642
Voltaire, 383, 615
Vrangel, Baron Aleksandr, 6, 149, 156-
    61, 164, 171, 181, 268, 270, 275, 279

War and Peace, 320, 383, 402, 497-98,
    500, 525
What's to Be Done, 243, 250-51, 265-
    66, 398n, 442

Wilhelm Meister, 182, 204
Woe From Wit, 212, 320, 513-14, 519

Yanovsky, Dr. Stepan, 6-7, 54, 56, 62,
   89, 149, 321, 543-44
Yanyshev, I. A., 271
Yastrzhembsky, 123, 134
Yevropeus, 116

Yeliseyev, 481, 592
Yerfimov, I., 635
Yermakov, Dr., 149
Yury Miloslavsky, 9, 266

Zenkovsky, 220n
Zhukovsky, Vasily Andreyevich, 9, 94
Zola, Emile, 560